JUGGLING WITH KNIVES

JUGGLING
with
KNIVES

SMART INVESTING IN THE
COMING AGE OF VOLATILITY

Jim Jubak

PUBLICAFFAIRS
New York

Published in the United States by PublicAffairs™, a Member of the Perseus Books Group

Printed in the United States of America.

PublicAffairs books are available at special discounts for bulk purchases in the U.S. by corporations, institutions, and other organizations. For more information, please contact the Special Markets Department at the Perseus Books Group, 2300 Chestnut Street, Suite 200, Philadelphia, PA 19103, call (800) 810-4145, ext. 5000, or e-mail special.markets@ perseusbooks.com.

Book Design by Trish Wilkinson
Set in 10.5 point Baskerville 10 Pro

Library of Congress Cataloging-in-Publication Data

Names: Jubak, Jim.
Title: Juggling with knives : smart investing in the coming age of volatility / Jim Jubak.
Description: New York : PublicAffairs, 2016. | Includes bibliographical references and index.
Identifiers: LCCN 2015040921| ISBN 9781610394802 (hardback) | ISBN 9781610394819 (e-book)
Subjects: LCSH: Finance, Personal. | Investments. | Stocks—Prices. | Bonds—Prices. | BISAC: BUSINESS & ECONOMICS / Personal Finance / Investing.
Classification: LCC HG179 .J773 2016 | DDC 332.6—dc23 LC record available at http://lccn.loc.gov/2015040921

First Edition

10 9 8 7 6 5 4 3 2 1

Contents

v

Chapter 1

An Age of Volatility

ON APRIL 24, 2015, police in London arrested a thirty-six-year-old independent trader and charged him with causing the May 2010 flash crash that took the Dow Jones Industrial Average down 1,010 points in thirty-six minutes. Twenty minutes after it bottomed at 2:47 p.m. New York time, the market had recouped almost 600 points of that loss. It was the largest intraday plunge in the more than hundred-year history of the index, and the loss—much of it temporary for anyone who held on but certainly not for those who panicked and sold—came to a trillion dollars.

How was this possible?

Two theories reigned after the arrest of Navinder Singh Sarao.

First: It wasn't possible for one person to take the markets down. Regulators, these theorists held, had fastened onto Sarao as a scapegoat for their own lack of oversight and inability, even five years after the flash crash, to explain how it happened. How likely was it, the scapegoat theorists asked, that a guy who traded using a customized version of off-the-shelf trading software from his modest home in a drab London suburb and with relatively modest capital could have taken down the US stock market?

Second: It was indeed possible. The market is so unregulated in some corners, so dominated by electronic trading platforms run by computers, and so illiquid these days that it doesn't take much to start an avalanche of selling or buying. Sarao could indeed have set the ball rolling and then watched it speed downhill.

That's not much of a choice. Either current markets are so complex that no one can explain why they behave the way they do—which means we could have another flash crash tomorrow—or markets are so structurally unsound that anybody with a terminal can crash them tomorrow, either intentionally or by mistake.

There is also a third theory, one that informs the spine of this book, to explain the flash crash: a combination of financial market causes—ranging from structural weakness in the markets to the effects of a tidal wave of central bank cash sent flooding through markets and economies to end the Great Recession—and real-life causes—ranging from the aging world population to hoarding economics for food, water, and energy—has created an Age of Volatility. It is an age characterized by rates of volatility significantly above the normal range of volatility cycles we have experienced in the more than thirty-five years since Federal Reserve Chairman Paul Volcker smashed runaway inflation by driving interest rates to double digits in the late 1970s and early 1980s.

This alternative is not especially cheerful, as there is no quick way to push financial market volatility back down to historical levels and because this volatility will be found in all parts of everyday life, from housing to jobs to education to what we eat and drink—and, of course, what we pay for it.

––––––

TO UNDERSTAND WHY THIS Age of Volatility will be so disruptive and so scary, we need to understand exactly what volatility is and isn't. Let's start with an analogy:

Which is faster: a bullet train or a roller coaster?

Easy, right? Bullet trains routinely travel at 200 miles per hour or more. And the fastest roller coaster in the world, the Formula Rossa in Abu Dhabi, comes in at a speed of 149 miles per hour.

Now, which is more volatile?

It takes an N700 Shinkasen bullet train in Japan two minutes to hit 170 miles per hour.

The Formula Rossa goes from 0 to 149 miles per hour in five seconds. No wonder riders are required to wear goggles so a random bug doesn't result in permanent eye damage. A hydraulic launch similar to those on aircraft carriers sends passengers on their way. And to make the ride even more of a thrill, after "takeoff" the cars climb a hill that reduces their speed to just 60 miles per hour before the Formula Rossa speeds up again.

But when it comes to volatility—the speed of a change in speed—maybe the Dodonpa roller coaster in Yamanashi, Japan, wins the prize. Although its top speed is only 107 miles per hour, it goes from 0 to 107 in just 1.8 seconds. It's no longer the fastest roller coaster in the world, as it was when it was built in 2001, but it still holds the record for the fastest acceleration.

In comparison to the Formula Rossa or the Dodonpa, a bullet train is smooth and unscary. As you roll through the Japanese, Chinese, or French countryside at 200 miles per hour, you don't have a sense of traveling all that fast. Even the acceleration into and out of train stations is gradual and gentle.

If you're looking for terror, for disorientation, for a mind-numbing concentration on the now, and for fear that makes you want to do the irrational (like release the safety harness), a roller coaster beats a bullet train hands down.

Volatility is scarier than speed. Whether it's roller coasters, social change, or financial markets, abrupt changes of acceleration and direction are much more emotionally draining and much more likely to produce irrational responses than mere speed is.

Unfortunately.

Because we're living through an era of extreme volatility in the financial markets and, I'd argue, in national and global economies as a whole.

And, unfortunately, because, as important as volatility is to financial markets—and, new neurobiological research says, to the way we think, the kinds of decisions we make, and how happy, stressed, rational, or fearful we are—our understanding of volatility is still rudimentary. That's true in the financial markets, even with all the work that analysts and statisticians have put in to develop indexes that track volatility. And it's even truer for life in general, where understanding volatility and its effects are largely matters of anecdote and feel.

This lack of an in-depth understanding of volatility hasn't been a big problem for a good piece of what we call the present. For twenty years, from about 1980 to 1999, speed dominated the markets and many global economies, translating into a steady, fast-paced trip uphill for most portfolios and many living standards. During that time understanding volatility and figuring out how to, if not master it, at least cope with its effects wasn't especially critical. You could have made very profitable investment decisions and intelligently planned your career, education, family—all the stuff we call "real life"—without spending much time thinking about volatility.

That, however, is certainly not the case for the Age of Volatility. The years from 1999 to 2000 marked the beginning of a transition from a period of steady, uphill speed to this Age of Volatility that hit its stride beginning in 2008 and still has years—a decade or two, in all probability—to run.

What we really want to know now is: What kind of volatility roller coaster are we riding? I think we can forget about the theory that we're not on a roller coaster at all: the four big volatility crises of the ten years beginning in 1997—the Asian currency crisis of 1997, the Russian crisis of 1998, the dotcom bust of 2000, and the global financial crisis of 2008—all convince me that we are strapped in for a ride.

But what kind of ride?

It could be the relatively predictable historical cycle between low volatility and high volatility periods, much like the roller coaster I rode at age thirteen, where I could see hills and valleys ahead and feel the cars strain to make the peaks.

At the other extreme it could be a supercharged roller coaster like the Fury 325 that debuted at Carowinds Park outside Charlotte, North Carolina, in March 2015, with a top speed of ninety-five miles per hour and brief calms before storms that make the descents even scarier and 360-degree turns designed to destroy the mind's ability to keep its terror under rational control.

Or maybe it's even worse. What if this volatility is enough to do what roller coaster riders fear at the scariest moments of the trip: to fling them off the tracks and into space?

After looking at all the causes and effects, I come down "at the other extreme" and just short of "maybe it's even worse." We're looking at something more than just a historical cycle, which can be scary enough, vacillating between periods of low and high volatility. And I think this "something more" will last a big longer than the three minutes of a ride on the Fury 325. Twenty years seems reasonable.

The good news, of course, is that the volatility in this Age of Volatility isn't likely to throw us and our lives off the track entirely. That means we do have a chance to do something to make it not just survivable and less scary but even profitable. But because we are looking at "something more" than the historical cycle and that it is likely to last for around twenty years—the period we commonly define as a generation—what evidence do we have to suggest a degree of volatility that is scarily above the norm but still short of a complete train wreck?

The easiest place to see this Age of Volatility at work and to gather evidence that it exists is the stock market. By no means is it the only or even the most important place where we can see volatility at work—just take a look at trends in everyday life in jobs, education, a global aging population, and climate change—but it is where volatility is most obvious and where we track it in the most detail. If you follow the financial markets at all or even if you just open your monthly statements for your 401(k) retirement plan, you know that stocks and bonds have been much more volatile than they used to be twenty or thirty years ago and that the volatility actually seems to be increasing. And, if you read even a bit of financial news, you know that Wall Street has focused a lot of time and energy recently on volatility and on inventing ways to profit from it—or at least to hedge against its worst damage.

It's not surprising that volatility has got Wall Street's attention. Just look at a brief chronology of crises that have sent volatility skyrocketing over the last two decades:

Asian Currency Crisis of 1997. Beginning with a speculative run on the Thai currency, the crises swept across Asia, sending financial markets plunging. The Thai market, for example, fell 75 percent.

Russian Ruble and Stock Market Collapse of 1998. In August 1998 the Russian stock and bond markets collapsed along with the ruble. With stocks down 65 percent, the stock market closed to trading.

The Dotcom Bust of 2000–2001. After hitting an intraday high of 5408.60 on March 10, 2000, the technology-heavy NASDAQ Composite index descended into a bear market that destroyed $5 trillion in stock market value over the next two years.

The Global Financial Crisis of 2008–2009. Initially limited to the US mortgage and housing markets, this crisis would eventually require the world's central banks to flood economies with cash to head off a global depression.

These were downside crises (for more details on this and other events and topics touched on throughout the book, see the Notes section at the end), but they are not the end of the story, as volatility isn't limited to the downside. How about the huge upside moves during this period?

In 1999 the dotcom bust had been preceded by a rally that took the NASDAQ Composite index up almost 100 percent in a year. And in 2009, once US stocks stopped plunging in the aftermath of the global financial crisis, they began a huge rally. The Standard & Poor's 500 stock index (S&P 500) climbed 213 percent from the postcrisis bottom at 676.53 on March 9, 2009, to 2117.69 on April 24, 2015.

These are examples of the kind of upward volatility that no one wants to miss.

But it is volatility nonetheless.

Big volatility events certainly aren't unprecedented in US financial history. On October 19, 1987, for example, the Dow Jones Industrial Average fell 508 points, a plunge of 22.61 percent in a day.

Nor is the occurrence of multiple big volatility events in a period of a decade or so unprecedented in US financial history. The historical record of the US stock market shows that volatility runs in cycles. Some periods have very low volatility, whereas others have extremely high volatility.

And right now, after a period—from 1981 to, say, 1997—of very low volatility, we are in a period of very high volatility, starting at 2008 and going to, well, whenever, with the years from 1999 to 2000 serving as the beginning of the transition.

This kind of volatility cycle certainly has its precedents. For example, from 1961 to 1981 volatility ran amuck, with bear market drops in the S&P 500 of 27 percent in 1961 to 1962, a 25.2 percent drop in 1966, and a 35.9 percent plunge in 1968 to 1970.

Now that's volatility.

And that volatility must have come as quite a shock because it was preceded by a period with an extraordinary absence of big-event volatility. From the end of World War II in 1945 to the technology bear of 1961–1962, US investors experienced just one big volatility event, which in fact didn't even quite qualify as a bear because it didn't tip the 20 percent threshold: from April 1956 to October 1957 the S&P 500 fell 19.4 percent.

As was the case with the 1961 to 1981 period of high volatility, the current period of volatility since 2008 was preceded by a very uneventful period of low volatility, even more uneventful than the period from 1945 to 1961. Once Federal Reserve Chairman Paul Volcker broke inflation in 1981 and the Reagan recovery began to take hold in 1983, US stocks moved steadily uphill until the short—two-month—stock market crash of August 25, 1987, through October 26, 1987. The next bump in the road on the way to the 1997 Asian currency crisis was another short three-month bear (21.1 percent decline), lasting from July 1990 to October 1990.

Except for that two-month crash and that three-month bear market, we're looking at a run from 1981 to 1997 without one volatility big event. And a US stock market, measured by the S&P 500 stock index, that gained 526 percent from 1982 to 1997.

The current period, however, represents a significant turn in the cycle. It's hard to put exact dates on the beginning and end of cycles like these. I see the low-volatility cycle running from 1981 to 1997. The Asian currency crisis, the dotcom bust, the Russian collapse, and the years leading up to the 2008 Lehman bankruptcy, which marked the turn from a US-centric mortgage crisis to a global financial crisis, strikes me as a transitional period. It's certainly characterized by two big volatility events, so I wouldn't argue too strenuously with anyone who wants to date the turn in the cycle to 1997 or 2000. But, to me, 1997 to 2000 constitutes a period when global central banks were moving toward the monetary policies that shaped the response to the 2008 crisis. In my reading of financial market history it was the Federal Reserve's intervention as a source of global liquidity in the Asian currency crisis that led to the hubris behind its attempt to repeal the business cycle in 1999. The Fed refused to restrict liquidity by enacting measures such as making it harder to borrow to buy stocks, a move that would have reduced the amount of cash available to buy financial assets in the face of an inflating asset bubble. By the time the 2008 crisis got really, really serious and global depression threatened economies across the world, the policies and mind-set that would release a flood of liquidity were in place. It's the attempt to cope with that vast addition of cash to the financial system and its consequences that provides the unifying causal foundation for the current high-volatility period.

It would be worth writing this book just to bring your attention to the cycles of high and low volatility in the stock market. Although investors do survive these cycles, the costs can be shockingly high. From January 1997 through the March 2009 post-financial-crisis bottom, the S&P 500 stock index gained a meager 1.14 percent. In other words, if you don't include dividends (and, thankfully, the S&P 500 stocks, as a group, does pay a dividend), the gain from US stocks during this period didn't even keep up with inflation. You can argue—and I will elsewhere in this book—that in a period of high volatility it would be smart to adopt strategies that might limit the downside and give you better-than-average returns for the downward part of the volatility cycle.

But in this book I propose an Age of Volatility that's something more, something different from these historical cycles of periods with lots of big volatility events in the stock market and periods with relatively few big volatility events.

Oddly enough, perhaps, the best evidence supporting that this is an Age of Volatility comes from the day-to-day moves—some spectacular, I grant you—in the stock market rather than from big volatility events such as those downward market moves of 20 percent or more that we label bear markets. Heightened volatility has become embedded in the stock market, and this pervasive volatility isn't limited just to those big moments like the technology crash of 2000 or the global financial crisis of 2008. It is embedded in the stock market on a monthly basis. You don't have to wait for a really big crisis to go for a roller coaster ride. To take just one example of many, in January 2014 the sky was falling. Again.

The US S&P 500 stock index had hit an all-time closing high of 1,848 on December 31 to cap a 2013 that had seen US stocks return 32 percent. We don't tend to think of market rallies as episodes of volatility, but they are, especially when the rally goes uphill this far and this quickly. Volatility isn't all on the downside. And in fact, the scariest volatility consists of rapid changes in direction from up to down.

Which is precisely what the US stock market proceeded to deliver.

After bobbing and weaving in early January—the index was still at 1,845 on January 22, 2014—US stocks decided to head for the canvas. By February 3 the S&P 500 was down 5.8 percent from its all-time high. And suddenly, after a 2013 when US markets never managed even a 5 percent drop, the financial press rediscovered the word "correction." CNBC, Yahoo Finance, *Forbes*, Bloomberg, and more all ran stories trumpeting the coming correction of 10 percent or more.

And the world's emerging markets could forget about the *coming* correction—they were already *in* a correction. The Brazilian stock market, for example, fell almost 15 percent from December 31 to February 3. You know it was serious because Wall Street had come up with a catchy name for the worst danger zones. Brazil, Turkey, South Africa, India, and Indonesia were the "Fragile Five"—those markets most likely to fall into chaos.

And then what happened?

The sky didn't fall.

US stocks recovered and, by the first week in March, were reaching new all-time highs. The S&P 500, for example, closed at 1,878 on March 7, 2014, wiping out the decline and tacking on another 1.6 percent from the December record high.

Those plunging "Fragile Five" markets? They recovered much of the early 2014 drop. Brazilian stocks, for example, climbed 9.5 percent from February 3 to February 27.

Did the rally then continue, with everyone living happily ever after? No, the porridge wasn't "just right," and stocks went back into decline: by March 14 the US S&P 500 gave back, again, all its gains for 2014. Brazilian stocks closed in on their February 3 low. Shanghai gave back much and Hong Kong all of their gains. Turkey managed to hold on to about half of its rally.

But what was truly remarkable about January through March of 2014 was how unremarkable this has become recently. Yes, in 2013 investors in US markets didn't experience this whiplash, but those markets were unusual among global markets. Investors in Brazil, China, Japan, Turkey, and others all rode markets where volatility was the rule and not the exception. Brazil, for instance, delivered not one but two bear markets, with a 39 percent drop from February 2012 to July 2013 and then a second bear of 20 percent from October 2013 to March 2014.

Go back a year or two, and it's clear that US markets haven't been totally exempt either. Join me for a brief tour of August 2011, in what had already been a volatile year by the time investors got to August:

- From April 29 through June 15 the US stock market, as tracked by the S&P 500 stock index, fell 7.3 percent.
- From June 15 to July 6 it climbed 5.8 percent. But the market was just getting warmed up.
- From July 6 to August 10 the S&P 500 fell 16.3 percent.
- Then from August 10 to August 15 it rallied to gain 7.4 percent.
- From August 15 to August 19 it fell 7.1 percent.
- Then it rallied again from August 19 to August 30, gaining 7.9 percent. The gods of volatility weren't done with 2011, though.
- From August 30 to October 3 the S&P 500 fell again, dropping 9.4 percent.
- Then, as you might expect by now, stocks rallied—big—climbing 22.1 percent from October 3 to October 26.
- Time for another drop after that, of course: the S&P 500 fell 6.8 percent from October 26 to November 25.
- The total net S&P 500 return for the year was a small but positive 2.1 percent.

Then, skip ahead to the early months of 2015, and you'll see this pattern of volatility continuing:

- Three times, January 6, 12, and 30, the S&P 500 fell, causing the index to be in the red for the year.
- And two times, on January 8 and 22, it rallied so strongly that stocks moved back into the black for the year.
- Contrast that with February, when, once the market rallied from the January 30 red ink, it didn't look back until it peaked on March 2 and began a month that looked just like January, with a move back into the red by March 11.

All the big stuff, the kind of big volatility events that gets investors' attention and draws the headlines, is taking place against a background of increased day-to-day little volatility.

To earn its claim to the title of Age of Volatility, this volatility can't be limited to the stock market. And it isn't. Even in just the past few years we've seen extraordinary volatility events in the currency markets and in the supposed ultra-safe market for US Treasuries. The Age of Volatility will include parts of the financial markets that we don't normally associate with volatility—or at least not with an extremely high degree of extremely short-term volatility.

Consider, for example, what happened in the currency markets on January 15, 2015. That morning the Swiss National Bank, the country's central bank, abandoned its three-year-old policy of capping the appreciation of the Swiss franc against the euro. That policy was costing the central bank billions because, to control the appreciation of the franc against the euro, it had to intervene in the markets to buy euros (supporting the price of that currency) and sell francs (depressing the price of that currency.)

The result of the bank's decision was massive losses in the currency markets as anyone short the Swiss franc took a bath on the jump. (Traders who go short something like Swiss francs borrow francs from another trader or institution at the current market price in the hope of repaying that borrowing in the future at a lower price. Those traders who lend Swiss francs to those shorts are hoping that the price of the franc will go up and that they will make a profit when those shorts repay their borrowings.) Bank currency desks were swamped with orders, and at least one electronic exchange halted trading. The big banks in the currency market—Deutsche Bank, Citi-group, UBS, and Barclays—stopped trading simply to try to figure out their net exposure to the move.

How wild did this market get? At one point in London the franc had climbed 41 percent against the euro. That was in a few hours within a single day.

Volatility reverberated from the currency market to hit every-thing from the housing market in Eastern Europe—because so many home owners in countries such as Hungary, Romania, and Poland had taken out low-rate mortgages priced in, you guessed it, Swiss francs—to the market for gold and gold mining stocks.

Another example comes from the Treasury market, which is nor-mally thought of, with good reason, as one of the most liquid, sta-ble, and low risk of all the world's financial markets. Historically you don't get moves in the price of Treasuries that even approach the price change on an average day in the stock market. But back on October 15, 2014, the Treasury market, the most liquid in the world, went through a one-day liquidity crisis that produced price move-ments so large that, statisticians say, they should happen only once every 1.6 billion years. (That may be an exaggeration, but you know what media hounds statisticians are.) That day the price of the ten-year Treasury, which is used to set the rates for housing mortgages and debt products, "soared." (Well, it "soared" in bond market terms.) The yield, which sinks as bond prices climb, plunged by 33 basis points (or 0.33 percentage points) to 1.86 percent before re-covering to settle at 2.13 percent. To understand how big that move was, don't compare it to the much bigger daily moves in stocks. Statistically, the bond market move was seven standard deviations away from a normal intraday move in the market for ten-year Trea-suries. (A standard deviation is a measure of how much the actual data differs from the expected projected data. A well-constructed political poll has a margin of error of about two standard devia-tions. What this measure tells us is that the Treasury market's actual results that day were about seven times less likely to have happened than our historical data would have predicted. That's a very unlikely outcome. It wouldn't normally be seen in the data in a year or a decade or a hundred years. On a graph of the data it would be an extremely unlikely data point—but one that could still occur sometime before the sun went nova.) As I noted above, a move of that kind could happen, statistics say, once every 1.6 billion years.

The infrastructure of the market was stunned. The human infrastructure of bond traders and dealers sat back to watch. The machine infrastructure of electronic pricing platforms came to a halt. Orders were canceled, and across the $12.4 trillion market, liquidity dried up.

Why? In retrospect some of the reasons for what happened on October 15 are pretty clear. In September, according to the US Commodities Futures Trading Commission, hedge funds had established a record net short position in interest rate futures. But between the end of September and the week ending October 21, traders fled that position.

It seems likely—or at least possible—that changes in financial regulations designed to make the financial system safer had made it less attractive for the big banks that once dominated trading in Treasuries to make markets in Treasuries. In retrospect it certainly looks like, in the face of this volatility, big dealers and market makers stepped back from the market that day.

Another possible explanation is that the rise of electronic trading has led to the exit of more experienced traders, from dealers to hedge funds and asset managers. That has left the big trading desks at the big banks in less experienced hands that might have shied away from the volatility on October 15.

And there's the possibility that the rise in electronic trading has moved an increasing part of the market's volume from primary Treasury dealers, who underwrote Treasury offerings and kept inventories of Treasuries, to broker dealers and high-frequency traders who don't keep inventories and are quick to abandon any market when trading trends turn against them. The machines that run big electronic platforms such as NASDAQ's eSpeed and ICAP's BrokerTec aren't market makers; they're market matchers of buyers and sellers. When there's a big mismatch between buyers and sells, as there was during a good part of October 15, the machines don't provide liquidity to the market. In fact, the easiest way for these machines' operators to cope with that trading imbalance is to simply turn off the machines.

If some or all of these explanations are correct, then we can expect other days of increased volatility on this historically least volatile of markets because increased volatility has now been built into
the structure of the Treasury market.

That's a sobering prospect as the Federal Reserve begins to reverse the falling interest rates of the last twenty years and starts to
raise rates so as to try to shrink its $4 trillion-plus balance sheet back
to something like the preglobal financial crisis $750 billion in order
to have some ammunition in hand for the next crisis. The more volatility there is in the Treasury market, however, the greater chance
that something the Fed does will turn out to be a big—not just a
small—mistake.

This degree of volatility is enough to earn this period the title of
the Age of Financial Volatility, but this spike in volatility isn't limited to the world's financial markets. Partly that's because the root
cause of much of the financial markets' volatility—the huge amounts
of cheap money from the world's central banks that have flooded
markets and economies—has real-world economic effects: just ask
anyone who owns a home or bought or sold a house during the
global financial crisis. But another big part of that heightened volatility is the way that real-world trends combine with this tide of central bank money to produce a big increase in real-world volatility.

- Demographic trends that point toward a rapidly aging world,
  for example, have placed huge demands on global financial
  markets that are already stretched from coping with the big
  debts that were run up to "fix" the Great Recession.
- An aging population, continued globalization of the world's
  economy, and disruptive Internet technologies have made the
  payoff from a college education less certain and have added to
  the volatility of career patterns.
- A long-overdue bill for environmental "externalities" looks
  likely to be presented for payment in national economies such
  as China and Indonesia and in the global economy as a whole.
- The coming Age of Volatility looks like it will stretch to include
  the housing market and the job market and the educational
  market and . . .

Well, you get the idea. Volatility won't be something we can neatly limit to the financial markets. We know, for example, that the global financial crisis had its roots in the US subprime mortgage crisis. But we also know that outside the financial markets, regular, everyday home owners saw huge losses in the value of their homes. In the twelve months that ended in February 2008, for instance, we know that housing prices fell 22.8 percent in Las Vegas, 21.7 percent in Miami, and 20.8 percent in Phoenix. And that was just the beginning of the bloodbath. By the end of March 2009 housing prices in the ten Las Vegas ZIP codes had plunged 60 percent from March 2008.

That—and the subsequent recovery in real estate prices—is real-life volatility.

Wall Street is guaranteed to come up with a raft of new products for coping with this volatility. But based on its record—Wall Street invented portfolio insurance in time to contribute to the 1987 crash, and derivatives powered the global financial crisis of 2008—I don't think anyone should count on Wall Street to fix financial volatility.

And we're looking at a period of intense volatility in our everyday lives that we'll all need to figure out how to manage as best we can. In many ways managing this real-life volatility is tougher than that faced by Wall Street professionals. Like passengers on Japan's Takabisha roller coaster—famous for its 121-degree drop—Wall Street professionals can simply decide to get off when the ride gets too scary. They can move to cash, for example. But that's not possible in the everyday economy. There's simply no way to call a time-out or to wait for the next car or to pass on the ride entirely if it gets too thrilling. You and I, in our daily lives, have to understand this Age of Volatility in real time and then decide how best to cope with it. The decisions in this realm are also frequently once-in-a-lifetime choices, so getting it at least sort of right is important.

Laying out the reasons for seeing the decade or two ahead as a period of high volatility in the financial markets is part of what this book is about. I cover this in Part I.

I've got two other goals in mind for this book as well.

Part II moves away from the focus on the financial markets to include the causes and effects of real-life volatility. One goal here is to keep this Age of Volatility in context. This isn't the first period of high volatility people have ever faced, and, as difficult and scary as it may be, it isn't the end of the world. Volatility also includes, as part of its promise of change, upside volatility, the possibility of profit, gains, and improvement. People did more than just survive the high volatility years of 1961 to 1981; they also raised families, bought houses, and saved for retirement. The world seemed disconcertingly different, sometimes from day to day, but it wasn't uniformly worse.

In fact, despite that volatility, many people in the United States saw their lives get quite clearly better. They could do things like travel to what were then exotic places, such as Paris, thus realizing what had only been a dream for their parents. Parents that had, maybe, finished high school were now sending their kids to college.

Although life didn't get better for everyone in the United States, and it didn't get better to the same degree for everyone, people who made reasonably intelligent decisions or were reasonably lucky did better than okay. And that's likely to still be the case, even if the period we're living through now turns out to be even more volatile than those twenty years. The purpose of Part II, then, is to provide the perspective needed to increase your chances of making the current period of extreme volatility turn out better than just all right for you. You will be respectful but not scared of market volatility. And if you understand the characteristic volatility of this period and where it comes from, you won't be quite so likely to react in exactly the wrong way. And you won't be quite so dependent on luck to do better than okay.

To help you get that necessary perspective, though, my explanation won't stick to just the narrow world of market volatility. If you lived through any part of 1961 to 1981, you know that volatility wasn't limited to bear markets in stocks. This was a time when the United States moved to a suburban way of life. When the personal computer started to transform work. When the rise of jet travel and the completion of the Interstate Highway System changed how fast we could get to places and where we could go. When the children of GI Bill soldiers began to believe that everyone was supposed to go to college.

Because it was a period of rising general prosperity, you did better than okay if you just avoided bad luck. But figuring out how to avoid bad luck and how to take control of your life by making "reasonably intelligent" decisions was a whole lot easier if you understood the changes going on with what we call "life in general." As someone born in 1950 and a child of the 1961–1981 volatility, I don't know if my parents made a conscious investment strategy based on an understanding of the way suburban growth made buying semirural land in New Jersey a smart move. (I'm from Eastern European peasant stock on both sides that has always thought buying land and planting fruit trees on it was an absolute good.) I am pretty sure that they never had a late-night talk about why changes in the nature of the global economy made saving to send their two sons to college an "appropriate adaptation to the changing global labor market." I also know that the Edison, New Jersey, public school system did decide that every kid—every kid in the academic track, that is—should start a foreign language in seventh grade and that my parents thought this was a smart idea, given how the world was trending. I do wish someone had thought enough about the way the world was trending to convince me to take something other than German. My attempt to teach myself Russian lasted about three weeks. But that's another story and an awful lot of foresight to ask for from parents and teachers.

No one can get right all the trends that make up the warp and woof of the volatility of any period. And I think a life lived with a constant worry that you might miss the main chance is likely to be rather narrow and anxious. But some degree of understanding of the trends driving the volatility of a period will make it easier to do better than okay. And that understanding might even make a high-volatility period less anxiety ridden and more—dare I say it—fun.

So Part II will also lay out ten trends that I see as the major sources of the volatility of our present period. They won't capture all of the sources of the current volatility, but they do capture the major reasons to think that we're living through a period of high volatility that isn't limited to the financial markets. And these ten trends add up to a unified picture that begins to suggest how individual trends can reinforce each other to produce more volatility than they otherwise might independently.

Part III will discuss investing solutions based on my thirty years observing Wall Street, picking stocks and mutual funds, and designing portfolios. I'll suggest strategies with concrete suggestions for how to implement them to profit from volatility and hedge against it. Because we can't jump off the roller coaster—at least I don't recommend it—we might as well see if we can enjoy it, even if we are afraid of heights.

PART I

VOLATILITY IN THE DECADES AHEAD

Chapter 2

The Volatility of Volatility

WHAT DO WE REALLY know about volatility? Quite a bit, though not as much as you might think.

The financial markets have developed myriad tools for measuring the volatility of the moment and, then, comparing it to historical averages in order to design products and strategies for protecting against or profiting from volatility.

And in the last few years neuroscientists have traced some of the chemical pathways that the brain uses to cope with volatility—as well as some of the behavioral consequences of those chemical pathways.

However, our understanding of the causes and consequences of the volatility of volatility are surprisingly limited, even in the financial markets. Most approaches to volatility treat it as if volatility were static and doesn't itself change over time. Even on Wall Street, which tracks volatility obsessively so that it can build (and sell) products to protect against or profit from volatility, there are major holes in our understanding of volatility and the volatility of volatility. In the everyday economy our ability to understand, track, and manage volatility and the way the volatility of volatility changes over time is even more rudimentary.

To show you some of the limits of Wall Street's approach to volatility, let me start with the most widely followed measures of stock market volatility, the Chicago Board Options Exchange Volatility Index, or VIX. The VIX, sometimes known as the "fear index," tracks the price of options on the Standard and Poor's 500 stock index. As the price that traders are willing to pay for these options rises—in order to hedge and reduce the risk of buying the index—so does the VIX. Options on the VIX allow you to buy or sell the index at a price fixed in the present. That gives the buyer of the option the chance to profit when the index rises above that fixed price or when it falls below that price. The present cost of buying that option rises or falls as traders decide they need more or less protection from future changes in price. And the VIX tracks the rise and fall of the cost of those options. Thus, it measures how much "fear" is in the market. When fear recedes, the price of these options falls, for example, then the VIX drops as well.

The VIX is one of the most followed market indexes. And it is certainly the most followed volatility index. You can buy exchange traded funds (ETFs) that track the VIX to the upside (they go up when market fear, as measured by the VIX, climbs), and you can buy inverse VIX ETFs that rise when the VIX falls. You can even leverage these bets using a 2X ETF, which is designed to rise by twice as much as the underlying index.

But what is clear from recent experience is that a static measure of volatility, one that doesn't take into account shifts in the volatility of volatility, isn't an adequate tool. For example, during most of 2014 absolute market volatility, as measured VIX, was well below the historic average. Even as the market climbed higher and higher, absolute volatility stayed low, signaling to investors that it was safe to stay on board the rally. On average in 2014 the VIX was a good 25 percent—or more—below the average of 20.09 for the index since its inception in 1990. (The numbers on the VIX are a way of expressing the price of S&P options. They don't represent units of anything. A trader knows from the index when the fear of volatility is high and when it is lower.) There were days in 2014 when the VIX was just 11 or so—far below the 20.09 historical average.

But that average was deceptive. What investors saw in the last half of 2014 were huge moves in the VIX that didn't take the index above the historic average but instead represented 40 to 80 percent moves from top to bottom. For example, the VIX was at 26.25 on October 15 when the market was in retreat and Wall Street had started to talk about a correction of 10 percent or more. But by December 5 the VIX was down to 11.82—a drop of 55 percent.

And then markets returned to relative turmoil again when oil prices plunged and there was a rout in the emerging markets. That moved the VIX in the other direction. And even more quickly.

From that low of 11.82 on December 5 to the December 16 reading of 20.86, the VIX moved a huge 76 percent.

On an absolute basis, volatility as measured by the VIX was still historically low. Looking at the volatility of volatility, however, this calm, complacent market was extraordinarily volatile.

What's going on? What explains the discrepancy between low absolute volatility and high volatility of volatility?

The guesses now—and here we're at the cutting edge of current research in financial market volatility—is that something has changed in the structure of the markets and the nature of trading. One possibility, one that makes sense to me, is that the low absolute readings on the VIX are a result of the easy-money policies of the Federal Reserve and other central banks—that is, the overall market, at its core, believes that the central bank cash will flood into any specific market that experiences a dangerous downturn. But this same high level of cash has led to a market that lacks conviction in any particular asset class and where huge amounts of portfolio money are in constant search of the next move, whether higher or lower.

This last observation might be testable by looking at the changes in volatility in the VIX in relation to indexes that track the volatility of other markets and other asset classes. It also leads to the idea of an interlocking landscape of volatilities—something that I'll explain later in this book. Work on describing that volatility geography is still in its early stages.

An added reason to put credence in this explanation is that it connects with the rise of ETFs that make it easy to move from buying the euro to selling the euro, from buying commodities to selling commodities, from buying Treasuries to selling Treasuries, all with a single trade. It makes sense to me that the added ease of trading short-term volatility would, of course, lead to more short-term volatility. (An ETF, an exchange traded fund, represents a basket of some underlying asset—stocks, bonds, a commodity such as oil, or options on an index—that can be bought or sold like a mutual fund but with the crucial difference that prices on an ETF change minute-to-minute [mutual funds price only at the end of the trading day] and that ETFs can be bought and sold at any time during the trading day at those changing prices [trades of mutual funds settle only once a day].)

Another very interesting and promising possible explanation is that changes in volatility actually cause changes in the way the brain functions. A period of high big-event volatility, like the global financial crisis and follow-on big interventions from the world's central banks, has changed brain chemistry in ways that lead Wall Street traders to seek out volatility and discount its dangers.

Work on this possibility is very thoroughly laid out in John Coates's 2012 book *The Hour Between Dog and Wolf: How Risk Taking Transforms Us, Body and Mind*. Coates, a former trader of derivatives for Goldman Sachs and manager of a trading desk for Deutsche Bank, is now a research fellow in neuroscience and finance at the University of Cambridge. In his book he describes our reaction to volatility in the financial markets, stating,

> Our defense reactions were designed to switch on in an emergency and then switch off after a matter of minutes or hours, or a few days at the most. But an above-average win or loss in the markets, or an ongoing series of wins and losses, can change us, Jekyll-and-Hyde–like, beyond all recognition. On a winning streak we can become euphoric, and our appetite for risk expands so much that we turn manic, foolhardy and puffed up with self-importance. On a losing streak we struggle with fear, reliving the bad moments over and over, such that stress hormones linger in our brains, promising a pathological risk-aversion, even depression, and circulate in our blood, contributing to recurrent viral infections, high blood pressure, abdominal fat build-up and gastric ulcers.

Volatility kicks off hormonal responses in the brain, Coates writes. In preparation for volatility, traders' metabolism speeds up and breathing accelerates. The release of multiple steroid hormones creates a surge of energy that increases traders' confidence and appetite for risk. Another steroid hormone, cortisol, travels to the brain, where it stimulates the release of dopamine. Together, corti-sol and dopamine deliver an addictive rush down the pleasure cir-cuits of the brain.

Cortisol also plays a key role in creating risk aversion. In an emer-gency our initial response is governed by adrenaline, a fast-acting, quickly dissipating hormone. Cortisol is the longer-lasting part of the body's response to danger, commanding the body to "Use glu-cose now" to respond to the threat. Its effects can last for hours, and when the emergency is over, the body's shift into overdrive in re-sponse to cortisol's commands can leave us feeling depleted and anxious.

Coates posits that the people who do well at high-stress trading desks are those most responsive to this short-term chemical ramp. They are able to muster reserves of energy by speeding up their me-tabolism at moments of market volatility, and they are also most likely to experience these trading emergencies as moments of plea-surable stress rather than moments of fear and anxiety.

The problem comes when this system, designed to help us escape the occasional charging lion, is forced into an environment of con-stant stress, where the body's chemical system for responding to emergencies is forced to operate without downtime. What happens then, Coates's brain research says, is that the brain habituates itself to the normal hormonal level of release. At that point two things can happen—and, indeed, probably both happen simultaneously. First, the brain's circuits can be sensitized to the "threat" so that lower levels of risk are required to set the hormonal system into motion. Second, the body, having become addicted to the pleasures of the cortisol-dopamine cocktail but also having become habituated to this drug, starts to require a higher level of volatility to push more of these hormones into the body.

Even this very brief summary of Coates's work has strong impli-cations for life in an Age of Volatility. For one thing, it suggests that part of what fuels financial bubbles is traders' chemical reaction, which can be summed up as "bubbles are fun." The earlier stages of bubbles, where big risks pay off big, make it chemically harder for traders to call it quits. Second, this description of the body's emer-gency response system argues that risk taking begets not only more risk taking but also bigger risk taking. One of Coates's research projects examined the chemical basis of the winner effect. In a fight between animals the winner emerges with a higher testosterone level. That then resets the animal's testosterone level so that it enters the next challenge already at a testosterone advantage. (Although that testosterone reset may help a baboon dominate a group, for traders, Coates's research shows, it leads to increased risk taking without an improvement in trading skill.) Third, the three factors that Coates identifies as most likely to lead to the long-term production of large quantities of cortisol—and, thus, risk avoidance behavior designed to minimize stress—include novelty, uncertainty, and uncontrollability. Those are factors that I'd closely connect with periods of increased volatility of volatility. "What we found was that their [traders] cortisol levels rose substantially with the volatility of the market, demonstrating that their cortisol did indeed increase with uncertainty. In fact, so sensitive were traders' cortisol levels to volatility that they displayed a remarkably tight relationship with prices of derivatives, the securities used to hedge volatility, a finding that raises the intriguing possibility that stress hormones form the physiological foundation of the derivatives market."

This approach to volatility in the financial markets is an impressive beginning, even if it is just a beginning. No, we don't have a measure of the volatility of volatility (although we do have the VVIX index, which measures the expected volatility of the 30-day forward price of the VIX)—or an explanation of why volatility changes. But we do have an index that measures volatility, a historical record of volatility built on this index, and a pragmatic understanding of the need to move beyond the static picture of volatility presented by the index to a view that includes the volatility of volatility. We have a theory of brain chemistry that might provide an explanation for the causes of the volatility of volatility. And we have an impressive toolbox for protecting against and profiting from volatility.

When we turn to the volatility of everyday life, we're moving to the realm of anecdote and impression. We say trends are "powerful" or "more powerful than," but we don't have much ability to quantify what that might mean. All too often in the realm of everyday life we find ourselves talking about the possible causes of volatility and then waving our hands to signify the vagueness of our understanding of the next step when we look at how these causes might actually generate volatility and how much and when.

But that isn't to say that we don't know anything about the volatility of everyday life. In fact, the volatility of everyday life supplies examples for important volatility concepts such as mooring and unmooring around benchmarks. And in everyday life we have much longer historical data sequences than we do for the financial markets. Combining anecdotes from everyday life with volatility principles and long historical data sequences gives us a very different approach to volatility but one with its own observational and explanatory power.

One of the conclusions that these observations and explanations point us toward is that the current period in everyday life is just as volatile as this period in the financial markets.

Think about the consequences of that. Financial market volatility and everyday life volatility are unlikely to operate in isolation. More likely they operate in combination with the effects of volatility in one system feeding into volatility in the other realm. If this is an Age of Volatility, as I believe it is, it's because that combination results in a volatility math that adds 1+1 and comes up with 3.

So let's take a look at what we know about the volatility of everyday life and some ways to measure it.

Chapter 3

The Volatility of Everyday Life

TO UNDERSTAND HOW WE can measure the volatility of everyday life and the kind of explanations that measuring the volatility of everyday life produces, I need to introduce you to my grandmother.

My grandmother was born in 1892. During the last years of her life I used to sit with her and ask about growing up on New York's Lower East Side in the early years of the twentieth century. To me, a suburban New Jersey kid, life as the daughter of recent Polish immigrants living in a tenement on Delancey Street was almost inconceivable. That was especially so because things I took for granted barely existed for her. As a young girl, my grandmother wouldn't have had a phone (invented in 1876) in her apartment or much acquaintance with electric lights (the first electric power station in New York City opened in 1882).

My grandmother rode a trolley to work in a factory, where she embroidered pillowcases, and when she and my grandfather moved out to New Jersey in the early 1920s, a local farmer picked up their friends on winter weekends in a horse-drawn sleigh.

Radio. Television. Computers. The Internet. My grandmother never took an airplane ride. I don't know whether they owned one of Henry Ford's Model Ts (Ford founded his car company eleven years after my grandmother was born), but I know they owned a Model A. I've seen the photos of my very proud grandparents standing with their car in front of the house they built in 1923.

If there was anyone entitled to feel she had lived through volatile times, it was my grandmother.

But her view of volatility wasn't what you might expect. The massive changes in her life—phones, electric lights, the car, the airplane, TV—my grandmother just saw as progress. That's how things were. Amazing stuff appeared every year. And every year life got better: the electric can opener (invented 1956) showed up on the kitchen counter, and a portable TV in her room let her watch her beloved Lawrence Welk without eye rolls from her grandchildren.

Amazing progress was my grandmother's idea of normal.

If you wanted to hear the tension rise in my grandmother's voice, you didn't talk to her about these things or the move to the suburbs— another expected trend, at least in retrospect. You wouldn't even hear it when she talked about World War II. (Her only child was a girl, so she encountered no draft dangers.)

My grandmother reserved her retrospective fear for the Great Depression. In 1933 she and my grandfather almost lost their house because my grandfather was out of work. They were rescued by friends who paid their $3,000 mortgage. That was the volatility my grandmother remembered, and years later, it still scared her. The emotions from that volatility were a key reason neither she nor my parents ever carried any debt. This was risk avoidance on a bedrock level. I still remember the arguments between my parents when my dad applied for a charge card at Sears (riding lawnmowers were my dad's major vice—we owned three) and the trepidation with which my mother applied for a gasoline credit card before we drove across country for a family vacation when I was fifteen.

I can see why it looks as though financial market volatility and real-life volatility are speaking past each other. The first seems dominated by historical data series and statistical measures such as the VIX, whereas the second seems to rely on narrative history and psychological anecdote. But the two perspectives on volatility actually form a surprisingly complementary and coherent way to look at volatility. For example, both make the point that the most intense sense of volatility comes at those moments of transition between rates of volatility that challenge the benchmarks we use to anchor our understanding of the world.

Let me use two volatility constructs, "benchmarking" and "unmooring," to show how our understanding of volatility in the financial markets and in everyday life share some fundamental underpinnings.

Out of their experience of the past, investors, specifically, as well as people who aren't wearing their financial market hats, create mental benchmarks that then serve as expectations for the future. (I'll have a longer discussion of benchmarking in the current period in my next chapter.) For example, the *Money 101* guide to gaining control of your financial life was a pretty good guide to the conventional wisdom for the low-volatility 1980s and 1990s. It was put together by *Money* magazine in 2011 and starts off by stating as incontestable fact that in the long run, investing in US stocks will return on average 10 percent a year and that bonds will return 5 percent a year.

That was indeed the conventional wisdom at the time, even after the bear market events of 2000 and 2008, and these numbers benchmarked expectations about future returns.

But where do these numbers come from? They are derived from the long-term historical record for a big chunk of market history. From 1926 to 2005 the average annual return (price appreciation and dividends) from large company US stocks (essentially the US S&P 500 stock index) was 10.4 percent, according to Ibbotson Associates. The return on long-term US government bonds (essentially US Treasuries with maturities of ten years or longer) was an annual average of 5.3 percent. Inflation averaged 3 percent during this period, so the real returns—that is, the return after subtracting inflation—on stocks and US government bonds were a very attractive 7.4 percent and 2.3 percent, respectively.

But these long-term benchmarks simply haven't held up very well since the end of that 1926 to 2005 period. As of the end of March 2014 the average annual return for the S&P 500 was 7.4 percent over the last ten years. A swing from 10.4 to 7.4 percent is meaningful. That's roughly 30 percent less a year on my stock investments for each of ten years. Go out fifteen years—back to March 2000 or almost the exact peak of the dot-com market—and the average annual return drops to 4.3 percent.

Whoa! That's lower than the benchmark return on long-term US Treasuries from 1926 to 2005. (And you thought the benchmarks said stocks were supposed to provide higher returns than bonds to offset their higher risk!)

But before you throw out the benchmarks with the bath water, please note that the average annual return for the S&P 500 over the last five years—which roughly corresponds to the bottom after the global financial crisis—is 19.8 percent. That's almost twice the long-term benchmark for stocks.

It's not only investors and financial markets that have benchmarks. Think back to my brief overview of my own family history—or think about your own. My parents, children of the Great Depression, derived a set of benchmarks about the riskiness of debt of any kind from their own parents' experience of the economy of that period. They didn't trust credit cards, the stock market, or mutual funds; the most arcane, newfangled financial innovation they ever tried were certificates of deposit and the US Treasury's Treasury Direct program for buying US government bonds.

I'd like to tease out a couple of key points from these two examples. First, benchmarks are tenacious. Investment advisers and guides used the old 10.4 percent figure for the average annual return on stocks for years after actual market performance showed that that figure was no longer a valid benchmark. Just as my parents refused to go into debt by using a credit card even though they lived in a house with a completely paid up mortgage.

Second, what succeeds a period of stable benchmarks is a period of unmooring, as actual observed volatility gradually erodes the consensus belief in the existing benchmark. But another stable benchmark doesn't immediately succeed the previous period of a stable benchmark; instead, we get a period when the most appropriate reaction might be to throw up your hands and yell, "Who knows?!"

In the relatively short time span from the *Money* guide in 2011 to March 2014, we've gone from a belief in a 10.4 percent benchmark

(1926–2005) for an investor in US stocks, to a 7.4 percent bench-mark (2005–2014), to an actual 4.3 percent (2000 to 2014) *and* an actual 19.8 percent (2009–2014).

What return can an investor in stocks expect? You can imagine the mental chaos.

In our attitudes toward debt in the same short period we've gone through the "nothing down" approach to real estate, to the cash is king, to the tentative reintroduction of subprime mortgage debt in the car and student loan markets.

And, importantly, the chaos isn't simply mental. We make deci-sions based on those benchmarks. In the language of behavioral fi-nance those benchmarks anchor our expectations for the future. So we put aside money for retirement based on a belief in 10.4 percent or 7.4 percent or 4.3 percent or 19.8 percent average annual returns. We not only decide to put different gross amounts away depending on whether we're expecting 4.3 percent or 19.8 percent returns; we also divide our money into different asset classes depending on those benchmarks. For example, an investor who now benchmarks a 4.3 percent annual return from US stocks but who still bench-marks the old 5 percent annual return on bonds would shift money into bonds. Contrast that with an investor who benchmarked re-turns on stocks at 19.8 percent.

The interplay of benchmarks and anchors and their ability to change behavior isn't limited to financial markets. Take, for exam-ple, where you might think about buying a house (assuming that appreciation in what is the largest financial asset for most families enters into your thinking) or the company or location you might target to look for a job. Once upon a time the benchmarks showed that the fastest growth in the United States was taking place in sub-urbs and that the most attractive job markets were in what the US Census Bureau calls "micropolitan statistical areas," population centers with an "urban" core of fewer than fifty thousand people. The "attractiveness" of suburbs is a long-term "fact" of thinking in the United States that dates back to the post–World War II housing boom, which was fueled by cheap government loans to the families of returning soldiers. And the "attractiveness" of small towns dates back even further, interrupted as it has been from time to time by voices such as Sinclair Lewis in *Main Street* (1920).

But new census data released in March 2014 from the period of July 1, 2012, to July 1, 2013, argues that our everyday anchors for thinking about the future of real estate need serious revision. In that July 2012 to July 2013 period almost all of the country's population growth took place in metropolitan areas—and most of that took place in areas clustered around the country's ten largest cities. In that year the number of people living in metropolitan areas climbed by 2.3 million, whereas the population in micropolitan statistical areas grew by just eight thousand people. (Population in rural areas dropped by thirty-five thousand, although I think that's an anchor that most of us expected.)

If you're like me, you're used to thinking that big cities are slowly losing population to the suburbs and smaller cities. For decades that's been true, so no wonder I believe it. For example, New York City, where I live, has lost population in a trend that stretches back to the middle of the twentieth century.

But for the three years, ending in July 2013, the city has gained people. With more foreigners moving to New York and with fewer New Yorkers moving to other states, in the twelve months prior to July 2013, the city added sixty-one thousand people, and the city's population moved above 8.4 million for the first time ever, with estimates saying that the city has grown by 2.8 percent since 2010. This growth in population was true in every one of New York's five boroughs, from wealthy Manhattan, to culturally hot Brooklyn, to the traditional laggard, the Bronx.

It's going to take me a while to get my head wrapped around that one. The Bronx adding population? I grew up in the era of mass demolition of whole neighborhoods in the Bronx, of every politician who wanted to prove "they cared" touring devastated neighborhoods, of endless stories about businesses closing in the borough, of the city papering over the windows of abandoned buildings with pictures of lace curtains and flowering planters.

All that was true. Which is why the benchmark belief is so strong in my head. But it's not true now.

And things have changed not just in New York. About one-third of the population growth in the United States from July 2012 to July 2013 came in just ten large metropolitan areas. That's extraordinary given that up until about 2005 the common belief was that big cities were losing population, and suburbs, small cities, and ex-urban areas were growing. Talk about volatility: the fastest-growing metropolitan areas over this twelve-month period have been tiny places such as Houston, New York, Dallas–Fort Worth, Los Angeles, and Washington, DC. The young and creative, the retired and wealthy, the hip and the want-to-be-hip, the "we'll always have Paris" crowd are all thinking, *Hey, maybe I'd rather live in Brooklyn or Manhattan than in the suburbs or the smaller cities that traditionally top the lists of ten best places to live now.*

But I'd point out here that the degree of volatility in our benchmarking and our anchoring—the change in the belief structures that guide how we make decisions—is actually greater than the volatility of the underlying numbers. The change in benchmark and anchor to "New York added population" from "New York has been losing population" is actually much bigger and more powerfully disruptive than the volatility in the trend that says New York added sixty-one thousand people over twelve months that ended in July 2013.

The volatility of the trend is itself rather gentle, stretched as it is over a period of time. The degree of volatility in the change in benchmarks and anchors is—or at least can be—relatively jarring. At its most jarring it's like waking up in a world that is suddenly unrecognizable to you.

Our appreciation of volatility and our reaction to it has a major subjective component. I certainly wouldn't go so far as to say that if volatility falls in the forest and no one hears it, then it hasn't happened, but the effect of real-world volatility is certainly amplified by the reactions of the observer who perceives it—or doesn't—and by the delays and unjustified leaps of logic she may add. I grew up outside Plainfield, New Jersey, in the 1950s and 1960s in what was, at the beginning of that period, a semirural area called Edison Township. In the 1960s, if you were paying attention, you could see that Plainfield was in decline. A couple of big stores had moved from Front Street to Route 22 or a mall. And you could see the relative rise of the suburban areas, like Edison, that ringed the older railroad-centric city. (My grandparents, in fact, had moved in 1923 to what would become Edison because the Jersey Central stopped in Plainfield, making it easy for their friends to make the weekend trip from the Eastern European enclaves on Manhattan's Lower East Side.)

But I didn't really become aware of Plainfield's decline until the racial riots of 1964 and 1967. I remember my shock when my Dad told me that he didn't know if he'd be able to get to work because his usual twelve-mile drive from Edison to Manville passed through parts of Plainfield that had erupted in violence. And I remember suddenly wondering whether it would be safe to go to the Plainfield public library. It was my home away from home, as Edison didn't have anything to match the Plainfield library, with its roots in the early-twentieth-century philanthropy of Andrew Carnegie. The Plainfield library was only blocks from areas of the city where fires raged. Within a few years after the riots you couldn't help but notice that Plainfield wasn't just in decline; the city had gone into freefall, and blocks of the Front Street business district had been turned into a giant parking lot.

On the other side of the volatility equation, it didn't really dawn on me that Edison was rising—rapidly—as Plainfield fell until I read a story my parents sent me about the 1990 census that listed Edison as the fifth-largest municipality in New Jersey. (Plainfield had tumbled to thirty-fifth.) This place where my grandparents had moved to because land was cheap would soon be ranked the twenty-eighth most livable small city in the United States by *Money* magazine (and number two in New Jersey). In 2009 *U.S. News and World Report* ranked the township one of the ten best places in the country to grow up. The public recognition of the changes in Edison actually sped up the pace of change in the township. The 2010 census found that 43 percent of the township's population was Asian, up from 29 percent in the 2000 census. When I was growing up, my Jewish friend Paul Pitel had been exotic to me: I hadn't had a Jewish friend until sixth grade. Later waves were very different. In the years when I visited Edison before my father died in 2008 it took me a while to realize that the doctors and dentists who had opened offices on every corner with names like Pitel, Patel, Pattel were all Indian. It's now way easier to get a good *biryani* in Edison than a good bagel. And who knows how far my parents would have to drive these days to get a good Polish kielbasa!

Because of that subjective element that we bring to our perception of volatility, our reaction to volatility depends on how much we're forced to pay attention to change, how available systems are to measure change, and then how much we are forced to pay attention to those available measurement systems.

Financial market volatility is a rather simple case. Because so much hinges on it—gains and losses in real money—Wall Street pays obsessive attention to it and devotes considerable time and money to track it. And we spend a lot of time and attention on financial volatility, even if we're not Wall Street pros. Modern financial planning is built on benchmarks that themselves are built around tracking volatility. Talk to your financial planner, and you'll wind up in a conversation about asset allocation and expected rates of return for stocks and bonds. Peruse the business section of your paper or any consumer financial website, and you can't escape stories about financial and economic change—inflation is going up or down, the Federal Reserve is raising or lowering interest rates, bonds are a good investment because interest rates are going down or a terrible investment because rates are going up, or stocks will/won't match their historical rates of return. Because we track these changes so obsessively, our sense of volatility in the financial markets and the related parts of the economy is high.

One effect of that, I'd argue, is that in the investment world we accept volatility as a part of the environment. It's the way things are and nothing special—most of the time. We don't react to this day-to-day volatility with shock or surprise. We are, to a degree, desensitized to volatility in this realm because we pay so much attention to it and track it so closely.

Our attention to everyday volatility, however, is all over the charts. Most of the time we don't pay any attention to it, not because we're desensitized but simply because it doesn't register. Except when something happens that forces us to pay attention.

For example, trends in real estate rank in most periods as low in subjective volatility because most of the time we don't track the price of our house or the direction of the real estate market very closely. We might notice if our local government changes its valuation of our house and we have to pay or appeal a tax increase. We certainly will notice if we refinance our mortgage or take out a loan against our house for college or some other big expense. But those are low-frequency events.

But when a seldom-tracked measure of volatility suddenly starts to get tracked, our subjective sense of volatility rises. This, of course, leads more people to act on their new sense of increased volatility. That, in turn, puts upward pressure on objective volatility. The subprime mortgage crisis that became the real estate crisis that became the global financial crisis is an excellent example of this. Suddenly every news outlet in every community experiencing a meltdown in real estate prices began reporting measures such as the Case Shiller Index of housing prices. Few home owners had even heard of the Case Shiller Index even though the index has been around, in one form or the other, since the 1980s. But now, even though this index gets reported with a substantial lag and covers only twenty cities, if you are—or were—a home owner in a deeply hit market such as Las Vegas or Florida during the US subprime mortgage bust, you suddenly feel that the moves in this index are—or were—important to you.

This change in the importance of measures of housing price volatility wasn't limited to individual home owners either. The Federal Reserve is a longtime student of housing prices and housing price volatility. But because the Federal Reserve had decided to stimulate the economy by pushing up housing demand and housing prices, economists in and outside the Fed moved housing market volatility higher up on their list of indicators to watch. And this focus then fed back into volatility in such assets as homebuilder company shares. For example, take a look at housing starts, a monthly number that got a whole lot less attention before this mortgage/housing crisis. After climbing in November and December 2013, in January and February 2014 the monthly starts fell back to their lower levels of April to October 2013. (Now remember that the data gets reported with a lag so that, for example, the February numbers were announced on March 24.) The shares of homebuilder KB Homes peaked at $20.67 on February 27—about the time when economists, Wall Street analysts, and investors would have been receiving the news that January wasn't going to show the strength of November and December. On March 26, just days after the report of the equally lackluster February numbers on March 24, the shares closed at $16.57. That's a 19.8 percent decline in a month. At least some of that volatility reflects how much attention economists, Wall Street analysts, and individual investors have invested in tracking the housing market after or during—depending on where you live—a housing crisis.

If you suddenly start paying attention to a kind of volatility that you've never or only sporadically tracked before, the subjective experience can be confusion and anxiety. That happens when you get numbers that experts, events, and markets tell you are important but that you don't have familiarity with and aren't sure exactly how to use. You've added data that should give you a better handle on what is happening and what might happen, so you should indeed feel more in control of that volatility, but the effect, at least initially, is feeling a lack of control.

The same thing happens to an even greater degree when a frequently tracked volatility measure, a familiar tool for figuring out how change works in the world, comes unglued from long-term, historical volatility benchmarks. I got my first job writing about the financial markets in June 1984. That's more than thirty years ago. And up until very recently the conventional wisdom about stock market volatility and returns has been remarkably constant. There's never been a rolling period, according to conventional wisdom, when a long-term investor who bought and held stocks for ten years or more had lost money. Stocks may go up and down way more than a certificate of deposit, to cite one example of a very low-risk asset, but because they return 10 percent on average annually, riding out that volatility is worth it.

So it's not surprising that investors now might feel a little unmoored. From August 2000 to August 2010—ten years, right?—the S&P's lost 28.2 percent. Add that to all the uncertainty that comes from having a bear market in 2000 and again in 2007—and that's just in the United States: investors in Brazil and China, for example, have seen two bear markets since the beginning of 2013.

What do you do when a benchmark comes unmoored? One common reaction is to ignore the unmooring and continue to use the old benchmark as an anchor. A common rationale—powerful because there's a solid element of plausibility to it—is that the current numbers are an anomaly and that they will soon revert to the old benchmark.

Others might posit conspiracy theories, claiming, for example, that inflation is really higher now than the official numbers say because "they" have rigged the numbers. Some simply play ostrich by avoiding the financial markets or the everyday situation until "it" is over. People search for new benchmarks, leading to a paradise for the sellers of data and explanations—and to some very important and useful rethinking of former truths. Right now, for example, there's very promising and important work happening that examines some of the mathematical tools of modern portfolio theory. Optimizing portfolio returns through picking the appropriate mixture of asset classes relies on historical returns for those classes and historical relationships between those classes. But this prompts questions: Should the math assume that those historical returns and relationships are fixed for all time? Should we somehow periodically reassess the historical returns and relationships for bonds and stocks, for developed market and emerging market assets, for gold and currencies because recent history indicates that those returns and relationships do indeed change decisively over time? And how do we differentiate between changes in those returns and relationships that are significant and those that are ephemera and can and should be ignored?

One of the perversities of volatility and our response to it is that an increased subjective sense of volatility can lead to behavior designed to reduce that perceived volatility—doing "something" can be powerfully soothing—but that actually has the effect of increasing volatility.

For example, the financial crisis that brought down Lehman Brothers and almost brought down American International Group,

Citigroup, and other global financial powers was particularly de-
structive because investors and traders who feared volatility—who
had a subjective sense that volatility was climbing but who, like one
of Coates's traders addicted to the brain chemicals released by risk
taking—had purchased insurance from other investors and traders
against that volatility. And because no one could be quite certain
who was on the other end of that insurance and didn't know whether
they would be able to pay on their claims, financial markets froze as
participants decided that hoarding capital was the smartest thing to
do. And this is why the Federal Reserve and other central banks had
to guarantee liquidity to the system when others wouldn't in order
to fight the crisis.

One way to think about "insurance" against volatility is that it
results in a delay in resetting benchmarks and anchors. It's a response to the unmooring of expectations about the future without
having to admit that those expectations require a complete "rethink." Perhaps you're wondering whether stocks have become so
expensive that they now fall outside historical benchmarks for risk
and reward. Well, of course, you could reexamine all your assumptions about the benchmarks you are using to make your decisions,
or you could simply buy what are called put options, which, as insurance, give you the right to sell the stocks in the S&P 500 at a
specified price at a specified date in the future. That way if stocks
fall in price, your puts climb in price, and you can use that gain in
the price of the options—or actually exercise the right to sell—to
offset any drop in stocks. You've put a patch on the problem and
postponed thinking about whether fundamental volatility has
changed in the market.

In everyday life—rather than in the financial markets—are you
worried that changes in the economy may well be making the connection between a college education and economic security more
tenuous? You could rethink your basic assumptions about the purpose of a college education, or decide to tell your kids to pass on
college, or admit that no amount of education is going to guarantee
the economic security of the 1950s or 1960s. Or you can simply decide to do the same thing—but more of it. The trends in the rising
number of colleges that individual high school seniors apply to, the

soaring number of applications received by "elite" colleges, the increase in spending on tutoring and test prep all tell us that the solution of choice has been, so far, more of the same.

We know from studies in behavioral finance that our tolerance for volatility isn't symmetrical. For example, we feel losses about two to two-and-a-half times as strongly as gains. In other words, we'd rather pass up a chance to gain $200 than run a risk of losing $100.

We also know that we have a bias toward believing that positive trends will continue to be positive for, well, forever. In a bear market we tend to look relatively quickly for the moment when the trend will turn. It is in fact our propensity to look for a bottom relatively quickly in bear markets that makes them especially devastating to investors. I speak here from experience—I got the break in the market just about right in the dot-com crash of 2000 and the post-Lehman crash of 2008. In both cases, however, I turned reasonably small losses into really big losses in my portfolios by calling the bottom too early and putting money to work after a 15 percent downturn just in time to catch another 25 percent drop in the markets. On the other side of the volatility spectrum our tendency to believe that markets that are climbing (upside volatility) will climb forever is so pronounced that it has led to a gaggle of investing clichés: "Acorns don't grow to the sky," for example, or, my favorite from Herb Stein, chairman of the Council of Economic Advisors under Presidents Nixon and Ford: "If something cannot go on forever, it will stop."

The reasons for this are pretty simple but still very important for figuring out what to do about volatility at any moment of time. I think we're pretty good at coping honestly with short-term volatility. Investors do move money to cash at times of market stress. We do go to the store to stock up on water and batteries when a hurricane is on the way. We do buy medical insurance against an unexpected illness.

These are, however, relatively easy decisions. We expect short-term volatility in financial markets and our lives—and the actual appearance of that volatility on stage isn't unexpected and doesn't threaten belief systems or assumptions about the direction of the world. We can and do indeed pass off this volatility by saying markets revert to the norm or pasting a sticker proclaiming "Shit Happens" to our bumper. Short-term volatility doesn't shock us into revising our beliefs (benchmarks) because we expect life to be volatile in the shorter run and that this short-term volatility will average out into a smoother long-term trend. In the financial markets that's the theory behind the old conventions of buy and hold—if you hold stocks for ten years or longer, the short-term volatility doesn't matter.

Volatility in the medium or, even worse, long term—is different. Some of that is because it is really, really hard to figure out what the long-term trend is. It's tough to separate the short-term grind of day-to-day events from the long-term trend. Did Jay Gould, my favorite nineteen-century robber baron, know that he lived during the great Victorian price equilibrium? Did any Florentine waiting to see the fiery priest Savonarola hanged and burned in 1498 say, "Hmmm, I think prices will climb for the next century about twice as quickly as they did in my great grandfather's time"? Most of us admit that figuring out the trends over this kind of extended period of time is beyond us—and we're especially willing to shrug our shoulders and say, "So what?"—because periods this long exceed our own lives by so much. Outside the pages of science fiction and the minds of conspiracy theorists, multicentury decisions and plans are rather rare in human history.

But that shrug of the shoulders is also an easy way out in dealing with volatility. It lets us escape the need to question our benchmark beliefs about the world. It gives us an excuse to avoid thinking about facts that suggest that our anchors have come lose and we're drifting in a scary realm of unpredictable change. If you put this tendency together with a bias toward an optimistic view of the future that has been characteristic of the American psyche, the shrug of the shoulders is profoundly comforting too. The future will be like the past—in the long run—and that's a pretty good thing because progress is gradually making everything better, little by little.

But think about the implications of all this for a period when volatility is actually on the rise, when benchmarks are actually under question, where there's a good chance that the future isn't going to look like some incrementalist version of the past. Our ability to ignore the evidence of short-term volatility that shows that long-term volatility is coming, our ability to rationalize holding on to the old benchmarks, and our preference for believing in the continuation of the current trends that bring order to our world means that we resist the conclusions short-term volatility has foreshadowed. We want to believe that the volatility is only a short-term phenomenon that will pass and then everything will revert to the mean. This isn't always easy, and sometimes eventually it may become impossible to hold to our belief that the long-term trend, the established benchmarks and anchors, are still intact. But establishing a new vision of the future isn't easy.

Here, I think, the study of volatility in everyday life—the stuff of such historical approaches as the history-of-everything Annales school, founded by Lucien Febvre and Marc Bloch—may have more to tell us than the number crunching of studies of volatility in the financial markets. Some of that is simply because of the very limited data sequences that we have on the financial markets. Depending on what year we peg as the beginning of financial markets, with something like the current structure of bond and equity markets, we have, say, a hundred years of data. I remember, as a very innocent financial reporter, asking the great economist Paul Samuelson about the long-term implications of the crash that sent the Dow Jones Industrial Average down 23 percent on *one* day in October 1987. "Did a crash like this mean that our assumptions about long-term returns in the market were wrong?" I asked. I could almost hear him shrug over the phone. "How can we know?" he said. We don't have enough data to know whether the last eighty years of the financial markets are a representative sample. They could be representative—or they could be from the narrow tail of the probability distribution at either the high or low end of a longer sequence.

The longer spans of economic history—price data for hundreds of years, for example—demonstrate both the persistence of volatility characteristics over long periods and the existence of changes in those long-term patterns. It's impossible to read this history and say that there aren't periods of transition when long-term anchors come adrift. These long-term data sequences also speak to the difficulty discerning changes in long-term volatility characteristics while we're living through short-term volatility. The challenge in figuring out what invalidates a benchmark and requires a new belief anchor and what is simply a meaningless piece of noise around the trend gives us plenty of reasons for not abandoning what has been a reliable long-term benchmark. For example, although the last half of the nineteenth century may be the Victorian Equilibrium in much of the world—in retrospect and to academic historians—to anyone living in the United States during the period it was a time of panics and depressions and violent worker protests over working conditions and pay. To the workers living through the Homestead Strike or the wars in the Colorado minefields, this certainly wasn't anything like the Victorian Equilibrium.

However, it is possible to identify an overall period of stable prices, economic progress, and calm that is different from the period before and the period after.

Looking at the data of everyday life with a long-term historical perspective and then trying to answer the question of what distinguishes one period from another and, indeed, what makes a period a period sends us back to look at the underlying causal structures of volatility. And that suggests a reason for talking about the current period as an Age of Volatility.

In the case of the period called the Victorian Equilibrium, for example, the US panics and depressions, the strikes and the bombings, and the armed repression of workers by government troops don't represent exceptions to the pattern of the longer period; instead, they reveal the tensions and contradictions that made that great equilibrium possible. It's the rise of the United States—and Argentina, South Africa, Canada, and Australia—and the incorporation of those frontier economies into the global economic system that sustained the extraordinary combination of rising wages, rising productivity, and stable prices that defines the longer period. But incorporating the production from those frontier economies into a global market was by no means easy, especially in an era when market information traveled so much more slowly than it does in our own times. Think of how long it took a cotton grower in Mississippi, a wheat farmer in Argentina, or a sheep farmer in Australia to get information on market prices and conditions. That's why the early panics and depressions in the United States in the nineteenth century all had triggers in the overproduction of commodities: The panic of 1819 was triggered by a collapse in cotton prices, and the deeper panic and depression of 1837, which lasted almost six years, was triggered by cotton (again), the failure of the US wheat crop, speculation in land—the key input in economies based on agricultural commodities—and a collapse in food prices that left farmers unable to buy much of anything, which, in turn, devastated the sales of anyone trying to sell goods to farmers. And the panic of 1857 is pivotal in the list of US panics and depressions, not because it marked a change in the frequency of these events—a pattern of 1819, 1837, and 1857 was followed by a pattern of 1857, 1873, and 1891—or a change in the longer-term trend of price equilibrium or even a change in the stress placed on the global economic and financial system by the need to integrate frontier economies into the global market; instead, the difference was in a shift in the triggers for panic and depression. The trigger for the panic and depression of 1857, for example, wasn't a collapse in the price of an agricultural commodity but the failure of the Ohio Life Insurance and Trust Company as a result of speculation in railroad stocks. (For those interested in the way financial history rubs up against other modes of history, the Panic of 1857 resulted in the bankruptcy of Ulysses S. Grant.) The panic and depression of 1873 (during Grant's second term as president) followed the same pattern: it was triggered by the failure of Jay Cooke and Co. as a result of speculation in railroad stock. The panic and depression of 1893—the worst depression in US history until the Great Depression, resulted from panic selling in the US stock market that led to the bankruptcy of 156 railroads. (Five hundred banks also failed in that depression, making 1893 a bellwether year in the shift from railroads to banks as the locus of speculation.)

There are similar causal factors that tie together our own period, the one I'm calling an Age of Volatility. Instead of the expansion of a global agricultural economy to new parts of the world, for example, the current period is characterized by an expansion of the global financial system to new parts of the world. Just as the panics and booms of that earlier period were caused, in part, by information lags as that global market for agricultural commodities grew in scope and reached for maturity, so our own period is coping with the challenges of sending information from one market to another and integrating that information in ways that don't create big-volatility moments such as the Asian currency crisis or the US subprime/ global financial crisis.

In the Victorian Equilibrium the heightened volatility that came with the expansion of the global economy to frontier markets and the inclusion of New York into a financial system dominated by London and, to a lesser degree, other European financial centers finds an echo not just in our own time but also in the period that witnessed the creation of the first global colonial empires. Trying— and failing—to incorporate vast additions to global cash flows from the New World crashed the Spanish economy. Despite the crown's huge cash flow, Spain was forced into bankruptcy in 1557, 1560, 1575, and 1596 because the global financial system was simply over- whelmed by New World silver. (One afternoon recently, when I learned that my son was on his way to Potosi in Bolivia, I did a back- of-the-envelope calculation that Spain had pulled 90.4 million pounds of silver out of just one mine during the centuries when Spain ruled Bolivia. To put that in context, the per capita GDP of Spain in 1700 was equal to roughly one pound of silver.) I don't think these historical rhymes (you know the Mark Twain quote: "History doesn't repeat itself, but it does rhyme.") should mark the limits of our search for the causes of volatility and its patterns. But they sure are a good place to start.

However, as we make that start, we need to remember the biases we bring to our search for the causes and patterns of longer-term volatility. We are biased in favor of believing in the continuation of existing trends. We are biased in favor of optimism about the future (at least we are in the United States). We anchor ourselves around existing benchmarks and have a hard time letting them go.

And these aren't merely psychological quirks in the way we inter- pret volatility. Our biases and attitudes toward volatility first de- press and then accelerate volatility itself. Because we are both observers and actors, the beliefs that govern our perception of vola- tility wind up feeding back into volatility itself.

One of the major results of that is that benchmarks and expecta- tions for volatility don't change smoothly—in contrast, they change jaggedly, in big lumps, and with considerable lags over time. The image that comes to mind is one of water building up behind a dam until it finally overflows and sweeps the dam away. But that's overly simplistic. The process of resetting benchmarks and expectations for volatility—and, hence, the rate of volatility itself—has a lot in common with the intellectual process laid out by Thomas Kuhn in his books *The Copernican Revolution* and *The Structure of Scientific Revolutions*. I'd certainly not claim that revising the benchmark assumptions for the rate of return on the long US Treasury bond represents anything like the difficulty in making the transition from Ptolemaic earth-centered astronomy to a Copernican sun-centered science, but the stages of what I'd call benchmark belief do resemble the path that Kuhn describes for science. Kuhn divides science into three stages: pre-science, which lacks a central paradigm; followed by "normal science," which consists largely of applying a paradigm to problem solving; and then, revolutionary science, after a crisis leads to the substitution of a new paradigm for the old framework. One of Kuhn's most important ideas is that in the period of normal science, when experiential results don't conform to the paradigm, the initial—and often very long-lasting—reaction isn't to throw out the paradigm but to blame the scientist for producing mistakes.

All this suggests that it is likely to be extremely difficult to get the timing of any transition in volatility right. And because—and in the financial world especially—being too early or too late is often equivalent to being wrong, that's a huge challenge in any attempt to successfully navigate an Age of Volatility. To see exactly how big a challenge it is to get the timing right, you don't need to look any further than the example of what happened to Bill Gross, a bond manager so central to his part of the money management industry that he was known as Mr. Bond, running the world's largest mutual fund, when he introduced the idea of "The New Normal" in 2009.

And that's the subject of my next chapter.

Chapter 4

Whom the Gods Would Destroy
They First Make a Pundit

IN SEPTEMBER 2009 BILL GROSS, then the portfolio manager at PIMCO's Total Return Fund, at that point the largest mutual fund in the world, wrote a piece called "On the 'Course' to a New Normal." After some extraneous comments about his golf game—the kind you're entitled to make when you manage a fund with more than $200 billion in assets—Gross laid down a serious challenge. For a long time—since 1982 at the least—it has paid to buy the dips because "markets, economies, profits, and assets always rebounded and went to higher levels," Gross wrote.

But, Gross went on to argue, this pattern isn't some kind of timeless, universal guarantee; it is the result of specific economic and financial conditions that have been in effect for a long time but are now changing. Because of leveraging, deglobalization (a shift to source manufacturing and capital locally rather than globally), and reregulation, Gross said, things are changing:

> If you are a child of the bull market, it's time to grow up and become a chastened adult; it's time to recognize that things have changed and they will continue to change for the next—yes, the next 10 years and maybe even the next 20 years. We are heading into what we [at PIMCO] call the New Normal, which is a period of time in which economies grow very slowly as opposed to grow-

ing like weeds, the way children do; in which profits are relatively static; in which the government plays a significant role in terms of deficits and reregulation and control of the economy; in which the consumer stops shopping until he drops and begins, as they do in Japan (to be a little ghoulish), starts saving to the grave.

There's certainly nothing very humble in Gross's piece. Besides the condescending characterization "children of the bull market" (really? You want to call the people who invest in your fund or who might invest in your fund "children"?), you come away from the article with the unmistakable impression that Gross thinks he's made an important discovery that no one else in the money management industry—or among economists—has had the brilliance to recognize.

Gross claimed that he had identified a big-volatility moment. All the old benchmarks need to go out the window. The future—or maybe it's the present—is going to be radically different from the past and different from the way we envision the future now. And to navigate that future, we've got to unmoor our thinking and create new benchmarks.

Wow!

I happen to think that Gross's argument, that we've entered a new era in the financial markets and the global economy, is correct. I agree that the old benchmarks aren't going to be useful guides to the period ahead. The case for the New Normal was strong in 2009 and has just gotten stronger.

It also happens to have been extremely premature. And, unfortunately, when you are trying to predict the moment when a series of long-accepted benchmarks gets thrown on the dust pile of history being really, really early is the same as being wrong.

Although I think it is possible to see that we're in a transition from the relatively low volatility period of 1981 to 1997 or so to an Age of Volatility that began, with a transition in 1999–2000, in 2008, I think we're so close to the transition that the new age is hard to see. As I noted in the last chapter, the study of everyday volatility—changes in price inflation, for example—argues that although periods with very different volatility characteristics do exist, it's easier to identify them in retrospect than in the moment. And in the moment our biases toward staying the course, toward a belief that everything will revert back to normal, toward a desire to hold onto the comfortable old benchmarks mean that we're likely to continue to behave as if the old benchmarks were still in place even after they have actually been superseded.

They call them "anchors" for a reason.

This means that when, eventually, the old benchmarks that have remained the foundation of expectations for the future are finally replaced, change will arrive not only with the volatility of these new circumstances themselves but also with the additional force of pent-up denial and delay.

The history of Bill Gross and his New Normal formulation is a good case study of this process at work, with all the frustration that comes from not only being right—quite likely, in my opinion—but also way too early. History tells us that the grander the theory, the bigger the big-volatility moment that it is trying to forecast, the harder it is to forecast when that big-volatility moment will arrive. Which leaves us with a practical problem as well as an intellectual conundrum: The grander the theory, the more profound the potential change and the greater the possibility for profit or the greater the need for protection from this big change. But at the same time, the grander the theory, the harder it is to project when the big-volatility moment will arrive. That suggests, to my mind, a need to try to match the timing uncertainty of the big-volatility moment with the longevity of the kind of options for volatility that you use in a portfolio or in everyday life. An option that expires in ninety days, as most purely financial options do, is much less useful in the case of a big-volatility moment than an option such as an ownership bet on the future of a stock.

That, in my opinion, is the crucial volatility lesson from this episode in financial market history.

This New Normal doesn't seem all that radical or threatening—although cumulatively it is. Instead of nominal (i.e., including inflation) global GDP growth rates of 6 to 7 percent driven by the world's emerging economies, in the New Normal investors can expect,

Gross said, nominal growth rates of 3 to 4 percent. The return on assets will be half of what it has been over the last twenty years both because of this lower rate of economic growth and because of the need to deleverage global economies and the global financial system after the excesses of the bubble that led to the global financial crisis. That translates, according to the New Normal, into average annual returns of 5 percent on equities. That's a huge drop from the 10.5 percent annual return that was the benchmark for investors and Wall Street for the lifetime of the children of the bull market. And bonds won't do any better. With the US deficit rising and with trillions in assets on central bank balance sheets that need to be resold to private markets, the New Normal says, global and, especially, US interest rates will need to climb to keep attracting foreign money. That will be especially the case in the United States, as the US dollar will be in decline, making dollar-denominated assets less attractive and requiring higher interest rates to attract overseas money. So don't count on the traditional 5 percent average annual return on ten- to thirty-year US Treasuries. How about 2 percent or 3 percent? And remember that this return includes inflation. If you think inflation will run at 2 percent a year, at the lower end of the benchmark range, bonds are only breaking even.

Unfortunately, the next few years after his 2009 pronouncement didn't prove Gross right. In 2009 the S&P 500 returned 26.5 percent. In 2010 the return was 15.1 percent, and in 2011 2.11 percent. The returns on the ten-year Treasury started off, in 2009, looking as if the data would demonstrate Gross's New Normal: that year ten-year Treasuries lost 11.1 percent. But then in 2010 they returned 8.5 percent, and in 2011 16 percent. At best Gross was early. And early, when you're trying to make money on a change in a big-volatility trend, isn't really all that different from being wrong.

Which led Gross to double-down in 2012.

By 2012 Gross had become even more pessimistic—not about benchmark returns but about the volatility ahead in markets and economies. Gross moved on from the New Normal to what he called the Paranormal. This condition, Gross wrote in his January 2012 investment report for PIMCO, was almost bimodal in its potential volatility. The world economy had an equal—if relatively small—chance of surging into hyperinflation (you know, like Germany after World War I, when people took wheelbarrows of money to the bakery to buy bread) or falling into prolonged deflation (like a global version of Japan's lost decades). Gross would still relegate those two possibilities to the tail ends of the statistical probability curve, but, he wrote, the tails that are home to unlikely events are relatively fat in the Paranormal economy.

In practical terms that's not very useful. Either the world economy would slide into hyperinflation or fall into hyperdeflation. Those are opposite ends of the possible spectrum of results, and it's hard to see how anyone could protect against that either/or or profit from it.

But for our purposes, what does Gross and the New Normal teach us about volatility? Three things, I think.

First, it is all too easy to underestimate the stickiness of the current benchmarks and their power to anchor behavior. The future, I would say, tends to arrive later than expected.

Furthermore, the bigger the difference between the present and the future, the larger the change we're predicting, and the larger the shift in volatility, the more likely it is that we will underestimate the stickiness of the present. Gross's new benchmarks would require a radical restructuring of lives and lifestyles. We'd have to buy less and save more. We'd have to do without the taken-for-granted five-thousand-square-foot house, the twice-a-year vacations, the $40,000 "family car," and the second and third cars too. Certainly given the dimensions of the change that Gross's scenario would require, it's only reasonable for people to want lots and lots of evidence that Gross is right.

There's an institutional element to this too. It's not just "people" who want to be convinced before they make big changes in behavior; benchmarks are also embedded in institutional practices and business models. Here we're talking about a widely accepted worldview—that stocks return an annual average of 10.5 percent and long Treasury bonds 5 percent—that is embedded in the practice of tens of thousands of financial consultants and money managers and is assumed in the reasoning behind the construction of millions of portfolios. It's embedded in the assumptions of pension funds and insurance companies, and it is built into the budgets of companies and governments on the cost of pensions and the price of insurance. If that conventional wisdom is wrong, if these portfolios can't count on 8 percent or 10 percent, then somebody—taxpayers or shareholders—is going to have to kick in more money to make the future books balance.

Second, we shouldn't underestimate the feedback loops between continued belief in the old benchmarks and the delay in the arrival of the future. The reluctance to abandon old benchmarks means that behavior tends to follow those benchmarks longer than the facts, the fundamentals, or whatever would predict.

For example, as the US stock market climbed to higher and higher levels—as measured by the S&P 500, anyway—in 2013 and then hit one all-time high after another in 2014, a hot argument raged on Wall Street about whether US stocks were overvalued or still reasonably priced. Both sides of the argument looked to history to prove its case.

One benchmark for deciding whether US stocks are over- or undervalued is simply to look at the unvarnished historical price-to-earnings (P/E) ratio. By this measure stocks—that is, the stocks in the S&P 500 index—were fairly valued, history since 1926 tells us, when they trade at fifteen to sixteen times earnings per share. They are cheap—buy 'em by the bushel!—when they trade at six to twelve times earnings per share.

But as the market climbed and climbed, valuation methods that didn't show stocks as overvalued and that didn't demonstrate the need for a big change in behavior and portfolios started to get a whole lot more pixel space. Instead of using past earnings, how about projected earnings to value a stock? That would seem to do a better job of capturing the future prospects of a company. How about adjusting the forward P/E to correct for the effects of the economic cycle? The Cyclically Adjusted Price-to-Earnings Ratio, or CAPE, uses rolling averages of the monthly closing P/E ratios of the entire S&P 500 for ten-year periods in an effort to take out the effect of economic cycles by using a long enough period so it should include both economic decelerations and accelerations.

Of course, the feedback from this belief that there was no need to do anything big and disruptive meant that money didn't move out of financial assets and the price of these assets continued to climb, further validating the decision to do nothing. See, anyone invested in stocks could say, methods that showed valuations to be reasonable must be right because stocks are still climbing.

This feedback effect is one of the things that bit Gross and the New Normal in the behind. To generalize, Gross looked at interest rates, the trillions that central banks had added to the global money supply, and massive deficits, both in annual budgets and accumulated, for governments around the world, and from all this he concluded that interest rates couldn't go any lower. The long decline in interest rates from 1981 was over—and because that decline had been a big part of the 10.7 percent annual average return on stocks and the 5 percent average annual return on Treasuries, the old benchmarks were finished—it was time for the New Normal.

You don't have to dig very deep to see why Gross reached this conclusion in 2009. Just take a look at the Fed Funds rate, the benchmark interest rate set by the Fed that determines what banks have to pay to borrow money overnight. At the end of 2008 the effective Fed Funds rate went from 2 percent in August to 0.97 percent in October to 0.16 percent in December. (For context, the Fed Funds rate peaked at 19.08 percent in January 1981.) It would not break 0.22 percent at any time over the next seven years. Much of that time it hovered near 0.1 percent. In February 2015 the rate was 0.11 percent.

Gross and a lot of other investment analysts and market watchers wondered: How long could that go on?

And the answer was: a lot longer than any of these folks imagined. In January 2011 the yield on the ten-year Treasury had tumbled to 1.91 percent. It fell as low as 1.65 percent in 2011 before rebounding: in February 2015 the yield on the ten-year Treasury was 1.98 percent.

All those bond market analysts and investors who asked, lightly, "How low can rates go? They can't go below 0 percent, right?" turned out to be wrong. In fact, negative yields have become common around the world. By the end of February 2015 $2 trillion in European bonds traded with negative yields. That's up from just $20 billion in a year. Five-year bonds from Germany, Denmark, Austria, Finland, and the Netherlands all traded with negative yields. As part of its effort to get banks in the EuroZone to lend, the European Central Bank, which in normal times pays banks interest if they store money with the central bank overnight or longer, started to *charge* interest on those deposits. A bank that wanted to keep its money on deposit with the European Central Bank would have to pay 0.2 percent interest for the privilege. The Swedish national bank, the Riksbank, cut its benchmark interest rate to a negative 0.1 percent in mid-February 2015.

The financial markets weren't quite ready to move on from the period of ever-lower interest rates that stretched back to 1981. The New Normal was still sometime in the future.

Which isn't to say that it isn't in the future, just that the big-volatility moment, when the markets move from a period of ever-declining interest rates to a period of rising interest rates hasn't arrived yet. But this was a problem for Gross and his mutual fund. Gross had done exactly what his belief in the New Normal/Paranormal paradigm said he should do. In 2011, worried about the huge buildup in US government debt and Congress's continued inability/unwillingness to address the US budget deficit in any serious way, Gross moved his bond portfolios away from longer-dated US Treasuries such as the five-, seven-, and ten-year notes. If interest rates started to climb, long-maturity US Treasuries would fall in price more than Treasuries with shorter maturities such as two-year notes or three-month Treasury bills. In the third quarter of that year, as a result of that decision—and as a result of getting the timing of the big-volatility moment wrong, the fund lost 1.1 percent.

Here we come to the third lesson that Gross and the New Normal teach us about volatility and protecting against it or even profiting from it. Gross and other market analysts were trying to call an inflection point in a long-term trend, one that had begun in 1981. That's always a challenge in the financial markets. By and large, trends to the upside and the downside tend to go on for longer than expected. It's one of the reasons calling a bottom—for the market in general or, in particular, for a commodity such as oil in 2015—is so hard and frequently produces significant losses for even experienced traders. On the upside, bull-market rallies last longer than expected, often long enough for traders and investors who had moved to the sidelines to get impatient at the lack of the predicted downturn and get back into the market just in time to get hit by exactly the sell-off they were hoping to avoid.

But I think there's an even more general point about volatility to make here: the grander and more encompassing a theory of volatility is, the harder it is to get the timing right.

It's one of the ironies of our understanding of volatility: our ability to predict and track volatility is relatively good for smaller-scale and shorter-term volatility. The further you go out, however, the less likely a grand theory of volatility will get the timing or the magnitude of change correct. And that's even if the grand theory is correct.

This isn't a problem limited to the financial markets or to volatility; you can find a good example of this predictive conundrum in the current debate in technology and artificial intelligence (AI) circles about the coming "singularity." Vernor Vinge (a very good science fiction writer, by the way—check out his *A Fire upon the Deep*) and Ray Kurzweil have argued that smarter and smarter AI machines are very close to being able to outsmart humans. At that tipping point, what they call a singularity, smarter machines will themselves build smarter machines without human intervention and control. That will leave human intelligence in the dust. The shape of the future after this singularity is impossible to predict, they say, because at that point the future will be driven by machine intelligence, which will render obsolete everything we know from human history about the velocity of change.

But it is possible to predict from the current rate of progress in technology and the acceleration of that rate when the singularity will occur, Kurzweil argues. Following what he calls the Law of Accelerating Returns, progress in the technologies needed to produce the singularity will accelerate at an exponential rate. Using his model of exponential change, Kurzweil pegs the arrival of the singularity for 2045.

What's interesting to me—and what's important for this discussion of volatility—is the degree of disagreement with the grand singularity theory. Of course, as you'd expect, there are those who say that the Law of Accelerating Returns doesn't work the way Kurzweil believes it does, that it's a misextrapolation from Moore's Law, and that the singularity won't arrive in 2045. There are also those, including Microsoft cofounder Paul Allen, who say the Law of Accelerating Returns doesn't even exist and that, in any case, there are huge technology hurdles that need to be jumped before machines can act as intelligently and independently as Kurzweil posits.

And, finally, there are those who disagree with Kurzweil's belief in an exponential acceleration of technological and scientific change. In general these critics fall into two camps: those who argue that the rate of technological change isn't accelerating fast enough to produce the kind of tipping point in human history represented by a singularity, and those who argue that the rate of technological change isn't accelerating at all and is actually declining. Some of these critics see the rate of change as slowing to a degree that suggests that, rather than moving toward a singularity, we're moving away from a singularity that may have already occurred. The argument here isn't about whether technological change is occurring—both sides agree it is—but about the velocity and rate of acceleration or deceleration of that change.

The idea of a singularity—to use a term from physics, the moment when existing trends trip a system into a state change—isn't limited at the moment to discussions of technology and artificial intelligence; the concept also shows up in discussions of world population growth, urbanization, and demographics. In each of those instances you can draw a chart, if you make certain assumptions about the data, that shows the same pattern of hyperbolic takeoff in which change goes essentially vertical that Vinge and Kurzweil see in the acceleration of technological change. (Systems theorist John Smart has argued—warning: radical simplification alert—that this kind of pattern of hyperbolic growth, clumping, and reorganization is built into the structure of the universe.)

And there is, at the moment, a very similar critique of these singularities in these other areas arguing that in the last thirty or forty years it looks like the acceleration in these systems is slowing as well and that we're moving away from singularity and not toward it.

Enough disagreement for you? It's clear to me from all these arguments and counterarguments that it's just about impossible to predict when the singularity, that big-volatility moment of all big-volatility moments (from a human perspective), will arrive. When you get into a grand theory that essentially posits the end of not just human history but of humans themselves, I think the possibility of scheduling the arrival of that moment is very, very small.

And this leaves us with this problem: if the grander the theory and the more profound the potential change, the more difficult it is to ascertain whether the theory is correct and the more difficult it is to get the timing right, then what do you do? What is the best stance for coping with the extreme uncertainty of results when those results will change "everything" coupled with the extreme uncertainty in the timing of this massive change?

A couple of ways of addressing this problem falls out of Gross's New Normal.

The first task is to see how possible it is to judge the probability that a grand theory is correct. Now, the New Normal isn't a theory with the grandness of Kurzweil's singularity—we're talking about bond yields here and not the cosmic future of human intelligence—so the task is relatively simpler.

I find the paradigms of Gross's New Normal or Paranormal absolutely convincing, and yet I find myself with significant reservations as a result of recent market behavior. I can't dismiss the possibility that, as complex as Gross's reading of the markets is, it has missed something. It is, after all, hard to argue that the Federal Reserve can buy another $4 trillion in Treasuries and mortgage-backed securities over the next twenty years rather than deleveraging its portfolio or that yields on the ten-year US Treasury—at less than 2 percent in March 2015—can fall 11 or more percentage points and set off a long bull market, as they did beginning in the early 1980s.

And there's a sound foundation in consensus economics that expanding the money supply should lead to higher rates of inflation and to a depreciation of the value of currencies, both of which eat into real returns. (And remember that that's the number we're talking about—the real return on investment after you subtract inflation. Real-return calculations normally don't factor into the appreciation or depreciation of currencies, but maybe they should, especially if currency volatility is climbing.)

But consensus economics—a term that I use to include Friedman-school monetarists, Keynesian advocates of demand side intervention, and advocates of supply-side intervention—doesn't encompass all possible models that have something useful to say about the current postglobal financial crisis market. For example, theories from the Austrian school of economics, which includes Friedrich Hayek and Ludwig von Mises, who focus on the effects of increases in bank credit, describe a crucial aspect of the current situation. The Austrian school points out that when banks extend credit at artificially low interest rates—such as the negative rates engineered by many of world's central banks currently—the result is that businesses misallocate resources. This misallocation, which von Mises called malinvestment, is a result of businesses borrowing at these low rates and overinvesting in capital goods and facilities, producing overcapacity. That seems a very apt description of what has happened in the iron ore sector, for example, where even as the price of ore fell from $140 to $70 a metric ton, big iron ore producers such as Vale and BHP Billiton moved forward with plans to spend billions on expanding capacity. The hope, the companies said, was that they would force less efficient Chinese producers to shut their mines. The problem with that strategy is that in a world of cheap money, a money-losing miner can always find a bank willing to lend in order to keep the company in business. (That's especially true in the Chinese system, where money-losing companies that produce lots of jobs can count on loans from banks or lenders affiliated with local governments.) And this malinvestment isn't limited to the iron ore sector. The US oil and natural gas from shale boom ran so hot and furious because companies that had not yet produced a profit could easily raise money to expand production.

Adding this approach to the consensus mix helps explain why inflation is so low—and shows no signs of moving up soon in most developed economies: Why should prices go up when so many companies, industries, and sectors are operating with excess capacity and are willing to sell their products at just about any price? It also suggests that the timetable for correcting this situation is rather long, as reducing this overcapacity will require the liquidation of significant amounts of capital malinvestment. Deepwater drillers, for example, will have to stack and store dozens of rigs to restore balance—and pricing power—to that sector, a process that has only begun.

So the first task, it seems to me, in figuring out the probability of any grand theory like the New Normal is to run it up hard against the data as it exists. How much does it explain? How close is the fit with reality as we can ascertain it? How major are the loose ends?

The New Normal's inability to explain how the world's central banks' massive money printing can result in negative interest rates counts as a major loose end in my book.

Second, there's the task of putting some kind of bound on the magnitude of the change that the grand theory projects. Are we talking about a six-month correction in the bond market or one that lasts for a decade or two? Is the volatility likely to be limited to a market niche or to spread across global asset markets?

Third, we need to put some kind of timetable together for when the change predicted by the grand theory will likely occur. Would the New Normal set in during 2014, 2015, or 2025? Does the failure of the predicted result to arrive on the projected schedule invalidate the entire grand theory?

Fourth, what other trends either support this grand theory or militate against its likelihood? In the case of the New Normal, for example, global aging is a definite and observable trend that supports a thesis of lower return on investment in the decades ahead.

And fifth—and this is probably the hardest part of the job—what's the probability that we can predict the timing of a big-volatility moment? The odds that the projections in any grand theory will be correct don't approach 100 percent until they stop being projections and are embedded in reality. My read of the New Normal: It is very likely that these projections will prove to be accurate. Picking a moment when this big-volatility moment will arrive isn't anywhere near as uncertain as putting a data to Kurzweil's singularity, but it is uncertain. Because of the effects of delay, denial, and extension, the New Normal didn't arrive on Gross's schedule. But I think the uncertainty is measured in years—maybe two, maybe five, but I'd be surprised at ten rather than decades.

Looking around the financial markets I can see signs of the kind of excesses typical of transitions from one volatility period to another. Investors—in this case, a category that includes individual investors using bond mutual funds and bond ETFs as well as institutional and professional money managers—have bought junk bonds by the carload, adding the riskiest kind of bonds to their portfolios in an attempt to extend just a little longer the old bond yield benchmark of better than 5 percent returns. That has led to an amazing drop in the yield paid by some very risky bonds. For example, on April 4, 2014, Wind Telecommunicanzioni, Italy's third-largest mobile company, sold $5.1 billion of junk bonds with a yield of 7.375 percent in the biggest high-yield bond sale since T-Mobile's US unit sold $5.6 billion in October 2013. Wind is rated four levels below investment grade by Moody's Investors Service. A 7.375 percent yield on a junk bond that's that junky is remarkably cheap money.

Or consider some of these recent bond durations. In January 2014 Electricite de France, Europe's largest operator of nuclear reactors, sold almost $3 billion in one-hundred-year bonds, with a yield of 6.125 percent. This comes after a year when the University of Pennsylvania, MIT, and Ohio State have all sold one-hundred-year bonds. Railroad Norfolk Southern and Mexico have done so as well. (Mexico's one-hundred-year bonds paid a yield of 5.75 percent when they were initially sold.) Buying a one-hundred-year bond seems risky under any circumstances—who knows what will happen to interest rates and inflation in a hundred years; whether the British pound, the currency in one of Mexico's hundred-year issues, will be worth anything; or if nuclear power will be a viable way to generate electricity or a source of employment for thousands of security guards manning the sites of decommissioned plants—but it does makes sense if you simply look at this as one of your last, best chances to lock in the old above 5 percent bond yields before they're gone.

I'd characterize the current period as the Wall Street version of St. Augustine's plea to God: "Grant me chastity and continence, but not yet." For investors you can rephrase that to "I recognize the risk in buying or holding this stuff. I really do know that the higher yields offered by these investments at the moment doesn't begin to justify the risk in the current environment. And I fully intend to sell them—but not yet."

And this is what produces the typical behavior we see at a moment, when volatility starts to creep up as we approach the turning point in a trend. We don't get either a gradual shift or a clear one-time move; instead, we get a series of tests of the hypothesis of change that are typically accompanied by a series of warnings about the change in the trend. If we regard Gross's New Normal in 2009 and his Paranormal of 2012 as two rounds of warnings about a shift in market return and risk, then the warnings that cropped up in 2015 as bond yields moved into negative territory, and when investors and traders piled into the riskiest parts of the bond market, were a third warning. In a March 2015 survey of three hundred global money managers, conducted by CFA in the United Kingdom, four out of five said that bonds were overvalued. The survey itself elicited mentions of the B-word: the bond market could be in a bubble.

I doubt that this round of warnings will do the trick either. But the warnings do add to the volatility of markets unsettled by changes in fundamentals such as shifts in central bank monetary policies or declining growth in China.

The hope, of course, in a period like this is that you'll be able to see the crash or whatever coming and hit the exits ahead of the crowd. Or that we'll be able to buy the right kind of financial insurance at the right time. That itself adds to volatility, as the hope that there will be a buyer in the market when you're ready to sell is accompanied with the fear that there won't be. From the chaos in the financial markets that followed after the collapse of Lehman Brothers and Bear Stearns in 2008 we know that this hope can be disappointed. The Federal Reserve and other central banks had to step in then because there weren't any buyers—at any reasonable price—and there weren't enough buyers even at unreasonable prices.

And we know from the October 2014 liquidity meltdown in the Treasury market that worrying about liquidity and the ability to sell is very, very reasonable right now.

What I've tried to do in this chapter is construct a framework that will let you come to a conclusion about the nature of current volatility, how important it is, and how you can reach a decision on what to do about it.

I've also tried to use the example of Gross and the New Normal to argue for the importance of timing. Especially in a period of heightened volatility—and in the next two chapters I'll lay out the biggest reasons for thinking we're in an Age of Volatility—when projecting the schedule for major volatility transitions becomes extremely difficult, I think giving yourself as much room for timing error as possible is a key strategy. Matching the volatility tools that you use to the likely "margin of error" in timing is also crucial. At moments of increased volatility, getting the timing wrong—being early or late—is as damaging as being wrong. That thinking is reflected in the investing strategies laid out in the last third of this book.

Chapter 5

Rollin', Rollin', Rollin', Keep Them Presses Rollin'

COMPARE FINANCIAL MARKET VOLATILITY since 2000 (the year I'd pick as the beginning of the transition to the current Age of Volatility) or since 2008 (the year I'd pick as the beginning of that Age) with the volatility of the early 1980s that ushered in the great bull market that ran from 1981 to 2000 (even as the economy struggled in those early years), and I think you'll find solid evidence that this current volatility unwinding is more volatile, more violent in its vacillation between ups and downs.

And, if you look at root fundamental causes for the volatility in these two periods, this is actually surprising. The volatility in both periods was rooted in central bank, particularly Federal Reserve, policy. Why, then, has the more recent period been so much more volatile?

Because cheap money moves markets up—big—and down—big. And in the current period global central banks have created unprecedented amounts of cheap money.

I vividly remember the early 1980s. (Yes, I'm that ancient—don't make fun of your elders.) Federal Reserve Chairman Paul Volcker had sent the Fed-controlled short-term interest rates up to more than 20 percent in an effort to break inflation, which was then running at 13 percent. The yield on the ten-year Treasury peaked at 15.84 percent in September 1981. My broker urged me to put everything I had in cash into zero-coupon Treasuries. Interest rates would be coming down and as they did, the price of bonds that had originally sold with a coupon rate, which promised to pay 12 percent, 10 percent, or whatever, would soar. What else would you expect? When an existing bond with a 10 percent coupon interest rate traded in a market where newly issued bonds carried a coupon of only 5 percent, the price of that bond would climb until its coupon payments were equal to the 5 percent of a newly issued bond. So if I bought now and held, my broker advised, I had the prospect of making a steady double-digit, low-risk profit for my retirement fund.

I was convinced and followed his advice. Unfortunately all the cash I had then was less than $5,000. If I'd understood the nature of that crisis and the historical opportunity it presented, I would have somehow found more cash. I would have convinced my parents—who never invested in anything more risky than CDs—to put money into Treasuries. I would have sold my autographed Yogi Berra baseball. I would have lived on ramen day in and day out.

But I didn't. I let the opportunity of that crisis pass me by while I worried about 10 percent unemployment and keeping my own job—not an unimportant worry, I'll grant you.

Why do I remember this so vividly? Because you have a certain regret when you miss out on a chance to turn a $10,000 Treasury bond purchase into what would be $59,104.48 as of the end of 2014. (This does assume that I'd found a magical way to hold that ten-year Treasury for thirty-three years. But, hey, if you're gonna eat your heart out over missed opportunities, you might as well go whole hog on the regrets, no?)

Are the circumstances different now? You bet. Yields on ten-year Treasuries aren't 15.84 percent. In June 2015 the yield was all of 2.3 percent. A year earlier it had been 2.73 percent, but despite that decline—or maybe because of it—it is extremely unlikely that over the next thirty years the yield on the ten-year Treasury will drop by 13.16 percentage points as it did in the years since 1981. It is extremely likely that, in fact, rather than falling for thirty years, the yield on the ten-year Treasury will rise. And because the price of existing bonds falls as the yield rises, it's extremely unlikely that a ten-year Treasury bond that you buy today will be worth more in five, ten, twenty, or thirty years than it is today.

Okay, so whereas the period of 1981 to 2000 was characterized by falling interest rates and bond yields and rising bond prices, the next twenty years will be characterized by rising interest rates and bond yields and bond prices. That's pretty clear. But why should this period of rising interest rates and falling bond prices be more volatile than a period of falling rates and rising bond prices?

There are three reasons.

First, because investors and traders know the bull market, supported by falling interest rates, is coming to an end, but they don't know exactly when. No one wants to leave money on the table if the end is delayed, but no one wants to be last one out the door either. Think of the strategy that some kids use in playing musical chairs: they'll lag behind until the chair ahead of them opens up and then rush for it to be sure they'll have a place to park. The result isn't a smooth progress around the circle until the music stops but instead a series of slowdowns and races as the parade continues. What we're seeing as investors worry about the end of the bull market's upward volatility trend is a similar panicky uncertainty.

Second, the monetary and fiscal fundamentals behind the coming increase in interest rates and falling bond prices are much less stable than the fundamentals of 1981 to 2000.

Third and finally, the dynamics of rising interest rates and falling bond prices have destabilizing effects on the economy and financial markets that falling interest rates and rising bond prices don't match. The two sets of conditions don't have mirror-image effects.

Start with just the issue of the Federal Reserve's balance sheet, the statement of the value of assets that the Federal Reserve owns. In 1981 the Federal Reserve's balance sheet showed $180.6 billion in the way of Treasuries, mortgage-backed securities, and other financial assets. Because the Fed buys the assets on its books by "creating" money, its balance sheet shows how much money the Fed has created and then pumped into the economy to stimulate, the Fed hopes, economic activity by lowering the cost of credit and, the Fed worries, to eventually produce inflation, as this created money then increases the money supply and thus reduces the value of existing money.

The Federal Reserve's balance sheet in April 2014 stood at $4.19 trillion. For all intents and purposes the Fed's balance sheet total in 1981 is a rounding error today: the increase over the last three decades is a little more than $4 trillion.

Nor was that $4 trillion increase created evenly over those years. At the beginning of 2011—on January 19, 2011—the Fed showed a balance sheet of $488 billion. That's only about $300 billion more than the Fed's balance sheet in 1981. Two years later—by January 10, 2013—its balance sheet stood at $2.92 trillion. And then, from January 2013 to January 2014, the Fed added more than another $1 trillion to its balance sheet. And created another $1 trillion in money that has been pumped into the US—and global—economy.

Which would be stunning enough if the US Federal Reserve were the only global central bank pouring money into the global economy. But it isn't. The Bank of Japan, the Bank of England, the People's Bank of China, and the European Central Bank are all on the money-creation bandwagon. The European Central Bank, despite its reputation as a hard-nosed inflation fighter, has been almost as active as the Fed. By June 2012 it had taken its balance sheet up to $4.15 trillion, an increase of $1.2 trillion from pre–financial crisis levels.

And in March 2013 the Bank of Japan announced that it would "create" money to the tune of buying—every month—$80 billion worth of bonds and other assets. The goal is to end the decades-long grip of deflation on the Japanese economy that has taught Japanese consumers—from farmers to CEOs—never to buy anything today because it will be cheaper tomorrow. This has led to annual economic growth that rarely hit 1 percent and was closer to zero—or in negative territory—all too often. Likewise, the Federal Reserve's most recent effort to stimulate the US economy saw the US central bank buying $85 billion in US Treasuries and mortgage-backed securities every month. (The Fed began to taper off these purchases at the end of 2013.) Adjusting for the smaller size of the Japanese economy, the Bank of Japan's purchases are equal to the US Federal Reserve buying $280 billion in assets every month, or about three and a half times the Fed's own aggressive program of money creation.

And don't forget the People's Bank of China. Quarter in and quarter out, it quietly grew the country's money supply by 15 percent, 17 percent, 20 percent. And the bank had plenty of help from the country's five big banks—owned by the central government—as well as from local lenders and the country's rapidly expanding, relatively unregulated shadow banking sector.

The effect of all this easy and cheap money was volatility—sometimes to the downside but also frequently to the upside. One of the reasons the current period is more volatile than the period of 1981 to 2000 is that cheap money, as I noted above, moves markets up—big—and then down—big.

There are examples of this in financial markets and economies all over the world, but one of the easiest places to see the volatility of cheap money at work is in China. For example, easy and cheap money in China led to such rapid expansion in "hot" industries that supply outstripped global demand. For instance, in the solar industry, banks and the local government in Wuxi threw money at Suntech Power Holdings. The company used $1.8 billion in short-term bank loans to double production from 2009 to 2011. By 2009 the company's stock, traded as an American Depository Receipt (ADR) on the New York Stock Exchange (NYSE), was valued at $2.7 billion.

Of course, the cheap money that was easy for Suntech to raise was also available to fund lots of other solar companies to expand production. What cheap money created, cheap money took away as prices in the solar industry collapsed. Suntech's solution to that was to borrow more money, first to expand production and then to pay its bills. By the end of 2012 the company's debt-to-equity ratio had climbed to 500 percent. Finally, in March 2013, the company's largest subsidiary filed for bankruptcy. All of which took investors on a wild ride: the New York–traded ADRs of Suntech Power, which had traded at $45.97 before the global financial crisis on September 25, 2008, and a postcrisis $18.03 on January 8, 2010, closed at 42 cents on March 22, 2013.

This kind of cheap money volatility was not limited to the Chinese solar sector or to China. Shares of European banks had been

crushed in the financial crisis initially caused when cheap money
from private sources overwhelmed the market for subprime mortgages. But when cheap money from global central banks rode to the
rescue, these bank stocks turned into very profitable bets. For example, the New York–traded ADRs of Spain's biggest bank, Banco
Santander, hit a low of $4.89 on July 24, 2012. The Spanish economy
was reeling after the country's own real estate bubble had burst and
as an austerity budget of spending cuts and tax increases pushed
Spain toward a recession with 25 percent unemployment. But from
that low the ADRs of Banco Santander soared 66 percent to $8.13 on
September 14, 2012.

Why? European Central Bank President Mario Draghi made a
promise on July 26, 2012, to do whatever it took to defend the euro.
Whatever it takes, the markets knew, would include massive infu-
sions of cash into the financial markets in support of bank balance
sheets and the sovereign debt of stressed countries such as Spain. A
66 percent gain in less than two months from buying a bank stock
just because the European Central Bank had announced that it
would supply the market with as much money as was needed to support the euro? Can you see why traders and investors might think
chasing central bank policies is a good way to make money?

Of course, the more times that investing to follow the central
bank cash works, the more traders and investors jump on even the
promise of central bank cash. And the earlier they do it, the earlier
investors and traders think they need to rush to capture the move,
then the more likely the rush will overshoot and the greater the possibility that the reality won't live up to the promise.

Can you say increased volatility?

For example, a huge rally in Japanese stocks began in November
2012, on speculation that after the December elections for Parliament, the Bank of Japan would move to pour cash into the economy
to drive down the Japanese yen. With a cheaper yen, exporters such
as Mazda Motor would be able export more because their products
would be cheaper to consumers who bought in Thai baht, Korean
won, euros, or dollars. And when those sales in strong currencies
were translated into yen on company books back home, Japanese
companies would get a second earnings boost. With the leading

prime minister candidate—and eventual winner—Shinzō Abe running on a platform that called for a weaker yen, the Tokyo stock
market began a huge rally on November 14. Abe wanted the Bank
of Japan to change its inflation target from a very conservative 1
percent to 2 percent. That would be accompanied with—and accomplished by—an aggressive program of the Bank of Japan buying assets. (The word "unlimited" floated through the campaign.) There
was even talk that the bank would target foreign assets, such as US
Treasuries, in its buying.

Now, you may hate Japanese stocks, assuming you think about
them at all after their twenty-year nap. You may think the long-term
prospects for Japanese companies such as Sony are grim. You may
think that Japan's political system, which caters to old and rural
voters, just about guarantees the country's continued economic descent into irrelevance.

But even traders who believed all that still piled into the yen and
Japanese stocks. They knew that the only principle that counted in
the global financial market at the moment was "Follow the central
banks." If Abe looked likely to win, then what else to bet on than a
weaker yen and higher yen-denominated revenue and earnings for
Japanese exporters? Forget the fundamentals and follow the money.

And you would have been spectacularly right. The Nikkei 225
index climbed 74.7 percent from November 14, 2012, to May 17,
2013.

And shortly after that, you would have been spectacularly wrong.
The yen stopped falling on a belief that the Bank of Japan would
weaken the currency and instead began to climb on fears that
changes in Federal Reserve policy would produce turmoil in the
global financial markets. To get ready for that turmoil—and in a
move that actually helped create that turmoil—traders bought yen,
the world's safe haven currency of the moment. Japanese stocks
went into a nosedive as the yen rallied. The Nikkei 225 index fell
17.6 percent from May 22 to June 7. That was what—a little more
than two weeks later?

Volatility begat volatility. Following central bank money as an
investment strategy as banks react to events and change directions is
a recipe for volatility.

Once you've identified central bank moves—and cash flows—as the key to market moves, you look more and more closely to find examples of those moves. Because each offers a chance for big profits—or the risk of big losses—it makes sense to focus on this part of the financial landscape. And remember, in this process you're not following any real conviction about what stocks are worth or the fundamentals of individual companies or sectors; you're just waiting on the next spin of the money policy wheel.

At the beginning of this "follow the central bank cash" trend, it might have been limited to professional investors and trading desk number crunchers, but very quickly the search for opportunities to execute these follow-the-cash strategies moved to individual investors. Everybody is doing it. And the trading strategies that "everyone" is following are pretty sophisticated.

For example, traders in China—and I'm talking here about both the professionals and individuals trading for their own accounts—now regularly bet on the cash flow policies of the People's Bank of China in the weeks surrounding the Chinese Lunar New Year. "Everyone" knows that the People's Bank, China's central bank, works to provide extra cash to the system in the weeks before the holiday and then withdraws that cash in the weeks after the holiday. Most years some of that extra cash, provided by the central bank so companies and consumers won't run out of cash during a period of extraordinary spending, finds its way into the stock market, so it pays to bet that the market will climb on that extra cash, or at least on the expectation that the extra cash will drive stocks higher. For example, in the weeks between December 5, 2013, and January 20, 2014, that bet on the People's Bank paid off with an 11 percent gain and then again, just before the Lunar holiday period, it produced a 9.9 percent rally from January to February 2014.

The problem is that once you think you've found a tradable pattern, your tendency—well, the tendency of all of us who aren't iron-disciplined, extraordinarily savvy traders, that is—is to see the pattern everywhere. Because the point is to arbitrage between rumor and fact, you wind up speculating on rumors.

Let's say you know the recent history of the connection between Chinese stock prices and government stimulus spending. So in early

March 2014 the average individual trader in China, listening carefully to speculation that officials in the Beijing government were worried that the Chinese economy was slowing too much, began to build positions in the shares of the kind of infrastructure companies that had been used to funnel money into the economy in previous bouts of stimulus. Buying soon focused on China's railroads and the shares of big, state-owned railroad construction companies such as China Railway Construction. Your confidence in this speculation rose when official news sources said that the government wanted to speed up railroad construction spending as a way to generate a bit more economic growth. Fortunately you weren't the only trader with this thought: From March 12 to April 9 money poured into shares of China Railway Construction, turning into a 32.9 percent gain in less than a month. But then those same official sources started to quote even higher-ranking government officials as saying that the economy didn't need a big stimulus program, that minor tweaks to the tax code would be sufficient, and that, in fact, the 7.5 percent target economic growth rate was "flexible." Shares of China Railway Construction began to give back some of their gains: in the next two trading days they retreated 6.8 percent.

It was still a very attractive 24 percent gain in a less than a month—if you sold. And why wouldn't you? It's not like you really know anything fundamental about China Railway Construction. It's just a lottery ticket in a drawing sponsored—the market believed—by the Chinese government. Cash out and wait for the next drawing. (And so what if cashing out added a big dose of downside volatility to the market? That's someone else's problem.)

Or consider this example closer to home. In May 2013 the US stock market was roiled by rumors that the Federal Reserve was about to begin to taper off its purchases of $85 billion a month in Treasuries and mortgage-backed securities. That wouldn't actually reduce the amount of money in the financial system, but the Fed would cut back on the number of new dollars it was pumping out. That would, the theory went, raise interest rates and be bad for stocks. On that rumor and that conclusion, traders sold US stocks, and the S&P 500 fell 5.6 percent in the month from May 20, 2013, to June 24, 2013.

It turned out, however, that the rumor wasn't true. The June 11 and July 31 meetings of the Federal Reserve's Open Market Committee passed without any action on reducing the Fed's purchases. And so the market said, "Oops, never mind." And the S&P 500 climbed 8.7 percent from June 24 to August 2.

It's tempting to think that it's only Wall Street traders or individual investors in markets such as China's that are notorious for betting on rumors (or the significance of the ticker numbers of Hong Kong and Shanghai stocks), but individual investors in US markets are by no means immune. For example, in the months before the European Central Bank launched a Federal Reserve–style program of asset purchases in March 2015, cash from US individual investors and Wall Street traders began to flow into ETFs that invested in European stocks. In the first week of March $3.9 billion flowed into European equities—a record. In the first two and a half months of 2015 the amount of money flowing into ETFs investing in European stocks doubled from the same period of 2014. Do the individual investors sending their money into Europe-focused companies want to invest in Deutsche Bank or Continental AG because they believe those companies' earnings and revenue growth stories? Or are they betting that Magic Mario—Mario Draghi, president of the European Central Bank—can elevate European stocks with his asset purchases in the same way that his promise to do whatever it takes to save the euro created a huge rally in European government bonds?

Either because they think they have to or because they're more accustomed to doing it or because Wall Street has created new mass-market vehicles such as specialized ETFs for executing these bets—or because of the combination of all three of these reasons—individual investors have jumped into trading on central bank cash flows big time. For example, investors in ETFs bet on the price of oil-held futures equivalent to 175 million to 180 million barrels of West Texas Intermediate crude oil, the US benchmark, for delivery in May 2015. That was about 30 percent of all the open interest in this contract on the New York Mercantile Exchange and the Intercontinental Exchange, the main markets for energy futures. Not every investor in these ETFs is an individual investor, but the bulk of the money in ETFs, such as the US Oil Fund (USO), comes from individuals. As of the end of March 2015 that fund owned contracts on 64 million barrels of West Texas Intermediate, a ten-fold increase from March 2014. Bets that oil prices will head up from mid-March's $45 a barrel are secondary bets on the world's central banks. If central bank cash succeeds in stimulating economic growth in the EuroZone, China, Japan, and the United States, then demand for oil will climb, and so too will oil prices.

I'd also argue that we've become convinced that everyday life is more volatile than it used to be, that this volatility is going to be with us for a while, and that we need to come up with ways to incorporate this increased volatility into our everyday decisions and behavior. As noted earlier (pages 24–27), John Coates's research into brain chemistry suggests that we first become sensitized to volatility and then, as we get habituated to the excitement and chemicals it releases, seek out more of it. Sensitization to volatility is even more powerful if, as in the markets right now, paying attention to volatility puts money in our pockets.

I wouldn't blame all of this change in our sensitivity to volatility in everyday life to global central banks, but I do think central bank policy, interest rates, and inflation projections have entered everyday thinking to an extraordinary degree.

In real life we discount much of volatility, as it is just "normal." If the bus scheduled to come in seven minutes comes in eleven minutes, we don't even notice on most days, and we notice even less if that level of volatility is an everyday occurrence. But I would notice if, instead of a bus arriving four minutes late, it didn't arrive until the following Tuesday. And we all would notice if, instead of a bus, an elephant with boarding ladder walked up to the curb. But in everyday life those things just don't happen.

"Normal" in everyday life isn't a fixed anchor. As a benchmark, normal varies over time as expectations change. For example, one recent winter my wife and I got worried here in New York when the bus my son was taking from Bolivia to Buenos Aires still hadn't arrived, even though it was fourteen hours after the bus company said it was due. But our friends in Argentina were remarkably *not* upset when we called them. Happens all the time, they said, but they did promise to call the bus company to try to find out what was going on. Our friend in La Paz, Bolivia, was even less concerned when we called him. He had actually taken the bus route in question, and in his experience a bus that arrived only fourteen hours late should be considered early. The bus finally got in eighteen hours late. My son, accustomed to the level of volatility of New York bus schedules, was the only passenger surprised, as far as I can tell from his account of the bus company's deceptive promises about "direct service."

Recent events in the financial markets, the housing market, the job market, and the retirement market have all increased our expectations about the degree of volatility in everyday life. To take one example, my dad worked at the same company in the same town from the age of seventeen until he retired. His job wasn't always the same, thank goodness; over the course of those years he climbed from sweeper to senior maintenance electrician. I certainly never had any thought that my work history would look anything like this. The longest I've ever worked for any company is twelve years, and one of the most important parts of any job I've ever had, once I understood how the current economy works, has been figuring what I can do in that job so that when it's time to leave—either by choice or through a corporate reorganization—I've got new skills that will help me find not just a better job but one that will open up new job possibilities. As I talk to my now twenty-year-old son, I realize that I think about my own career as a model of stability in comparison to the work world he will likely face. Thinking about realms in everyday life, such as where to live or how to prepare for retirement, I realize that I don't have any pat solutions because I assume that the future world will look radically different in ways that I can't currently imagine from the world I live in now.

If you're familiar with the idea of decision landscapes, this rise in unexpected outcomes isn't unexpected. A decision landscape models the paths that a system uses to reach equilibrium. Think of the model as a landscape of mountains, hills, plains, and valleys, where the valleys represent a decision or equilibrium in the system. In this model you can imagine a decision as the path that a ball bearing would follow if it were dropped in this landscape on its way to a decision or equilibrium. When a system has relatively low energy—when volatility is low—most decisions follow well-worn paths. In this system state you can think of a decision as a river flowing down a deeply cut channel. Raise the energy in the system as a whole—add more water to the river until it hits flood stage—and the odds that the river/decision will break over the banks of the channel go up. When a river floods, it cuts new channels, and sometimes rivers don't return to the old patterns. Likewise, in times of high volatility, financial systems and everyday life can carve out new outcomes.

As comforting as it may be to think of volatility as producing a continuum of results, the evidence is that at some point an increase in volatility produces a big jump in outcomes with previously low probabilities. As energy levels in a decision landscape increase modestly, most decisions follow well-worn paths. But at some point, with the addition of energy to the system, the chance increases that a decision will jump off that path to carve a new channel. If it's only a modest thunderstorm, the odds are that rivers will stay in their channels. If it's the kind of deluge that accompanies a tropical storm, the river will likely jump its banks and carve a new channel.

This is just another way, one that I find visually easy to understand, to explain the difference between expected volatility and big-event, state-changing, new-channel-carving volatility of the sort described earlier as the New Normal.

The addition of huge amounts of money to the global financial system by the Federal Reserve, the Bank of Japan, the People's Bank of China, and the European Central Bank certainly qualifies as a big addition of energy to the world's financial and economic systems of the sort that can take a system to new outcomes. And once the addition of significant new energy destabilizes a system, it can take quite a while for the system to settle into a new equilibrium state.

In early April 2014 the International Monetary Fund (IMF) published one of its regular reports on global financial stability. The IMF knew, of course, that the world's central banks had been busy creating trillions of dollars, yen, yuan, and euros in the years after the onset of the global financial crisis. The authors of the report knew that this flood of cash had had some effect, and they suspected that the effect on emerging markets, on the relatively small and illiquid financial markets of the world's developing economies wouldn't be good. Reading the opening pages of the report, I came away convinced that the IMF's experts expected to see market distortions in prices and in the allocation of capital in many of these emerging financial markets. The worst damage, I expected them to report, would be to the markets of those countries that had done the least to control their deficits, to improve their labor markets, and to make the price of money responsive to market forces.

As I read deeper into the report, however, I realized that this isn't what the experts found and that what they had found had surprised them. Global cash flows from the world's central banks—and from retail investors through mechanisms such as ETFs—had overwhelmed distinctions among developing economies. Countries that had developed sound fiscal policies, countries that had maintained a tight watch on inflation and current account balances, countries that had let the markets set exchange and interest rates so that pressure didn't build up in the system for sudden changes, and countries that had done none of the above—they all experienced the same ebbs and flows of cash as central banks tightened, loosened, tapered, or whatever the opposite of a taper is. And the advent of ETFs, which had made it easier for retail investors to put money into heretofore-exotic markets and instruments, was actually making the situation worse, the IMF found. For example, the emerging market bond funds retail investors used were more sensitive to global market (and, hence, central bank) sentiment than institutional bond vehicles such as pension funds and sovereign wealth funds. The volatility of the financial system as a whole had increased for all the players.

If you combine the IMF report's perspective with the idea of how extra energy—in this case, trillions in cash—works in a decision landscape, you have to conclude that the likely outcomes aren't merely "more" but are indeed "different." Perhaps perversely on the fundamentals but absolutely logically from what the IMF experts had found, when the US Federal Reserve announced in December 2013 that it would reduce its program of bond buying by $10 billion a month beginning in January, emerging financial markets fell and financial markets in the United States rallied. A trader who had bet that US markets in stocks and bonds would fall—because reducing the Federal Reserve's monthly asset purchases would cause the US economy to slow, thereby reducing company profits, and because winding down the Fed's program of asset purchases brought closer the day when the US central bank would finally begin to raise interest rates from the current 0 percent level—would have been right logically and dead wrong in practice. The logic would have been based on the historical record and the dynamics that have ruled past markets and past reversals in Federal Reserve stimulus. The actual moves in the market, however, suggested that, for the moment, it would be more profitable to throw the historical record onto the trash bin of history.

Why didn't the past provide a useful guide to current market volatility? Because the degree of money creation by the world's central banks had forged new pathways in the decision space, resulting in breaks with past pathways.

The likelihood that the system will continue to throw up historically unusual decisions persists too. You could say that once the system has become destabilized, it continues in that condition and is capable of producing surprising decisions—or at least decisions that violate historically based expectations—for years.

So, for example, in Japan in 2015 the financial system, rather than settling down toward either past patterns or some new but predictable pattern, showed a profound tendency to head in unexpected directions. After the election of Shinzō Abe to prime minister in 2013, the Bank of Japan launched its own version of quantitative easing. Like the program at the Federal Reserve, the idea was for the central bank to buy massive quantities of government bonds in order to drive down interest rates. That would translate into faster economic growth—in the United States through the mechanism, again, of a housing market revived by lower mortgage rates and, in Japan, through an increase in exports thanks to a cheap yen.

But, strikingly, that Japanese program looks like it is headed into unexpected territory. Although the Bank of Japan has kept to its public goal of increasing inflation to 2 percent in order to break the long grip that deflation has had on the Japanese economy, it has not actually engineered a significant and sustained increase in either inflation or growth. The collapse in oil prices has pushed down inflation, and an increase in the national sales tax has slowed growth. Rather than the two-year program originally envisioned, the Bank of Japan now seems embarked on a permanent effort to hold down interest rates so that the Japanese government can continue to run huge budget deficits without running up an even more crushing interest bill. As of March 2015 the Bank of Japan owned 23 percent of all government debt, and with monthly purchases of 80 trillion yen, it is buying twice as many bonds in the market as the government is issuing. The government's interest rate bill, because interest rates are so low, has dropped to 10.1 trillion yen. That, the *Financial Times* has noted, is less than the government paid in interest in 1986, when the government's accumulated debt was 20 percent of today's total.

The fear among fiscal conservatives in the United States has long been that the Federal Reserve and the US government have no intention of ever paying back what the government owes. Instead, critics say, Fed policies are designed to monetize the debt so that, through inflation and permanently super-low interest rates, the debt and debt payments would gradually fade away.

Although that fear remains real, it is still just a fear in the United States. Japan, however, looks like it has embarked on a path that winds up with the Bank of Japan monetizing the government's debt. That, I think, would qualify as an unexpected, big-volatility, "different" decision.

As this example from Japan shows, volatility puts extraordinary stress on institutions—which is one reason high volatility can produce unexpected decisions. In Japan we're seeing the long-recognized weakness of the Japanese political system, biased as it is toward the country's more rural and older voters, turning into a perhaps fatal inability to reduce government deficits and pursue long-term growth policies. We're seeing the inefficiencies of the Japanese economy, which were certainly present during the decades of Japan's economic miracle, move from quaint anecdotes to the deep cause of Japan's inability to generate 2 percent economic growth.

It makes you wonder what weaknesses in US, EuroZone, and Chinese institutions will be exacerbated by heightened volatility. China has faced challenges of managing a huge expansion of the money supply, done to prevent the global financial crisis from crashing the Chinese economy, and then figuring out what to do with the resulting explosion in debt and bad debt. This has resulted in a quiet but bitterly fought battle between the People's Bank and the China Banking Regulatory Commission over the goals and direction of China's banking system. The solution to that, the central bank feels, is to tighten up lending standards at regulated banks and reduce lending by unregulated shadow banks by making it harder for these companies to get capital. That effort, the People's Bank feels, is being hampered by the China Banking Regulatory Commission. The central bank sees the China Banking Regulatory Commission as too close to the state-owned banks it is supposed to regulate and too lax with the smaller lenders who currently pose the biggest bad debt risk to the system. The People's Bank would like to see the commission implement a long-discussed system of deposit insurance and move more quickly toward interest rates for deposits set by the market instead of regulatory fiat.

In turn the China Banking Regulatory Commission believes, according to officials from that commission and the central bank who have recently discovered a new interest in talking to the press, that the People's Bank created the current problems by failing to address growing risks in the banking system years ago. And now the People's Bank is unfairly blaming the commission for a problem that the central bank created.

Because the two agencies are barely speaking to each other, the policies being thrown at the financial markets often seem more like one-upmanship in this turf battle than considered efforts to address the problems in the system. The liquidity freezes of 2014 by the People's Bank, for example, which suddenly starved the banking system of the overnight loans banks need to balance the cash flows in their lending units, sent the price of overnight money soaring to all-time records, above 20 percent—yes, 20 percent interest on an overnight loan. Worse yet, when considering the working of the system as a whole, some medium-size and small banks couldn't find overnight funds at all; parts of the banking system simply froze in place. Faced with that reality, the People's Bank had to quickly reverse course and restore liquidity—only to starve the system again in a few weeks. And only to have to backtrack again.

Of course, the effect on the markets was to make all lenders and borrowers aware of exactly how precarious the supply of funds was.

In the second round of the liquidity events it actually took less of a move by the central bank to create more chaos in the system because banks and lenders started to hoard cash as soon as they sensed a repeat of the liquidity event that had only recently been so painful.

And it's not just financial institutions in developing economies that can find themselves taking steps under stress that increase volatility in a crunch. The US Federal Reserve was founded in 1913, so it's not exactly a kid anymore. However, in light of the extraordinary steps it had taken in the aftermath of the financial crisis—adding $3 trillion to its balance sheet, launching three rounds, more or less, of unprecedented asset purchases, and holding short-term rates at 0 percent for six years and counting as of 2015—the Fed decided it would be a good thing to communicate its policy intentions to the financial markets as clearly as possible.

- In December 2008 the Fed said it would keep interest rates exceptionally low "for some time."
- In March 2009 it changed that statement to "for an extended period."
- In August 2011 that became "exceptionally low levels for the federal funds rate at least through mid-2013."
- In January 2012 the Fed changed "mid-2013" into "late 2014." In September 2012 "late 2014" turned into "mid-2015."
- In December 2012 the Fed said forget the calendar and watch the unemployment rate. The US central bank would keep rates at 0 percent until the unemployment rate hit 6.5 percent.
- And then in January 2014 the Fed threw that formula out the window too. Because the US recovery had been so slow and enough people had dropped out of the workforce, the unemployment rate was falling toward 6.5 percent, even though the number of people actually working wasn't changing much.
- The new policy hinged on the word "patient," as in the Federal Reserve would be patient before beginning to raise interest rates.
- That word then disappeared from the Fed's postmeeting statement in March 2015 and, despite much premeeting speculation, financial markets didn't tumble or soar.

As you might expect, the markets have become confused by this changing formulation and staged significant rallies or drops as investors interpreted and misinterpreted the Fed's intentions.

All this volatility has emphasized a couple of key contradictions in the very makeup of the Fed. First, the Fed has a conflicted relationship with Wall Street and the financial industry that it is supposed to regulate. The Fed conducts that regulation with at least one eye at all times on the way the financial industry can slow or speed up economic growth. If the financial industry is in a snit about the extent of new regulations, it can, consciously or unconsciously, cut back on lending and other forms of financing to slow the economy. If you're a financial conspiracy fan—and I am—you'd say that Wall Street has frequently done just that in response to the wave of post–financial crisis regulations.

Second, in 1978 Congress added a second set of tasks to the Fed's mandate in the Humphrey-Hawkins Full Employment Act. The Fed, according to those marching orders, is supposed to manage the money supply both to assure the soundness of the financial system *and* to maximize employment in the economy. Leaving aside the question of how to do either job adequately, it's not at all clear how one institution is supposed to do both adequately. In a normal economy the conflict between those goals isn't especially intense, but in a crisis it comes to the fore, as the Fed's shifting guidance on when it will start to raise rates from 0 percent might suggest. And in a crisis, when the market has both ears cocked in an effort to hear the slightest sound of a policy change, that conflict adds volatility to the market, as the Fed produces messages that can be read in too many ways, even when the poor wordsmiths at the Fed thought they were being perfectly clear and consistent.

The global financial crisis and the task of managing the huge wave of cash that central banks created to "fix" that crisis would, by itself, be enough to propel the global financial system and global economies into a very "energetic" decision space. This is, of course, likely to produce lots of decisions that deviate from past history. But this isn't the only crisis that the world's systems are facing right now. The world's central banks have had a relatively large amount of experience in dealing with global recessions and depressions—although it isn't clear that this experience has translated into a well-defined consensus on how to react to this kind of crisis. But they have much less experience with the crisis that the unprecedented aging of the world's population has created.

In many ways it's a good crisis to have, as living longer is, I've heard, generally preferable to the alternative. But there still should be no doubt about how big a dose of volatility an aging world—a world that is older than it has ever been—adds.

I think that some of this talk about volatility landscapes and central bank policy can sound pretty abstract. What's the point? How is this all going to help me earn a better return on my portfolio or figure out where and when to buy a house? I promise that the last third of this book will get very concrete indeed and that I'll give you five investment strategies built on this approach to volatility.

But let me also give you a preview in the next chapter of how my analysis of volatility—which I'm still in the process of explaining—can make you money. I'll use a concrete strategy involving dividend income stocks to show why incorporating volatility into your thinking is a profitable thing to do in the Age of Volatility. After that diversion into concrete investing strategies, I'll then continue my exploration of the volatility landscape and my explanation of how to think about and use volatility by describing how the shape of the unexplored territory of demographics adds volatility to the system.

Chapter 6

A Strategy Appetizer

Dividend Stocks as a Way to Beat Market Volatility

MANY INVESTORS ALREADY USE dividend stocks as a way to control volatility. The theory is that stocks that pay a dividend—offering a yield of, say, 3 percent, which is way more than you get on a ten-year Treasury (2.13 percent in May 2015 and 2.52 percent in May 2014)—provide a buffer in volatile markets. Investors who, for example, bought chip maker Intel for its 3 percent dividend yield would hold even if the stock dropped in price because that 3 percent dividend, short of a meltdown in Intel's business, would continue to be paid despite the drop in price.

That theory actually works, in my experience, as long as the volatility isn't too extreme. In practice, if we're looking at day-to-day volatility—those effectively random daily moves or a modest 3 percent or 5 percent decline in the indexes—then, yes, buying a stock with an attractive dividend will damp volatility. That's a reason that, like Intel, other stocks with 3 percent or so yields in 2014 and 2015, such as Microsoft and Procter and Gamble, were measurably less volatile than the market as a whole. The beta on these three stocks was in each case below 1—0.93 for Intel, 0.88 for Microsoft, and 0.87 for Procter and Gamble. (Beta compares the volatility of an individual stock to the market as a whole. By definition, the market has a volatility of 1. Stocks with a lower volatility than the market as a whole show betas below 1, whereas stocks with a higher volatility than the market as a whole show a beta above 1. So Google, which does not pay a dividend, has a beta of 1.06. Palo Alto Networks, a fast-growing cyber-security stock that also pays no dividend, has a beta of 1.24.)

But any investor who has suffered through the bear markets of 2000 and 2008 knows that when general-market volatility climbs above 15 percent or so, even dividends won't protect a portfolio. In a bear market everything falls, as even the least volatile stock seems risky in comparison to cash. As a bear drags on, traders need to meet calls on the margin loans they used to buy stocks, so they sell what has fallen the least to raise cash. In this kind of market the degree of volatility overwhelms a dividend's ability to protect against a decline in the price of a stock.

But in the Age of Volatility I think we can—and, indeed, should—go beyond this traditional strategy for using dividends to manage volatility. And I have two suggestions for an improved dividend strategy that uses volatility to score higher dividend yields for your portfolio rather than simply using dividends to dampen the effects of volatility in some markets.

The first suggestion relies on long-term volatility in dividend payout rates across stocks. It turns out that just as "financial engineering" tools such share buybacks or highly leveraged private equity buyouts have trends, so do dividend payouts, the percentage of cash flows that companies pay out as dividends.

The second is built on the observation that if interest rates in the United States are set to rise beginning late in 2015 or sometime in 2016, the bond market is likely to turn more volatile. (Remember that bond prices fall as interest rates and yields rise.) That will give an edge to dividend-paying stocks over bonds because companies can raise dividends to keep pace with rising interest rates, whereas bonds are stuck with the coupon interest rate they were born with. I think this will make dividend-paying stocks, especially those from companies with a tradition of raising payouts, an attractive asset versus bonds.

A dividend strategy for the Age of Volatility would, first of all, take into account long-term dividend cycles. For example, Microsoft paid a quarterly dividend of 31 cents a share in April 2015, whereas in 2008 its quarterly payout was 11 cents a share; Intel's quarterly dividend in 2015 was 24 cents a share, but in 2006 it was 10 cents a share; and Apple paid a quarterly dividend of 47 cents a share in 2015 plus a special dividend of $3.29 a share in May 2014, though in 1995 the dividend was 10 cents a share.

Today's relatively high-dividend payouts and yields came after a long period of companies paying almost nothing. Intel's dividend in 2004 was a token 2 cents a share—just enough to let those money managers who were limited to buying shares with dividends buy Intel stock.

Why the change? In part it's a result of Intel's and Microsoft's maturation from technology growth stock "rockets" owned by earnings momentum investors into stocks owned by growth at a price investors, value investors, or income investors. These mature companies went out to recruit a new investor base to replace those who had moved on to, say, Amazon.com or Palo Alto Networks.

In part it's a result of activists and other investors demanding that companies return a higher portion of their cash to shareholders. That has certainly been the case for Apple, which has even been adding debt to enable it to pay higher dividends. Higher dividends are a price that companies are paying right now so activist investors such as Carl Icahn will leave them alone to take care of business as they see fit.

And in part it's a turn in the cycle. The previous trend emphasized big buybacks of shares because reducing the share count spread earnings over fewer shares and made the remaining shares more valuable. And profited executives with compensation packages linked to earnings per share. Companies believed that's what investors wanted to see. But in the last few years—sometime after the end of the worst of the global financial crisis but while the slow growth of the Great Recession was still with us—companies came to believe that investors were more impressed by dividends because they actually put cash in their pockets. (Some of that was a result of a growing cynicism about buybacks. Investors recognized that announcing a plan to buy $6 billion in shares wasn't a guarantee that a company would actually buy back $6 billion in shares.)

Whatever the reason, dividends have been in favor recently. In the first half of 2014, for example, 422 out of the 500 companies in the S&P 500 paid a dividend, the highest percentage since September 1998.

What does this mean for you, the investor? It means that this is the time to lock up the relatively high dividends that come with dividends being again in favor. However, with US stocks near all-time highs in 2015, you can't just drive up to the market window and say, "Fill 'er up with 5 percent yields."

Yields that high are few and far between, but they do exist, as well as 4 and 3 percent yields on stocks that used to pay just about nothing. As long as the fashion stays tilted toward dividends, you'll be able to find a small but steady supply of stocks offering dividend yields above the long-term average.

In the post–World War II US stock market, from roughly 1958 to 1974, the "fashion" for dividends fluctuated around a 3 percent yield for the stocks in the S&P 500. The high-inflation and high-interest period from 1974 to 1983 saw the yield on the S&P 500 peak at a little over 6 percent. Since then it's been pretty much downhill, with a low of just above 1 percent in 1999, and then a very modest rally to just short of 2 percent in 2015. That suggests that if you can find a yield above the 3 percent level—which seems to be a market default for much of the postwar period—and then lock it in by buying shares of a company that looks to stand a good chance of growing the cash flow it has available to pay dividends, then you'd be well served.

Paying this much attention to one or two percentage points might seem piddling, but you'll understand why it's not if you look at Robert Shiller's data for price appreciation on the S&P 500 against price appreciation with dividends reinvested. Shiller is the 2013 Nobel laureate in economics and, more germane here, the author of *Irrational Exuberance*, a book published in 2000, that is indispensable for understanding the last two bear markets and the nature of the current market. He found that from July 1999 to April 2012 the price appreciation of the S&P 500 produced a gain of just 0.4 percent. With dividends reinvested, the return came to 26.3 percent. This is especially amazing when you see that the dividend yield for that period was almost always below 3 percent and frequently below 2. Reinvesting dividends during this period meant you were putting new money to work at a bottom in stock prices—hence the large gain.

Yield makes a difference. And the longer the period, the greater the difference. It seems like trying to lock in yields above 3 percent now, when the long-term volatility wheel has turned in favor of dividends, would make a big difference to anyone investing for a long-term goal such as retirement, a house, or a kid's education.

The second part of an Age-of-Volatility "improved" dividend strategy attempts to use short-term volatility to pick up dividend yields of 5 percent or so—frankly, I'd take anything that rounds up to 5 percent—when market sell-offs or sector panics produce them. Remember that if Bill Gross's projections for his New Normal scenario are correct, 5 percent a year in yield is going to be above the benchmark for most income investments in the period ahead. What the improved dividend strategy tries to do is to keep that goal in sight during all times of volatility and to snap up solid, sustainable 5 percent or better yields when fear stalks the financial markets.

Let's stick with Intel as an example. Remember that in recent years Intel has been raising its quarterly dividend rather aggressively. In 2015 the quarterly dividend had climbed to 24 cents. That's up from 22.5 cents a share in November 2012 and 21 cents a share in August 2011.

But Intel's share price has climbed during that period from the double lows of 2011 and 2012, when the entire market struggled back at those points. In April 2015 the stock traded in the neighborhood of $32 a share, but back in November 2012 the share price was $19.57, and in August 2011 it was just $19.19.

The math says that despite its bigger-dollar dividend in 2015, 24 cents in the first quarter of 2015 versus 21 cents in August 2011, Intel's yield was higher back then because of the stock's lower share price. The yield then was a little over 4.5 percent, more than the slightly under 3 percent yield in 2015.

My improved dividend strategy would have said, "Back up the truck" in 2011. You would have locked in a 4.5 percent yield. Even if the stock price didn't go higher, you still had only paid $19.19 in 2011 and assured yourself of a yield of 4.5 percent on that money.

And if the share price went higher, Yippee! Icing on the cake of that 4.5 percent yield.

And, of course, your $19.19 a share price back in 2011 wasn't just buying the current dividend payout; you were buying the increases— if any—in the cash payout by Intel too. So for your $19.19 in 2011 you were also buying the 93 cents a share annual payout in the twelve months ending in May 2015. That's a 4.8 percent yield, with the prospects of the income from that initial purchase at $19.19 climbing even higher in the years ahead if Intel continues to raise its cash payout.

Where you set the dividend yield that triggers your "buy" decision comes down to personal choice and subjective judgment. In a context of very low overall interest rates and yields—less than 2.5 percent on a ten-year US Treasury, for example—I would set my trigger a bit lower, at, say, 4.5 percent rather than an ironclad 5 percent. I'd also set a somewhat lower cutoff—4.5 or maybe 4 percent— in the case of a company with a strong record of increasing dividends. Another reason to set my trigger at 4.5 percent for Intel is that the company has grown dividends at a 9.6 percent annual rate over the last five years. That's better than PepsiCo at 7.8 percent or Procter and Gamble at 7.9 percent annual growth.

However, what I don't want to do is set a lower trigger for a company with shaky growth prospects going forward. I'd buy Intel back in 2011 at a 4.5 percent yield because this is the world's best chip manufacturer with a long-term technology advantage in that aspect of its business, because the company looks to have a solid growth path in chips for the servers that run the cloud, and because Intel will, in my belief, eventually gain a bigger share than its current tiny slice of the market for chips in mobile devices. In contrast, I wouldn't stretch to buy Procter and Gamble now, with its 3.21 percent yield in April 2015, because the company is struggling with slow growth in developed economies and with lower-than-expected growth in developing economies. The company faces a strategic restructuring to fix those problems, and I'd like to see the plan before I put my money on the line.

Pursuing this improved dividend strategy requires three disciplines from an investor. First, the investor needs to know where we are in general market cycles. For example, if the market is selling off, you can expect dividend yields to be rising as share prices fall, so this is a good time to go on the hunt as long as you believe the market isn't headed into an extended bear. If a sector is out of favor, it can also be a good time to go on the hunt as long as you don't think prospects for the sector are permanently impaired. ("Permanently" is a subjective term that means "Longer than a specific investor can stand.") It also helps to have a feel for whether dividend-paying stocks are in or out of favor. They tend to rise in price when the market is nervous and investors are looking for a bit of safety. They tend to decline, usually modestly, in price when the market is brimming with confidence and everybody wants to own momentum stocks.

Second, our investor has to run a computerized screen, looking regularly for higher-dividend yields on an Internet site—once a week strikes me as reasonable—to see what names pop up to the top of the yield list because of changes in share prices. You can find simple screeners on Morningstar, Yahoo Finance, or on specialized sites such as Dividend.com.

Third, an investor has to perform the same research into company and industry fundamentals before buying any stock that will be held for a while. A 5 percent yield is great, but it won't offset a steady or rapid drop in the share price if the company is losing market share, does business in a declining industry, or is in the hands of entrenched idiots in the executive suite.

And please, when pursuing any dividend strategy—mine or any other—learn to look at dividend record dates before buying and, especially, selling. The record date is the day that entitles the owner of shares to the dividend on the payout date. Buy after that date, and you don't get this dividend, although you'll get the next one. Sell before that date, and you'll lose that dividend payout.

This chapter has, as promised, gotten very nitty-gritty and concrete. You can expect more of the practical of this sort in the last third of this book, where I'll give you five more investing strategies for *Juggling with Knives*.

In this chapter I've applied some of what I've highlighted earlier about volatility and the opportunities—as well as dangers—it presents. This dividend strategy, for example, seeks to profit from the difference in long- and short-term volatility and tries to incorporate the probability that the next couple of decades will offer much lower returns on assets such as stocks and bonds than we experienced in the period from 1981 to 2000.

It also foreshadows such volatility ideas as the likely change in the correlations among asset classes that will likewise change how we build portfolios—the standard 60 percent–40 percent equity-to-bond ratio isn't likely to be so standard in the future given the likely changes in the volatility landscape.

Now it's time to turn back to the big trends that drive this Age of Volatility and to develop some of those so far only foreshadowed ideas, using those trends as examples. And of those trends, none are bigger than the demographics of an aging world, the subject of my next chapter.

Chapter 7

Older, Yes, but Wiser?

IT'S IRONIC THAT MOVES designed to take volatility out of the financial markets wound up at the core of the greatest big-volatility event since the Great Depression.

But it makes perfect sense. The huge wave of cash created by global central banks added enough energy to the system to push it into very unexplored territory. The aging of the world's population added more energy—in the forms of greed, delusion, biased decision making, and political expediency—to truly unmoor the system from historical norms and expectations.

Imagine it's January 2005—years before the Lehman bankruptcy of September 2008 that is usually tagged as the beginning date for the global financial crisis—and you're a portfolio manager at a pension fund or an insurance company. The yield on the ten-year US Treasury has fallen to 4.23 percent, and there's a good chance it will move even lower over the next year or two or three. That 4.23 percent yield is a problem for you.

A big part of your job is to match the maturities and cash flows from the investments the portfolio owns with the projected cash flows out of the portfolio as it meets its obligations to retirees, in the case of a pension fund, or to policyholders. Using actuarial projections, you know roughly how long retirees will live and how long you'll need to send them a monthly check. Using similar projections you also know about how many will get sick in any given year, and thus need their insurance to pay hospital bills, and how many will die, leaving their beneficiaries to collect on their policies.

At the moment you're getting very uncomfortably squeezed from a number of different directions. Yields on the safest investments, such as Treasuries, are low and look set to go lower. (In fact, in May 2015 the yield on a ten-year US Treasury was down to 2.13 percent.) If you can't find a way to improve those yields, the pension fund will have to ask the sponsoring corporation or government to increase its contributions to it. Ask taxpayers for more money? Yipes! That's a good way to end a career in fund management. Ask a corporate client to up its contributions? Another stellar career move.

And even finding enough safe assets to buy seems to be a bigger and bigger challenge. Only a handful of companies now earn an AAA credit rating from S&P or the equivalent from Moody's Investors Service or Fitch Ratings. Even the number of local and state governments with AAA ratings has been in decline, and it's even possible that the biggest bond issuer of all, the United States, might someday lose its AAA rating. Japan lost its AAA rating in 2001, so a downgrade for the United States certainly can't be ruled out. (The United States would, indeed, lose its AAA rating in August 2011.)

But maybe the biggest squeeze is coming from rising life expectancies. The life expectancy at birth in the United States had climbed to 77.5 years in 2005. (That's the average for both sexes and all races.) In 2000 it had been 76.8 years and in 1995 75.8 years.

Now, certainly you're in favor of people living longer and expiring later, but it still makes your job tougher. If you're a portfolio manager at a pension fund, every extra month of life expectancy means another month of pension payouts. And it's not like you can go ask retirees to put in more cash to make up for living longer.

The problem is different but equally thorny for portfolio managers at insurance companies. People aren't simply living much longer in general; they're particularly living much longer once they get to be old. Life expectancy at sixty-five had climbed to 18.4 years in the United States by 2005 on average for both sexes. In 2000 it had been 17.6 years, and 17.2 years in 1990 and 16.4 in 1980. And although people may have more years of life after sixty-five than ever before, there's no getting around the fact that the last years of life can be very expensive medically, as chronic conditions worsen or as measures to prolong life get more extreme.

Any portfolio manager facing this crunch—low yields, diminishing AAA supply, rising payouts—would have been willing to listen in 2005 when Wall Street came calling with a new product. The housing boom was old enough so that it wasn't about to generate a big increase in AAA-rated mortgages, and with mortgage rates following the yields on ten-year Treasuries as they crept lower, the kind of mortgage-backed debt instruments that portfolio managers were used to buying from Wall Street houses, which had first bought them from banks and then bundled them into securities, didn't seem like a way out of the portfolio manager's crunch.

But Wall Street had come up with a new wrinkle. The mortgage lenders that had most aggressively ridden the housing boom—companies like Countrywide Financial and Washington Mutual—had expanded the pool of potential homebuyers by approving mortgages for buyers with less-than-sterling credit ratings. By offering what were called subprime mortgages, these lenders were able to keep feeding the big mortgage engines they had built. But, as a result, they were producing huge volumes of subprime mortgages that would lock up their capital as long as these mortgages stayed on lenders' books. Portfolio managers were used to buying securitized bundles of AAA-rated mortgages from lenders, but these subprime loans presented a problem. By definition they didn't carry AAA credit ratings, and the ratings they did carry flagged them as carrying too much risk for many portfolios.

Which is where Wall Street rode to the rescue. What if, the new product developers on Wall Street asked, we bundled those subprime mortgages? A few mortgages could go bad, but the whole pool would be big enough that those defaults wouldn't matter, they argued. And further, if the bundles were divided into pieces, called tranches, with different credit ratings, it would be possible to create a mix of bundles in which the highest-quality subprime mortgages would insulate the lower-quality ones. Even if the lower-quality subprime mortgages defaulted at a higher rate, the ownership of the higher-quality tranches would provide a big buffer.

And these bundling tactics gave the new product a very high credit rating. Credit rating companies such as the S&P and Moody's Investors Service looked at Wall Street's models and agreed with their number crunchers that the best of these tranches of subprime mortgages did indeed deserve AAA ratings. And because the borrowers who were signing up for these subprime loans were paying more for their mortgages, as they didn't have the world's greatest credit ratings, even the AAA-rated tranches paid higher yields than ten-year Treasuries.

It was the best of all possible worlds—higher yields and comparable safety.

You might think that there would have been more resistance to this product than there was. After all, isn't the financial industry home to hard-nosed cynics who firmly believe that if a deal is too good to be true, it is indeed unlikely to be true?

But that ignores a truth well known and cherished by the practitioners of scams and frauds for a millennium. The best scam is one in which the potential victim already believes—he wants the scam to be true. And it's even better if the potential victim believes that he is smarter than the person running the game. The sheep that believes it's smarter than other sheep is so much easier to sheer. And those sheep that believe they are smarter than the wolves are by far the easiest to devour.

I don't know whether you've ever spent much time watching a street game such as Three-Card Monte, sometimes known as Find the Lady because a queen is often the card the mark needs to find in order to win. (I grew up in an era in New York when Times Square was full of Three-Card Monte games on any sunny afternoon, and I used to love to watch them.) The dealer always worked with a shill whose job was to convince the mark he would win because either he—and Three-Card Monte victims, in my experience, were almost always guys—was smarter than the dealer and, therefore, would be able to find the queen easily despite the dealer's effort to obscure its position among the three cards of the game, or because he was smarter than the guy who was currently beating the dealer on every second or third hand. (This winner would also be a shill working with the dealer.) To get the mark to bet, the shill had to convince the victim that he was sure to win. Little remarks belittling the dealer, the second "winning" shill, and pumping up the potential victim's ego were the successful shills' tools of the trade. Don't think for a moment that this formula doesn't work: Three-Card Monte has been around since at least the fifteenth century.

I don't want to carry my Three-Card Monte analogy too far but, if you'd like to cast the parts, pick your favorite Wall Street rocket scientist at Goldman Sachs or JPMorgan Chase as the dealer and the rating agencies as the shills. It's pretty clear that the victims were all the money managers who bought this stuff thinking that they were smart enough to beat the dealer.

And those portfolio managers were, of course, only the first level of victims. A lot of people who never even met the dealer or saw the cards being shuffled lost their homes and retirement portfolios and jobs because of the actions of that first level of victims. There's a lesson here about how to navigate the period of heightened volatility ahead. Certainly it's pretty clear that trusting the smart guys and gals isn't a good idea; they have their own institutional goals and biases that don't have much in common with yours, and they're going to have their hands full getting through this period with their own skins intact. Their interests may, from time to time, correspond with yours—and then they may be worth listening to. But most of the time I wouldn't count on them for advice that's got a whole lot of value for you.

The story of how the financial crisis unfolded has been told a number of times by now, and the story of what financial companies, central banks, and national governments have done to fight the Great Recession is still unfolding, is still contentious, and despite that—or because of that—it too has been told over and over again.

But let me make a couple of important points from the perspective of volatility so we can understand where we've come from recently and what we're likely to wind up facing.

From a volatility perspective much of the recent finger pointing about who was more at fault—greedy bankers or greedy homebuyers—is largely beside the point. The whole episode is a gigantic and scary example of how volatility begets volatility. Once the bankers, portfolio managers, credit rating companies, and deregulating politicians had let the housing boom build up momentum, it would have required a truly courageous central banker or politician to put a foot on the brakes hard enough to stop the economy as it hurtled, at ever higher speeds, toward disaster. Could someone have stepped on the brake that hard? It is difficult to imagine but certainly possible. But as the crisis built up speed each month, stepping on the brake got harder and more unlikely.

As the crisis unfolded, we moved from the unmooring of benchmarks and expectations into complete fantasy worlds. But because, as in some huge game of Three-Card Monte, the victims wanted to believe, it's hard to see how, short of a crash, it would have been possible to restore some rational sense of risk and reward. Again from a volatility perspective, casting the people who lied on their mortgage applications as victims is beside the point. Many of these folks, on some level, knew what they were doing was over the line. But they wanted to believe. They wanted to be a part of the profits. They wanted to think that for them it would be different this time.

And the workers—hardly bankers in any traditional sense—who "helped" borrowers fill out their mortgage applications? Many of them also knew that something was wrong, that faking an ID wasn't how the process was supposed to work, that making up income numbers quite probably constituted fraud. They too wanted to believe that what they were doing would work out, that the people signing those forms would be able to pay and not only keep their houses but also sell them at a profit.

It's important to ask how you get a crisis that requires this degree of unmooring from reality, legality, and any sense of how the world really works. Yes, you can chalk it up to greed, but then you have to ask: What brought out the greed at this moment? If greed is always with us and is one of the classic seven deadly sins, why did we have an outbreak at this particular moment? (And once we figure that out, we sure should ask: Can this happen again? The answer to that is a very depressing: Of course.)

Think of how unhinged this crisis was. In *The Unwinding* George Packer describes a Tampa real estate boom in which a buyer named Sonny King had been able to sell houses he had bought for a few hundred or thousand dollars to front buyers who were drug dealers, arsonists, or mentally ill. These buyers paid $200,000 to $300,000 or more, which they had borrowed from a local bank that was a subsidiary of the national Washington Mutual. The bank had asked very few questions, did not attempt to verify incomes, perhaps did not even visit the properties being purchased, and certainly required no down payment. Although it may be true that there are operators like this in any market, the question remains: Why did we get to this scale of fraud in this market at this time?

I'd isolate two factors. First, you need to have a really, really strong motivation that will make people step up to the Three-Card Monte table and play. That motivation can be arrogance—a belief that you're smarter than the rubes who have been winning the game so far—or it can be desperation: the chance to beat the dealer out of $20 bucks is very important. (Do you think the people who play Powerball when the pot gets to be $100 million don't know that the odds of winning are very, very small?) But to get a crisis like the subprime mortgage debacle, you need something that unmoors people from how they know the world really works and from what they know is right.

And second, you need to have some amplifier that turns a run-of-the-mill crisis, in which a few cities get sucked down the drain, into a national or, indeed, global big-volatility event. You need leverage to turn the US (and Irish and Spanish) real estate boom and subsequent bust into a crisis capable of threatening the entire national and then global financial system, one that required innovations in Wall Street financial engineering that let leverage build up, that disguised the institutions that were in trouble, and that then let the weakest parts of the system endanger the whole.

You don't have to look far for the source of that leverage, for the motivator, for the amplifier capable of throwing country after country into crisis and of sending the global financial system careening toward yet another cliff. It's called aging. I don't think it's the only cause of volatility over the next few decades, but it's certainly a major one and one that was at the heart of the motivation of the money managers that led to the global financial crisis.

In 1982 12 percent of the US population was sixty-five or older. By 2012 that percentage had climbed to 14 percent. And anybody running money at a pension fund or insurance company knew the projections for the next twenty years by heart: by 2030 the percentage of the US population sixty-five or older will climb to 20 percent.

If you don't think that's a big deal, consider the following.

In February 2014 the Congressional Budget Office issued a report looking at big multi-employer pension funds. These huge plans, sponsored by a collection of companies in the same industry and often administered through a union—the Teamsters' Central States pension fund with four hundred thousand members is a good example—have been thought to be too big to fail. But now dozens of these multi-employer plans that cover 10 million US workers and retirees are teetering on the edge. If they fail in the number that the Congressional Budget Office fears, their failure will completely wipe out the federal government insurer that covers these plans. The causes of that potential failure were low returns on investments (a result of big losses in the dot-com and global financial crises, plus the low interest rates prevailing as the Federal Reserve kept short-term interest rates at near 0 percent) and the increase in life expectancy. People who had reached sixty-five were living for more years after sixty-five and collecting more pension benefits. In 1990 the life expectancy for men reaching sixty-five was 15.3 years and for women 19.6 years. By 2012 that had climbed to 19.1 years for men and 22 years for women. Plans based on male workers collecting benefits for 15.3 years after they retired just weren't funded for male workers who lived almost an extra 4 years. (And a life expectancy of 22 years after sixty-five for women was a total horror show. Is it really surprising that when Congress passed legislation in 2006 that let pension funds cut the benefits paid to retirees, gutting one of the central guarantees of the 1974 Employee Retirement Income Security Act [ERISA], one of the key groups whose benefits were now okay to cut were widows?)

I think the odds are that the US pension crisis won't turn into a big-volatility event. So far the mechanism is absent for amplifying the disaster and then spreading the pain across the financial markets until the crisis finds a weak link ready to collapse—and take a big chunk of the pyramid down with it. Pension funds will go bust and retirees will suffer huge pain, but so far I don't see the interlocking leverage that turned the subprime mortgage crisis into the global financial crisis.

Not that Wall Street hasn't helped pension funds, companies, and city and state governments dig themselves a deep, deep hole. It has invented products that justify claims from money managers that they would earn 10 or 12 percent on the pension fund's money—enough to keep the pension fund in the black in fantasy accounting world. If a pension fund manager would put the fund's money into a hedge fund instead of the usual fixed-income portfolio, Wall Street was willing to promise 12 percent returns. (Of course, the argument got a lot more convincing if somehow fees found their way to politically connected law firms or contributions went into political campaigns, as they did in some combination in the case of state pension funds in Rhode Island, New Jersey, and Illinois.) Wall Street was also glad to design programs of derivatives to either insure against losses from a pension fund taking on more risk in a hedge fund than it would have if it just bought bonds or to give the fund leverage in order to increase its gains from market moves. And certainly everything conspired to suggest that looking the other way was a more tolerable situation than actually facing up to the reality of a declining pension fund. But the results of these maneuvers have been the failure of individual pension funds or local governments—local rather than global pain.

But don't worry. An aging world has other tricks up its sleeve. At best these will add to the financial and everyday volatility of the current period and, at worst, might even turn into another big-volatility event capable of shaking the global financial market.

Reverse mortgages, for example, are too small—so far—to lead to a global crisis, but the product is still young. Reverse mortgages, which allow home owners to take money out of their houses even if they still owe on the house and then live there until they die, are growing at a frantic rate. In 2013 reverse mortgage borrowers took out $15.3 billion in such loans, up 20 percent from 2012, according to Inside Mortgage Finance. About ten thousand baby boomers turn sixty-five each day, and almost half don't think they'll be able to cover all their expenses in retirement, according to a survey by Fidelity.

Reverse mortgages can be toxic under the right—or wrong—circumstances. Reverse mortgages are based on expectations that inflation will remain relatively contained. When you take out a reverse mortgage, the monthly payments to you are fixed. From those monthly payments you have to pay your living expenses in retirement in addition to such things as taxes on the house, home owners insurance, flood insurance, and utilities. If any of those critical payments are missed, you can then go into default and lose your home—reverse mortgage or no. The longer you live, the greater the chance that inflation will fall outside your current projections. As of February 2013 the Consumer Financial Protection Bureau reported that nearly one in ten reverse mortgage borrowers were at risk of foreclosure as a result of failing to pay real estate taxes and insurance.

The odds of foreclosure go up, the Consumer Financial Protection Bureau noted, for those borrowers who took their reverse mortgage as a lump-sum payout instead of monthly checks. A lump sum payout is a good way to up your risk because you now have to manage the lump sum so that it lasts as long as you expected. In the twelve months leading up to September 2011 73 percent of reverse mortgage borrowers took lump-sum payouts, an increase of 30 percent since 2008. Part of that might be an unintended consequence of newer low-cost, government-backed reverse mortgage options that offer only a single fixed-rate choice—with a lump-sum payout. Fixed-rate reverse mortgages are popular with consumers, so the effect may well be to push more people into the lump-sum option. (Lump-sum-payout reverse mortgages are also more profitable for lenders, which gives loan officers an incentive to recommend these deals over adjustable-rate loans.)

But this still isn't likely to rise to the level of a big-volatility event. Reverse mortgages won't be geographically concentrated, so default won't produce ghost towns, which means that housing prices aren't likely to fall so far and so quickly that banks won't be able to recoup their loans. And so far, despite the fast growth in this product, the total size of this market is relatively small, at less than $20 billion in 2014.

The dangers of increased volatility from an aging population aren't limited to the United States and the developed world; some of the biggest impacts will be felt in developing economies with vulnerable financial systems, rudimentary retirement programs, and economies that have been built around a young and relatively cheaper workforce.

We're used to thinking that the United States is a quickly aging society—and bemoaning the "fact." But like many of the things we call "facts," this one isn't especially true. Certainly the United States is getting older, but this is occurring in a pattern that's unlike what's happening pretty much anywhere else in the world.

The United States is indeed aging. In 2012 14 percent of the US population was aged sixty-five years old or older, according to the World Bank. That is up from 1982, when only 12 percent of the population fell into that age bracket.

And by 2030 20 percent of the US population will be sixty-five years old or older. Then, the projections say, the percentage of sixty-five-and-olders stabilizes at the rough 20 percent level until 2050. (At which point the projections stop because the margin for error just gets so large as to overwhelm the data.)

The US pattern bears very little resemblance to that of any other developed country. Take that in, please. The United States is, in this context, exceptional. We're the City on the Hill of Aging, if you will.

Japan, of course, we know about: 10 percent of the Japanese population was sixty-five or older in 1982—that's less than in the United States. By 2012, however, the percentage was up to 24 percent, and by 2030 it's projected to hit 33 percent. At the same time, the absolute number of Japanese is projected to drop to 95 million by 2050 from 128 million in 2012.

Japan is an extreme case among developed countries. But the general pattern, if you look at less extreme cases such as Germany, France, Italy, Spain, and Finland, is that in 1982 the average developed economy started with something like the US level of sixty-five-year-olds but then aged much faster. So Italy, which we think of as an old country now, started with just 13 percent of its population at sixty-five or over in 1982. But by 2012 that percentage had climbed to 21 percent.

Compare that to the US pattern of 12 percent in 1982 and just 14 percent in 2012. Italy's economy and society has been more stressed by an aging population during those thirty years than has the US equivalent. France went from 13 percent in 1982 to 17 percent in 2012. Germany started at 15 percent in 1982 and reached 21 percent in 2012. Portugal traveled from 12 percent in 1982 to 19 percent in 2012. And Spain was at 12 percent in 1982 and then 18 percent in 2012.

If you're looking for stability of a degree greater than what the United States can offer, you'll have to look to Sweden, which although it was extraordinarily old in 1982—with 17 percent of its population sixty-five or older—it didn't get a whole lot older by 2012 (19 percent). (The other, stranger outlier is Russia, where 10 percent of the population was sixty-five or older in 1982 and only 13 percent is sixty-five or older today. But I think here we're looking at the result of the collapse of the Soviet health care system—and plunging life expectancies—after the breakup of the Soviet Union.)

The developing world is the source of real aging volatility. From 1982 to 2012 many of these countries fit our stereotype of extraordinarily young societies that somehow stay extraordinarily young. Mexico starts in 1982 with just 4 percent of its population sixty-five or over, and that figure climbed only to 6 percent by 2012. Indonesia went from 4 percent in 1982 to just 5 percent in 2012.

But there were rumblings even in the 1982 to 2012 data of aging still to come. China went from a Mexico-like 5 percent of its population sixty-five or older in 1982 to 9 percent by 2012. Brazil's sixty-five-and-over population increases from 4 percent in 1982 to 7 percent by 2012.

Want a shock? Go out further. Brazil's population of sixty-five and over is projected to hit 13.6 percent by 2030. Indonesia will likely reach 9.6 percent in 2030. And China, thanks to the long-lasting effects of the one-child policy—will move from that 9 percent of its population sixty-five and over in 2012 to a projected 16 percent sixty-five and over by 2030 . . . and to 24 percent of its population sixty-five and over by 2050.

The world as a whole will double its older population, moving from 8 percent sixty-five and over in 2010 to a projected 16 percent in 2050.

Those absolute percentage changes are, in many cases, stunning. As hard as it may be to imagine a United States with one-fifth of its population sixty-five or older, I'm pretty sure that the average Chinese on the *hutong*, China's traditional narrow allies, or the government planners trying to plan for this change—hah!—can't begin to conceptualize a China with nearly a quarter of its population sixty-five and over.

But remember this is a book about volatility, and as overwhelming as the absolute measure of the change may be (the bullet train), the acceleration of the transition (the roller coaster) is even greater. The volatility of this transition, especially in developed countries, is completely off the scale of human experience.

Most developed nations have had decades to adjust to their changing age structures. It took a hundred years for the percentage of people sixty-five and older in France to go from 7 to 14 percent. In contrast, many countries in the developing world will see that degree of change in a single generation. Brazil, for example, will take two decades to go through the demographic changes that took a century in France. The number of Chinese sixty-five and over will go from 110 million today to 330 million by 2050 . . . 330 million. That's roughly the population of the United States now. The last time the US population was just 110 million was in 1922. China's population of sixty-five and over will replicate the entire population growth of the United States from 1922 to 2014—and the total change that took ninety-two years in the United States will take place in China's sixty-five-and-over population in just thirty-six. (By 2050 China will have almost as many people over eighty—100 million—as the total population of the United States in 1922.)

Even countries that don't get as old in percentage terms as China are looking at a huge increase in the number of people over sixty-five. India, where a much smaller percentage of the population will be sixty-five or over by 2050 (just 14.9 percent), will still see huge population-shift volatility in the next thirty-five years. The number of Indians sixty-five and over is projected to explode to 227 million in 2050 from a mere 60 million currently. That's a 280 percent increase.

The volatility of this change jumps upward when you consider some important multipliers. For example, even as populations are aging, they are shrinking in absolute terms. For example, the three-fold jump in China's sixty-five-and-over population will occur even as the country's population will peak at 1.46 billion in 2030 and then begin a very slow decline to 1.41 billion in 2050. The sixty-five-and-over population is growing even as the number of children is remaining relatively constant. Somewhere before 2020 the number of people in the world aged five and under will fall below the number of people sixty-five and over. This has never happened before in the known history of the world.

Half of all the population growth will be concentrated in a handful of countries so that increases in the sixty-five-and-over populations will be, in percentage terms, less drastic in those countries. In most of the world, however, the number of people over sixty-five will be growing within a context of relatively slow growth in the overall population—or no growth at all. (Japan, the most extreme case among large countries, saw its population peak at 128 million in 2008. Its population—and the forecasts show a huge difference in results—is projected to fall to 50 million [National Institute of Population and Social Security Research] or to 90 million [United Nations] by 2050.) Half of the world's population growth from 2013 to 2021 will take place in just eight countries: Democratic Republic of the Congo, Ethiopia, India, Niger, Nigeria, Tanzania, Uganda, and the United States. Think that group might exhibit a bit of diversity in its response to aging?

Even if you live in a developed economy with a relatively developed pension and retirement system, you have some sense of how disruptive an aging population can be. In the United States, for example, state and local governments are engaged in bitter fights over pension benefits for retired public-sector workers. Some state governments increasingly resemble laughing-stock countries such as Argentina. You know the ones that say inflation is only 10.9 percent

(Argentina's official annual inflation rate in 2013) when in reality inflation is 28 percent, according to private economists. For example, Illinois faces a shortfall of $97 billion in its state pension fund because for years state leaders have decided to paper over deficits rather than put more actual dollars into the funds. The result is that since 2009 Illinois has suffered thirteen downgrades from S&P, Moody's Investors Service, and Fitch Ratings. The state's A– credit rating from S&P (down from A+ as recently as April 2012) means the state will pay $450 million more in interest over the twenty-five-year life of a $1.3 billion bond for highway repair and construction than will a highly rated state such Virginia or Maryland.

The problem is by no means limited to feckless states with Democratic governors. S&P cut New Jersey's credit rating one step to A+ on April 10, 2014, in the wake of yet another state budget miss. State revenue collections have fallen short of revenue projections for three straight years, and to close a midyear gap, the state will use $94 million in "savings" gained by recalculating the state's required pension contribution for the fiscal year that ended on June 2014. The state's pension system is underfunded to the tune of $47 billion, and the most recent "rob Peter to pay Paul" move won't make that any better.

On the national level the US government is wrestling with the need to find more revenue to keep the national pension system, Social Security, solvent. And you know how loud the yelling is on that (because it is a great political issue for both parties) even though the fix is relatively simple—as it was in 1983. The most recent report from the Social Security Board of Trustees says that beginning in 2021, costs will exceed income. That will shrink the Social Security Trust funds until they're exhausted in 2033. After that, income from Social Security taxes will be sufficient to cover only 77 percent of scheduled payments.

How hard is that to fix? Not very—the 1983 experience says. In that year the Trust funds faced insolvency in July 1983 until, on April 20, 1983, Congress finally got its act together and, by cutting some payments and raising payroll taxes and the income ceiling for paying those taxes, put the Trust's funds back on a solid foundation projected to last until 2033.

What's most amazing about 1983 is how good that projection was. The Trust funds are now projected to be exhausted in 2033—just about where the 1983 fix projected. Congress could duplicate the 1983 fix by raising payroll taxes and the income ceiling again and by cutting some payments to higher-income beneficiaries or by modestly raising the retirement age. That's what Congress will finally wind up doing, but not, of course, until our politicians wring every ounce of political advantage they can out of yelling at the top of their lungs, "They want to destroy Social Security; we want to save it!"

Unfortunately other problems that the aging US population is creating aren't nearly as easy to solve. Take the rising cost of health care. That's driven at least in part by the increase in the sixty-five-and-over population. The Congressional Budget Office estimates that 25 percent of the increase in health care costs comes from the growing number of people who have health insurance under the Affordable Care Act. (Strangely enough, people who have the ability to pay for health care because they have insurance consume more health care. Go figure.) Another 40 percent, the budget office calculates, comes from cost increases in the health care sector. The final 35 percent is—you guessed it—a result of an aging population.

Health care spending actually fell in 2012 to 17.2 percent of GDP from 17.3 percent of GDP in 2011, according to the federal Centers for Medicare and Medicaid Services. That's the first, very modest break in a rise that has taken health care from 16.2 percent of GDP in 2006 steadily higher year after year. (It climbed again in 2013 to 17.4 percent.)

It is projected to keep climbing. The Centers estimate that health care spending will increase by an annual average of 5.7 percent a year from 2012 to 2022 and then accelerate, growing 6 percent from 2015 to 2023. That will, the statisticians say, take health care spending to 19.9 percent of GDP in 2022. Projections from the Congressional Budget Office go out a bit further: by 2038 health care spending will hit 22 percent of GDP.

Even if we could pay for this increase, would we? Already in 2010 health care spending soaked up 26 percent of the federal budget. By 2016 it is projected, at 28 percent of the budget, to exceed all the discretionary spending in the budget. Unless we somehow increase government revenue—I think the process is the very popular one called "raising taxes"—paying for health care means cutting spending on education, environmental protection, defense, national parks, the National Institutes of Health, food stamps, and more and more and more.

The process is a cruel crowding out that has already earned the title of the War Between the Young and the Old.

On the surface that seems an apt description. For example, in New Jersey the state plans to sell $197.5 million in revenue bonds through the state Educational Facilities Authority to be repaid from annual appropriations from the legislature. S&P, taking what seems to me a deliberately naïve view of how things work in the state capital of Trenton, has given these bonds an A rating. Besides the extra interest payments that come from the state's credit downgrade because it can't/won't meet its obligations to its pension funds, there's simply a question of whether the state, when push comes to shove, will pay the bill on these bonds without resorting to another round of gimmicks. The record $2.5 billion pension fund payment that's included in the state's budget plan for the fiscal year that began on July 1, 2014, crowds out other spending. "How long do you all think we can keep this up?" Governor Chris Christie asked a town hall meeting in Fairfield.

There's certainly another way to look at this problem, one that doesn't paint it as a war for limited resources between generations. There is, of course, the issue of why resources are so limited and why growth has slowed and why economies around the world seem so unresponsive to the traditional methods for goosing growth. I'm going to explore one of these explanations in the next chapter and examine what I call the "collapse of the growth consensus" of the last twenty years as a result of volatility that will add to volatility.

But that's the next chapter. To finish this look at the relationship between global aging and financial and economic volatility, I'm going to turn to the nexus of the crisis: China.

Earlier I noted that it took a hundred years for the percentage of sixty-five-and-olders in France to go from 7 to 14 percent. The percentage of the Chinese population sixty-five and over will climb to

24 percent by 2050. The United States, in contrast, went from 12 percent sixty-five and over to 14 percent in the thirty years from 1982 to 2012. And then it will take the United States another thirty-eight years for the sixty-five-and-olders to hit 20 percent of the population.

But it isn't just the speed of the Chinese transition in comparison to that of the United States that will add to volatility; China is a much less wealthy country than the United States. All the recent headlines about the size of China's economy surpassing that of the United States—when measured using purchasing power parity that takes China's lower prices into account—is largely beside the point from this perspective. Even using purchasing power parity calculations, which I think overstate the size of China's economy, per capita GDP in the United States was $51,000 in those latest calculations, whereas China's is just $11,000. (Using the official exchange rates, China's economy was about 60 percent the size of the US economy in 2014.)

The worry that China's planners have had—that China will become old before it becomes rich—seems dangerously accurate. And if a more gradual aging in a much richer United States is producing political turmoil, think of the effect on a much more quickly aging and poorer China.

For example, China's government pension fund was only put in place in 1997. According to Dai Xianglong, head of the National Council for Social Security Fund, pension reserves equal just 2 percent of GDP in China. That compares to an inadequate 15 percent in the United States and a slightly less inadequate 25 percent in Japan. As you might imagine, benefits are very low—the pension fund covers only about one in three of China's sixty-five-and-olders, and the monthly benefit is only $12.

An aging China is going to hit other walls besides a simple lack of funding. The infrastructure—inadequate and expensive as it may be—that we take for granted in the developed world, even in the United States, doesn't exist in China. Estimates say that currently nearly 23 percent of China's elderly need help to take care of themselves. Because traditionally the country has relied upon children to take care of elderly parents, the country doesn't have anything like a network of retirement homes, nursing homes, rehabilitation facilities, and the like. Currently less than 2 percent of the elderly in China use institution-based care. Estimates say that about 22 million elderly Chinese will be able to afford institutional senior housing by 2020, which is an impressive number until you remember that China's sixty-five-and-over population numbered 110 million in 2012 and is projected to hit 330 million by 2050.

A rising population over sixty-five in China also means, as in the United States and Japan and wherever, an increasing population suffering from the diseases of old age. And these alone would be a crushing burden on China's financial resources. Take a look at just one chronic disease that increases in incidence and the severity of its complications with age: diabetes.

In 2014 China passed the United States in the incidence of diabetes. Compared to 11.3 percent in the United States, 11.6 percent of Chinese adults have the disease, although in 1980 the figure in China was only 1 percent. (More disease or more disease testing?) About 25 percent of Chinese have the abnormal levels of blood sugar that are the common precursor to adult-onset diabetes.

Diabetes is a global scourge, with 380 million people globally living with the disease. One-third live in China. (No one knows why the Chinese population seems to be so susceptible to diabetes. Theories that make sense to me include the rise of US-style fast food, the prestige accorded to Western-style sweets by the newly wealthy, the tendency to indulge children in one-child families with more sweets, and a decline in exercise that's the result of a move from the country to the city, where air pollution discourages even such modest exercise as walking and biking. There may even be a genetic factor, as studies seem to show that weight gain leads to Type 2 diabetes in Asians at a lower body-mass index than in whites and blacks.)

No country in the world really does a good job at focusing its health care spending on diabetes prevention; instead, most spending goes toward treating the complications of the disease, which include stroke, heart disease, and kidney failure. China spends about 80 percent of what it spends on diabetes now on treating complications of diabetes.

But if you're looking for a set of multipliers that will increase the social volatility of aging in China beyond that in even Japan, let alone the United States, look at the combined effects of the one-child policy, the country's dependence on a displaced population of migrant workers for much of its industrial workforce, and the increasing urbanization of the country planned by China's leaders. One projected—and honestly feared—result is something out of the *Mad Max* movies, with roving migrant gangs of unmarried and resentful bachelors setting off waves of unrest in China's cities. This isn't some vision from a childhood spent reading too many comics and too much science fiction (to both of which I plead guilty, by the way). It comes from presentations by Valerie Hudson, professor at Texas A&M, and Andrea de Boer, senior lecturer at the University of Kent, at a conference called Beyond the Pivot: Managing Asian Security Crises, held in Washington, DC, in April 2014.

This scenario begins with the current gender imbalance in China that has resulted from the government's one-child policy and the cultural preference for sons. In 2010, according to China's census, men outnumbered women in China by at least 34 million. The imbalance will continue to worsen until it peaks sometime between 2030 and 2045. The effect will be that at least 20 percent of men of marriageable age will not be able to marry. By midcentury China will have a surplus of 40 to 50 million bachelors.

China's poorer provinces and the poorer villages in those provinces have a higher concentration of bachelors, or "bare branches," as they're called in China. And it already looks like the country's migrant workforce also has a higher concentration of these unwed-despite-their-desires males. It seems only logical that men with lower status, less income, less opportunity to meet women, and difficulty forming lasting relationships due to their working and housing conditions would have less success in competing for China's relatively scarce female population.

The current migrant worker population, denied permanent urban status by China's *hukou* household registration system, is young and relatively undereducated: 62 percent are under thirty-five, with the majority holding only a high school education. This, plus a lack of marriage partners, isn't exactly a recipe for social stability. An

estimated 10 to 30 percent of the floating migrant population partic-
ipates in criminal gangs—either the relatively organized black societies (*heishehui*) or the more loosely organized dark forces (*e'shili*).
The most recent government ten-year plan aims to increase urbanization to 60 percent by 2020 and sets a goal of ensuring that 45 percent
of those in cities have official urban status. (This means, according to
my math, that 55 percent won't.) The ten-year plan envisions adding
massive levels of social infrastructure to cities in order to accommo-
date this growth and to catch up with current unmet needs. So far,
however, the actual money spent on this infrastructure—as opposed
to that promised to be spent—hasn't made much of a dent in the
backlog of services that aren't provided to migrant workers.

This all makes China seem like a gigantic social experiment. The
world's fastest-aging society, a hugely inadequate pension system,
an underfunded health care system, a massive gender imbalance
and huge surplus male population, the continued rush to urbanize—
what could possibly go wrong?

And just for fun, add in a relatively underdeveloped financial system that nonetheless plays a critical role in the global economy and
financial system.

Don't count on being able to sit back on your front porch and
watch from a distance. Thanks to the magic of global financial markets, China's volatility will be the world's volatility.

Let me be clear: I'm not making some gloom-and-doom forecast
for China's next forty years. I think China has immense challenges
to meet, but it's quite possible the country will meet them. But even
if it does, even if it succeeds in rising to the top of the global economic heap, there's no reason to think that this ascent will be any
less tumultuous, any less likely to produce big volatility than the
rise of the United States in the nineteenth century. In fact, I think
it's likely that whatever struggles, wrong turns, and missteps China
makes will be even more likely to move from domestic big-volatility
events to global big-volatility events because of how China is
integrated—and not—into the global financial system.

To see how this might work, let's turn to Chapter 8: The World's
Largest Game of Three-Card Monte.

Chapter 8

The World's Largest Game of Three-Card Monte

THE GREATEST PENDING SOURCE of global risk—in financial markets and in the global economy—in the next few decades is China.

It may seem like an exaggeration to compare China's financial system to a game of Three-Card Monte. But remember that, as the US subprime mortgage debacle demonstrated, financial con games these days are run by folks in suits working out of offices where the carpet is color coordinated with the company logo and with nary a shifty confederate hanging around, ready to yell, "Run! It's the cops!"

Instead, today's financial confidence games are run by financial institutions such as the state-owned China Construction Bank, with carefully constructed walls of deniability, of course. The con game that brought a crowd of about sixty masked demonstrators into the street in Beijing at the end of April 2014, for example, was only "sold" by the bank on "behalf" of (state-owned) Jilin Trust. And in China these games come with innocuous and auspicious-sounding names such as Songhua River Number 77 Opulent Blessing Energy Project. (In the United States the conventions of believability require names like Enron.)

The demonstrators, several in their sixties, wanted their money back. They targeted China Construction Bank because, they said, the bank sold them the Songhua River Number 77 Opulent Blessing

Energy Project trust promising "no risk, only high returns," one pro-
testor told the *Financial Times*. The several million yuan he had invested in this trust is now lost because the trust has defaulted. That
makes the Songhua River Number 77 Opulent Blessing Energy
Project a trail-blazing financial product in China. Other trusts have
gone bust in the past, but the government has always made up investors' losses. Since 2012 more than twenty investment trust products,
including Opulent Blessing, totaling 24 billion yuan ($3.8 billion),
have run into trouble. The government arranged a bailout in every
case—until 2014. Opulent Blessing is the first trust to default in
which investors will actually lose their investments.

It's easy to understand why the people demonstrating outside the
bank put their money into this trust. At a time when the Construction Bank of China was paying 3.25 percent on deposits—at that
time the Chinese government would not allow banks to pay depositors any higher interest rate on deposits than that—the trust promised to pay 12 percent on a minimum investment of 1 million yuan,
about $160,000, and said that investors would not lose their money.
(According to many accounts, the promises went even further, including a "guarantee" of those 12 percent interest payments.)

Remember why Three-Card Monte and other confidence schemes
work: victims want to believe in the scam. They want to believe they
are smarter than the average player and can beat the game. You
might even say that they are confident that they can out-trick the
tricksters.

I have a sneaking suspicion that few of the Opulent Blessing investors looked very closely at the details and logic of this trust. There
is, of course, the basic issue of what their money would go into that
could possibly justify a 12 percent risk-free interest payment when
bank deposits were paying 3.25 percent. In this case the money that
Jilin Trust raised through China Construction Bank was lent to a
large, privately owned coal mining company. If you thought about
it for a moment, you'd be left wondering why a coal miner had to
pay 12 percent to private investors to raise money when solid Chinese companies were raising cash at half that cost directly from China's big banks. Could it be that the coal company was sinking under

a mountain of debt so large that China's banks wouldn't lend to it? The coal company did indeed collapse.

But that kind of analysis is really beside the point when you think you understand the game and are smart enough to beat it. The investors who went into the Opulent Blessing trust were rich enough to meet the 1 million yuan minimum. They knew this wasn't the kind of deal being offered to just anybody and that they were a cut above the suckers who had to put their money into the bank at 3.25 percent. These investors were, indeed, "privileged" by the government.

Which is one reason the investors protesting that day in Beijing were so angry at the government-owned China Construction Bank and at the Chinese government. They thought they had a sweetheart deal sanctioned by the Beijing government that was so attractive because it wasn't available to just anybody. Consider what one of the protestors said: "The bank marketed this to high-income customers, not the wider society and if they want to use my money they should bear responsibility [for losses]."

And you know what? This privileged, wealthier-than-most investor, so obnoxiously impressed with his own importance, has a point. The rules of the game until the Opulent Blessing trust was allowed to default, rather than being bailed out by the government, were that trusts like this were guaranteed. The government had, in fact, set up a special class of investment with returns four times what the banks paid to the hoi polloi and had guaranteed those returns.

How dare the government decide to change the rules now?

A very, very astute investor sensitive to every shift in the policy winds from Beijing might have seen this change in the rules coming months earlier, but I doubt it. In the last few years the government had made the same pronouncements over and over again about the need to rein in lending from the trust sector and to reduce the role the country's big banks played in selling these trust products. Government financial market regulators had flagged the surge in risky loans and warned that some borrowers wouldn't be able to pay back what they had borrowed, but banks, local governments, and the largely unregulated market for nonbank lenders such as Jilin Trust kept rolling over these loans and even making new ones in sectors that everyone knew were operating at a loss. Too big to fail in China was known to mean "too many jobs to lose" by forcing a company into default.

How was anyone to know that this time the government was serious? And how, even after the first-ever default on a trust product—which followed, by a matter of weeks, the first-ever default on a corporate bond in China—could anyone be really sure the government meant it? Maybe these were just warning shots fired for political purposes. Surely the government didn't mean to introduce a new program of financial reforms that would open up part of the financial market to a greater degree of market risk?

The answer is that the Chinese government is indeed serious. It really doesn't have any other choice. That doesn't mean, however, that the timing of these reforms is obvious now or predictable, that this recent decision to let a corporate bond and a trust fund product default isn't mostly political posturing, or that the road to more market-based returns and risks won't be marked with sudden shifts into reverse, hard stomps on the brakes, and then reckless pressure on the accelerator.

It does mean, however, a huge step up in financial market volatility in China along with the rest of the world, as China's markets now determine such a large percentage of global cash flows. It's an exaggeration to say that when the butterfly of Opulent Blessings flapped its wings in Beijing, it created the financial weather in New York, Tokyo, and London—as well as Sao Paulo, Mumbai, Jakarta, and Istanbul—but it's not totally wrong either. The volatility that these policy changes will introduce in China will result in volatility across the rest of the global financial market and economy.

The Opulent Blessings default could mark the opening of a very big can of worms in China's financial sector. The government's decision to slap such a low ceiling on the interest rates that banks can pay to depositors has created a vast industry of nonbank—officially, anyway—trust companies that package loans to companies and then, usually using banks as agents, sell them to individual investors. Assets invested in trusts grew by 8 percent in the first quarter of 2014 to reach 11.7 trillion yuan ($1.9 trillion). That's about four times as much as assets in trust products by the end of 2010.

But trust products are only part of a vast shadow banking sector in China that functions to keep China's credit-creation machine humming while also keeping many of the loans being created off the official books of China's big state-owned banks. Officially China's banks have extremely low levels of bad loans, even though those levels have been rising relentlessly. In the last quarter of 2013, according to the China Banking Regulatory Commission, bad loans at China's banks rose for a ninth straight quarter to the highest level since the 2008 financial crisis. But that still took bad loans—officially, that is—up to just 1 percent, an increase from the 0.97 percent of the third quarter. For 2014 the Agricultural Bank of China, the country's third-largest bank, reported that the percentage of bad loans at the bank had climbed to 1.54 percent from 1.29 percent at the end of September.

Of course, nobody believes the official numbers, but even the official trend is headed in a bad direction. S&P said that it expects loan quality to continue to decline in 2015.

The reason no one believes these numbers is because everyone knows that China's banks have systematically moved loans—assets in bank accounting—off their books. For example, an increasingly popular financing structure called trust beneficial rights allows a bank to buy the cash flow of an asset—say, a corporate loan or bond—in what is effectively a loan. But because it isn't actually a loan but rather an investment—it's officially an interbank asset—it gets booked with a lower risk weighting than a loan would have. Then when it comes to calculating the bank's capital at risk, this interbank investment gets assigned a lower capital adequacy ratio so the bank needs to put less money aside in reserve against potential losses. As you might imagine, these trust structures are especially popular when banks have a distressed loan, one that hasn't yet gone bad but might be headed in that direction. If that loan is rebooked as trust beneficial rights, the bank doesn't have to take money out of earnings to set aside as a loan-loss provision.

But the biggest problem in the Chinese financial system, one where bad loans probably dwarf those at the big state-owned banks, comes from another set of incentives. The officials who run local governments have a vested career interest in producing growth and jobs in their jurisdictions. That means providing low-cost financing, even for projects that banks have turned down because their potential profitability simply isn't high enough to cover the interest on the loan and eventually repay it. Because local government officials' goal is to create growth and jobs rather than generate a profit or even to see a loan get paid back, local governments have been financing hundreds of residential and commercial projects, factories, rail hubs, and airports that are clearly never going to repay their borrowings.

Well, sort of.

Because, you see, most of China's local governments legally can't issue debt. (The country did begin a pilot program that would allow a few local governments to issue debt in 2015 and expanded a program of local debt swaps.) They have very small revenue streams from taxes and fees because all that money flows, initially, to the national government. Some does come back, but often with attached demands and programs for spending. Although those programs may fit national requirements, they often don't match up well with local priorities.

And this is why any local government run by officials with any ambition has set up one or more affiliated financial institutions. These affiliates do what the local governments themselves can't do: borrow on revenue streams generated by the sale of land to developers, often land that officially is allotted to local farmers, and then lend to developers and companies that are going to create jobs in the local area. (If a good part of this cash flow seems circular with money from developers being used to fund loans to developers, that's because it is.)

How much money have local governments—excuse me, I mean affiliated financial companies—lent out? A government audit in June 2014 showed that China's local government debt climbed to 17.9 trillion yuan ($2.9 trillion). That's an estimated 67 percent increase from 2000 and an estimated 30 percent of China's GDP, up from 23.4 percent in 2011.

Putting the debt levels in China's shadow banking system together, you start to get some real money: 17.9 trillion yuan ($2.9 trillion) in local government debt and 11.7 trillion yuan ($1.9 trillion) in trust lending with the total amount of wealth-management products (a category that includes but isn't limited to trusts) that reach, Fitch Ratings estimates, 13 trillion yuan ($2.1 trillion) at the end of 2013.

Bank credit—that is, credit in the regulated part of China's financial system—was equal to 135.7 percent of China's gross domestic product at the end of 2012.

Add the shadow banking figures to the regulated banking figures, and the total, Fitch estimates, is around 198 percent of GDP. Other estimates are even higher. According to Partners Capital, for example, the debt load is $23.3 trillion, which the private investment bank calculates as being equivalent to 260 percent of GDP. The total of $23.3 trillion is up $15 trillion in five years.

That's a lot of debt. Especially when all the signs indicate that a lot of those loans extended to the corporate sector aren't going to be repaid—ever. Anne Stevenson Yang, cofounder of J Capital Research in Beijing, estimates that about 60 to 70 percent of new lending is going to service old loans. In other words, the system is only kept upright by the willingness of lenders to keep rolling over what they are owed.

If you're looking for the source of volatility in China's economy and financial markets, you don't have to look any further than this mountain of debt and the potential wave of crashing bad loans. According to the China Banking Regulatory Commission, Chinese banks added 89 trillion yuan ($14.67 trillion) of assets, mostly loans, over the last five years, whereas US commercial banks held a total of $14.6 trillion in assets at the end of the third quarter, according to the US Federal Deposit Insurance Corp. In other words, China's banks have added new loans over the last five years that equal the total loans at US commercial banks.

This level of debt and the potential for loans to turn into bad loans is exactly what makes any slowdown, even a minor one, in China's economy a really big deal. Liabilities at nonfinancial companies hit 139 percent of GDP at the end of 2012 and are likely to climb to 150 percent by the end of 2014, according to Haitong Securities. That means that any slowdown, even a drop to the 6.8 percent GDP growth rate for 2015 projected in January 2015 by the International Monetary Fund, has the potential to set off a wave of defaults at overextended companies.

I don't think the result of all this bad debt in the Chinese financial system is one big implosion in China's economy; the reality is likely to be a lot more complicated than that and to produce an extended period of volatility in China as well as globally rather than one big crash toward the bottom in some Chinese replay of the US subprime debt crisis that peaked in 2008.

I feel reasonably confident about that prediction because China has been here before in the Asian currency crisis of 1997. And that crisis presents a very attractive road map to the Chinese government and China's banking authorities.

Why is it so attractive? Because it worked.

In the run-up to the Asian currency crisis and in the fall-out from it, nonperforming loans at China's banks soared to at least 25 percent of bank loan portfolios, with some estimates putting the number at 40 percent. In early 1999 Guangdong International Trust and Investment went bankrupt, leaving investors holding $4.4 billion in worthless loans. Many predicted that China's financial system would collapse and take the Chinese economy with it.

But it didn't happen. Banks wound up being recapitalized by selling $32.5 billion in bonds. Bad debt was removed from bank balance sheets and transferred to the books of newly created asset management companies. China's economy did slow, with GDP growth falling to 7.6 percent in 1999 from 13.1 percent in 1994. But by 2003 growth was back above 10 percent again.

What was the magic plan?

One of the advantages of running a relatively closed, relatively responsive, top-down command economy—and China's financial system more closely fit that description in the 1990s than now—is that no company or bank is bankrupt unless the government says it's bankrupt. No set of books gets branded a tissue of lies unless the government agrees with that assessment. No company or bank ever really runs out of the ability to borrow unless the government decides to close the money tap.

The Chinese government responded to the crisis of the 1990s by setting up financial companies that would buy bad loans from China's banks. That removed these bad loans from bank balance sheets and miraculously restored insolvent institutions to health. Where did these new bad banks get the money to buy those bad loans? They sold bonds to China's banks, securities companies, and life insurance companies. Even overseas institutions wound up on the subscription list. And why would anybody buy these bonds? After all, on paper they were backed only by the bad loans that these companies had bought from China's banks. Because the Chinese government backed these bonds, told state-controlled financial institutions to buy, and then made it clear to privately owned companies, both domestic and overseas, that participation in these bond sales was the price of doing business in China.

In theory the bonds sold by these bad debt financial companies were to be paid off in ten or fifteen years. In actual practice many of these bonds simply reached maturity and then disappeared. After all, what state-owned bank was going to raise a fuss over not getting paid on a bond after the government had arranged this bailout scheme? Other bonds were "kicked down the road" when these bad debt financial companies went public in the 2000s by selling shares to—can you guess?—China's big state-owned banks and privately owned financial companies, both domestic and overseas, that wanted to do business in China. Many of the bad-loan financial companies from the crisis of the 1990s still exist, and I'm sure that the Chinese government could mobilize these companies—and create others—to implement an updated version of this solution if the current situation threatens to head south.

Of course, the solution wouldn't be exactly the same. The fix that worked in the 1990s would need to be updated and not just slavishly duplicated, as China is actually in a much deeper credit hole now than it was in the 1990s. At that time China's debt-to-GDP ratio was 25 percent, far lower than the ratio for most developed countries. Today no one is certain exactly how high China's debt-to-GDP ratio is—198 percent? 260 percent? But it is clearly higher than the ratios for most developed economies.

Of course, China is also much richer in foreign exchange reserves than those developed economies or than it was in the 1990s. China's reserves, by far the largest in the world, were worth $3.9 trillion at the end of 2014.

But the biggest change is in China's economy and the government's recognition that it has to respond to the big demographic challenges spelled out in my last chapter as a result of a rapidly aging population in an economy with inadequate retirement plans, a health care system that isn't prepared to cope with a surge in age-related illnesses such as diabetes, and a lack of institutions that can make up for the decline in family-provided elder care that is the result of one-child policies. The responses that differentiate China's economy from what it was in 1997 include new retirement plans, an extension of residence rights to more of the migrant worker population, and an attempt to shift away from an investment-based economy to a consumer-based economy. Some of those changes will make solving this bad debt problem easier than it was in 1997. Some, however—most, in my estimation—will make it tougher.

For example, take a moment to think about the implications of that last response, the attempt to shift from an investment- and infrastructure-based economy to a consumer economy, and about how China accumulated that $3.5 trillion in reserves. Countries don't put that much money in the bank simply by getting rich. If a country's citizens are getting richer but spending as much as they're taking in, the country isn't putting anything in the bank. Foreign exchange reserves and savings reserves accumulated by individuals and companies are the difference between what a country creates in wealth and what it spends.

On average Chinese citizens saved 30.6 percent of their disposable incomes in 2012. (In comparison, US citizens finished 2013 with a 4 percent savings rate.) And in fact, the Chinese savings rate is actually an increase from the 23 percent savings rate of ten years ago. That savings rate has contributed to one of the world's most lopsided economies. Consumption accounts for only 35.7 percent of China's economic activity. That's way behind the 50 to 60 percent in most other countries. In the United States, for example, consumption makes up about 70 percent of GDP.

Why do the Chinese save so much? The reasons include the lack of health insurance and pensions. If there is no safety net standing between you and disaster if you get sick or when you get old, then you save more. But in China conscious government policy has also played a key role. By keeping the value of its currency low, the Chinese government has kept the price of imported goods high, which has discouraged consumption. (And it has also led to annual trade surplus after annual trade surplus, each one adding to the country's huge foreign exchange reserves.) And by keeping official interest rates so low—capped at just 3.25 percent for bank deposits—the government has forced the average person in China to put a huge percentage of income away as savings in order to build up anything like a sufficient retirement nest egg.

In the United States, where we worry about our low savings rate, we don't spend a lot of time thinking about the "costs" of a high savings rate like that of China. But there are costs. A big one is that China has developed a grossly inefficient capital market. The country just doesn't do a very good job of putting its money into projects that will generate a positive rate of return, and the problem is getting worse.

On a microlevel that means that China has done a very poor job of shutting down inefficient companies to funnel capital to more efficient companies. Entire sectors of the Chinese economy operate at a loss because companies have found it so easy to raise capital that they have kept expanding—adding jobs was a major goal, even if the resulting operation didn't make money—and because companies producing nothing but losses were easily able to stay in business by raising more capital to cover operating losses. For example, in the first half of 2014 the profit margin for China's steel industry, the largest steel industry in the world by capacity, was a scant 0.3 percent and 80 percent of the industry's profit came from government subsidies. For all intents and purposes, Chinese steel companies made nothing—no profit, nada, zilch. In its rhetoric the government talks about the need to shut down inefficient steel producers to reduce capacity and raise prices, and in 2014 the government actually ordered the closing of eighty of the least efficient producers. Despite that order from the central government, however, production barely fell in 2014, going from 68.84 million metric tons in April 2014 to 68.09 million in December.

There are obviously limits to the power of commands in this command economy. The traditional Chinese adage "The mountains are high and the emperor is far away" comes to mind.

The problem exists across the Chinese economy, whether in steel or solar cells or real estate. Estimates are that it now takes $3 in new credit—new lending by financial institutions—to create $1 in economic growth. In 2006, those estimates say, it took just $1.20 in new lending to create a dollar of GDP. With 60 to 70 percent of new lending now going to service existing debt, China has to expand credit at an annual rate of greater than 20 percent a year to keep the Chinese economy growing at the target 7.5 percent rate.

And because of the way China's financial markets are structured, the economy faces a kind of negative leverage that makes this already grim situation even grimmer—and potentially even more damaging.

To understand how the system works, let's stick with the steel industry for a moment. On March 31, 2014, Haixin Steel defaulted. On the surface the company's failure to repay loans due at the end of the month wasn't a particularly big deal; after all, Haixin Steel doesn't even rank among the top thirty steel mills in China. With nobody in the steel industry making much profit, it's not surprising that Haixin had been relying on new loans to stay afloat and that it would hit the wall when it found itself unable to raise new cash. In 2013 the company sold off a mining subsidiary to raise cash, but that only delayed the March default on the company's debt.

But strangely enough—and absolutely normal in China's financial system—Haixin, despite its own struggles, was somehow a lead investor in a credit guarantee company that backed other companies' debts for a fee. Haixin's partners in this deal were other local private companies, and the credit guarantees were extended to companies, such as coal miners, with their own debt problems. The rules say that credit guarantee companies are supposed to keep enough capital on hand to cover multiple defaults from creditors. But many of these companies have extended so many loan guarantees that they are clearly overcommitted. An example from 2012 shows the danger: local governments and banks near Hangzhou had to offer bridge loans to sixty-two companies after the collapse of a single property development company that had been at the center of a local credit guarantee network.

The cascade of defaults that this kind of network of guarantees makes possible is why financial markets shudder at any default, no matter how innocuous it might seem. No one really knows how any specific default might ripple through China's financial system. It's just about impossible ahead of a default to disentangle the network of guarantors and guarantors of guarantors to know what entities are actually holding the bag. (If this sounds similar to the problems in the credit default derivatives market in the United States heading into the subprime mortgage crisis, that's because it is. And we all know how well that turned out.)

Even without other factors, such as a slowdown in growth in the Chinese economy, this situation isn't sustainable. Each year the economy loads up with more debt from increasingly less creditworthy sources like Haixin Steel, each year more of that debt is applied to support existing debt, and each year the financial system needs to grow credit at a slightly higher rate just to keep the economy running at the same speed.

But the Chinese economy does include other factors. What might be slowly unsustainable without demographic change, to take just one factor, threatens to become speedily unsustainable. China's rapid aging means the country simply can't afford this increasingly inefficient allocation of capital. Next to demographics, the most important factor in China's potential financial and economic crunch is the country's growing environmental crisis. China needs to make a huge investment in improving air and water quality, for example, and to seriously enforce existing laws, which will raise costs at many Chinese companies. Exactly where does that money come from?

The demographic and environmental crises in China are related in another way: they both show signs of the potential to move from strictly financial and economic crises to become the basis for a serious political challenge to the Communist Party's effective monopoly on power.

For example, consider the pension fund protests that broke out in the spring of 2014 at Yue Yuen Industrial, a company in Gaobo that makes running shoes for Nike and Adidas. Workers there had discovered that the company was stiffing them on contributions to their accounts with the national pension fund established in 1997. The company would make payments to the fund, for instance, based on worker earnings that excluded overtime, used a lower hourly wage rate to calculate earnings, or included only part of the company's workforce. Obviously, as the forty thousand workers who went on strike concluded, the company wouldn't have been able to get away with these practices if local government officials hadn't given their okay. For example, government officials told the company that it could use an artificially low hourly wage rate in its pension calculations as long as the rate was above the legal minimum wage. As one worker stated, the government "did not want to put too big a burden on the factory since it wants foreign investment."

The company's defense has been very simple: everybody does it. (In early May the municipal government declared in favor of the workers and ruled that Yue Yuen should have based pension contributions on higher pay levels. The company estimates that it will have to pay an extra $31 million in 2014.)

What I find most interesting about this specific strike is how it highlights the generational divide among China's workers and the connection between aging and social volatility. As one worker in his twenties put it, "I really don't care about the pension issue, as I'm really young. I won't spend my whole life in a factory." A friend added, "Most young workers think the same way, which is why nobody at Yue Yuen checked their pensions."

There's significant evidence that China's current leadership team understands that the current situation isn't sustainable. The current ten-year plan, adopted in November 2013, calls for rebalancing the economy toward consumption, and thus China has committed to raising the minimum wage by 13 percent a year, increasing government spending on health care and education, and extending social benefits to more of the migrant worker population.

This new direction has China's leaders talking about the need to reform the country's financial system and let some companies default. Premier Li Keqiang has said that financial defaults are "unavoidable" if the country hopes to force borrowers and lenders to price market risk into their decisions.

I think China's leaders are absolutely serious about the need for financial system reform, but they're serious within a Chinese context. They realize that although China is by no means a democracy and the Communist Party is perfectly willing to use force to maintain its grip on power, it is preferable to recruit the "consent" of China's political and economic elite to that rule. Reform to maintain the party's long-term grip on power can never go so far as to alienate the elites that provide the base of the party's support.

Reform in this context will follow the 1997 model of state intervention in the banking sector to prevent too much reform but with a dash of harsh market truth served out to a select group of examples in the economy and financial system. The odds are this group of examples will be relatively light on companies and financial players connected to the elites.

I think you can see this model of reform at work in the first-ever default of a corporate bond in China in March 2014. Shanghai Chaori Solar Energy Science and Technology was unable to pay an 89.8 million yuan ($14.4 million) coupon due on March 31 on a bond issue. I'd argue that this default is a big deal—in the long term. It inches China's financial markets closer to pricing risk into stocks, bonds, investment trusts, and other financial products. With very few exceptions, China's markets behave as if the government will bail out any company that gets in trouble and will make investors whole. An event like this default suggests that this might not always be the case. And the default will blaze new pathways as China continues to develop legal processes for dealing with default and bankruptcy.

Shanghai Chaori is not a major player even in the Chinese solar energy sector. It was definitely a three-strikes-and-you're-out story. The company only avoided default in 2013 after a local government in Shanghai pulled strings to get its bank to defer claims on overdue bank loans. At the end of June 2013 Shanghai Chaori had failed to pay 1.5 billion yuan in loans to twelve banks on time. In November the Bank of Tianjin said it was shopping for buyers for 52 million yuan in loans to the company after having already extended the loans once. And Shanghai Chaori operates in a sector that the Beijing government has targeted for a "reduction" in suppliers: the government has made it clear that it would like to see some solar companies go out of business or merge so that the sector could start to make money again.

But most important Shanghai Chaori is a small operator without sufficient political connections. From this point of view the default is a "show trial." By letting Shanghai Chaori default, Beijing gets to make the point that investors shouldn't assume the government will always ride to the rescue. But that doesn't mean that Beijing wouldn't bail out a more politically connected company. In China's politically cynical markets the default actually reinforces a perverse point: if you want to avoid risk, the trick isn't to invest in solid balance sheets but rather in superior political pedigrees.

The logic here can get a bit circular. It's easy to assume that because Shanghai Chaori was allowed to default without a bailout, it must not have any political clout. (And it's hard to follow the political DNA in China's often-opaque ownership and management family trees.) But the history of Shanghai Chaori and its president and chairman, Ni Kailu (who, together with his daughter, Ni, owned 44 percent of the company) suggest a company with limited clout. For example, in January 2014 the press was reporting a bailout through an ownership transfer from Ni to the state-owned Qinghai Muli Coal Development Group. That deal fell apart when some official or official body refused to approve the involvement of a state-owned company in the transfer. It also doesn't smack of clout to have to look for a rescue from a state-owned coal company; that sector is up to its eyebrows with its own financial problems. Or go back to the company's 2010 initial public offering (IPO) on the Shenzhen market. That listing was originally scheduled for 2009 but regulators refused to approve it because they found the company's expansion strategy too risky. Shanghai Chaori only got its listing after working to increase its capital base. That isn't the kind of objection regulators make to companies with political clout. Object to listing a solar company because it's too risky? In China? The interest rates Shanghai Chaori was paying on its debt also make me question the quality of its political connections. The 1 billion yuan of five-year notes the company sold in March 2012 carried a variable coupon rate that started at 8.98 percent. In a country where the price a company pays for money is determined by connections, this indicates that Shanghai Chaori was a very small fish indeed.

The problem—for investors and traders in and outside China and for the average person in China simply trying to navigate the Chinese financial markets—is that the Chinese government and its regulators are trying to walk a very fine line indeed. If the examples are too clearly contrived and too clearly intended to have effectively no wider impact beyond the small fish caught in the net, then this effort won't produce any of the intended reforms. I'd argue that this was exactly the problem with the Shanghai Chaori example. On the day it was announced that the company's bond issue would be the first corporate bond to ever default in China, the Shanghai Shenzhen 300 index fell all of 0.24 percent. Nobody was impressed. Nobody thought this "example" meant much of anything.

Swing too far in the other direction, however, and there's a danger that markets and economies will be overly impressed, to the extent that the example produces volatility that threatens to escape officials' preferred bounds. I'd argue that's what happened in the financial markets in general in January and February 2014.

The People's Bank ended 2013 and began 2014 fighting to constrain new lending by China's banks. One way the bank sought to do that was by withdrawing money from the financial system. (If a central banks sells debt—say, thirty-day paper—in the open market, it has the effect of reducing the money supply, as the money used to buy that paper is now sitting at the central bank and is out of circulation.) In January, however, the bank's efforts to reduce the money supply and, thus, reduce the amount of money banks could lend ran straight on into market expectations that the central bank would, as it does every year, supply extra liquidity to the banking system in the run-up to the Lunar New Year holiday that, in 2014, fell on January 31. Individuals and businesses tend to hoard cash in the days and weeks before the holiday so they won't run short, and usually the People's Bank sends extra cash into the banking system to balance that hoarding.

But not that January. The bank, in fact, continued to keep liquidity on a tight rein. And people—well, banks and businesses anyway—noticed. Because this refusal to provide liquidity at this time of year ran so contrary to the accepted practice, everyone decided that it had to be a big deal. So banks and businesses that might have otherwise hoarded some cash instead started hoarding a lot of cash. Banks with extra short-term cash decided they'd rather keep it in their own vaults rather than lend it even for just a few days to other banks with short-term cash needs.

The result was a brutal liquidity crunch that in one day pushed up the interest rate on a seven-day repurchase agreement, a benchmark for liquidity in the banking system, by 1.53 percentage points to 6.32 percent.

The People's Bank immediately reversed course. Overnight it injected 255 billion yuan ($42 billion) into the banking system. The rate on the seven-day repurchase agreement fell back to 5.44 percent, and the Shanghai stock market rose 0.86 percent on the day.

The problem, however—and the important point when it comes to market and economic volatility—is that once you've demonstrated that a move and countermove like this are on the table, markets start to watch for repeats of the move and react even more strongly on the next go-round. Using the terms I introduced earlier to describe how volatility begets more volatility, once the People's Bank demonstrated that it will move to decrease and increase short-term liquidity like this—and will react with a quick course correction to the market's reaction—investors and traders have lost a key benchmark. The bank didn't do this in the past; it now will do this . . . so what will it do in the future?

Should an investor ignore any action that involves a company with only modest political clout? Should you buy on any dip after a central bank move because the dip is a guarantee that the bank will quickly reverse course? After all, you could decide that all the government's talk about market-based financial reforms was just talk.

You could decide that your new rule or benchmark was to ignore any default at a company like Shanghai Chaori. In fact, the smart thing to do, your new benchmark for market expectations would tell you, would be to buy on any dip that results from less sophisticated traders selling on fear. (Three-Card Monte rides again!)

But notice all the assumptions in that benchmark. You would be betting that you would be able to correctly tell the difference between an insignificant default (of a Shanghai Chaori) and a significant one. You'd be betting that the important distinction as far as the government's decision on whether to bail someone out is the individual company's political clout and that the aggregate status of a sector won't, at some point, override the profile of individual companies in a sector.

We'll get a lot of chances to test these conclusions. Total debt at publicly traded nonfinancial companies in China and Hong Kong stands at $1.98 trillion as of the end of 2014, up from $607 billion at the end of 2007, according to Bloomberg. Sixty-three of those publicly traded companies have debt-to-equity ratios above 400 percent, with many companies in sectors with big over-capacity problems such as solar, steel, and shipbuilding.

In some sectors I've got to wonder—and to wonder how long it will be before the financial markets as a whole start to wonder—whether the correct benchmark belief is that big state-owned and politically connected companies are "safe" because the government will bail them out before they officially default. In some sectors there may be so much bad debt at so many individually unimportant companies that the collective danger is enough to spread fear of some systemic default. For example, although everyone believes that China's five big state-owned banks will get whatever government support they need with their bad debt problems, smaller Chinese banks, which individually don't have that guarantee, have, as a group, built up enough bad debt to stress the system. A *Financial Times* analysis of ten unlisted banks—banks without publicly traded shares—that are important in their local markets but don't have much of a national profile found that at the end of 2013 shadow banking products such as investment trusts, for example, made up 23.3 percent of bank assets. That was an increase from 14.3 percent at the end of 2012 and is far larger than the 1.7 percent of assets at China's big banks that are in shadow banking products according to

Deutsche Bank. The four largest banks in China account for nearly half of the assets in the banking sector, so from that perspective these smaller banks aren't a problem; a default or two or three among this group isn't likely to produce significant market volatility. But if the problem is indeed as widespread among this group as it seems and if these local banks are as important to local companies in China's second- and third-tier cities as we know they are, then I have to think that the benchmark belief about how the Chinese market, economy, and government operate is in need of fundamental revision.

As the example of bonds and the Paranormal economy in the United States (pages 48–61) suggests, that kind of fundamental revision of a benchmark belief can produce a lot of volatility, which is likely to be the case in China—and by extension in the global financial markets and economy—over the next decade or more. This is because there's a lot of evidence that China's leaders are playing a different game from what the markets think they are playing. The rules and the goals assumed by the two groups are not congruent in important ways.

The focus of this incongruence is China's extraordinary foreign exchanges reserves, the world's largest at $3.9 trillion as of the end of 2014. The financial markets and China's traders think of this $3.9 trillion as a source of strength. Those reserves are a guarantee that whatever China's bad debt problems, the government has the means to bail out the system. They guarantee that if China's economy falters, the government has the means to reaccelerate growth. They guarantee China's ability to project power in the world and to gain access to the raw materials that its extraordinary economy needs.

Increasingly, though, China's leaders—central bankers crucially among them—have a more ambivalent position. Yes, everything China's traders and financial market believe is undoubtedly true, but . . .

- China's huge financial reserves keep China uncomfortably pinned to US financial policy. Anything that hurts US Treasuries, such as a rise in the yuan versus the US dollar, takes a huge bite out of the value of China's foreign reserves because so

much of them are invested in dollars and dollar-denominated
assets such as Treasuries.

- China's huge financial reserves are at least partly a function of
central bank intervention to keep the value of China's currency
low versus the currencies of its trading partners. (This is one
reason China's reserves peaked in the middle of 2014 and retreated slightly in the second half of that year.) Whatever the
benefits of that currency intervention to China's exporters, it
comes with costs too. The intervention requires the People's
Bank to constantly mop up some of the extra supply of dollars
that results from China's trade surplus with the United States.

- Mopping up dollars requires the bank to issue yuan to buy
them. The resulting constant infusion of yuan into the Chinese
economy feeds inflation and growth in the money supply. It is
arguably impossible for China to get its money supply—and its
resulting bad debt problem—under control until it radically di-
minishes the amount of money it pumps into China's economy
as a result of this currency intervention.

- And, finally, the controls on cross-border money flows necessary for the People's Bank to control the value and supply of
the yuan mean that China's currency does not have anywhere
near the financial presence that the size of its economy would
justify. The yen, the currency of a smaller Japanese economy,
plays a much bigger role in the global economy because it is
free to respond to market forces and demand-and-supply across
national boundaries. No trader in yen, no company hedging in
yen, no buyer and no seller in yen has to worry that government rules won't allow the currency flows necessary to close a
position, execute a trade, or settle a transaction. In the last few
years China has moved to sign bilateral agreements with individual countries such as Brazil and Australia to allow trade to
be settled in yuan. Although those agreements have expanded
the presence of the yuan in the global currency markets, the
need for those deals has also drawn attention to the distance
the yuan still has to travel to become a fully convertible global
currency. And turning the yuan into a global reserve currency
is clearly a major Chinese policy goal.

The United States derives substantial advantages from the dollar's role as the dominant global currency, and anyone who thinks that China's leaders haven't studied those advantages or targeted the duplication of those advantages as future government goals is guilty of thinking that China's leaders know far less economic history than they do and have far less ambitious global goals than they do. (The recent initiative by China to create a Chinese-led Asian infrastructure bank to offset the existing World Bank and Asian Development Bank testifies to China's goals.) Getting the yuan to a point where it can seriously challenge the dollar as the dominant global currency is by no means impossible, but it will require major changes in China's foreign exchange regime and in the openness of its economy to the rules of the global market. That won't happen without major challenges to the consensus benchmarks that currently govern assumptions about how China will solve its bad debt problems.

Chapter 9

The End of the Debt Model of Growth?

THE GLOBAL ECONOMY HAS seen a remarkable period of growth over the last decade that has lifted billions of people out of abject poverty and created hundreds of millions of new consumers. I don't think this growth is coming to a halt. But the methods for creating it seem to have run into at least some short-term obstacles, and the sustainability of those methods is in serious doubt. Growth looks like it's going to be a lot less predictable and consistent over the next decade or two compared to the previous ten to twenty years.

This, of course, will contribute to global volatility. China is the most important story here as the world's leading practitioner of the debt/growth strategy. It has used debt to become the engine of global growth, creating global businesses and lifting hundreds of millions of Chinese people out of poverty. The debt load from that growth, however, is now so large that it threatens the economy's ability to grow in the future.

It is, of course, not the only country to have followed a debt model of growth. China's emphasis, though, has been on infrastructure and fixed-asset investment rather than the dominant model of expanding consumer credit.

For example, Brazil's economic growth in the last decade or two has been built on debt that accrued to consumers rather than to businesses, local governments, or banks, as in China. But the slowdown in Brazil's economic growth in 2013, 2014, and 2015 was, to a great degree, connected to Brazil's use of consumer credit to fuel growth. The result was an accumulation of choking levels of debt that left consumers unable to service that debt load, let alone continue to spend.

Although there are differences in the Brazilian and Chinese models of debt-fueled growth, the similar results—a slowdown in growth and the need to pile up ever-larger amounts of debt to get the same growth bang for the real or the yuan—suggest that the economic practice of using debt to create economic growth may have reached its limits. This is not just the case in Brazil and China but also across the globe in countries as different from China and Brazil as the United States and Spain.

Credit for the incredible reduction in poverty in Brazil rightly goes to government programs initiated under President Luiz Inácio Lula da Silva and extended under the current president, Dilma Rousseff. By the World Bank's count, in 2012 15.9 percent of Brazilians lived below the national poverty line, down from 18.4 percent in 2011, 21.4 percent in 2010, 22.6 percent in 2009, and 24.2 percent in 2008. (By comparison, the official poverty rate in the United States in 2012 was 15 percent.)

The foundation for the progress in reducing the number of Brazilians living in poverty was laid in the Federal Constitution of 1988, but the programs that did the bulk of the heavy lifting date to Lula da Silva's presidency. According to Brazil's Institute of Applied Economic Research, social spending in Brazil went from 19 percent of GDP in 1990 to 21.9 percent of GDP in 2005.

The Bolsa Familia, launched in 2003 by President Lula as part of the Fome Zero program, gives cash payments to poor families under the condition that they keep their kids vaccinated and in school. Extensions such as Brasil Sem Miséria (Brazil Without Destitution) added 2.8 million extremely poor people to the country's welfare lists beginning in June 2011. A total of 22 million people have been given cash benefits to bring them above the absolute poverty line (currently 70 reais a month, or $35 per family member.) President Rousseff's effort reached the remaining 2.5 million extremely poor people whom the government knows about and asked mayors to help identify an estimated additional 2.5 million people sunk in extreme poverty who aren't on any government rolls.

However, much of the next stage of Brazil's growth story—moving millions of Brazilians into the middle class—is connected to the growth in the country's availability of consumer credit. The World Bank defines middle class in Latin America as that portion of the population that earns between $10 and $50 a person per day. By that definition 15 percent of Brazil's population was middle class in 1980, and that number had risen to nearly 33 percent by 2012. In a country of 190 million people that's a swing of roughly 32 million additional middle-class consumers ready to buy cars, TVs, yogurt, and chicken. (The government's definition is somewhat broader. In 2013 the Secretaria de Assuntos Estratégicos [Strategic Affairs Secretariat] categorized 50 percent of Brazilians as middle class. By the Secretariat's definition, people who live in households with a per capita monthly income of 291 reais [$145] to 1019 reais [$500] are middle class.)

Because a massive expansion of consumer credit further boosted middle-class purchasing power, more people in Brazil qualified for credit and more products were sold on credit. I don't think you can underestimate the effect of that credit expansion on consumer spending. Plane tickets are now commonly purchased on credit, for example, and, according to Data Popular in São Paulo, between July 2011 and July 2012 9.5 million Brazilians flew for the first time.

The rise in the availability of consumer credit also expanded demand by enabling Brazil's new middle class to buy things they couldn't afford on their current income. It was as if the cynical joke about the country—Brazil is the country of the future . . . and always will be—had become bank loan officers' motto. As of the end of 2013, consumer loans had more than doubled to $600 billion from five years earlier. Consumer lending rose at an annual average rate of 25 percent in the four years after the global financial crisis of 2008.

But you could see the trouble coming. From 2008 to 2013 the ratio of outstanding debt to GDP jumped from 31 to 56 percent. In 2013 more than 20 percent of household income went to pay off debt; in the United States the comparable rate is 10 percent. The Brazilian debt load is an even bigger burden when you consider that the interest rate on the average loan is 37 percent. (The Banco Central do Brasil raised its benchmark Selic interest rate to 11 percent in

April 2014 and to 12.75 percent in March 2015; the Federal Reserve's interest rate benchmark at that time was 0 to 0.25 percent.) Part of the reason for that sky-high 37 percent rate is that very little of Brazil's household debt is secured by a residential mortgage. Most of the borrowing went to buy assets such as cars or TVs, items that begin to lose value from the moment they are purchased. A house, in contrast, is a relatively secure, appreciating asset.

All these caveats aside, the credit boom worked to increase consumer purchases and to accelerate growth in the economy as a whole. Between 2005 and 2010 auto loans more than tripled to $70 billion a year. In 2012 Brazilian drivers registered 2.9 million new cars, a 130 percent increase over a ten-year period.

With consumer credit providing the fuel for a surge in consumer spending, Brazil's GDP growth soared. According to the World Bank, from an annual growth of 0.3 percent in 1999, a year when China's GDP grew by 7.6 percent, growth in Brazil inched upward to 1.3 percent in 2001, 2.7 percent in 2002, 3.2 percent in 2005, 4 percent in 2006, and then up to 7.5 percent in 2010.

But the slowdown in global growth, especially the slowdown in China, the major market for Brazil's commodity exporters, has been especially cruel to Brazil's indebted consumers. Brazil's economic growth dropped back down to 2.7 percent in 2011 and then, despite initial government forecasts for 4.5 percent GDP growth, plunged to 0.9 percent in 2012. Then 2013 was a recovery, of sorts, as growth returned to the 2.3 percent of Brazil's preboom days. But growth soon fell back to just 0.1 percent in 2014.

Lower GDP growth isn't just a statistic in this situation; it translates into fewer hours worked, fewer jobs, and more time unemployed. (It hasn't helped that Brazil's consumer boom sent inflation toward the top of the central bank's comfort zone of 4.5 percent, give or take two percentage points. With inflation at 6 percent, the Banco Central do Brasil raised rates nine times in 2013, sending its benchmark Selic interest rate benchmark back into double digits.) It's no wonder that Brazil's consumers began defaulting on their credit cards and loans. By mid-2012 the default rate on consumer loans had climbed to 8 percent, and on credit card debt it was a whopping 27.3 percent.

As you might imagine, there's a considerable negative feedback loop here for the Brazilian economy. As more consumers cut back on spending to avoid default or go into default and stop spending entirely, the economy slows. When the economy slows, more people see their work hours cut or lose their jobs entirely, which then makes it more likely that they'll default on their loans.

This problem isn't by any means limited to Brazil, just as the use of consumer credit to boost economic growth wasn't a strategy limited to Brazil either. In Thailand, government programs designed to stimulate spending, with an emphasis on buying a car, sent household debt up 56 percent. Russian consumers put 80 percent more on their credit cards in 2013 than they did in 2012.

The reliance on consumer credit for growth can be a sign of an economy with deeper economic problems. South Africa faces a declining mining industry. Russia's economy is almost totally dependent on the energy sector and global energy prices. Growth in Thailand has been all over the block, from 2.5 percent in 2008, to a drop of 2.3 percent in 2009, to an increase of 7.8 percent in 2010, and then back down to 0.1 percent in 2011 before a rebound to 6.5 percent in 2012.

What does all this have to do with volatility?

It's not that Brazil is about to go bust. Whatever the shortcomings of Brazil's economic policy, the Banco Central do Brasil has steadfastly built up reserves of $372 billion. That's ten times more than a decade ago and pretty good insurance against the worst kind of a crisis.

And even if Brazil were to go bust, to default, for example, like Argentina, I think the resulting crisis would be relatively limited in scope and duration. It certainly wouldn't send waves of volatility through the global economy for a decade or more.

No, the source of global and long-lasting volatility here isn't the danger that this or that individual country could default but rather current global worry that these consumer-debt growth strategies have produced economic growth that might not be sustainable.

The global problem—and the potential source of significant global volatility—is that the middle-class status achieved by so many of the recent poor is so fragile that a slowdown in growth and a contraction of credit will be enough to send hundreds of millions of those recently promoted to the middle class back into the ranks of the poor.

There's no agreed upon income level that defines middle class, and the calculations required to turn incomes and prices in one country into comparable figures for another country are rife with assumptions and subject to massive revisions. But one common definition is that earning $2 to $10 a day pushes you—just—into the middle class in most developing economies. Globally 40 percent of the world's population—that's 2.8 billion people—fall into that income band. The extreme lower end of that band—$2 a day, adjusted for purchasing power in developing economies, that the Asian Development Bank uses as its definition of the line between poverty and the middle class—makes up a huge percentage of that $2 to $10 a day group. The *Financial Times* calculates that almost a billion people—952 million—in the developing world make between $2 and $3 a day.

It's this group that is most in danger of slipping back into poverty from the "middle class" with any slowdown in economic growth.

It is very possible that, at minimum, the 952 million most vulnerable or the larger class of 2.8 billion that includes people farther away from the minimum level for entry into the middle class that have recently emerged from poverty to join the middle class might slide back out of the middle class. And this possibility contributes to global volatility in financial markets and political and economic systems on three levels.

First and simplest, there's the financial market volatility that results when companies that pegged their strategy to this growing population of consumers discover that the demand this group was supposed to provide isn't materializing as expected. Companies such as consumer giants Nestlé, Unilever, and Procter and Gamble have been expanding in developing markets with products targeted at this new middle class—laundry detergent sold in small sizes to fit the very modest incomes of these consumers or instant noodles that are cheap enough for these budgets but are a step up in calories and convenience. Expanding in these markets has been a way for these companies to make up for slowing growth in the mature markets of North America and Europe.

But at the end of 2013 and into 2014 and 2015 growth in these emerging markets lagged expectations. For example, Nestlé announced first-quarter 2014 sales growth of 5.4 percent, up from the first quarter of 2013. Within that, Nestlé's revenues barely grew in Europe—up 1.5 percent—but were a pleasant surprise in the Americas: sales of dairy products and ice cream in Mexico grew faster than expected. But some emerging markets experienced what Nestlé called a "softening" that was significant enough to put the company's target of 5 to 6 percent sales growth for 2014 at risk. The shares dropped on this news, falling 5.93 percent from January 23 to February 4, a decline of almost 6 percent in about two weeks.

And Nestlé and its food-industry peers aren't the only companies showing the effects of a slowdown in spending by developing market consumers. For example, the damage included France's Publicis Groupe, which handles consumer advertising in emerging markets. Liquor companies such as Pernod Ricard and Diageo, which sell what I'd call aspirational brands of scotch and cognac in emerging markets, saw sales growth in those economies slow in 2013 and 2014.

As you might imagine, this slowdown in sales growth in developing economies has produced significant weakness in the shares of companies that have pegged their growth strategies to emerging consumers in these economies. The question, of course, is whether this slowdown is a blip of a few quarters or perhaps a couple of years or the beginning of a longer trend. At this point I think it's extremely hard to tell, and given how long it takes to put a strategy in place at a company such as Nestlé or Unilever or McDonald's, the logical and reasonable reaction is to let the strategy ride for a while. But if—to take the most important global example—growth in China continues to show a downward trend from 7.4 to 7.2 percent and a projected 6.8 percent in 2015, then at some point companies will revise their growth strategies and assumptions. The point at which they make that revision will introduce a new level of uncertainty and volatility into global stock prices.

A transition from a world economy where every economy was growing to one where some economies are growing much faster than average makes up my second level of volatility. The huge May 16, 2014, election victory of prime minister by Narendra Modi and his Bharatiya Janata Party in the Indian elections was largely a vote by Indians tired of the corruption and slow economic growth produced by the incumbent Congress Party. Bharatiya Janata, even without the votes of likely allies, wound up winning an absolute majority of 282 seats in the 543-seat Parliament. That was the biggest win by a single party since 1984.

The discontent with the economic policies of the Congress government is easy to understand. Economic growth in India had fallen—and then stayed—at the lowest rate in a decade as the Reserve Bank of India raised interest rates to fight Asia's second-highest rate of inflation. (India's inflation rate was 8.6 percent in April 2014.) India's GDP growth had slowed to 4.5 percent in the country's fiscal year that ended in March 2013, and the economy was on track to turn in growth of just 4.9 percent in the year that ended on March 31, 2014. These recent rates are a solid increase from the 3.2 percent recorded in fiscal year 2012, but they are nonetheless a huge drop from the 9.1 percent growth in fiscal year 2011.

But although 4.5 percent growth would be greeted with cheers in any EuroZone economy, in Japan, or even in the United States, it just doesn't cut it in India. India, like China, needs high growth rates to provide jobs for its growing population. But India's population is growing faster than China's and is projected to exceed China's by 2025 at 1.45 billion, up from 1.29 billion today. And India's population is younger than China's, with half of India's population under the age of twenty-four. That means that every year produces a huge new crop of young people who need to enter the workforce, so India needs a growth rate in the range of 7.5 percent, estimated as the break-even rate in China to keep up with population growth. Estimates are that each one percentage point of growth in India adds about 1.5 million jobs. With about 9 million people entering the workforce each year, that works out to a minimum of 6 percent growth just to break even. From 2005 to 2010 economic growth in India averaged 8.7 percent a year, but even that stunning growth didn't make a huge dent in the number of India's unemployed and underemployed.

Long before the actual election the Congress government knew it was in trouble. In mid-2013 it pushed through Parliament a program to guarantee cheap food grains. Everyone saw the measure as an attempt to bolster the party's standing ahead of the May 2014 elections. Moves like this had certainly worked for the party before.

But not this time. It was perhaps too cynical—even some of the poorest Indians who would have benefited most from the guarantee found it an offensively naked attempt to buy power using government funds. But more tellingly, the effort proved just how out of touch with Indian reality Congress had become. Since Congress had returned to power in 2004, by the government's—quite possibly overly optimistic—count, 935 million Indians have escaped from the most abject poverty of less than $2 a day. For these Indians the goal wasn't a food subsidy but rather more and better jobs that would move them farther away from the $2 a day threshold. The Congress food guarantee missed that point completely, and Congress's recent record on economic growth struck many of these voters as a threat to their hard-won but tenuous achievements.

It's not overstating the case to say that this fear of slipping back into poverty and the hopes for climbing farther into the developing world's middle class powered Modi's huge election victory over Congress. It created a wave of optimism. The can-do First Minister of Gujarat would dismantle red tape, cut a growth-hobbling bureaucracy, and reduce corruption to unleash the full potential of the Indian economy. And in 2014 GDP growth rebounded to 7.5 percent rate.

Now, 7.5 percent growth is a good thing for India. But even good things contribute to volatility in the Age of Volatility. The higher growth rate for 2014 couldn't have come at a better time for Modi because it gave him extra momentum in his efforts to reform the Indian economy. It also led to a rash of headlines pointing out that, at 7.5 percent growth for 2014, India edged out China (at 7.4 percent growth for 2014) as the global growth king. It was then only to be expected that this would lead to stories predicting that India would grow faster than China for the foreseeable future.

Of course, stock markets didn't wait for the April 2014 election to push Indian shares to record highs. That enthusiasm kicked in with local elections in December 2013 and then ratcheted upward to all-time highs in the weeks before first-round voting. By May, when the

first results from the final round in the election came in, the Mumbai
stock market was already up 13 percent for 2015. That didn't stop a
5 percent rally on the day the first results came in, showing a sweeping Modi victory.

Overseas investors moved even faster. By December 2014 they
had put $43 billion in India's financial markets. The move made
sense even though the track record of India's stock market shows
that it is one of the world's most volatile. (The standard deviation, a
measure of the volatility of returns, of India's stock market over the
last five years is 25 percent. That's roughly double the standard deviation of the US S&P 500.) Think about the way that a lack of alternatives created by the faltering of the standard debt-based economic
growth model makes putting money into one of the world's most
volatile markets a sensible move.

In a world where emerging market stars of past financial markets
are faltering—China is slowing, and Brazil is near recession—and
where new growth champions are emerging, even perhaps temporarily, you wind up with increased volatility as investors chase
growth from one market to another. And when central banks are
adding big dollops of cash to the global financial system, that adds
up to my third level of volatility.

India is a prime example of this third level: the effect of global
central bank cash on the developing economies and emerging markets of the world. The recent record prices of stocks on the Mumbai
market haven't removed the historical volatility of Indian stocks. In
fact, they should be seen as confirmation of that pattern and to raise
the possibility of even higher volatility in the future.

Like many developing economies—Turkey and the Philippines
come to mind—India isn't self-sufficient in capital. Because the country runs a trade deficit in most years and the government runs a budget deficit, the country is dependent on flows of capital from outside
India. A 2014 report from the International Monetary Fund noted
that India isn't unique among the world's twenty biggest economies
in running a big government deficit or a big trade deficit; it is, however, the IMF noted, the only country in the group to run big deficits
on both measures in 2013. For the full year of 2013 the trade deficit

came in at \$138.6 billion; remarkably this was a big improvement from the 190.3 billion trade deficit racked up the prior year.

In March 2014—March marks the end of India's fiscal year—India's monthly trade gap widened to \$10.5 billion, the highest level since October 2013, and it looked like the country was headed to another huge trade gap. And then came the plunge in oil prices at the end of 2014. Because India imports almost all of its oil, the drop in global oil prices produced a big drop in India's import bill. For March 2015 oil imports were down 55 percent in US dollars from the same month in 2014.

The Modi government had inherited a persistent government budget deficit that had run north of 4.5 percent of GDP a year in recent years. For the 2014–2015 fiscal year the government's budget showed a 4.1 percent deficit, a major part of which is debt incurred to provide food and fuel subsidies to India's poor. This number is down from 4.9 percent in fiscal year 2013–2014 and from 5.2 percent in fiscal year 2011–2012. What's more, for 2015–2016 the government's budget projects a 3.9 percent deficit. That improvement assumes economic growth of better than 8 percent and continued low prices for oil that will cut fuel subsidies to the poor by a projected 8.6 percent.

In other words, on both the trade and budget deficit much of the recent improvement depends on a continuation of current good fortune. Despite the hoopla and hopes for economic change that followed Modi's election, the new administration introduced relatively modest changes in the way the economy and government work. Absent those larger changes, the country will remain dependent on overseas cash whenever current good fortunes turn a bit sour. Of course, when those outside conditions look a little less favorable and India again needs an infusion of outside cash to balance its accounts, that overseas hot money may well have already headed off in chase of the next hot story.

(Just in case you are wondering why the United States can run persistent budget and trade deficits and India can't, the answer is that we can't in the long run. The United States is currently dependent on Japanese, German, and other savers to finance its deficits by purchasing US assets such as government bonds. Over the long term that's not sustainable, but unlike India, the United States owns the world's current exchange currency, the dollar, and that gives the United States sizeable protection from short-term outflows of cash and extends the amount of time before the country's dual deficits result in some kind of reckoning.)

This is, of course, a high-altitude view focused on financial markets and macroeconomies. The volatility that I'm sketching here has effects beyond the price of stocks in Mumbai or how the relative popularity of developing- and developed-market financial assets influences global cash flows, currency prices, and interest rates.

The success or failure of Modi's government will determine how easy it is to get around a very congested Mumbai and where people choose to live. It will influence how much money young people are willing to sink or will have to sink into often fly-by-night schools that promise a better job. It will influence how quickly India's increasingly huge second-tier cities such as Pune grow and how quickly—and whether—they are integrated into corridors with existing megacities such as Mumbai.

In other words, there is one world of volatility connected to financial markets and global macroeconomics, and there is another where the volatility is expressed in people's everyday lives. The changes in this everyday economy determine the success or failure of strategies that we don't normally think of as investing, such as decisions about education or what house to buy. And these changes create investing opportunities through traditional and untraditional markets and assets.

The next part of this book looks at this larger world of volatility in ten parts of our everyday lives with an eye toward what will create that volatility and how much of it we can expect. When it's applicable, I'll also discuss investing opportunities that these volatility trends will create and include advice for navigating that volatility to make the smartest decisions on everyday issues that constitute the future for us and our families.

PART II

THE VOLATILITY OF EVERYDAY LIFE

Chapter 10

Volatility Trend No. 1
Houses as Financial Assets

ONCE UPON A TIME we all thought of our homes as our castles. The quiet, solid shelter from the turmoil of the larger world. The nest where we raise our young. Of course, we knew—or hoped—that this house would be our physical and financial shelter in our old age, but that was largely a far-off conclusion that we didn't think about much.

That way of thinking about a house still exists. Realtors, for example, still get questions about the quality of local schools and how long it takes to commute to work.

But the opening decades of the twenty-first century have chipped away at this vision. Partly that is a result of the boom and bust of the US (and Irish and Spanish and . . .) housing market that culminated in the subprime mortgage crisis that led to the global financial crisis that hit full force in 2008. It's hard not to think of a house as a financial asset if you've seen its value rise and then fall by 30 or 40 percent or more.

Part of it is a result of the not-so-slow demise of the traditional defined pension plan. Defined contribution plans such as 401(k)s were supposed to take up the slack, but for many retirees the reality is that their house is their major retirement asset.

And part of it is a result of the increasing role of central bank money in the global market and economy. In the attempt to recover from the global financial crisis, many central banks—certainly the

Federal Reserve—treated housing prices and demand as the key tool in managing the economy. It's hard not to be influenced by that thinking and its power in the economy.

It's not remarkable that the US Federal Reserve, along with central banks in the United Kingdom, China, and Australia, has concluded that the easiest way to turn interest rate changes into economic growth is by manipulating the yield on the seven- to ten-year Treasury notes that serve as the benchmark for mortgage rates. Lower the benchmark interest rates—using, say, a massive program to buy Treasury notes of these maturities—and a central bank could lower mortgage rates and, thus, stimulate demand for houses and increase economic growth.

That increased demand for houses would also lead to an increase in the prices of existing houses. Which, given the central role that houses play in most Americans' portfolios, would lead to increased confidence in the financial markets and, thus, create an increase in consumers' willingness to spend.

If you look at the concentration of wealth in real estate in most American households' net worth, it's easy to understand why concentrating on housing prices would strike the Federal Reserve as a good method for moving the economy. According to the US Census Bureau, the median net worth of a household in the United States was $68,828 in 2011. Most of that median net worth and more is wrapped up in the family home. Even after the US mortgage crisis and the subsequent housing bust, the median household, with its $68,828 in net worth, owns a house with $80,000 in positive equity. That dwarfs the $30,000 in the median 401(k) or the median $20,000 in stocks and bonds. (Because of household debt, the total value of the median portfolio is less than the median positive equity in the family home.)

The Census Bureau's assessment in 2011, its last regular ten-year report, shouldn't surprise anyone. "Did you know," the Census Bureau asked, "that changes in overall median net worth observed over the past decade have been driven primarily by changes in one of its major components—equity that American households hold in their homes?" Median net worth fell by 35 percent from 2005 ($102,844)— that is, before the mortgage crisis—to 2010 ($66,740)—that is, after the crisis and before the recovery in housing prices. This drop in median household net worth came about, even though household net worth, excluding home equity, increased by 8 percent from $13,859 in 2009 (the stock market bottom) to $15,000 in 2010.

However, there's a volatility cost to treating real estate as a tool for managing the economy. If housing prices are subject to manipulation by central banks, if they rise and fall with interest rates, then in what sense does a house have a "real" price?

In March 2014 the interest rate on a thirty-year fixed-rate mortgage had climbed to 4.4 percent. A few months later mortgage lending giant Freddie Mac reported that the recovery in many of the country's housing markets was stalling. Freddie Mac's Multi-Indicator Market Index found that only four of the fifty metro areas in that index—San Antonio, New Orleans, Austin, and Houston—fell into the stable category. For the rest of the country the trend was bleak: less than half of the metro areas were showing an improving trend. A year earlier 90 percent of metro areas had ranked as "improving."

A year later, though, economists and financial markets were surprised when sales of new homes rose 7.8 percent in February 2015 to a seasonally adjusted annual rate of 539,000, the highest rate since February 2008. (Sales of new homes in any month are turned into an annualized rate—this is how many houses would be bought over a year if sales continued at the current month rate for a year. That gives a rate that is more meaningful for the economy as a whole than a single monthly number.) The median sales price in the month climbed 2.6 percent.

The difference between the sagging market and lagging market prices for houses in 2014 and the surprisingly strong market and higher prices of 2015? Interest rates that had climbed to 4.4 percent in March 2014 had dropped back to 3.7 percent in 2015.

At 4.4 percent a $300,000 mortgage results in a monthly payment of $1,502, whereas at 3.7 percent the monthly payment is only $1,380. At 3.7 percent a buyer would pay $1,518 a month—roughly the same as at 4 percent for a $300,000 mortgage—for a loan that is 10 percent bigger at $330,000. If you're in the housing market and you've calculated what you can afford to buy, 3.7 percent means you can afford 10 percent more house.

This, of course, increases demand. Lower mortgage rates plus higher demand result in higher home prices. Thus, changes in interest and mortgage rates result in housing market volatility. And uncertainty about interest and mortgage rates add to volatility as well, as buyers move to buy before mortgage rates climb and sellers delay selling in the hope that mortgage rates will fall. The truth is that rather than being shelter from the storm, our houses are wrapped in the winds of the storm. The image that comes to mind is Dorothy spinning through the air on her way from Kansas to Oz. And who knows where that house will land—or on whom.

In *Pudd'nhead Wilson* Mark Twain writes, "Behold, the fool saith, 'Put not all thine eggs in the one basket'—which is but a matter of saying, 'Scatter your money and your attention'; but the wise man saith, 'Put all your eggs in the one basket and—WATCH THAT BASKET.'"

With the family home being by far the largest asset for most families, watching that basket would seem to be imperative. But what does that mean in an Age of Volatility?

My wife works as a real estate agent in New York—Manhattan, no less. I know this is a rarified real estate market, and I certainly wouldn't extrapolate every trend from Manhattan to the rest of the country, but putting together what I see as I watch her work and what the data about national and regional markets show me, I have to conclude that savvier real estate buyers seem to have changed attitudes and behavior in the three following ways.

First, more buyers are moving from thinking of housing as a long-lived asset that is a once-in-a-lifetime purchase to thinking of a house as a financial asset that is some combination of an ATM and a seven- to ten-year option on the economic cycle.

Second, because buying a house isn't just a once-in-a-lifetime purchase, a buying—or selling—decision needs to include an estimate of where the housing market and the economy are in their cycles. To play the boom-and-bust cycle in a home purchase, you have to be willing to contemplate new strategies such as selling near the top and then renting until prices fall. I know people who have adopted just that strategy recently. In the odd real estate market that is Manhattan this has the added advantage of giving you lots of cash

that will give you an edge in the inevitable bidding war over anything with space and light. It also has the advantage of giving you
cash to clean up your personal balance sheet so you can earn a
higher credit score and procure a lower mortgage rate.

Third, we're seeing an expansion in information that can provide
alternative values for real estate that might function independently
of prices that fluctuate with interest rates or economic cycles. For
example, both the St. Louis Federal Reserve and the Brookings Institution have recently published studies of the relationship between
school quality and home value. The conclusion is that, yes, a house
near a good school is indeed more valuable in the market place, but
as I read the studies, we're still at a point where there is major disagreement about how big a jump in value a good school can bring—
and how good a good school has to be before the bonus kicks in.
This kind of research is no longer of just academic interest, as real
estate websites now allow for property searches by school district,
and other sites, such as greatschools.org, allow for searches to identity good schools on various metrics. (What the best metrics are and
whether any of these metrics mean anything is an ongoing debate.)
Using these information sources, I can see a day when it is possible
to arbitrage the price of a house calculated by the market against the
price calculated by some other valuation system.

How far we go down this road toward strategies based on economic and interest rate cycles and alternative valuation models depends largely on how convinced we have become that the recent
volatility we're seeing in real estate during this latest boom-to-bust-
to-recovery cycle is here to stay. If it were a one-time thing and we're
now back to normal appreciation and depreciation, then these
trends toward developing alternative strategies for buying and selling real estate probably won't go much farther. Another boom-and-
bust cycle, however, would convince more real estate owners and
investors that it would be worthwhile to put time and money into
strategies to cope with this volatility.

I certainly don't have a real estate crystal ball, but it is likely that
a global financial system that creates lots of cash, promotes ultra-low
interest rates, and then provides incentives for that money to flow to
the next hot market will lead to a continued increase in volatility.

In some real estate markets you can already see signs of a new boom in prices not so long after the latest bust. In London, for example, 2014 brought a huge surge of leverage that only makes sense if buyers think they're seeing the beginning of a new boom. In the first three months of 2014 prices for first-time buyers rose to a record eight times their income. (The average since 1983 has been 4.9 times income.) But if you have selling on your mind—and mortgage money costs just 4.4 percent on a variable rate loan—that kind of leverage isn't really a negative. Price gains on the average London house over the 2014–2015 year were almost double the £34,200 ($57,668) median annual income of a full-time London worker.

That's a more-than-reasonable return for taking on the risk of going so deeply into debt. Or at least that's what a big part of the home-buying population in London believes—again.

You don't have to wade across the pond to see reasoning that might form the foundation for a new boom. For example, there's the argument that we're about to see a big surge in home buying as millennials, who have put off household formation and home buying during the Great Recession, move out of their parents' basements and rental apartments. A March 26, 2015, report from real estate site Zillow.com argues that affordability now favors buying over renting. And that's especially true in the metro areas, such as San Francisco and New York, which are most attractive to professional millennials. When stocks hit new highs, Wall Street responds with research to explain why stocks can go even higher. Stories about the soon-to-be-released buying power of millennials fulfill a similar function in the real estate market right now. They may not be wrong, and buying may make more sense than renting, but the argument is still a justification for buying at higher prices now—because prices will be even higher tomorrow.

Will markets, thinking, and behavior snap back to normal? In other words, will all parties involved decide that the crisis was just an episode, now over, and we can resume our regularly scheduled programming? Or will those parties decide that the new normal is a constant stream of crises and that heightened volatility is the rule going forward?

I call this the Flitcraft dilemma in honor of a character in an anecdote that Dashiell Hammett's detective Sam Spade tells in *The Maltese Falcon*. Spade and Flitcraft don't have any interest in the housing market of our time or theirs, but the story is about how the "rational actor"—a mythic creature much beloved by rational market economists—copes with a world that is at least intermittently irrational.

Spade tells the Flitcraft story to Brigid O'Shaughnessy as they wait around for the next outbreak of chaos to move them along in their search for the Maltese Falcon.

Some time before the action in *The Maltese Falcon* Spade had been hired by Flitcraft's wife to find the successful Tacoma real estate agent who left his office one day and never came home. Flitcraft wasn't in financial trouble, was on good terms with his wife and their two young sons, there was no evidence that he had set his affairs in order to prepare for vanishing, and there was no evidence that he was having an affair.

Five years after Flitcraft had disappeared, Spade found him, following a tip, in Spokane. He had a new wife, a baby son, a house in a Spokane suburb, and owned an auto business. As he had in Tacoma, he frequently took afternoons off to play golf.

In fact, the most remarkable thing about Flitcraft's life in Spokane was how closely it resembled his life in Tacoma.

Why had he done it? Flitcraft was eager to explain himself to Spade. As Spade remarks to Brigid, his disappearance and new life make perfect sense to Spade but, Flitcraft suspects, not to most people. Perhaps he senses that Spade, accustomed to a world where the irrational acts far outnumber the rational, is the best audience he can ever expect to have; certainly, Spade notes, the wife he left behind in Tacoma finds his behavior baffling.

Going to lunch on the day he disappeared, he told Spade, a steel beam fell ten stories from a construction site, grazed his cheek (leaving a scar), and punched into the sidewalk next to him. Suddenly the life Flitcraft thought he could count on seemed a lie. Men died by chance in the new world the falling beam had revealed to him. Life was random, and to cope with that new understanding, Flitcraft decided he would do something random and abandon his ordered life.

After wandering aimlessly for a few years, he'd gotten married again to a woman who didn't look much like his first wife but who, like his first wife, played decent games of golf and bridge. His new business was selling cars instead of real estate, but it was otherwise much the same.

Steel beams had stopped falling, Flitcraft concluded, and he went back to something resembling his old life. He had adjusted to a world where random steel beams came crashing out of the sky, and then he'd adjusted to a world where the beams had stopped falling. That world was just like the old world that existed before that midday moment in Tacoma. So Flitcraft went back to living the life he'd lived before.

So do home owners and investors decide that the steel beams have stopped falling? Or do they conclude that an irrational and volatile world remains irrational and volatile?

It's hard for me to call an "all clear" on plunging steel beams when I look at how far central banks still have to go in order to reverse or even control the flood of cheap money that they created in their efforts to fix the Great Recession. Home owners and investors who saw how cheap central bank money created the housing bubble that peaked in 2005–2006, depending on where you live, are all too aware that central banks have been creating money to raise housing prices.

And, gee, you know what? Home owners and investors don't trust the world's central banks not to leave them hanging out to dry again. Will the Federal Reserve continue to support housing prices, even after it starts to raise interest rates, by increasing rates very, very gradually? Remarks by Federal Reserve Chair Janet Yellen in May 2015 pointed toward a process so gradual that it could take until 2018 to normalize interest rates. Or will central banks, either through calculation or a policy mistake, wind up creating a surge in the seven- to ten-year government notes that serve as benchmarks for mortgages and, once again, crash the mortgage and housing markets?

The key point I make here is that we don't know, but in contrast to earlier periods, we track housing, mortgage, and Treasury markets and think we ought to be able to figure out—and then act—on the answers to these questions. Some of those answers will be wrong and some right, but the impulse to act itself increases the volatility of this market.

Add that to other factors such as worries about aging populations resulting in the formation of fewer new households and a logical conclusion that high unemployment among younger workers isn't encouraging home buying, and I think you can understand why, unlike Flitcraft, home owners aren't willing to conclude that everything is back to normal.

This trend of treating houses as financial assets isn't the only big trend that I will explain in the next few chapters. The very next chapter, for example, explains why I think we're facing a period of increasing volatility in the job market, with big consequences for everything from housing prices to, well, jobs.

As I've promised, this book will lay out strategies for coping with or even profiting from these trends. That's the subject of the third part of this book. If you want to skip ahead—or skip around—you'll find the relevant strategies for coping with volatility in the housing market in Chapter 21: A Strategy for Bonds, which begins on page 277.

Chapter 11

Volatility Trend No. 2

The Job Market Feels More Volatile as Economies Slow

HERE'S THE GREAT PUZZLE of the current economic recovery in the United States: the US economy is creating jobs at a decent rate, but what's known as labor force participation remains steady around a thirty-seven-year low. The labor force participation rate—the percentage of the country's civilian population over sixteen, not in the military and not in school or other less voluntary institutions, either working or looking for work—has been stuck between 62.7 and 62.9 percent in the eleven months ending in February 2015, even as the official unemployment rate has dropped to 5.5 percent. The last time the participation rate was under 63 percent was March 1978, when it stood at 62.8 percent.

There have been lots of guesses at a cause. The aging Baby Boom generation is one possibility, according to the Bureau of Labor Statistics. From the ages of thirty-six to fifty-five the Baby Boom cohort had an incredibly high participation rate of 84 percent. As this population ages, however, its members go from a high participation group to a lower participation group. There's some evidence that low wages and a lack of support, such as low-cost childcare, have discouraged some potential workers. With the federal minimum wage stuck at $7.25 since 2009, in terms of purchasing power adjusted for inflation, it is worth less than the $1.60 an hour ($10.88 in 2014 dollars) minimum wage of 1968.

And there's evidence that workers who were out of work during the Great Recession for long enough to count as long-term unemployed or who were out of work for so long that they dropped out of the workforce completely and no longer count as looking for work have seen their job skills erode so much that they aren't a good match for available jobs in the current economy.

In an aging world, that first cause, the aging of the Baby Boomers, accounts for a big part of this problem. The Congressional Budget Office calculates that roughly half of the three-percentage-point drop in the labor participation rate since 2007 is due to the aging workforce.

But it's that last group, the long-term unemployed, that interests me most because it suggests that the job market is becoming structurally more volatile just as we hit a patch of slow growth in the global economy. It also suggests that even normal cyclical slowdowns in growth are likely to make the job market more volatile.

Think of the kind of economy and job market that the world has built out of its abundant supply of cheap capital. It's based on identifying immediate profit opportunities and then investing in them until enough—or more than enough—competition has been attracted to the opportunity so as to kill the profit margins that attracted capital to the opportunity in the first place.

The economic boom—now turning to bust in Mississippi's casino industry—is a good example of the job-creation process in the age of cheap global cash. The casinos started arriving in Mississippi's economically depressed Mississippi River counties in 1992. There wasn't any particular draw to these counties other than cheap land, cheap labor, and a very receptive state government that saw casino taxes as a way to put more money into the state treasury without raising taxes. Of course, although the pioneers had to work hard to convince investors that this was a viable opportunity, the proof of concept was certainly in place by the time capital went from inexpensive and available to super-cheap and super-abundant. By 2013 the state's nontribal casinos recorded $2.1 billion in gross gambling revenue. At its peak Mississippi was the third-largest casino market in the United States.

Not bad for a start from zero. But now some of these casinos are closing and taking their relatively well-paid jobs—$13.80 an hour for a cook—with them. That's a big deal in a state with a 7.7 percent official unemployment rate in April 2014, a month when the national unemployment rate hit 6.3 percent. (Mississippi's unemployment rate then was higher than that of every state in the country except for five: Kentucky, California, Illinois, Nevada, and Rhode Island.)

The Mississippi casino industry didn't do anything wrong—except to succeed. By growing to $2.1 billion in 2013 revenue from a standing start, the Mississippi success demonstrated to other states—and other casino operators—what could be done. If you count tribal casinos, forty states now offer casino gambling. And there's clear evidence of a glut, with revenue falling in markets such as Missouri and Atlantic City and state officials in New York and Iowa scaling back projections for revenues from casinos still on the drawing board. The two biggest causes of the problem? First, states competed to see who could grease the wheels the most because taxes on casinos were an all too attractive "free lunch" for states and communities that didn't want to raise taxes. Second, in an era of cheap money, any sector that promised—and for a while, at least, delivered—growth found it very easy to raise money in the financial markets. The boom-to-bust cycle isn't an example of capitalism not working: it's supposed to work that way, with initial high returns for first entrants attracting new competitors, resulting falling margins that wash out the weakest and least efficient competitors and leave only the most efficient standing. But the cycle isn't supposed to move quite this quickly—twenty-two years is awfully fast, and it doesn't leave communities and workers with much time to adjust.

The story of Mississippi's casinos isn't any different from the story of China's solar sector or the US oil and natural gas sector from shale boom. The states at the top of the list for job creation in April 2014—that is, those with the lowest rates of unemployment—were North Dakota, Vermont, Nebraska, Wyoming, and South Dakota. Three of those five were the hot bed of the hottest industry in the United States up until the end of 2014. The ability to unlock oil and natural gas deposits from tight shale formations has revived US production. The US Energy Information Administration reports that US production of crude oil averaged almost 8.7 million barrels a day in 2014, up 1.2 million barrels a day from 7.5 million barrels a day in 2013 and only 0.9 million barrels a day below the all-time peak for US production in 1970. With production continuing to creep higher in 2015—projections are calling for 9.5 million barrels a day—there's a good chance of an average annual record. Much of this production from shale is coming from geologies in unlikely places, sending North and South Dakota and Wyoming into the top tier of US oil-producing states.

However, three things about the US shale energy boom are paradigmatic to the current model of job creation. First, the industry was able to raise a gusher of cash. The lowest-rated energy producers, those with junk-bond ratings, were able to sell $90 billion in junk bonds in the three years leading up to December 2014.

Second, these companies raised all this cash, even though they weren't actually profitable—all it took was the promise of future profits. In a February 2015 presentation EOG Resources, one of the biggest and most efficient producers of oil from shale, told Wall Street that it earned 12.4 percent on its capital in 2013 and 13.7 percent in 2014, and it estimated that its US exploration and production peers had, on average, done much worse, with a return of just 3.4 percent in 2013 and 4.3 percent in 2014. Many of the biggest and most recognizable names in the sector were investing more in exploration, production, and development than in generating cash from operations. Continental Resources, for example, recorded cash from operations of $3.36 billion in 2014 but spent $4.59 billion on capital investment.

And third, even though the return on capital is miniscule and so many companies weren't generating enough cash to cover capital budgets, the sector was able to raise enough money to expand production to such a degree that it helped fuel a collapse in oil prices as global supply overwhelmed global demand. In June 2014 crude oil peaked at $115 a barrel. By the end of the year US benchmark West Texas Intermediate had tumbled below $50 and was threatening to fall to $40. Despite this price crash on slowing global demand growth, US oil production continued to climb into 2015.

This part of the economic character of the capitalism of our time certainly isn't limited to Mississippi's casinos or the Dakotas' oil and gas fields. Apple makes it clear with the success of its iPhone that there are big profit margins available in smartphones, and the company draws the competition not just of Korea's Samsung but also of China's Lenovo and HTC. And like Mississippi, only the most efficient companies, in this case Samsung and Apple, actually make any money. In 2013 and 2014 almost all of the profits in the smartphone sector went to Apple and Samsung. In servers, the machines at the core of the Internet, ARM Holdings saw that Intel was making a pretty good buck and decided to launch its own chip for servers, with one of its first customers being Google. Intel, not to be left out, decided that Qualcomm's margins in the market for smartphone chip sets were attractive and set out to conquer that business.

There are still barriers to entry—if you don't have the intellectual property to make chip sets for smartphones, you have a problem, although you can license that intellectual property from ARM Holdings or Qualcomm. But a lack of capital sure isn't among those barriers.

But if capital is more globally fluid than ever, labor isn't. Labor isn't very geographically mobile, and it isn't very mobile from hot sector to hot sector.

One of the stranger statistical patterns from the Great Recession in the United States and from the slow recovery from that slump shows that the Great American Moving Van is picking up fewer households than it did before the global financial crisis. You'd expect that any trend that had more homeowners in United States thinking about their houses as if they were options on seven- to ten-year Treasury bonds would drive the notoriously high moving rate for US householders even higher. If, after all, you're tracking buy-versus-rent strategies as a way to figure out when to buy and sell in the price and interest rate cycle, wouldn't that drive households to move more frequently?

You might think so, but that trend doesn't show up in the most recent US Census data from 2012–2013. In fact, they show just the opposite.

In 2013 36 million US residents—11.7 percent of the US population—moved. That's down from the 12 percent rate in 2012 and is barely above the 11.6 percent record low set in 2011. That's a huge drop from the 20 percent of Americans who moved during the 1950s and 1960s and the 14 percent rate before the housing bubble.

That result, though perhaps initially surprising, actually makes sense—if you look at the figures solely from a housing perspective. Considerable numbers of US home owners live in regions where housing prices haven't yet recovered to their 2006 peak. Remember that, on average, US housing prices in March 2014 were still 13 percent below the 2006 peak, and in places such as Las Vegas and Orlando they were still 30 to 40 percent below their peak.

If you are underwater on your mortgage or looking at a big loss on selling your house, even if only a paper loss, it's a considerable disincentive to selling and moving, even on the prospects for a new job.

That's especially the case if the jobs in the new hot sector are radically different from the jobs in the old hot sector. Very few people are moving from a job in a Mississippi casino to a job on a South Dakota oil rig.

And moving a long distance for a new job isn't the historical pattern in the United States anyway. The American pattern of moving is odd in its extremely local nature. Historically and currently most of the trips that the Great American Moving Van takes are very, very short. About two-thirds of people who move stay in the same county, according to the US Census Bureau's Journey-to-Work and Migration Statistics Branch. Of those who did set off into the great unknown by leaving their county, a full 40 percent moved less than fifty miles away, and only 24.7 percent moved five hundred miles or more. A booming job market a thousand miles away might as well not exist.

I think there's also a volatility effect at work here. Moving isn't easy. People don't move farther for several reasons: they don't want to leave friends and family, they're scared of leaving the familiar, and moving itself is expensive. No one wants to go through that experience for a job in a booming job market if it might not be booming by the time they get there. There's no point in moving if the job you do manage to land is going to vanish in a matter of months or a year or two.

Your willingness to move for a job, then, is related to your belief in the security of the job market. If you think you've been laid off because of bad luck, because your supervisor doesn't like you, or because your particular company has been badly managed, then you're likely to believe that the job market is volatile but really no more so than it has ever been. People lose jobs every day—it's just part of the churn in the economy and is no big deal. Moving to find a new job is just what everyone does—or at least considers.

If, however, you believe that you lost your job because of some structural problem in the economy, you're less likely to move. If you think that unfairness with the way the game works is rampant, that your entire industry is in decline, or that "they" took your job, you're less likely to move.

The more you feel you are a victim of big volatility, the less likely you are to move.

If you think back to John Coates's research (see pages 24–27) on volatility, risk, stress, and brain chemistry, this reaction makes sense. Coates's work focused on Wall Street traders and their reactions to the stress of market events. In the short term, volatility and heightened risk produced a chemical cocktail that was both useful in coping with the event and actually pleasurable. In the long term, however, that same chemical response system led to decreases in response effectiveness and a negative emotional response.

It's only reasonable to think that this same chemical response system works in a similar way on the downside too. The challenge of finding a new job, though stressful, in the short term can produce an effective burst of energy. Stretched out over a longer term, however, the reaction will be similar to what Coates described: the longer downside stress lasts, the less effective we are likely to be in coping with it and the more it weighs on the chemical responses of our brain.

Although the degree of volatility in the job market isn't totally subjective, there is nonetheless a subjective element to it. The longer you're out of work, I'd hypothesize, the more discouraged you're likely to be *and* the more likely you are to feel like the victim of something other than normal, everyday volatility.

It may seem far-fetched to think that repeated volatility over the long term could result in something like depression. But that's what I think Japan's experience over the last two decades suggests—in this as well as in so many other prospects Japan serves as a great real-life laboratory of large-scale behavioral economics. Why has it been so hard to reignite growth and inflation in Japan? Prime Minister Shinzō Abe, acting as national therapist, said in his first policy speech after winning election that the answer might be that Japan is psychologically depressed. "I propose," he said, "that the great issue here is the fact that the Japanese people have been robbed of their confidence." A lack of confidence makes it more difficult for the Bank of Japan to create expectations for future inflation, which would, finally, break Japan's long period of deflation. But getting people to believe that prices will be even modestly higher in the future (modest inflation in this context is a good thing) requires them to believe that the future will be better and that their actions can influence that future.

There may be a similar dynamic at work in the job market that explains part of the drop in the labor participation rate, the (declining but still) stubbornly high level of discouraged workers, and the near-historic lows in the American moving rate: some part of the workforce shares that feeling of volatility and stress-induced depression.

This isn't something made up out of whole cloth by these workers; it's a reflection of their experience in the real job market. As Mark Zandi, chief economist at Moody's Analytics, sums up, "There's a mismatch between the skills of the unemployed and the skills required by employers. The people stuck in unemployment are often those in construction, old-line manufacturing, and other industries that aren't doing as well, and they can't make the transition to another."

For example, remember that the current oil and natural gas job boom comes freighted with its own history. That boom has driven North Dakota's population from 620,000 in 2000 to 730,000 today. But in at least part of the region the companies, the workers, and their families remember the events of thirty-five years ago, when the oil boom of the 1980s had started to fade by 1982. The hope now is that the current boom will last, as it's built on the discovery of a new resource base rather than tax subsidies and what turned out to be a relatively temporary bump in oil prices. But nobody really knows. The data on how quickly an unconventional well drilled in shale will start to decline are very patchy. Right now oil companies don't have enough experience with shale wells to make their projections of depletion rates anything more than educated guesses. And, of course, if worst comes to worst and the predictions of a 2015 peak in the North Dakota oil boom turn out to be accurate, then workers from North Dakota can take their skills at welding and heavy equipment operation down to the next regional boom along the Gulf Coast, where projections say $64 billion will be spent to build facilities to export liquefied natural gas (LNG). From 2014 to 2016 that effort is projected to increase the LNG workforce from 62,000 to 103,000.

Even before the first exports have left the new LNG export facility, scheduled for late 2015, there are fears that this boom might also be within sight of a peak. Recent projections say that if the Department of Energy approves all the export licenses submitted, it would add up to 25 percent of all US natural gas production. That seems unlikely to happen, although I don't expect that global capital markets will slow down the enthusiasm before the boom turns to a glut.

This kind of rotating regional boom is great for workers who can move from one boom to another. But, as Zandi points out, not just anybody who walks in from the employment office can do that.

Do a search for jobs in North Dakota to see what I mean.

One that runs under the title "Laborer" requires recent equipment operating and maintenance abilities, and a welding certificate is preferred. Or one for a truck driver/treater, to mix and deliver fracking chemicals to the oil field, invites applications from high school graduates with a current Class A commercial driver's license and two years of commercial driving experience; experience with oil and gas wells and with forklifts and chemical pumps as well as the ability to operate a computer, including web-based programs, is preferred. Each job description also requires applicants to be able to lift heavy weights.

A fast-growth economy creates lots of jobs, and the mix is likely to include one that matches up reasonably well with somebody in the unemployment pool. A slow-growth economy still creates jobs, but with fewer openings, it's more likely there will be a mismatch between openings and potential workers. Take the numbers from Massachusetts: at the end of 2013 unemployment in the state was near 7 percent, and more than 250,000 workers were officially unemployed, with many more discouraged workers no longer counted in the official numbers. But the state had thousands of unfilled openings for health care workers such as lab technicians. And manufacturing companies were looking for workers who could run computerized machinery.

Slow economic growth, then, exposes the effects of some long-standing trends in the US economy. Jobs are getting more specialized, and the number of jobs that are, by convention, called unskilled is falling. Companies looking to squeeze out a profit in this slow-growth economy shed workers and then shed some more. The result is that it can take longer—much longer—to find a job. Even the normal churn in the economy of workers being laid off for whatever reason likely sees an increase in the time spent looking for work between jobs, with all the extra stress—and chance of volatility-related depression—that results. And with higher job market volatility, it's probable that those job search periods will themselves be more frequent.

This mix is by no means unique to the United States or to the world's developed economies. In fact, as developing economies climb the value-added ladder, the skills required by their workers not only increase but also get more specialized. For example, in 2006 Mexico added more than 1 million jobs as the economy expanded at a 4.5 percent rate. More than half the jobs were in construction, a sector with lots of relatively unskilled jobs.

The construction sector was one of the hardest-hit parts of the Mexican economy in the financial crisis. Housing construction ground to an almost complete halt, and Mexico's economic growth fell to 1.1 percent in 2013.

Growth picked up in 2014 to 2.1 percent and, despite the plunge in the price of Mexico's oil, was forecast to climb to 2.5 to 3.5 percent in 2015 and to 2.9 to 3.9 percent in 2016. The driver in that improved growth comes from the manufacturing sector, where the growth revival started with a pick-up to 3 percent growth in 2013 and has continued with strength in industries such as automotive parts and appliances. In 1994 manufacturing accounted for 20 percent of GDP; in 2013 it made up 36.6 percent of GDP.

But there's an important change going on within that manufacturing sector too. In labor-intensive manufacturing, Mexico, like China, is losing market share to countries such as Vietnam and Bangladesh. But in more highly automated sectors such as transportation equipment and parts, where capital investment is more important than the cost of labor, Mexico has picked up market share against China.

China's economy and job market is changing too. As you might imagine, if Vietnam is taking market share in labor-intensive manufacturing because of rising wages in China, and if Mexico is taking market share in more capital and productivity sectors, China is looking to move even farther up the value chain. China doesn't aspire to assemble motor bikes (that has gone to Vietnam) or to build drive trains for Chrysler and General Motors (that has gone to Mexico); instead, it wants to make cell phones (and not simply assemble them either), telecom equipment, and solar modules in highly automated factories.

One result? In 2013 China bought one in five of all the robots sold in the world. That's correct: China, the global cheap manufacturing platform, bought more robots than Japan for the very first time. China bought 36,560 industrial robots in 2013, almost 60 percent more than they had in 2012, according to the International Federation of Robotics. That was way ahead of Japan's 26,015 robots purchased, and the United States was in third place, with 23,679. Robot sales to China have a lot of headroom: in 2012 China had just 23 robots for every 10,000 people working in manufacturing; in Korea the figure was 396 per 10,000 workers. Although the number of robots in use in China is steaming ahead, the country still has a long way to go to catch up to the 310,000 robots in operation in Japan or the 168,000 in the United States. China's robot population at the end of 2012 was just 96,000.

From one perspective this investment in robots makes perfect sense: China has to increase the capital intensity of its industry in order to offset rising labor costs. To compete globally, China needs to invest so that it can gradually match the productivity of the United States and Japan.

From another perspective, however, this investment makes no sense. The long-term benchmark has established that China needs 7.5 percent economic growth to create enough new jobs for a growing workforce. With growth at 7.4 percent in 2014 and projected to fall below 7 percent in 2015, investing in robots that replace workers would seem to add to the country's job-creation challenge.

But the official data says that China doesn't have a job-creation problem, even at 7.5 or 7.2 percent growth. The Ministry of Human Resources and Social Security says that 13.1 million new jobs were created in urban areas in 2013—that would be an all-time high and would argue that the job market in China is stable.

That figure would underline a remarkable achievement. As the ministry notes, in 2010 China created 11.7 million new jobs in urban areas, with a national GDP growth rate of 10 percent. In 2011 GDP growth fell to 9.2 percent, but the country still added 12 million new jobs in urban areas. In 2012 GDP growth fell even more, to 7.8 percent, and yet job growth hit that record high of 13 million.

These stats would be amazing—if they were true.

Unfortunately there's good reason to think they're not. (Which may actually be a good thing in the long run because a country that is putting an extra 13 million people to work but is seeing economic growth rates slow would seem to be in the midst of a collapse in labor productivity.)

Working from another data series at the Ministry of Human Resources and Social Security, Morgan Stanley's Ruchir Sharma, the *Wall Street Journal,* and *Forbes* have calculated that 767.04 million working-age Chinese (aged fifteen to fifty-nine) had jobs in 2012. That's 2.84 million more than in 2011.

This is way short of the totals for urban job creation in urban areas the ministry touted—12 million new jobs in 2012.

We're left with two potential explanations.

First, the 12 million new jobs created in urban areas isn't actually a net increase in jobs because many of these "new" workers actually had jobs in the rural areas before they migrated to cities as part of China's urbanization drive.

Second, the job-creation figures that show China adding more jobs in urban areas even as the economy slows are simply lies intended to make someone in government—everyone in government, actually—look good.

I suspect that the answer is all of the above. But what's really important for this chapter on volatility in the job market when it comes to China's decision to invest in robots is that China's economy is gradually starting to look like the world's developed economies. In 1978 agriculture accounted for 69 percent of all jobs in China, but by 2007 that sector accounted for just 26 percent of jobs. Because labor productivity in sectors other than agriculture was on average six times greater than productivity in agriculture, that shift in jobs meant a huge increase in productivity.

The increase in productivity that resulted from this shift initially fueled a big jump in Chinese wages without pricing China out of world markets. In 1978 the annual wage of an average Chinese urban worker was $1,004 in 2010 US dollars. By 2010 that wage had climbed to $5,500. But because China as a whole was increasing productivity as workers moved from farms to cities, that absolute wage increase didn't make China much less competitive.

That now seems to have changed. With fewer underemployed potential workers in agricultural regions to draw from, China's economy can't increase its productivity simply by moving vast numbers of workers from agriculture to manufacturing. The moment when moving workers from agriculture to manufacturing no longer produces economic gains is called the Lewis turning point, after Nobel-winning economist Arthur Lewis. It's likely that China still has a way to go before it actually reaches its Lewis turning point, but given the drop in the agricultural supply of workers and China's aging population, it is possible to see the Lewis turning point from here. The IMF says that China will reach its Lewis turning point somewhere between 2020 and 2025.

But the competitive pain for China cuts in well before 2020–2025 because many of the low-labor-cost economies that China competes with still have bigger agricultural workforces to draw from and are demographically advantaged—that is, they're younger—than China. That's why projections from the Organization for Economic Cooperation and Development and other international economic think tanks say that both India and Indonesia will post better economic growth than China after 2020.

Does China's rising imports of robots start to make sense then? If China hopes to escape the middle-income trap—developing countries' tendency to get stuck in a stage of development that leaves them richer but still far poorer than countries in the developed world—it has to find a way to replace the productivity gains that it had previously been getting from the migration of all those farmers to China's urban areas. Adding more robots to Chinese factories until the level approaches that of Korea, the United States, or Japan is one possible solution.

It's also a solution to the country's productivity problem that exposes China to developed economies' job-market volatility. The addition of these robots is going to require a higher skill level among workers than most recent migrants to China's cities have. It will result in layoffs and less job security. In the aggregate those changes at individual factories will mean more churn in the labor force and more workers who move from farm to city and back to farm as jobs materialize and then vanish.

The challenges to China's economic and political systems will be huge. The guarantee of a job and the promise of a better job tomorrow is a major foundation of the Communist Party's monopoly on power. To remain in control without needing to increase the level of coercion while coping with the higher levels of job-market volatility typical of developed economies will require a very thrilling tightrope walk. China wants to introduce capital-market reforms that make the allocation of capital more efficient, but it doesn't want to give the market so much power that it shuts job-producing—if inefficient—companies. China wants to create a greatly expanded social safety net that will make workers feel secure enough to spend more and save less, but it doesn't want to burden China's companies with big new costs that destroy profits in the hardest-pressed sectors. It wants to increase labor "mobility," but it doesn't want to make workers so unhappy that they organize and head to the streets.

These challenges aren't unique to China. You can find them in all economies that moved into the middle tier—or beyond—of economic development. You can find versions of these tensions at Korea's giant industrial *chaebol*, such as Samsung. You can see them in the growing dissatisfaction in Japan with the increase in part-time positions and in the United States in the battles over pensions for public-sector workers and the efforts to add to the roll of right-to-work states.

It's sure a lot easier to paper over these tensions when economic growth is higher, when jobs are abundant, when the time between jobs is short. But that doesn't seem to be the economy the world has right now. Just as China is coming out of a period when growth was "easy" and fast growth papered over a lot of problems in China's economy, the global economy is seeing the end to a period of easy fast growth that papered over big and still unresolved problems. The global financial system, to take one example, doesn't do a much—if any—better job of recirculating financial surpluses now than it did during the days when all the world's cash looked like it was going to wind up in the OPEC countries. It's unclear how the financial system might integrate the yuan into what is, currently, in essence a dollar-based system. Tensions over China's control of the exchange rate of the yuan and its manipulation of that exchange rate to further domestic economic goals are certainly not going to lessen if growth slows in China, the United States, or Japan. The world is also looking at a transition from a global economy in which China's cash surpluses funded US deficits to one in which China will need a bigger share of that surplus to meet the requirements of its own aging population.

Everything goes better with growth. A spoonful of growth makes the medicine go down. Pick your cliché.

I didn't pick the image of China walking a tightrope during this period at random. My thought was both to capture the possibility of a successful trip across the wire without a fall as well as to suggest that a mistake on the tightrope has the potential to produce not just a stumble but also a long dive into the net below.

There is a net, right?

Chapter 12

Volatility Trend No. 3

Volatility Rises when There Is No Place to Hide

RIGHT NOW WE'RE AT the end of a period of historically high correlations among asset classes. Why is that important? Because the projected direction of asset correlations from here—the propensity of an asset class (e.g., bonds versus stocks) to zig when others zag—points to an intrinsically more volatile market.

Volatility doesn't occur in some Platonic ideal space.

It is the volatility of something, and that something shapes the character of that volatility. That something influences how quickly volatility increases or decreases. It sets the scale of inertia and momentum—how much energy it takes to change direction and how long a trend will persist.

In *Juggling with Knives* that something is most often a market. To a degree a "market" is a subjective construction. We talk of bond markets and then divide that market into government and corporate, junk and investment grade, long and short term. On the other side of the great divide we can talk of the "stock market" and mean the US stock market or the global stock market. Going in the other direction and dealing with increasingly smaller discrete units, we have markets for sectors, such as technology, and individual commodities. Even that term can be divided further into markets for energy, industrial metals, or agricultural products.

Despite the subjectivity of these constructions, markets do have real existence and real features that shape the character of volatility.

Markets have more or less trading and liquidity, for example. They have more or less volume, speed, and transparency. They have more or less—sometimes too much and sometimes not enough—regulation.

Those real features aren't static over time. China's markets in Hong Kong, Shanghai, and Shenzhen have all grown immensely in size over the last few decades, and they're in the process of changing again in profound ways as it becomes easier for overseas investors and traders to buy and sell in what were once, in the cases of Shanghai and Shenzhen, forbidden markets. The role of London's financial markets is up for grabs as the UK struggles to find a place (or not) among the markets of a unified Europe. In the United States the rise of the ETF, the exchange traded fund, has enabled individual investors to easily buy and sell assets—gold, for example—that once required complex contracts and to hedge risk or leverage the upside of a rally with the ease of buying a mutual fund or individual stock.

For better or worse all these changes have had and continue to have profound effects on the volatility of financial and other assets. We're in the middle of a huge change in the features of global financial markets and economies that will increase the volatility of volatility over the next decade or two.

The easiest way to track that change is by looking at the correlation among asset classes before the US subprime mortgage crisis, during the great age of central bank cheap money, and now in the post–financial crisis markets.

In an effort to limit the damage in the subprime mortgage/Lehman bankruptcy financial crisis, the world's central banks acted together to flood global financial markets with cheap cash. In the years devoted to preventing the Great Recession from turning into a second Great Depression, central bank policy wasn't always completely coordinated: the European Central Bank moved to reduce the size of its balance sheet while the US Federal Reserve was still implementing a policy of financial asset purchases. But by and large the central banks pursued a common policy that had the global effect of driving down interest rates and inflating asset prices.

During the financial crisis and the Great Recession the different classes of financial assets—stocks, bonds, gold, real estate—showed a remarkable degree of correlation. When bonds went up—because interest rates were going down—so did stocks. When stock markets in developed economies soared on cheap money, so too did stock markets in developing economies. When cheap money sent stock prices soaring, gold prices—historically the great hedge against cheap money—climbed too.

This isn't the normal pattern in financial markets.

Remember that before the financial crisis, investors and money managers built portfolios that mixed stocks and bonds because the two asset classes didn't rise in lockstep. Owning both reduced a portfolio's volatility.

Real estate—a house or an investment in rental property—was a good way to diversify a portfolio and, thus, lower its volatility because real estate and stocks, for example, showed patterns of returns with decent independence.

But for a great while after the financial crisis and the Great Recession everything rose together under the influence of central bank cash.

It's logical—and optimistic—to think that as the overwhelming power of central bank cash becomes a little less overwhelming, the correlation of returns from different asset classes is likely to fall. As the crisis passes and central bank policies become increasingly idiosyncratic, the correlation of returns is likely to show wider separation, as anyone who believes that the financial world is returning to normal would say. As the timing of central bank policies diverges, the correlation of return is likely to fall, and correlations among asset classes will go back to normal.

Logical and optimistic, yes. But true?

If you look only at the daily flow of financial news, central bank policy is indeed less coordinated among the Federal Reserve, the Bank of Japan, the European Central Bank, the People's Bank of China, and other major global players than it was, say, in 2009. The Federal Reserve looks, as of October 2015 when I wrote this, to be poised to raise interest rates in late 2015 or early 2016, for example, whereas the Bank of Japan and the European Central Bank are still committed to cutting interest rates. That often has produced a strong dollar and policies pointing toward a weak euro and yen. The

People's Bank seems to be walking its own road with a policy that attempts a perhaps impossible blend of monetary stimulus to prop up economic growth and periodic jolts of monetary restraint intended to keep the yuan/renminbi relatively stable in value as the country pursues its long-term goal of turning the yuan/renminbi into a global reserve currency.

So on days when the economic news points to an earlier-than-expected initial interest rate increase from the Federal Reserve, the dollar climbs and the yen and euro fall. Because higher interest rates would divert some money from equities to bonds, prices of US stocks decline and European and Japanese stocks rise on the belief that a cheaper yen and euro will increase sales for Japanese and European exporters.

But this day-to-day volatility is deceptive. Much of this belief in the return of a period when some assets will zig as others zag is due to the apparent emergence of a difference in timing between the Federal Reserve and the world's other big central banks. After years of all the global central banks being on the same campaign to expand the economy by printing money, the Fed has indicated that it will move to increase interest rates in 2015 or 2016, even as other central banks continue to lower rates and print money. And this has started to create the potential for a separation in returns among asset classes.

From a slightly longer view it's not clear how much has changed from the era of central bank cheap money. Yes, the Federal Reserve will almost certainly raise interest rates sometime soon and do so ahead of the Bank of Japan and the European Central Bank, but that initial increase or two may be the only increases for quite a while. At the end of May 2015 Fed Chair Janet Yellen said that interest rate increases could well be so gradual that the financial markets won't see normalized interest rates until 2018.

And exactly when might the financial markets see the Fed begin to reduce the size of its balance sheet? Before the US central bank even begins to reduce the size of its portfolio, it needs to stop rolling over maturing Treasury notes and bonds. And as far as we can tell from the Fed's minutes, that preliminary move hasn't been on the agenda at recent central bank meetings.

In other words, despite the impression you'd gain from a focus on just the daily news flow, this is still a period characterized by cheap central bank money. And that has major implications for patterns of correlation among asset classes until the Federal Reserve actually starts to reduce the size of its $4 trillion balance sheet and the other major central banks—the European Central Bank, the Bank of Japan, and the People's Bank—end their stimulus programs.

What does all this say about volatility for the years ahead? It describes a market with structural features, visible in the patterns of correlation among asset classes, that increase the potential for volatility in the market.

How? Let me show you three structural features that point toward the potential for higher volatility.

First, there's the high level of correlation in this market's big asset classes. In 2015, as central banks and their cheap cash remain the dominant driving force in asset prices, the biggest asset classes in the market remain highly correlated. Look at the reaction in early 2015 to every rumor and economic sign that had a bearing on when the Federal Reserve would announce its initial increase in interest rates. When a piece of news suggested that growth was faltering in the US economy or inflation was slumping and that, therefore, the Federal Reserve would hold off on its initial interest rate increase— pushing it out from June to September, for example—stocks and bonds would climb, and the trend in housing prices would point more strongly upward as the promise that the 0 percent Federal Funds rate would last a little longer.

That meant that instead of investors being able to hedge their portfolio risk from stocks trading at all-time highs by moving into bonds, for example, they were faced with the very real possibility that bonds—especially corporate and junk bonds—were also fully valued and would rise or fall in lockstep with stocks. Previously there were periods when at least some significant asset classes showed relatively low correlations with the market as a whole or with other significant asset classes, and these periods experienced relatively lower volatility and a relatively lower tendency toward bubbles and blow-off tops. When traders and investors are able to move from an asset class signaling a top to an asset class that has lagged the market or to an asset class with the potential to zig when an asset class near a top zags, this drains money from the surging asset class before an extreme bubble forms.

Second, it's not that there weren't any asset classes showing low correlations with these big asset classes or with the market as a whole; it's just that they were relatively smaller in size. That had the effect of quickly drawing so much cash to any small but promising asset class that might provide a hedge to dominant market trends that this asset class quickly moved from promising to overpriced. The only investors or traders who made any money from hedging using one of these smaller asset classes were the very early movers, and this, of course encouraged traders and investors to jump on any promising asset class as quickly as possible. For example, in 2014 and 2015 the fate of airline stocks—quickly seen as a way to hedge against falling oil prices but also quickly bid up—or of the shares of oil refiners were seen again as a way to hedge against falling oil prices.

The relatively small size of these low-correlation or even anticorrelated asset classes made sure that they would be quickly bid up to levels where they weren't hedges on the general market but became instead their own overvalued assets that needed their own hedges. And the speed of this process encouraged quick trigger trading— and then profit taking in these sectors.

Third, it's not that we can't see asset classes that are now uncorrelated with the market or the market's biggest asset classes, and it's not that we can't see these classes producing big returns someday when the current trends turn or fail; it's that the day of the turn seems so far off and the current punishment for holding these asset classes so great that holding these uncorrelated assets is just too painful.

Gold is the great example. If inflation rises to the 2 percent level now targeted by pretty much all of the world's major central banks and then proceeds, as trends usually do, to overshoot that target so that developed economies show 4 percent inflation, then gold will rally, causing bond prices and the value of currencies such as the dollar to fall. At that point you'd want to be in gold to hedge your bond holdings, to make up for your exposure to currencies such as the dollar in your stock portfolio, and to profit from the rally in gold and shares of gold mining companies as they climb off the floor.

But that was the thinking in 2013: the SPDR Gold Shares ETF, which holds physical gold, dropped by 28.33 percent that year. In 2014 the loss was only 2.19 percent. For five years, ending in May 2015, the average annual loss was 10.46 percent. You would have done even worse with shares of a gold mining company such as Newmont Mining. That stock fell 47.77 percent in 2013 and 16.96 percent in 2014.

I don't know many investors or traders who would be willing to put up with those losses to build a hedge for some point in the future.

The consequence is that a lot of traders and investors have now given up on uncorrelated or anticorrelated asset classes, hoping that they will be able to buy into these assets closer to the turnaround. That's a familiar recipe for volatility.

Does correlation and the volatility from changes in correlation—and assumptions about correlation—have an everyday life as well as a financial markets component?

The most obvious everyday-life arena is the housing market. In the era of cheap money that produced the US subprime mortgage crisis, the housing boom and bust, and now the housing recovery, housing prices were extremely closely correlated with interest rate policies. That meant that, because the bond and stock markets were also very closely correlated to interest rates, the housing market was itself very closely correlated to the financial markets. I don't think that housing prices will become uncorrelated from interest rates because mortgage interest rates are a major factor in setting housing demand. But the degree of correlation is likely to shift, especially in the United States, as the Federal Reserve starts its very modest initial increase in interest rates. The result would be a change that sees other factors that set housing prices, such as demographics and the job market, gain strength within the mix of forces that influence housing prices. And that shift of causal emphasis would give housing prices more independence from the financial markets.

I don't think we're looking at housing becoming an asset with so much independence that it could act as a hedge against stock and bond market volatility, but anything that increases the independence of returns in the housing sector will help reduce the variation of returns in the overall portfolio of wealth in the United States.

A housing sector with significant causal independence from the stock and bond market could provide a huge economic cushion to stock- and bond-market volatility as the Federal Reserve begins to raise rates and starts to cut into the $4 trillion balance sheet it built up as it fought to stimulate the US economy.

I have a feeling that we're going to need all the cushion we can get as that process unwinds. It could even help reduce the anxiety we all feel as we look forward to a remarkably uncertain future. One part of that anxiety—whether the kids will be all right—is the subject of my next chapter.

Chapter 13

Volatility Trend No. 4

The Anxiety of Affluence and Soaring Spending on Education

EDUCATION IN THE AGE OF Volatility is a case study in how fear of volatility and its effects can change behavior. The willingness of a parent to pay $8,000 for tutoring so a child can get into a school costing $50,000 a year speaks to our anxiety that the job market described two chapters ago won't make the American Dream available to our children. If the legitimacy of the Communist Party in China rests on the promise of a job that brings a better life for the next generation, so too does the US system rest on the historical promise that each generation will have a better life than the one before. The economic data of the last thirty to forty years that shows stagnant real incomes for the US middle class argues that this promise can no longer be taken for granted.

If you look at the averages, the outcomes for our children don't seem all that different from what they were thirty or forty years ago. But studying volatility shows us that it's not the average outcome that matters but rather the likelihood that your individual outcome will fall either near or far away from that average. The spread of outcomes includes some in which our children don't do as well as we have. Outcomes that once seemed guaranteed are clearly no longer so, and the number of outcomes that fall along the tails of the distribution—either much lower or higher than the average—have increased.

When an investment goes sour, often the best solution is to take your losses and sell. That's not possible when we're talking about education. You don't get a do-over with your kids. You can't sell and put together a new family. Instead, the effort is to attempt to guarantee what can't be guaranteed. In this case parents' response to the volatility of results and the inability to control that volatility isn't the kind of depression that seems to rule discouraged workers; rather, their response is to double-down and invest even more in an attempt to control the uncontrollable.

When my son was two, we joined the parade of parents looking for the right preschool. All these years later I still vividly remember one parent, a dad, because his anxiety was so palpable and so painful. We were only half an hour into our group tour of the Barnard Center for Toddler Development, one of the premier preschools in Manhattan, and we already knew that this dad was divorced, had graduated from Harvard, and had worked as an investment banker. And then he asked *the* question: What percentage of toddler "graduates" goes on to Harvard?

The Barnard Toddler Center, run by the psychology department of Barnard College, is by no means the most expensive preschool in Manhattan; tuition for its two-mornings or -afternoons-a-week sessions for two- and three-year-olds costs *just* $3,800 a year. The Toddler Center, with its focus on serious academic research into early childhood development, is actually relatively sane in the context of a preschool system that will quickly expand your vocabulary (Do you know what "exmission" is?) and give you a first taste of the anxieties of education in the Age of Volatility. (Advice we received included this suggestion for gaming the system: you won't get in any place really "excellent" if you don't tell the school that it's your "first choice," but you can get blackballed if you tell more than one school it's your first choice. So, we were told, use the words "first choice" in only one letter and find ways to suggest that other schools are your first choice in those application letters without ever using those exact words. As you might imagine, this system overwhelms preschools with applications. And one school took a step not all that long ago that we might previously have viewed as nutty but now seems perfectly rational: the preschool at All Souls was the first in Manhattan to introduce a lottery to receive application forms.)

Preschool is just the first step in a system that can include tuition at a private school that rivals that at the most elite colleges—with less financial aid and for way more than four years—that may also include tutors to help your child learn how to organize homework hours, subject-matter tutors not just to avoid failing a course but also to earn a better score on the SAT, tutoring for the SAT itself, and often the price of extracurricular activities and summer trips designed to fill out a student's résumé for college. All this is before college itself, which can easily run $50,000 a year at the most prestigious schools.

All this might make sense for the 5 percent or so of Americans who can afford to pay these bills if paying $50,000 a year in college tuition actually guaranteed a $200,000 annual income. But it doesn't. The data does indeed show that college graduates earn more during their working years than just high school graduates, so it still pays to go to college: a college graduate can expect to earn $1 million more over a working life than a high school graduate, a 2014 study for the Federal Reserve Bank of New York calculates.

But part of that seemingly rosy set of data is a result of some far less rosy trends. Average wages for college-educated workers have been stagnant since the early 2000s and have actually declined since the Great Recession. But so have wages for those with only a high school degree. Between 2001 and 2013, the Fed's data shows, the average wage of workers with a bachelor's degree fell 10.3 percent, whereas the average wage for a worker with only a high school education dropped 7.6 percent. Thus the premium that accrues to a college degree remained relatively constant.

Data from the Pew Research Center covers a longer period, and the results are actually more depressing. Currently someone with only a high school diploma earns just 62 percent of what someone with a college degree earns. That gap has widened from 1965, when the person with only a high school diploma earned 81 percent of what those with a college degree earned. Just as the New York Fed's data says, the Pew numbers show that this trend isn't a result of college graduates doing so much better than they did back in 1965; workers with only a high school diploma are actually doing so much worse. From 1965 to 2013 median annual earnings for full-time workers aged twenty-five to thirty-two with a bachelor's degree grew by almost $6,700, to $45,000. During that same period median annual earnings for high school graduates aged twenty-five to thirty-two fell by nearly $3,400, to $28,000, according to the Pew Research Center.

So the rate of return on a college education holds steady at 15 percent for the last decade or so. That's better than the average rate of return of about 9 percent in the 1970s, but it's lower than the 16 percent rate of return for the investment required to earn a college degree in 2001.

That 15 percent is a great rate of return when you remember that, on average, the stock market, from 1981 to 2000, returned 10 percent.

So why doesn't everybody just relax? Why the angst about preschools, about test scores that can lead to $2,000 for twenty hours of tutoring to get a 730 on the SAT biology achievement test instead of a 620, or about getting into Harvard, Brown, or wherever so you can be a success in life—whatever that means?

Why the willingness—which sometimes reaches the level of mania—to spend whatever it takes on education? And I'm not talking here about just the top 5 percent in the economic pyramid. The price points might be lower, but the parents who send their kids off to learn Mandarin at their public school on Saturdays, who scrimp to save money to send their kids off to Model UN, or who cough up not much less than $100 an hour to have the college kid next door tutor Johnny or Katie in math for the SAT all are acting out their own anxieties about the uncertainty of outcomes in the current economy.

To understand the extent of anxiety you have to go back to a point I raised in passing earlier: it isn't the average that counts. Parents are going to the lengths that they are, spending the sums that they are not because the average outcome has changed so much. The difference between a 15 and a 16 percent return on investment for a college education isn't significant for anyone's life; the fear that counts is that, unless you spend whatever you can, the results for your child will fall below the average. And it's the hope that if you spend all you can, you can move the outcome for your child above the average.

In other words, this anxiety is being driven by our appreciation of two different sets of data. The first shows that the average—which used to mean a pretty good life in the US middle class—is under pressure. For decades middle-class incomes haven't risen significantly in real terms—that is, after accounting for inflation. Average isn't good enough. The second data set shows that, with income inequality on the rise in the US economy, the relative reward of making it into the upper 5 percent or 1 percent or 0.1 percent is greater than it was when being at the fiftieth percentile was just fine.

From the point of view of volatility, averages don't mean very much; what drives our fears and hopes is the deviation around that average, the odds that your result will fall somewhere near the average. How fat are the statistical tails of the bell curve that contain the unusually high or low results? And how easy is it to wind up in the tail? It's this perspective on the volatility of results that explains the intense anxiety and the massive expenditures that currently characterize education in the United States.

Once upon a time the promise of the US economy was that each generation would be better off than its parents were. My dad went to high school; his father didn't. My mom went to college; her father had a year of training as a draftsman. I went to college and then graduate school.

And my peak earnings were way higher than anything my parents achieved.

Not everyone got to achieve that result, of course. And it didn't come without lots of hard work by the parents and kids of that generation. (My summers in high school—and this is way before E. D. Hirsch or Allan Bloom waged their war to make sure every child knew the great works of Western civilization—were ruled by a reading list that my mother had found or compiled of the four hundred books that you should have read *before* you started college.) But it wasn't all that hard for most outcomes to cluster around the US economy's promise. (It was a lot harder in the 9.3 percent of

American families below the $4,275, for a family of four, poverty line in 1972, the year I finished college.)

My kids, I regularly suspect, are smarter than I am. They certainly know more about math and science and literature than I did at their age—and possibly than I do now. My son is way better at languages than I'll ever be. My daughter's robotics team won the sixth-grade Lego League robotics championship for Manhattan. (They got killed in the regionals, which is what happens when your team is made up of twelve-year-olds who lose three parts of their robot on the day of the competition.)

Do I think they'll be better off economically—certainly not the only measure, I know—than I am? I worry about the answer. I even worry about their ability to find a job, a career path, and a stable life when they get to that point in their lives. I know a lot of truly bright, well-educated, socially adept kids who are still drifting five or six or more years after college. And I know a lot of adults who don't seem to be able to nail down what passes for a career path these days—a progression of jobs that leads to a decent income and some stability and predictability of outcomes.

The data on educational results says that parents aren't being crazy when they worry about a greater spread of outcomes from their investment in education. The spread on return on investment differs significantly among majors, the New York Fed data shows. The average return on investment may be 15 percent, but it ranges from a high of 21 percent for engineering majors to 12 percent for liberal arts and 9 percent for education majors. The number of college graduates with bachelor degrees who are underemployed—that is, working in a job that typically doesn't require their degree—has climbed, and the New York Fed estimates that about one-third of college graduates spend much of their careers in jobs that don't typically require a bachelor's degree. For this group the return on a college degree is lower—12 percent on average, with a bottom rate of return at 8 percent for architecture and 7 percent for education majors. (I have one methodological problem with the New York Fed's calculations. They include an opportunity cost for going to college, which is the potential income foregone during the time it takes to earn a degree. One result of that is to drive down the opportunity cost of college in a recession period when what a worker might have made during those years not in college is relatively low. That has the effect of taking some of the bite out of recent increases in college tuition.)

And what do I do with my perhaps well-founded anxiety about the increasing uncertainty and spread of outcomes from the average? I do what a lot of parents do—indeed, I suspect most parents in the United States and in other economies who have room in their own lives to think beyond putting food on the table tomorrow. I scrape together as much as I can and spend it on education and testing and tutoring and extra activities and hope that my kids test well so that I don't have to pay for tutoring on how to take a standardized test. Anything that might give a kid an edge in a world where I suspect there are no guaranteed edges.

I double-down on education.

In a world where job growth will be slow, where jobs will be less certain, and where employment will be less predictable, parents will try to do everything they can to make sure their children will have the best future possible.

It's pretty clear to me that in the volatility ahead there is no way to guarantee that future.

But that won't stop people from trying. And the people who have the most resources to devote to that effort are those who are relatively well off already. They're affluent themselves, but instead of feeling reassured by that affluence, they're made even more anxious at the thought that if they spend yet another dollar, they might be able to guarantee that better future for their kids as well.

You can track this trend and that anxiety by following one statistic: the number of colleges and universities that US high school seniors apply to.

In 1990 only 9 percent of students applying to college applied to seven or more schools. By 2003 that percentage was up to 16 percent. In 2010 it hit 25 percent and in 2011 it was 29 percent. Estimates are that the figure is even higher now.

That has driven application numbers at colleges ever higher and the acceptance rate ever lower. Stanford, arguably the hottest college application ticket at the moment, saw 32,022 applications in

2010 and admitted 7 percent of those students; by 2014 the total was up to 42,267 and the acceptance rate was down to 5 percent.

Everybody wants to go to Stanford right now and be the next Sergey Brin or Larry Page—or at least get in a self-driving, all-electric car to a job at Google. (One in twenty Google employees went to Stanford.)

I don't expect this trend to stop anytime soon. The anxiety parents and students feel isn't likely to recede, and by now the game has become part of the system. Colleges and universities get rated by surveys such as that produced by *U.S. News & World Report* on measures that include not only yield—what percentage of those accepted actually attend—but also the acceptance ratio.

And these rankings are even embedded in the bond ratings awarded to colleges and universities by ratings agencies such as S&P. The ratings companies want to see rising or at least stable indicators that schools are attracting future donors before they award their highest ratings on a debt offering. In the aftermath of the global financial crisis S&P and other credit-rating companies cut credit ratings for universities that were forced to borrow in order to fund capital spending plans that were cut after their investment portfolios took a ding. Absolutely reasonable. For example, in 2012 S&P cut its credit rating for Amherst College in western Massachusetts to AA+ from AAA as the school prepared to borrow $100 million for capital projects it had postponed during the crisis. In 2012 Amherst charged $55,510 for tuition, room, and board and had a $1.6 billion endowment, the forty-second-largest among North American colleges and universities.

But basing credit ratings on how selective admissions are and how much demand there is for a specific college? Brown University got a AA+ bond rating from S&P in 2011 in part because, as S&P put it, "Brown's impressive student demand demonstrated by highly selective admissions and generally impressive demand."

Can you design a rational system for investing in an education in this world? (I'm assuming that you are willing to give $0 value to any of those old-fashioned and hard-to-quantify goals of a liberal arts education such as learning how to think.) There's certainly plenty of advice out there in media land to tell you how to do it—and do it better.

For example, you would use the best system you could find to rank institutions by return on investment while making sure that the system uses net rather than gross costs—a new wrinkle in college-planning advice—because some of the seemingly most expensive universities are actually quite reasonable in price because they give such generous aid packages. For example, after a 3.5 percent increase for 2014–2015, total annual gross costs at Stanford climbed to $58,386. (That's $44,184 in tuition, $13,631 in room and board, and $573 in student health care fees.) But financial aid knocked that down to a net cost of $37,357 for a family with an income of $110,000. (And Stanford has recently become even cheaper, with an offer of free tuition for families making less than $125,000.)

Once at Stanford, you'd then major in something sporting the highest rate of return. Computer science might be a good bet because Google is just down the road.

Of course, you can't just get into Stanford because you want to.

So in an effort to pursue your rational plan, you'd hire a writing coach to work on the Stanford application. You'd hire test tutors for the SAT and other achievement tests. You'd move to a school district with the best public schools or somehow scrape up enough money to send your kids to a great private school. You'd do everything you can to burnish that résumé with extracurriculars. (Think Stanford might need a French horn for its orchestra?) That's after, of course, paying a preschool with a great exmission record.

To me this best system sounds like the current system—but more so. It's a doubling-down like deciding the best way to show a profit in your portfolio is to buy twice as much Apple or Shell Oil, even through the results haven't been particularly good on those investments recently.

Instead of one internship, you encourage, arrange, and pay for your kid to go on two internships in high school, and one of them should demonstrate a social commitment to fighting poverty or disease or something. Instead of just playing team sports in your town's league, you encourage, arrange, and pay for your kid to play on a traveling team. Oh, and it's Mandarin lessons on Saturday and science camp in the summer at Johns Hopkins and . . .

A commonsense definition of insanity is trying the same thing twice and expecting a different outcome. A "better" college plan that really boils down to doing more of the same isn't quite insane, but this strategy produces what the financial markets call a crowded trade, and it doesn't address the problem of variation in outcome.

In a crowded trade everyone, for example, buys US Treasuries and, thus, drives down the price of the asset, making it hard to make a profit, and the number of people in the trade makes it very hard to sell without a big loss because everyone who bought is now selling. So the best college plan drives kids to apply to seven schools and then eight and then fourteen. It assures that the "best" or "hottest" schools receive so many applications that they accept just 5 percent, as Stanford and Harvard did in 2015. It means that if everyone is doing one internship, you encourage, arrange, and pay for your kid to do two. And if everyone does two, then your kid does three.

Nothing can reduce the variation in outcome to zero, as much as we might hope. We can add all the correct inputs—tutoring, right high school with great academics and a solid exmission record, internships, language lessons, whatever—but the results that come out are still subject to accidents, to the volatility of the world—will Google and computer science still be "hot" when your eighth-grader graduates from college?—to sudden shifts in trend, and to the intractability of human nature. If your kid is not interested in or good at math or has a passion for sea turtles, there's just no way that any college plan will have much luck guaranteeing a successful career designing traffic-maximizing algorithms for Uber.

Nor should it. I think we'd all like our kids to be happy, to follow their passions, to spend their work lives doing something they find worthwhile or interesting or maybe even fun as well as something that pays enough to support a life. When we focus so much attention on the economics of education, it's our anxiety speaking, and we need to find some way to let go of at least part of it. Is that easy? I've got a twenty-year old and a fourteen-year old, and I know how hard it is not to go berserk with anxiety about their futures. I've been lucky enough to have John Katzman, the founder of the Princeton Review, as one of the parents in my son's school cohort. To my mind, more valuable than any of John's perspectives and expertise on the nuts and bolts of the college admissions process has been his repeated conviction that "the kids will be all right."

Okay, but this isn't a "you must feel the power of the Force" kind of book, so let's move on to my second point and the analogy with a crowded trade.

I've outlined some of the perverse outcomes of this "best college plan" strategy above in terms of more effort, but the crowd's pursuit of similar best strategies in an effort to guarantee an average or better outcome—the Lake Wobegon result, where all the children are above average—actually winds up increasing the variation of outcomes and the unpredictability of outcomes. In other words, when everybody in the crowd pursues a similar strategy, volatility goes up.

It's easy to understand why. In the good old days, when it was only the exceptional application that included an internship spent opening the first ice cream store in Rwanda, that internship made the application stand out. It caught the eye of the admissions officer, and odds are that it significantly raised that applicant's chance of admission. And in a fairly predictable manner.

Now, though, when every application to an elite school has at least one internship and frequently two, the significance of that experience in winning admission declines. Applicants then respond to general parental anxiety and to an increase in the number of peers who recognize what gives an application an edge and seek to duplicate those factors, and they do so by ratcheting up the "investment" in those factors: they add another internship or another term abroad or more extracurricular activities. (And not just any extracurricular activity, but those that the experts tell students are important factors in the admissions process in general or for specific schools in particular. Want to go to Yale? The advice floating around my son's high school said, "Do model UN and edit the newspaper.")

Although the pursuit of common strategies by the crowd means more students are doing X and Y, the crowding of this strategy reduces the predictive value of X and Y. Is the admissions office looking not just at the number of internships but for some specific magic characteristic of the internship? Is the university looking for not just a student athlete who demonstrates what in my college application days was called "well roundedness" (which is why I became a mediocre but determined soccer player in high school) but also for someone who plays a specific sport and a specific position in that sport?

For most of us, the college admissions process never becomes transparent at that level of granularity—we don't know whether a university is seeking harpists or kids who belonged to championship robotics teams. And we certainly don't know the important factors far enough in advance to do anything about it. Your junior year in high school is a little late to decide that it's important to become a nationally ranked fencer.

What we're confronting in this education example is actually a fairly common problem in designing a system to reduce the variability of outcomes and, thus, to reduce volatility. Solutions that don't consider the correlation of strategies often increase volatility in the ways that I've noted above. To reduce the volatility of outcomes, you need to apply a mix of strategies, some of which are uncorrelated or even anticorrelated, so that some zig when others zag.

For example, if one worry about the outcome of an educational strategy is that when your kid graduates from college—with $100,000 in debt—there won't be any jobs in his or her field and that the post-college income will be lower than expected, then doing all you can to get your kid into an elite college with the right major and the right postgraduation reputation doesn't really reduce that risk. When I graduated with my PhD in English in 1977, it really didn't matter that I'd graduated from one of the best American literature programs in the country or that, as advised, I had published and that I had letters of recommendation and support from some truly big guns in my field. There simply weren't any jobs that year. Or the year before or the year after. My peers who had done the same "right" things weren't employable either.

So what do you do? Find an uncorrelated strategy to add to the mix. This is going to require some real outside-the-box thinking because neither we nor the experts think about everyday life in terms of correlated and anticorrelated strategies. But how about, to take an off-the-wall thought, if a parent who was worried that the economy might be in the dumpster when Bobby or Mary was set to graduate, passed on a tutor or two or a writing coach or a second internship and instead bought a modest portfolio of gold mining stocks? If the economy went south with a period of a weak US dollar and higher inflation, that portfolio would score a solid return that could be used to reduce the variation of results for that graduate. Or how about taking some cash from those sources again and sinking it into a two-week or a monthlong boot camp during the college years so that the art history major would learn how to digitize images and use Photoshop or the business major would learn how to blog and market using social media?

You can probably think of lots of specific examples of uncorrelated or anticorrelated strategies that won't occur to me. And that's as it should be, because the more specific and less crowded these alternatives are, the more useful they will actually be in reducing the volatility of outcomes that any individual will experience. (And listen to your kids and respect their enthusiasms, not just because you're a great parent but also because they probably think outside the box better than you do—or at least differently.)

I think some of the specific investment strategies you'll find in the last part of this book will jog your thinking. And please try to use them that way: as clues that lead to your own outside–the-box thinking in everyday life rather than as cookie-cutter strategies that lead to crowded trades.

Meanwhile, in the next chapter I'll take a look at a very different part of everyday life, the real estate market, and the way that an increase in the variation of returns at the extremes—the key driver in anxiety over our kids' futures—can lead us to overgeneralize about volatility. It's very important, it turns out, to understand how volatility itself can vary wildly in what we think of as a single sector, market, or facet of everyday life.

Chapter 14

Volatility Trend No. 5

*Real Estate Boom and Bust and
the Volatility at the Extremes*

WHAT OFTEN DRIVES VOLATILITY, as I argued in the chapter on education, isn't a significant change in the average result; rather, it is an increase in the probability that the result a single individual achieves will fall a significant distance either above or below that average. In real estate even more than in education what matters is the gain or loss at the extremes and the likelihood that your experience will wind up at an extreme.

Now that we can step back from the excitement of the real estate boom and the fear of the real estate bust, we can see that whole swaths of the real estate market weren't caught up in the cycle. There were indeed big bulges that represent extreme results, and those bulges drove our perception of volatility. But the results for many home owners in the middle were by no means as volatile.

Why? We need to be very careful in looking at what seems to be a uniform and unified market to see exactly where the causes of volatility begin and end. What we now know about the housing boom and bust is that the cycle wasn't something that sucked everyone in and that the results were sufficiently varied across the sector that there was the possibility of winning and losing strategies in response to the volatility. This would seem to suggest that in other cases of extreme volatility, including those that are still to come, it's important to

- first understand what is causing the volatility,
- then map the power of those causes across the sector
- to see where those causes are operating and where they are now
- so you can devise strategies to take advantage of that volatility or find safe havens to stay away from it.

What matters most for our experience of the housing market over the next decade isn't the volatility of the average—which is likely to change relatively slowly and relatively modestly—but instead the volatility at the extremes. The driver of housing-price volatility over the next decade or two will be determined less by the national median change of 11.5 percent in 2013 or the projected 2.1 percent national median annual change from 2015 to 2018 and more by the change in extremes at the fast-profits and big-losses ends of the barbell in places such as San Francisco and Nevada.

That doesn't mean, however, that we need to let that perception of volatility, drawn from our reaction to variation at the extremes, determine how we react to the actual volatility across a sector or market. Sometimes fear is just fear.

Which was the better real estate investment in the recent boom-bust-recovery cycle: Miami, Florida, or Elmira in upstate New York, located in what's called the Southern Tier, just a short distance from the Pennsylvania border and about 230 miles west of New York City?

No brainer, right? Well, no.

Elmira's golden age was the nineteenth century when the construction of canals and railroads put the city on major east-west transportation routes and led to the development of major manufacturing industries. The city population peaked in 1950 at just under fifty thousand, though, as suburbs in surrounding Chemung County siphoned off growth, railroads declined in importance, and manufacturing moved to cheaper sites in the United States and overseas.

Still, Elmira real estate wasn't a terrible investment during the 2000 to 2006 boom. And it was a very good investment during the real estate bust. According to the New York Fed, home prices in Elmira rose an average of 4.5 percent a year from 2000 to 2006. Because Elmira wasn't a hot spot in the real estate boom, it didn't attract much of the subprime mortgage hot money that drove up housing prices in the boom, and consequently, prices in Elmira didn't fall as hard during the bust. From 2006 to 2009, in fact, housing prices rose in Elmira by an average of 3 percent a year.

What you got with your investment in Elmira real estate was steady appreciation at a low rate that still beat inflation or the yields on Treasury notes without a big drop in the bust. From the perspective of Elmira, the residential real estate boom and bust of 2000 to 2009 didn't happen. Volatility? What volatility?

Contrast that to an investment in Miami real estate. From 2000 to the peak in 2006, Miami housing prices rose by 184 percent, or an average of 19 percent a year. That's a lot better than the 4.5 percent gain in Elmira. From the peak in 2006 to the trough in 2011, however, housing prices in Miami fell by 55 percent. As of February 2014 Miami housing prices had only recovered to 60 percent of their peak levels.

What you got with your investment in Miami real estate was a huge gain in the boom—a $300,000 house bought in 2000 was priced at $550,000 at the 2006 peak. And then a stomach-churning drop that sent the price of that $550,000 house back down to $305,000 by 2011. The recovery through February 2014 would have brought the price back up to $330,000. Your gain from 2000 to 2014 was $30,000 on a $300,000 investment. That works out to about 1.2 percent a year compounded.

In contrast to Elmira, what you bought in Miami was volatility. If you owned a house in Miami, you understood exactly all the hoopla in the national press about a housing boom and bust. If in Elmira the story might have seemed to be flying over home owners' heads, in Miami a home owner was on the front lines.

So which was the better investment?

It turns out those numbers—the 4 percent compounded return in Elmira and the 1.2 percent return in Miami—don't really answer that question. Those numbers do indeed define the trend in those two places, and they do tell you in retrospect how a hypothetical home owner who saw their house in Elmira or in Miami as an investment— would have answered the question. But it doesn't tell you which house was the better investment for any specific home owner because it doesn't match the trend in the market place with the strategy that a particular home owner might have followed. A buy-and-hold home buyer who would have ridden the whole boom-bust-recovery cycle from 2000 to 2014 would have done better in Elmira. And done better with very little anxiety—assuming that home owner could have tuned out the national meltdown—and very little work. A home-and-hold buyer in Miami would have had a much worse case of anxiety and much worse results. Conversely, a buyer in Miami who saw the top and sold at something near the top would have crushed the returns of those friends living in Elmira and would have had plenty of cash to fly them down to share the beachfront rental where they lived while waiting for the market to bottom. Obviously that Miami buy-sell-buy home owner would have had to do a lot more work than the Elmira buy-and-hold home owner in order to rack up that higher return.

In the example of the US real estate boom and bust, the volatility of the world around you and your financial experience of that volatility depends on the volatility of a very specific piece of that world and on how well your volatility strategy matches not the volatility of the world in general but rather your specific piece of it.

In many ways, then, real estate presents us with a fairly typical volatility scenario. Volatility isn't uniform across a market or sector of everyday life; it is, in fact, sensitive—either somewhat or violently—to your specific position in the sector. Somewhere in the sector there is likely to be a haven of lower volatility. At the extremes, where the causes of volatility operate most fiercely, we're likely to find extreme gains or losses. The distribution of that haven and those extremes of volatility vary in real life and across market sectors. There is no one-size-fits-all volatility distribution. And your success in coping with any specific volatility scenario hinges on figuring out a map of this volatility distribution, even in relatively general terms, and then matching a strategy to the specific place where you stand on this volatility map.

The first two steps in constructing that volatility map are figuring out what causes drive the volatility and then to see how the power of those causes varies across a market or everyday-life sector. By now the number crunchers at the Federal Reserve and elsewhere have convincingly demonstrated in more detail what we already knew from experience: the volatility in housing prices in the boom-and-bust years correlates strongly with the number of subprime mortgages written during the boom in any specific market and that the correlation is particularly strong with subprime mortgages that originated from 2005 to 2007 toward the very end of the boom. The amount of cheap money made available to marginally qualified (or absolutely unqualified) buyers in these markets added to the demand that drove up prices during the boom. And it was these buyers' inability to make their mortgage payments during the Great Recession that led to a surge of selling and foreclosures that made the bust so much worse in these markets.

What isn't so clear from experience but is apparent from the Fed's data is that the number of subprime mortgages written as a percentage of all housing units—what the Fed calls the penetration rate—varied widely among real estate markets. A study published by the Federal Reserve Bank of New York in 2010, for example, found that the national average penetration of subprime mortgages in 2006 was 55.5 per 1,000 housing units. In Elmira the penetration rate, however, was just 24.7. That's low even for the nationwide grouping of real estate markets that the New York Fed called "modest or no boom, no bust," which nationally had a subprime penetration of 47 out of 1,000 housing units in 2006. (Other areas that fit in this group include much of the noncoastal South, Illinois except Chicago, Texas, and western Pennsylvania.)

Locations such as Miami, however, fall into the New York Fed's boom-bust group. The penetration of subprime mortgages in that group was 81.6 per 1,000 housing units. That's above the national average of 55.5 and more than three times the penetration of Elmira's 24.7.

The results, when you look at delinquency rates and foreclosure rates, are predictable. At the national average of 55.5 penetration, the result was a delinquency rate of 13.2 percent and a foreclosure rate of 12.6 percent. For the boom-bust group at its 81.6 per 1,000 housing units penetration, the delinquency rate was 14.3 percent and the foreclosure rate was 17.1 percent. For Elmira, at 24.7 penetration, the delinquency rate was just 9.4 percent and the foreclosure rate was only 7.1 percent.

These figures deepen our understanding of the causal dynamics of volatility in the real estate boom and bust, but they leave an important question unanswered: Why was subprime penetration so much lower in a town such as Elmira than in the boom-bust towns and the national average?

The New York Fed takes a stab at answering that question: "It is likely that causation runs in both directions—an increase in nonprime lending led to more significant home price appreciation, and more rapid home price appreciation led to a rise in nonprime lending." Obviously the greater availability of cheap mortgage money to more buyers would have led to rising housing prices, and those rising prices would, in turn, have encouraged lenders to make more loans and to refinance existing mortgages for higher amounts.

Lenders were more willing to make loans on properties whose values were increasing and were expected to continue to rise, especially when the price increases were rapid. Under these circumstances loans on properties with rising values would appear less risky. One primary determinant of risk from the lender's perspective is the balance of the loan relative to the value of the property, often referred to as the loan-to-value ratio, or LTV. As the value of a home rises, the LTV falls, and a low LTV loan is considered less risky than a high LTV loan.

Here's where we reach step three on our volatility map: at this point we try to connect similar examples or locations with one another to draw a contour map of volatility. The maps from the US Geological Survey that hikers use connect all the elevations at 2,180 feet with each other and all the locations at 1,440 feet with each other with what are called contour lines. By looking at the lines we can figure out whether we are about to walk up hill or down and whether the climb or descent is gentle or rapid. Hikers, in my experience, don't think of contour lines this way but instead as a measure of the power of the landscape.

For our step three we want to build an analogous map of how the power of the causes of volatility varies across the landscape that we're studying, in this case the residential real estate market.

I don't think there's a single causal map that you can draw that will cover every volatility situation. Cash flow, as in my current example of central bank cash flows, is a powerful shaper of causal landscapes but not the sole determinant of volatility. Demographics in our aging world is another powerful one. But some market sectors and some parts of everyday life have their own causal dynamics. In real estate one of the keys to why banks lend money in some places and not others is the presence or absence of a "story." A good story is one that promises rising property values by offering a narrative that explains why prices "must" go up. A strong story is one that supports a belief that the future will bring rising prices that will lower loan-to-value ratios and make current mortgages—even if they are a little risky now—less risky in the future.

The idea of a "story" as a powerful causal force may seem vague or weak, but my experience in the stock market, for instance, convinces me that when it comes to money, we tend to go with the narrative first. We invest because of the story that might be developed for an Apple production of a car or because Alibaba is the Amazon of China. The numbers may not support the story—General Motors makes 1 percent operating profit and Toyota 10 percent (in contrast to Apple's 30 percent), so how an Apple car would make sense as a good use of Apple's cash would indeed be puzzling. But for most investors—and I include professional investors in this group—stories sell stocks.

Likewise, stories sell real estate.

If you look at the boom-bust markets outlined by the New York Fed, most of them have this story element. They are on the coast—and everybody knows beachfront property can only go up in value—at least until it's under water, anyway. They are urban areas with a limited supply of real estate, such as Manhattan or San Francisco, that are attractive to young professionals or creatives with rising incomes who value the urban experience of hanging out with other people just like them. These are areas that are attractive to the demographic bulge of retiring Baby Boomers looking for the amenities that will keep them feeling young-ish without such disadvantages as higher property taxes to pay for schools.

Take a walk in Brooklyn's Williamsburg or a drive in Florida's Sarasota to see what I mean by the power of story. It's hard to imagine two more different places, but I think Williamsburg and Sarasota lie on the same real estate volatility contour line.

Last winter my son and I went to the Nitehawk Cinema in Williamsburg, the "capital" of Hipster Brooklyn. (It's hard to define "hipster." In Brooklyn I think it would include a disdain for Starbucks and the ability to conduct a passionate and heated debate about the virtues of Brooklyn Roasting Company [recycled roasting machines] vs. Oslo Coffee Roaster [coffee chaff for compost] vs. West Coast transplant Blue Bottle [all coffee roasted no more than forty-eight hours in advance of sale] and a belief that Williamsburg is over, too expensive, and too touristy.)

We were there to see a documentary on New York street photography. We had passed up a chance to have lunch at the movie theater—a kale salad and a duck confit sandwich with what they call a driver but what I call a dark and stormy with Gosling's rum and ginger beer. Table service. Reclining seats. Specialty menus. (At the NiteHawk's screenings of *The Chef*, they served El Jefe's Cubano sandwich with twelve-hour roasted pork and Negra Modelo with an optional shot of el Jimador tequila.) Instead, on the way back to the subway, we suffered near-paralysis standing on Metropolitan Avenue as we tried to decide between eating at St. Anselm, Spuyten Duyvil, or Fette Sau.

The streets were jammed on a sunny but coldish day with guys who could have been software geeks or members of a punk band and gals with stunning tats and hair of all colors. It felt like the community was all out to do whatever.

A few weeks later I found myself in Sarasota, Florida, at the other end of the demographic and cultural curve. Sarasota has built a national reputation as a city with a vibrant cultural scene for a somewhat older population than you'll find on Bedford Avenue. In the 2000 census 22 percent of the city was sixty-five or older. By 2007 that percentage was up to 30 percent. By 2012 the population of sixty-five-and-olders was 32.5 percent.

It's not hard to see why the city is so attractive to this age group. So much that is hard elsewhere, even if you're an active sixty-five-and-older is easy—or at least "easier" here. The escalators in the airport, for example, are wider than normal, so getting a walker on board is easy, and they move a little bit slower, so getting on and off is simpler if you move a little slowly. The weather, of course, is sunnier and warmer than I'm used to in New York.

And the city has cultivated an arts scene of which it is justifiably proud. There's the Sarasota Orchestra, with its three-week-long music festival. The John and Mable Ringling Museum of Art, the Florida State University Center for the Performing Arts, the Sarasota Ballet, the Sarasota Opera, and the Sarasota Film Festival. Many of these institutions have adapted to the city's demographics, Ted Fishman notes in his book on aging, *Shock of Gray*, by adding more restrooms with automatic soap dispensers and towel dispensers at every sink to minimize the distance that older patrons have to move. Performances tend to be conservative, Fishman reports, so that opera- and theatergoers see versions of works that remind them of past productions they have seen.

The two "communities" couldn't have much less in common. I suspect that a restaurant that worked in Williamsburg wouldn't work in Sarasota and vice versa. I doubt that movies that sell out at the Nitehawk would get an audience in Sarasota and vice versa. The music scenes in the two are both vibrant but totally different. Even the baristas at the coffee bars look different.

But both Williamsburg and Sarasota are magnets. The biggest complaint I hear about Williamsburg is that it's so popular that no one can afford to live there anymore. Townhouses on Bedford Avenue have sold for $2 million. In the second quarter of 2013 the median home price in the Williamsburg and Greenpoint neighborhoods jumped 24 percent from a year earlier, according to realtor Douglas Elliman.

In Sarasota, in May 2014, the median home price had climbed 13.2 percent from a year earlier, according to Zillow. Of course, that hasn't taken prices back to their 2006 peak. In February 2014 the median value of a home in Sarasota was still just 59 percent of its peak value.

But what you note if you compare Sarasota to other Florida cities is that it had a bigger run-up than most cities from 2000 to the peak, a big fall, and then a faster-than-most recovery. As of February 2014, for example, from 2000 to the peak, Sarasota prices rose 153 percent. That's more than in Tampa (140 percent) just up the coast, Orlando (137 percent) just halfway across the state, or Jacksonville (103 percent) in the northeast corner of the state. The damage in the bust was tremendous, with a 53 percent drop from peak to trough, but the year-to-date appreciation, as of February 2014, was 15.7 percent—better than Jacksonville, Ft. Myers, or the Florida average as a whole, of 14.2 percent.

If you had wanted to avoid volatility, clearly you shouldn't have bought in Sarasota.

Or Williamsburg in Brooklyn either. Despite clear differences in housing stock—there are no brownstones in Florida—and the demographics of the market, Williamsburg and Florida real estate followed a similar pattern. A *New York Magazine* piece in July 2009, "The Billyburg Bust," even made the comparison explicit, comparing the real estate boom and subsequent bust in Williamsburg to Miami. In 2009 sales in Williamsburg had fallen 57 percent from the year earlier, and the area was dotted with unfinished or unoccupied condominium projects that had been pitched to the young and wealthy who had worked on Wall Street before the financial crisis.

At the height of the frenzy, luxury projects were being marketed at prices of $1,000 a square foot. That was a huge jump from the $500- to $600-a-square-foot prices in early projects. (Even those early prices seem insane in retrospect in a neighborhood where the median income was $25,892 in 2005.) At $1,000 a square foot, developers were pricing their buildings above Manhattan, which averaged $800 a square foot.

Who wouldn't want to live in Williamsburg if you were young and hip and worked at Goldman Sachs but wanted to be as hip as a coder for Google or one of the other companies that made up New York's Silicon Alley? Who wouldn't want to live in Sarasota, with the art, theater, music, and good food on a par with what they enjoyed back home when they were working and now had time to enjoy— with better weather? What bank wouldn't lend to places with quality stories like these, even if the stories were totally different?

All that speculation came crashing down around developers when the global financial crash led banks to tighten their credit checks and made money more expensive and harder to get. The decrease in financing was a disaster for developers carrying huge loans with huge monthly payments. It didn't help, either, that banks that had been willing to lend to just about anyone with a blueprint now decided that they wanted to see actual sales before letting developers off the hook for charges that cut into cash flow.

The recovery that began in 2011 has sent prices up in Brooklyn just as it has in Florida. In the second quarter of 2013, for example, the median price of condominiums, co-ops, and one- to three-family homes was up 15 percent from a year earlier, according to brokerage Douglas Elliman Real Estate. The median price of $550,000 was even slightly above the 2007 peak in Brooklyn of $540,000. In Brooklyn's hot neighborhoods of Williamsburg and Greenpoint the year-over-year gain in the second quarter of 2013 was 24 percent.

You can say—and I'd agree—that these stories are backward looking. In fact, the whole volatility map that I've sketched here is backward looking. (History tends to be like that.) To work from that backward-looking volatility map to one that tells us something about the shape of future volatility, we need to reverse the steps we took to build this map.

So first we have to begin with what was our last step and see how likely it is that the stories that help determine bankers' decisions will remain in place. Remember that those stories helped draw a volatility map by providing a narrative that justified cash allocation decisions. Only if these stories remain convincing to buyers as well as to the bankers who put up the cash to start a boom and willingly bend the lending rules to keep a boom going will the historical volatility map have any relevance for future volatility.

I think those stories remain intact for places like Williamsburg and Sarasota, and this tells us something important about the future trajectory of real estate and housing prices. As long as the stories that set the volatility contours remain in effect, Williamsburg and Sarasota will remain high-volatility boom-and-bust real estate markets.

But those stories and the volatility contour lines they support are subject to change. It's important to check out the continuity of any volatility cause before projecting the future. At the moment the real estate market presents a good case study on how important that is—and how difficult.

Where will we want to live in the future? That's a key element to the Sarasota and Williamsburg stories. One projection, laid out in Alan Ehrenhalt's 2012 book *The Great Inversion and the Future of the American City*, sees recent growth in urban centers as a sign of a big long-term change in attitudes toward cities and suburbs. The effect, driven by changes in demographics and the kinds of jobs being created by the US economy, will be increased population growth and rising real estate prices in urban centers as well as in smaller cities and suburbs that can reconstruct themselves to mirror the higher densities, the intellectual resources, and the pedestrian/public transportation orientation of these urban centers.

Not everyone agrees with this projection, however. The other side of this debate—Joel Kotkin's book *The Next 100 Million: America in 2050* is a reasonable standard bearer—sees the changes we're now seeing in urban centers as essentially a blip in the long-term trend that leads from post–World War II suburban developments such as Long Island's Levittown to what Kotkin calls Greenurbia, the suburbs of the future. In this vision the central urban centers will thrive where they serve as important poles of a multipolar region. San Francisco, for example, is a center of the Bay Area, but Silicon Valley is the economic center, and Berkeley and Palo Alto are the educational centers. Central cities will be niches, Kotkin says, with 10 to 20 percent of the population living there—recent immigrants, young people, the very wealthy, and those who serve the very wealthy.

One thing about those two competing visions of the future is that they are both strongly supportive of the Sarasota and Williamsburg stories—maybe with an edge to Williamsburg on the "very wealthy and young" side of the story and to Sarasota to the "very wealthy but more traditional suburban amenities" side. And these two competing visions also suggest that Elmira isn't about to generate a strong new story, so it's not about to move to a high-volatility contour on the map. But the important question, if you own a house in Elmira, is whether Elmira will remain a buy-and-hold, low-volatility market and whether that low volatility will remain low volatility to the upside.

Because low volatility isn't good if it means that instead of the slow and steady ascent that Elmira experienced in 2000 to 2010, a real estate market is in a slow decline. That would still count as low volatility, but it would be directionally low volatility of a very unpleasant kind. It's better, of course, to lose 2 percent in the value of your real estate gradually each year rather than taking a 40 percent beating in one lump sum, but it still can't be called a good thing.

The trends for many of the country's older suburbs aren't especially positive. A big portion of today's older suburbs have become poorer during the last Census period as the less well off and the working poor move out of central cities they can no longer afford to suburbs that offer cheaper housing and the promise of more jobs for workers with modest educations and training. US Census data released in 2011 show that in the first decade of the twenty-first century poverty increased by 53 percent in US suburbs, compared to a 26 percent increase in the nation's cities.

Some older suburbs will clearly escape that negative trend. Some will be able to reinvent themselves by, for example, building cores that offer the central urban qualities of density, diversity, cultural access, and pedestrianism (yes, there is such a word, derived from a nineteenth-century form of competitive walking that evolved into modern race walking). Moreover, the demand for those qualities will drive the redevelopment of some older suburbs to include centers that resemble, in some ways, the bigger urban centers. There will also be rebranding of older, smaller urban points as the next hot place, in much the same way that the *New York Times* these days seems caught up in trying to figure out which relatively undiscovered neighborhood in Brooklyn will be the next Williamsburg or what small city—perhaps the mid–Hudson River town of Hudson located 125 miles north of New York—will be the next Brooklyn.

Now, Elmira isn't really a suburb of anywhere, but some of the same factors that will influence housing prices in the country's suburbs will play important roles in deciding the direction of real estate prices in Elmira and small cities like it. Deciding whether a small city such as Elmira will see a change in story that moves it from the stable middle, with its steady appreciation of housing prices, to a negative narrative that puts it into a new declining group is somewhat harder than judging the prospects of a Williamsburg or Sarasota. In those instances we can count on the higher-level story to carry those places along. In the case of Elmira we have to take a more detailed look at the pluses and minuses of the specific place and decide what story might be spun out of those details. Elmira still has, for example, a substantial manufacturing base that includes Anchor Glass Container; a subsidiary of a Spanish maker of passenger rail equipment; Hardinge, a manufacturer of precision turning machines that has been expanding by acquiring international competitors; and Hilliard, a maker of filters, brakes, and clutches. That's enough to support a solid base of blue-collar employment—if the global economy cooperates. The city also has Elmira College; a minor league baseball team; the Arnot Art Museum; the Clemens Center for Performing Arts (Mark Twain is buried in Elmira); the restored Eldridge Park carousel, the fastest carousel in the world; and a historic district with the largest concentration of Victorian homes in New York State. Those resources aren't enough to guarantee the stability of Elmira's story, but they certainly do constitute significant resources to work with.

So much for the stories behind the historical volatility map. How about the cheap money that drove the boom and bust? Most projections I've seen assume that interest rates won't climb significantly in the relative near term from their current historically low rates. That's not an outlandish assumption. In March 2015 a consensus of the members of the Federal Reserve thought the US central bank would raise interest rates in 2015, with fifteen out of seventeen coming down on the side of a 2015 increase, with two advising to wait until 2016. But the end of the year consensus was for a short-term interest rate increase to just 0.625 percent by the end of 2015, from 0 to 0.25 percent in March. Projections for how fast the Fed will increase rates have fallen from the end of 2014 as the US and global economies have slowed. In December 2014 the Fed consensus was for interest rates of 1.125 percent; the consensus projection for the end of 2016 was just 1.875 percent as of March 2015.

From these assumptions most projections I've seen about returns—and, thus, volatility—in the housing market over the next few years look very much like those of the housing boom but without the bust. For example, by 2018 the median price of a single-family house will continue to recover and climb close to the peak reached in 2006 before the housing bust, according to a study from the Demand Institute, a think tank operated by the Conference Board and Nielsen. That median will encompass a big spread, but it will be nowhere near as large as that in the boom cycle. The top five of the fifty largest metropolitan areas will show a gain of 32 percent, versus an average gain of only 11 percent in the bottom five. The top five, the study projects, will be Memphis, Tampa, Jacksonville, Milwaukee, and St. Louis. The five markets showing the smallest appreciation will be Washington, DC; Oklahoma City; Denver; Minneapolis; and Phoenix.

I'd probably tweak that projection a bit to give more emphasis to demographics—San Francisco and the near–San Francisco Bay cities, Austin, and Brooklyn, for example, have strong millennial stories at their backs. I'd also give more weight to warm and cheap areas for the Boomers' retirement. But this projection doesn't seem totally off base, and it isn't an unreasonable volatility map.

Of course, "not totally off base" or "not unreasonable" isn't exactly an overwhelming endorsement. Before we put money into a house or make a life decision about where to live or make an investment in the housing sector, we'd like to get a bit more precise than "not totally off base."

To get to something more exact and more useful, we're going to have to dig a bit deeper into the dynamics of the causes of volatility in this sector. Saying the housing boom and bust was driven by cheap money is a good first approximation of fundamental causes, but it's not particularly exact. That level of explanation doesn't look at how sensitive cash flows into mortgages are to changes in market conditions or what kinds of changes might be most powerful in producing changes to our volatility map over time. Nor does it tell us which of those changes are more or less likely.

For that we need to do a deeper dive into the trends in the fixed-income market and, in particular, into the trends in the market for debt issued by US cities and states as well as by sovereign countries.

That's the subject of my next chapter.

Chapter 15

Volatility Trend No. 6
The Shortage of High-Quality Debt

I'VE SEEN THE FUTURE of the bond market, and it's New Jersey.

For the fifteen-year period that ended in 2013 the average annual return on the Barclays U.S. Aggregate Bond Trust, a benchmark for returns on US Treasury bonds, was 5.55 percent. That, in fact, outstripped the average 4.4 percent annual return for stocks in the S&P 500 stock index. The driver here was a steady decline in interest rates, as the yield on a ten-year US Treasury bond fell from a high of 13.92 percent in 1981 to less than 2 percent at the beginning of 2015.

For much of this period the market behaved as if credit quality didn't matter very much. Oh, sure, if it became clear that a specific, high-profile issue such as Argentina or Greece might not be able to repay a bond, the price of the bond would fall and the yield would rise because buyers of the bond would want higher compensation for taking on the extra risk—12 percent on a two-year Argentine note or 48 percent on a Greek ten-year bond, when US Treasuries of similar maturities were paying 1.93 percent.

But for most issuers, even relatively risky ones, central bank cash and low and falling interest rates overwhelmed credit quality. When the S&P cut the US credit rating from AAA to AA in the chaos of congressional threats to refuse to raise the debt ceiling, US bond yields actually fell because the liquidity of the US Treasury market was seen as quite valuable to investors. When US oil and natural gas from shale producers issued junk bonds to expand production, the yields on those junk bonds fell to a very narrow premium over "risk-free" Treasuries because the US energy boom promised to revolutionize the US economy. And those yields fell even though these producers weren't actually generating profits big enough to cover the costs of expanding production.

But that world is now coming to an end, and to understand the new world and what it will mean for volatility, we need to take a trip to New Jersey. Next stop, Exit 7. (I grew up at Exit 10, so I can make Turnpike jokes.)

Since Chris Christie became governor of New Jersey in November 2009, ratings companies have cut the state's credit rating eight times. The most recent downgrade came on September 10, 2014, when the S&P, citing recurring revenue shortfalls, a reliance on gimmicks to fill budget gaps, and a minuscule rainy-day fund, cut the rating on the state's bonds to A. That downgrade followed a similar cut on September 5 from Fitch Ratings that cited the state's refusal to pay a promised $1.6 billion to close a gap in New Jersey's pension fund. (The state paid just $696 million.) Among US states only Illinois has a lower credit rating. California, which has a rating equal to New Jersey's, is in line for a credit upgrade after making progress on its budget.

Down where New Jersey and Illinois live is the really nasty part of the credit rating neighborhood. In the case of Illinois, the state owes so much money to its underfunded pension plans that if it were a company, it would have filed for bankruptcy reorganization.

I've already developed the story that explains what's happening in these markets (see pages 105–108), so I'm simply going to summarize here. Cheap money from global central banks encouraged state and city governments to overextend their finances and for a while offered an easy way—more borrowing at very cheap rates—to plug the financial gaps that undisciplined spending created. Add in the effect of an aging population on such liabilities as pension funds and public employee health care, and you had a recipe for budget disaster. At the end of 2013, for example, Illinois faced $100 billion in unfunded pension liabilities, while New Jersey's pension hole was $46 billion. Just for comparison, New Jersey's entire proposed state budget for 2015 is either $32.7 billion or $53 billion or $70 billion, depending on what spending and revenue streams you include.

I'd note that, as is the case with the federal budget, the inability to come up with a definitive spending total with a "margin of definition error" of less than 100 percent is an indication of how deep the financial doo-doo is.

But what's of interest here from a volatility perspective is how little damage this financial doo-doo did to the ratings of New Jersey, Illinois, and California. Sure, these states have fallen from AAA to AA or A, but A doesn't sound especially dire. Here's how the S&P defines an A rating: "A strong capacity to meet financial commitments, but somewhat susceptible to adverse economic conditions and changes in circumstances."

"Somewhat susceptible?" New Jersey faces a pension hole that's about the size of an entire year's budget. The hole for Illinois is twice as large. California got a credit rating upgrade to A from A– from the S&P in January 2013 on a state budget that started to eat into a huge backlog of internal transfers, deferred payments, and other gimmicks that the state had used in recent decades to "balance" the budget. At the end of fiscal year 2015, however, the state, by its own projections, would still carry $13.1 billion in unpaid budgetary borrowing. In August 2013 Fitch Ratings also upgraded California to A from A–.

This, I might remind you, is all taking place during an economic recovery, even if not a terribly strong one. Think what these budgets would look like in tough times.

What we're seeing across the debt markets is a lag between a decided decay in creditworthiness and actual downgrades that mark that decay. The actual state credit grades are striking enough. In mid-2014 Moody's Investors Service gave fifteen states its highest rating, one equivalent to the S&P's AAA. That means that thirty-two states earn lower ratings. (Three states don't get a rating because they don't issue general obligation bonds.)

The situation is even worse in the corporate sector. In 2014 only three companies—Johnson and Johnson, ExxonMobil, and Microsoft—earned AAA ratings from S&P. Back in 2008 eight of the companies in the five-hundred-company index had AAA ratings. In 1980 the figure had been sixty of five hundred.

And the situation isn't much different in the market for sovereign government debt. In 2014 there were only nine countries in the world that held top ratings, equivalent to AAA from the S&P from all three major debt rating companies—S&P, Moody's, and Fitch Ratings: Australia, Canada, Denmark, Germany, Luxembourg, Norway, Singapore, Sweden, and Switzerland. In the last few years the United States, France, the United Kingdom, and Finland had all lost their places on this list.

I'd argue that as striking as these changes have been, they still significantly lag the realities of a global financial system where central banks are looking for ways to shrink their balance sheets—someday—so that they don't enter the next financial crisis so leveraged that they can't respond. These ratings certainly don't take into account the realities of an aging world where governments, companies, and countries already strapped for cash flow have to find a way to fund retirements and health care. Japan, the financial canary in the global economy in so many ways, is a sign of exactly how stressed the system is and how determined it is to avoid recognizing that stress. S&P rates Japan's government debt AA, which is defined as "having a very strong capacity to meet its financial commitments. It differs from the highest-rated obligors only to a small degree."

Really? The fastest-aging developed economy in the world? With the highest debt-to-GDP ratio of any developed economy in the world? With a shrinking population of all kinds and an especially quickly shrinking working-age population? Where some economists have started to think the Bank of Japan is pursuing a policy of monetizing government debt because there is no way Japan will even be able to pay what it owes?

That Japan is an AA credit?

Why is any of this an important source of volatility and an important predictor of investment returns for your portfolio? And why is it especially important to the volatility of housing prices?

Before I get to that, I want to give a very quick refresher course on the relationship between bond prices and bond yields because understanding that is crucial to understanding what is happening in the cases of New Jersey, Japan, and corporate debt. All things being equal, as the yield on newly issued debt falls, the price of existing bonds rise. Think of it this way: bonds are issued with a coupon interest rate that doesn't fluctuate during the life of the bond. The effective yield, though, does change with the price of the bond. A $1,000 bond with a coupon of 4 percent pays the owner $40 a year. If the price of that bond stays at $1,000, the yield is the same as the coupon—$40 divided by $1,000, or 4 percent. But if the price of the bond climbs to, say, $1,200, the yield drops to $40 divided by $1,200, or 3.33 percent.

When interest rates change, the coupon that the government or any other issuer has to put on a bond issue in order to sell that bond changes too. If the ten-year bonds that the US government wants to sell you this Tuesday pay a coupon of 3 percent, why would you buy those new bonds if existing bonds, issued, say, a year ago still pay 4 percent? The price of those existing bonds needs to climb until the higher price for the bond reduces that 4 percent coupon payment of $40 to an effective yield equal to the 3 percent coupon on the Treasury's newly auctioned bonds. To take the 4 percent coupon payment on a Treasury selling for $1,000 down to 3 percent, the price of the bond in the market has to climb to $1,333. At $1,333, that $40 coupon payment works out to an effective yield of $40 divided by $1,333, or 3 percent.

You'll remember—if you think back to my earlier discussion of the causes that helped fuel the global financial crisis—the need for pension funds, insurers, and other money managers to find high-quality, relatively high-yielding long-term debt investments. Money managers wanted to believe that Wall Street had found a way to spin risky subprime mortgages into AAA-rated debt. A lack of AAA-rated debt paying more than the extraordinarily low interest rates paid by five-year Treasuries (1.55 percent) and ten-year Treasuries (3.69 percent) in September 2008, for example, made it attractive—and profitable—for Wall Street to create those instruments, and a lack of AAA-rated debt at higher interest rates made it attractive to believe those Wall Street promises. If the supply of creditworthy debt faces even more contraction as credit ratings catch up with global trends and as central banks in the EuroZone and Japan continue to buy the debt with high credit ratings as part of their plans for boosting growth and inflation in their economies, we can expect those pressures on both the selling and buying side of the debt market to increase. The result will be more volatility rooted in the same causes as the global financial crisis.

We're looking at a huge shift in where investors look for profits in the debt markets. Instead of finding profits from the gradual reduction in interest rates across the entire debt market, investors will look for specific types or sources of debt, where an improvement in credit quality will drive bond prices higher. Investors who now spend their time scouting for the highest yields will wind up devoting more time looking for countries about to experience a credit rating upgrade.

Consider Colombia, for example. In 2011 the country earned its first investment-grade credit rating in a decade as a reduction in the intensity of the country's long-time battle with FARC guerillas brought a record tide of overseas investment to a country starved of infrastructure investment. In April 2013 the country received a one-step upgrade to BBB from the S&P.

With the upgrade the yield on Colombia's ten-year peso bond dropped another 4 basis points (100 basis points equal 1 percentage point) to bring the total drop in yield for the year to that point to 82 basis points. At that point the yield was 4.84 percent.

A drop to a 4.84 percent yield from a 5.66 percent yield results in the price of existing bonds climbing. In this case the price appreciation amounts to $116.90 on a $1,000 bond—11.69 percent. Given that the yield on this bond produces just $56.60 a year—at the original 5.66 percent coupon interest rates—the gain from price appreciation is a very important component of the 17.35 percent one-year total return. And in a world where yields are still microscopic, that 17.35 percent total return looks especially luscious.

That capital gain from an improving credit rating and falling yields becomes even larger if a country, state, or municipality can generate a string of credit upgrades on the basis of a continued improvement in its finances. California is an example of that process.

But predicting this kind of steady and long-lasting improvement in credit rating isn't easy. Economies can go south, with budgets following along. Politics can shift, derailing forecasts for financial progress.

Go back to Colombia for a moment. For a while it looked like investors could count on a trend of long-lasting credit rating upgrades in Colombia. But with inflation picking up and a bitterly contested election in June 2014, fought in great part on the issue of whether to continue the peace process with the FARC guerrillas, yields on ten-year peso bonds moved back up to 6.44 percent on June 16. Bond prices then went in the opposite direction, erasing all the gains from the drop to a 4.84 percent yield—and more.

The suggestion from this example is that gains from credit-quality improvements are more volatile than gains or losses from changes in interest rate trends when those trends are part of a long-term change in economic conditions. Interest rate trends have more momentum and don't change direction nearly as quickly.

Let me tease out the major volatility points from these three observations both for the last chapter's look at volatility in the real estate sector and for our study of volatility as a whole.

One, the fundamentals of the debt market—when added to such factors as global demographics and government debt at all levels—argue against smooth growth in housing prices. The same dynamic that fed the subprime mortgage boom and bust is still in place.

Two, there's a considerable likelihood that interest rates—or at least mortgage interest rates—won't behave in the way the consensus expects. Projections that are based on steadily increasing or stable interest rates stand a substantial chance of being wrong.

Three, the question in any projection isn't binary—it's not just right or wrong. The market prices in volatility itself so that the chance of being right or wrong is itself investible. (I'll have more on this idea when, in Chapter 24 in the third part of this book, I'll talk about options and the option market.)

It's often not clear how to invest in volatility instead of in an outcome. I'd suggest that in the debt and housing market I've sketched out in this chapter and in the last one it would be a good idea to hedge against volatility and to look for ways to profit from changes in volatility. Buying into improving credit-rating situations strikes me as one way to do this because a change in credit rating is essentially a judgment call on the likelihood of a change in a borrower's ability to pay back a loan. From this point of view, buying California or Colombian debt on a belief in a future credit upgrade is a bet not on volatility itself but on the probability that the projected volatility will be correct.

In the last part of the book I will come back to the idea of the two components of investing in volatility: investing in what you believe will be the correct outcome of the volatility and investing in the changing probability of that projected outcome—and the market's fears and hopes of that outcome—being correct. In the next two chapters, though, I want to add additional complexity to the process of drawing up a volatility landscape. So far, in the case of the housing sector, for example, that landscape has been about charting the effects of a single causal parameter such as the supply of cheap cash, with, perhaps, a wrinkle or two thrown in. In the next two chapters on energy and climate change I'm going to look at volatility landscapes in complex systems with way more than one or two causal parameters.

That task is much more complicated and difficult. And the results are much less certain and much more volatile. That is, of course, frustrating if your goal is to determine a projection of the future with absolute certainty—it just isn't gonna happen.

But if the goal is, instead, understanding the way everyday life will unfold in all its messiness and coming up with strategies to invest in the midst of that messiness, I think we can draw some useful conclusions and outline some valuable processes from the next two chapters.

Chapter 16

Volatility Trend No. 7
The Age of Energy Uncertainty

AND YOU THOUGHT THE volatility landscape of the housing market was complex.

Here's the energy future—well, for the next twenty-six years for oil and natural gas anyway—projected by the US Energy Information Administration in its 2014 annual energy outlook, as published in May 2014. US production of natural gas continues to soar, fueled by increasing production from the shale geologies of the Dakotas, Texas, Ohio, Pennsylvania, and Oklahoma. Natural gas production grows, according to this projection, at an average rate of 1.6 percent a year from 2012 to 2040. That so completely outstrips the 0.8 percent annual growth in US consumption that the United States becomes a net exporter of natural gas before 2020. In 2012 the United States imported a net 1.5 trillion cubic feet of natural gas. By 2030 net US exports will climb by 88 percent, and by 2040 US net exports will reach 5.8 trillion cubic feet.

Or maybe not.

In the same report the same government energy agency notes that because production of oil and natural gas from shale geologies is such a recent development, no one is sure what the depletion rate on these wells will be over time. The resource, in other words, could be much smaller than currently projected. Low global oil and gas prices as a result of lower demand than now expected could slow exploration and development, as began to happen in the first half of 2015, even in the heart of the US shale boom. If everything breaks in the right way, the agency calculates that total natural gas production would climb to 45.5 trillion cubic feet a year. However, if low demand and low prices inhibit development, if depletion rates are faster than expected, if the resource is smaller than anticipated, then, the agency forecasts, US natural gas production would plateau at 29 trillion cubic feet from 2027 to 2036 and then decline to 28.1 trillion cubic feet in 2040.

That's almost 40 percent lower than production under the more optimistic scenario. And the uncertainty about natural gas production isn't limited to the United States.

In 2014 the International Energy Agency said in its annual survey that the US natural gas and oil from shale story wouldn't just be matched by production from countries such as Russia, Argentina, Mexico, and Canada; production from those countries would be so large that the United States would make up barely 15 percent of the world's total resources of oil from shale geologies.

Or maybe not.

A year earlier, in its 2013 report, the agency said, "Little is known at this point about the size and quality of the global tight oil resource, and . . . it seems unlikely that shale plays or other tight oil formations will be developed outside of the U.S. before the end of the [five-year] forecast period."

And then, of course, I've got my own back-of-the-envelope calculations. From my perspective the picture in areas outside the United States has gotten darker since 2014, not rosier, as the IEA suggests. Major potential resources have been downgraded or abandoned (Poland) or slowed by a lack of necessary infrastructure such as pipelines (China) or put on hold by local politics (Argentina).

The international oil majors that flocked to Poland have largely pulled out as test wells have been hugely disappointing. China's shale geologies, on an aggregate level once thought equal to those in the United States, now look so twisted and jumbled that exploiting them is going to be much more expensive than the market will currently support. Argentina, which does, it looks right now, have big natural gas deposits in shale formations that look geologically feasible to develop, keeps chasing international partners out of its markets with threats of—or actual—expropriation.

My point, though, isn't that my back-of-the-envelope calculations are superior to those produced by the legions of economists at the IEA; rather, all projections, from those produced by legions of analysts to those scratched on the back of envelopes, result in forecasts with huge swings due to basic uncertainty.

And mind you, that's not the end of the uncertainties in the oil and gas sector. A brief list would have to include questions about the condition of the Saudi oil reservoirs, when and if Iran will get back into the global export market, how quickly Mexico can revive its oil industry, and so on.

And this uncertainty isn't limited just to natural gas and oil production from shale geologies or to just oil and natural gas production as a whole. The same degree—or perhaps even more—uncertainty can be found in forecasts for nuclear power, for alternatives such as wind and solar, for coal, and for technologies such as ethanol. (Remember the days when ethanol seemed a legitimate future energy source and not just a gift from the farm lobby to the country's largest corn producers?)

Despite the ads that lobbying groups for such industries as natural gas are running right now, the story for the next decade or two isn't one of certain expansion of supply; supply projections and actual supply are very likely to be extremely volatile during this period—and not just for natural gas.

Even on those internal grounds alone, uncertainty about energy prices and energy sources would be a major source of financial and everyday-life volatility during the coming decades. But questions about energy impinge on pretty much every aspect of our lives. Gasoline prices affect decisions on where to live and work, for example. Energy costs help determine the relative competitiveness of national economies, sending chemical companies rushing to open plants in the United States because of low natural gas prices, for example. And energy costs influence how much money consumers have in their wallets to spend at Walmart and Costco.

The volatility in the energy space is so far reaching and so complex that it just about defeats any conventional approach to investing in or living with volatility. Volatility events like the collapse in oil prices in 2014 that cut the price of a barrel in half over the course of six months seem almost random. We can construct an explanation after the fact, but it seems suspiciously inadequate. The slowdown in the Chinese growth rate from 7.4 to a potential 6.8 percent, the rise of US oil production from shale to near-historic peaks, increasingly strict mileage standards for cars in the world's developed and in some developing economies—all of this led to a market oversupplied with oil by 2 million barrels a day, from a global supply of 95 million barrels a day. And this 2.1 percent oversupply led to a 50 percent drop in the price of oil in six months. Why didn't I see that coming? (Imagine me slapping my head in punishment right about here.)

But I think the complexity of the energy space defeating conventional approaches to volatility is actually a good thing—as long as we don't simply throw up our hands in despair but instead seek for a new approach. I hinted at the direction of that approach in the last chapter: in thinking about volatility—and how to profit from it, how to avoid losses from it, how to plan for and around it—we've got to move away from an approach that simply tries to come up with the best guess on the correct outcome of that volatility. You can think of this approach as the "Will home prices soar or crash over the next decade?" approach.

It's not simply an issue of getting on the right side of a trade in the "winning trend"; instead, we need to consider volatility itself and the uncertainties about the nature of that volatility as a source of prices in the financial markets and in everyday life. As uncertainties about the volatility of housing prices climb, then, all else being equal, housing prices will fall as well. As uncertainties about inflation or the soundness of the US dollar increase, then, all else being equal, the price of gold will climb too.

This approach to volatility begins with an understanding that investments in, on, and against volatility are options on different volatility probabilities. As such, we need to not only consider the "rightness" of the option but also the price of the option. If the price is low enough and the uncertainty high enough, even an option on a result that turns out to be incorrect can be profitable. Conversely, an option that is too expensive can turn out to be only minimally profitable, even if it is ultimately correct about the trend.

Traders in formal options markets understand this, but this approach to volatility isn't limited to buying put-and-call options on the S&P 500 index or the euro. From this larger perspective buying gold is an option on inflation and the dollar. Purchasing a house is an option on interest rates, demographics, and energy prices. Deciding to major in computer science is an option on the direction of the economy and its growth prospects.

The task, then, is to find the options that, for the lowest price, give you the most leverage—either up (profits) or down (protection)—on volatility.

This is all rather abstract, I know. So let's dive down into the details of volatility in the energy sector to see what this means on a concrete basis.

We're in a period of extreme—and interlocking—energy uncertainty because of uncertainties in energy sources that include but aren't limited to oil and natural gas from shale and conventional sources, electric cars, solar, wind, and nuclear power. The volatility caused by uncertainty in those energy sources provides the raw materials for five different—and, of course, interlocking—volatility landscapes.

There is, first of all, uncertainty about the amount of recoverable fossil fuel resources. Because the Saudis, for example, play the condition of their oil reservoirs so close to the *thawb*, we're missing key information that would let us predict what percentage of oil from Saudi Arabia's biggest fields is actually recoverable. We don't, for example, have good data on how much damage has been done to oil reservoirs in the Middle East by injecting water to increase pressure after extracting oil has led to a drop in oil field pressure. We do have studies that indicate a likely recovery rate for oil in models of these oil fields, but we don't know for sure what the recovery rate will ultimately be in these fields or how expensive the methods for increasing the recovery rate will be.

If we have that uncertainty about the recovery and depletion rates from conventional oil fields, our uncertainties about recovery and depletion rates from wells in US shale geologies is even greater. We don't have a long history for oil and natural gas production from shale, so we don't know the depletion rate for US production from those geologies. Well costs have dropped in these fields—at an amazing 15 percent a year in 2014 and 2015—and the injection of more fracking material has led to increases in production to a surprising extent. Those surprises have been a key reason production in the US shale fields has remained stubbornly high, even as oil prices have plunged. Because many countries are really only starting to gather the detailed geological information we need, it's hard to predict how much of the oil and natural gas locked up in the shales of China or Europe, for example, is actually accessible and recoverable. Already, in the last five years, Poland has gone from being a hot bed of shale drilling to a bust. But the range of estimates for how much oil is in the Bakken formation should give us pause before we write off Poland and other European shale geologies. In April 2008 a US Geological Survey report estimated the amount of technologically recoverable oil in the Bakken at 3 to 4.3 billion barrels. That same year the state of North Dakota reported an estimate of 2.1 billion barrels of technologically recoverable oil, and in 2013 the US Geological Survey released a new estimate of 7.4 billion barrels of recoverable oil. What we know about China suggests that the country has vast potential natural gas and oil reserves in its shale geologies, but extracting it is going to be very difficult and expensive.

A second source of uncertainty is financial. Will government-owned oil companies be able to raise the cash they need to invest in new-production technology? Government policy is critical over the next decade, and national policies are all over the block and seem to change as quickly as the direction of the wind. Brazil, for example, has put huge obstacles in the way of efforts by the government-controlled oil company Petrobras to exploit its deepwater discoveries far, far beneath the waters and salt formations of the South Atlantic. As long as the government insists that Petrobras's refinery operation must sell gasoline in Brazil at subsidized prices, Petrobras is going to have trouble raising the money it needs to develop these fields. In February 2014 Petrobras cut its capital-spending plan for 2014 to 2018 to $221 billion from $237 billion. (It doesn't help that in

2014–2015 Petrobras was at the heart of an investigation into a huge scheme to bribe government officials, making it impossible for the company to raise money in the international financial markets.) Mexico, to take another example, is trying to revive its flagging oil industry by making it possible for national oil company Pemex to share revenue with overseas oil companies in exchange for investment and technology. Oil production has dropped in Mexico because the government has starved Pemex of the investment capital needed in order to upgrade pressure, pumping, and collection systems and to begin production from the shale formations that stretch across the border from Texas. Russia's oil companies need $600 billion in investment capital over the next twenty years in order to develop new fields to replace production from older wells. Output from brownfield sites in Western Siberia has decreased from more than 20 million metric tons at its peak in 2006 to just four hundred thousand barrels in 2013.

A third source of uncertainty and volatility is changes in government policies favoring one energy technology or another. Which sources will governments favor? And will they favor those sectors with enough consistency to permit companies in those sectors to raise capital, cut costs, and reach economies of scale? Remember when Canada's oil sands were the key to North American energy security? Remember when turning corn into ethanol seemed to make sense? (Well, to US agribusinesses anyway.) Remember when subsidies and generous mandated payments from utilities to producers of electricity from solar and wind sources supported the rapidly expanding solar and wind industries in the United States, Spain, and Germany? Remember when there was serious talk about reducing the subsidies in the form of favorable accounting treatment and tax breaks for master-limited partnerships that tilted the playing field toward fossil fuels? (As we began 2015 the IRS actually looked to be moving on these tax breaks.) Anybody want to bet what government energy policy will look like in the United States, Germany, Japan, or China in ten years?

When I look at the uncertainties surrounding nuclear energy in France, I'd have to say I wouldn't put much cash on my ability to predict any government's energy policy over the next ten years. If ever there were a country where the future of nuclear power looked absolutely predictable, it was France. The country currently gets 75 percent of its electricity from nuclear power plants, more than any developed economy in the world. Consequently, France has escaped most of the uncertainty about energy supply that hits Eastern Europe, Germany, and the rest of the European Union so hard whenever Russia threatens to cut off supplies of natural gas. And at a time when European companies worry that high energy prices are going to raise costs and price European exports out of the global marketplace, France, thanks to its fifty-eight nuclear plants, charges among the lowest price for electricity in Europe.

Yet the government of President François Hollande has called for a cap on nuclear power plant capacity that is likely to lead to the closing of some older nuclear plants as early as 2016. Renewable sources are to provide 40 percent of electricity by 2025, up from 15 percent today, at the same time as consumption of fossil fuels is to be cut by 30 percent by 2030, the Hollande government says. Offshore wind power generation is to grow to three thousand megawatts by 2020, the equivalent of four nuclear power plants. A government subsidy will pay anyone trading in a diesel for an electric car up to €10,000. And France, if the proposed energy transition law passes, will install 7 million electric vehicle–recharging points by 2030.

As policy, it's not clear how much of this is simply the triumph of one lobbying effort over that of another. French carmaker Renault has invested heavily in electric cars. Renault is part of the Renault/Nissan alliance, which is the world's leading manufacturer of plug-in electric vehicles, with global sales of 134,000 electric cars (Nissan's Leaf) from December 2010 through 2013.

Fourth, what technologies will see costs fall fastest? The future of electric cars—and, to a degree, solar and wind power—for example, depends on how fast the price of rechargeable batteries falls over the next decade. Tesla founder Elon Musk claims that his company's battery technology, which relies on using seven thousand small lithium rechargeable batteries to make up a battery pack instead of a smaller number of larger batteries, gives his electric car a huge cost advantage over rivals such as Nissan's Leaf. Tesla calculates that its battery packs and their power-management and cooling systems cost less than $300 per kilowatt-hour of storage capacity—that's about half the cost of rival companies. Tesla has announced plans for a battery gigafactory, which by 2017 will produce batteries for five hundred thousand cars a year. That mass-mass production will eventually cut battery costs by another 30 percent, Tesla believes. Investment research company Sanford C. Bernstein calculates that when costs for battery storage of electricity drop to around $200 a kilowatt-hour, battery-powered cars will start to become competitive, without subsidies, with conventional cars. And that is key to Tesla's hopes of producing a mass-market electric car sometime after 2017. Let's count the uncertainties in that plan.

- First, what will gasoline cost in 2017? That's crucial to figuring out at what point Tesla's cars become price-competitive with conventional cars.
- Do current improvements in energy efficiency for gasoline and diesel engines and vehicles continue at recent rates?
- What will a hybrid, with its batteries, cost in 2017?
- What continued improvements in energy efficiency in conventional vehicles will add to the cost of those cars and trucks?
- What subsidies will go to electric cars and/or hybrids?
- Will Musk's projected 30 percent drop in costs from his gigafactory materialize? (UBS figures that raw materials such as lithium for the cells make up 70 percent of the price of a lithium battery. Manufacturing at a larger scale will have a minimal effect on the cost of raw materials—that is, if lithium technologies remain the technologies of choice.)
- Is concentrating on battery technology even the best way to get increased energy storage at a lower cost? (Some energy researchers think that cutting the size and price of the electronics that manage the power systems in an electric car—and in a hybrid—would produce as much of a gain in energy efficiency range and vehicle cost as an improved battery would.)

And as big and uncertain as those questions and answers are for electric cars, they are by no means the only big energy questions we'll see answered in the next decade. Battery technology is almost as crucial for solar and wind as it is for electric cars. Reducing the cost of storing electricity when the sun shines and the wind blows for times when they don't will turn solar farms and wind-generating turbines into something closer to base-load power plants and reduce the need for utilities to build peaking power plants (e.g., using natural gas turbines). This will have a major effect on the real-life cost of solar and wind-generated electricity.

Fifth and finally, the biggest uncertainty—because it has the biggest potential effect on not just energy prices but also on global inflation and deflation, living standards in the developing world, and national competitiveness—is whether the stunning drop in the cost of solar-generated electricity will continue, and at what rate? It's important not to make either too much or too little of recent drops in the price of solar panels and solar cells. For example, although it's true that the cost of solar photovoltaic models fell 75 percent from the end of 2009 to the end of 2014, and although in January 2015 Deutsche Bank predicted another 40 percent decline in the cost of generating power from the sun, it's hard to say exactly what that actually means in terms of real improvements in the sector's efficiency. A severe glut of solar-manufacturing capacity has sent prices plunging, especially in China, as companies have elected to sell products at just about any price in order to bring some amount of revenue in the door. Current solar prices have been radically depressed by that overcapacity, and it's not clear how much prices will rebound when that glut of capacity is over, or at least reduced from glut to modest oversupply. However, solar companies are improving the power conversion from sunlight to electricity in their solar cells, and those very real changes in technology are driving very real reductions in the cost of producing a kilowatt-hour. For example, in June 2014 China's JA Solar announced that it had started mass producing its PERCIUM solar cell, with a conversion efficiency of 20.4 percent, and 25 percent is within sight. (Conversion efficiency is a measure of how much of the sunlight falling on a solar cell is converted to electricity.) The world record for conversion efficiency in 2014 was 44.7 percent but that record was set in a lab, not in mass production. Solar researchers believe that 50 percent efficiency is a reachable goal, and as those lab efficiencies enter mass production, the cost of solar-generated electricity will fall. If solar costs fall far enough and fast enough, it will be a massively disruptive technology. Already solar-generated electricity is cheaper than diesel and kerosene alternatives in off-the-grid locations in developing economies. If costs fall only modestly quickly, within a decade, money manager Bernstein calculates, it will be competitive with liquefied natural gas in many parts of Asia and with conventionally generated electricity in high-intensity solar regions such as the Southwest United States and parts of California. If it falls faster than that, it will compete effectively with high-cost fossil fuels from the Canadian oil sands or Brazil's South Atlantic deepwater reserves. Obviously the rate at which solar costs fall is extremely important to the return on investment in projects such as facilities for the export of liquefied natural gas in the United States and Australia or for the future of nuclear power.

But the competitive pressure of rising solar efficiencies will have even wider economic effects. It could radically reduce energy costs in regions or countries with lots of sunshine, and this might produce something like the economic boom set off by natural gas from shale production in the United States. With enough competitive pressure, solar power could put a cap on energy costs in general and from fossil fuels in particular. Under some scenarios for rapid reductions in the cost of generating electricity from sunshine, the global economy could see deflationary pressures from the energy sector within a decade. And that could go a long way toward overturning current assumptions that the biggest danger to the global economy comes from inflation rather than deflation. At the least, even if falling solar costs weren't enough to push the global economy into deflation, they would certainly lower global inflation rates, and this would work to keep future global interest rates lower than what is now expected.

See, I told you that the trends, uncertainty, and volatility in the energy sector reach across the global economy and the global financial market.

I hope that this discussion of uncertainty in the energy sector has removed any notion that the way to manage volatility caused by energy trends is simply to *get it right* by correctly forecasting the future. Given the causal complexity of this space and the way uncertainty piles on uncertainty, nailing the future in your forecast seems unlikely.

At the same time, I hope the discussion has convinced you of the extreme uncertainty in the energy sector; the high likelihood of extreme volatility in the sector, in the financial markets, and in everyday life; and, therefore, of the need to do something and the opportunity to, possibly, profit from doing that something.

So how do you approach a volatility landscape—or, in truth, an interlocking collection of volatility landscapes—of this complexity?

Start by simplifying the number of volatility landscapes you need to consider. Because these landscapes are interlocked, your "solutions" don't need to address every volatility situation and source individually. Some of these volatility sources are, in fact, parts of inverse pairs. You don't need to come up with an independent solution for potential nuclear and solar volatility because you can solve the volatility of this pair by investing in one of the two. Investing in solar, for example, is a bet that the technology problems with storage batteries that prevent solar power from taking on a base-load role in the power system will be solved. If it is, then nuclear becomes a much less necessary part of the energy mix. One bet will address both sources of volatility.

Then look at the interlocking relationships of these volatility landscapes to see which have the most influence over others. You're not likely to find any one landscape in a complex system that determines another; after all, you've done your best to find independent sources of volatility. But you are likely to find that some landscapes are more dominant than others and that you can capture 50 or 60 percent of the volatility of one landscape by focusing on just the more dominant partner in an interlocking pair.

In these energy-sector volatility landscapes I'd say, for example, that you can cover most of your volatility needs with positions— long or short—in natural gas and solar. Natural gas is the great bridge fuel, and the longer that progress in wind, solar, batteries, and so forth takes to move beyond uncertainty to a part of the volatility landscape, where the trend is relatively predictable, the more valuable natural gas will be as an energy source and an investment and the more its price will reflect the volatility of these other energy sources. Natural gas will also pick up much of the slack, if there is any, if oil supplies turn out to be more limited than the consensus now projects.

Solar is the great independent disruptor. If solar can reach non-subsidized cost parity with conventional sources of power generation, then it disrupts the entire price structure of the sector—nothing more or less volatile than that. Solar is not yet at the point at which news about a gain in solar efficiency moves the market for oil or natural gas, but I would be surprised if that doesn't become the case sometime in the next decade. Solar power is such an important source of volatility that I think you have to make a bet on it.

An investment perspective isn't the only important take on these energy landscapes. From an everyday life perspective, oil prices are incredibly important because they influence everything from the cost of commuting to work to how fast the economy will grow. At the moment our transportation system is extremely oil dependent and will likely continue to be so for the next decade. I'd overweight oil volatility in this system for that reason and make sure I factored in oil price volatility into decisions such as where to live and work and how much extra value there is in easy access to public transportation, even if you have no intention of using it now.

The last stage in "solving" the volatility of a complex interrelated system of volatility landscapes is concretely figuring out what to do. Here I think you need to apply my analogy to options to figure out what alternatives give you the most potential protection and/or potential profit. That involves analysis that looks at the price of each alternative and the leverage of that alternative to volatility as well as such factors as ease of trading and liquidity. (Houses, for example, aren't a good option on oil prices because they are so illiquid and hard to trade. However, shares of auto suppliers working on solutions that extend the efficiency of internal combustion engines are more liquid, but they are an order of causation removed from changes in home prices related to the cost of a commute.) I'll get to some specifics of these changes and suggest some sources of options on these sources of volatility in the third part of this book.

In the chapter after next I'll look at volatility from food and water supply and demand. The total volatility landscape here is less complex because it is composed of fewer individual volatility landscapes. But it nonetheless has its own challenges for investors in and navigators of volatility: food and water volatility is a case study in how volatility doesn't need to be continuous and how volatility systems are subject to big tipping-point effects, in which a slight move in the underlying cause of volatility produces a big change in the volatility itself.

But before I get to food and water, I'm going to take a technology stop in the world of Big Data to look at how our ability to track risk affects volatility and changes our conception of risk.

Chapter 17

Volatility Trend No. 8

Big Data and the Reinvention of Risk

WUTHERING HEIGHTS, THE STORY of the tortured love of Cathy and Heathcliff, is a more absorbing story than, say, *Rebecca of Sunnybrook Farm* because Emily Brontë imagines the grand disasters of the human soul. It's not that nothing bad or painful happens in Kate Douglas Wiggins's 1903 novel—Rebecca's father dies and the family faces poverty—but no one's soul is in danger of damnation, no passion threatens anyone's sanity, no revenge reverberates with a challenge to God.

Face it: reading about disaster, disaster on a really cosmic scale, appeals to us. This is true in literature, and it's true in investing disaster books—*The Great Bust*, *The Coming Bust*, *The Doom*, *The Great Doom*, *The Great Busted Doom* all have a huge audience that seems as delighted to be scared as those who gobble up Stephen King.

Throughout this book I have stressed that volatility is a phenomenon that has both a downside and an upside; a bear market is volatile, but so too is a bull market. But so far I've focused mostly on the downside. We'll drive ourselves into bankruptcy paying for college, even though there are no jobs, and then in our endless impoverished old age we'll shuttle from house to house in an endlessly declining real estate market. And that's before I get to the next two chapters on the scarcity of food and water and the chaos of global climate change. But let's break out the good cheer and look at Big Data, the new technologies for gathering unprecedented amounts of information on who we are, what we buy, and how we behave. Big Data has the potential to completely rearrange the volatility landscape for investing, home buying, education, and jobs. Although we're still early in the Big Data game, it's already clear that, like a big bulldozer, it will push around the "dirt" in the volatility landscape, creating new hills and valleys. Big data will produce major shifts in the trade-offs in risk and reward across the landscape—for those who understand this revolution. And the likely effect of that rearrangement will be a big increase in our ability to manage volatility.

Eventually.

This, from the perspective of *Juggling with Knives*, is a good thing. Of course, on the road to that good thing, the transition to Big Data markets will introduce new sources of volatility. But you can't make an omelet without breaking a few eggs, right?

I'm pretty sure that you, however, don't think about Big Data this way but instead more as a social trend that attacks your last shreds of privacy or in terms of individual products and services. If I asked you to think about how Big Data affects your life, you might mention Google's ability to serve you more relevant ads; Uber's ability to figure out how to price its rides while factoring in congestion, construction, and fluctuating demand; or the potential to design drugs that take into account a patient's genetic profile. All true. But these are likely to have less of an impact on our daily lives than what we'll feel from Big Data's ability to slice and dice price risk and volatility.

Of course, the potential effect of Big Data on volatility isn't all to the upside. There's the possibility that some of Big Data's views of the financial markets or of the everyday world will get the risk-reward trade-off wrong or miscalculate the volatility in the existing landscape. And there's the possibility that a Big Data product designed to more precisely control risk and volatility will change the underlying structure of a market or a real-life trend in a way that adds unpredictable volatility. We know that's a possibility because it has already happened in the financial markets—repeatedly.

Let me start explaining why Big Data has the power to change the volatility landscape. AirCare, a truly revolutionary product, has been rolled out by Berkshire Hathaway—yes, Warren Buffett's Berkshire Hathaway. For $25 a trip you can buy AirCare insurance that will pay out fixed amounts for travel snafus. Delayed on the airport tarmac for two hours or more? AirCare pays you $1,000. Lose your luggage? $1,000 to you. Luggage delayed for twelve hours or more? $500. Miss a connecting flight? Collect $500. Flight delayed two hours or more? Here's $50.

Big Data makes AirCare possible. To make this kind of insurance work and to decide what a policy will cost and how much it will pay out for what kind of incident, you have to be able to put together enough data on delays—for example, what's the incidence of delays on an airport tarmac versus a delay of two hours or more in the terminal?—and then be able to crunch that data to put together patterns that show how many travelers might think this insurance is worth buying, on what routes you might want to market this, and what routes you'd like to avoid with any big marketing campaign.

It's revolutionary from an air traveler's perspective. A frequent and creative flyer who pays attention to the readily available numbers on on-time performance for a specific flight can now use Air-Care as a hedge on that delay. If a flight that's $70 cheaper comes with a 20-percentage-point greater chance of a delay, buying Air-Care insurance for $25 gives you a shot at picking up not only the $70 price differential but also good odds of collecting at least the $50 payment for a two-hour delay.

In other words, in some situations AirCare makes accepting the risk of a delay a smart play on the volatility of airplane delays.

Don't think about AirCare as a product for the air travel market or as an example of innovation in the insurance industry; instead, think of it as an example of how Big Data has created a new tool to manage volatility. Big Data sliced and diced and priced risk so that it's possible to move the impact of that risk around in the market.

Monsanto's 2013 purchase of Big Data weather startup Climate Corp. for $930 million provides another example of the way Big Data can be used to manage volatility—and the way it changes how we can manage volatility too. Founded in 2006 by two Google engineers, Climate Corp.—then called Weatherbill—collects weather data from 2.5 million locations and 150 billion soil observations. It then crunches that data to provide 150 trillion weather-observation data points that it then plugs into its models. The company's original product provided weather insurance for ski resorts, outdoor venues, and farmers. Then, in 2010, Climate Corp. decided to focus on farmers and launched its Total Weather Insurance Product, which offers insurance to cover losses to farmers that the US government's crop insurance program doesn't cover. Unlike the federal crop insurance program, payments from Total Weather Insurance aren't based on an estimate and verification of actual damage to a crop; instead, the insurance is based on weather targets. For example, Total Weather would pay out if rain on an insured farmer's acres didn't meet a target, regardless of whether that lower or higher rainfall damaged a crop. From the company's perspective, the key, of course, is being able to predict rainfall accurately enough to set the premium on your insurance high enough so that it can make money over the long term, even in a market as volatile as weather and climate. From a farmer's perspective? Well, it's more complicated. A policy that paid off on low rainfall could become a profit center for a farmer who had invested in technologies that reduced the water necessary to grow a crop, for example. How about the profits from being the first to switch away from a high-water-intensity crop such as alfalfa? Or from adopting more expensive but more drought-resistant seeds?

In other words, Total Weather isn't just insurance; it's also a way to create profits from volatility.

Monsanto, the seed and agricultural chemical giant, bought Climate Corp. for its data-crunching capability but with a different product in mind than crop insurance. In the press release announcing the deal Monsanto didn't even mention the insurance business until well down in the text; instead, it said that it was acquiring Climate Corp. because the company's Big Data capabilities—hyper-local weather monitoring, data modeling, and high-resolution, extremely detailed weather simulations—would enable Monsanto to tell farmers how to tailor their applications of herbicides and pesticides to local, near-term weather. Farmers will be able to use less or more agricultural chemicals and fine-tune the application of those chemicals by using data on things like current soil moisture and forecasts for future growing conditions such as temperature. Using this knowledge, they'll also be able to tailor the timing of planting and the types of seed they buy from Monsanto. Think of it this way: having this data and having someone interpret it for farmers makes the application of chemicals much less of a brute-force, one-formula-fits-all business. In some years that may actually reduce the amount of chemicals farmers need to buy from Monsanto, but I'll bet you that the knowledge that the company provides along with the chemicals it does sell will be valuable enough to make farmers willing to pay a little more for chemicals combined with that knowledge. Monsanto would wind up manufacturing and selling fewer tons of chemicals but making more money on each ton it does sell.

But take a step back and look at the similarities in AirCare and what Monsanto proposes to do with Climate Corp. Applying pesticides and fertilizers in a brute-force way is like buying a very clumsy insurance product. By applying tons of pesticides and herbicides, a farmer is insuring against the risk of an outbreak of wheat rust or corn borer, even if the actual risk of those pests is low in a particular year. And in a tough year, when farm incomes are stretched, farmers are tempted to go bare and forego this chemical insurance, taking the risk that these pests won't strike that year. The same goes with seeds: maybe this year precipitation will be ample enough to avoid buying more expensive genetically engineered drought-resistant seed strain from Monsanto or competitors DuPont and Syngenta.

Add more information on weather and soil conditions, as Monsanto will be able to do as a result of the Climate Corp. acquisition, and a farmer can fine-tune that insurance to buy only what is needed in a particular year and place. The Big Data from Monsanto enables the farmer to get a more specific read on risk and its potential volatility and then buy a product that is more tightly tailored to that risk.

The kinds of volatility-management products that Big Data is making possible aren't new; the financial markets have had them for years. You can lay off the risks of a bond default with a credit default option. You bet on the upside or downside volatility of oil or Treasury bonds in the futures market. Even individual investors can go long or short on currencies, commodities, and stock indexes by using leveraged or unleveraged ETFs.

What has made these volatility-management products possible is a mountain of data on how these various assets behave in different

circumstances. A market for laying off the risk of a Greek debt default exists because we have agreed-upon methods for pricing that
risk, given our past experience with conditions like those that now
obtain in Greece and the EuroZone. We can hedge against a farther
fall or we can bet on a rally in the euro because of all the data we
have on how the euro has behaved in the past when the Federal Reserve is raising rates, when economic growth is slow but picking up,
or when interest rates are near zero. (Conversely, we have very little
data on how any currency or other asset behaves when interest rates
are below 0 percent.)

Big Data is really about two things: first, collecting enough data
from everyday life to make this kind of volatility pricing and analysis possible in new realms, and, second, speeding up the collection
and analysis of this data so that we have something like the real-time
data routinely provided by the financial markets.

Speedy, real-time data collection is everywhere in daily life now.
For example, at its annual developers' conference on June 25, 2014,
Google announced a new attempt to crack the TV market with a software platform and hardware device it is calling Android TV. Android
TV is intended to provide an easy-to-use interface that works with a
directional pad and voice commands to replace the confusing and
time-consuming current menu interface. It will let a user watch movies and TV shows available through the Android marketplace and to
access select Android apps and games, including multiplayer games.

The financial media's dominant reaction to the product was: Why
bother? Android TV will be Google's third shot at the TV market
after Google TV and Chromecast. The effort faces major competition from Amazon, Apple, Roku, and Microsoft. It's too soon for
sales numbers on the recently launched Amazon Fire TV, but Apple
TV sales are near 20 million as of mid-2014, and Roku has sold
8 million units. That's both a measure of a decent user base and a
sign that the category hasn't yet set consumer hearts aflutter. Most
reaction to the announcement went on to conclude that Android TV,
even if successful, won't sell enough units to make a significant impression on Google's top or bottom lines.

I think that reaction misses the point. Android TV's value isn't as
a product but as a Big Data collection method. It isn't supposed to

make money on the device or even on advertising that runs on the device or in the device space. If even reasonably successful, it will capture huge amounts of data on viewing habits that can then be used to create even more accurately targeted ads. Highly targeted ads—ads that go just to men who watched *Game of Thrones*, for example, are more valuable to an ad buyer selling rugged SUVs—can you imagine the targeted Toyota RAV4 campaign with the car driving through the snow while the voice-over intones, "Winter is coming"? And Google, of course, has the ability to put data from TV viewing together with the data they have on Internet searches on Gmail subject lines to create even more segmented audience data and even more precise targeting.

What does this have to do with risk and volatility? The ability to collect immense amounts of data on narrower and narrower vertical markers enables the creation of insurance products that target very specific market and population segments. Using existing data, you can create an ETF, for example, designed to hedge the risk of stocks in the S&P 500. Using Big Data collected and analyzed at near real-time speeds, you can create an S&P 500 hedge that measures investor buying and only kicks in when the levels of short selling exceeds the volume of long buys in the half hour before the close of trading on the New York markets. Or you could design a product for just that part of the investor universe that was within two years of retirement and invested mostly in stocks.

Logically the ability to segment risk and then lay off exactly that piece of it that's important to you should lower volatility. After all, there will be less need to make portfolio-changing buys and sells when you can hedge your risk and still hold on to what you own. And the ability to segment and then hedge that targeted risk should reduce the kind of fear that can lead to quick and not especially well-thought-out shifts in portfolio positions.

But from our limited experience with risk-management products such as portfolio insurance or bundled subprime mortgages, the changes in volatility from the future application of Big Data are by no means actually heavily weighted toward reduction. The result of a simple reduction in volatility is, instead, a shifting of volatility, the creation of new sources of volatility, and the reshuffling of the time tables at which volatility operates. For example, the subprime deba-cle provided a crash course in counterparty risk—the danger that the party paid to guarantee against some part of the risk in an in-vestment would be unable to uphold that guarantee and that the guarantors' questionable solvency could cascade through the mar-kets. We've learned in quick one-day crashes that the peace of mind resulting from purchasing such hedges can turn the release of risk from a gradual month- or quarter-long process into something more akin to the bursting of a dam.

But perhaps ironically the biggest changes in volatility are likely to be a result of how little data we actually have on the effects of Big Data. For example, someone you know, even if you don't know who exactly, is a shopper who visits retailers to enter the price of a Cham-pion sweatshirt or Bose Noise-Canceling Headphones into a data-base that then powers one of a number of comparative-shopping engines. How does the existence of that database, those shopping engines, and the near real-time availability of that information to consumers change behavior and the volatility of that behavior? Will it lead to an Internet version of the post-Thanksgiving Black Friday crowd madness? Will it lead to a convergence of prices around those in the database? Will it create one great, big market or lead to the emergence of smaller niche markets, each with their own pricing systems?

We simply don't know. Yet.

Big data is still in its relative infancy, and the basic standards for crunching data are still in flux. At its June 2014 developer's confer-ence, for example, Google declared an end of Big Data operating and processing software running Hadoop in favor of Flume, Mill-Wheel, and Google Cloud Dataflow (naturally). We don't know—and I doubt most of us care—which of these pieces of software will end up defining the standards for this market. What we do know is that the direction of Big Data is toward speed, speed, and more speed. With Google's new approach, for example, a Big Data user won't have to wait around for computers to complete a batch opera-tion on a hunk of data before performing analysis on that data. Google says that its Cloud Dataflow service, using internally devel-oped tools named Flume and MillWheel, can analyze data without

waiting for batch operations as it pours into a database. At the conference Google demonstrated an instantaneous analysis of tweets
about World Cup matches.

Instantaneously.

The Holy Grail is in sight: real-time analysis of Big Data. And that
means that the speed of innovation in Big Data applications is only
going to get faster.

Does this add more volatility or smooth it out? My guess is that
speed—which stresses the humans' and human systems' ability to
respond to data—will add volatility. At the least we can expect more
volatility as the system settles down and learns to cope with all this
speed.

Where is all this going in terms of slicing and dicing and moving
around volatility risk? A couple of trends look likely.

First, more peer-to-peer networks that spread risk across a larger
pool of risk takers and that spread a bigger net to collect nontradi-
tional data. An example here is Vouch, a lending startup that lets
borrowers use their social networks to prove their creditworthiness.
Friends and contacts can become part of a borrower's Vouch network and "sponsor" a borrower. A sponsor agrees to pay something—
the average was $110 in 2015, the company says—if the borrower
falls behind in a loan payment. The system is sort of like a group-
sourced version of cosigning a loan. After that, a potential lender
still does the conventional lender things like checking a FICO score,
but the system spreads the risk, taking some away from the lender
and distributing it among a group of limited cosigners.

The second trend is modeled on Kickstarter and other similar
crowd-funding efforts, but here, thanks to Big Data, the effort will be
to fund not a project but what I'd call life risks. Yale economist Robert Shiller has suggested, for example, a kind of career futures market
in which buyers of the future would be purchasing a piece of potential earnings of, say, a promising painter, violinist, poet, or video artist. A lot of projects get funded on Kickstarter not because they are so
attractive as investments but because they are things that some group
of people would like to see created in the real world. Buying a piece
of an artist's career could work the same way, especially if we had
some data on what that career might cost and the likelihood that it

might result in increased income. Right now there are networks to fund the purchase of a "name" violin with a historic pedigree for young violinists, so why not do the same for the violinist?

And, of course, there's no reason that this career futures market would need to be limited to elite choices such as violinists or film-makers. Right now we have a kind of career futures product called college scholarships, but the money in this pool could be expanded if it didn't have to come from alumni and rich donors—and if it came with some kind of potential return other than feeling good. If you pitched money into a pool that educated computer scientists or engineers in exchange for a piece of future earnings, would that produce enough to compete with a return on a Treasury bond? And is that the appropriate rate of return given the risk of the investment? Big data could tell us. Such a futures market would go a long way toward reducing the uncertainties—and, thus, volatility—in the education market.

A third trend is the creation of new markets. Not new products, mind you—although that is a crucial step—but entirely new markets for the pricing and trading of volatility products that don't yet exist. I see the beginning of this trend in things like Stubhub, which allows the trading of tickets from existing holders to new buyers. An extension of this, a smaller market so far but one with deeper Big Data roots, is the nascent market for paid dinner reservations. The thought is to go from a system in which those with speed dial can cop a reservation at a busy restaurant, but no one else can, no matter how strong their desire. Restaurant owners see the squandered revenue this represents: if someone really, really, really wants to eat at Red Rooster in Harlem, why shouldn't there be a market that prices and then maybe trades reservations at Marcus Samuelsson's always-booked restaurant? Other markets that seem in the midst of formation include efforts in education, such as John Katzman's education search and aggregator site, Noodle.com, and LinkedIn's recent purchase of online training, education, and how-to site Lynda.

The fourth and last trend I see, even in these early stages of Big Data, is disintermediation. Disintermediation got its legs as a trend in the financial markets in the late 1960s when consumers, using everything from Treasury Direct to buy government bonds to self-directed brokerage services such as Charles Schwab, began to cut out the Wall Street middleman so they could buy and sell without brokers and banks. The two keys to disintermediation were, first, finding a way to cheaply reach the potential customer directly and, second, discovering enough information to know how to price a piece of what was formerly a unified collection of services or products. For example, once upon a time you walked into a calm, wood-paneled office and met with a broker, who might hand you a bit of research, make a recommendation or two, and then charge a 6 percent commission. One of the great discoveries was that there was a very large customer base who didn't care about wood-paneled offices, face-to-face contact, or research recommendations, people who would gladly give up all of that in exchange for trades priced at $29.95 (then—it's $8.95 now).

You can now find disintermediation throughout the economy in big names such as Amazon.com and in more niche services such as online grocery ordering and delivery services such as Fresh Direct. (Look, Ma, no grocery stores!) The trend is still accelerating as computers, the Internet, and Big Data make it ever easier to cut out the middleman. Uber is an example of disintermediation as it cuts out cab companies as middlemen and makes it possible for drivers to deal directly with consumers looking for a ride from point A to point B. The prices for those rides are set by Big Data about factors such as demand and congestion.

Universities are ripe for disintermediation. If you think about it, a university is actually a bundle of services: classes, of course, but also a social experience, housing, food services, counseling, and so forth. Already we're seeing disintermediation in classes where various kinds of online education models are asking: What's the product we need to deliver and at what cost in order to attract a significant portion of the current university market and to attract a new market currently not served for whatever reason by the traditional university product?

The effect of disintermediation on volatility is not entirely clear because it is difficult to tease out its effects from other factors. More of the difficulty in measuring its effects is due to sector dependence and each sector's very different market structure.

But it is clear there is some effect. Disintermediation on Wall Street has diminished the role and numbers of market makers, and the performance of the bond market in 2014 and 2015 suggest that a reduction in the liquidity provided by market makers can significantly increase volatility. This decline of market makers—in the face of questions from market makers about the profitability of this function in the face of regulatory demands for more capital—looks like it was behind the one-day Treasury market "flash crash" in October 2014 and the one-day global stock market "flash crash" in April 2015.

In all the instances of Big Data at work you need to be very careful to distinguish between the eventual volatility in a mature market made possible by Big Data from the volatility in a new or transitional market. Disintermediation in the form of online education markets is likely to produce years of accelerating chaos for existing educational players and patterns before settling into a stable pattern with a predictable volatility landscape. We're not even sure at this point how new financial risk products such as inverse ETFs (designed to rise when markets fall) and 2X or 3X ETFs (designed to go up two or three times as fast as the market) will work until they are, relatively, developed. We know that a system in which shoppers standing in a store aisle but able to check prices at competitors within a three- to ten-mile radius should have some effect on behavior, but we certainly don't know the details of those changes in behavior. How do electronic markets for life insurance or real estate change the power of word-of-mouth recommendations? We've got guesses, but I suspect that the fields of venture capital will be piled with a lot of corpses of failed Big Data businesses. After all, remember Webvan, an online grocery delivery startup, and its $800 million in venture capital before its 2001 bankruptcy?

Data will eventually be a boon to those looking to manage volatility. The road to getting to that point, though, is going to be marked by potholes and downdrafts.

Now on to an emerging trend that we know is going to produce volatility. And then, for the last of my ten volatility trends, I'm going to look at one real-world change that could throw all Big Data modeling—in the financial world, at least—into chaos.

Chapter 18

Volatility Trend No. 9
The Economics of Hoarding Food and Water

THE MARKET MECHANISMS THAT are supposed to send price signals that help regulate supply and demand don't work very well under conditions of scarcity or when people are worried about scarcity. We can see this in everyday life when people rush to stores and strip shelves ahead of a storm or even just the prediction of a storm.

The odds of a storm crashing the food supply system so that there isn't any food in the stores may be small, but the personal consequences for not preparing for that possibility are so dire that it makes sense to hoard.

The same thing is true on a macroscale: if you're in a situation in which future global supplies of food and water might not be sufficient to meet demand, it makes sense to spend whatever you can to make sure that if the worst happens, your country, company, town, or family won't be without. For the last two decades, for example, China has pursued a policy of buying energy resources—making more than $30 billion in investments in Canada's oil sands sector from 2006 to 2012—at prices that were often at peaks for the sector or at significant premiums compared to the prices that other buyers were willing to pay. The country has made similarly large and similarly priced purchases in strategic materials such as thermal and metallurgical coal as well as in pigs, which are considered one of the country's "strategic" agricultural commodities. The impetus is the same fear that empties supermarket shelves: there won't be any supply of a crucial something at any price. And if that's what you're afraid of, then buying everything you can in the market makes sense.

Of course, hoarding plays havoc with the market. It drives up prices of critical goods to insane levels. It even drives up prices of goods that aren't in short supply or aren't related to the current emergency. And it produces exactly the shortages that everyone was afraid of to begin with. Hoarding produces extreme price— and supply—volatility, even if the extremely unlikely worst doesn't happen.

Not all fear sets off hoarding. Initially people are likely to ignore warnings. Then they might act with foresight and buy an extra pack of batteries or two and some jugs of bottled water. It's only when fear reaches a higher level, often increased by feedback from the market—what do you mean, you don't have any flashlights?—that the irrational volatility of hoarding kicks in.

Over the next decade or two worry over supply and demand for water and food is likely to add a big dose of volatility to the global economy. And according to current evidence, there is a strong possibility that we'll see more and longer-lasting outbreaks of hoarding of the sort that we've already seen when Ukraine and Russia clamped export controls on wheat in the face of tight wheat inventories and when Thailand and India took similar measures to ban rice exports. The world, on paper, has the capacity to produce enough food if it fixes the inadequate transportation and storage infrastructure that now serves as a black hole for more than 30 percent of food produced in a country such as India before it even gets to market. Regardless that there is enough food for all, what we're seeing is almost classic hoarding behavior.

Major world regions are simply running out of water. Countries have polluted existing sources or are seeing the effects of climate change on supply. That has set off a rush by upstream countries to lock up water supplies flowing out of the world's mountains. China, in fact, seems to be pursuing a "dam them all" strategy on the rivers that flow out of its mountainous regions and then down to the sea through Vietnam, India, Cambodia, and Laos.

The big question here isn't whether feared shortages of food and water will lead to global volatility—I think that's certain. The question is whether those fears will be enough to tip the system into that extreme state of volatility characterized by hoarding.

It also turns out that it matters who does the hoarding. You or I can go to the local Piggly Wiggly and buy a couple of gallons of water without moving prices or supply much. A government, though? That's another order of volatility. Government hoarding really cranks up the volatility engine.

What has happened in the pork market in China over the last decade shows how a government determined to avoid market shortages can actually jumpstart hoarding volatility.

China accounted for about half of the 109 million tons of pork consumed worldwide in 2014. Pork is an iconic food commodity in China, and increased consumption serves as a symbol of the country's economic progress and growing wealth. Per capita annual pork consumption climbed from 70 pounds in 2002 to 86 pounds in 2012, and projections are that it will rise an additional 14.6 pounds by 2024.

Because of its place in both kitchens and politics, pork is the single-most important item in China's food inflation: nothing raises public discontent faster than rising pork prices. The government tries to maintain stable prices by maintaining a frozen pork strategic reserve that it can release onto the market when prices threaten to rise too quickly. I think it's safe to say that no other central bank in the world pays as much attention to pork prices as does the People's Bank—certainly I know of no other country in the world that maintains a strategic pork reserve.

Until very recently Chinese pork production, an estimated 54.7 million metric tons in 2014—compared with 10.8 million metric tons in the United States—had managed to keep up with consumption. Imports have started to rise, however, and the government started to respond to the "crisis" that erupted based on fears that China's pork producers had hit a wall.

In 2007 record pork prices in China prompted a big step-up in government intervention in the market and a surge in investment in the industry. That led to depressed prices in 2010 due to a surge in supply from domestic sources as well as from imports. Pork imports then nearly doubled in 2008, which was followed, in 2011, by new

highs for pork prices as the government cut back its market intervention and producers cut back their expansion plans.

I hope you can treasure the irony—the Chinese government, intending to avoid a shortage of pork, had increased volatility in the
pork market because of lags between efforts to expand supply and
the signals that prices sent through market mechanisms. For example, the high prices of 2007–2008 reflected supply shortages in China.
By themselves, those high pig and pork prices—hog prices in China
went from 52 cents a pound at the beginning of 2007 to $1.08 a
pound in April 2008—would have produced an increase in supply
from domestic producers and imports. But the government, driven
by a fear of scarcity and a desire to dampen the price swings that
have always been present in the market, stepped in to increase that
dynamic. A temporary cut in China's pork tariff and a big contract
from a state-owned company to build up pork reserves ahead of the
August 2008 Olympic Games added to domestic supply beyond
what price signals by themselves were doing. By May 2009 hog prices
were back down to 61 cents a pound. (A drop in pork demand on
fears among Chinese consumers that swine flu could be transmitted
by eating pork also added to the rapidity of the drop in demand.)

Think about the signal sent by government intervention, especially government intervention in an economy with limited market-
pricing mechanisms and strong top-down controls. Government
intervention signals that there is a real danger of supplies running
short, which sensitizes the market to short-term fluctuations in supply and price. By saying, in essence, that everybody needs to watch
the price of this commodity, government intervention increases the
reaction to normal price fluctuations. And the volatility gets worse
if the sector is one characterized by long lead times before investments in supply actually result in increases in supply. (The longer
the lead time, the more likely it is that investments in supply will
overshoot, leading to oversupply sometime in the future. Chicken
markets, because of the short time it takes to get a commercial
chicken to market [six to fourteen weeks to maturity] are less volatile than commercial pig [twenty-two to twenty-six weeks to slaugh-
ter] or cow [steer, actually, require fifteen months to maturity]
markets.) And if the source of those investments, such as a govern-

ment watching its unrest indicators, is relatively price insensitive, then the price volatility will be even more extreme. Like the hoarder, driven by fear of a shortage of water, who will pay $20 for a gallon of water, a government afraid of a supply-and-demand crisis in pork will cough up money for a pig supply deal at a price that the market will later reject as excessive.

For example, in September 2013 Shuanghui International paid $7 billion in a Chinese-government-sponsored deal—including the assumption of debt already on the books at the time of the acquisition—to buy Smithfield Foods, a US producer of pork and other protein. After the purchase Shuanghui International renamed itself WH Group in preparation for what was eventually a failed effort to go public. The public financial markets voted No on the deal when WH Group attempted to raise 41.2 Hong Kong dollars ($5.3 billion) on the Hong Kong stock exchange. The problems, as far as the markets were concerned, were the huge increase in debt to $7.4 billion from $194 million at the end of 2012 that the company took on to pay for the deal and the structure of the initial public offering in Hong Kong that would have sent all proceeds from the IPO, except for a maximum of $4.2 billion, to existing investors in the company, including Goldman Sachs, CDH Investments, Singapore's state investment fund Temasek Holdings, and New Horizon Capital. (New Horizon is a private equity investment company cofounded by the son of former Chinese prime minister Wen Jiabao.)

But this doesn't mean the company had any trouble raising the money from another source—the Chinese government. The Bank of China, one of the country's big government-controlled banks—approved a $4 billion loan in a single day. The rest of the financing came from other government-controlled financial institutions or overseas investors that wanted to score points with China's government.

From the perspective of the public financial markets, the deal wasn't cheap. It valued Smithfield at about almost seven and a half times annual earnings before interest, taxes, depreciation, and amortization (a measure called EBITDA often used by highly indebted companies to "express" their "true" earnings.) That compares with a median EBITDA multiple of seven for twenty similar deals, according to Bloomberg. The acquisition price of $34 a share was about

31 percent more than the closing price of shares the day before the deal was announced.

But from the perspective of a government worried about running out of pork or seeing pork prices rise quickly, this was a very good deal. Smithfield is the world's largest hog producer, raising about 15.8 million hogs a year. By buying Smithfield, China gets not just pig capacity but also an entire take on raising pigs. To a hoarder, that's a huge and comforting assurance that adequate supplies will be there, no matter what.

And currently that's extremely important to the Chinese government. In the not-so-good-old days, before the market revolution started by Deng Xiaoping, pig production in China was dominated by small holdings in which a family raised a pig or two every year in the backyard and fed it whatever food waste was available.

Those days are long gone—and China's appetite for pork has far outrun the capacity of backyard pig producers. Chinese pig "farms" are much bigger than they were in the days before Deng's economic reforms, which began in 1978. In the United States, farms with an annual production of three thousand pigs or more account for 83 percent of total production. Today the comparable figure in China is just 2.5 percent. Of course, in the days before 1978, the number of pig farms of that size was effectively zero.

Hoarding economics isn't especially discriminating—fear of an oncoming storm can empty the shelves of directly useful items like batteries and jugs of water. But if the fear rises high enough, the shelves will be stripped of everything from toothpaste to Jell-O. *Buy something!*, our psychology screams.

So it shouldn't be surprising that a country already inclined toward hoarding would easily apply that same psychology and policy to things besides pigs.

Like water. The one huge difference between a food commodity such as pork and water is that water is, by and large, unpriced around the world. Only 40 percent of homes in the United Kingdom, for example, had water meters in 2012—and without meters, pricing for volume used is impossible. In India the only consumers who pay for water by volume used are the very poor who have to buy their water from the local water man.

You might think that the unpriced nature of water would reduce hoarding psychology, but you would be wrong; instead, because water usage isn't metered, it lets consumers' and governments' imaginations run wild. This unrestrained imagination tells us to "dam everything," resulting in water hoarding on a massive scale, as China tries to address its fear of running out of water by emptying Southeast Asia's rivers before they ever reach Cambodia, Laos, and Vietnam.

Hoarding economics take over, remember, when the possible negative consequences of running out make buying at any price seem like a reasonable response. In this instance the price includes rising tensions with China's downstream neighbors (such as Vietnam, which has fought wars with China not so long ago and which is now at loggerheads with China over oil in the South China sea), massive environmental degradation from dam projects, and huge renminbi costs for building these dams.

Most discussions of those possible negative consequences focus on drinking water and the current and future lack thereof. And that makes sense, given the high profile of that part of the crisis and the truly scary trends.

Let's use Beijing as an example. Annual water consumption in the city reached 3.6 billion cubic meters in 2013. That's a whopping 71 percent more than the 2.1 billion cubic meters available locally, according to the Beijing Water Authority. This means that Beijing has a more severe water scarcity problem than some countries in the Middle East. Water supplies from surface and underground sources have tumbled by 38 percent in the last few years as the city's growing population has drunk aquifers dry. The city's water resources are sufficient for a city of 12 million, calculates Xu Xinyi, director of the Beijing Normal University's College of Water Sciences. But Beijing's population now tops 20 million.

Solutions? Well, the Chinese government could try to limit Beijing's growth, but that goes against the urbanization goals in the government's latest five-year plan. Officials could try to encourage more efficient use of water, but that's hard when most water consumption is both free and unmetered. Or you could build the huge South to North Water Diversion Project, which is designed to bring

1 billion cubic meters of water to arid Beijing from the water-richer south, at a projected cost of $81 billion. (Do note that it will take an extra 1.58 cubic meters to fill the current gap between consumption and local supply.)

The diversion project also runs into the problem of growing water pollution in China. For example, the Danjiangkou Reservoir, a critical source of water for the diversion, is facing problems with pollution in the five rivers that flow into the reservoir.

A water pollution plan issued by the State Council, China's cabinet, requires that the water quality for all five rivers that flow into the Danjiangkou meet a Grade III standard by 2015.

But four of those rivers are now rated Grade V, "for agricultural use only," and the fifth is rated "for industrial use only." Local governments are responsible for the costs of sewage-treatment plants, including 687 miles of sewage pipes to collect waste water, but they simply don't have the money to clean up the 1.3 million tons of wastewater discharged directly into the five rivers each day. It sure looks like the diversion project could deliver 1.58 billion cubic meters of polluted water to the parched north of the country.

But the consumer drinking water problem is only part of what scares China's leaders when they look at the future of water for their country. China's "Dry 11" provinces, according to China Water Risk, cluster around Beijing and Shanghai. In total the provinces are home to some 510 million people and to almost half of China's GDP. And much of that GDP is at risk in any water shortage.

China's electricity comes predominantly from water-intensive sources such as coal, nuclear, and hydro. Mining coal and then using it to generate electricity consumes 17 percent of China's water supply, and that percentage will go up if China follows through on a plan to reduce air pollution in the eastern provinces by expanding coal production in drier western areas such as inner Mongolia.

And it's not just agriculture or electricity production or even old-line industries such as coal mining that have been put at risk by China's water shortage; new industries such as chip and solar cell manufacturing—anything that uses silicon—are huge consumers of water, and the growing shortage of clean water poses huge problems for these industries.

Okay, we all get that rising population increases demand for water. China's municipal water use will climb to 133 billion cubic meters in 2030 from 77 billion cubic meters in 2010, according to the Water Resources Group. That's an increase of 72 percent. But because very few of us know much about the industrial processes that create the products of our technological civilization, most of us don't have a clue about the industrial demand for water.

But the demand is huge. A large chip factory that might process forty thousand silicon wafers a month can use 4.8 million gallons of water a day. That means a chip factory can, in one day, use as much water as a small city of sixty thousand people consumes in a year. Strikingly, though, when China's Ministry of Industry and Information Technology published a list of targets for water conservation in industry, it included iron and steel, textiles, chemicals, and oil refining, but not semiconductors. This is particularly surprising given that in 2011 79 of China's 160 semiconductor plants were located in areas that are running water supply deficits, such as the Yangtze River delta, and another 31 plants are in water-scarce regions near Beijing, Tianjin, and Hebei. (And the situation is even worse than the raw supply-and-demand figures say because we know from the industry's US experience that semiconductor plants produce wastewater that contains nasty pollutants such as arsenic, antimony, and hydrofluoric acid that can all too readily pollute groundwater.)

China brings together many water supply problems on a scale big enough to be readily visible, but the same problems exist in most of the world's developing economies. In India, for example, groundwater levels are falling at startling speeds, and chemical pollution of groundwater supplies from everything from agricultural pesticides to mercury is further reducing the supply of clean groundwater. The World Bank concluded in a recent report that, without major changes in water policies and markets, most major Indian cities would run dry by 2020. One of those major changes would need to include shifting water supplies from agriculture, which now uses about 80 percent of available water, to consumption in cities and by the industrial sector, which now uses only 10 percent of available supply. Without more water for its industries, India can kiss plans of a China-like boom in manufacturing—and manufacturing jobs—good-bye. The water is there—globally agriculture wastes 60 percent of the water that it uses each year—but reallocating that water from India's farmers is a huge political problem in a country where cheap or free water is assumed as a fundamental right. Required change would include massive investments in more efficient irrigation systems and in reducing leaks in the distribution system. It would also require a shift in what farmers grow away from thirsty crops such as cotton, rice, sugar cane, and wheat. A World Wide Fund for Nature (WWF) report, "Thirsty Crops," figures that these four crops account for 58 percent of the irrigated farmland in the world.

Think how easy that will be. Cotton, to take just one of these crops, is a major source of cash for many of the world's small farmers. It also accounts for 24 percent of insecticide use. Let's see—so all a government such as India has to do is go up against rural voters and the big money of the global agricultural chemical industry.

Piece of cake.

Just as I don't want to suggest that the water crisis is limited to China, I also don't want to argue that it's just a developing-economy problem.

The United States, for example, has its own set of "foibles" that range from growing cotton in the desert or near-desert of Arizona, to the expansion of water-intensive almond cultivation in drought-ravaged California, to my favorite bit of water "management": the Colorado River Compact.

The compact is a 1922 agreement among the seven states in the Colorado River Basin on how to divvy up the water that flows down the river, across Mexico, and then to the Pacific Ocean. (The signing of the compact didn't end all disputes over Colorado River water in the Southwest. In 1935, unhappy with California's decision to dam the river, Arizona called out the National Guard and commissioned a two-boat state navy.)

The trouble with the compact is that its architects had to forecast a base flow for the river. They looked at the rainfall patterns in the years 1905–1922 before the compact and concluded that the river's average flow was 16.4 million acre feet a year. It turns out, however, that this benchmark period included years of extraordinarily high rainfall. New studies of tree rings have come up with significantly reduced historical estimates such as 13.2 million acre feet per year, 13.5 million acre feet, and 14.3 million acre feet.

Reducing those allocations wouldn't be a huge problem except that once this 16.4 million acre feet were allocated to the states, they used them. Growth in the region has soaked up every bit of that water and more so that, many years, the Colorado no longer manages to reach the ocean. Those years, which have been called "drought years," are, many water scientists have concluded, actually representative of normal rainfall. Huge federally funded projects such as the Hoover Dam (formerly the Boulder Dam) and the Glen Canyon Dam, Lake Powell and Lake Mead, and the Central Arizona Project, although they may not be quite as ambitious individually as China's South to North Water Diversion Project, in the aggregate are just as grandiose and productive of perverse incentives and consequences: because there was plenty of water, local officials encouraged water-intensive community development, which they now need to either scale back or "borrow" water for from other sources, such as cotton and alfalfa farming. Water levels have dropped so far in Lake Powell, created by the Glen Canyon Dam in 1963, that flooded canyons that environmentalists thought were lost forever have again seen the light of a desert day. There are even calls to decommission the dam and let the Lake Powell reservoir gradually dry up entirely.

Just fifty years after water engineers thought they were building a long-term solution to the water supply problems of the Southwest, it's clear that we've constructed no such thing.

This makes the US Colorado River Compact experience a good model for the kind of volatility we get when hoarding economics are added to an already volatile supply-and-demand equation. It's not that hoarding economics alone create volatility; the supply-demand imbalance in water, for example, would lead to massive volatility on its own as farmers shifted crops, as governments imposed rules that restricted farming in general, and as water-intensive industries have to decide to spend money on increasing access to supplies of industrial water.

But hoarding behavior increases volatility by substituting big projects for smaller incremental change, by pursuing policies based on a belief that throwing enough money at a problem can fix the supply-and-demand imbalance, and by mobilizing all the forces of a national government—including financial and military—to impose a solution. The hoarding behavior that is manifest in China's decision to dam the upstream sources of water that feed the Mekong River, for example, could easily turn into an armed conflict following a pattern that is currently being blazed by competition over control of the South China Sea's potential energy resources.

Food and water volatility also show the way that increased scale leads to increased volatility. Larger capital-intensive "solutions" require more lead time than do small projects. We can see that in the recent volatility in the iron ore market, where companies have to make investment decisions five or ten years in advance on whether to develop a new mine. It's hard to know that far into the future whether a project is needed, and the long lead time, shared with multiple players, creates huge opportunities for unforeseen effects as independent decisions turn out to reinforce each other, either positively or negatively. It's also harder to fine-tune large-scale projects—you can't build just half a dam or half a pipeline—and this increases the chance of an overshoot. The scale of these projects means that governments will have committed substantial resources, making it harder for leaders, politicians, and officials to admit mistakes and reverse a course. And finally, the scale of the resources that has to be mustered for a big hoarding "solution" creates inertia on both the "Let's get it going" end and the "Do we still need this?" end. The battle over the Keystone XL Pipeline is a good example of this inertia effect in large-scale "solutions."

The food and water commodity space is so dominated by situations of extremely tight supply and growing demand that it's safe to expect frequent examples of enhanced volatility because of hoarding behavior. Take corn, for example. In 2012 corn prices rose to $8 a bushel as extreme heat during the pollination period devastated the corn crop. Tight global inventories prompted hoarding psychology and a fear that the world was "running out of corn." In June 2014, however, corn for December 2014 delivery fell to $4.40 a bushel and threatened to go lower.

This volatility in corn prices—a swing from $8 to $3.85 a bushel—is what I'd expect from a commodity that is moving through the supply-and-demand equilibrium point so frequently as well as getting an additional volatility push from hoarding economics.

You will find similar dynamics in primary food commodities such as wheat, soybeans, and rice. The supply-and-demand balance in these commodities is so tight that it doesn't take much to tip markets into a hoarding psychology. For instance in the 2007–2008 crisis traditional exporters such as India, Thailand, and Vietnam restricted or banned rice exports in an effort to dampen domestic price increases. This led to perfectly understandable riots in importing countries such as the Philippines and much less understandable hoarding from exporters such as Vietnam. At the height of the crisis frightened consumers in Ho Chi Minh City had emptied store shelves of rice, even though Vietnam is the world's second-largest rice exporter.

So far in this section I've gradually built up an increasingly complex view of volatility in a system—or related systems—and in the resulting volatility landscape. However, I've saved the best—that is, the most complex—for last. Global climate change combines powerful volatility leverage with a system so complex that predicting what the local effects will be is just about impossible with our current state of modeling. (By local, I mean something as large as the state of California or the British Isles.) Let me explain what I mean by that in the next chapter.

And then I'll move on to some concrete investment strategies for the Age of Volatility.

I promise.

Chapter 19

Volatility Trend No. 10

Climate Change as Pure Volatility

THE YOUNGER DRYAS IS my favorite geological period.

About 1,300 years long, it was a brief period of cold and drought that occurred between 12,800 and 11,500 years before the present. The Younger Dryas interrupted the warming trend that had been in place since the last glacial maximum 20,000 years ago. What fascinates me is that the Younger Dryas represents a turn in the global climate, from warming to colder, in a period far shorter than had long been assumed possible. And although no one knows what caused the shift, there is a hypothesis that this shift in global temperature trend was a result of a stalling of the Gulf Stream brought on by the melting, in the warm period, of the great North American ice sheets in what is now Canada. (Other theories point to volcanoes, a strike by a meteor, a shift in the jet stream, or solar flares, but the evidence tilts toward the melting ice sheets.)

Warm temperatures, this hypothesis goes, melted the great ice dams in North America, thereby redirecting massive amounts of freshwater that had previously flowed into the Gulf of Mexico down the St. Lawrence River instead and into the North Atlantic. That freshwater was enough to disrupt the Gulf Stream's great conveyor belt of warm water from the south along the eastern coast of what would someday be the United States and up past Iceland to the British Isles and northern Europe. The result was a drop in the mean temperature in the United Kingdom to 23 degrees Fahrenheit (−5

Celsius). Forests in Scandinavia were replaced with glacial tundra. Glaciers returned to near their previous greatest extent.

I like the Younger Dryas because it's a reminder of exactly how complex the global climate is and how difficult coming up with a correct projection is. The global climate went from warming to cooling in just seventy years and then reversed in fifty years either because the warm period melted a giant ice dam or because of some random event such as a meteor or volcanoes.

And this doesn't begin to deal with the question of local effects either. Predictions of an average increase in global temperatures of somewhere between 2 to 11.5 degrees Fahrenheit by 2100 don't tell us what we need to know locally. Will California enter a permanent drought? Will the Midwest grain basket become too hot and dry for corn? Most disturbing of all, will Italy and France become too hot to produce great wines?

We know, as I read the evidence from scientists, that we're looking at a period of massive climate change in a relatively short period—in other words, a period of extraordinary volatility in local and regional outcomes. But we don't know with any degree of certainty what the specific results of this climate change will be. Will wheat production become economically viable in Canada all the way to the Arctic Circle? Will average global warming unmoor the jet stream in North America, resulting in an increase in the bone-chilling weather episodes, now called polar vortexes, that struck the eastern half of the United States in the winter of 2014–2015? Will Sydney's water supply, already stressed, collapse with a plunge in winter snowpack? Will one of Antarctica's great ice sheets begin a mad dash to the sea, lubricated by a layer of meltwater?

I think the result is a situation of almost pure volatility. We have only very limited ability to predict the actual outcome for any local situation. (There are exceptions—we do know that sea levels will rise and, therefore, that the lowest-lying areas of Florida and island systems such as the Seychelles will be underwater.)

If we live in San Diego, however, we don't know whether the weather will get even drier. If we live on Long Island, we don't know how much worse winter storms will become or how frequent the worst will be. If we produce champagne in Champagne, France, we know that we face a heat challenge, but we don't know whether the increase in temperature will be enough to make buying land in the chalk lands of southern England the best path to survival.

That doesn't mean, however, that we don't know anything. Or that we can't do anything. It just means that what we are most sure of comes from our study—at this stage in the evidence and the science—not of concrete predictions but of volatility itself. We do know something useful about how people respond to volatility at different levels of volatility, and this points us toward actions that will hedge us against the risks of global climate change, even if we don't have the ability to accurately predict specific outcomes.

Does that sound paradoxical? Something like the sound of one hand clapping?

Well, let me show you what the knowledge of volatility, gleaned from chapters so far, tells us about how we can approach this mind-numbingly complex system and the changes it will bring to our world.

For example, we know that we need a considerable amount of volatility to overcome inertia in financial markets and in everyday life—and that volatility needs to go on for quite a while before most people begin to act on it. Behavior is anchored to long-term benchmarks—either financial, such as stocks returning 10 percent a year, or everyday life, such as it's safe to build on the beach behind the first set of dunes. And we only grudgingly give up on these anchors. Initially that leaves us unmoored in a psychologically uncomfortable state. Eventually we revert to the old benchmark—when, in Flitcraft's world in *The Maltese Falcon*, steel beams stop falling (see pages 155–156)—or construct a new benchmark, such as Bill Gross's New Normal (pages 48–63).

In the case of global climate change much of the world is still sticking with the old benchmarks. Some places—an increasing number—have decided that the benchmark has changed enough to require some action. But the scope of that action is still relatively small.

In California, for example, a five-year-old drought has finally led to a mandatory 25 percent cut in urban water use. The mandatory restrictions will replace voluntary measures that have failed to produce big results. In the last seven months of 2014, for example, water use in California under the voluntary measures fell by only 10 percent. With groundwater levels in California at all-time lows—or at least as far back as records go—and the mountain snowpack at just 6 percent of the long-term average, the new rules don't seem draconian. Other water use restrictions in the state come with a very relaxed schedule. For example, new restrictions on agricultural water use, which accounts for 80 percent of water consumption in California, went into effect on January 1, 2015, and call for reaching sustainability in the state's groundwater supplies by 2040.

I guess a five-year drought isn't enough to build a strong political consensus for change.

That shouldn't be surprising. As the examples (pages 217–227) of volatility in the oil and iron ore sectors argue, volatility is related not just to the rate of change in the real world but also to the availability of mechanisms to act on that volatility. There is no market in global temperature. As I discussed in the last chapter, there really isn't much of a market in global water, as so much use is unpriced. There is no (primary) market in drought. There is something of an insurance market in floods and fires. All of which means that there are very limited ways to express volatility in those areas short of big actions such as restricting any further expansion of the acreage devoted to growing almonds, which has doubled in the last twenty years, because by some estimates it can take up to a gallon of water to grow one almond, or building plants that turn seawater into drinking water.

Part of the problem with desalination plants is that they're big ticket/big unit solutions that are very expensive and take a long time to build. Santa Barbara, for example, spent $40 million to build a desalination plant twenty years ago in an earlier drought. The plant has been mothballed for most of the last twenty years because that drought wasn't permanent. But the city is now thinking of reactivating it.

The nature of the markets for expressing volatility goes a long way toward determining the dimensions of that volatility. For example, commodity markets for wheat and corn, say, lay off the risk of the next harvest—three months to a year is the time frame here. That makes them relatively responsive to shorter-term phenomenon such as the El Niño/La Niña oscillation. However, if the only way to respond to water volatility is by building a desalination plant with a $40 million price tag or prohibiting the expansion of the California almond industry, then responses to change will be postponed, thus allowing the pressure for those changes to build up and, ultimately, result in more violent volatility.

At the same time, the value of existing infrastructure guarantees that we will eventually respond to climate change—quite possibly with a crash program with all the volatility that comes with delayed action and potential overshoot. Because global climate change includes huge swings in not only where the rain falls but also how much rain falls, in the long term it's likely that states such as California, Arizona, Oklahoma, and Texas are going to need to create new water supplies. Politics will trump any economic analysis. We're not going to abandon San Diego or Perth, for example, even though these cities were built in virtual deserts.

Water is subject to hoarding behavior: when people believe they are about to run out, they rush to stock up and are willing to spend just about anything to secure a supply. But hoarding psychology produces exceptionally big volatility when a commodity or good trades in very expensive single units. Water supply from desalination runs in units of $10 million to $40 million or more, not in jugs that cost $1.99. One huge challenge in global climate volatility is the relative absence of markets with low unit costs to express long-term volatility.

For example, in Australia the response to the drought that ended in 2010 was a crash program to build desalination plants, creating a huge "Who cares what it costs?" bill. By the November 2014 election the bill for the desalination plant southeast of Melbourne had climbed to $1.2 billion. Plants in Victoria, New South Wales, Adelaide, and on Australia's Gold Coast cost $10 billion to build.

Like the Santa Barbara plant discussed above, the Melbourne plant hasn't produced water since 2012. The other plants are effectively mothballed. The problem was, of course, that by the time the decision had been made to build them and they were built, the drought was over.

California could be headed down the same path now. The costs of doing nothing—a growth moratorium in San Diego, for example, or fallowing huge acreage of farmland—have finally trumped the costs of being wrong. So Carlsbad, a city of 110,000 people north of San Diego, is building a $1 billion desalination plant that could open as early as November 2015. It would be the biggest desalination plant in the Western Hemisphere. Florida, with one plant already in operation, is looking at building more. Texas is thinking about joining the trend. More than a dozen California cities are looking at desalination plants.

From a volatility perspective, incrementalism would be better. If we could get people to implement significant changes in water use, energy efficiency, carbon emissions, and so forth year in and year out, we'd face fewer lags from big-project hurdles, and we'd probably stand a better chance of getting the solution right with fewer white-elephant, big-ticket construction projects and there would be less likelihood of bad and expensive decisions based on hoarding psychologies.

The current California experience with water politics, however, suggests that significant incremental changes are at least as tough to sell politically as big-ticket construction solutions. Everybody is happy with incremental solutions as long as they don't add up to significant changes to behavior or costs. No glass of water in a restaurant unless you ask, and don't wash my hotel towels every day are fine because they don't cost us much in time or effort or dollars, but they also don't make a real dent in the problem. Requiring home owners to gradually reduce the water appetite of their landscaping by replacing grass with desert plants is a tougher sell politically. (Half of municipal water use in California goes to lawns.) How tough? Just note that one of the reasons for turning California's voluntary plan for water reduction into a mandatory program is that it will make it possible to fine all those folks who have figured that if everybody else cut back on watering their lawns and washing their cars, they wouldn't have to.

Knowing these things about how volatility works and knowing what we do about the likely approaches, how do we invest in global climate change, and how do we hedge against that change in everyday life?

In your investing strategy, embrace the perversity of human behavior: it may make far less sense to spend $10 billion on flood walls to protect New York than to invest $1 billion in marshland restoration projects, but I'll bet you dollars to donuts that we'll go for the big capital-intensive project, and probably on a crash schedule: water desalination companies, big construction and engineering companies, and big centralized, utility-scale solar operations to "remediate" the carbon emissions from these big capital- and energy-intensive projects. The pressure of our politics, where big-project companies donate big money to politicians, certainly suggests that efforts to reduce carbon emissions will be done with big projects to reduce emissions and then more big projects to balance the carbon emissions from those emission-reduction projects. Show me the big profits from building a marsh to recycle gray water or to reduce coastal flooding.

That doesn't mean you have to embrace this perversity in your everyday life, especially if you live in a community with a record of democratic (small "d") activism. Fight for that marsh project to recycle wastewater because it will save you and your fellow citizens money in comparison to the costs of building a big wastewater treatment plant for gray water. Support rules that make it easier to build and finance green roofs.

Act locally—as in the above examples—but invest globally. We can't know where the impacts of global climate change will fall, so we don't know whether building a desalination plant in Sydney or Carlsbad makes more sense—if either does—but a company that builds desalination plants around the world doesn't care about the where. That kind of investment hedges the specific "where" risk.

Realize that the primary effects of global climate change are likely to show up most powerfully in our everyday lives in secondary markets. The volatility of global climate change—the difficulty in predicting where local effects will fall—means that things like food production, which require predictability, will be a major attractor of volatility. For investors, food commodity producers (again, with global footprints or in a portfolio with a global footprint unless you know how the climate change will break in Russia, Canada, the Midwest, China's and India's wheat belts, and Brazil's soy regions) will rise or fall with volatility—just look at corn prices in the last five years, with a swing from $8 a bushel to below $4. One advantage here is that you can buy and sell volatility in food commodities in units that sell for well below the $1 billion cost of a desalination plant.

Plan your own incrementalism in everyday life—even if our politics won't respond to that approach on a larger scale. Join a community garden (my son even found us one in Manhattan) or a local community-supported agriculture (CSA) farm to create your own hedge against rising food costs and the energy and transportation stresses built into our large-scale system of food production and delivery. Add triple-insulated windows whenever you replace a window. See if you can replace an incandescent or fluorescent bulb with an LED, especially now that cost of the newest generation bulb is $5 or less at Home Depot. (How about that next set of Christmas tree lights?) Your individual contribution won't fix the problem—and maybe not enough of your neighbors will join in the effort to produce a significant effect. But even if you don't manage to reduce the volatility in global climate change, you will reduce the volatility in your own family budget.

I've tried in this middle section of *Juggling with Knives* to focus on what we might know about volatility in chunks of our everyday lives. It's not always been easy or desirable to avoid following those descriptions of how volatility works in these particular instances with concrete investment strategies. In the last third of this book I'm going to throw out any attempt to avoid investment strategies and go for the brass—or better—ring. So bring on the concrete, the money-centered—those portfolios in need of a new strategy.

PART III

INVESTING SOLUTIONS FOR
AN AGE OF VOLATILITY

Chapter 20

Improving a Traditional Stock-Picking Strategy

SINCE MAY 1997 I'VE run a public online stock portfolio on my website, JubakPicks.com. The return on the portfolio, with dividends reinvested when market conditions said putting that cash to work made sense, was 445 percent through the end of 2014. During that same period the return on the S&P 500 stock index was 238 percent with dividends reinvested. (As you know from Chapter 6 where I told you about a dividend-income strategy for the Age of Volatility, dividends are extremely important for investors in the S&P 500. Without reinvested dividends the return for the S&P 500 drops to 147 percent during this period.)

I have no complaints about that return. I do, however, have a suspicion that I could have done even better if I'd been a bit smarter about calling the bottom after the big market drop at the end of the dot-com boom, which peaked in March 2000, and during the bear market called the global financial crisis of 2008.

But what I have noticed in the last couple of years is that the strategy behind this portfolio and its picks has shifted.

That's not terribly surprising to me. I follow a school of investing that I call tactical stock picking. The idea is to follow macrotrends, such as rising or falling interest rates, a stronger or weaker dollar, and an aging world, and then pick stocks that capture the gains in those trends. For example, I've owned shares of:

- Novo Nordisk, a Danish company that specializes in diabetes drugs and insulin, because an aging population means a higher incidence of diabetes.
- Cummins, a maker of diesel truck engines because the company's newest engines run considerably cleaner than older engines, and that's a big thing in a world that's trying to cut pollution and, especially, carbon emissions.
- Fertilizer maker Yara International during a time of rising farm commodity prices.
- India's HDFC Bank when that country looked like it would actually grow faster than China.

These kinds of holdings aren't different in strategy from picks early in the life of the portfolio, such as communications chipmaker Broadcom during the days of accelerating growth in smartphone use or Cisco Systems during the headiest days of traffic growth on the Internet.

But in the last couple of years I've also found myself adding an ETF, a basket of stocks, focused on German equities to pick up the growth in exports that is supposed to follow from a cheap euro against a strong US dollar. The ETF is hedged, by the way, against damage to the returns that a US-based investor gains from a fall in the euro against the dollar.

I also added an ETF that specializes in Indian infrastructure plays when interest rates in India started to fall and the Indian government started to talk about investing more in India's airports, ports, and roads.

I added shares of two airline stocks when oil prices dropped because lower oil prices results in cheaper fuel, which means rising profits at airlines such as American Airlines Group and United Continental Holdings.

In other words, I was investing not just in macrotrends but also with an eye toward volatility. ETFs were an attractive choice from a volatility point of view because it's a big advantage to be able to quickly buy or sell a whole basket of stocks in a market in which volatility, as measured by the VIX, or the "fear Index," was moving up or down 40 percent or more in a matter of a few weeks.

That same attention to volatility drove my airline picks. My first move in that sector was to add shares of American Airlines because the company had ended all of its own hedges on fuel prices in July 2014. By going naked in this way, American would get all the advantage of any fall in fuel prices—and take the biggest hit if fuel prices climbed.

Did I see something I particularly liked in the operational fundamentals of American Airlines? Nothing that set my heart aflutter: decent opportunities for cutting costs, of course, as well as a strengthening balance sheet. But my primary reason to buy the stock wasn't fundamental; this was a pick based on chasing volatility in the price of oil.

In other words, I have started to tweak a relatively traditional system of stock picking to take account of an Age of Volatility.

Investing during an Age of Volatility takes courage. This is especially so during stomach-churning drops when there is plenty of opportunity to underperform market indexes such as the S&P 500 by selling low in a panic and during bull market booms when it's hard to resist buying high when you're afraid you will be left behind as the market soars. We've had huge plunges and recoveries like that in the years since the dot-com boom peaked in March 2000. For example, the S&P 500 stock index fell 22.6 percent in the fourth quarter of 2008, 11.7 percent in the first quarter of 2009, 11.9 percent in the second quarter of 2010, and 14.3 percent in the third quarter of 2011.

Those are drops in a quarter—not a year.

The traditional investing response to volatility like that has been either to just tough it out—buy and hold means buy and hold—or to try to time the tops and bottoms of the market.

Toughing it out is a good strategy for a year like 2010, when the 14.3 percent drop in the second quarter was followed by a 10.7 percent gain in the third quarter and a 10.2 percent gain in the fourth. One of the strongest arguments for buy and hold is that this strategy avoids the chance that you'll get out too early or too late after the peak and then miss getting back in at the bottom. That argument applies extremely well to a year like 2010. Research has repeatedly shown that most investors underperform the mutual funds they invest in because of their emotional reaction to volatility. They sell low in a panic, when volatility sends the market plunging, and then buy high in a panic when volatility sends the market soaring. In a year like 2010, buy and hold would have avoided that problem.

Of course, buy and hold wouldn't have worked so well in the multiyear bear market that began in 2000 when the S&P 500 fell 9.1 percent. That drop was followed by an 11.9 percent tumble in 2001 and a 22.1 percent plunge in 2002. On March 24, 2000, the S&P 500 stock index had peaked at 1,527 after a huge run-up in anything connected with technology, from America Online to Nortel Networks. And then came the bust. By April 4, 2001, the S&P was down to 1,103—a 28 percent drop. That's real honest-to-goodness bear market territory.

And that wasn't the bottom. On September 24, 2001, the S&P 500 hit 1,003, and the actual bottom wouldn't come until September 30, 2002, at 801 for the index.

The traditional solution in a bear market like this is a market-timing strategy that uses some combination of indicators to move out of stocks near a peak and into stocks near a bottom. Where do you move to? Typically cash, as that adds a very low volatility asset to your portfolio and because you then have money to put back into stocks when they are at much lower prices at the bottom.

My record over the years shows that I am not a particularly good market timer. But I am a bad market timer in very specific ways.

I'm actually pretty good at getting out somewhere near the top. The Jubak's Picks portfolio sold heavily in the first half of 2000, close enough to the beginning of that three-year bear market for me to count the move as a success. And I came reasonably close to getting out in the early stages of the bear market that followed on the Lehman Brothers bankruptcy in the fall of 2008.

I am, however, terrible, the record says, at deciding when to get back in. In what would turn out to be the 2000 to 2002 bear market I actually called a bottom around the middle of 2000 and made a round of picks that continued to sink until the actual bottom in 2002. In the global financial crisis I made the opposite mistake: I waited and then waited and then waited too long to get back in. For example, in 2013 the return on my Jubak's Picks portfolio came to 19.66 percent. Certainly not bad. But the S&P 500 stock index returned 32.39 percent for the year.

How come? Pretty simple. My cash position for the year averaged 30 percent of this portfolio, with a high of 34.59 percent at the end of the June quarter and a low of 23.51 percent at the end of the December quarter. My coulda, woulda, shoulda calculations show that if I had invested all of the portfolio at the same return that I earned on the 70 percent of the portfolio that was invested, the total return for the year would have been 29.62 percent. Of course, I can't take that 29.62 percent to the bank, but this calculation is nonetheless important because it tells me that the major "mistake" I made in 2013 wasn't in the stocks I picked but in the cash I held.

Why was I holding so much cash? As the stock market recovered from its bottom in 2009, I got progressively more nervous about another drop. That anxiety turned out to have been absolutely misplaced, but it is completely understandable after a huge bear market. Drops like that of 2008, when the S&P 500 fell 36.81 percent for the year, do tend to leave investors fearing the worst after any return of good future.

In 2009, while the S&P 500 was moving off the March 2009 bottom on the way to a 26.37 percent return for the year, I was gradually reducing my cash position to 19 percent by December 31, 2009. In 2010 I continued reducing my cash position, hitting just 5 percent cash by December 31, 2010, while the index returned another 15.10 percent.

But in 2011 the market, already up so far off the bottom, looked rocky again. That year the S&P 500 would return only 1.89 percent, and I moved the portfolio heavily back into cash, at 37 percent by December 31, 2011.

The problem after that was that, as the US stock market moved ever higher and, in fact, put in one all-time high after another, it became increasingly hard for me to put that cash to work. Some of that was fear that the market was getting more and more ahead of itself. Part of it was a reluctance to admit that I'd missed a big leg in the rally and worry that I was about to buy at a top, just as the market decided to turn down again. In fact, I wasn't able to bite the bullet and put most of that cash back to work until January 2014, after the lagging performance of 2013 convinced me that I just couldn't keep so much on the sidelines anymore. Fortunately, in 2014 the US markets continued to march upward, and my decision to allocate cash to stocks turned out to be a profitable one.

Yep, for me traditional market timing is hard.

But in the last few years I've also become convinced that this kind of market timing, when it is used as a way to cope with volatility, is a misreading of how volatility works and especially of how volatility works as financial markets gradually stop moving in a single block, driven by global cash flows. As we slowly see a return to financial markets with varying correlations—and lack thereof—among asset classes (see Chapter 12 on the return of varying correlations among asset classes), I think a volatility strategy beyond market timing is absolutely crucial. At the least, any market-timing strategy needs to recognize that as global central banks start to reduce the flood of cash they've unleashed on the markets, asset classes will start to show a spread of changing correlations and anticorrelations again. Any market timing strategy needs to consider that the possible strategies aren't just questions of simply more or less cash—because all other assets move in lockstep.

What's wrong—or at least less than optimally useful—about thinking about volatility in the way most people think about market timing? First, it falls into a trap of thinking that the way to win the contest with volatility—the way to profit from it and to avoid getting hurt by it—is to guess the correct answer to the volatility question. The purpose of employing the very useful but by no means infallible tools of technical analysis, this way of thinking says, is to figure out when the market is going to rise or fall—and rise or fall dramatically—and then to position your portfolio either long or short (or neutrally in cash). To this way of thinking you make money—or lose less of it, which is in many ways the same thing—by knowing where the market will wind up after the volatility winds have stopped blowing.

And second, much of the effort of market timing goes into picking the moments and the direction of big moves in the market—the bear markets (when markets, by definition, fall 20 percent or more), the recoveries from market bottoms (when stocks and bonds and other financial assets can take off like rockets), and the peaks that mark the time to get out.

But these are exceptional—and rare—moments in a constant stream of volatility. Most volatility happens in smaller increments and in almost incidental moves as markets or everyday life settle toward their eventual goals. And there's enough volatility in that settling, the jostling from temporary highs or lows before the market gets to its ultimate destination, to provide significant opportunities to make and lose money.

Consider, for example, the incredible plunge in oil prices in 2014 and 2015. West Texas Intermediate, the US crude oil benchmark, traded near $105 a barrel in July 2014 and then fell and fell and fell to below $50 a barrel in January 2015. That was certainly a big volatility event, and you would have made a lot of money if you managed to call the top in July and then held on through all the rallies and drops until January. At each one of those rallies and drops you would have asked yourself whether this was a bottom, was the drop over, and was it time to go long? The answer to each of these questions, as the long plunge continued, was no. You wouldn't have needed to answer all of those questions correctly to make money, but each one you got wrong would have cut into your profits. Along with the giant investment companies on Wall Street, you would have put together your own opinion on the correct final—well, temporarily final—price of oil.

The volatility sketched out as of this writing in 2015 in any chart for oil prices looks, at first glance, to be a whole lot less promising for making a profit on the decline or rally in oil. Instead of the long and pretty clear downward march of oil prices from July to January, the chart for February and March 2015 showed a market stuck in a rut. West Texas Intermediate traded at a low near $43 a barrel in both February and March of 2015 and at a high near $53 a barrel during those same months.

This small volatility is characteristic of the very unsettled conditions in our Age of Volatility. You can find patterns that look like this in the S&P 500 stock index in early 2015, with lots of movement for not much net gain, for example, or in the price of the euro against the US dollar.

Here's another example of big and small volatility. Back in July 2014 the euro traded at $1.35 to the dollar. It then began a long and steady descent—looking much like the descent in the price of a barrel of West Texas Intermediate in 2014—that took the euro down to $1.125 in January 2015. That's the big volatility trend.

The small volatility events are the drop from $1.13 to $1.05 in late February to mid-March, the bounce back from $1.05 to $1.10 in March and then the resumption of the drop in April.

In the Age of Volatility you need to include both big volatility trends and small volatility events in your portfolio from a number of independent asset classes in which volatility operates in (potentially) different directions and on different time scales. The same July–March period that saw oil plunge from $105 to $45 and the euro from $1.35 to $1.05 saw the S&P 500 stock index climb from 1,975 in July 2014 to 2,100 in March 2015—with, of course, a substantial number of little volatility moves along the way.

I have an opinion on where oil will bottom. We've already seen it at $40—before making a turn upward. And I certainly have an opinion on whether the euro is heading for parity or even lower against the dollar. I certainly don't have any problem with backing those opinions—with my dollars. The best way to profit from that kind of long-term trend, with volatility measured out in multiple quarters or even years, is with individual stocks or baskets of stocks—through an ETF—that give you not only decent leverage on this volatility but also the longest time scale for volatility to play out. I think you can get more leverage from individual stocks than from the basket of stocks in an ETF if you pick the individual stocks most "responsive" to this trend. Oil services leader Schlumberger, deepwater drillers Seadrill and Ensco, leading US natural gas from shale player Chesapeake Energy, and global extreme conditions producer Norway's Statoil are examples. But an ETF still gives you good participation in longer-term volatility with the right long-run time frame.

But I also don't want to concentrate just on getting to the final destination for this volatility; rather, I also like to put some money on volatility itself, on the recognition that a price that seems to be a bottom near $40—say, $45—increases the number of people willing to go long, and a price near $55 brings out the sellers who want to protect profits. This volatility trend won't last forever, so you can't lock it into place or fall in love with it. This is why ETFs are so useful: they enable an investor or trader to get in and out very quickly—much more easily than with a bucket of individual stocks—and they are far harder to fall in love with an individual stock because they feel rather mechanical and amorphous.

But even better for making this kind of short-term trade on volatility itself is the option market, which gives you more leverage to pure short-term volatility than stocks do. I'll have more on options in Chapter 24.

This allocation between long-term plays on the long-term destination of volatility and short-term plays on volatility itself can sound a lot like the old traditional asset-allocation advice to mix 60 percent stocks with 40 percent bonds to reduce risk to a portfolio and then to divide up those allocations themselves among asset classes such as emerging market equities and junk bonds.

But we're talking about three significant differences from that approach. First, the asset class net is cast a lot wider. I'd argue that you should look well beyond stocks and bonds to include much more of the financial and nonfinancial universe. Second, even within the asset classes that you wind up including when you cast your net so widely, you should wind up slicing and dicing those asset classes into finer segments and be prepared to shift among those segments as the characteristics of those subclasses also shift in this very volatile market and global economy. And third, some portion of the resulting portfolio(s) might well be called a trading portfolio because you would move in and out of that asset class with relative frequency. With this strategy you'd consider not just stocks and bonds and subunits of those asset classes but also currencies and commodities and, using ETFs, real estate, and infrastructure. (You can find a portfolio built along these lines, with updates on the topics in this book and other portfolios from a later chapter in this section of *Juggling with Knives* on the website, JugglingwithKnives.com, I've built for readers of this book. You can use this code—daggers2016—to gain a year's free access to what is, for everyone else, a paid subscription site.)

In this Age of Volatility the correlations between these assets can change relatively quickly—but not overnight. You need to follow the development of such trends that I have outlined thus far and in the chapters still to come to track the shifting volatility landscape. Then use the shifts in that landscape to revise the portfolios and strategies that I'm going to lay out in this section. (And, of course, don't forget the dividend strategy covered earlier [pages 84–91].)

Because I don't know you, it's up to you to pick a strategy—or combination of strategies—that matches your own investing psychology. Some investors get so nervous at even a modest market fluctuation that they aren't likely ever to make a profit trading—and they certainly shouldn't build their strategy around trading. Some investors like the end result of investing—profits, we hope—but hate the close tracking and constant attention that some of the strategies in this section require for success. If you can't, won't, or don't want to put in the time and attention required by a specific strategy, forget about pursuing strategies that require that discipline. Strategies that are built on a certain degree of attention to financial markets on a daily or weekly basis won't work if you only sort of pay attention. Conversely, the obsessives among you—please send me the list of typos in this book that you've collected so we can correct the next printing—especially if they combine obsessiveness with a certain trading bravado, should think twice about any of the more aggressive of these strategies. You should invent some "governor rule" that will kick in if you start to get too impressed with your own cleverness.

In other words, pick a strategy that not only makes sense to you but also is one you stand a chance of executing successfully.

And with that caveat, let's begin our walk—or maybe a run, as we're talking about volatility—down strategy lane with a look at bonds and why tweaking traditional bond strategies isn't enough for an Age of Volatility.

Chapter 21

A Strategy for Bonds

IF WE'RE TO HAVE any hope of knowing where we're going, we need to know where we've been.

For investors that means knowing that we've come to the end of an extraordinary period, one when we could count on a steady decline in interest rates. From the monthly high on ten-year US Treasuries of 15.32 percent in September 1981 to the 1.53 percent in July 2012, we've lived in a financial market and economy of falling interest rates. We've been able to count on interest rates being lower tomorrow than they were yesterday.

That's over. It's a new age for bonds and bond investors, so it's time for a new strategy for using bonds in a portfolio. The rise in the yield on the ten-year Treasury certainly hasn't been quick or large from the July 2012 1.53 percent level, but by July 2013 the yield was up to 2.58 percent. From then until May 2015 the yield has dropped as low at 1.9 percent and climbed as high as 2.9 percent, but yields don't show any signs of falling below that 1.53 percent from July 2012 on a consistent basis.

For bonds the period from 1981 to 2012—interrupted by events such as the dot-com crash and the turmoil at the beginning of the global financial crisis—represented the best of all worlds: low risk and the traditional low volatility of bonds with returns that, on average, nearly matched the returns of riskier equities and, in some periods, exceeded those returns.

Just how extraordinary was the combination?

In the 1950s investors could count on interest rates on a ten-year Treasury of 2.3 to 3.8 percent pretty much for the whole period. And because interest rates were relatively stable during those years, investors in bonds reaped that 2.3 to 3.8 percent coupon interest payment from the bonds but not much else. Contrast that with the returns for the fifteen years from 1998 to 2013, when, thanks to the rising price of a bond as interest rates and inflation continued their fall from the double-digit highs of 1981, the average nominal annual return on that Treasury was 5.5 percent. In the latter period a bond investor made twice as much a year as one made in the stable 1950s.

It's tempting to think that the investing rules that run around in our heads—from parents, from wise Uncle Joe (the family's Oracle of Great Neck), from *Money* magazine and Internet gurus, and, of course, from any financial adviser you've ever had—are timeless, like gravity and Murphy's Law. But they're not. Advice that made sense in the 1950s in an environment of low and stable interest rates and low inflation wouldn't have worked very well in the 1970s, 1980s, or 1990s. Advice that worked during what I'd call, looking backward, the Golden Age of Bonds, from 1981 to 2012, wouldn't have worked very well in the 1950s. And that advice also isn't likely to work very well over the next twenty-year bond cycle.

We don't know exactly what the next big period will be like. We are certain that the next decade won't see a 10 to 15 percentage point drop in the yield on a ten-year Treasury from the current rate just above or below 2.4 percent as of May 2015. I think it's a good bet that we won't see anything like the stability we saw in the US financial markets in the 1950s. (Being the only major global industrial power that hadn't seen a major part of its industrial base destroyed in a world war does wonders for your economy.) And I think it's likely that we'll see more inflation than there was in the 1950s and less than the 1970s, as all the excess capacity created with cheap money dampens the inflationary effects, at least somewhat, of all that created cheap money.

Trying to invest for the period ahead, then, isn't like sailing totally blind in a fog off the Grand Banks; we can figure out things to do that will increase our odds of success—and limit the odds that we'll take a huge downside beating.

But if we're looking for a bond strategy that will deliver something better than 0.7 percent or so—the yield on a two-year US Treasury in May 2015—or better than the 0.83 percent yield at that same time on a ten-year German Bund, we're going to have to try something different.

If, in the years from 1981 to 2012, the way to make money in the bond market was to ride the downward volatility in interest rates, then over the next twenty years the way to profit in the bond market will be from both the long-term downward volatility in bond prices, as interest rates and yields rise in a reversal of the 1981–2014 trend, as well as from the shorter-term volatility in credit quality.

My "improved" bond strategy for an Age of Volatility is in many ways similar to my "improved" dividend stock strategy; it's built on a recognition of long-term volatility and a strategy for profiting from it—and, likewise, a recognition of short-term volatility and a strategy for profiting from that as well.

To get to a place at which you can profit from those two dimensions of volatility, you'll need to jettison the traditional rules about the role of Treasury bonds in our portfolios. The key to asset allocation and risk reduction for the next decade is likely to be the exact opposite to the rules of the last period. Previously, the advice to keep 40 percent or so of your portfolio in bonds (and 60 percent in stocks) to reduce the risk and volatility in your portfolio made a great deal of sense. And it worked. (Although not, I believe, for the reasons most advice givers expected.)

That allocation—and the tweaks to it, such as the rule of thumb calling for older investors to start adding to bond allocation as they aged—was designed to reduce portfolio risk. A mix of more volatile (and risky stocks) and less volatile (and less risky bonds) would reduce the volatility (and risk) of an overall portfolio. Bonds would keep chugging along, adding their 4 percent or whatever yield to your portfolio, even in years when stocks fell. Part of the advice was also based on historical patterns that showed bond prices tending to rise when stocks stumbled. Investors in periods when there was worry about stocks tended to move to the safety of bonds, giving bond prices a boost when share prices faltered. And bonds and stocks tended to move in opposite directions as well because a stronger economy was good for earnings (a plus for stocks) but also tended to bring on higher inflation (bad for bonds).

But in recent years this relative pattern, in which stocks zig when bonds zag, has disappeared as all markets danced to the tune of central bank cash. When the economy weakened, for example, bonds would climb in price because a weaker economy meant lower interest rates and a higher probability that central banks would add more cash to the financial system in an effort to boost growth. But when the economy weakened, stocks would rise as well on the same expectation of lower interest rates (good for stocks) and increased central bank cash (good for stocks).

You might think that change in the relationship between stock and bond returns would have led to a revision of the standard wisdom about asset allocation in a portfolio. But it didn't. When I was a pup, just starting off covering the financial markets in the 1980s, the traditional wisdom, as I said, began with an allocation of 60 percent stocks and 40 percent bonds and then modified a portfolio from there for variables such as individual age or risk tolerance. This hasn't changed. For example, the "neutral" allocation for Wells Fargo's Index Asset Allocation Fund in 2014, according to the fund's website, was still that same 60/40 ratio of stocks and bonds.

The outsized returns earned by allocations to bonds—remember that from 1998 to 2013 bonds returned 5.5 percent a year—removed any real pressure to rethink this allocation advice. Putting 40 percent—or more—in bonds was a great decision simply because bonds performed so well. Who cared if the underlying logic of that asset allocation had vanished?

I don't think investors can put off rethinking that conventional wisdom much longer. Interest rates have indeed fallen for longer than expected: Who would have imagined that yields on US ten-year Treasuries could drop to 2 percent and then drop farther? Or that bond yields in Germany, Denmark, and Sweden would all go negative? Or that the European Central Bank would begin charging member banks to hold their cash—and that banks would gladly pay.

But if we're not yet at a turning point for interest rates, we can see the turning point. As of this writing, the Federal Reserve is expected to raise interest rates in late 2015 or in 2016, probably not aggressively, but nonetheless, it will mark the first increase in rates since 2006. European central banks will look to end the current experiment in creating ultra-low or negative interest rates as soon as their economies and currencies will allow. At some point the shrinking pool of global savings—we can already see the leading edge of that trend in Japan—will lead to higher interest rates, even in Japan.

And at that point the conventional wisdom will run into a huge challenge: Does it make sense to stick with the 40/60 base formula when bonds have switched from a long cycle of falling interest rates and rising bond prices to a period of rising—even if only slowly— interest rates and falling bond prices?

Put that baldly: it's hard for me to see "Yes" as an answer.

That doesn't mean that US Treasuries and other bonds don't have a central role in portfolio construction; it's just that instead of being long on these bonds, all the time in an unchanging allocation in order to go with the long upward volatility trend in bond prices, your portfolio should on be at least occasionally—and perhaps frequently— short on these bonds, as I show below. Unlike the years from 1981 through the present, when Treasury returns were positive in most years and the investment decision was how big a long position in Treasuries made sense, in the period of increased volatility that I see ahead, the big investment decision, the single-most important asset allocation decision in controlling portfolio risk, will be how big a *short* position in Treasuries an investor should hold in a portfolio and when.

Being long Treasuries means that you buy the bonds, stuff them in your portfolio, and then wait to collect your interest coupons and any price appreciation that results from an increase in bond prices as interest rates fall.

For the fifteen-year period that ended in 2013, for example, the average annual return on the Barclays U.S. Aggregate Bond Trust, a standard sector benchmark, was 5.55 percent, as the long-term trend in bond prices was solidly upward as interest rates on a ten-year US Treasury bond fell from a high of 15.23 percent in 1981 to 2.9 percent in December 2013.

Being short means borrowing the bonds, selling them, and then rebuying them to return them to the original lender at some point in the future. The hope is to make a profit by borrowing bonds, selling them at a relatively high price, and then buying the bonds to cover the short at a relatively lower price. In a short you're betting that bonds will fall in price because interest rates rise, and you then make your profit from that fall in price.

It's unlikely that shorting Treasuries and the bonds of other governments will prove to be anywhere near as profitable compared to the fifteen-year period that began in 1981—and the gains from this strategy will certainly prove to be more volatile. The movement in interest rates during this period just doesn't have the magnitude of the 11.4 percentage point drop in interest rates that took place between 1981 and 2014. At the beginning of 2015 economic forecasts were calling for an increase in the Federal Reserve's benchmark short-term interest rate, from 0 percent to less than 2 percent at the end of 2016 to maybe near 3 percent or 4 percent in 2018. The direction of that move is important, but interest rates are, according to the consensus at the beginning of 2015, just not going to move higher very aggressively.

The turn in the long-term bond cycle certainly argues that you should have a short bond presence in your portfolio, but the relatively modest returns likely from shorting Treasuries says it should certainly be less than the 40 percent of the traditional asset-allocation model. (Short strategies also cost more to execute because the options and other instruments used by ETFs and individual investors to execute short strategies expire and then need to be rolled over to keep the trade in place. That expiration and then renewal costs money.)

Dividend stocks, the subject of Chapter 6, are a better bet for income in a period of rising interest rates because companies can raise their payouts. So if you're looking for more income, add more dividend-paying stocks and fewer bonds. If the global economy is headed into a period of very modest growth, which certainly looks possible, shorting bonds could still produce positive returns on a normalization of interest rates, but they won't be huge. If inflation should step up, which is relatively unlikely if growth stays low, then gold is likely to be a better hedge than bonds. If currencies head into a period of depreciation, then bond shorts will show positive returns as bond prices fall when their currencies sink in value.

The one situation in which shorting bonds will pay off with higher-than-expected returns is a gloomy economic future in which inflation kicks up, currencies sink, government budgets go into crisis, and economic growth goes into a tailspin. If you think that scenario is relatively likely, then you should short more bonds than someone who thinks the future will be a period of simply muddling through.

I am a member of the muddling-through camp. What makes Treasuries so interesting to me as a short position in a portfolio with a considerable allocation to long positions in, say, US stocks, is that Treasuries are, potentially, uncorrelated with other asset classes and the potential trends that might move those assets. In other words, a short Treasury position would play exactly the role in lowering risk and decreasing volatility that a long position in Treasuries was supposed to provide. For example, if or when the Federal Reserve moves to—finally—increase interest rates, stocks will face downward pressure, bond prices will fall, and a short position in Treasuries would be profitable.

A short position in Treasuries would also be a good hedge against a slowdown in the housing sector and a pause in the rise of housing prices because such a slowdown would be most likely the result of rising mortgage rates. (In other words, shorting Treasuries hedges the risk of a decline in real estate prices.)

I'm not suggesting that shorting Treasuries is a risk-free bet. Weaker-than-expected US economic growth could lead to a rally in bond prices if that slower growth raises the odds that the Fed would delay any interest rate increases.

And, perversely, a stronger-than-expected US economy that led to fears of a faster-than-expected increase in interest rates might actually lead to at least a temporary rally in Treasuries. The US Treasury market, because it is the world's most liquid market, remains a safe haven in turmoil, even if the turmoil is rooted in the United States. That can lead to the seemingly counterintuitive result that Treasuries go up in price as a result of a debt-ceiling crisis in the United States or a cut in the US credit rating. A political or economic crisis overseas could trigger the safe haven in US Treasuries response, which would lead to an increase in Treasury prices and a loss for anyone shorting Treasuries as well as a substantial drop in the prices of "riskier" emerging market bonds.

Thanks to the wonderful world of ETFs, it's now very easy for individual investors to short Treasuries. I'd check to see how a short ETF did against a long position in bonds as part of any due diligence on a short ETF. For example, a short-bond ETF such as ProShares Short 20+ Year Treasury (TBF) did fine in 2013, with a total return of 11.95 percent, when a long-bond ETF such as iShares 20+ Year Treasury Bond (TLT) fell 13.37 percent.

You've got a lot of choices for short vehicles. There are, of course, the inverse ETFs that build portfolios designed to go up when Treasuries—usually a Treasury index or a Treasury ETF is the benchmark—go down. Examples include ProShares Short 20+ Year Treasury (TBF) and Direxion Daily 20+ Year Treasury Bear 1X (TYBS).

Some short ETFs use leverage—they borrow money—to try to deliver twice or three times the downside profits in the case of a Treasury decline. Frankly the volatility of these leveraged ETFs scares me to death—the Direxion Treasury Bear 3X (TMV) lost 68.54 percent in 2011, and that's just too much volatility when what I'm looking for is a way to lower a portfolio's risk.

You can also decide to avoid the inverse ETF route entirely by directly shorting long-only Treasury ETFs yourself. (Because ETFs price with market moves, you can short these vehicles, unlike mutual funds, which price only at the end of the day.) For example, you could buy put options on the iShares 20+ Year Treasury Bond (TLT) ETF. A put option would give you the right to sell the ETF at a specified price, a right that would become valuable if Treasury prices and the price of the ETF shares fell. Using options to short has the added advantage of limiting your losses to the amount that you've put up to buy the option. (I'll have more on options in Chapter 24, so hold on if this reference is all Greek to you.) If you short, however, and the price of what you've shorted goes up, the size of your losses is limited only by how much the asset climbs in value. The iShares 20+ Year Treasury Bond ETF has a very long average maturity of twenty-eight years, which gives the ETF strong leverage to any change in interest rates without the need for any leverage from borrowing. (As a rule of thumb, the longer the maturity of the bond, the more it moves with changes in interest rates.) You can find a listing of all the prices and dates in the options chain for these ETFs at NASDAQ.com.

I'd also probably wait to make a major commitment to a short strategy until I actually saw the Federal Reserve make not one but two increases in benchmark interest rates. You want to see more than a token gesture from the central bank at the front of any cycle of higher interest rates.

Everything I've written in this chapter so far is about making money from the long-term volatility cycle of rising interest rates and falling bond prices. However, as I noted when I began this chapter, short-term volatility—or maybe, better yet, shorter-term volatility—also offers its own profit opportunities.

First, there's the opportunity in the market's oscillation between conditions that we've learned to call risk-on and risk-off. In this pattern, when the bond—and stock—market gets spooked by, say, a rising threat of a Greek default or the possibility that the Federal Reserve will move more aggressively than expected to raise interest rates, bondholders and other investors and traders sell the most risky and least liquid assets in their portfolios and put that cash into the world's most liquid asset. In this move—called risk-off—they sell Brazilian bonds or Indonesian stocks, for example, and buy anything denominated in very liquid currencies such as yen and dollars. In the risk-on part of the cycle, investors and traders sell their yen and dollar positions to raise cash and buy those risky emerging market assets they sold in the other half of the cycle. Trading this risk-on/risk-off cycle can be very profitable, but it *is* a trading strategy. As such, it depends on your ability to call the turns in this pattern of volatility. If you want to pursue this risk-on/risk-off trading strategy, I would again suggest using ETFs. You'll have to decide on a dollar-denominated ETF or one in local currencies (more on currencies later). Among dollar-denominated emerging-market bond ETFs, take a look at the iShares JPMorgan USD Emerging Markets Bond ETF (EMB). Among local currency ETFs, look at iShares Emerging Markets Local Currency Bond ETF (LEMB), Market Vectors EM Local Currency Bond ETF (EMLC), or WisdomTree Emerging Markets Local Debt ETF (ELD).

I prefer another shorter-term volatility strategy because it is not nearly as dependent on calling the shifts in market emotions; instead, it relies on trends in bond issuers' credit quality. I'm agnostic about what kind of bonds you use in this strategy—this is more an issuer-specific strategy than one that depends on larger trends in sectors or markets.

This strategy requires you to get familiar with momentum trends in credit ratings and learn how to look for turning points in those trends as you now might be doing with momentum indicators in the equity market. This strategy focuses on relatively short-term trends—one to three years—in bond credit ratings and looks for situations in which improving credit ratings will push up the price of a bond. Let me show you how this strategy works using bonds issued by the state of Kansas.

The state's budget woes are a widely known story. In 2014 state tax revenue fell by 3.8 percent to $7.3 billion from 2013's $7.6 billion. The decline, despite growth in the US economy that pushed up state tax collection in most states, was a result of big tax cuts sponsored by Republican governor Sam Brownback. The cuts were, according to supply-side tax theory, supposed to create enough extra growth so that applying lower rates to a bigger economy would actually result in higher receipts. It didn't happen. In January 2015 projections showed the state facing budget shortfalls of $710 million in the fiscal year's 2015–2016 two-year budget.

The decline in revenue had already prompted S&P and Moody's Investors Service to cut the state's credit rating. In August 2014, for example, S&P cut the state's rating to AA from AA+ with a negative outlook.

And in February 2015, looking at a new forecast of a negative $280 million general fund balance at the end of fiscal 2015—about 4 percent of budgeted spending—S&P warned that the state's outlook continued to deteriorate. The rating company wasn't especially thrilled with the Brownback administration's proposals for a mid-2015 correction to eliminate the general fund deficit. Proposals included $201 million in one-time transfers from other state funds, $41 million from a delay in a scheduled increase in contributions to the state's pension funds, $5 million from delays in hospital expansion,

$3 million in savings from a bond refinancing, $5 million in reduced transfers for capital construction, and 4 percent in spending cuts at state agencies. S&P rightly pointed out that most of these were one-time gimmicks and didn't address the revenue shortfall, pending court-ordered increases in state education spending, or the long-term shortfall in pension contributions. "Although the proposed mid-year corrective actions could eliminate a year-end deficit position, they do not appear to significantly address the mismatch between recurring revenue and expenditures," S&P wrote in February 2015.

The market has already begun to reflect the likelihood of another cut in the state's credit rating by pushing up the interest rate that Kansas has to pay to sell its bonds. And the state legislature knows it. Although the BVAL Muni Benchmark for thirty-year debt showed a yield of 3.07 percent in April 2015, when the state legislature passed a bill in April authorizing the sale of bonds to reduce the unfunded liability to the Kansas Public Employee Retirement System to $6.28 billion from $7.26 billion, the legislature was clearly worried about the interest rate Kansas would have to pay to sell its debt. In the legislation the body capped the interest the state was willing to pay at 5 percent.

I'm not suggesting that you buy Kansas state bonds even if they carry a 5 percent yield; that yield isn't some magic "buy" signal under all circumstances. Even a quick look at the numbers makes a strong case that the state's general fund problem is going to get worse because the current shortfall in revenue has depleted general fund balances and the current raft of one-time fixes to the current budget gap means that those one-time fixes won't be available for use next year. I think Kansas could easily follow the path blazed by New Jersey, plagued by its own pension-funding shortfalls, to an A rating from the current AA rating. That, of course, would force Kansas to pay more to sell new debt, and it would drop the price of existing bonds so that their coupon rates would rise to match the new higher yields.

What I would suggest—and here Kansas is a template for my shorter-term bond volatility strategy—is that Kansas's falling credit rating is an opportunity worth watching. That credit rating is likely to fall farther in the shorter term, which would push the yield on Kansas bonds up and the price down. But then Kansas bonds are likely to recover. (Brownback's second term runs through 2018, by the way.) Before this debacle Kansas had an above-average credit rating, according to S&P. The revenue shortfalls of the Brownback administration will bring that rating below average. But there's no reason that the rating shouldn't bounce back under a more fiscally prudent governor. For a model of this move, take a look at California: the state saw its credit rating pummeled but has now started to move back to average. In January 2013 S&P raised California's credit rating to A from A− in the first upgrade since 2006 after Democratic governor Jerry Brown proposed a balanced budget with spending cuts and a $6 billion tax increase. To give you an idea of how bad things had become in California, in October 2010 the state sold six-month revenue anticipation notes, debt backed by revenue the state hadn't yet collected, at a tax-free yield of 1 to 1.5 percent. At the time, a one-year Treasury bill paid 0.2 percent. But then again, at the time California was facing a projected $25.4 billion budget shortfall by the middle of 2012.

So what's the profit potential from the shorter-term volatility in the Kansas credit rating?

Let's say that state finances continue to deteriorate in Kansas, that the state's credit rating continues to erode, and that things finally get so bad that Kansas winds up paying not the 5 percent worst-case cap envisioned by the state legislature on in its debt authorization but instead 4.5 percent.

And then let's envision the day that Kansas, like California, gets its financial act back together, the state's credit rating improves to something like average, and the rate the state has to pay for money drops back down to just 3 percent. A bond paying a 4.5 percent coupon purchased for $1,000 when the state's credit rating was dismal would rise in price until that coupon of 4.5 percent was equivalent to the 3 percent on new Kansas bonds. That would result in price appreciation of a $1,000 bond until it was selling at $1,500 in the secondary market.

I'm sure you see the potential opportunity in this volatility: the potential for a 50 percent gain on the change in price of the bond, some interest payouts at a relatively hefty rate, and the chance to increase the effective annual return from this opportunity by cutting the time your money has to be locked up in these bonds—the longer you can hold off buying to the point at which the state's credit rating turns the corner, the fewer months and years that price gain gets spread over. And the quicker you can sell and move on to another opportunity of exactly the same sort.

Because this certainly isn't a buy-and-hold strategy; it's more like a wash, rinse, spin, and repeat strategy. It's based on my read of a fundamental change in the volatility landscape for bonds away from the landscape of steadily falling interest rates steadily pushing up bond prices—with the occasional peak or valley of volatility when external events create a bond-market panic or an upward spike— that has defined bond volatility from 1981 to 2014. And toward a landscape where the long-term trend in bond prices is likely to be downward, although not savagely so. Economic growth is likely to be relatively weak, and therefore, yields are likely to be low. Further, a combination of trends such as aging populations and global climate change in addition to slow growth are likely to present a constant diet of challenges to bond-issuing entities. Those challenges won't be insurmountable, but it's likely that a significant number of bond issuers won't be up to the challenge at least part of the time. And this will provide bond investors with a constant stream of volatility opportunities to exploit as bond issuers cycle between higher and lower credit ratings.

I used Kansas as my example of such a bond volatility opportunity because Kansas is more familiar to most bond investors in the United States—and in many other developed economies—than, say, Senegal or South Africa or even Mexico or Brazil. But there's no reason you should limit yourself to any one geography of volatility opportunity in global bond markets. Anywhere you've put in the time to understand the economy and the politics is a place to look for volatility opportunities in bond markets.

Bond issuers among emerging markets that I'd target as potential volatility opportunities include Mexico, where a recovery in oil prices would have a huge positive effect on government finances, and Brazil, where a recovery in commodity prices (e.g., oil, iron ore, and soy beans) and a change in government would reignite economic growth and confidence.

The comparison of the two provides a template for prioritizing debt-market volatility opportunities. The Mexican volatility opportunity is the easier to track of the two—what Mexico needs is rising oil prices, pure and simple. But Brazil's is larger: the country's credit rating has been cut to BBB- by S&P, just one notch above junk status. That puts the country's prized investment grade rating, finally achieved in 2008, at risk. Economic growth has slowed until it was barely positive in 2014. Inflation is projected to peak at 8.3 percent in 2018, way above the government's target of 4.5 percent, give or take 2 percentage points. A scandal involving government officials and bribes from Petrobras, the government-controlled oil company, is gradually working its way higher and higher toward President Dilma Rousseff. Brazil could well lose its investment-grade rating, in contrast to Mexico, where S&P calls the country's BBB rating stable. This increases the potential payoff from any turn in Brazil's credit rating, although all the chaos in Brazil makes calling the turn harder. Of course, you could do both of these volatility opportunities sequentially because chances are that Mexico will bounce, whereas Brazil is still stuck in the quagmire.

This bond market volatility opportunity strategy is appealing for one other reason: it isn't all that closely correlated with assets such as stocks. Yes, for this strategy to yield good profits it does need decent economic growth so that revenue streams at bond issuers are improving. But it doesn't need great growth or extremely loose monetary policies at central banks. I wouldn't say it is uncorrelated with stocks, but I would say that it has considerable independence.

This, of course, brings me to a good point for looking at another strategy for building portfolios during an Age of Volatility.

Chapter 22

Portfolio Construction

BEFORE I CONTINUE WITH my recommended strategies for one asset class or another, we need to take a glance back at the lessons about complex systems of volatility in my trend chapters on hoarding food and water and anticipating global climate change. The takeaways I would apply to investing strategies in this section of *Juggling with Knives* include, of course, the necessity and importance of formulating strategies for individual asset classes such as stocks and bonds that take into account altered volatility landscapes for those assets. But that alone isn't sufficient. As well as looking at the volatility landscape for each separate asset class, we also need to look at the way all these volatility landscapes fit together into a complex system of volatility and recognize that the way they fit together changes over time too. An increase in the volatility of those changes in the way the system fits together—and rapid shifts in the way those changes work to affect each other in the system—is a major characteristic of this Age of Volatility.

In thinking back to those business school courses that introduced me to the foundations of modern portfolio theory, what strikes me as oddest is how ahistorical they were. The embedded assumption was that the relationship among asset classes didn't change much from market period to market period, despite huge moves in asset prices. In seeking to identify the efficient frontier—the optimum mix of assets—to maximize the returns from a portfolio while minimizing risk, I don't remember ever asking how the relationship between asset classes might change over time. Bonds were always less volatile than stocks, always carried lower returns than stocks, and always could be added to a position in stocks to reduce a portfolio's risk. Emerging market stocks and bonds could be added to a portfolio to increase returns without blowing out the risk as long as they were added in moderation and the portfolio owner could be counted on not to panic in the face of these markets' huge swings. Relatively under-followed and under-researched assets such as timberlands could be added to a portfolio to increase returns. Further, because they weren't correlated with larger asset classes such as stocks or bonds, they could be counted on to reduce portfolio risk, as they would zig when other asset classes zagged.

In practice the folks who manage money for a living know that the formulas and abstractions they were taught in Capital Markets 101 aren't true. In fact, they spend their professional lives trying to make money from the ways in which they aren't true. They hunt to discover new under-researched asset classes and then the best managers dump them when they see that everyone else has discovered those classes. (The Yogi-ism about a restaurant sums up the situation: nobody goes there anymore—it's too crowded.)

But you don't have to be a Wall Street professional or have an MBA to know the assumption in this model of unchanging relationships among asset classes isn't true. (And just so no one accuses me of résumé padding, I don't have an MBA, though I did take MBA classes at Columbia as part of a fellowship in business journalism.) If you step back from the day-to-day news on the market, you too will recognize that over the last ten years bonds don't behave the way they once did, that emerging markets have sure kept the extra volatility but can't be counted on to beat stocks from developed economies, and that gold and commodities such as oil aren't the hedges against currency risk that they used to be.

And if you continue your step back, you may notice that the ETF phenomenon is a double-edged sword when it comes to building portfolios. On the one hand, the ability to easily trade baskets of assets makes it easy to construct a portfolio with a dash of S&P 500, a soupçon of Treasuries, a pinch of China or Brazil, and a sprinkling of emerging market debt. On the other hand, the sheer variety of offerings in the ETF world and the ease of trading them tempts the individual investor toward fine-tuning—how about adding a bit of MOO (the Market Vectors Agribusiness ETF) to overweight fertilizer (Potash of Saskatchewan), seeds (Monsanto and Syngenta), tractors (John Deere), and chicken (Tyson)? And if you like Treasuries at the moment because you think interest rates are headed down before they head up, how about an inverse ETF that shorts the Treasury market? At their best, tweaks like this can capture temporary outperformance in a specific asset class or avoid temporary underperformance in a portfolio that is otherwise constructed around more stable relationships among asset classes. At their worst, however, these kinds of tweaks grow until they aren't tweaks anymore, and then you wind up owning not a portfolio built around the relationship of asset classes but around fashions and whims.

There's nothing wrong with intelligently breaking the rules—going against the herd is, when you're right and the herd is wrong, a way to outperform the market. But to intelligently break the rules, you do have to know what the rules are.

To tweak the correlations between asset classes when you build your portfolio, you need to know what those correlations are. That's especially difficult at a time like this, when correlations among asset classes are showing the same high degree of volatility that we see in those asset classes themselves.

But just because it's hard doesn't mean we should not take a shot at figuring them out. And this is precisely what I'll try to do in this chapter. Please be aware that although this isn't akin to trying to capture lightening in a bottle, the correlations that obtained when I wrote this book are volatile and aren't going to stay the same forever. In fact, the more accurate I am that this is an Age of Volatility, the more likely that these correlations will themselves change fairly rapidly—think instead of trying to capture lightning bugs in a bottle.

I'm going to start with an examination of the volatility of the connections between individual volatilities: how the relationship between the movements of stocks and bonds, for example, changes over time and the speed of changes in those movements among asset classes either speeds up or slows down. For my examination I'm

going to focus on shares of commodity producers. Commodities'
failure to work the way they're supposed to in portfolios has been
one of the stranger and more painful examples of the volatility of
correlation in financial markets from, say, 2010 to 2015.

There are two reasons to own shares of a commodity company
such as oil producer Chevron (CVX), natural gas producer Chesapeake Energy (CHK), copper producer Freeport McMoRan (FCX),
iron ore miner Vale (VALE), or fertilizer producer Potash of Saskatchewan (POT).

First, you're hoping for commodity prices to climb and the prices
of these stocks to soar. That was certainly true during the glory days
when commodity stocks—and the shares of the companies that sup-
plied commodity producers, such as John Deere, Joy Global, and
Schlumberger—led global equity markets. And the returns from
those years—128 percent in 2009 and 70 percent in 2010 on Joy
Global, or 229 percent in 2009 and 53 percent in 2010 on Freeport
McMoRan, respectively—are indeed something to look back upon
with longing.

Second, you're looking for diversification for your portfolio. Historically we know that commodity stocks rise if inflation kicks up
because the price of a barrel of oil or a pound of copper, as a concrete thing, will climb with inflation. Historically we also know that
if the dollar sinks, the prices of a barrel of oil or a pound of copper
will rise. These commodities are priced in dollars, so a cheaper dollar
means purchasers of these things will have to use more dollars to
buy them. Commodities and commodity stocks are, therefore, historically a good hedge against a weaker dollar. Unlike some other
hedges against inflation and a weaker dollar, historically commodities and commodity stocks will rise if the economy picks up, as that
will mean more buying of oil and copper. That gives them more upside in a strong economy than does a hedge like gold, for example.

At least that's been the historical pattern.

Only not this time.

This time the vast expansion of mines and of drilling capacity,
made possible by cheap central bank money and made attractive by
projections of steadily growing demand, wound up producing inflation at commodity producers at a time when inflation in the econ-

omy as a whole was just about nonexistent. Costs at gold and iron miners and oil producers rose as they competed for skilled workers, as the price of things such as giant tires for mining trucks rose, and as services such as the lease of drilling rigs as well as seismic data collection and analysis soared. At the same time, extraction costs rose because, as ore grades fell, miners found themselves moving more rock to get at a pound of copper and as oil producers came to rely on more expensive technologies for producing oil such as fracking in tight shale geologies.

The result has been a shift not in the potential profitability of investments in shares of commodity producers. When demand catches up with supply and then, again, passes it when economic growth picks up, these will be very profitable shares to own. The trend is still—long term—toward higher commodity prices as more and more people, globally, are able to afford houses built with steel rebar and appliances with copper wiring. Instead, the volatility in that trend has increased, I believe, because commodity sectors are struggling to cope with big additions to capacity during a time of muted demand growth. But is it still a sector to include in a long-term portfolio.

What has changed is the connection of that trend and the volatility of that trend in relation to other parts of your portfolio. As hedges against inflation and dollar weakness, commodity stocks are less useful right now—and quite possibly will continue to be less useful—than they once were because of structural changes in the industries that make up the commodity sector.

The correlation between commodities and commodity stocks and the other parts of your portfolio have changed.

Why is this important?

In your attempt to build a portfolio with the best mix of risk and return, you're looking for low correlations between asset classes or an actual negative correlation. Correlations between asset classes can be calculated over time. We can know what the historical correlation is, for example, between US stocks and emerging market stocks, between global equities and gold, between bond and stocks, or between commodities and stocks or bonds or cash or whatever. Portfolio strategists have used these historical correlations—high, low, or negative—to build portfolios that, in the past, hug what's called the efficient frontier, that place where, in theory and based on historical relationships, a portfolio will get the most return for a specified degree of risk.

Unfortunately right now those historical correlations aren't very useful guides to future correlations. And some correlations show even more volatility than asset prices themselves.

For example, sticking to commodities stocks, Freeport McMoRan Copper and Gold showed a reasonably close correlation with the S&P 500 stock index between 2012 and 2014, of roughly 0.70, when a correlation of 1 would indicate that the stock moves in perfect sync with the general market index. In the last year, however, the correlation between shares of Freeport McMoran and the US S&P 500 stock index has collapsed to a -0.65. That does argue that, beginning in November 2014 and extending through the spring of 2015, holding shares of these copper and gold miners would indeed have added diversification to a portfolio of US stocks. That rapid change in the correlation of this individual stock and the S&P 500 index as a whole is an example of the very rapid shift in the correlation of assets typical of the current volatile market. The disappointing thing about this drop in correlation, however, is that although it shows that the performance of this stock does deviate from the index, it also shows that the deviation in early 2015 was all to the downside—Freeport McMoRan falls harder than the index. That's not very useful because nobody tries to add losses greater than those of the index to their portfolio. Without a comparable upside deviation, this commodity stock doesn't look like a promising correlation-building block for a portfolio.

Natural gas producer Chesapeake Energy, however, shows a promisingly different pattern. The stock has roughly the same correlation with the S&P 500 in general—at 0.78—from 2012 to 2014, as Freeport McMoRan Copper and Gold. But in analyzing the moments when the stock showed a big drop in correlation with the index—in November 2014, for example, when the correlation turned to a -0.50—the performance of this stock has a huge degree of independence from the index. The November 2014 drop in correlation, for example, is a result of shares of Chesapeake Energy climbing in price just after a drop in price in the S&P 500. This independence is what you might expect because Chesapeake's share price responds to the price of natural gas rather than interest rates or economic growth. If you are looking for an asset with upside and enough correlation independence to add diversification to a portfolio, then Chesapeake Energy is certainly a better place to start than Freeport McMoRan Copper and Gold, even though both stocks belong to the commodity sector. (By the way, you can see correlation graphed as an indicator on charts at StockCharts.com.)

Most institutional investors and money managers don't look for correlations one stock at a time. I happen to follow Chesapeake Energy and natural gas prices very closely because the shares have been a member of my online Jubak's Picks portfolio for a number of years. (It's also one of my favorite trading positions because natural gas prices show a very strong seasonal pattern that provides very strong markers on when to trade.)

Most correlation, as used in building portfolios, makes use of asset classes—such as S&P 500 stocks—for entire sectors. The preferred vehicle here is a basket of stocks, either built by hand by a portfolio manager in the good ol' days or, now, represented by an ETF that follows a sector index. For example, Market Vectors Gold Miners ETF (GDX), which holds Goldcorp, Barrick Gold, Newmont Mining, Randgold, and pretty much everything else in the gold mining sector in positions weighted by market capitalization, provides a portfolio with a one-stop diversification. For most of 2012 through 2014 the Gold Miners ETF showed a correlation to the S&P 500 of -0.50. Unfortunately, for most of this period the Gold Miners ETF also woefully underperformed the S&P 500, falling -54.02 percent in 2013 and -12.42 percent in 2014, versus a 32.31 percent gain for the S&P 500 ETF in 2013 and a 13.46 percent gain in 2014. In other words, as in the case of Freeport McMoRan Copper and Gold, by owning Gold Miners ETF, you would indeed have added diversification to your portfolio but at the cost of a big hit to performance.

Not exactly what we're hoping for.

And this leaves you with two choices in terms of using correlations to add diversification and at least the potential for decent returns to a portfolio.

First, you could watch the Market Vectors Gold Miners ETF and look for a period when this low or negative correlation asset starts to show better performance. That possibility emerged for this ETF in early 2015, when the Gold Miners ETF gained 6.53 percent for the year through May 31, versus a 3.18 percent gain for the S&P 500 ETF. (That also pushed the correlation between these two assets to a positive 0.78 in early 2015. Although it remains to be seen if this asset can deliver higher returns and a lower correlation to the market index, it was an intriguing development.)

Second, you could look for an asset class with a low or negative correlation to the market index but with a relatively long-term record of outgaining the S&P 500. In a financial market where cash flows from global central banks still dominate market trends and frequently overwhelm trends in individual asset classes, this isn't exactly easy. Adding diversification to a portfolio by buying an asset class that loses money while the rest of your portfolio gains isn't exactly the ideal solution in any market. But it's an especially bad idea in a volatile market, where assets can fall into and out of favor so quickly and so hard. For example, while SPDR Gold Shares (GLD), an ETF pegged to gold bullion rather than to shares of gold miners, is a great diversification pick on the basis of its negative 0.11 correlation with the S&P 500, it's a terrible portfolio addition because it is so out of favor with the financial market in general. Over the twelve months ending on June 12, 2015, the S&P 500 gained 10.6 percent; GLD, however, fell 7.67 percent.

Yep, you got diversification—and a sizeable loss.

But if you were willing to roll your own by picking individual stocks to represent an asset class rather than using ETF market baskets, you could have found some promising low-correlation assets to use in constructing your portfolio. For example, although the US Natural Gas Fund ETF (UNG) showed a correlation with the S&P 500 that was generally in negative territory from 2012 to 2014, the fund also showed a horrific loss of 28.61 percent in 2014. Conversely, an individual natural gas stock, Cheniere Energy (LNG), an exporter of liquefied natural gas that is set to make its first exports in 2016, showed a correlation to the S&P 500 in 2014 concentrated in the range from 0.5 to 0 but with a gain of 63.27 percent in 2014.

I won't kid you: finding a diversification/high-gain combination isn't easy. But it sure is worth looking for them.

One other place I would look for the elusive combination of low correlation and solid returns includes agricultural commodities, a sector facing constraints that make adding new capacity difficult. China, to take an example, may want to create a domestic dairy industry, but given the limits on the supply of water and land, that effort is likely to be as ultimately quixotic as are the Saudi efforts to create a domestic wheat industry. Possible portfolio candidates for diversification in this sector include nonpotash fertilizer makers such as Yara International (YARIY), which move with the price of core raw material natural gas more than with the S&P 500 as a whole, and protein producers such as Mexico's chicken and beef processor Industrias Bachoco (IBA). (Both companies trade as ADRs in New York. In 2015 through June 15 the two ADRs were up 10.95 percent and 12.32 percent, respectively, against a 2.21 percent gain for the S&P 500 in that period.)

In an Age of Volatility it has definitely become harder to find asset classes that do the job you want in building a diversified portfolio. If your idea of owning uncorrelated asset classes was to own vacation real estate in Florida and emerging market stocks in 2008, then you quickly discovered, to your intense pain, that the flood of cheap cash that had pushed up asset prices in both classes had now given way to a panic in both asset classes.

And that has driven some investors ever farther afield into what are called "alternative" investments. It's a huge, catch-all term that's far less rigorous than the late Supreme Court Justice Potter Stewart's 1964 definition of pornography: "I know it when I see it." At least Stewart thought he'd know it when he saw it—the problem with defining alternatives is that what is alternative at one moment may be absolutely mainstream the next. Although pornography is a term subject to certain rough kinds of empirical testing, "alternative" investing isn't. Nothing makes that clearer than the brief history of the "alternative" investments that drove the Yale University endowment to a gain of more than 100 percent in a decade that included the dot-com and the subprime mortgage booms and busts and the global financial crisis.

The best place to start working toward a definition of alternative investing is to see where the Yale portfolio wasn't. In 2012 only 6 percent of the Yale portfolio was invested in US equities, according to Bob Rice's 2013 book *The Alternative Answer*. The rest—the overwhelming majority—was in real assets such as timberland, in "risky" emerging markets, and in hedge funds and other vehicles pursuing strategies that were far from any index.

If all these different assets and strategies had one thing in common, it's that they managed money as if the efficient market theory—you know, markets are rational and prices accurately express all information—was absolutely, 100 percent, iron-clad true . . . except in the part of the market universe where these money managers operated. In these inefficient parts of the market it was possible, these managers maintained, to deliver outsized returns that weren't correlated to the larger markets because information was difficult to obtain and analyze, because the number of real experts was so limited that it was possible to "corner" knowledge, because the general market relied on outdated or inexact tools, because buying and selling an asset in this market was difficult and subject to significant lags, because the general market and the average investor was subject to extensive prejudices, because . . .

In other words, these alternatives were everything mocked in the joke about two rational-expectations economists walking down the street and passing a $50 bill lying on the sidewalk without picking it up. After all, if that really were a $50 bill, someone else would have already picked it up. Managers and investors in alternative strategies pick up that $50. Over and over again. For as long as the supply of $50 bills lasts.

For example, the Yale portfolio and its peers following alternative strategies invested an unconventional amount in timberland. Wood. Trees. That stuff. Partly that was a call on economic growth—more growth means more houses means more demand for lumber. Partly it was a call on a booming real estate market that was hungry for the land adjacent to developed areas that many forest owners were sitting on.

And partly—crucially for the success of this strategy as an alternative—it was a call on an underfollowed, underresearched, inefficient piece of the market. Timber companies themselves were only gradually waking up to the value of some of the land they held. What was known as higher-better-use land, land that, because of its location, could be sold off to developers or used to form the core of a timber company's own new real estate development business, was a whole lot more valuable than the average acre growing yellow pine. Early analysts faced skeptical audiences who were uncomfortable with research that divided the holdings of timber companies such as Weyerhaeuser, Plum Creek, St. Joe, or Rayonier into standard timberland good for producing timber and higher-better-use land that could be turned into houses, commercial business parks, and entire planned developments. One reason for the skepticism was that the results of this analysis were so outlandish. Cranking the numbers often yielded investment recommendations that calculated that a company's higher-better-use land was worth so much that an investor got the rest of the company—and its timber land and trees—for free.

And if analyzing big public companies that did get some attention from Wall Street pointed to overlooked opportunities, digging deeper into the sector but looking at smaller public companies, relatively large but still private companies, and small family-owned companies showed even more $50 bills—and sometimes $100 bills—lying on the sidewalk.

Timberland worked spectacularly well for these portfolios—until it didn't.

For a number of reasons.

Timberland might have been only loosely correlated with, say, the trend in IBM or the NASDAQ technology market or even US stocks in general, but it was closely correlated with the real estate market. When the subprime mortgage crisis took down real estate prices and then when the global financial crisis took down real estate prices some more, timberland prices fell too. Ironically the timber stocks that did best during that real estate downturn were those such as Rayonier, which had thriving non–real estate businesses producing, in Rayonier's case, cellulose fiber for things like cigarette filters.

Just as important—and more important for any understanding of how to invest in or define "alternatives"—the more analysts followed the sector, the more consultants beat the woods and then pitched to endowment funds, the more endowment and pension funds put money into the asset, the less alternative it become. The supply of $50s lying on the sidewalk didn't go down, but there were definitely more people looking for a chance to scoop one up. And that meant your chance of scooping one up went down. And so did the returns from this alternative investment.

From this let me suggest a few rules of thumb for finding alternatives with the biggest chance of yielding a steady supply of neglected $50s.

First, be at least slightly early—and be right, of course. By the time the consultants are hanging out their shingles, the best returns are gone.

Second, neglected markets are good. Hated markets are better. The biggest profits come from trades in assets that no one wants.

Third, structural "problems" in a market that make it difficult to collect information are great, but structural problems that make it difficult to buy the asset are even better. One reason timberland worked so well is that transferring title, for example, to put together a big enough collection of assets to make buying and selling attractive is time-consuming and requires specialized skills.

This last point is the reason behind two of my favorite alternative investments right now.

The first is farmland. The supply is limited, obviously, and need for more in the future is clear. But beyond that, it's still early. We're just starting to get private investment trusts, such as the American Farmland Co., which are buying up US farmland. Farmland Partners (FPI) and the Gladstone Land (LAND) have just listed. But we're still talking about relatively small portfolios considering the size of the market. American Farmland owns 131 farms and eleven thousand acres. Farmland appreciated by 8.4 percent in the twelve months to June 2014 and 4.7 percent annually since 1990, according to the farmland index compiled by the National Council of Real Estate Investment Fiduciaries. Adding in the income produced by crops raised on the farmland brings the total average annual return to 11.9 percent a year since 1990.

It's even easier outside the United States, where the structural barriers in the market are even higher. For example, Cesky Fond Pudy, the first investment company targeting Czech farmland, among the cheapest in Europe, has just started raising money for a second fund. (Potential returns at Cesky Fond and other farmland funds in the Czech Republic are pegged at 6 to 8 percent annually.) Besides the obvious geopolitical worries to the East, structural problems include a highly fragmented ownership structure leftover after state ownership ended, making putting together efficient farms a long struggle.

In Asia HAGL JSC, a Vietnamese real estate developer, is in the midst of transforming itself into Vietnam's biggest listed farmer by acreage. Most of the company's revenue still comes from real estate and plantation crops such as rubber (74 percent of revenue from these two sources in 2012), but the company is adding corn acreage. In 2015 the company's commodity harvest included corn in Cambodia and Laos, plus sugar cane, palm oil, and rubber from its overseas plantations. The company is now listed in London as well as in Vietnam.

Climate change is likely to make the farmland cycle longer and less certain. There are investment companies now at work trying to identify those marginal agricultural regions that will be less marginal when temperatures climb. Although it's too early to sink my kids' college funds into that one, it's still very interesting.

My second favorite is non-Chinese and especially Indian e-commerce companies. Here the barriers to purchase are very different but just as important. Many of these companies are still private and at the venture capital stage. Even when they're public, they'll trade on the relatively difficult-to-access (for non-Indian investors) Mumbai stock exchange. So far the only way I've found to get around this problem—and remember that the problem creates the opportunity—is to buy shares of Japan's Softbank (SFTBY). Softbank was an early investor in China's Alibaba, where a $20 million investment in 2000 resulted in a 32 percent ownership stake in the Chinese Internet giant now worth some $65 billion. Since then Softbank has announced plans to put $10 billion into India's Internet and e-commerce sector. It owns stakes in India's and Indonesia's big-gest e-commerce companies, Snapdeal.com and Tokopedia, in addi-tion to pieces of companies in advertising, media, gaming, and real estate. It's hard for individual investors to get in on venture capital stage companies anywhere, but to find a basket that gives you expo-sure to Asia's next generation?

With these suggestions for finding profitable assets for portfolio diversification, I'm going to leave correlation behind. My next chap-ter is a return to the simpler world of stocks for the long side of your portfolio.

Chapter 23

A Not-So-Random Walk on the Long Side for Stocks

SELLING SHORT AND OTHER hedging strategies aren't worth pursuing if you don't have a portfolio worth protecting.

In fact, the point of diversifying a portfolio and adding asset classes that zig enough to give you some overall downside protection is so that you can invest in asset classes that zag so that you make bigger profits on the upside without adding a disproportionate amount of risk.

And when we're talking about assets that profit to the upside in most portfolios, we're talking about stocks. They're easy to trade, they seem to have an easily understood relationship to economic growth, and they're familiar. The historical record even says that stocks are a good choice for the core long position in a portfolio.

And from the volatility perspective of *Juggling with Knives*, in an Age of Volatility stocks are an especially good match for trends that develop over long periods of time.

This, in fact, is a good time to remind you that when we talk about volatility, we're not just talking about big, rapid moves to the downside. Volatility includes at least the possibility of big, rapid moves in the other direction, toward the profitable upside. Those big upward moves have, in fact, been key to setting up those big downward moves. If not, for example, for the 95 percent boom in

NASDAQ shares in general and technology shares in particular in 1999, the bust in 2000 would not have been nearly so painful.

Making money on the upside in a period of high volatility isn't nearly as easy as it may sound. The point of volatility—at those moments when the market does indeed seem to be out to get you—is to shake you out of the long positions that you should be holding for their upside potential before you have a chance to realize that potential. The gods of volatility are even happier if they can shake you out of those positions and then entice you into building them again—over and over again in a churning pattern of buying high and selling low.

This effect of a high-volatility market has been demonstrated in academic research that shows that the average investor in a mutual fund underperforms the fund itself because that investor tends to put money in near the top of markets, when enthusiasm for markets runs high, and to take money out near the bottom of markets, when fear is at its height. The result of that is, of course, a kind of perverse, reverse-dollar cost averaging in which investors buy more shares when they're expensive and fewer shares when they're less expensive.

How do you reverse that so that an investor will be able to look past current volatility and the greed-chasing/fear-avoiding emotions to a strategy that will use the volatility in the market to repeatedly buy low and sell high in the long portion of your portfolio? The key, I believe, is to rope the stocks in your portfolio, the long part of most portfolios, to trends that you're convinced have considerable longevity. That way you're more likely to keep your eye on the far horizon when fear is climbing. You know that you want to own these trends for the long haul and that this minimizes your tendency to sell on a temporary upsurge of fear. What trends will do that for your long portfolio—and your sanity? Well, that's the subject of this chapter.

My strategy for building the core long part of your portfolio has three parts. First, you should use a hedging strategy like the one outlined in the first half of my last chapter on going short on US Treasuries to reduce your worst fears about Big Volatility. Although a shorting strategy won't eliminate the damage that a true bear market in stocks will do to the long portion of your portfolio, it should put enough distance between the worst of a bear market and your portfolio returns so that you can think clearly. It's quite remarkable how knowing that you did something that's working to some degree to avoid the worst damage to your portfolio can keep you from panic in a bear. Call it Investing Schadenfreude 101: being down only 15 percent when the world is down 25 percent can be remarkably reassuring and empowering. Your goal from this part of your strategy is to preserve your ability to think clearly enough to identify opportunities and act on them.

Second, you want to use the volatility themes in Part II of this book to identify stocks that have strong long-term trends at their backs. Such trends won't prevent these stocks from going down in strong, market-wide downdrafts during a bear market, nor will they remove short-term volatility. But the fact that these stocks are backed by strong, long-term trends that you've identified and understand means that you recognize these stocks as targets of opportunity in a sell-off. These are exactly the stocks you want to buy low—and sell high—over and over again. Volatility here is your friend—or at least that's the goal.

And third, you want to use the valuations of those core stocks as indicators—much in the way that I suggested using dividend yields as indicators (pages 85–90) for adding exposure to more volatile stocks that will give you more leverage from these themes when the likely direction is upward and will also let you lighten up your exposure to these trends when the direction is downward.

Let me show you what I mean by using the trend (pages 248–254) for the growing demand for—and the shrinking supply of—water.

Water is notorious among sector and trend investors for being frustratingly hard to invest in. Water utilities are a possibility, but as regulated utilities, the return from these stocks on the water supply/demand trend is limited. You can buy water "makers" and distributors such as Nestlé or Coca-Cola, but although water is a growing part of these large food companies, it is only one part of a diversified business. For example, even though Nestlé's water portfolio of fifteen brands includes such global names as Perrier, Poland Spring, and Pellegrino, water sales made up just 7.8 percent of the company's global revenue in 2013.

No, if you want to build a core position that is long on rising water demand and prices, with the additional potential of riding the water regional shortages likely to result from global climate change, then you've got to go with water infrastructure companies.

Why? Well, partly because I'm extremely cynical about how global governments are going to respond to falling supply and rising demand over the next few decades. We could institute water conservation measures, address leaky local infrastructure, reduce the waste in the way we irrigate, and re-engineer industrial processes to use less water and produce less pollution. All those are cost effective and would go a long way toward addressing the problem. And eventually those solutions will need to be a big part of the mix.

In the nearer term—say the next twenty years—though, all the evidence suggests that the world is going in a very different direction. To many experts that direction is, well, stupid. But that doesn't mean we aren't headed that way. This won't be the first time in economic history that a stupid set of decisions won out for a considerable length of time.

I've already sketched in one big example of this direction in water supply-and-demand economics—China's South to North Water Diversion Project. At $62 billion—and counting—the project's goal is to build a system of long canals and pipelines, giant aqueducts, and massive pumping stations to move more water than is in the River Thames every year from China's relatively water-rich south to its parched north. At twenty-seven hundred miles, it is the world's longest and largest water-transfer project. The fact that it's also likely to be an environmental and public health disaster is, so far, beside the point.

Lest, however, any investor looking at this project thinks it's a uniquely Chinese form of lunacy, I draw your attention to the latest plans by the Indian government for its own version. The National River Linking Project (the South Asian Water Grid, to its friends), would send water from the north and east of India, where rivers such as the Indus are fed by (shrinking) Himalayan snowfields through a network of over ninety-three hundred miles of canals and reservoirs to the drier south and west at a cost of $168 billion (assuming no cost overruns, and there are always cost overruns in India) over twenty-five years. The goals are stunningly ambitious: expand arable land by one-third, add thirty-four gigawatts to India's hydroelectric capacity (the equivalent of twenty nuclear plants), and mitigate the country's horrendous seasonal floods. India currently supports 17 percent of the world's population on 4 percent of the world's water, so it is certainly necessary to do something. I would question, however, whether this something is the best solution to the problem or, rather, a political calculation by the new government of Narendra Modi, who wants to be seen as doing what the defeated, dithering, doddering Congress government couldn't or wouldn't do. (One advisory committee to Manmohan Singh, the leader of that Congress government, called the project "against the forces of nature.")

These Chinese and Indian projects are immensely ambitious and would require massive commitments of capital, labor, and engineering. And, looking at them, you might think there has to be a simpler way to achieve these goals. But one of the reasons these projects are moving ahead as the first response to these countries' massive water needs is that, looked at in a context that includes all factors—especially the political realities—these are the easy solutions.

That should be apparent from a US experience that includes the draining of the Owens Valley in the Sierras to feed Los Angeles's water appetite. (For a brilliant introduction to US water politics, download *Chinatown*, Roman Polanski's deeply cynical and remarkably realistic film about this bit of California water history with one of my favorite Jack Nicholson performances.) That includes the bitterly fought but ultimately losing battle against flooding Glen Canyon to feed the water appetite of Arizona and the other states in the Colorado River Compact. Or the many versions of the plan to ship water from Northern California to Southern California or the Central Arizona project or . . .

Well, you get the idea.

From a long-term perspective, looking at either capital costs and returns or environmental pluses and minuses, these projects don't pass muster. There are cheaper and more effective ways to accomplish these goals. A project, as the Central Arizona Project does, that results in growing alfalfa in the desert and then sends the water in that forage to Asia either in the form of alfalfa or milk or meat, doesn't make dollars-and-cents sense. Much better, in capital accounting terms, is to raise water prices or cut water allotments so that alfalfa farming is curtailed in the desert and shifted to a wetter part of the country or world.

But if you look at the political accounting, it's clear why these projects got built, why China's South to North Water Diversion Project will get built, and why India's massive proposed diversion stands a good chance of being built. The political pluses are immense—votes and money from cotton growers, dairy farmers, water-intensive industries, suburban and urban populations, and governments all argue for building these projects. The minuses include opposition from relatively marginal and politically less powerful groups such as rural communities facing flooding, small-scale farmers who stand to see their water supplies shipped elsewhere, environmentalists who argue positions based on the beauty of Glen Canyon or the potential for the spread of disease, or conservationists and fiscal conservatives who point out the waste of dollars and the existence of more efficient alternatives. The fight is hardly fair. All the money and most of the votes are on the side of "Let's build." (Close to forty years ago I was involved in a fight to stop a dam project in Washington County in Southwest Virginia. One day I asked a particularly honest and totally disdainful utility company official why the company had decided to put the dam there. "Hell," he told me, "these folks can't even get their county board of supervisors to listen to them." They didn't stand a chance of stopping this dam, he just about chortled. He turned out to be wrong in that case, but most of the time that logic is absolutely correct.)

Add in a second factor—the all-too-human propensity to send good money after bad—and I think you'll have a strong sense of the direction of the trend in global water supply and demand over the next twenty years or so. At least enough so that you can see why this is a place to put a good chunk of your portfolio that's devoted to long-term and low-risk growth.

Generals are told to never reinforce failure. It may be extremely difficult not to try to rescue troops in an untenable position by sending in more troops, but military history says it's almost never a good idea. Portfolio managers and company CEOs are told to forget about sunk costs when making a decision about where to allocate new money. Putting new cash into a failing venture because you have already invested so much in the effort doesn't pay off.

But that is exactly what we will do over the next twenty years with our investment in global water supply and demand.

No one is going to be willing to write off Perth or San Diego just because they happen to be built in near-deserts without the ability to beg, borrow, or steal enough water to support their growth or to support their current population if—as looks likely—climate change deals them a losing hand in future rainfall.

Nor do I expect China to write off its silicon-based manufacturing industries just because they happen to be incredibly water hungry and located in parts of the country with dwindling supplies of water clean enough for industrial purposes. Nor will India, Saudi Arabia, or China write off their investments in wheat farming.

At some point I expect that rising costs, changing patterns of rainfall, population growth, and water pollution from farms, industries, and cities will make it clear that some—if not most—of these projects aren't sustainable. And then we'll enter a new stage, as we have in the United States, with conversations about undoing and abandoning some of these efforts and finding other, politically more difficult but economically and environmentally more sustainable ways to approach global water needs. After all, in the United States we're now starting to talk about unflooding Glen Canyon because the great dam projects that created Lake Mead and Lake Powell are facing the realities of falling water supplies.

But that reimagining of solutions, that turn in the cycle, is a good twenty years or more away in much of the world. And in the meantime we'll go on building dams, digging canals, pumping billions of acre feet of water, constructing desalination plants along with the power plants to provide the energy needed to create usable water for San Diego and Perth and, most of all, the Middle East.

In other words, here you've got a long twenty-year trend that you can count on to provide long-term growth for your portfolio. Stocks that represent this trend include General Electric (GE), Xylem (XYL), and Keppel (KEPLY in New York or KEP in Singapore) in water desalination and pollution reduction; Flowserve (FLS) in water pumps and fluid controls; and Chicago Bridge and Iron (CBI) and Fluor (FLR) in engineering and construction.

The most volatile part of this group are the shares of engineering and construction companies because the market sees their backlog of projects as subject to the rising and falling economies of developing countries in the Middle East, Asia, and Africa.

So a volatility portfolio built around this theme might consist of, one, a core position in General Electric, Keppel, Xylem, and Flowserve, where you pursue a volatility version of a dollar-cost-averaging strategy in which you buy more shares of these core stocks over the long term whenever a plunge in the market makes them temporarily cheaper, and, two, a trading position in the more volatile engineering and construction "edge" stocks, where you buy shares on a market plunge and then sell them when the market looks fully or overvalued, with the understanding that you will play this cycle again (and again and again—wash, rinse, spin, repeat) on the next plunge and boom.

To implement the third part of my strategy, I suggested using the core stocks in any trend portfolio as indicators for buying and selling either more of the core stocks or for trading in and out of the more volatile "edge" stocks. One way to construct this indicator is to use the Bollinger Bands indicator on a technical chart to indicate when a core stock is overbought or oversold. Bollinger Bands, invented by John Bollinger, create a constantly updated channel that uses average measures of volatility (standard deviation) to indicate when a stock, based on recent history, is over- or undervalued. Or you can track historical high and low price-to-earnings multiples on core stocks to tell you when to add or subtract from these positions or when to sell or rebuy completely.

There are additional themes from Part II that are also good candidates for this kind of core and volatility strategy. Food, for example, might see you building a core that consists of New Zealand

dairy producer Fonterra (FSF.AU in Sydney), Mexican and Brazilian chicken producers Industrias Bachoco (IBA) and BRF (BRFS),
Norwegian natural-gas-based fertilizer maker Yara International
(YARIY), and French dairy products company DANONE (DANOY
in New York) with volatility positions in potash fertilizer–mining
stocks such as Potash of Saskatchewan (POT) and Mosaic (MOS).

Energy infrastructure would not include the producers of oil and
natural gas, where costs, commodity prices, and accessibility are
moving against many of the international majors; it includes the
companies that are making it possible to find and extract unconventional sources of oil and gas as well as the companies that are building the new pipelines, storage terminals, and processing facilities
needed as unconventional sources of production disrupt traditional
systems of transportation and distribution. A core portfolio might
contain oil and gas technology company Schlumberger (SLB), rail
tank-car maker Greenbrier (GBX), advanced pipe maker Tenaris
(TS), and oil and gas producer and natural gas transportation company Statoil (STO). Volatility positions might include shares of liquefied natural gas exporter Cheniere Energy (LNG), US natural gas
producer Chesapeake Energy (CHK), and global energy infrastructure ETF Macquarie Infrastructure (MIC).

Other trends such as education are still developing. Although the
education trend itself is promising, the investible names are still
very thin on the ground. Beyond Brazil's Kroton Educacional
(KROT.BZ in São Paulo) and Korea's Megastudy (072870.KS in
Seoul), I don't have stocks to recommend.

Other trends that might seem like good candidates for this strategy aren't as suitable as they may seem. Health care spending is indeed going up in an aging world, but so are efforts to cut the costs
of providing care to an aging population. This means there will be
battles over payments for expensive new drugs and efforts to cut
reimbursement schedules for chronic diseases such as diabetes. It's
clear to me that although spending on health care will continue to
climb, it's by no means certain that profitability in the sector will
continue to grow. In general, though, drug stocks for the diseases of
old age, such as diabetes specialist Novo Nordisk (NOV), are a better bet because they're less exposed to this effort to control costs

than are service providers such as dialysis center operator DaVita Healthcare Partners (DVA). And you might look at the recent acquisition of Omnicare by CVS Health (CVS) that has created a powerhouse of pharmacy benefit management for eldercare institutions.

Implementing this strategy is more difficult than executing the dividend strategy with which I started this section. It also presents more exposure to volatility but with, I believe, a higher return that outweighs the added risk.

The next chapter will present a short-term complement—options—to this long-term strategy for an Age of Volatility. Then I'll move on to a strategy with even more exposure to volatility, with an even higher risk/reward ratio, I believe. Adding exposure to emerging markets and developing economies using the strategy I suggest will fill out the long, riskier growth portion of your portfolio. After that, I'll end this section with a final chapter with some concluding thoughts about strategies for reducing risk in volatile markets.

Chapter 24

The Option of Options

NO BOOK ON VOLATILITY would be complete without at least one chapter on options.

But before going into why that is so, let me answer a few questions about options themselves—beginning with what they are.

Options are a form of what's called a derivative because their value and their price movement up or down is derived from the value and pricing of an underlying asset. An option on ExxonMobil, for example, is based on shares of that oil company.

At its simplest, owning an option gives you the right to sell (called a put option) or buy (called a call option) a specific quantity of a specific stock (e.g., ExxonMobil) at a specific price (called the strike price) in a specific time period. After that time period is over, the option, if it hasn't been exercised, expires worthless.

You buy a put option if you think the price of the underlying asset will fall relative to the strike price. For example, on July 3, 2015, when shares of ExxonMobil closed at $83.14, you could have bought a put option on ExxonMobil that would give you the right to sell a hundred shares of ExxonMobil until July 10 for $82.50 a share. That put on a hundred shares would have cost you $120 on July 3. If shares of ExxonMobil were to fall to $77.50, $5 a share below your strike price, you'd have the right to sell those shares at $82.50 to the trader or institution that wrote the put option you own. That would give you a profit of $5 times a hundred shares, or $500. The put option itself on a hundred shares would have cost you

$120 on July 3. So your profit on that $120 purchase would come to $500 minus $120, or $380. Not a bad return on that $120 purchase.

Now, of course, the odds of shares of ExxonMobil falling to $77.50 a share from $83.14 at the time of your July 3 purchase of these puts to their expiration on July 10 are pretty small. Which is why the options themselves were so cheap on July 3. If you get to July 10 and ExxonMobil is still trading above $82.50, the options would expire, worthless, and you'd lose your entire $120 purchase price.

A call option, on the other hand, gives the owner the right to buy a stock at a specific price at a specific date. A call is a bet that the price of the underlying stock will go up. For example, on July 3, when the stock had closed at $83.14, you could have bought a call option on ExxonMobil with a right to buy, for $390, a hundred shares at $87 by July 3. If the stock hit $92 by July 3, you would be able to buy those hundred shares at $87 and then sell them in the market at $92 for a profit of $5 a share, or $500. Subtract your $390 cost for the call options, and your profit on that $5 move would have come to $110 on a $390 investment, or 28 percent. This is nowhere near the 316 percent you might have made on a call if ExxonMobil dropped to $77.50 but still a very good return for a less-than-two-week investment.

Of course, if ExxonMobil shares didn't climb over $87, your call option would have expired worthless, and you would have lost all of your $390 purchase price. Now, let me explain why options are important and useful in an Age of Volatility.

If you decide to attempt to profit from or hedge against short-term volatility, options offer unmatched leverage. Nothing but options gives the individual investor—you know, someone who isn't George Soros and can't borrow billions to leverage a bet against the pound or for US Treasuries—a tool to multiply an overnight 0.25 percent move in the dollar into a 2.5 percent gain.

And options illustrate three of my most important observations about volatility.

First, volatility comes in different time spans. Most of *Juggling with Knives* has been about long-term trends and the volatility that goes along with those trends as well as the strategies you can use to profit from or hedge against that long-term volatility. But long-term volatility is only one kind of volatility.

In fact, the long-term trends that produce long-term volatility are accompanied by big surges in instances of short-term volatility. Because long-term volatility produces change that operates in fits and starts as it moves toward a new equilibrium, accelerated long-term volatility results in an increased frequency of bouts of short-term volatility.

Second, you should match the duration of the volatility strategies you use to the likely duration of the volatility trend itself. When you're looking at a volatility trend that is unwinding over a course of multiple years and possibly over the course of a decade or two, you should look for investment vehicles with matching effective lifetimes. If you're waiting for the withdrawal of cheap central bank cash to play out or looking to profit from trends in water or food, you'd like to use a vehicle for your strategy that doesn't expire in months, doesn't charge a set of fees every time it renews, and doesn't present you with a new mixture of price/reward every month or two. This is why, for playing long-term volatility trends, I like strategies that use stocks and bonds. Those asset classes have long lifetimes that match the duration of the volatility trends that you're trying to profit from or hedge against.

But not all volatility operates on those kinds of time scales. As I noted in example after example in these pages, the current financial market is also the home to short-term and sometimes very violent moves up or down that take place over the course of weeks or months. Strategies that rely on changes in the price of these long-maturity assets don't have the leverage to make short-term volatility pay. But options do.

And third, options illustrate my observation that although you can certainly profit from volatility by accurately predicting the end point of a trend—such as that oil will be $87 a barrel in December 2016—you can equally profit from calling the rise or fall in volatility and betting on effects of that volatility trend on asset prices itself. You don't need to be able to predict the date when the euro and the dollar will reach parity for the first time since 2002 to make a profit on the volatility trend; you can also profit from volatility itself as asset prices fluctuate on expectations, fears, and anticipation of the trend. You can make those profits from the short-term fluctuation in the prices of assets themselves or from the movement in the prices of options leveraged to those changes in asset prices.

The examples above assume that the buyer of the put or call actually exercises the option by buying or selling shares of Exxon-Mobil on the July 10 expiration date. Most explanations of how options work stress that assumption.

But, according to the Chicago Board Options Exchange (CBOE), in real-world markets only about 10 percent of options are actually exercised. Another 30 percent expire worthless.

And 60 percent are traded out before their expiration date.

It's this group that is, from a volatility perspective, most interesting because it is an illustration of how you can profit from shifting expectations on volatility without having to predict the projected end point of that volatility correctly.

Let's take a look at the action around the June 17, 2015, meeting of the Federal Reserve's Open Market Committee, the body at the Fed that sets interest rates. As the meeting approached, speculation among traders soared: Would the Federal Reserve raise interest rates for the first time since 2006? Would the short-term interest rates that the Fed controls finally climb from 0 percent, where they've been stuck since 2008? Would the Fed, looking at uncertainties in the US and global economies, decide to put off any increase until its December meeting or even until 2016?

From the perspective of the long-term volatility trends that I've written about in much of *Juggling with Knives*, this move by the Fed would be just the first step—of many—to unwind the cheap-money policies of the Federal Reserve and other global central banks. In these pages I've given you strategies for profiting from that long-term trend—you might have built a short position in US Treasuries or bet against an index of corporate or emerging market bonds.

Over the long term that's likely to pay off handsomely, just as a bet purchased in 1981 or 1982 on falling interest rates and rising bond prices would have.

But that's the long term. The long-term trend is actually going to be composed of lots of short-term volatility events like the June 2015 meeting of the Federal Reserve. Or the September 2015 meeting of the Fed. Or the December meeting. Or the January 2016 meeting. At each one of these meetings traders will bet on whether the Fed will act at that particular meeting and how the financial markets will then react.

You could see that short-term speculation at work as we drew nearer and nearer to the June 17 meeting of the Fed. Option volumes on the VIX, the Chicago Board Options Exchange Volatility Index (also known as the fear index), started to rise as June 17 approached. (Yes, there are options on the VIX, the S&P 500 stock index, and on the Bloomberg Commodities Index.)

If the Fed unexpectedly raised interest rates, fear and the VIX would climb. In fact, the VIX would start to climb even before the date, as some traders started to worry that the Fed just might raise interest rates.

Betting on a rise in the VIX, on market fear, would be a good way to capture the short-term volatility in the markets.

So how did options on the VIX move as the markets approached the June 17 meeting?

The VIX climbed 7.2 percent on Friday to 13.78. Five of the ten most owned VIX contracts were call options, according to Bloomberg. Remember that a call is an option that pays off if the underlying asset (in this case, the VIX) climbs in price. The highest strike price in that group was at 23 for an option expiring on June 17. Those were very strong bets on a big jump in the VIX because those options would only pay off if the VIX climbs above that level. (A call option gives the holder the right to buy the index at the strike price. So if the VIX were to climb to 28, say, an option to buy at 23 would turn a very nice profit.) The VIX climbs as fear of market volatility increases, so these traders were betting that the market would get very, very worried and volatile in the days leading up to the Fed meeting.

But the VIX actually stalled well short of 23 and the level that would have moved these options into the money. The VIX hit 15.39 on June 15 before retreating to 13.19 on June 18 and then moving up a bit to 13.96 on June 19. If you had bought those call options on the VIX in the hope of seeing the index climb to 23 or higher and then held until the expiration date, you would have lost money when they expired, worthless.

Bad trade, no?

It depends. If you didn't hold until expiration but instead traded out during the rise in volatility, the gain or loss on the trade would have depended on what you paid for the option and what strike price you'd picked—if you paid little enough and picked a strike price offering protection that looked attractive as the VIX moved up to 13.78 from 12.85 in a single day. After all, if the upward trend in the VIX was strong enough, it would certainly suggest that the VIX could climb farther, maybe all the way to 28 by the time the option expired.

And, of course, if you paid a premium of just $80 or so for that call option with a strike of $25, you would only have to see a move in the VIX from $12.85 to $13.65 to put your call in the money. You could sell at a profit with the VIX at 15 or 16, as the market began to worry that volatility was moving higher.

I like a short-term volatility trade like this using options off a very solid long-term trend because you can repeat it over and over again without the need to learn new tricks each time while also gradually learning more about the ins and outs of a pattern.

For example, the next important Federal Reserve meeting after that was the one held in September. Looking at Federal Reserve comments and trends in the US economy after the Fed's June meeting, it appeared more likely that the Fed would raise rates in September rather than in June.

Not that the market consensus was voting overwhelmingly for a September interest rate increase. At the beginning of July the probability of an interest rate hike in September was 11 percent. And that probability climbed to 42 percent in December and 58 percent in January 2016 ahead of the Federal Reserve meetings for those months.

You might think that, with the probability so low on a September rate increase, you should look right past the VIX options set to expire on September 16, just a day before the Fed would speak on interest rates. But remember that although you'd love to be able to accurately predict what the Fed will do on September 17—"Fed raises interest rates by 0.25 percentage points," for example—by purchasing call options and trading them before they expire, you're really trading shifts in market sentiment. A consensus that points to a very low chance of a rate increase in September means there's a very good chance the odds will shift enough in the time before the options expire to make the market swing to a belief in a greater probability of an interest rate increase. There's not much chance that the July probability of 11 percent will sink sufficiently to turn an option bet on a falling VIX (a put) into a profitable trade. But with the consensus so low, buying a call could be very profitable on a turn in sentiment even if, ultimately, the Fed didn't raise interest rates on September 17.

With the consensus pointing so clearly to "no increase," there's a very good chance that something will happen sometime during that period to shift the odds, even if only slightly toward an increase. A move to a 22 percent probability wouldn't be a stupendous improvement in odds, but it would be a huge move from that 11 percent probability.

And that shift in probability would likely be enough to create buyers for call options who are looking to profit from or protect themselves against an increase in volatility.

On July 7, for example, when the VIX was at 16.09, you could have bought call options with a September 16 expiration date and a strike price of $25 to $28 for a price of anywhere from $85 to $105 for a hundred options. My opinion at that point in July was that it was unlikely the VIX would break 25 before these options expired. The 2015 high on the VIX was just 20.97, after all, and you would have had to go all the way back to October 15, 2014, to see the VIX above 25, and then it only hit 26.25.

But what you're buying with those options isn't just the September projected endpoint but also the volatility in the days and weeks leading up to that event.

So, for example, on July 7, when the VIX fell 5.4 percent to 16.09 from the previous day's 17.01, the VIX option for September 16 with a strike price of 26 dropped 13.04 percent, as traders turned optimistic that global financial markets might be stabilizing. The day before, those same options had climbed nearly 12 percent. And on the day after that 13.04 percent tumble, these options gained almost 14 percent as pessimism overwhelmed hope.

I'm not suggesting that you try to guess these day-to-day moves. What I would suggest, however, is a short-term trade on volatility that starts from a relatively extreme consensus (that 11 percent probability of an interest rate increase) with options that sell for a modest price ($105 to $85 for a hundred) and where the long-term trend (the Fed will raise interest rates sometime in the next six months) provides a steady trend behind the day-to-day gyrations of the VIX.

It's unlikely that you'll find a trade that has just one driving trend. For instance, my July 7 example isn't just a reflection of the rising and falling fear surrounding the Federal Reserve's first interest rate increase since 2006. On that day and the days around it the VIX was also responding to fears that Greece would default and exit the euro and that the bear market in stocks trading on the Shanghai and Shenzhen markets in China would spread to other Asian markets and then to the economies of China's trading partners.

And I'd use this context to point out how difficult it is to predict the daily moves in the markets in general and the VIX in particular. I would have thought that the fear in the market would have climbed on a day when Greece moved ever closer to leaving the euro and when Shanghai and Shenzhen stocks continued their plunge. But, nope, the VIX fear index fell. And this is why I'd like to have a long-term trend moving in my favor.

The examples I've used in this chapter barely scratch the surface of the strategies you can build with options. The option itself is conceptually pretty simple, but on that foundation traders have built structures of amazing complexity—for instance, covered calls where you give up part of your profit to hedge against a loss and guarantee that you will, at least, earn the premium that the creator of an option generates. There are also combinations of options—call on this and put on that—that arbitrage pricing and differences in the sensitivity to volatility of different options built on different asset classes.

I'm not even going to pretend that I can teach you everything you need to know about options in one chapter of this book. My goal is more modest: I'd like to tell you enough about options in an

Age of Volatility so you can decide whether this strategy is something you want to work to master. If you want to go farther down that road, I'd recommend a book such as Sheldon Natenberg's *Option Volatility and Pricing: Advanced Trading Strategies and Techniques*.

Don't let the math throw you. And remember that you don't need to master every option in the market. Just pick a few that respond to market moves in ways you understand and then use them as tools for making a profit or hedging against short-term volatility.

Chapter 25

A Tisket, a Tasket, an Emerging Market Basket Strategy for an Age of Volatility

IF OVER THE NEXT decade there is an asset class that is likely to outperform on the long side of stock and bond markets of the United States, Japan, and the EuroZone—the world's developed markets—it's the equities of the world's emerging markets. The reasons are fundamental and the case solid—in the long run. (The emerging markets and economies do need to get past China's slowdown in growth.)

First, there are superior demographics: more of these economies are younger and near the age distribution that has more workers and fewer dependents (children and oldsters) that give an economy a boost. Second, there is the creation of a consumer market: a huge surge in growth as a result of rising incomes that push more of the population into the consumer market as daily incomes cross the $2-a-day figure. Third, there are productivity gains from increased education and worker training as well as from better health care. And finally, we have integration into the global economy as additional countries become part of the global market.

In the long run those trends all point upward. However, increasing volatility in the short run will—repeatedly—make the long-term trend a very bumpy ride.

For example, in the summer of 2014 it looked like China's Shanghai stock market might be staging a sustained rally. From June 19 to August 4 the Shanghai Composite Index climbed 9.9 percent.

And then volatility struck. On August 5, 6, and 7 the index went into reverse, and traders began to wonder whether the Shanghai market wasn't about to give back all of its gains.

Anyone who sold on those fears, however, would have sold just in time to miss a massive rally of 152 percent for the twelve months leading up to June 15, 2015. An outbreak of speculative fever among highly leveraged individual retail investors in China fueled this rally.

That's the kind of volatility that makes it hard to hold onto positions and drives lots of investors to chase rallies when they're carried away by the gains in the upside of the cycle and then sell at or near bottoms, fearful that modest losses will turn into big losses that more than wipe out prior gains. Yes, emerging market stocks do have the potential to outperform, but that doesn't make it easy to reap that outperformance.

The volatility in emerging markets is also likely to get larger rather than smaller over the next decade. And the balance in that volatility—between big upward surges and big downward plunges—isn't going to be as clearly slanted in favor of the upside as it has been during the decades characterized by the rise of China. In the period ahead I think we're likely to see more downside episodes that cause lots of traders and investors to doubt the basic premise of emerging market outperformance.

The problem is China.

The easiest part of China's growth is over. The growth of China's economy that lifted hundreds of millions out of abject, grinding poverty; that saw the country become the factory for the world; that led to the creation of a new consumer class that was bigger than the total population of the United States was hardly inevitable. China could have stayed poor. And it certainly wasn't easy, as the hard work and sacrifice of hundreds of millions of Chinese citizens testifies.

But we know from the history of economic development that, as difficult as this stage has been, it is easier than the next stage. The difficulties China now faces are so well known that they have their own name: the middle-income trap.

The very forces that allowed a developing country to reach this stage now have to be painfully redirected. Export economies need to become domestic consumer economies. Top-down command economies have to become somewhat less top-down and somewhat less command so that market forces can set prices and eliminate the worst waste in the way in which an economy allocates capital. The big stakeholders who have won vast wealth in the growth of the economy so far have to be persuaded or cajoled or forced to give up some of that economic power to make way for new players and new markets.

That's where China stands now. And right now it is in China where it is easiest to see the magnitude of the task ahead and to doubt: China has built vast ghost cities of apartments and empty industrial parks that stand as monuments to the misuse of capital; whole sectors of the economy that bleed red ink because they are unable to compete in a global market still find it easy to raise capital from state-owned banks and local governments while potentially more innovative smaller companies without political connections are starved for investment cash; whole industries are reorganized overnight to protect vested interests or a bureaucrat's definition of the national interest; Chinese consumers are forced to accept interest rates barely over inflation so that they can, in effect, subsidize the country's exporters; China's domestic consumer economy has been deliberately stunted so that the country can continue to record trade surpluses; and not the least of all, the Communist Party, whatever its revolutionary roots, has become a profoundly conservative economic machine designed to pass down wealth and the economic benefits of power to the children and families of party leaders.

It's certainly not guaranteed that China will be able to surmount all of these challenges and move from an economy that provides a better life for hundreds of millions to an economy that provides something like the economic benefits of the world's developed economies to hundreds of millions of people. I think the odds are that China will succeed, but the ticking bomb of China's demographics—the country's population is on track to be as old as the United States's within the next twenty to thirty years—means that China doesn't have unlimited time. And there is a real danger, as manifested in recent Chinese politics, that the country will return to the days of purges of political opponents and embark on an expansionist, xenophobic military program designed, in part, to diminish the likelihood of domestic dissent.

In other words, even if China does make it, if it does manage to move past the middle-income trap, it's not going to be easy or pretty.

This, given China's critical role in the global economy and its role in setting the direction of emerging financial markets, means a bumpy ride for the stock markets and economies of its big trading partners, countries such as Brazil, Indonesia, and Australia that are the sources for the commodities that fuel China's factories and meet its consumers' needs and demands. When construction slows in China, for example, the world's copper producers in Chile, Peru, and Indonesia feel the pain because China consumes more than 40 percent of the world's copper.

Given that potential reward from investing in emerging markets and the likely extreme volatility of those markets over the next decade or more, can we find a volatility-investing strategy that will enable us to reap more of the rewards and experience fewer of the losses? My suggestion for that strategy is the topic of this chapter.

Because we know what happens when China sneezes, we have a huge edge in designing a volatility strategy.

We could adopt something like the core-and-trade combination that I suggested in Chapter 23 for taking advantage of long-term trends in sectors such as water and food during short-term volatility.

Emerging markets, however, just aren't very liquid in most cases, and this presents an extreme challenge to any attempt to hold onto core positions during downside volatility. Because these markets lack liquidity, overseas investors who want to put money into any emerging market tend to be concentrated in a relatively few, more easily traded names. The result is that core stocks—the ones you might call global blue chips—that you might expect would hold up best in a downside plunge often lead the market downward during these periods simply because they're the easiest positions to get into and out of during volatility.

For example, you might expect China's HomeInns Group (HMIN), currently the subject of a proposal from insiders to take the company private, to show less volatility during a plunge in China's stocks than an index such as the Shanghai Composite stock market index. After all, the company, the largest operator of budget and midmarket hotels and motels in China, doesn't have any exposure to the ups and downs of China's exports and is positioned to benefit from the long-term growth of travel in China as income levels rise. Yet although the Shanghai Composite fell 11 percent from December 4, 2013, to May 19, 2014, the New York–traded ADRs (American Depositary Receipts) of HomeInns (then known as Home Inns and Hotels Management) plunged 38 percent in the shorter time period of December 31 to May 8. And I think the reason HomeInns Group followed the Shanghai market down and then picked up even more downward momentum as the correction in Shanghai continued is that, for traders wanting to sell China and for investors scared into selling, China's HomeInns was a very easy sell. It trades in New York, volumes are decent, trading costs are low, buy/sell spreads (most of the time) aren't horrendous, and once you were out, getting back in promises to be equally easy and low cost.

That's actually a bigger drop than China's instant messaging giant Tencent Holdings showed in roughly the same period in either New York or Hong Kong, where the stock shows roughly fifty times the trading volume that it does in New York. Tencent's worst period took the shares down 27 and 23 percent in New York and Hong Kong, respectively. This is not low volatility by any means, but nonetheless, this Internet stock, with its price-to-earnings ratio of 47, fell less than what you might have thought would be the less-volatile consumer-sector stock. (A price-to-earnings ratio of 47 is about four times the P/E ratio of Intel, to take another technology sector stock.)

In comparison with Tencent and then HomeInns, fundamentally a "core" stock is, ironically, a great trading vehicle in times of volatility.

Which does suggest the need for some creative thinking about how core and trading baskets might work in emerging market stocks.

I'd still divide my emerging market exposure into baskets as I did in the previous chapter, but I would utilize and define those baskets differently here.

First, I'd create a basket that consisted of stocks that are correlated to the long-term upward trend in developing economies and emerging markets but are relatively uncorrelated to the kind of short-term yips—those 6 to 7 percent drops that I cited at the beginning of this chapter—that are characteristic of China and other emerging markets. Many—if, indeed, not most—of the stocks in this basket would be those with big exposure to China and other emerging markets but aren't themselves the shares of Chinese companies. A stock such as London-based insurance company Prudential (PRU. LN), with big exposure to China's economy and long-term trends such as the growth of life insurance sales as incomes rise, would make it into this basket. I might even look past the current campaign against conspicuous gift giving to include shares of luxury goods makers such as LMVH Moët Hennessy Louis Vuitton (MC. FP in Paris).

My second basket would be what I'd call blue chips—and, increasingly, global blue chips—located in emerging economies but that so far largely trade on emerging market exchanges. Tencent Holdings, as I've noted, would be one of these. I'd also include Chinese insurer Ping An (2318.HK in Hong Kong), South Africa's hidden Internet gem Naspers (NPN.SJ in Johannesburg), Mexico's corn meal and tortilla giant Gruma (GRUMAB.MM in Mexico City), Asian water utility Manila Water (MWC.PM in Manila), or Brazil's Avon-like Avon-killer Natura Cosmeticos (NATUR3.BZ in Sao Paulo). Here you're getting a buffer from emerging market volatility from the relative difficulty in trading these stocks because they are only listed on emerging market exchanges and from the fact that revenues in these companies are increasingly spread across multiple economies.

My third basket would be composed of what I'd call emerging-market volatility indicator stocks. This basket corresponds to the "edge" trend stocks discussed in this last chapter. These are the shares of companies that are especially susceptible, for one reason or another, to shifts in relatively short-term trends in their home or the general developing economy universe. I'd put HomeInns in this category because of the way this stock is positioned in its owners' portfolios and minds. Brazil's Itau Unibanco (ITAU in New York) seems to occupy a similar position in portfolios looking for Latin American exposure: with one buy of the New York–traded ADRs, a portfolio manager can get the banking sector and general economy of Brazil as well as much of the rest of South America. This basket would also include stocks that are, for specific reasons particular to each company, especially sensitive to short-term economic moves. For example, Brazil's Localiza Rent a Car (RENT3.BZ in São Paulo) is extremely sensitive to interest rates, as rates determine whether buyers will be able to afford to buy the used cars that Localiza, the biggest rental car company in Latin America, sells out of its fleet. Staying with Brazil, I'd also put Vale (VALE) and Petrobras (PBR) in this group because both of these companies with extensive government stakes are extremely sensitive to changes in government policy toward capital investment and fuel prices, respectively.

Once you've got your baskets set up, trade them in a pattern that takes advantage of their volatility differences. On the downside the idea is to begin by trading basket three, as those are the stocks most likely to be moved by short-term trends, and then, if that indictor basket shows a drop extending much beyond 7 percent, begin to trade basket two stocks because at this point owners of emerging-market portfolios are likely to begin getting nervous. And finally, if volatility has continued to the point at which we're looking at something like a 10 to 15 percent or more correction, you begin to sell basket one stocks.

The same order works in reverse on the upside, with buys going first into basket one stocks and then into basket two and finally basket three. The idea is to produce enough selling to give you downside protection in markets that can fall by 30 percent without driving yourself crazy with trades on those 6 to 7 percent yips. On the upside I'd like you to put money to work first in those stocks that were most attractive as long-term propositions to begin with and that often drop the most if downside volatility goes on long enough because they are often the most liquid among emerging market shares.

You will note that you can't execute this strategy by using ETFs. ETFs are indeed often the cause of volatility in big-cap individual stocks in emerging markets because those are the equities most represented in indexes weighted by market capitalization. Those vehicles are organized around indexes that represent regions or individual country markets or sectors. I'm looking to create baskets based on the volatility potential of groups of individual stocks.

Fortunately, these days just about every brokerage worth their name allows you to define your own basket of stocks and then buy or sell the names in that basket with one trade: Fidelity does. Charles Schwab does. E-trade does.

But look carefully at how these basket services are priced. Some are structured as conveniences—you can sell or buy the group with one trade—but priced as if you were executing individual trades in every name in the basket. That can make a basket-buy or -sell easy but pricey. Remember that you'd like to pay as little to efficiently execute any strategy as you can because each dollar saved on costs is a dollar less than you need to figure out how to earn with your investing strategy.

Look for one of the brokerage houses that specializes in basket trades, as these have annual flat rates for all the basket buys and sells you execute. FolioInvesting.com, for example, prices a year of basket creations and trades at a flat $290.

Conclusion

Summing Up:
Why Volatility Is Too important to Ignore

THE STORY GOES THAT J. P. Morgan was walking down the street one day, shortly after he'd bailed out the US government with an emergency shipment of gold, when a stranger intruded on the great man's solitude. "Mr. Morgan," he asked, "What is the market going to do?" With a smile Morgan said, "It will fluctuate."

It's one of the great smart-ass bits of financial advice of all time, exactly the kind of remark you can get away with if you're the financial master of the universe who will motivate Congress to pass the Federal Reserve Act because the government is afraid you won't be around—or that your successor as most powerful man on Wall Street won't be as public spirited—the next time Washington needs a rescue.

But J. P. Morgan's answer is, from the perspective of this book, even less useful than it first seems. I've argued that it's not just the fact of volatility that matters but also its character and speed. Yes, the market will fluctuate, but it's critical to know how fast it will fluctuate, to take just one variable. How quickly high-volatility episodes follow one another, the degree to which volatility undermines accepted benchmarks, and the extent to which volatility makes investors feel unmoored in a "new" future all matter as well. How the market fluctuates is as important as the fact that it does.

Fluctuation is, after all, the accepted condition of market life. Extreme fluctuation is an unusual condition.

From our own experience of volatility over the last twenty years of financial market history, from the research of behavioral economists and neuroscientists, and from projections about the period ahead, we know that volatility in the financial markets, in the national and global economies, and in everyday life is important.

We know from that evidence that extreme volatility and, especially, repeated periods of extreme volatility changes the behavior of individuals and markets.

As I've noted in earlier research reported or conducted by John Coates, a Wall Street trader turned academic neuroscientist, that repeated exposure to high volatility and the emotions that come with coping with an environment of extreme risk and reward resets the body's flight-or-fight mechanisms so that future episodes of volatility produce a different and exaggerated response.

The slightest bit of introspection into our own investing decisions shows the effects of volatility. I don't know anyone who puts money into any financial asset today without some mental reference to the dot-com boom and bust and the global financial crisis and subsequent Great Recession. When US stocks move up to a new all-time high, we think about that move with reference to the busts we've been through. When a stock falls 20 percent, we don't think of that as truly extraordinary, as we've invested through periods of much worse downside volatility. We find it harder to be a contrarian and buy our favorite bargains because of our experience of those two big busts. Worries about trying to "catch a falling knife" are all too real after our recent experience. (Hence the title of this book, *Juggling with Knives*. But I'd guess you've figured that out by now.)

In our everyday economic lives recent extreme volatility has left us with a sense of being adrift. Old patterns about how to save for retirement—buy a house—or a belief that a college education will guarantee children a better economic future than their parents seem up for grabs.

And looking ahead at trends in demographics, climate change, resource scarcity, and the change in global incomes, we have a sense that the future isn't going to be less volatile than the last twenty years. In fact, it will likely be even more volatile.

I don't think assuming the ostrich position is a viable response to this volatility. The changes I've sketched out in this book are too big and too all-encompassing to ignore. They won't simply go away if you close your eyes. And, besides, I don't even think it's possible to play the ostrich when volatility is changing the way we react to volatility. To paraphrase Pogo, we have met the volatility, and it is us.

As I've argued in this book, the challenge, then, is both external and internal. We need to understand the scope, direction, and sources of this volatility so we can build the most sensible external solutions possible to limit the downside damage and increase the upside potential from this volatility in our portfolios and our lives. The most concretely financial of those solutions are the investing strategies in Part III of this book, but earlier chapters suggest more general "life decisions" for coping with volatility.

Understanding the scope, direction, and sources of recent and future extreme volatility has an internal goal too. If bouts of extreme volatility change the way we respond to volatility—and not always for the better—because they reset our flight-or-fight response, then we need to do everything we can to consciously and unconsciously resist that instinctual reset. If that flight-or-fight reset makes us more likely to be euphoric near market tops so that we stay in the game longer than is wise or if it makes us so risk adverse that we can't take advantage of buying opportunities near the bottom, then understanding volatility can give us the perspective to change these automatic, first-level responses. I wouldn't go so far as to equate the level of understanding of volatility that might come from reading this book with the calming effects of mediation—I doubt you'll see that all market volatility is merely an illusion, and I'm not sure that's a useful stance for anyone intending to make money in the financial markets anyway. But I would like to think that an understanding of the sources of volatility might make you feel less out of control and less a victim of cosmic forces beyond your ken and more like a captain who, because of an ability to read the waves, knows how to steer a ship safely through dangerous storms. Sure, that captain's adrenaline will be flowing when the waves are crashing and the wind is howling, but that captain won't have succumbed to panic and stands a good chance of reaching port with the ship's cargo and recording a profitable voyage, despite the storms.

And that would be a good result in the nonmetaphorical financial and economic storms ahead. This book will have achieved my goal if it makes you a better, less panicky, and more successful captain of your own financial and economic ship.

Jim Jubak
New York and Tuscany, August 2014
New York, April 2015

Acknowledgments

Bricolage: something constructed or created from a diverse range of available things.

It's one of my favorite words and a very apt description of the process of creating *Juggling with Knives*.

This book wasn't so much reported over a limited period of time as constructed from what I've learned about investing and markets and economies over past thirty years or so.

As I've edited and re-edited and then reviewed the edits of others over the past year of this book's growth, I've found myself repeatedly stopped by the echoes in my text of voices from those three decades.

I've heard the words my grandmother about growing up on the Lower East Side of New York City at the end of the nineteenth century, and I've heard my father's stories of joining the New Deal's Civilian Conservation Corps during the Depression, and I remember talking with my mother while we pasted Gold Bond Stamps into booklets before turning them in for the sleeping bags we'd use when we drove cross country on our 1965 family camping adventure.

In my chapters on work I can hear the satisfaction of the guys on the night shift in the Johns Manville powerhouse during the summer of Boris Spassky–Bobby Fischer whenever one of them beat "the college kid" at chess (which was frequently, I might note).

I remember protesting to the libertarian king of Spain that lending his umbrella to the libertarian Holy Roman emperor in exchange for betraying the sultan in the diplomacy game we all played at the University of Chicago seemed like mixing ducats and dollars. (All I got was a scornful smile.)

I remember trying to explain the meaning of the Flitcraft story to my students at the University of Virginia the first time I taught Hammett's *The Maltese Falcon*. The idea that life might be capricious and random isn't easy to accept at twenty.

I remember trying to explain how much they'd taught me—the college professor—about community and the love of place to the leaders of a community group from the backwoods of Washington County, Virginia, who were in the process of stopping the efforts of one of the biggest U.S. utilities to flood their valley for a pumped storage reservoir.

I remember excitedly buttonholing everybody I could find in the offices of *Venture* magazine when I finished an interview with a venture capitalist who became the twentieth really, really smart guy with lots and lots of money to invest to tell me that the disk drive company he had just backed only needed 10 percent of the market.

I remember a series of conversations I had with Walter Russell Mead in my office at *Worth* magazine about how a family making $200,000 a year but trying to educate two kids could feel overwhelmed with economic anxiety.

I remember wondering why my editor at *Worth*, John Koten, was so eager to accept my promise to build him the world's greatest mutual fund rating system over the summer. (I do get it now, by the way.)

I remember hearing the amazement and enthusiasm in Ted Fishman's voice as he told me he had seen the future of an aging America and that it was Sarasota.

And woven inextricably among those voices, I hear those of my extraordinary family—my all-too-frequently right spouse Marie D'Amico, my sarcastic son Finn, and my daughter Luna with her fourteen-year-old's take on the world—and my wonderfully contentious group of friends—especially Josh, Ellen, Mark, Susan, Viveca, and Bob—with whom it's been my privilege to discuss and experience life.

Socrates declared that the unexamined life is not worth living. As far as I'm aware, though, he never noted how much one can learn from the examined life—or how much fun the process could be. I hope some of that comes through to you in the pages of *Juggling with Knives*.

Notes

Chapter 1: An Age of Volatility

5   **fell 75 percent:** Beginning with a speculative run on the Thai baht in May 1997, which saw the baht lose half its value and the Thai stock market plunge 75 percent, the Asian currency crisis swept across Asia to engulf Indonesia, the Philippines, Taiwan, and Korea. In Indonesia the rupiah plummeted from 2,600 to a US dollar to a low of 14,000 to a dollar. (When a currency falls against the dollar, it takes more of it to buy a dollar.) Indonesia would lose about 13.5 percent of its GDP in 1998. In Korea, KIA Motors, the country's third-largest car maker, had to ask for emergency loans, and the national debt-to-GDP ratio more than doubled. The Chinese government launched a huge program of buying bad debt from banks and then burying it in special-purpose financial vehicles created for this event. It was a stunning act of chutzpah. These entities raised capital to buy bad debt from the banks by issuing bonds that were purchased largely by the banks in question, with the effect of removing the debt from bank balance sheets. Those "clean" banks then bolstered their balance sheets by going public in stock offerings led—you guessed it—by government institutions, other state-owned banks, and overseas institutions looking to score points with the government. How big was huge? In 1998 Beijing injected $30 billion into the country's four largest state-owned banks. That was followed by another injection of $170 billion in 2000 to 2001 and a third cash contribution of more than $100 billion in 2004.

6   **closed to trading:** Maybe the Russian crisis of 1998 should get lumped in with the Asian currency crisis that began in 1997, as the plunge in demand for metals and oil, Russia's two biggest sources of

overseas cash, resulting from the Asian crisis certainly played a key role in bringing on the Russian debacle. But the declining productivity of the Russian economy, massive internal corruption (about $5 billion of the first rescue package put together by the International Monetary Fund was simply stolen), and a domestic political crisis all played a role in undermining faith in the central government. Even after the government hiked interest rates on government bonds to 150 percent, banks refused to buy—inflation was only 10 percent or so—because they didn't trust the government to repay any borrowings. In August 1998 the Russian stock and bond market, along with the ruble, collapsed. With stocks down 65 percent, the stock market closed to trading. The final loss from January 1998 to August 1998 was more than 75 percent. On August 17 the government devalued the ruble, defaulted on its domestic debt, and declared a moratorium on payments to its foreign creditors. At the end of the month the government abandoned all attempts to defend the ruble and let it float freely. The currency dropped to 21 rubles to a US dollar, a decline of two-thirds in a month. Just as a drop in oil demand and prices had helped bring on the crisis, a recovery in demand and prices in 1999 brought it to a close—although not until forcing Russian president Boris Yeltsin to resign in favor of Vladimir Putin in 1999. Russia ran a large trade surplus in 1999 and 2000, aided by the devaluation of the ruble, which crushed domestic demand. Eventually, as Russian businesses paid off back-wages, domestic demand began to recover.

6   **the next two years:** On March 10, 2000, the technology-laden NASDAQ Composite hit an intraday high of 5,408.60. Over the next two years of the dot-com bust, a bear market destroyed $5 trillion in stock market valuations. Some established technology companies such as Cisco Systems survived, although it lost 86 percent of its stock market valuation at the worst point in the bear market. Some established technology giants such as Nortel Networks didn't—it eventually went into bankruptcy in 2009. The dot-com companies that had been the stars of the great bull market—the NASDAQ almost doubled in 1999—cratered spectacularly. Lycos, an Internet search engine startup, had previously sold to Spanish telecommunications company Telefonica for $12.5 billion in 2000; in 2004 the Korean company Daum Communications bought it for $95.4 million. On March 10, 2014, fourteen years after the NASDAQ Composite peaked at 5,408.60, it closed at 4,333.45. If you'd had the misfortune to buy at the March 2000 peak, fourteen years later you were still below water and looking at a 19.9 percent loss. For all intents and purposes, as the definition of a bear market is a loss of 20 percent, you would still be stuck in your own individual bear market.

6   **a global depression**: The global financial crisis of 2008–2009 began slowly. It was initially limited to the mortgage and housing markets in the United States, then quickly spread to the mortgage and housing markets of Ireland, the United Kingdom, and Spain. It then gradually turned into a crisis that forced major financial powers such as the Lehman Brothers investment bank into bankruptcy and, finally, threatened the global financial system. There were massive bailout packages from national governments, and US, Japanese, and EuroZone central banks decided to roll the printing presses 24/7, managing to save the global financial system from total collapse and prevent a worldwide recession. The Federal Reserve grew its balance sheet to $4.1 trillion, from $785 billion before the crisis. The Bank of Japan's balance sheet soared to $2.1 trillion, equal to 43 percent of the country's GDP. At the European Central Bank the increase was 240 percent to $3.1 trillion. The resulting recession, however, was virtually indistinguishable from a depression in countries such as Spain, Italy, Portugal, Greece, and Ireland, where general unemployment soared to 25 percent or more, and unemployment rates among younger workers moved above 40 percent. But for much of the global economy the massive intervention of governments and central banks meant a long and grinding recession rather than a depression. The US unemployment rate peaked at just above 10 percent at the end of 2009, and the US stock market, as measured by the S&P 500 stock index, fell 51.93 percent from 1,565 on October 9, 2007, to 752.44 on November 20, 2008. US stocks wouldn't recover their October 2007 levels until April 2013.

7   **plunge in 1968 to 1970:** From November 1961 to June 1962 there was what we can call the first tech-bubble bust (IBM traded with a price-to-earnings ratio of 80 at its prebubble peak), with a 27 percent bear market drop in the S&P 500. And then there was the 25.2 percent first Vietnam War–related bear from February 1966 to October 1966, the 35.9 percent second Vietnam War–related bear from November 1968 to May 1970, and the 44.97 percent oil shock bear of January 1973 to December 1974. Stretch the period from twelve years to twenty, and you can include the second 26.9 percent oil shock bear from September 1976 to February 1978, and the 24.6 percent bear from April 1981 to August 1982, when Federal Reserve Chair Paul Volcker finally broke the back of double-digit inflation.

9   **to fall into chaos:** The Brazilian market fell 14.9 percent from December 31 to February 3. South Africa tumbled 13.9 percent during that same period. Turkey, which began its decline earlier, plunged 27.4 percent by February 3. Shanghai dropped 11.6 percent from December 4 to January 20, and Hong Kong retreated 14.4 percent from December 6 through February 3.

18   **afraid of heights:** My editor keeps cutting this joke (which I made
      up and am very proud of) out of the book, but he finally agreed to let
      me put it in the Notes: I hate books that tell me there's a big crisis
      coming but don't tell me what do about it. It's like the joke about the
      two dinosaurs just before a giant comet is about to strike earth and
      wipe them all out 65 million years ago. (Stop me if you've heard this
      one.) The Stegosaurus runs up to the Apatosaurus and says, "I've just
      discovered that a comet is about to strike earth—it could wipe out 70
      percent of all species on the planet." The Apatosaurus is understand-
      ably concerned: "What can we do? What can we do?" His friend
      shakes his spiked tail. "Nothing, I'm afraid. If we'd evolved oppos-
      able thumbs a few million years ago, maybe we could have built
      rockets, invented Bruce Willis, and sent him to space to divert the
      comet. But now? I can't think of anything to do." To which the Apa-
      tosaurus says, "What's a Bruce Willis?"

Chapter 2: The Volatility of Volatility

24   *Us, Body and Mind:* John Coates, *The Hour Between Dog and Wolf: How
      Risk Taking Transforms Us, Body and Mind* (New York: *Penguin Books,*
      2012).

Chapter 3: The Volatility of Everyday Life

42   **Victorian price equilibrium:** The Victorian Equilibrium shows how
      hard it is to define a volatility period and how important the observer
      position is. Although it does make sense, in my opinion, to treat this
      single period as a characteristic level of (very low) price volatility,
      this long period is clearly broken by shorter periods that interrupted
      the trend. Prices surged in Germany, for example, in the 1840s as the
      result of bad weather and disastrous harvests and again in the 1860s
      as a result of the Danish War (1864), the Austro-Prussian War (1866),
      and the Franco-Prussian War (1870). In the United States the Civil
      War resulted first in a period of rising prices, especially in the South,
      during the war and then a period of rapid deflation that lasted until
      1880. Financial panics and depressions took place in the United
      States at almost exactly twenty-year periods: 1819, 1837, 1857, 1873,
      and 1893. It's tempting, at least to those of us who enjoy toppling
      historical structures, to see all that short-term volatility—the US pan-
      ics and depressions of those years, for example—as evidence that
      characterizing the years 1820 to 1900 as a period of low volatility is
      simply wrong: How can you have a low-volatility period with panics
      every twenty years? If you're doing so much averaging and

smoothing to make the period look like the Victorian Equilibrium, then you're doing so much statistical manipulation that you're wringing out all the meaningful texture of the time. But if you're trying to characterize the volatility of a period, I don't think that the most useful course is either throwing out the big trends in favor of a view limited to an endless succession of short-term ups and downs or bulldozing those ups and downs flat in favor of a big-picture trend with more explanatory power. I think you need both the long-term and local perspectives at once—or, "alternatively," if "at once" makes your head hurt. And you especially need both perspectives if you are an investor or trader trying to profit from or not get hurt by volatility. My suggestion is, instead, to look at the conflict and the contrast between the long and the short term as itself a meaningful measure of volatility as well as a guide to the causes and characteristics of that volatility. I think you'll see why that dual perspective can be especially valuable for investors and traders. See Chapter 24, which discusses options, for an example.

43 **and Marc Bloch:** The Annales school, founded by Lucien Febvre and Marc Bloch, and carried to its greatest glory, in my opinion, by Fernand Braudel, emphasized the use of social structures as explanatory forces. Its greatest glory, as well as, again in my opinion, its greatest weakness, was a failure to limit what social structures to examine. The result was what I call a history of everything.

47 *Scientific Revolutions:* Thomas Kuhn, *The Copernican Revolution: Planetary Astronomy in the Development of Western Thought* (Cambridge, MA: Harvard University Press, 1957), and *The Structure of Scientific Revolutions* (Chicago: University of Chicago Press, 1970).

Chapter 4: Whom the Gods
Would Destroy They First Make a Pundit

53 **earnings per share:** The problem with the standard P/E benchmark, however, is that it's not especially useful as a predictive tool at certain points—well, at most points, to be honest—in the economic cycle. At the bottom of the cycle, when the economy is struggling, the market will show a high P/E because earnings are depressed. In reality stock prices are often cheap at this point because, although stocks have been hammered by tough economic times, the denominator—the E in P/E—falls harder at the bottom of the cycle than the P does. This means that on a pure P/E measure stocks will look expensive at the very point in the economic cycle when they aren't. A pure P/E benchmark will show stocks to be overvalued, even though the bottom of the economic cycle is exactly when you want to buy shares that are

looking forward to the coming improvement in earnings as the economy picks up.

53   **decelerations and accelerations:** Of course, the market has frequently moved from overvalued to way overvalued and then to super-overvalued. The high CAPE during the technology bubble in December 1999 was 44, an all-time high. In contrast, the high in 1929 just before the crash that ushered in the Great Depression was a mere 32.6. The problem with CAPE is that it has been above its historical range for years, basically since the mid-1990s. For example, CAPE moved above 24, at 24.35, in November 1995 and then stayed above 24 until February 2008, when it dipped to 23.49. That means that by the CAPE measure, the market was overvalued—very overvalued—for thirteen years.

55   **longer than expected:** This "problem" has led some people to suggest that CAPE isn't very useful. Robert Shiller, who developed this ration with John Campbell, himself says that it's not a tool for timing the market. Other financial analysts and economists say that the problem with CAPE is that it assumes that the definition of earnings is consistent over time. In 2001 the definition of earnings got a huge revision with FAS 142. The Financial Accounting Standards (FAS) Board decides what constitutes Generally Accepted Accounting Principles, or GAAP. Before 2001 and FAS 142, GAAP required goodwill to be deducted from earnings over a forty-year period. Goodwill can be created by many events; for example, if a company acquires another for more than the pre-acquisition market price of the acquired company's stock, the difference is accounted for as goodwill. In 2001, however, FAS 142 eliminated the amortization of goodwill entirely. This means that earnings before 2001, when the lax pre-FAS 142 standards were in effect, and earnings after 2001 aren't comparable and that any ratio that, as CAPE does, uses earnings from both before and after 2001 to create long-term averages is fundamentally flawed.

56   **hoping to avoid:** This has led some Wall Street analysts and economists to another benchmark called the Q ratio. This one, devised by economist James Tobin, compares the total market capitalization of the stock market to the total replacement value of the economy's underlying assets. (Shiller won the Nobel prize in 2013 and Tobin in 1981, so we're talking real heavyweights here.) Right now the Q ratio shows that the stock market is about 70 percent overvalued. One problem with the Q ratio is that, like CAPE—and like P/E ratios themselves—it depends on assuming that key relationships remain constant over time. In the case of Q the key is the relationship between stock market capitalization and the replacement value of the

market's assets. If, for example, something changed the nature of that relationship—by, let's say, requiring fewer assets for a given level of production or by changing the life of those assets and, thus, their replacement value—then the Q ratio itself wouldn't be an unchanging measure but rather one subject to change with shifts in the economy. What might produce those changes? Oh, say, the Internet might change the useful life span of productive assets or, as recent Internet initial public offerings (IPOs) have demonstrated, reduce the amount of assets required to produce a certain level of revenue. If that's the case, then the Q ratio is itself time and condition bound. And to figure out whether the stock market is overvalued, we first need to figure out whether economic conditions have changed, how they have changed, and to what degree.

62   **insurance at the right time:** Financial insurance, which played such a big role in the 2007 debacle, has a history of not performing as expected. I remember the shock in the market during the 1987 crash when even stocks such as Procter and Gamble couldn't find ready buyers. Prices that day in October frequently fell $5 a share between trades. Portfolio net wealth was disappearing in a matter of minutes as sellers searched for buyers, any buyers. Financial insurance is only as good as the insurer's ability or willingness to pay off the risk. That's true of all insurance, of course: when events move not just in unexpected directions but also result in low-probability events that produce big losses that insurers are supposed to cover, insurance pools' ability to cover the risk can come into question. That's why insurance markets such as those for property damage have developed a second level of risk absorbers: reinsurers buy risk from primary insurers at a price, thus spreading the risk beyond the original insurance seller. And this is true of the market for financial insurance too: a bank may buy a derivative such as a credit-default swap to insure against the possibility that Italy will default on its government debt. That derivative contract might have another bank or insurance company on the other end. The seller would guarantee to pay if the price of Italian government bonds fell to X. That seller of insurance then might lay off part of that risk to another party, who would write a contract to pay the bank in case the price of Italian government bonds fell to X-1 so that the original seller wouldn't be on the hook for all of a disastrous decline in the price of Italian bonds. The seller of that secondary insurance might then, in turn, lay off part of their risk by buying a derivative that would deliver a profit if, say, the Japanese yen climbed, as this safe haven currency well might if an Italian debt crisis rocked the euro. The key difference and the key problem here is that the trail in financial insurance is a lot longer than that from

insurance company to reinsurer, and the credit quality of the parties on the other end of this reinsurance is a lot murkier than it is in the relatively regulated world of insurance and reinsurance companies. The bank that bought the original insurance against an Italian government default on its debt doesn't know who bought part or all of the risk, how many parties hold pieces of that risk farther downstream, or what the credit quality of all those parties might be. It's probably an overstatement to say that any insurance stream is only as good as its weakest player, as strong intermediaries would certainly try to honor their commitments. But it is true that if there is a weak hand or two somewhere in the risk stream unable to pay, this can jeopardize even the strong hands' ability to pay their obligations, as they themselves are counting on the parties to whom they sold risk to pay off that insurance so they can pay off on their own commitments.

Chapter 5: Rollin', Rollin', Rollin', Keep Them Presses Rollin'

65 **circumstances different now:** It's customary on Wall Street and in the financial press to adopt a posture of superior cynicism whenever someone says anything like, "It's different this time." It's different this time, and the Dow Jones Industrial Average will triple to hit 36,000. (A book of that title hit the stores in 2000 just in time to catch the dot-com bust.) It's different this time, and you really can take risky, subprime mortgages and, by bundling them together, create AAA-rated paper just as good as US Treasury bonds. It's different this time, and Bernie Madoff really does have a black-box strategy that will let him reap gains of 10 to 12 percent year after year with no risk.

I certainly understand the skepticism. "It's different this time" has been the marketing cry of enough scoundrels and frauds to keep Hollywood screenwriters in business for decades. But that doesn't mean it can't ever be true, especially if we keep our claims for how it's different very carefully delineated and very bound up in history.

66 **mortgage-backed securities:** A good stock market rumor is a terrible thing to waste. After the Taper Tantrum in the spring of 2013, by August financial markets were again awash in rumors that the Fed was about to begin tapering off its monthly Treasury purchases. Now the Federal Reserve, the rumor had it, would announce the beginning of a taper at its September 18 meeting. The S&P 500 went back into retreat, falling 4.5 percent in the days from August 2 to August 30. That rumor also turned out to be wrong. The Fed said at its

September 18 meeting that it wasn't ready to taper just yet, and the market went back into an uptrend—a big uptrend. In fact, if you'd bought at the depths of that rumor-created downtrend on August 30, 2013, and held until the end of the year on December 31, you would have seen a gain of 16.4 percent—one final volatility irony. The Federal Reserve actually did announce the beginning of the taper at its December 18 meeting. By this time, however, traders had been through this routine so many times that stocks moved only slightly lower in the days before the December 18 meeting and then proceeded to rally on December 19 through the end of the year on the actual announcement.

Chapter 6: A Strategy Appetizer:
Dividend Stocks as a Way to Beat Market Volatility

87 **Irrational Exuberance**: Robert Shiller, *Irrational Exuberance* 3rd ed. (Princeton, NJ: Princeton University Press, 2000, 2015).

Chapter 7: Older, Yes, but Wiser?

98 *The Unwinding*: George Packer, *The Unwinding: An Inner History of the New America* (New York: Farrar, Straus and Giroux, 2013).

Chapter 8: The World's
Largest Game of Three-Card Monte

130 **0.86 percent on the day:** That was the biggest jump in seven months. And on the jump in the repurchase interest rates, the Shanghai Composite Index, which had been struggling in 2014 as the People's Bank kept money tight, dropped below 2,000 for the first time since July 2013.

So in mid-February 2014, just after the People's Bank released data showing that new bank lending in January had increased threefold from December, no one was terribly surprised when the People's Bank moved to withdraw liquidity from the banking system. And the financial markets were prepared to take the central bank's move seriously. The Shanghai Composite index fell 6.8 percent from February 19 to March 11. You can also bet that traders were ready, even while stocks were still falling, for the People's Bank to reverse course, which is exactly what they got in mid-March. By April 10 the Shanghai market had tacked on a 6.8 percent gain, and stocks had climbed to within hailing distance of their February 19 level—down 6.8 percent and lots of profit if you had been able to short the move, then up

6.8 percent and lots of profit if you caught the recovery. Volatility can be a beautiful thing if you're prepared to move with it. Want to bet that the traders who missed the move quickly swore that they wouldn't miss the next one? Which arrived in short order as the Shanghai index fell 6.1 percent from April 10 to April 28. It's certainly not as clear-cut and numerical as the examples I've discussed earlier in this book, but for all intents and purposes China's financial markets and its traders and investors have established a benchmark. That was even clearer in the bear market in the Shanghai and Shenzhen markets that started on June 12, 2015: when the index had fallen below 3,500 and seemed poised to drop farther, regulators told company executives not to sell stock until the Shanghai index returned to 4,500.

Chapter 11: Volatility Trend No. 2:
The Job Market Feels More Volatile as Economies Slow

168   **36.6 percent of GDP:** Growth picked up in 2014 to 2.1 percent and, despite the plunge in the price of Mexico's oil, was forecast to climb to 2.5 to 3.5 percent in 2015 and to 2.9 to 3.9 percent in 2016. The driver in that improved growth came from the manufacturing sector, where the growth revival started with a pickup to 3 percent growth in 2013 and has continued with strength in industries such as automotive parts and appliances. Exports of factory goods grew 7.1 percent in April 2014 from April 2013. (Manufactured goods make up more than 80 percent of Mexico's exports.) This strength in manufacturing resumes a long-term trend in the Mexican economy. In 1994 manufacturing accounted for 20 percent of GDP; in 2013 it made up 36.6 percent. But there's an important change going on within that manufacturing sector as well: in labor-intensive manufacturing, Mexico, like China, is losing market share to countries such as Vietnam and Bangladesh. But in more highly automated sectors, such as transportation equipment and parts, where capital investment is more important than the cost of labor, Mexico has picked up market share against China. The record level of foreign direct investment—$35.2 billion in 2013, double the level in 2012—says that at least foreign companies think that export growth is likely to continue. And the effect on job growth? It's too early to tell, but the pattern is pretty clear: when Mexico's economy grows at 3.5 percent or better, the country creates jobs, even with its persistent disadvantages of a workforce with too little education and too few skills. In 2006 the economy added more than 1 million jobs as the economy expanded at a 4.5 percent rate. In 2010 the Mexican economy created 730,348 new

jobs as the economy rebounded from the worst of the global financial crisis. There's nothing terribly profound in this observation: when the economy grows, it creates jobs. When it grows faster, it creates more jobs.

But think for a moment about what happens from the point of view of the volatility that individual Mexicans experience when the economy grows more slowly. With faster national economic growth, regional booms and busts matter less because workers have an easier time finding a new job when an old one disappears. The standard churn in an economy, as workers constantly lose jobs and then find new ones, matters less because the time between jobs is relatively low. The kinds of problems economists write about, such as skills gaps, inadequate education, and infrastructure bottlenecks, don't loom nearly as large.

Chapter 14: Volatility Trend No. 5:
Real Estate Boom and Bust and the Volatility at the Extremes

202 **Shock of Gray:** Ted C. Fishman, *Shock of Gray: The Aging of the World's Population and How It Pits Young Against Old, Child Against Parent, Worker Against Boss, Company Against Rival, and Nation Against Nation* (New York: Scribner, 2010).

205 **Future of the American City:** Alan Ehrenhalt, *The Great Inversion and the Future of the American City* (New York: Deckle Edge, 2012).

205 **America in 2050:** Joel Kotkin, *The Next 100 Million: America in 2050* (New York: Penguin Books, 2010).

Chapter 16: Volatility Trend No. 7:
The Age of Energy Uncertainty

217 **in other words:** Of course, falling solar costs aren't the only thing that's pushing the global economy toward deflation. It's true of many commodities where the availability of cheap cash has created massive supply-and-demand imbalances that don't look likely to go away soon. A commodity such as iron ore is a good example of the problem and why financial markets and economies are likely to spend much of the next decade bouncing back and forth between fears of inflation and then deflation. In May 2014 the price of 62 percent iron ore, a global standard for iron content in iron ore, delivered in China, fell to $97.50, the lowest price since 2012—it had been $120 a metric ton as recently as April 9. The immediate culprits in the price drop were something old—a big drop in demand from China as the Chinese economy slowed—and something new—a fear that China's steel

makers had been importing more iron ore than they actually needed
in order to use those supplies as collateral on loans. China's steel
makers were searching everywhere they could for cash because most
were running at a loss and faced the need to refinance piles of existing debt. In a world of perfectly rational supply and demand, the
longer-term price signals being sent on demand—that demand will
be lower—would result in supply reductions that would eventually
bring supply and demand back into line and result in relatively stable prices. The first reductions in supply would take place as lower
prices told iron ore miners to cut back on plans for opening new
mines, the second as miners shut their least-efficient mines and reduced operations at others, and the third would see the least-efficient
iron ore miners go out of business. Although big low-cost producers
such as Vale, BHP Billiton, and Rio Tinto were profitable at these
prices (Morningstar estimates that Vale's cost is $22 a ton and that it
costs another $20 a ton to ship ore from Brazil to China), you'd cer-
tainly expect even these companies to reduce expansion plans. Further, many of China's small producers weren't making money at these
prices, so you'd expect that many of them would be shutting down
individual mines and maybe even exiting the business completely.
Currently some of these reactions to price signals are indeed taking
place, but the response is more muted than you might expect. And in
other cases there seems to be no reaction at all—or one pointed in an
entirely perverse direction. For example, estimates say small Chinese
miners will close 40 to 50 million metric tons of higher-cost, lower-
quality mines in 2014, and this would rise to as much as 80 million
metric tons if iron ore prices stayed low in 2014—as they did. That
would be almost 25 percent of China's total domestic production of
350 million metric tons.

At least the direction of the response makes sense. If prices are too
low to make money, then shut down some production. The closure of
this much capacity in China would be enough to send iron ore prices
higher over the next few years—except that the big global miners are
in the midst of increasing production. Vale, for example, is scheduled
to increase production to 450 million tons a year by 2018 from 300
million tons in 2013. As early as 2018 iron ore miners may be producing between 5 and 6 percent more capacity than demand, according
to Vale's José Carlos Martins, the head of Vale's ferrous metals unit
until 2014. "We will probably start to have some surplus capacity
around 2015," Martins said at the World Steel Association's 2014 annual congress. "Peak prices are unlikely to happen again. Nobody
can grow at the pace that China has been growing in the last 10, 15
years. At some point you will have a slow down. But there won't be a

reduction." Given those sentiments, why is Vale expanding production so rapidly in a surplus? To a degree this is because it can raise the money now at really low rates: the company has received a $2.8 billion loan from Brazil's national development bank, BNDES. And it is also because the mining industry is on the edge of a huge wave of innovation: Serra Sul will be the world's first truckless mine, using conveyor belts to automate production processes. That means falling costs—and few jobs for miners—and the ability to grab market share, Vale hopes. It sure raises the possibility of falling iron ore prices—and one more force for global deflation.

Chapter 18: Volatility Trend No. 9:
The Economics of Hoarding Food and Water

245   **14.6 pounds by 2024:** China will consume about half of the 109 million tons of pork that will be eaten globally in 2014, the US Department of Agriculture projected at the end of 2013. In 2012 per capita annual pork consumption climbed from 70 to 86 pounds. Projections from the USDA say that per capita pork consumption will rise an additional 14.6 pounds by 2024.

Until very recently Chinese pork production had managed to keep up with pork consumption. Pork production in China dwarfs that of the rest the world, with its projected production for 2014 an estimated 54.7 million metric tons, according to the US Department of Agriculture. (US production is projected at 10.8 million metric tons.) But China also consumes more pork than the rest of the world combined—55.4 million metric tons for China and 53.5 for the rest of the world, according to the USDA. Imports have started to rise, however, and there is fear that China's pork producers have hit a wall.

Chapter 19: Volatility Trend No. 10:
Climate Change as Pure Volatility

257   **layer of meltwater:** The earth's climate passed an important milestone in June of 2014. For three months in a row the planet's average carbon dioxide levels were above 400 parts per million. Concentrations of this greenhouse gas haven't been this high in somewhere between 800,000 and 15,000 million years. (How's that for a "precise" estimate?) Achieving this milestone is not, to state the obvious, a good thing. The current scientific consensus projects that this increase in the atmospheric concentration of CO_2, plus contributions from other more potent greenhouse gases such as methane, will increase average global temperatures by 2 to 11.5 degrees Fahrenheit

by 2100, depending on whether the world gets greenhouse gas emissions under any kind of control and on tweaks to current models of global climate. This degree of average warming will send big chunks of the Antarctic and Greenland ice caps plunging into the sea, leading to a rise in the average global sea level of two feet by 2100. As warmer ocean water absorbs more CO_2 (a good thing), oceans will become more acidic (a bad thing). Compared to preindustrial levels, on average, oceans are expected to be 170 percent more acidic by 2100, making them less habitable for ocean life. But did you notice all the volatility that surrounded this major climate change milestone? No? You didn't because there wasn't any. And here you have the huge challenge that climate change presents to anyone trying to predict the dimensions and focus of future volatility: we have solid numbers that argue that the world is headed toward climate change that will have a major effect on everything from air conditioner use (and thus the demand for electricity) to the viability of Miami, the entire state of California, and the inhabited parts of Australia—and almost nothing and nobody reacts. If climate change is such a big thing—and I believe it is—then where's the volatility?

Chapter 20:
Improving a Traditional Stock-Picking Strategy

275   **paid subscription site:** You can find that portfolio with my current stock picks on my JubakAM.com site. That site is by subscription only ($199 a year) for most of the world. But readers of *Juggling with Knives* can find a portfolio built along these lines—with updates on the topics in this book and other portfolios from later chapters in this section of *Juggling with Knives*—on the website, JugglingwithKnives .com, that I've built for readers of this book. You can use the code daggers2016 to gain a year's free access to what is, for everyone else, a paid subscription site. If you have trouble signing up, send me your e-mail address and the secret code above at jjubak@JubakAM.com, and I'll get you a fix for your problem.

Chapter 21: A Strategy for Bonds

277   **That's over:** The issue of how much "financial constants," such as correlation and rates of return for different asset classes, change over time and what to do with those changes is one of the most contentious subjects in the investing literature at the moment. Classic models of how to maximize return and minimize risk—a practice called finding the efficient frontier—assume that future correlations and

rates of return will resemble those in the historical record. Over some time scales, this is clearly not true; however, deciding what to do about the historical variation depends on what time scales are being considered. If the variation is small enough and quick enough, investors might be best off ignoring it and adopting something like the old buy-and-hold perspective—that if your holding period was ten years or longer, you could or should ignore short-term volatility. If, however—as in the period from the peak of the dot-com boom in March 2000 to the slow recovery off the bottom over the next fifteen years—the evidence points to long-term shifts in these important relationships, then we do need to figure out some way to plug that volatility into the classic formulas. (In case you're still in doubt at this point in *Jugging with Knives*, I'm in the camp that believes the market's constants do change over certain time scales, making it important to factor that change into investment decisions.)

278   **But they're not:** Some economists argue that the extraordinary period of US prosperity in the 1950s and 1960s was an anomaly created by the destruction of other economies in World War II and the US position as the sole intact global economy following the war. On that basis they argue that this period can't be used as a baseline for projecting future growth trends, as it is unlikely that the postwar circumstances will be repeated. That leads them to see the post–Vietnam War period not as a decline from greatness or evidence of some failing of character but rather as a return to an economic normal in terms of productivity growth, economic growth, wage growth, and so forth. I'd actually take that a step or two further to argue that the future we're now facing shows a major break with that post–Vietnam War normal due to forces such as aging, global climate change, and the need to unwind the huge portfolios of the world's central banks.

284   **wonderful world of ETFs:** One sign of how much the financial markets have changed and are continuing to change is the plethora of new products from Wall Street for dealing with those new circumstances, although I think it's debatable how much of this is a response to actual changed market conditions and how much is simply a recognition of a good marketing opportunity. One of the biggest categories of new products is exchange traded funds, or ETFs, that allow you to buy and sell baskets of stocks during market hours rather than only at the end of the day, as with mutual funds. One point I'd like to draw your attention to by using the example of ETFs is that these new tools, as much as they might resemble products you use already, require their own course of study. With an ETF, for example, you need to understand what index it tracks (and whether it is actively or

passively managed) and how the ETF's holdings are weighted (most are weighted by market capitalization and, therefore, focus on the biggest stocks in a sector or national market). Take some time with the nuts and bolts of a new Wall Street product before using it, and keep your eye out for changes in how that product is built. For example, the trend in ETFs is toward actively managed baskets of assets.

Chapter 22: Portfolio Construction

300   *The Alternative Answer*: Bob Rice, *The Alternative Answer: The Nontra-ditional Investments That Drive the World's Best-Performing Portfolios* (New York: HarperBusiness, 2013).

Chapter 23: A Not-So-Random Walk on the Long Side for Stocks

305   **Long Side for Stocks:** If the title of this chapter is puzzling to you, you need to bone up on the argument between those who see (and then invest) as if the market were efficient, and those who see the market (and invest following that belief) as a landscape riddled with inefficient information and pricing. The classic book on the efficient market is Burton Malkiel's *A Random Walk Down Wall Street* 15th ed. (New York: W. W. Norton & Co., 1975, 2015). A book that sums up, convincingly to me, the other side of the argument is Andrew Lo and Craig MacKinlay's *A Non-Random Walk Down Wall Street* (Princeton, NJ: Princeton University Press, 2002).

312   **John Bollinger:** See John Bollinger, *Bollinger on Bollinger Bands* (New York: McGraw-Hill, 2001).

Chapter 24: The Option of Options

323   **Trading Strategies and Techniques:** Sheldon Natenberg, *Option Volatility and Pricing: Advanced Trading Strategies and Techniques*, rev. and exp. 2nd ed. (New York: McGraw-Hill Education, 2014).

Chapter 25: A Tisket, a Tasket, an Emerging Market Basket Strategy for an Age of Volatility

324   **very bumpy ride:** In my opinion the best daily source for news on emerging markets and emerging market stocks is London's *Financial Times*. And it's way shorter and quicker to read every day than the *Wall Street Journal*.

Conclusion: Summing Up:
Why Volatility Is Too Important to Ignore

333 **"It will fluctuate.":** We're not certain Morgan actually said this. He lived in a period when newspaper reporters didn't hesitate to make up the quotes that the source is attributed to have said. Consequently the period is also the source of some of the best quotations about the financial markets.

Index

The Godfather Returns

The
Godfather
Returns

Mark
Winegardner

RANDOM HOUSE
NEW YORK

Copyright © 2004 by The Estate of Mario Puzo

Published in the United States by Random House,
an imprint of The Random House Publishing Group,
a division of Random House, Inc., New York.

RANDOM HOUSE and colophon are registered trademarks
of Random House, Inc.

Library of Congress Cataloging-in-Publication
data is available.

ISBN 1-4000-6101-6

Random House website address: www.atrandom.com

Printed in the United States of America

246897531

FIRST EDITION

Book design by Carole Lowenstein

alla mia famiglia

*Whoever forsakes the old way for the new
knows what he is losing, but not what he will find.*

—Sicilian proverb

They were killing my friends.

—AUDIE MURPHY,
most decorated U.S. soldier of World War II,
when asked how he had found the courage to fight
an entire German infantry company

Contents

Timeline

	The Godfather Returns (1955–1958)		The Godfather Returns (1959–1962)**	
The Godfather (1945–1954)		The Godfather II (1958–1959)*		The Godfather III (1979–1980)

* *The Godfather II* also covers the early life of Vito Corleone (1910–1939) in flashback scenes.

**The second half of *The Godfather Returns* also covers the early life of Michael Corleone (1920–1945) in flashback scenes.

Cast of Characters

THE CORLEONE FAMILY

Vito Corleone, the first godfather of New York's most powerful crime family
  Carmela Corleone, Vito Corleone's wife and mother of their four children
Sonny Corleone, Vito and Carmela Corleone's oldest son
  Sandra Corleone, Sonny's wife, now living in Florida
  Francesca, Kathy, Frankie, and Chip Corleone, Sonny and Sandra Corleone's
    children
Tom Hagen, *consigliere* and unofficially adopted son
  Theresa Hagen, Tom's wife and mother of their three children Andrew,
    Frank, and Gianna
Frederico "Fredo" Corleone, Vito and Carmela's second-born son (underboss
    1955–1959)
  Deanna Dunn, Oscar-winning actress and Fredo's wife
Michael Corleone, Vito's youngest son and the reigning Don of the Corleone
    Family
  Kay Adams Corleone, Michael's second wife
  Anthony and Mary Corleone, children of Michael and Kay Corleone
Connie Corleone, Vito and Carmela's daughter
  Carlo Rizzi, Connie Corleone's deceased husband
  Ed Federici, Connie Corleone's second husband

THE CORLEONE FAMILY ORGANIZATION

Cosimo "Momo the Roach" Barone, *soldato* under Geraci and nephew of Sally
    Tessio
Pete Clemenza, *caporegime*
Fausto Dominick "Nick" Geraci, Jr. (aka Ace Geraci), *soldato* under Tessio, later
    caporegime, later boss
  Charlotte Geraci, Nick's wife
  Barb and Bev Geraci, Nick and Charlotte's daughters
Rocco Lampone, *caporegime*
Carmine Marino, *soldato* under Geraci and third cousin to the Boccicchio Family
Al Neri, head of security for Family hotels, other security details as needed
Tommy Neri, *soldato* under Lampone and nephew of Al Neri

Richie "Two Guns" Nobilio, *soldato* under Clemenza, later *caporegime*
Eddie Paradise, *soldato* under Geraci
Salvatore Tessio, *caporegime*

RIVAL CRIME FAMILIES

Gussie Cicero, *soldato* under Falcone and Ping-Pong; owner of L.A. supper club
Ottilio "Leo the Milkman" Cuneo, boss, New York
Frank Falcone, boss, Los Angeles
Vincent "the Jew" Forlenza, boss, Cleveland
Fat Paulie Fortunato, boss of Barzini Family, New York
Cesare Indelicato, *capo di tutti capi,* Sicily
Tony Molinari, boss, San Francisco
Laughing Sal Narducci, *consigliere,* Cleveland
Ignazio "Jackie Ping-Pong" Pignatelli, underboss and later boss, Los Angeles
Louie "the Face" Russo, boss, Chicago
Anthony "Black Tony" Stracci, boss, New Jersey
Rico Tattaglia, boss, New York (succeeded by Osvavldo "Ozzie" Altobello)
Joe Zaluchi, boss, Detroit

FRIENDS OF THE FAMILY CORLEONE

Marguerite Duvall, dancer and actress
Johnny Fontane, Oscar-winning actor and probably the greatest saloon singer
    who ever lived
Buzz Fratello, nightclub entertainer (usually with his wife, Dotty Ames)
Fausto "the Driver" Geraci, a trucker in the Forlenza organization and father of
    Nick Geraci
Joe Lucadello, friend of Michael Corleone's youth
Annie McGowan, singer, actress, and former hostess of puppet show *Jojo,*
    Mrs. Cheese & Annie
Hal Mitchell, retired Marine and front for Corleone-owned casinos in Las Vegas
    and Lake Tahoe
Jules Segal, head surgeon at Corleone-owned hospital in Las Vegas
M. Corbett "Mickey" Shea, former bootlegging partner of Vito Corleone's;
    ex-ambassador to Canada
    James Kavanaugh Shea, governor of New Jersey and son of the Ambassador
    Daniel Brendan Shea, assistant attorney general of New York and son of the
    Ambassador
Albert Soffet, director of the Central Intelligence Agency
William Brewster "Billy" Van Arsdale III, heir to the Van Arsdale Citrus fortune

BOOK I

Spring 1955

Chapter 1

O N   A   C O L D spring Monday afternoon in 1955, Michael Corleone summoned Nick Geraci to meet him in Brooklyn. As the new Don entered his late father's house on Long Island to make the call, two men dressed like grease monkeys watched a television puppet show, waiting for Michael's betrayer to deliver him and marveling at the tits of the corn-fed blond puppeteer.

Michael, alone, walked into the raised corner room his late father had used as an office. He sat behind the little rolltop desk that had been Tom Hagen's. The *consigliere*'s desk. Michael would have called from home—Kay and the kids had left this morning to visit her folks in New Hampshire—except that his phone was tapped. So was the other line in this house. He kept them that way to mislead listeners. But the inventive wiring that led to the phone in this office—and the chain of bribes that protected it—could have thwarted an army of cops. Michael dialed. He had no address book, just a knack for remembering numbers. The house was quiet. His mother was in Las Vegas with his sister, Connie, and her kids. On the second ring Geraci's wife answered. He barely knew her but greeted her by name (Charlotte) and asked about her daughters. Michael avoided the phone in general and had never before called Geraci at home. Ordinarily, orders were buffered, three men deep, to ensure that nothing could be traced to the Don. Charlotte gave quavering answers to Michael's polite questions and went to get her husband.

Nick Geraci had already put in a long day. Two heroin-bearing ships, neither of which was supposed to arrive from Sicily until next week, had shown up late last night, one in New Jersey, the other in Jacksonville. A lesser man would be in prison now, but Geraci had smoothed things over by hand-delivering a cash donation to the pension fund of the International Brotherhood of Teamsters, whose men in Florida had performed like champs, and by paying a visit (and a sizable tribute) to the Stracci Family *capo* who controlled the docks in north Jersey. By five, Geraci was exhausted but home in his backyard in East Islip, playing horseshoes with his two girls. A two-volume history of Roman warfare he'd just started reading sat next to the armchair in his den, in position for later that night.

When the phone rang, Geraci was a few sips into his second Chivas and water. He had T-bones sizzling on his barbecue pit and a Dodgers/Phillies doubleheader on the radio. Charlotte, who'd been in the kitchen assembling the rest of the meal, came out on the patio, carrying the phone with the long cord, her face drained of color.

"Hello, Fausto." The only other person who called Nick Geraci by his given name was Vincent Forlenza, who'd stood as Geraci's godfather in Cleveland. "I'd like you to be a part of this thing Tessio arranged. Seven o'clock at this place called Two Toms, do you know it?"

The sky was blue and cloudless, but anyone watching Charlotte rush to herd the girls inside might have thought she'd learned that a hurricane was bearing down on Long Island.

"Sure," Geraci said. "I eat there all the time." It was a test. He was either supposed to ask about *this thing Tessio arranged* or he wasn't. Geraci had always been good at tests. His gut feeling was to be honest. "But I have no idea what you're talking about. What thing?"

"Some important people are coming from Staten Island to sort things out."

Staten Island meant the Barzinis, who had that place sewn up. But if Tessio had set up peace talks with Michael and Don Barzini, why was Geraci hearing it from Michael and not Tessio? Geraci stared at the flames in his barbecue pit. Then it came to him what must have happened. He jerked his head and silently cursed.

Tessio was dead. Probably among many others.

The meeting place was the tip-off. Tessio loved that place. Which meant that most likely he'd contacted Barzini himself and that either he or Barzini had set up a hit on Michael, which Michael had somehow anticipated.

Geraci poked the T-bones with a long steel spatula. "You want me there for protection," he said, "or at the table or what?"

"That was a hell of a long pause."

"Sorry. Had to get some steaks off the grill here."

"I know what you're worried about, Fausto, but not why."

Did he mean Geraci had nothing to worry about? Or that he was trying to figure out what if any role Geraci had played in Tessio's betrayal? "Well, pilgrim," Geraci answered, in his best John Wayne, "I ain't so much worried as I am saddle sore and plum tuckered out."

"Excuse me?"

Geraci sighed. "Even in the best of times I'm a worrier." He felt a tide of gallows humor rise in him, though he spoke flatly: "So shoot me."

"That's why you're so good," Michael said. "The worrying. It's why I like you."

"Then you'll forgive me if I point out the obvious," Geraci said, "and tell you to take a route there you'd never ordinarily take. And also to avoid Flatbush."

Now it was Michael's turn for a long pause. "Flatbush, huh? How do you figure that?"

"Bums're home."

"Of course," Michael said.

"The Dodgers. Second game of a twin bill with Philadelphia."

"Right," Michael said.

Geraci lit a cigarette. "Not a baseball fan, eh?"

"Used to be."

Geraci wasn't surprised. Seeing the business side of gambling ruined sports for a lot of the smarter guys. "This could be the Bums' year," Geraci said.

"That's what I keep hearing," Michael said. "And of course you're forgiven."

"For what?"

"For pointing out the obvious."

Geraci lifted the steaks off the grill and onto a platter. "It's a gift I have," he said.

An hour later, Geraci arrived at Two Toms with four of his men and positioned them outside. He took a seat alone and sipped an espresso. He wasn't afraid. Michael Corleone, unlike his brothers—the brutish Sonny and the pathetic Fredo—had inherited the old man's deliberate nature. He wouldn't order a hit on a hunch. He'd make sure, no matter how long it took. Whatever test was coming, however galling it was to be tested by the likes of Michael Corleone, Nick Geraci would respond with honor. He was confident he'd emerge unscathed.

Though he'd never heard Salvatore Tessio say a bad word about Michael, Geraci didn't doubt that Sally had thrown in with Barzini. He *had* to be angry about the nepotism that made a Don out of a greenhorn like Michael. He *had* to see the folly of cutting the organization off from its neighborhood roots to move west and become—what? Geraci had taken over countless once-thriving neighborhood businesses built by industrious, illiterate immigrant fathers and ruined by American-born sons with business degrees and dreams of expansion.

Geraci checked his watch, a college graduation gift from Tessio. Michael certainly hadn't inherited the late Don's legendary punctuality. Geraci ordered a second espresso.

Time and time again, Geraci had proven himself a loyal member of the Corleone organization and, still shy of his fortieth birthday, maybe its best earner. Once he'd been a boxer, a heavyweight, both as Ace Geraci (a boy-

hood nickname that he let stick, even though it mocked him for acceding to the American pronunciation of his name: *Juh-RAY-see* instead of *Jair-AH-chee*) and under numerous aliases (he was Sicilian but fair-haired, able to pass as Irish or German). He'd kept his feet for six rounds against a man who, a few years later, knocked the heavyweight champion of the world on his ass. But Geraci had hung around gyms since he was a little kid. He'd vowed never to become one of those punch-drunk geezers shuffling around smelling of camphor and clutching a little bag of yesterday's doughnuts. He fought for money, not glory. His godfather in Cleveland (who was also, Geraci gradually learned, *the* Godfather of Cleveland) had connected him with Tessio, who ran the biggest sports gambling operation in New York. Fixed fights meant fewer blows to the head. Soon Geraci was called on to give out back-alley beatings (beginning with two kids who'd assaulted the daughter of Amerigo Bonasera, an undertaker friendly with Vito Corleone). The beatings punished deadbeats and loud-mouths who had it coming, and earned Geraci enough money to go to college. Before he was twenty-five, he'd finished his degree, left the enforcer racket, and was a rising man of promise in Tessio's *regime*. He'd started out with some dubious qualities—he was the only guy hanging out at the Patrick Henry Social Club who hadn't been born in Brooklyn or Sicily; the only one with a college degree; one of the few who didn't want to carry guns or visit whores—but the best way to get ahead was to make money for the people above him, and Geraci was such a gifted earner that soon his exotic flaws were forgotten. His most brilliant tactic was to exaggerate his take on every job. He handed over sixty or seventy percent of everything instead of the required fifty. Even if he *had* been caught, what were they going to do, whack him? It was foolproof. His overpayments were an investment with jackpot-level payouts. The more he made for the men above him, the safer he was and the faster he rose. The higher he rose, the more men there were underneath him paying *him* fifty percent. And if the greedy morons held out on him, he was smart enough to catch it. It became clear all over New York that there was a difference between getting hit by the toughest guy you ever fought and having your eye socket flattened into a bloody paste by a blow from a former heavyweight prizefighter. The threat of what Geraci *could* do became a part of the mythology of the street. Soon he rarely needed to do anything to get his money but ask for it. If that. Intimidation is a better weapon than a fist or a gun.

During the war, Geraci mastered the ration-stamp black market and held a draft-exempt civilian position as a loading-dock inspector. Tessio proposed him for membership in the Corleone Family, and at the ceremony his finger was cut by Vito himself. After the war, Geraci started his own shylock operation. He specialized in contractors, who at first never realized how front-loaded their expenses were and underestimated how

tough it was, at the end of jobs, to get everyone who owes you money to pay (here, too, Geraci could be of service). He also targeted business owners who were degenerate gamblers or had any other weakness that made them seek quick cash. Before long, Geraci was able to use those businesses to launder money and give wiseguys something to put on their tax returns—at least until the time came to bust the place out. For thirty days, deliveries would stream through the front door and go straight out the back: presents for wives and girlfriends, gestures of friendship to cops, but otherwise sold to bargain hunters from the neighborhood. Once the bills came, so, too, would a mysterious fire—*dago lightning*. Geraci hated both the term and the crude endgame strategy, and he put it to rest by working on a night school law degree and supplanting the fires with perfectly legal bankruptcy proceedings. He incorporated every business in question (Geraci had a guy in Delaware), sheltering the owner's personal assets. If the owner was a good sport, Geraci tossed in a thousand bucks and some land in Florida or Nevada. When Michael Corleone took advantage of his father's semiretirement and covertly got involved with prostitution and narcotics, the businesses Vito had refused to enter, he'd put Geraci in charge of narcotics and let him hand-pick several men from Tessio's *regime* and what was left of Sonny's. Within months, Geraci worked some things—with the great Sicilian Don Cesare Indelicato, with the powers-that-be on the docks in New Jersey and Jacksonville, and with airports in New York and the Midwest, where he operated several small planes owned by companies the Corleones controlled but did not on paper own. The Corleones, unbeknown to most of the men in their organization, were making as much from narcotics as anybody in America. Without that money, they could never have amassed a war chest big enough to go after the Barzinis and the Tattaglias.

Finally, just after nine o'clock, Peter Clemenza and three bodyguards walked into Two Toms and sat down at Geraci's table. Geraci took it as a bad sign that Michael hadn't come, that he'd sent his *caporegime* instead, the one who'd over the years supervised the family's most important hits. Which sealed it: Tessio was dead.

"You eat?" Clemenza asked, wheezing from the effort of the walk from his car to the table.

Geraci shook his head.

But Clemenza waved a meaty paw to indicate the restaurant's aroma. "How can you resist? We'll get a little something. Just a snack." Clemenza ordered and devoured an *antipasto crudo*, a plate of caponata, two baskets of bread, and linguine with clam sauce. Last of a breed, Clemenza, almost literally so—the last *capo* Michael had inherited from his father, now that Tessio was dead.

"Tessio's not dead," Clemenza whispered to Geraci on the way out.

Geraci's stomach lurched. They were going to make him pull the trigger himself, a test of loyalty. Geraci's certainty that he would pass was no solace at all.

Darkness had fallen. He rode in the backseat with Clemenza. On the way, Clemenza lit a cigar and asked Geraci what he knew and what he could guess. Geraci told the truth. He did not know, yet, that earlier that day the heads of the Barzini and the Tattaglia families had both been killed. He couldn't have known that the reason Clemenza was late was because he'd first had to garrote Carlo Rizzi, Michael Corleone's own brother-in-law. These and several other strategic murders had all been made to look like the work of either the Barzinis or the Tattaglias. Geraci didn't know that, either. But the things Geraci *had* been able to surmise were in fact correct. He took the cigar Clemenza had offered him but didn't light it. He said he'd smoke it later.

The car pulled into a closed Sinclair station just off Flatbush Avenue. Geraci got out, and so did everyone in the two cars that had pulled in beside them, one bearing Clemenza's men, the other Geraci's. Clemenza and his driver stayed in the car. When Geraci turned and saw them there, an electric ribbon of panic shot through him. He looked for the men who would kill him. Trying to guess how it would happen. Trying to figure out why his own men were standing by passively watching. Why they'd betrayed him.

Clemenza rolled down his window. "It ain't like that, kiddo," he said. "This situation here is just too—" He put both palms to his jowly face and rubbed it fast, the way you'd scrub a stain. He let out a long breath. "Me and Sally, we go back I don't want to think about how long. Some things a man just don't want to see. You know?"

Geraci knew.

The fat man wept. Clemenza made very little noise doing it and seemed unembarrassed. He left without saying anything more, waving to his driver and rolling up his window and looking straight ahead.

Geraci watched the taillights of Clemenza's car disappear.

Inside, toward the back of the first filthy service bay, two corpses in jumpsuits lay in a heap, their blackening blood oozing together on the floor. In the next bay, flanked only by Al Neri, Michael's new pet killer and an ex-cop Geraci had some history with, was Salvatore Tessio. The old man sat on a case of oil cans, hunched over, staring at his shoes like an athlete removed from a game that was hopelessly lost. His lips moved, but it was nothing Geraci could understand. He trembled, but he had some kind of condition and had been trembling for a year now. There was only the sound of Geraci's own footsteps and, wafting in from another room, thin, distorted laughter that could only have come from a television set.

Neri nodded hello. Tessio did not look up. Neri put a hand on the old warrior's shoulder and squeezed, a gesture of grotesque reassurance. Tessio fell to his knees, still not looking up, lips still moving.

Neri handed Geraci a pistol, butt first. Geraci wasn't good with guns and didn't know much about them. This one was heavy as a cashbox and long as a tent spike—a lot more gun than seemed necessary. He'd been around long enough to know that the weapon of choice in matters like this was a .22 with a silencer—three quick shots to the head (the second to make sure, the third to make extra sure, and no fourth because silencers jam when you fire too many shots too fast). Whatever this was, it was bigger than a .22. No silencer. He stood in that dark garage with Tessio, a man he loved, and Neri, who'd once cuffed him, chained him to a radiator, punched him in the balls, and gotten away with it. Nick Geraci took a deep breath. He'd always been a man who followed his head and not his heart. The heart was just a bloody motor. The head was meant to drive. He'd always thought there'd come a time, when he was old and set, when he would move down to Key West with Charlotte and play the affluent fool.

Now, looking at Tessio, he realized that would never happen. Tessio was twenty-some years older than Nick Geraci, which until that moment had seemed like a long time. Tessio had been born in the last century. He would die in the next minute. He'd lived his life governed by his head and not his heart, and where had it gotten him? Here. A man who loved him was about to reduce that same head to blood and pulp.

"I'm sorry," Tessio muttered, still looking down.

This might have been directed at the Corleones or Geraci or at God. Geraci certainly didn't want to know which. He took the gun and walked around behind Tessio, whose bald spot, lit only by streetlights, gleamed in the darkness.

"No," Neri said. "Not like that. In front. Look him in the eyes."

"You're fucking kidding me."

He cleared his throat. "I don't suppose I look like I'm kidding you."

"Whose idea is that?" Geraci said. Neri didn't have a gun in his hand, but Geraci could not leave this scummy garage alive if he shot anyone but Tessio. From that back office, the television set erupted in a gale of tinny applause.

"Don't know, don't care," Neri said. "I'm just the messenger, sir."

Geraci cocked his head. This dumbass didn't seem witty enough to make a joke about shooting the messenger. But he did seem sadistic enough to take it on himself to make the killing as cruel as possible. And *sir*? How did he mean that? "Salvatore Tessio," Geraci said, "no matter what he's done, deserves more respect than that."

"Fuck youse!" Tessio said, loud now, but eyes still on the slimy floor.

"Look up," Neri ordered Tessio. "Traitor."

Trembling no worse, the old man did as he was told, eyes dry, staring into Geraci's but already far away. He muttered a rapid string of names that meant nothing to Nick Geraci.

Geraci raised the gun, both sickened by and grateful for the sight of his own steady hand. He pressed the barrel gently against the old man's soft forehead. Tessio did not move, did not blink, did not even shake anymore. His saggy flesh pillowed around the gun sight. Geraci had never before killed a man with a gun.

"Just business," Tessio whispered.

What made my father great, Michael Corleone had said at his father's eulogy, *was that nothing was ever just business. Everything was personal. My father was just a man, as mortal as anyone. But he was a great man, and I am not the only person here today who thought of him as a god among men.*

"What are you waiting for?" Tessio whispered. "*Sono fottuto.* Shoot me. You pussy."

Geraci shot.

Tessio's body flew backward so hard his knees made a sound like snapped roof shingles. The air was filled with a glowing pinkish gray mist. A yarmulke-sized piece of Tessio's skull caromed off the wall of the garage, smacked Neri in the face, and clattered to the floor. The tang of Tessio's airborne blood mixed with the smell of his shit.

Nick Geraci rubbed his shoulder—the pistol kick was like a savage right cross—and felt a wave of euphoria wash over him, obliterating the hesitation he'd felt. He felt no remorse, no fear, no disgust, no anger. *I am a killer,* he thought. *Killers kill.*

He spun around, laughing not out of madness but joy, more intense, *better* than the rush he'd gotten the time he sampled his own heroin. He knew what was happening. This was not the first man he'd killed. Sometimes when he killed he felt nothing at all, but even that might have been a lie, he told himself. Because the plain truth was that killing people felt good. Anyone who'd done it could tell you that, but they won't. They won't! A book Geraci had read about the First World War had a whole chapter on the subject. Hardly anyone would talk about it because for most people the bad feeling that came later, after the good feeling, shut them up. Plus, any shithead could guess that everything that would happen after a person proclaimed that it felt good to kill people, and after he convinced his listeners that he was serious, would be entirely bad. Still. It felt good. Almost sexual (another thing any shithead could guess would be bad to admit). You're powerful and the dead guy's not. You're alive and the dead guy's dead. You've done something that everyone on earth has at

some heated moment wanted to do but most never will. It was easy, and it felt *magnificent*. Geraci practically skated across the scummy floor of that garage, certain that, this time, the bad feeling would *not* come later. There would *be* no later. Everything would always be now. Everything is *always* now.

Geraci wanted to give every live man there a bear hug and a highball, but he settled for striding toward them, raising his pistol before they could raise theirs. Being the cowardly cocksuckers that at heart they surely were, they hit the ground, which gave him a clear shot through the doorway to the office at his target: the rectangle of hazy blue light behind them. Geraci fired. The shock he felt at the recoil (was Neri really stupid enough to give him a gun with more than one bullet? what a dumbass!) giving way a split second later to a dull pop, a puff of toxic smoke, a belched little fireball, and a tiny and satisfying afterglow of falling glass. Human beings have never built a machine more satisfying to destroy than a television set.

And then silence.

For Geraci, it seemed like an awfully long silence.

"Hey!" shouted a raspy-voiced man, one of Geraci's guys. "I was *watching* that."

It cracked everyone up. Just what the doctor ordered. Neri patted Geraci softly on the back. Geraci handed him the gun. Then everyone went to work.

Clemenza's men used a bone saw on the two corpses who'd been assigned to kill Michael Corleone. Geraci sat on the case of oil cans and watched, so flooded with ebbing adrenaline that everything seemed like the same thing. Grimy window. Calendar with topless wrench-wielding dairy maid. Fan belts on metal hook. Friend's corpse. Button on cuff. A universe of undifferentiated equivalency.

When the men finished, Neri handed Geraci the bone saw and pointed to Tessio's head. Around the gaping entry wound, the dead man's flesh was already proud.

Numb, Geraci took the saw and dropped to one knee. Later, he would look back on this moment with fury. But at the time, Geraci could have been checking the pH in his pool. When a man sees things for their essential literalness, how is sawing off the head of a dead father figure so different from separating a succulent turkey leg from the carcass? A thicker bone, true, but a bone saw is a better tool than some knife your brother-in-law got you as a wedding present.

Nick Geraci closed Tessio's bulging eyes and drew back the saw. Later had come—sooner rather than later, which in a moment of clarity Geraci recognized as later's way.

Neri clamped his hand on Geraci's forearm and took the saw.

"That was an order, too."

"What was an order?" Geraci said.

"Seeing how willing you were to do it."

Geraci knew better than to ask how willing he'd seemed or, worse, who'd given the order. He merely stood and said nothing, went blank and revealed nothing. He motioned toward the pocket of his bloodied suit jacket. Neri nodded. Geraci took out the cigar Clemenza had given him, a Cuban the color of dark chocolate, and sat back down on the oil cans to enjoy it.

Clemenza's men stripped the assassins naked and stuffed their clothing and the ten severed body parts into a suitcase. Tessio's corpse was left alone.

Which was when Geraci figured everything out.

There was no need to send a message to the Barzinis. Everyone involved with Tessio's betrayal was already too dead to benefit from messages. And of course the Corleones wanted Tessio's body found. This part of Brooklyn was identified with the Barzinis. The cops would presume that was who ordered the hit. The detectives would puzzle over the unidentifiable corpses of the assassins, and none of the conclusions they'd draw would involve the Corleones. The Corleones wouldn't even need to trouble their judges or their people in the NYPD. And it wouldn't take the usual forgiven gambling tabs and extended grace periods on loans to get the newspapers to fall in line. They'd play this just the way Michael Corleone wanted and feel virtuous about every squalid inch of type.

It was, Geraci had to admit, brilliant.

With a final glance back at the corpse of his mentor, Geraci got into the back of a car with Al Neri. Geraci wasn't afraid or even angry. For now he was only a man, staring straight ahead and ready to confront whatever came next.

In the weeks that followed the killings, Geraci worked closely with Michael Corleone. As he saw and helped administer the details of the ongoing war, Geraci learned how badly he'd underestimated his new Don. The Corleones had safe houses in every borough and a dozen suburbs, a constantly rotating inventory. They had underground garages full of cars and trucks with phony licenses and registrations. Some were armored and/or souped up with engines that could compete at Le Mans. Others were deceptively sound junkers that could break down at the flick of a hidden switch, snarling traffic and blocking pursuers. Some were destined to be crashed or fished out of rivers and swamps. Several were exact replicas of cars driven by high-ranking members of the Family, poised to mislead witnesses, enemies, or the police. They had arsenals of weapons all over the city: behind a rack

of clothes at a dry cleaner's on Belmont Avenue, underneath bags of sugar and flour in the back rooms of a bakery in Carroll Gardens, inside crates at a coffin warehouse in Lindenhurst. Michael Corleone was out to gain full political control of a state (Nevada) and a country (Cuba), and the more Geraci learned, the more plausible such things began to seem. The Corleones had more law enforcement agents on their payroll than the FBI, and they had pictures of the FBI director in a dress, sucking the penis of his top assistant.

Michael's grand, intricate plan was this: peace, coupled with massive expansion and relocation, then organization of the crime families throughout the country, better than before, while at the same time strengthening and expanding business ties with Sicily, all on the way to legitimacy, complete with utter control of Cuba and access to the White House and even the Vatican. Everything new would be built with other people's money: "loans," much of it from the pension funds of various unions. Those truck drivers, electricians, and jukebox stockers would receive a greater rate of return than they'd have ever gotten from a racket like the stock market. The Corleones would put more and more layers between themselves and anything like street crime. Before long they could stop using fronts and operate in the open, indistinguishable from any of the master criminals known collectively to suckers everywhere as the Fortune 500.

The plan wasn't unworkable, Geraci thought. Merely unnecessary. They were already in the only business in the history of the world that turned a profit every year. But he went along. In the short run, he had no choice. In the long run, he couldn't lose. If things worked out, he'd get what he really wanted, which was to run Tessio's old *regime:* a traditional operation with roots in the neighborhoods. If the Corleones spread themselves too thin and fell apart, Geraci could just grab what was rightly his and take it from there.

He forced himself not to think about Tessio. A boxer learns quickly to put things out of his mind. Otherwise he's a sitting duck. Geraci had hated boxing the whole time he was doing it, but ten years after his last fight, he had to admit that it had served him well.

Over the course of that summer, Nick Geraci and Michael Corleone became something like friends. Had a thing or two gone differently, they might have stayed that way.

For example: If only Michael hadn't decided in August to make his brother, Fredo, his underboss, a position the Corleones had never used and that Michael intended as symbolic, a way of bringing Fredo, a good-hearted bumbler, back into the fold. If only Michael had let the top people in his organization—rather than no one at all—*know* it was only symbolic.

Or: If only Geraci had been from New York and not Cleveland. If only

he hadn't had such ties to Don Forlenza. If only he'd been less ambitious. If only he hadn't, upon getting the news that Michael had appointed Fredo *sotto capo,* respectfully asked Michael if he'd lost his mind. If only his subsequent apology had made his intemperate remark go away.

If only *Fredo* had known his new job was symbolic, he might not have been so driven to have a piece of action that was all his. He might not have tried to create his own city of the dead in the swamps of New Jersey. He might have lived to celebrate his forty-fourth birthday.

If only Tom Hagen had been more involved with all aspects of the Family business, instead of being removed as *consigliere* so that he could try to become the governor of Nevada.

If only, twenty years ago in Cleveland, after Don Forlenza had been shot for the second time but before his first heart attack, he hadn't anointed a man his own age as his successor. If only one of Forlenza's many afflictions had killed him. If only Sal Narducci, a man of moderate ambition otherwise, hadn't had to spend two decades ready to take over any minute now.

If only Vito Corleone hadn't observed Narducci serving as *consigliere* at a dozen Commission meetings. If only, not long before Vito's death, he hadn't suggested to his son that installing Narducci as Don, rather than waiting for nature to take its course, would eliminate the Barzini Family's biggest ally outside New York.

Change one or two of those things, and—who knows?—maybe, as you read this, Nick Geraci and Michael Corleone would be out there somewhere, side by side, two leathery old goats beside a swimming pool in Arizona, toasting a life well lived, eyeing a couple sixty-something babes across the way, and busting out the Viagra.

History is a lot of things, but one thing it's not is inevitable.

Vito Corleone often said that every man has but one destiny. His own life was a powerful contradiction of his own cherished aphorism. Yes, he fled Sicily when men came to kill him. Yes, when a young neighborhood tough named Pete Clemenza asked him to hide a cache of guns, Vito had little choice but to comply. And, yes, when Vito committed his first crime in America, the theft of an expensive rug, he thought at the time that he was just helping Clemenza move it. All of these things had found him. This is not unusual. Bad things find everyone. Some might call this destiny. Others might call it chance. Tomato, tomahto. But Vito's involvement in his next crimes—hijacking trucks along with Clemenza and another young tough from Hell's Kitchen by the name of Tessio—had been a willful act. When they invited Vito to join their band of thieves, he could have said no. Saying yes, choosing to become a predatory criminal, sent him down one path. Saying no would have sent him down another,

perhaps a family business his three sons would have been able to join without first becoming murderers.

Vito was a skillful, intuitive mathematician, a brilliant assessor of probability, and a man of vision. Believing in something as irrational and unimaginative as destiny was out of character. It was beneath him.

Still, what human being is above rationalizing the worst thing he ever did? Who among us, if directly and indirectly responsible for the killing of hundreds of people, including one of his own children, might not tell himself a lie, something that, unexamined, might even seem profound?

Both Nick Geraci and Michael Corleone were young, smart, creative, careful, and tough. Each had a gift for reinventing himself, at contriving to be underestimated and then taking advantage of it. It has often been said that they were too similar and destined to become enemies. It has often been said that wars are waged to create peace. It has often been said that the earth is flat and that this way demons lie. Wisdom is a thing rarely said (the late Vito Corleone often said) and less often heard.

Michael Corleone and Nick Geraci might certainly have made other choices. Better things could easily have happened. They were by no means destined to destroy each other.

Chapter 2

THE CREMATORY was owned by none other than Amerigo Bonasera. Neri had his own key. He and Geraci went right in the front door, and stripped out of their bloody clothes and into the best of what they could find in a back room. Geraci was a big man. The closest thing to a fit was a linen suit the color of baby shit and two sizes too small. Bonasera was semiretired, living most of the time in Miami Beach. His son-in-law took the suitcase and the wad of bloody clothes from Neri and didn't say a word.

One of Geraci's men drove him home. It wasn't even midnight. Charlotte was still wide awake, sitting up in bed, doing the *Times* crossword puzzle. She was good at crossword puzzles but did them only when something was eating at her.

Nick Geraci stood at the foot of their bed. He knew how he looked in that suit. He cocked his head, arched his eyebrows in a way he hoped was comical, and thrust out his arms the way a vaudevillian would as he said "Ta-da!"

His wife did not laugh or even smile. The "gangland-style slayings" of Phillip Tattaglia and Emilio Barzini had been on the television news. She tossed the *Times* aside.

"Long day," Geraci said. "Long story, okay, Char? Let's leave it at that."

He watched her size him up. He watched her face go slowly slack, watched her make herself not say she wasn't going anywhere, watched her swallow her desire to ask to hear the story. She didn't say a word.

Nick Geraci got undressed, tossing the suit over a chair. In the time it took him to piss, brush his teeth, and put on his pajamas, Charlotte managed to make the suit disappear (Geraci never saw it again), turn off the lights, get back into bed, and pretend to have fallen asleep.

In New Hampshire, in her parents' house, Kay Corleone lay next to her sleeping children in the same double bed she'd had as a girl, trying to concentrate on the Dostoyevsky novel in her hands, dogged by the questions

she hadn't asked, and knew she couldn't ask, about why Michael had not only suggested this visit but picked the dates.

In Las Vegas, in a darkened hotel suite on the top floor of the first high-rise in Las Vegas, the Castle in the Sand, home of the buck-fifty steak dinner and the nickel cup of coffee, Connie Corleone Rizzi clutched her newly baptized baby boy to her breast and stared out beyond the lights of the city. The last light of day drained from the desert. She was happy. Connie was not, as a rule, a happy person. She had not had an easy day, getting up so early for that flight and then having to contend the whole way with her six-year-old son Victor's epic squirming and resourceful misbehavior while her mother, Carmela, barely lifted a finger to help and just nattered on and on about how this trip had made her miss Mass. But the baby—Michael Francis Rizzi, christened yesterday, named after her brother Mike, who'd stood as the boy's godfather—had been a perfect angel, sleeping and cooing and burrowing that little nose into her. Somewhere over the Rocky Mountains, for the first time, he had laughed. Now, every time she blew on his forehead, he'd do it again. It was a sign, she thought. Babies bring their own luck. The move out here would be a new start for everybody. Carlo would change. He *had* changed. He hadn't hit her once since she'd gotten pregnant with this baby. Mike was going to give Carlo a lot more responsibility in the family business now. Carlo had been supposed to make the flight, too, to look at houses and help shop for other things they'd need, but at the last minute Mike had said he needed Carlo to stay. Business. Neither her father nor any of her brothers had ever done that before, made Carlo feel like he mattered. She moved her infant son to her other breast and stroked his soft, fine hair. He smiled. She blew on his forehead. He laughed, and she did, too.

In the next room, Vincent started jumping on the bed, which he'd been told countless times not to do. The phone rang. Connie smiled. That would be Carlo. She let Victor answer.

"Mo-om!" the boy called. "It's Uncle To-om!" Hagen.

Connie stood. The baby began to scream.

On the street below, draped in a long black shawl, Carmela Corleone emerged from the hotel, head down, shielding her eyes from the glare of the neon lights, muttering to herself in Italian. She started down the Strip. It was after nine, too late for services anywhere, especially on a Monday, but in a town with all these wedding chapels, how hard could it be for a

determined widow to find a priest? Or at least a man of the cloth. If all else failed, a quiet and holy place where she might escape these garish lights and fall to her knees and seek intervention on behalf of the souls of the damned, humbly beseeching the Virgin Mary, as she did every day, one suffering mother to another.

BOOK II

September 1955

Chapter 3

FOUR MONTHS LATER, early Sunday morning of Labor Day weekend, Michael Corleone lay in his bed in Las Vegas, his wife beside him, his two kids right down the hall, all of them sound asleep. Yesterday in Detroit, at the wedding of the daughter of his late father's oldest friend, Michael had given the merest nod toward Sal Narducci, a man he barely knew, putting in motion a plan designed to hurt every formidable rival the Corleones still had. If it worked, Michael would emerge blameless. If it worked, it would bring lasting peace to the American underworld. The final bloody victory of the Corleone Family was at hand. A trace of a smile flickered on Michael Corleone's surgically repaired face. His breathing was even and deep. Otherwise, he was motionless, untroubled, basking in the cool air of his new home, enjoying the sleep of the righteous. Outside, even in the pale morning light, the desert baked.

Near the oily banks of the Detroit River, two lumpy men in silk short-sleeved shirts—one aquamarine, the other Day-Glo orange—emerged from the guest cottage of an estate belonging to Joe Zaluchi, the Don of Detroit, the man who'd saved his city from the arbitrary violence of the Purple Gang. The one in orange was Frank Falcone, formerly of Chicago and now the head of organized crime in Los Angeles. The one in aquamarine, Tony Molinari, was his counterpart in San Francisco. Behind them came two men in overcoats, each carrying two suitcases, each suitcase containing, among other things, a tux worn to last night's Clemenza-Zaluchi nuptials. The surface of the water was awash in dead fish. From the barn-sized garage, a limo came to get them. When the limo pulled out onto the street, a police car followed it. The cop was on Zaluchi's payroll.

At Detroit City Airport, they turned down a dirt access road and drove alongside a fence until they got to a gate marked EMERGENCY VEHICLES ONLY. The police car stopped. The limo kept going, right onto the tarmac. The silk-shirted men got out, sipping coffee from paper cups. Their bodyguards practiced karate moves.

A plane taxied toward them, bearing the logo of a meatpacking con-

cern in which Michael Corleone had a silent, controlling interest. The logo featured the profile of a lion. The name on the pilot's birth certificate was Fausto Dominick Geraci, Jr., but the license clipped to the visor read "Gerald O'Malley." The flight plan he'd turned in was blank. Geraci had a guy in the tower. At airports all over America, Geraci had the use of planes that did not on paper belong to him.

Under his seat was a satchel full of cash. Storm clouds filled the western sky.

Across the river, just outside Windsor, the door to Room 14 of the Happy Wanderer Motor Inn opened just a crack. Framed there was Fredo Corleone, his brother's new appointed *sotto capo,* a man shaped like a bowling pin and dressed in last night's rumpled shirt and tux pants. He looked out to the parking lot. He didn't see anyone walking around. He waited for a piece of junk car to chug by. It was loud enough to wake a person up. Fredo was aware of some stirring on the bed behind him, but the last thing he was going to do was look back.

Finally the coast was clear. He pulled a porkpie hat low, over his eyes, eased the door closed behind him, and hurried around the corner, down an embankment, and across a drive-in theater, filthy with discarded cups and popcorn buckets. The buckets were adorned with fat blue clowns— heads cocked, faces contorted into gruesome, knowing smiles. The hat wasn't his. Maybe it belonged to the man in that room or else came from one of Fredo's many stops last night. It may have even belonged to one of his bodyguards. They were new, strangers to him. His head pounded. He patted his shirt pockets, his pants pockets. He'd left his smokes back in the room. His lighter, too. The lighter was a present from Mike: jeweled, from Milan. It was engraved CHRISTMAS 1954 but with no name, of course. Never put your name on anything, his old man always said. Fredo didn't even break stride. Fuck it. He jumped a muddy ditch and jogged across the parking lot of an apartment building. He'd hidden the car, a Lincoln that Zaluchi had lent him, behind a trash incinerator. The coat of his tux was balled up in the backseat, along with a yellow satin shirt, which wasn't his, and a whiskey bottle, which was.

He got in. He took a drink and tossed the bottle onto the passenger seat. *It may,* he thought, *be time to take a break from the booze.* And the other thing. Jesus. How can a thing you want so bad seem so repulsive right after you do it? He'd quit that, too. No more after-hours clubs. No more paying for it from junkies too messed up to know whose dick they sucked. Easy enough to start today, heading home to Vegas, where he was a known ladies' man, where the town was so small he couldn't get the

other thing anyway. He put the car in gear and drove away as if he were someone's pious Canadian grandpa on the way to Mass. Though he did— at a stoplight—finish off the whiskey. He hit the main drag and sped up. At this pace, he'd make the plane to Vegas, easy. It started to rain. Only when he flicked on the wipers did he notice that there was a piece of paper under the passenger-side blade, a handbill or something.

Back in the darkness of Room 14 of the Happy Wanderer, the naked man on the bed awoke. He was a restaurant supply salesman from Dearborn, married, two kids. He moved the pillow from his crotch and rose. He smelled his fingertips. He rubbed his eyes. "Troy?" he called. "Hey, Troy? Oh, hell. Not *again*. Troy?" Then he saw the lighter. He saw Troy's gun. Troy struck him as the kind of guy who'd carry a gun, but not this kind. This was a cowboy gun, a Colt .45, its grip and trigger covered with white adhesive tape. The naked man had never touched a real gun before. He sat back down on the bed. He felt faint. He was a diabetic. Somewhere, there should be oranges. He remembered Troy giving a bartender fifty bucks to go to the kitchen and get a bag of oranges. He ate three right at the bar, while Troy walked to the door and looked out into the street, waiting until he'd finished eating and the peels were gone. The man could not remember what happened to the rest of the oranges.

His heart revved and sweat poured out of him. He called the front desk and asked for room service. "Where you think you are," said the desk clerk, "the Ritz?" Good question. Where *was* he? He wanted to ask, but first he had to do something about his blood sugar. Was there any food at all? he asked. A vending machine or something? Any way he could get the clerk to bring him, let's just say, a candy bar? "Your legs busted?" the clerk asked. The man said he'd pay five bucks for a candy bar to be delivered to his room. The clerk said he'd be right there.

The man needed to call his wife. This had happened before. He'd said it was with a secretary, a woman. He'd promised his wife it wouldn't happen again. He started to dial, then realized he'd need the clerk for an outside line. The clerk must have been off getting the candy.

The man had a good job, great wife, great kids, nice house. He was a newly initiated Rotarian. Yet here he was, after a night with some street tough, doing *those things*, waking up on a Sunday morning *in a place like this.*

He got up again to look for the oranges. No luck. He saw his pants but not his yellow shirt. He couldn't find his porkpie hat. He didn't know the name of the dive where he'd left his car. He'd have to take a cab home, shirtless, then have his wife drive him around seedy neighborhoods, looking for it. It'd be easier to just buy a new car.

He picked up the gun.

The Colt felt even heavier than it looked. He ran his finger along the barrel. He opened his mouth. He rested the end of the gun on his tongue and held it there.

He heard the squeal of tires outside. It was a big car, he could tell from the sound of the slamming door. It must be Troy. Coming back for him. Then a second car door slammed.

Two men.

They'd come all the way from Chicago. They weren't coming for him, though the naked man didn't know that. They'd been following him for hours, which he also didn't know. The naked man pulled the Colt out of his mouth, stood, and trained it on the door. "See you in Hell," he whispered. He'd heard someone say it in a movie. He wasn't a tough guy, but with his fingers curled around the pearly butt of that six-shooter he sure as hell felt like it.

In Hollywood, Florida, under the carport of the coral-colored house where she'd lived since her father, Sonny, died in that car wreck (she had no reason to believe it was anything other than what she'd been told), Francesca Corleone honked the horn of her mother's station wagon for a good ten seconds. "Stop it," said her twin sister, Kathy, sprawled across the backseat, reading some French novel, in French. Kathy was headed off to Barnard. She wanted to be a surgeon. Francesca was going to Florida State, in Tallahassee, and wanted, mostly, to be on with it: out of the house, on her own. Though with all this horrible business in New York and how that side of the family had gotten the family name in the papers, even if it was all lies, this might not be the easiest time to start a new life. Kathy had wanted to go to school in New York, partially to be close to all their family up there. Now, of course, everyone had moved away except for Grandma Carmela and their horrible Aunt Connie. Apparently Uncle Carlo had simply disappeared—one of those jerks who went out for cigarettes and never came back: a lousy thing to do, even for a creep like him, but Francesca had to admit that anyone married to Aunt Connie would have had to consider it. Kathy, especially up there, would probably get asked every day, even by her professors, if she was any relation to those notorious gangsters, the Corleones. If the past few months in Hollywood were any indication, Francesca would have to be braced for this, too, even in Tallahassee.

Her mother, the controlling shrew, was driving them both. *Driving!* To New York! Thank God Francesca would get dropped off first. She honked again.

"That's very annoying," said Kathy.

"As if you're really reading that book."

Kathy answered in what was either French or fake French.

Francesca hadn't taken a language and planned to evade the issue either by taking Italian—which, in truth, she didn't know all that well—or by majoring in something with no language requirement. "We're Italian," Francesca said. "Why aren't you learning Italian?"

"*Sei una fregna per sicuro*," Kathy answered.

"Nice mouth."

Kathy shrugged.

"You can swear in Italian," Francesca said, "but you can't *read* Italian."

"I can't read at all unless you shut up."

Their mother was next door at their grandparents' house, and had been there for ages, laying down last-minute care-and-feeding instructions for Francesca's brothers, Frank, fifteen, and Chip, ten. Chip's real name was Santino Jr., and, until he had come home from baseball practice one day this summer and announced that he would henceforth answer only to "Chip," had been called Tino. Francesca could probably do that. She could go to college and take on another name. *Fran Collins. Franny Taylor. Frances Wilson.* She could, but she wouldn't. They'd already Americanized the pronunciation, from *Cor-le-o-nay* to *Cor-lee-own*, and that was change enough. She was proud of her name, proud to be Italian. She was proud that her father had rebelled against his gangster father and brothers and become a legitimate businessman. Anyway, Francesca's name would change in good time, when she found a husband.

Francesca honked again. What was taking so long in there? Nonna and Poppa would ignore every word Francesca's mother said. Those boys got away with *murder*, especially Frankie, especially once the football thing started. Francesca honked once more. "You're making it *much* easier," said Kathy, and Francesca finished the sentence: "—for you to leave. I know." Kathy sighed as only an American girl can. Moments later, she stroked the back of Francesca's hair, softly. The twins had never in their eighteen years spent a night apart.

Hal Mitchell's Castle in the Sand Hotel and Casino never closed. Neither, these days, did Johnny Fontane, who'd done his two shows (eight and midnight) and been up all night, showing the swells and pallies a good time, then, for luck (since he had a session today), to his suite, where there were two chicks. One was a blond French girl who danced at the casino across the way and said she'd had one line ("Gosh, look!") in that Mickey Rooney picture they'd filmed here last year, the one where Mickey's a prospector in the desert and there's a bomb test and the dose of radiation he gets makes it so any slot machine he touches pays off (there's no scene

with wiseguys beating the shit out of Mickey Rooney). The other one was a luscious brunette with a C-section scar who was probably paid to be there (fine by him; by Johnny's stars, the worthiest of human attainments was to be a professional). When he'd asked, a total gentleman about it, if either of them had a problem going to bed—y'know? all three of them?—they'd laughed and started to strip. The brunette, who'd said her name was Eve, had a flair for it, knowing just when it was the blonde's turn to suck Johnny's dick (when she saw the size of it, she grinned and whispered, "Gosh, look!") or when it was her turn to do it up against that fountain in the middle of the room while the blonde rubbed his back. Eve knew the perfect time to push Johnny down on his back and maneuver the blonde onto his cock and for the first time in the whole deal to start pawing the blonde's tits and kissing her, which sent Johnny off in a matter of seconds. It was a gift. A lot of women didn't have it. The blonde—her name was Rita, short for Marguerite; he never forgot their names in the morning—was still there, asleep, when he'd left to come up here to the roof, to the pool. He hated men who tested the water with their pinky toe. He tossed off his heavy robe and jumped into the deep end. When the shock wore off, he went under again, holding his breath and counting to two hundred.

His head pounded, and not from the depth of the water. He didn't drink as much as people thought, at least not anymore. The secret? Go from table to table, joint to joint, leaving half-finished drinks everywhere, which no one notices, while at the same time accepting every new one that comes his way, which *everyone* notices. Any poor mook who tried to match him drink for drink got folded into the back of a cab and sent home, courtesy of Johnny Fontane. He controlled his drinking. He controlled what he did and who he did it with.

He surfaced. He swam a couple laps to limber up, then took a deep breath and went under again. He repeated the drill three more times and got out. At the end of the deck, on the far edge of the roof, was a billboard: HAVE A BLAST! BEST VIEW OF THE BOMB IN LAS VEGAS! Underneath a painting of a purple-orange mushroom cloud, on movable letters, was a time, tomorrow morning. *Early* tomorrow morning. Johnny had heard they were going to set up a bar, a breakfast buffet, even crown some broad Miss Atomic Bombshell. What sort of sucker would get up at dawn to watch a bomb go off sixty miles away? Maybe they think they'll start to glow and set off the slot machines. People want to pay to watch a bomb, they ought to go see Johnny's last picture. He grabbed his robe and took the stairs two at a time, down to his room.

She was gone. Rita. Good kid. The room still smelled like whiskey, smokes, and pussy. The statue of the naked lady in the fountain, whose

outflung arm had seemed at the time like it was made to hold on to, needed repairs. He got dressed and—just to make sure he didn't nod off on the way to L.A.—took one of the little green pills Dr. Jules Segal had prescribed.

Johnny Fontane emerged into the brutal sunlight of the Castle's VIP parking lot and did not flinch. He grabbed his lapels, so sharp they could cut meat, straightened his jacket, and climbed into his new red Thunderbird. The cops here knew this car. He had that 'Bird going over a hundred before he even left town. He checked his watch. In a couple hours, the musicians would start trickling into the studio. They'd spend an hour tuning and gassing, then for another hour or so Eddie Neils, his musical director this time out, would have them rehearsing. Johnny should make it in time. Lay down the first few tracks, get to the airport by six, hop on the charter along with Falcone and Gussie Cicero, and be back here in plenty of time for the private show he said he'd do for Michael Corleone.

It wasn't until four in the morning—after he arrived, exhausted, at the guest suites at the Vista del Mar Golf and Racquet Club—that Tom Hagen realized he'd forgotten his racquet. The pro shop didn't open until nine, the same time Hagen was supposed to meet the Ambassador on Court 14. Hagen couldn't bear to be late. He asked the desk clerk if he might borrow a racquet, and the clerk looked at him as though he'd tracked mud on the lobby's white carpeting. He told the man he had an early court time and asked if there was any way to get in the pro shop now, and the clerk shook his head and said he didn't have a key. Hagen asked if there was anything that could be done, either now or at some time before eight-thirty tomorrow, and the clerk apologized and said no. Hagen took out two hundred-dollar bills and told the clerk he'd be grateful if there was anything humanly possible that could be done, and the man just smirked.

Hagen had begun yesterday in his own bed in Las Vegas, then, before dawn, flown with Michael Corleone to Detroit, first for a meeting with Joe Zaluchi on his daughter's wedding day, then the wedding itself, an appearance at the reception, and finally a flight back to Vegas. Mike had been able to go home and go to sleep. Hagen went to the office for an hour of paperwork and then a quick stop home, to change and to kiss his sleeping daughter, Gianna, who'd just turned two, and his wife, Theresa, who'd become an art collector and was excited about a Jackson Pollock that had just arrived from her dealer in New York. His boys, Frank and Andrew, were teenagers, each behind a closed door in a bedroom strewn with science fiction paperbacks and records by Negroes, both of them unkissable now.

As Tom Hagen packed his tennis gear, Theresa walked around their

new house holding the gorgeous, paint-splattered thing in front of various white walls. She'd taken advantage of the move to Las Vegas and the expanses of blank surfaces to go on a buying spree. The paintings were worth several times more than the house itself. He loved being married to a woman with taste. "What about opposite the red Rothko in the center hallway?" she called.

"What about the bedroom?" he said.

"You think?" she said.

"Just a thought," he said. He met her gaze and cocked an eyebrow to indicate that it wasn't the location of the painting he was talking about.

She sighed. "Maybe you're right." She set down the painting and took his hand.

Marriage.

But he'd been far too tired, and things hadn't gone particularly well.

Hagen was no longer the Corleone *consigliere,* but with the death of Vito Corleone—who'd succeeded Hagen in the job—and with Tessio dead, too, and Clemenza in the process of taking over in New York, Michael needed an experienced hand. He was waiting to announce a new *consigliere* until he felt sure the war with the Barzinis and Tattaglias was definitely over. Michael had something up his sleeve, but all Hagen had been able to figure out was that it had something to do with Cleveland. In the meantime, Hagen was still doing his old job and trying to move on to his next thing, too. He was forty-five years old, older than either of his parents had been when they'd died and definitely too old for this shit.

Now he rose to the knock of the room service he'd had the foresight to order before going to bed. He downed the first cup of coffee before the door closed behind the bellboy. Weak. The way it was everywhere out here. Hagen congratulated himself for guessing beforehand that he'd need two carafes. He took the first one out on the balcony. Eight A.M., the sun barely over the mountains, and already it was baking hot. Who needed a sauna? By the time Hagen finished the first pot of coffee—ten minutes, give or take—the robe that had come with the room was soaked.

Hagen shaved, showered, dressed in his tennis clothes, and was standing outside the pro shop at eight-thirty, waiting for someone to arrive. After a few interminable minutes, he went back to the desk. A different clerk said that the manager was here now and he'd page him.

Hagen went back outside the pro shop. The wait was excruciating. If there was one thing he'd learned from Vito Corleone—and what *hadn't* he learned from him?—it was promptness. He paced back and forth and dared not go to the men's room for fear he'd miss the manager or some other arriving employee. When finally someone came to open up—a Slavic woman who looked more like a masseuse than a manager or club pro—it was nine on the dot.

Hagen grabbed a racquet, slapped two hundred dollars on the front counter, and told her to keep the change.

"We don't take cash," she said. "You have to sign for it."

"Where do I sign?"

"Are you a member? I don't recognize you."

"I'm a guest of Ambassador Shea's."

"He needs to be the one to sign for it. Him or a family member or his valet." She pronounced it to rhyme with *mallet*.

Hagen took out another hundred and said that if she could find it in her heart to straighten all this out, there was more than enough money here for the racquet and her time.

She looked at him the same way last night's clerk had, but she took the money.

Hagen thought his bladder would burst, but by now it was five after nine. He tore the cardboard off the racquet and broke into a dead sprint. Those exact words occurred to him—*dead sprint*.

When he got to Court 14, ten minutes late, there was no one there. He was so rarely late that he had no idea what to do. Had the Ambassador already been here and left? Was he late, too? How long should Hagen wait? Would it make sense to go take a leak and come back? He looked around. A lot of bushes, but this wasn't the sort of place where a guy ought to be pissing in the bushes. So he stood there, hopping from foot to foot, holding it. Surely, the Ambassador had come and gone. Finally, he couldn't take it anymore, and he ran to the nearest men's room. When he got back to the Court 14, a note was pinned to the net. *Ambassador Shea—unable to play tennis this a.m. Late brunch? 2. Poolside. A man will pick you up.*

The note didn't say where.

Kay Corleone pointed back toward the road to the Las Vegas airport. "He missed our turn," she said. "Michael, we missed our turn."

Next to her in the backseat of their new yellow Cadillac, Michael shook his head.

Kay frowned. "We're *driving* all the way to Los Angeles? Are you out of your mind?"

It was their fifth anniversary. She and the kids and even her mother and Baptist pastor father had already been to Mass. Michael had business tonight, before, during, and after the private show Johnny Fontane was doing as a favor for the Teamsters. But he'd promised her that the whole day up until then would be one long date—like old times, only better.

Michael shook his head. "We're not driving. And we're not going to Los Angeles."

Kay turned around in her seat, looking back toward the road not taken, then turned to her husband. Abruptly, she had what felt like a block of ice in her guts. "Michael," she said. "Forgive me, but I think this marriage has withstood about all the surprises that—" She made circles with her hands, like a sports official signaling improper movement of some sort.

He smiled. "This will be a good surprise," he said. "I promise."

Soon they came to Lake Mead, near a dock with a seaplane moored to the end. The plane was registered to Johnny Fontane's movie production company, though neither Fontane nor anyone who worked there knew anything about it.

"Surprise number one," Michael said, pointing to the plane.

"Oh, brother," she said. " 'Number one'? You've counted them up. You really should have become a mathematics professor." The illicit thrill she'd once gotten from what he'd become instead had waned enough that she might actually have meant this.

They got out of the car.

"That's counting," he said. "At most *accounting*. Not mathematics." He held out his hand toward the dock. "M'lady."

Kay wanted to say she was afraid but did not, could not. She had no reason whatsoever to think that he might do her harm.

"Surprise number two—"

"Michael."

"—is that I'm flying."

Her eyes widened.

"I started pilot training in the Marines," he said, "before I was, you know." *Sent to fight in 120-degree heat for tunnel-riddled coral islands ladled with a maggoty stew of mud and corpses.* "For some reason flying relaxes me," he said. "I've been taking lessons."

Kay exhaled. She hadn't realized she was holding her breath. She hadn't realized that, in all those unaccounted-for hours the past few weeks, she was afraid he was having an affair. *That's not true.* What she was afraid of was worse. "It's good you have a hobby," she ventured. "Everyone needs a hobby. Your father had his garden. Other men have golf."

"Golf," he said. "Hmm. You don't have a hobby, do you?"

"I don't," she said.

"There's always golf." He was wearing a tailored sport coat and a stark white shirt with no necktie. He hadn't slicked his hair. A light wind tousled it.

"Actually," she said, "what would you think if I went back to teaching?"

"That's a job," Michael said. "You don't need a job. Who'd watch Mary and Anthony?"

"I wouldn't start until we're settled. By then your mother will be here and she could do it. Carmela would be *thrilled* to do it." Though Kay actually dreaded hearing what her mother-in-law would say about Kay working outside the home. "Really, all it would be is a hobby."

"Do you want a job?" Michael said.

She looked away. A job wasn't exactly the point.

"Let me think about it." His father wouldn't have approved, but he was not his father. Michael had once, like his father, been married to a nice Italian girl, but Kay did not know that and was not that girl. What concerned Michael was security, even though it was part of the code that the risks to her were slight. Michael put a hand on her arm and gave it a gentle squeeze.

Kay put her hand on top of his. She took a deep breath. "Well, look," she said. "I'm not getting in that contraption. At least not until you tell me where we're going."

Michael shrugged. "Tahoe," he said. A grin flickered on his face. "*Lake* Tahoe." He gestured to the seaplane. "Obviously."

She'd told him once she'd love to go there. She hadn't thought he'd been listening.

He opened the door to the plane. Kay got in. As she did, her dress both hiked up and stretched taut across her ass. Michael felt a wild impulse to grab her hips from behind but instead just let his eyes linger. There was nothing better, nothing sexier, than looking at your wife like this without her knowing it.

"Now, the only tricky part about floatplanes," Michael said as he got in and started the engine, "is that they sometimes flip."

"Flip?!" Kay said.

"Rarely." He stuck out his lower lip, as if to indicate the lightning-strike unlikelihood of such a thing. "And if a floatplane flips, guess what? It floats."

Kay regarded him. "That's comforting."

"I do love you," he said. "You know that, right?"

She tried for the expressionlessness Michael had mastered all too well. "That's also comforting."

Their takeoff was so smooth that Kay felt her every muscle relax. She hadn't been aware that they were clenched. She had no idea for how long.

Chapter 4

OVER LAKE ERIE, the small plane flew into the teeth of a thunderstorm. The cabin was hot, which suited Nick Geraci just fine. The other men in the plane were sweating just as much as he was. The bodyguards had already blamed it on the heat. Tough guys. He'd been one of them, once, written off as a big dumb ox, both relied upon and disposable.

"I thought the storm was behind us," said Frank Falcone, one of the silk-shirted men, the one in orange, the one who didn't know who the pilot really was.

"You said a mouthful," said the one in aquamarine, Tony Molinari, who did know.

The hits on the top men in the Barzini, Tattaglia, and Corleone crime syndicates had aroused the interest of law enforcement everywhere, from local-yokel hard-ons to the FBI (though the agency's director, supposedly because the Corleones had something on him, continued to maintain that the so-called Mafia was a myth). For most of the summer, even corner-bar shylocks had had to close things down. The other two New York Dons, Ottilio "Leo the Milkman" Cuneo and Anthony "Black Tony" Stracci, had overseen a cease-fire. Whether this would mean an end to the war, no one knew.

"Excuse me, but I meant the real storm," said Falcone. "The storm out there. The fucking storm."

Molinari shook his head. "Jokes are wasted on you, my friend."

Their bodyguards, noticeably more pale now, looked down at the floor of the plane. "Lake effect," said Geraci. "The way it works is that the air and the water are sharply different temperatures." He tried to make his voice sound the way a pilot's would, in a movie where the pilot was the lead. He relaxed his grip. "That's what makes it possible for storms to come from any direction, and all of a sudden. Keeps things interesting, eh?"

Molinari put a hand on Geraci's shoulder. "Thank you, Mister fucking Science."

"You're welcome, sir," Geraci said.

Falcone had been a top connection guy in Chicago—buying politicians, judges, and cops—and now ran his own thing in Los Angeles. Moli-

nari had a four-star dockside restaurant in San Francisco, plus a piece of anything there he wanted a piece of. According to the briefing Michael had given Geraci, Falcone and Molinari had always had their differences, particularly when it came to the New York Families. Falcone saw them as snobbish, Molinari as recklessly violent. Molinari had also felt a personal attachment to the late Vito Corleone that Falcone had never shared. But the last few years, the two West Coast Dons had forged a wary, effective allegiance, particularly in organizing the importation and distribution of narcotics from the Philippines and Mexico (another reason, Michael did not have to say, that Geraci was being sent to meet them). Until Michael had taken over the Corleone Family, they'd been the two youngest Dons in America.

"O'Malley, eh?" said Falcone.

Geraci nosed the plane up through the thunderhead, seeking better air. He knew what Falcone meant: the name on his pilot's license. The flight was obviously challenging enough that Falcone accepted it when Geraci didn't answer. It's not the eyes that see, it's the brain. As Michael had predicted, Falcone put an Irish name together with a broad-shouldered, fair-haired Sicilian, a man he naturally presumed worked for the Cleveland operation, and what he saw was an Irishman. Why not? Cleveland worked with so many Jews, Irish, and Negroes that the men in it called it the Combination. People outside of it called its Don, Vincent Forlenza, "the Jew."

It was a necessary deception. Rattlesnake Island was not an easy place to get to. Falcone might not have boarded a plane owned by the Corleones. Don Forlenza had hoped to come to the wedding, but his health had precluded it.

The plane finally rose above the clouds. The men were bathed in blinding sunlight.

"So, O'Malley," Falcone said, "you're from Cleveland, huh?"

"Yes, sir, born and raised." Misleading, but true.

"Guess our DiMaggio and his Yanks were too much for the Indians this year."

"We'll get you next year," Geraci said.

Molinari started talking about watching DiMaggio play for the San Francisco Seals and how even then he was a god among men. Over the years Molinari had made a bundle fixing Seals games, but never once the whole time DiMaggio had been there. "People have these ideas about Italians, am I right, O'Malley?"

"I'm not sure I have any ideas at all, sir."

"We got us a *cacasangue*," Falcone said.

"Pardon me?" Geraci said, though he knew full well what the word meant.

"Smart-ass," said Falcone's bodyguard.

"*Wiiiiise guy, eh?*" said Geraci, in the manner of Curly from the Three Stooges.

Molinari and the two bodyguards laughed. "That's pretty good," Molinari said. Geraci obliged him with a perfect *nyuck-nuck-nyuck* laugh. This, too, amused everyone but Falcone.

The conversation was sporadic, inhibited by the bumpy flight and the name on Geraci's pilot's license. They talked for a while about restaurants and then about the title fight at the Cleveland Armory that they were planning to attend tonight instead of going to Vegas to see Fontane—an invitation-only show, courtesy of Michael Corleone, to kick off a Teamsters convention. They talked, too, about *The Untouchables,* which they both liked, though partly because they found it funny. Geraci had heard it on the radio and been irritated by the stereotypical straight-arrow cops and spaghetti-slurping, bloodthirsty Italians. He'd never seen the television show, though. He was a reader. He'd sworn never to own a television set, but last year, Charlotte and the girls had worn him down. He knew a guy—Geraci always *knew a guy* or *had a guy*—and one day a truck pulled up and two men in suits unloaded the biggest one anybody made. Before long, Charlotte was serving meals on TV trays. Saturday became "TV dinner night," an abomination Geraci was glad his mother never lived to see. Geraci would've liked to drag that television to the curb, but a man must pick his battles. A week later, a contractor Geraci knew pulled a crew off the parking garage they were building in Queens and had them dig up the wild mulberry bushes behind Geraci's in-ground swimming pool. A couple weeks after that, Geraci had his own little house back there, his den: a refuge from the noise and the zombie feeling he got when he used that goddamned television to watch anything but sports.

Geraci nosed the plane down into the clouds. "We're beginning our descent."

The plane was bucking. The passengers eyed every strut, every bolt, every screw and rivet, as if they expected it all to break apart.

Geraci tried to trust his instruments and not his eye or his anxieties. He breathed evenly. Soon the shit-brown surface of the lake came into view.

"Rattlesnake Island," said Molinari, pointing. "Right?"

"Roger that," said Geraci, using the voice again. "That's pilot talk, fellas."

"We're landing on that?" Falcone said. "That fucking little landing strip?"

The island was only forty-some acres, a fifteenth the size of New York's Central Park, and most of it, from the air, seemed to be taken up by

a golf course and an alarmingly small landing strip. A long dock protruded north from Rattlesnake Island so far it was practically in Canadian waters, which of course, during Prohibition, had been useful. The privately owned island was so tangentially a part of the United States that it issued its own postage stamps.

"It's a lot bigger than it looks from up here," Geraci said, though he wasn't so sure about that. Not only had he never landed on the island; even though his *padrino* for all intents and purposes owned it, Geraci had never been there.

Molinari patted Falcone's hand. "Relax, my friend," Molinari said.

Falcone nodded, sat back in his seat, and tried to coax a last drop of coffee from his cup.

Moments before they were about to touch down, the plane caught a downdraft, as if it had been slapped out of the sky by a giant hand. It plummeted toward the surface of the lake. Geraci could see the froth of the waves. He pulled up, got control, leveled the wings, buzzed a cabin near the shore.

"Oooo-kay," Geraci said, yanking back the stick. "Let's try that again."

"Jesus, kid," Molinari said, though he was only a few years older than Geraci. Softly, Geraci muttered the Twenty-third Psalm, in Latin. When he got to the part about fearing no evil, instead of "for Thou art with me," he said, "for I am the toughest motherfucker in the valley."

Falcone laughed. "Never heard that in Latin."

"You know Latin?" Molinari said.

"I studied to be a priest," said Falcone.

"Yeah, for about a week. Don't distract the pilot, Frank."

Geraci flashed a thumbs-up.

He found a pocket of smooth air, and his second attempt to land was improbably soft. Only now, the flight over, did one of the bodyguards start to vomit. Geraci caught a whiff of it and stifled the gag it provoked. Then the other bodyguard threw up on himself. Moments later, men in yellow slickers appeared on the end of the runway to meet them.

Geraci sucked fresh air from his window, and his passengers got out. Men opened umbrellas for them, put chocks behind the wheels, lashed down the wings, and took all but one of the suitcases. A big black carriage, lined in red velvet and drawn by white horses, waited for them onshore, to carry them up the hill—a hundred-yard journey, tops.

Geraci watched the Dons and their puke-stained men rush to get into the carriage. Once they were inside the lodge, Geraci lugged his suitcase up the hill alone, opened the cellar doors, and disappeared down the steps, into the remains of what was once a thriving casino, past the bandstand

and the cobwebby bar to the dressing room. He flicked on the light. The rear wall was made out of the kind of sliding steel door he associated with automotive garages in Brooklyn, but otherwise the room looked like a high-roller suite in Vegas: king-sized bed, red velvet everywhere, elevated bathtub. Behind the steel door was a room full of canned goods, gas masks, oxygen canisters, generators, a water-treatment system, a ham radio, and a bank vault. Underneath, carved into the bedrock, was a gigantic fuel oil tank and, supposedly, other rooms and more supplies. So long as Don Forlenza had any warning at all, whatever happened—if the state police staged a raid, if strange men came to kill him, if the Russians dropped the bomb—he could hide down here for years. Forlenza controlled the union that worked the salt mine under the lake near Cleveland; rumor had it that a crew did nothing day and night but dig tunnels to and from Rattlesnake Island. Geraci had to laugh. A kid like him, son of a truck driver, standing inside the kind of place a regular person would never even hear about. He carried the bag of money into the other room. He set it down in front of the vault.

He stood there, staring at the bag.

Money was an illusion. The leather of the bag had more inherent value than the thousands of little slips of paper inside it. "Money" is nothing more than thousands of markers, drawn up by a government that couldn't cover one percent of what it had out on the street. Best racket in the world: the government puts out all the markers it wants and passes laws so they can never be called in. From what Geraci understood, those slips of paper *represented* a month's worth of the skim from a Las Vegas casino in which both the Corleones and Forlenza had points, along with a sizable gift in consideration of Don Forlenza's hospitality and influence. Those stacks of bills *represented* the labors of hundreds of men, reduced to scrip, to wampum, exchanged for the negotiating power of a few, the actions of fewer yet. Worthless paper that Don Forlenza would accept unthinkingly. Just markers.

Minchionaggine, his father would say. *You think too much.*

Fredo rolled down the window and handed the customs agent his driver's license. "Nothing to declare."

"Are those oranges?"

"Are what oranges?"

"In the backseat. On the floor there."

Sure enough, there they were: a mesh bag of Van Arsdale oranges. They weren't *his* oranges per se. Fredo wouldn't eat an orange if it were the last fucking morsel of food on earth.

"Sir, could you just pull your vehicle over to that lane there? Next to that man in the white uniform?"

"You can have the oranges. Keep 'em, toss 'em, I don't care. They're not mine." His father had been buying oranges the day Fredo saw him get shot. One of the bullets pulverized an orange on the way into the old man's gut. A lot of things from that day were fuzzy. Fredo remembered fumbling with his gun. He remembered watching the men run away up Ninth Avenue, leaving Fredo unfired upon, too insignificant for even a single bullet. He remembered that orange. He did not remember failing to check to see if his father was dead and instead sitting on the curb weeping, even though the picture of him doing so had won the photographer all kinds of prizes. "I forgot they were even there."

"Mr. Frederick." The agent was studying Fredo's driver's license. It was under a fake name, Carl Frederick, but it was real, right from the Nevada DMV. "How much have you had to drink this morning?"

Fredo shook his head. "Over there, huh? By that guy?"

"Yes, sir. If you will, please."

Two men dressed like Detroit cops were making their way toward the man in white. Fredo pulled over and reached around to the backseat, grabbing the yellow shirt and draping it over the whiskey bottle. The man in white asked him to please step away from the car.

This was more or less exactly how it had happened to his brother Sonny. If this *was* a setup and they were there to kill him, the only chance he had was to reach under the seat, *right now*, get his gun, and come out of the car shooting. But what if they were for real? In which case he'd have killed a cop or two and might as well be dead. Though Mike had gotten away with it.

Think.

"Sir," said the man. "Now, please."

If they were for real and they found the gun there, he'd get arrested. Which someone, probably Zaluchi, could fix. No way to get rid of the gun now anyway.

Fredo palmed one of the oranges. He opened the door and got out slowly. No sudden moves. He flipped the orange to the man in white and braced himself for death. The man just stepped aside. The cops grabbed Fredo by the arms before the orange hit the ground.

"Shouldn't you fellas be Mounties?" Fredo's eyes darted, looking for the men with tommy guns.

"You're coming *into* the United States, sir. Please come this way."

"You know, that car?" Fredo said. "It's Mr. Joe Zaluchi's, who as you probably know is a pretty important businessman in Detroit."

Their grip loosened, but only a little. They took him behind the road-

side A-frame customs building. Fredo's heart knocked against his rib cage. He kept looking around for the men with guns, listening for the sounds of cocking hammers, inserted clips. He considered shaking himself free and making a run for it. Just as he was about to, the men pointed to a line on the ground and asked him to walk it.

They *were* real. They weren't going to kill him. Probably.

"Mr. Zaluchi is kind of eager to get his car back," Fredo said.

"With your arms out like this, sir," said one of the cops. He said *out* in that funny Canadian way. That accent always struck Fredo as comical.

"Sure you're not a Mountie?" Fredo asked, but he did as he was told.

So far as he could tell, he walked the line perfectly, but these jokers were unimpressed. They had him recite the alphabet backward, which he did perfectly. He looked at his watch.

"If you fellas give me your names," he said, "I'm sure Mr. Zaluchi would be happy to make a donation to your retirement fund or something. Whatever he does, I'll do, too."

Each man cocked his head, the way dogs do.

Fredo was getting the giggles.

"Is something funny, Mr. Frederick?"

Fredo shook his head. Betrayed by his own nerves, he tried, literally, to wipe the smile from his face. Nothing was funny.

"I apologize if I misunderstood, sir," one of them said. "Did you offer us a bribe?"

He frowned. "Wasn't the word I used *donation?*"

"That was the word all right," said the other one. "I think Bob thought you were proposing a sort of quid pro quo."

A cop learns some lawyer words, he gets assigned to cream puff duty at the border. *Cream puff duty:* the thought forced the corners of his mouth up, though he was furious at himself, not amused. *Cream puff.* Not Fredo Corleone, who'd knocked up half the showgirls in Vegas and was on his way back there to take care of the other half. He took a deep breath. He was not going to laugh. "I don't want no trouble. I don't want to assume anything, but"—and here he had to fight the giggles again—"did I pass the test or not?"

They exchanged a look.

The man in white came around the corner of the building. *Here it comes,* Fredo thought. But he wasn't carrying Fredo's gun. Instead, he had that wet, mangled piece of paper, the handbill, spread out on a clipboard, dabbing at it with a handkerchief. "Mr. Frederick?" he said. "Can you explain this?"

"What's that?" Fredo said. Which was when he remembered: *he'd left his gun back in the room.* "I never seen that."

The man put his face close to the note. "It's signed 'Forgive me, Fredo,' " he read. "Who's Fredo?"

Which he pronounced to rhyme with *guido*.

Which caused Fredo, finally, to erupt in laughter.

The warm-ups his doctor had prescribed took half an hour, tops, but Johnny Fontane was taking no chances. He started them in the desert, stopped in Barstow for a steaming mug of tea with honey and lemon, and was going through the regimen of humming and ululations for maybe the fiftieth time when he blew through a red light a couple blocks from the National Records Tower. An LAPD motorcycle cop swung behind him. They came to a stop together, near the back entrance of the building. Phil Ornstein—second in command at National—stood alone at the curb, pacing, smoking.

Johnny ran his fingers through his thinning hair, grabbed his hat from the seat beside him, and got out of the car. "Take care of this," Johnny said, jerking a thumb toward the cop. "Will ya, Philly?"

"Got that right." Phil put out his cigarette. "We thought you were driving down here after your midnight show. There's a room at the Ambassador Hotel we paid for and you never checked into."

The cop took off his helmet. "You're Johnny Fontane," he said, "aren't you?"

Without breaking stride, Johnny turned, flashed a million-dollar grin, made his fingers into six-shooters, winked, and fired off a few imaginary shots.

Phil, on his way to talk to the cop, stopped, sighed, and ran his fingers through his hair.

"The wife and I loved your last picture," the cop said.

It had been a Western, a real piece of shit. As if anyone would believe a guy like him on a horse, saving decent folk from desperados. Johnny gave the cop the autograph he wanted, right on the back of his ticket pad.

"Making records again, huh?" the cop asked.

"Trying to," Johnny said.

"My wife always used to love your records."

That's why none of the record companies in New York would give him a contract—no singer who'd ever been more popular with women than men (said some *pezzonovante* at Worldwide Artists) had ever managed to change that. But what Johnny hated even more was the past tense: not *loves* but *used to love*. Movies were fine, though even now, with his own production company and an Academy Award (currently swaddled in his daughter's toy crib at his ex's house), the people who ran things out here

still made him feel like some dumb Guinea who'd crashed the party. The long waits on the set bored him silly, and he'd had about enough of smart-asses calling him One-Take Johnny. From here on, if he could get the right part, swell, but he was moving on. It just wasn't where his heart was. He wasn't really an actor, not really a hoofer, not really a teenster idol or even a crooner. He was Johnny Fontane, saloon singer—a good one and, if he gave it his all, which this contract with National gave him the chance to do, maybe one of the best who'd ever lived. Maybe *the* best. Why not? It's hell when the person you know you are isn't the person people see when they look at you. Not that he was going to say anything. You don't say anything bad to or about anyone who's been loyal to you. "What's your wife's name?" Johnny asked.

"Irene."

"You and Irene ever get over to Vegas?"

The cop shook his head. "We've talked about it."

"You got to see it to believe it. Look, I'm at the Castle in the Sand all month. Classy joint. You want to come, I'll get you in."

The cop thanked him.

"Fucking guy," he said to Phil in the elevator up to the studio. "Bet he pulls over all your talent, eh? Bet he's got an autograph collection that'd fill a garage."

"You're a cynical man, Mr. Fontane."

"Loosen up, Philly, you're too serious." Though Johnny caught sight of his own mug in the shiny steel walls of the elevator, and he looked nothing if not serious. He took off his hat, ran his fingers through his hair, and replaced it. "Everything all set?"

"For over an hour now," Phil said. "There's just one thing. Hear me out, okay?"

Johnny poker-faced him and said nothing, but he'd listen. It was Phil Ornstein who—after every other major label had passed—had given Johnny a seven-year contract (for lousy dough, but so what? dough wasn't an issue). It was Phil Ornstein who had insisted that Johnny Fontane's voice was back and that his public image as a boozing, brawling thug was both unwarranted and would only enhance sales.

"I know you wanted Eddie Neils for musical director, and if that's what you really want, fine, we'll try it."

Johnny hit the *stop* button on the elevator. Eddie Neils had arranged and recorded Johnny the last time he'd had any hits. Johnny went to his house and wouldn't leave until the old man gave him an audition right in his marble-floored hallway, among statues of eagles and naked people, and, when Johnny overcame the shitty acoustics and sounded like a little bit of something, Eddie had finally agreed to work with him again.

"You're telling me Eddie's not here?"

"That's what I'm telling you," Phil said, tapping his gut. "Bleeding ulcer. Had to go to the hospital last night. He'll be fine. But—"

"He's not here."

"He's not. Right. Here's the thing, though. He was never our choice for you anyhow."

That Phil was classy enough to say *for you* instead of *for your comeback* wasn't lost on Johnny. "You always wanted the other guy," Johnny said. "The kid. Trombone man."

"Yes. Cy Milner. He's not a kid. He's forty, forty-five years old. We took the liberty of hiring him to write a couple new charts."

Milner had been a 'bone man with Les Halley, but after Johnny had left the band. They'd never met. "Since when? Since yesterday?"

"Since yesterday. He works fast. He's a legend for the fast-working."

The kid's a legend, and I'm One-Take Johnny. "What about the charts Eddie already did?"

"We can use those, too. Either way."

Phil ran his hands through the hair he mostly didn't have. He was the sort of man who unconsciously took on other people's mannerisms.

"What do you think I am, difficult?" Johnny yanked the *stop* button. "C'mon, Philly. I'm a pro. We'll give old Cy a whirl, try some things, see if we can kick up a little magic, eh?"

"Thank you, Johnny."

"I always liked a Jew with manners."

"Fuck you, Johnny."

"And guts."

Johnny got off the elevator and strode down the hall toward 1A, the only studio big enough for the string setup he wanted. He burst through the doors and made a beeline to the gray-blond man across the room. He had on a British tweed suit and horn-rimmed glasses, one lens so thick it made the eye look funny. Broad-shouldered, like someone who'd played football, not what you expected from a man with a baton. He looked like a kindly headmaster from some movie. Johnny and Cy Milner made each other's acquaintance with the bare minimum exchange of words. Johnny jerked a thumb toward the microphone, and Milner nodded.

Milner mumbled directions to his engineer and then took the podium. The musicians reached for their instruments. Milner took off his coat, raised his brawny arms, and flicked his baton. Johnny was in front of the mike and ready to go.

"C'mon, gents," he said. But that was all he said.

Johnny hit the song hard from the first note, and the orchestra— Eddie Neils's people every one—surged lushly behind him. It was like old

times. He felt himself riding over the top of the song. He could still do this. Just like riding a bicycle.

When they finished, the people in the booth clapped soundlessly.

Milner sat down at a stool. Johnny asked him what he thought. Milner said he was thinking. Johnny asked if he thought they should do it again. Milner said nothing. He just stood and raised his arms. They did it again. Milner sat back down and started making notes.

"What are you doing?"

Milner shook his head but said nothing else. Johnny looked at Phil, who got the message and brought them all into the booth together.

"We're getting rid of two thirds of the orchestra," Milner said.

Not "we should" or "maybe we should"; just the flat statement. Johnny snapped. This was exactly the kind of orchestra he'd used on his biggest hits, exactly the sound people yearned for.

Milner stood his ground, expressionless, absorbing Johnny's tirade.

Finally Milner handed Phil a slip of paper. On it was the list of people to take off the clock and send home. Phil arched an eyebrow, then pointed at himself. Milner said he didn't care who did it.

"Hell," Johnny said. "Do what you need to do." He sat down heavily on a leather chair.

Milner was the one who sent the men packing. Johnny sat and looked over the list of songs he'd chosen, compared the charts Neils had done and the ones Milner had done. Milner's were written fast, dotted with sloppily filled notes. There was nothing like the old days about this.

Moments later, Johnny was back behind the microphone, staring down at the sheet music on the stand in front of him. Milner's this time. An old Cole Porter number that he'd recorded once before, way back when. He wanted to both kill this Milner and hug him. He'd love to prove the man wrong. He prayed that the man was right.

People who'd seen Johnny Fontane in clubs, or even those who'd seen him record ten years ago, wouldn't have recognized the coiled, brooding man now breathing evenly behind the microphone. The remaining musicians took their places. The engineer wanted a mike check. Just as they were getting ready, some kid came in and asked where he should put Mr. Fontane's tea. Johnny pointed but did not talk, rocked slowly in place but did not otherwise move, kept his eyes fixed on the music but did not really look at it. This all took only a few moments, but to Johnny it felt like hours and also like no time at all. He closed his eyes. The last time he'd sung this song, his voice had been as clear as rainwater and, as far as he was concerned, about as interesting.

Johnny was hardly aware of the song starting. His breath control was so built up from all that time in the pool, he was barely aware he was

singing. The arrangement was everywhere and nowhere, kicking in when he wanted it, staying out of his way without needing to learn how. One verse in, and all Johnny was aware of was that bum in the song, trying to use pretty words and jokes to convince himself he could survive without the woman who'd left him. By the time Johnny hit the first chorus, he *was* that bum. He wasn't singing to the other people who might be hearing him, in the studio, on the radio, in the privacy of their living room with a bottle of whiskey emptying out far faster than it should. He was singing to and for himself, telling truths so private they could burn holes through stone. There was nothing that anyone who really heard the music could do except look upon all the pretty words and false fronts lost love inspired, upon all the blame lavished on everyone who did the right thing and left you, and despair.

The song finished.

Milner lowered the baton and looked to the engineer, who nodded. The people in the studio—even the diminished band—burst into applause. Milner headed toward the booth.

Johnny stood back from the microphone. He looked around at the smiling faces of all these yes-men. Milner returned from the booth and started repositioning microphones. He said nothing. You'd swear the guy was Sicilian, for how little he said, and how much.

"No," Johnny said. "Thank you all very much, but no. You fellas were great, but I can do better. Let's give it a shot, okay?"

Milner repositioned another mike.

"That eighth bar, Cy," Johnny said. "Can you do that up like Puccini?"

Milner fished a wrinkled piece of paper from his shirt pocket, a dry-cleaning receipt it looked like, and sat down at the piano bench, noodled around a bit, scribbled a few notes, gave a few brief directions to various men in the band.

Johnny wouldn't be working with Eddie Neils anytime soon.

He'd been somewhere, gone somewhere, singing that song, and he could go there again, he was absolutely sure of it, and go deeper, and then do it a dozen more times. He could fill a whole long-playing record with songs that took people out of their lives, and deeper into them, and—it came to him, in a flash—sequence the songs the way Les Halley did back when Johnny was his singer, only all together on a record, so that everything plays off of everything else, in a way and to an extent that nobody, not even the best jazz cats, had ever quite done before.

Phil Ornstein kept congratulating everyone. Philly wasn't going to be happy to have them spend the whole session on just this one song, but too bad. Johnny Fontane would defy you to show him a record shop where

people walked in asking about the new releases from National Records. It was the songs they wanted. It was the singers.

Milner climbed to the podium. His glasses made it look like his regular eye was on the orchestra and his huge eye was on Johnny. Johnny looked down, and again they began.

Eight bars in, Puccini's ghost somehow cracked the song open even farther, and Johnny filled his lungs with air and swam right in.

Michael and Kay spent the first hour of the flight in relative silence. Once Kay marveled about the startling beauty of the desert, comparing it to the work of abstract painters Michael knew he should know. He pretended to, and she talked about art for a while, and he sat there wondering why, about something so trivial, he hadn't just been honest.

Michael asked about the move. Kay considered telling him about the day last week when the Clemenzas had shown up at his parents' old house, which they'd already bought, and found Carmela Corleone standing at the window of her late husband's office, a room she'd hardly set foot in over the years. She was drunk and mumbling prayers in Latin. *This is my home,* she'd announced. *I'm not moving to no desert.* He'd hear about that soon enough. Who was she kidding? He must already know. "It's going fine," Kay said. "Connie's been a big help."

Even that neutral comment was loaded. Michael didn't react to the mention of his sister, but he knew Connie still blamed him for the death of her husband, Carlo, even though an assistant D.A. he knew from Guadalcanal had charged a Barzini button man with the murder.

"Strange," Kay said after another long silence. "Flying over the desert in a seaplane."

In every direction, desolate, unpopulated sand and scrub stretched to the horizon. Eventually shapes that turned out to be mountains emerged from the haze to the north.

"How are the kids getting along?" Michael finally asked.

"You saw them this morning," Kay said. Mary, who was two, had cried and chanted, "Daddy, Daddy," as they'd left. Anthony, who this time next year would start kindergarten, was sitting under a box on the floor, watching television through a hole. It was a program in which clay figures confront life's problems: the temptation not to share one's red wagon or the virtues of admitting one's role in the shattering of Mom's sewing lamp. Safe to say the little clay boy would never have to contend with two of his uncles being murdered. His cardigan-sweatered clay daddy would never be called an "alleged underworld figure" in *The New York Times.* His svelte clay grandfather was unlikely to drop dead at his feet. "How did you think they were?"

"They seemed to be making out fine. Do they have friends yet? In the neighborhood?"

"I'm still unpacking, Michael. I haven't had time—"

"Right," he said. "I'm not being critical."

He was close enough to Reno airspace to check in.

"Your parents had a nice trip?" he said.

"They did." Her father had taught theology at Dartmouth long enough to have a small pension from that, too, augmenting the one he'd been drawing since he'd retired as a pastor five years before. He and Kay's mother had bought a travel trailer and planned to see America. They'd arrived yesterday, to help Kay get the house together and see their grandkids. "They said the trailer park was so nice they might never leave." The Castle in the Sand had its own trailer park.

"They're welcome to stay there as long as they like."

"That was a joke," she said. "So what do you have planned? What's to do in Tahoe?"

"What would you say to dinner and a movie?"

"It's not even eleven o'clock."

"Lunch and a movie. A matinee. There's got to be a matinee we can catch."

"Okay. Oh, God, Michael, look! It's beautiful!"

The lake, much bigger than Kay had imagined, was dotted with fishing boats and ringed by mountains. Around most of it, thick dark pine forest extended to the banks. The surface of the water looked as smooth as a lacquered table.

"It is," he said. "I've never seen a more beautiful place."

He glanced at her. She was swiveling around in her seat, craning her neck to see the splendor into which they were descending. She seemed happy.

Michael came in low, near the shore, and landed the plane not far from a dock and boathouse. There seemed to be nothing else around but woods and a clearing nearby, where a point of land jutted into the lake.

"This is pretty far from the town part," Kay said.

"I know a great place for lunch," he said, "right near here."

As the plane approached the dock, three men in dark suits emerged from the woods.

Kay drew in a breath and pulled back in her seat. The men came out on the dock, and she called her husband's name.

Michael shook his head. The implication was clear: *Don't worry. They work for me.*

The men climbed out onto the floats and tethered the plane to the dock. The one in charge was Tommy Neri, Al's nephew. Al—who, in his old NYPD uniform, had emptied a service revolver into Don Emilio

Barzini's chest, and who, with a steak knife taken right from the man's kitchen, had disemboweled Phillip Tattaglia's top button man and urinated into the man's steaming body cavity—was in charge of security for all of the Family-controlled hotels. Like Al, Tommy had been a New York cop. All three looked to be barely out of high school. They said almost nothing and headed back into the woods.

As they did, Kay faced Michael at the foot of the dock. There was both a world of things to say about that and nothing whatsoever.

"Wait right here," Michael said. He touched the side of his face where it had once been crushed, which he did, probably unconsciously, when he was nervous. For years after that cop had punched him, he'd done nothing, blowing his nose constantly and talking about his ruined looks until finally, for Kay's sake, he'd had it fixed, after which he'd looked better, but not exactly like before, never again exactly like himself. She had never once told him this.

He walked to the door of the boathouse, reached up onto a ledge, found a key, and went in.

Kay both did and didn't want to ask whose boathouse this was. What stopped her wasn't fear of the answer. It was fear of Michael not wanting to be asked.

A moment later, he emerged, thrusting a dozen roses toward her. She moved backward a step. Then she reached forward and accepted them. They kissed.

"Happy anniversary," Michael said.

"I thought this trip was my present."

"All part of the same package."

He ducked back into the boathouse and came out carrying a striped beach blanket and a huge picnic basket covered with a red-checked tablecloth. Two long loaves of Italian bread poked out of the basket, like crossed swords. "Voilà!" he said. With his head, he pointed toward the clearing. "Lunch at the beach."

Kay led. She set down her flowers and spread out the blanket.

They sat down Indian-style, facing each other. They were both overcome by hunger, and they dug in. At one point Michael dangled a bunch of grapes over Kay's head.

"All right," she said, "I'll bite." She bit off a grape.

"Nicely done," Michael said.

She looked into the woods but could not see the men. "That wasn't what I meant. That wasn't *only* what I meant." She paused. But why not ask? It wasn't a question about business. He'd brought her here on a date. For their anniversary. "Where'd this food come from?"

He pointed across the lake. "I had it delivered."

"Whose land is this?"

"This land? Here?"

She frowned.

"Oh," he said. "I guess it's yours."

"You guess?"

"It's yours." He stood. He pulled a piece of paper from his back pocket. It was a photostat of the deed. Like everything they owned, it had her name on it and not his. "Happy anniversary," he said.

Kay picked up her roses. That they could afford this, on top of the house in Las Vegas, both appalled her and thrilled her. "You sure know how to show a girl a good time," she said.

Michael knew he shouldn't have called this land an anniversary present, too. He was overdoing it. "Your last present," he said. He put his right hand on an imaginary Bible and raised his left. "I swear. No more surprises."

She looked up at him. She ate a strawberry. "You bought land here without telling me?"

He shook his head. "I have an interest in a real estate company that bought it. It's an investment. I was thinking we could develop the land here, for us. For the family."

"For the family?"

"Right."

"Define family," she said.

He turned around and faced the lake. "Kay, you have to trust me. Things are in a delicate place right now, but nothing's changed."

Everything has changed. But she knew better than to say this. "You move us to Las Vegas and then, before we even unpack, you move us again, up here?"

"Fredo already had things set up for us in Las Vegas. But in the long run Lake Tahoe is a better opportunity. For *us,* Kay. You can work with the architect, build your dream house. It may take a year, even two. Take your time. Get it right. The kids can grow up swimming in this lake, exploring the woods, riding horses, skiing." He turned to face her. "The day I asked you to marry me, Kay, I said that if everything went right, our businesses would be completely legitimate in five years."

"I remember," she said, though this was the first time they'd spoken of this since then.

"That still holds. We've had to make some adjustments, it's true, and not everything went right. I hadn't counted on losing my father. There were other things, too. A person can't expect everything in a plan that features human beings to go right. But"—he held up his index finger—"but: We're close. Despite some setbacks, Kay, we are very, very close." He

smiled and went down on his knees. "Las Vegas already has a certain reputation. In any version of this plan, we'll retain our hotel and casino businesses there. But Lake Tahoe is different. This is a place that can work for us all, indefinitely. We have enough land here to build any kind of house you want. My mother, your folks if they want. Anybody who wants to be here, there's room."

He did not mention his sister or his brother. Kay knew him well enough to be sure this was probably not an accident.

"I can fly the seaplane in and out of here, and any size jet can fly into Reno, which is just up the road. Carson City is less than an hour from here. San Francisco is three."

"Carson City?"

"The capital."

"I thought Reno was the capital."

"Everyone thinks that. It's Carson City."

"Are you sure?"

"I've been there on business, to the capitol building itself. You want me to prove it?"

"Sure."

"It's Carson City, Kay, believe me. How do you propose I prove it?"

"You're the one who proposed proving it."

He picked up an egg. He held it like a dart and flicked it at her.

She caught it and in the same motion threw it back at him. She missed. It sailed past him and two-hopped into the lake, and he laughed.

"It's nice to see you like this," she said.

"What do you mean?"

"I can't explain it."

He sat down beside her. "There's a lot I can't explain, too, Kay. But I have a vision. It's the same vision I always had, only now it's a hell of a lot closer to reality, with our children growing up more the way you did than I did, all-American kids who can grow up to be anything they want. You grew up in a small town; so will they. You went to a good college; so can they."

"You went to one, too. You went to a better one."

"You finished. They won't need to leave for any reason, and certainly not to help with my business. They won't be influenced by me the way I was by my father, and living here will be a part of that. We're distancing the family—"

Kay arched an eyebrow.

"Define it however you want, all right? The family. Our family. Ourselves. We're distancing ourselves from all the"—he picked up a half-empty milk bottle and chugged the rest of it—"from let's just say New

York. That *alone* is going to chart a new course for us. Our holdings in the state of Nevada—this isn't a very populated state, Kay, not yet—our holdings here will give us a means of reorganizing my business in ways that would have been impossible in New York. We're already done with the hardest part of this. Mark my words: five years from now, the Corleone Family should be every bit as legitimate as Standard Oil."

"Should be," Kay repeated.

He sighed. If this was what she was like as a teacher, her students had been both lucky and doomed. "I apologize for it not being one hundred percent certain. What in life is?"

"Family, right?"

Michael chose to take that as playful. "What else can I do? Walk away? Even if I could do that and not make a widow out of you, what then? Take a job selling shoes while I go to night school and finish college? People depend on me, Kay, and while you and the kids come first and always will, I have other people to consider, too. Fredo, Connie, my mother, and that's just the immediate family, not the business. We sold the olive oil company because we needed a sizable and completely government-approved amount of cash, but even after that we still have controlling interests in all kinds of other completely legitimate businesses: factories, commercial real estate, dozens of restaurants and a chain of hamburger joints, various newspapers and radio stations and booking agencies, a movie studio, even a Wall Street investment firm. Our interests in gambling and lending money can all be operated where it's legal. As for what we spend to help get politicians elected—that's no different from what any big corporation or labor union does. I suppose I could stop and sit back and watch it all fall apart, watch us lose everything. *Or.*" He raised an index finger. "Or. Instead, I could take a few more calculated risks and try to bring about a plan that's already, I would say, eighty percent implemented. You know I can't tell you the specifics of it, but I will tell you this, Kay: if you can just have faith in me, five years from now, we'll be sitting on this very spot, watching our kids—Mary and Anthony and maybe a couple more—swimming in the lake, and Tom Hagen, my brother Tom, will be two months away from getting himself elected governor of the great state of Nevada, and the name Corleone will have started to mean the same sort of thing to most Americans as the names Rockefeller and Carnegie. I want to do great things, Kay. Great things. And the main reason for that, first and foremost, is you and the kids."

They gathered up their lunch. Michael whistled, and Tommy Neri came out of the woods. He said he and the guys had already eaten, but a snack would be great, thanks.

Michael showed Kay into the boathouse. Inside was a Chris-Craft,

aquamarine with spruce panels. He extended an arm. Kay got in. She expected Tommy Neri to follow her, but he released the boat and stayed behind.

"I was wondering," Michael said, backing the boat out into the lake. "What's the traditional fifth-anniversary present, anyway?"

"Wood. Which reminds me." She pulled a card out of her purse and handed it to him.

"Really?" he said. "Wood?"

"Really," she said. "Open that."

Michael smiled and pointed at the tree-lined banks of the lake. "Behold," he said. "Wood."

"Open the card," she said.

When he did, a brochure tumbled out. He picked it up.

"Behold," she said. "Woods."

It was from the pro shop of a country club in Las Vegas.

"Woods and irons both. I got you a set of golf clubs," she said. She squeezed his right bicep. "You have to go in to get measured for them."

"Golf, huh?"

"You don't like it? You don't want to take it up?"

"I do," he said, rubbing the side of his face. "It's perfect. Golf. Like any all-American executive. I love it. I do."

Michael put the boat into gear, and they started across the lake to town. Kay slid next to him on the bench seat, and he looped his arm around her. He opened the throttle all the way. She lay her head on his shoulder and kept it there for the twenty-minute trip.

"Thank you," she said when they got to shore. "I love the lot. I love your plan." She leaned toward him. "And—" She kissed him. Michael did not usually like to show his emotions in public, but something in her kiss shot right through him, and as she started to pull away he pulled her back toward him and kept kissing her, harder now.

When they finally separated, breathless, they heard applause. It was two teenage boys onshore. They were each with a girl. The girls apologized. "They're retards," one said.

"Can't take them anywhere," said the other.

They were all dressed as if they'd just come from church.

"No apologies necessary," Michael said. "Say, is there a movie theater around here?"

There was, and they got directions. The boys lagged behind the girls, laughing and punching each other on the arm.

"I was going to say—" Kay said.

"You love me," Michael said.

"You're as bad as those boys," she said. "And you love me, too."

The theater was closed. The picture they were showing was one pro-

duced by Johnny Fontane's production company, which was sixty percent owned by a privately held Delaware-chartered corporation in which the stock was held by fronts for the Corleone Family. At some point, Michael would (for a purchase price of symbolic money) buy the whole shebang. That's if there was anything worth buying. The company had once been fairly profitable. This picture, like most of the recent ones, did not star Johnny Fontane. Michael rapped on the window.

"It's closed, Michael."

He shook his head. He knocked harder. Before long, a bald man in a cowboy shirt and dungarees came into the lobby and mouthed that they were closed. Michael shook his head and knocked on the door again. The man came to the door. "Sorry, mister. Sundays all we got is the one show at seven-thirty."

Michael motioned for the man to open the door, and he did.

"I understand," Michael said. "It's just that my wife and I are on a date, and this"—he turned and glanced at the movie poster—"Dirk Sanders, he's just about her favorite movie star in the world, isn't that right, honey?"

"Oh, yes, that's right."

"Well, you can see it tonight. Seven-thirty."

Michael looked at the man's left hand. "You see, though, we need to be home by seven-thirty, and this, today, is our anniversary. Our fifth. You know how it is, right?"

"I'm the owner," he said, "not a projectionist."

"Which makes your time all the more worthwhile. I wouldn't expect you to do a favor like this for a total stranger. You know how to operate the projector, though, am I right?"

"Of course I do."

"Could I just have a word with you, then? Alone? Just for a second?"

The man rolled his eyes, but Kay could tell there was something in Michael's cold stare that affected the man. He let Michael in. They exchanged some whispered words. Moments later, Michael and Kay sat in the middle of the theater as the movie started. "What did you say to him?"

"Turns out we have some mutual friends."

A few minutes in, as the lead characters literally bumped into each other in a Technicolor soundstage version of Paris, the theater owner brought them two sodas and a bucket of fresh popcorn. The man and the woman in the movie took an instant dislike to each other, signaling the dull inevitability of their falling in love. Soon Kay and Michael began making out in the dark, like kids. They couldn't leave, not after getting the owner to show the movie just for them. They kept at it. Things escalated. "Behold," Kay whispered, grabbing his cock. "Wood."

Michael burst out laughing.

"Shhh," Kay said.

"We're alone," Michael said. "All alone."

A year ago, one of the two men pacing near the ticket counter at Gate 10B of the Detroit City Airport was a barber on Court Street in Brooklyn who made book on the side, reporting to a guy who reported to a guy who reported to Pete Clemenza. The other one had been a goat farmer in Sicily, near Prizzi. In the intervening years, loyalty and battlefield promotions and a frank shortage of labor had caused them to come up through the ranks more swiftly than a person could in times of peace. The barber was third generation, with terrible Italian; the goatherd still struggled with English. Their flight to Las Vegas was boarding now. There was no sign of Fredo Corleone. The goatherd held a phantom telephone to his ear. The barber sighed and nodded. What choice did he have? He went to a pay phone and started dumping quarters into it.

"Service," said the voice in Las Vegas. Rumor had it that the girls at the phone service, this one and the one in Brooklyn, were nieces of Rocco Lampone's, all of them gorgeous, but no one ever saw them or knew for sure.

"This is Mr. Barber calling," he said.

"Yes, sir. And your message, Mr. Barber?"

"Our luggage," he said, "has been misplaced." He almost said *lost*, but *lost* would have been taken as *killed*. "It won't be on the scheduled flight."

"Yes, sir. Is that all?"

Is that all? When Don Corleone hears that Fredo's new bodyguards lost him in a casino somewhere in the wilds of Detroit, yes, that'll be all, all right. "Just say that me and Mr.—" The barber blanked. *Goat* in Italian was what? He put his hand over the phone. The goatherd was across the hall, getting coffee. "*Come si dice* 'goat'?"

"*La capra,*" said the goatherd, shaking his head.

As if, growing up on Court Street, the barber had ever seen a goat, had ever had an occasion to learn that fucking word. "Mr. Capra and me are looking for it. We hope to be on the next flight out, luggage and all."

"Yes, sir. Thank you, sir."

Sandra Corleone parked her Roadmaster wagon on the grass near Francesca's dormitory.

"Oh, Ma," Francesca said. She slipped into her stylish new raincoat. "You're not going to park here, are you?"

All the other cars were squeezed onto the pavement of the street and the loading zone.

"I'm sure it's fine," Sandra said, turning off the car and reaching into the backseat to wake Kathy. As if on cue, two other cars followed her lead. "People have to park somewhere."

They opened the gate of the wagon, and Kathy loaded Francesca and Sandra up with boxes, which were all from the liquor store her mother's fiancé owned. Most of the other kids had moving company boxes or steamer trunks. Kathy took only a table fan and Francesca's Bakelite radio. "Someone has to get the door," she said.

The front doors were wide open. Kathy punched the elevator for them. Already, their mother was drenched in sweat. She set her boxes down in the elevator. "I'm fine," she said, too winded to say anything more. She was thirty-seven, ancient, and had gained a lot of weight since they'd moved to Florida.

"I can't believe you're making Ma carry the heavy stuff," Francesca said.

"I'm not feeling that great." Kathy smirked. "I can't believe you're wearing a raincoat."

"You never know when it might rain," Francesca said. Kathy knew full well it was the dress code. Francesca was wearing Capri pants. Female students in anything other than a dress were required to cover themselves. Most, Francesca had been told during orientation, chose raincoats. The dress code probably didn't apply on moving day, but Francesca wasn't taking any chances. She was the kind of person who followed rules.

When they got to Francesca's room, Kathy set down the fan and the radio, flopped down on the bare twin bed, curled up, grabbed her abdomen, and moaned.

Francesca rolled her eyes. Because she rarely got cramps, she was skeptical about her sister's ongoing problems with them. But complaining about it was as useless as Kathy was.

"Where are the sheets?" Sandra said.

"On the other bed," Francesca said.

"Not those." She pulled out a nail file and started slicing open boxes. Francesca made a trip by herself. When she got back upstairs the bed was made with pink sheets, and Kathy was propped up on the pillows from both beds, the fan trained on her, her eyes closed, a wet washcloth draped on her forehead, sipping a Coke through a straw, listening to jazz on the radio.

"Where'd you get the soda?"

"The dorm mother came by with them," Sandra said. "To welcome you."

"I said I was you," Kathy murmured.

Francesca was, for a split second, furious. But it probably wasn't a bad idea. It was just a soda. And as for Kathy's pretending to be Francesca, it was efficient and would hardly cause trouble in the long run. Just like Kathy herself. "Thanks," Francesca said.

Kathy waved a hand. "Don't mention it."

"I won't. You going to share that Coke?"

"That's Charles Mingus there."

"Wonderful. You going to share that Coke?"

Kathy handed it to her. "Charles Mingus plays bass. Wild, huh?"

Francesca took out the straw and drank as much of the soda as she could, hoping to finish it, but the fizz in her nose overcame her. She handed the bottle back to her sister.

On the next trip down, her mother stuck her head into the common living room, grabbed a delicate-looking wooden chair, and motioned Francesca down a dark hall to the side door. Classes didn't start until Tuesday, and, thanks to her mother, Francesca had already broken two cardinal rules from orientation—*Never leave the side door open* and *Never take furniture from the living room*. Other girls and their parents immediately benefited from this, too, of course.

Her mother took three heavy boxes and could barely walk. Francesca set her load down on the steps to the side door, waiting for her mother to catch up.

"Why couldn't you have gone to a girls' school?" called Sandra Corleone, breathing heavily, pointing with her head toward the next building, where dozens of young men and their parents were moving in. Her mother was a loud talker. "Like your sister is?"

Her mother's sundress was so drenched with sweat that in places Francesca could see her dark-colored bra and underpants. She was not a slim woman, but her underwear seemed unnecessarily gigantic. "How are you possibly going to unload Kathy's stuff all by yourself?"

"Don't worry about Kathy. She'll be fine. You know, no one said the boys' dormitory would be right next door." Her voice grew even louder. "I don't like the looks of that."

People were looking, Francesca was sure. Francesca was tempted to correct her and say *men's dormitory*, except that that would have made things worse.

On the next trip, her mother took a lighter load. Still, by the time they got to the side door, she was huffing and puffing and had to stop. She plopped down on that wooden chair, which made a splintery sound. People are supposed to move to Florida and be out in the sun all the time and slim down so they'll look good in tennis clothes and at the beach. Her mother was getting bigger all the time. This summer, Francesca had

caught Stan the Liquor Man pinching her mother on the ass and saying he liked her *caboose*. Francesca shuddered.

"How can you possibly be cold?" her mother asked.

"I'm not."

"Are you sick?"

She looked at her mother, who was practically having a heatstroke in that straining chair. "No," Francesca said. "I'm fine."

"Right next door," her mother repeated, pointing at the men's dorm with her thumb this time. "Can you believe it? Because I can't."

Why she was talking so loud, who knew?

"So why *didn't* you want to go to a girls' school?"

She said this loud enough that Francesca was sure people in the men's dorm could hear. "This is a good school, Ma, all right?" She extended a hand to help her mother up. "C'mon."

When they got to Barnard, Francesca knew, all Kathy would hear was "Why did you have to go so far from home?" Anything Francesca did was found wanting for not being enough like what Kathy did and vice versa. Before the homecoming dance, her mother had pulled Francesca aside to extol the virtues of Kathy's date, whom she later that night dumped. Then Francesca asked him to the Sadie Hawkins dance. The next day, her mother started listing all the things wrong with him. *He's changed,* Sandra said. *Anyone with eyes can see that.*

Francesca took another trip by herself. It was only then that she noticed how many doors were festooned with Greek letters. Her mother and Kathy had talked her out of coming up the week before, in time for sorority rush, her mother because she had her heart set on the convenience of making one big hoop-de-doo car trip and Kathy because she said sororities were great for WASPs, sluts, or dumb blondes, but not for any sister of hers, who already *had* a family and who certainly didn't need to pretend she was the *sister* of a bunch of slutty blonde WASPs. Francesca had said that cinched it, she was rushing. But she hadn't. Only now did it occur to her that the friendships made last week might already mark Francesca as a loser, an outcast: as *different*.

By the time she got back to her room, her mother had opened her boxes and suitcases and begun putting things away. She'd also produced a small Madonna print and a set of red bull horns, neither of which Francesca would leave up after her mother left. "You don't need to do that," Francesca told her.

"Bah," Sandra said. "It's no problem."

"Really," Francesca said. "I can take care of it."

Kathy laughed. "Why not just tell her you don't like her going through your stuff?"

"I don't like you going through my stuff, Ma."

"I go through your *stuff* at home. *Stuff*? I hope this good school here will teach you not to talk like a dirty beatnik. And anyway, what are you trying to hide from me, eh?"

"Nothing." *Beatnik*? "And in case you haven't noticed, we're not *at* home."

Sandra looked up as if startled by a loud noise.

Then she sat herself down at Francesca's desk and burst into tears.

"Now you've done it," Kathy said, sitting up.

"You're not helping any."

"I wasn't talking to you," Kathy said, and of course she was right: it's not just yawning and laughter that can be contagious.

The twins teared up, then began to cry, too. They all three huddled together on the bed. It had been a terrible year. Grandpa Vito's funeral, which had been rough on everyone. Then Uncle Carlo's bizarre disappearance. Chip, the sweetest one in the family, getting called a name at school, snapping, and breaking the kid's skull with his thermos. Yet there was only one other time the three of them had ever been like this: united, embracing, sobbing. The girls had been in Mr. Chromos's math class. The principal came to get them and took them to his office without telling them why. Their mother was in there, her face red and puffy. She said, "It's your father, there's been an accident." They all fell onto the principal's smelly orange couch and sobbed for who knows how long. Now, sobbing together again, they must have thought of that day, too. Their sobs got louder, their breathing more ragged, their embrace tighter.

Finally they calmed and released their grasp. Sandra took a breath and said, "I only wish—" She couldn't say the rest of it.

A sharp knock came at the door. Francesca looked up, expecting this to be the true first impression her dorm mother would have of her. Instead it was a couple, he in a powder blue suit and she in a poodle-cut hairdo, both smiling and sporting HELLO, MY NAME IS name tags.

"Excuse us," said the man, whose name tag read BOB. "Is this Room 322?"

The number was painted in black on the door. His index finger was actually touching it.

"Yes, pardon us," said the woman. They both had an extremely thick southern accent. Her nametag read BARBARA SUE ("BABS"). She was looking past them to the Madonna and frowning. "If y'all'd like us to come back later—"

"This is her room," the man said, stepping aside and gently pushing a dark-skinned girl across the threshold. The girl kept her eyes on her Mary Janes.

"I believe we're interrupting," the woman said.

"Are we interrupting?" the man asked.

Sandra Corleone blew her nose. Kathy wiped her face on Francesca's pillow. Francesca used her hand. "No," she said. "No. Sorry. Come in."

"Fantastic," the man said. "I'm Reverend Kimball, this is my wife, Mrs. Kimball, this is our daughter Suzy. With a *Z*. Not short for Suzanne. Just Suzy. Say hello, Suzy."

"Hello," the girl said, and then looked back down at her shoes.

"We're Baptist." The man nodded toward the Madonna. "We have Catholics in Foley, though, the next town over. I played golf once with their leader. Father Ron."

Francesca introduced herself and her family—pronouncing it *Cor-lee-own*, which even her mother did lately—and braced for a question about her name. It didn't come.

Suzy looked from one sister to the other, visibly confused.

"Yes, we're twins," Kathy said. "That one's your roommate. I go to another school."

"Are you identical?" Suzy asked.

"No," Kathy said.

Suzy looked even more confused.

"She's kidding," Francesca said. "Of course we're identical."

The man had noticed the bull horns. He touched them. Sure enough, they were real. "Suzy is an Indian," he said, "like you folks."

"She's adopted," whispered the woman.

"But not a Seminole," he said, and laughed so loud everyone else in the room jumped.

"I don't follow you," Sandra said.

With a whiny sigh, the man stopped laughing. Suzy sat at what would be her desk and stared at its Formica top. Francesca wanted to give her flowers, wine, chocolate, whatever it would take to make her smile.

"Florida State," the man said. "They're the Seminoles." He pantomimed throwing a football. He laughed again, even louder, and stopped laughing, even more abruptly.

"Naturally they are," Sandra said. "No, I mean about being an Indian. We're Italian."

The man and the woman exchanged a look. "Interesting," he said. *Inner-esting.*

"Yes," said his wife. "That's different."

Francesca apologized and said her mom and sister had to go but she'd be back in just a sec to help Suzy with her stuff.

Her mother flinched slightly at *stuff*, but of course did not correct Francesca in front of the Kimballs.

Francesca and Kathy held hands on the way out to the car. Neither one of them could, or needed to, say a word.

"Want me to drive, Ma?"

Sandra opened her purse, took out a handkerchief and her keys, tossed the keys to Kathy.

"Don't get pregnant," Kathy said.

Their mother let this go, did not even express feigned decorous shock.

I won't become a WASP either, Francesca thought. *Or a dumb blonde. Or anyone else's sister.* She squeezed Kathy's hand. "Don't wreck your eyes reading," Francesca said.

"Don't do anything I wouldn't do," Kathy said.

"Maybe I *am* you," Francesca said.

It was an old joke. They'd always wondered how their mother had kept them straight as babies, always presumed they'd been mixed up a few times until they were old enough to assert their own identities.

They kissed each other on both cheeks, the way men would, and Kathy got into the car.

As Francesca hugged her mother good-bye, Sandra managed it at last. "I only wish," she whispered, "that your father could be here to see this." Sandra stepped back, triumphant. She looked from one daughter to the other. "His college girls." She blew her nose. It was very loud.

"Pop never liked us to cry," Francesca said.

"Who likes to see his family cry?" Kathy said.

"He wasn't exactly one for tears himself," Francesca said, wiping her face on the sleeve of her raincoat.

"Are you *kidding?*" her mother said. "Sonny? He was the biggest baby of us *all.* At movies he'd cry. Corny old Italian songs made him blubber like a baby. Don't you remember?"

Seven years later, and Francesca was already starting not to.

She watched the Roadmaster nose its way through the clogged, narrow, palm-lined drive. As the car pulled around the corner, Francesca silently mouthed the word *good-bye.* She had no way of knowing this for sure, but she'd have bet her life her sister did the same.

Chapter 5

Nᴵᴄᴋ Gᴇʀᴀᴄᴵ heard footsteps coming from across the darkness of the abandoned casino. A heavy limping man in squeaky shoes. "Sorry to hear about your ma, kid," a voice called.

Geraci stood. It was Laughing Sal Narducci, Forlenza's ancient *consigliere*, dressed in a mohair sweater with diamond-shaped panels. When Geraci was growing up, Narducci was one of those guys you saw sitting out in front of the Italian-American Social Club, smoking harsh black cigars. The nickname was inevitable. A local amusement park had this motorized mannequin woman at the gate called Laughing Sal. Its recorded laughter sounded like some woman who'd just had the best sex of her life. Every Sally, every Salvatore in Cleveland, and half the Als and Sarahs, got called Laughing Sal.

"Thanks," Geraci said. "She'd been sick a long time. It was kind of a mercy."

Narducci embraced him. As he let go, he gave Geraci a few quick pats, though of course Falcone and Molinari's bodyguards had frisked him back in Detroit. Then Narducci opened the wall. Laughing Sal saw the bag, lifted it, and nodded. "Arizona didn't help her none, huh?" He put the bag down without even opening it, as if he could count money purely by weight. A half million in hundreds weighs ten and a quarter pounds. "Bein' away from this fucking weather?"

"That definitely helped," Geraci said. "She liked it there. She had a pool and everything. She was always a big swimmer."

Narducci closed the wall. "Her people were from by the sea, you know. Milazzo, same as mine. Me, I can't swim farther than from here to the far side of a whiskey glass. Ever been?"

"To the far side of a whiskey glass?"

"Milazzo. Sicily."

"Sicily yes, Milazzo I never quite made it to," he said. He'd been in Palermo only last week, working out minor personnel issues with the Indelicato clan.

Narducci put a hand on Geraci's shoulder. "Well, like they say, she's in a better place."

"Like they say," Geraci said.

"Jesus Christ, look at you." Narducci squeezed Geraci's biceps, as if they were fruit he might buy. "Ace Geraci! Looks like you could still go twenty rounds in the Garden."

"Nah," Geraci said. "Probably just ten, eleven."

Narducci laughed. "You know how much money I lost on you over the years? A bundle, my friend. A bundle."

"Should have bet against me. That's what I usually did."

"I tried that," Narducci said. "Then you'd always win. And your father? How's he?"

"Getting by." Fausto Geraci, Sr., had been a truck driver and a Teamsters official. Connected but never inducted, he'd driven cars and done various favors for the Jew. "He's got my sister there." *And the Mexican woman on the other side of Tucson he thinks no one knows about.* "He'll be fine. He misses going to work, if you want to know the truth."

"Retirement don't suit some people. But he should give it time, the retirement."

Not a problem Nick Geraci ever expected to face. *You come in alive,* Vito Corleone had said at Geraci's initiation, *and you go out dead.* "We ready?" Geraci said.

"Ready." Narducci slapped him on the ass and escorted him back through the casino. Geraci looked for an exit route, a flight of stairs. Just in case.

"How long since that casino was in business?" Geraci asked.

"Back in the Italian navy days," Narducci said, meaning the fleet of speedboats they'd operated on the Great Lakes during Prohibition. "Now we got these ships. Best things to have. No local fuck has the resources to raid ships. Plus, your guests are stuck out on the lake all night. Give 'em a show, set up a few rooms with some girls, then drop 'em back off at their cars. You've taken all their money, and they're happy you did it."

The Stracci Family had huge secret casinos in the Jersey Palisades, but as far as Geraci knew, none of the Families in New York had gambling ships like that. Maybe he'd look into developing a few, once the peace was solid and things cooled down.

"Other than legal joints in Vegas and Havana, we're out of the on-land stuff altogether," Narducci said. "Except down in West Virginia, which don't really count. You can buy off that whole state for less than the heating bill on this place here."

He ushered Geraci into a dank room and pulled open the door to an old cage elevator.

"Relax, kid," Narducci said. "Who's going to kill you here?"

"I get any more relaxed," Geraci said, "I'll need you to tuck me in and read me a story."

They got in. Narducci smiled and hit the button. He'd called it right, though; it was how Geraci had been trained: elevators are death traps.

"Changing the subject," Narducci said, "I gotta ask. How'd a big *cafone* like you get through law school?"

"I know people." He'd done it on his own steam, night school, busted his ass. He still had a few classes to go. But Nick Geraci knew the right answers to things. "I have friends."

"Friends," Narducci repeated. "Attaboy." He put his hands on Geraci's shoulders and gave him a quick rub, the way a cornerman might.

The door opened. Geraci braced himself. They stepped into a dark, carpeted hallway crowded with chairs and settees and little carved tables that were probably worth a mint. At the end of the hall was a bright marble-floored room. A young redheaded nurse pushed Vincent "the Jew" Forlenza toward them in a wheelchair. Narducci left to go get Falcone and Molinari.

"*Padrino*," said Geraci. "How are you feeling?" His speech and probably brain were fine, but he wasn't going to walk again.

"Eh," Forlenza said. "What do doctors know?"

Geraci kissed Forlenza on each cheek and then on his ring. Forlenza had stood as godfather at his christening.

"You've done well, Fausto," Forlenza said. "I hear good things."

"Thank you, Godfather," Geraci said. "We hit a rough patch, but we're making progress."

Forlenza smirked. His disapproval might have been gentle, but it registered; a Sicilian doesn't have the American faith in progress, doesn't use the word the way Geraci just had.

Forlenza motioned to a round table by the window. The storm raged even stronger now. The nurse pushed Forlenza to the table. Geraci continued to stand.

Narducci returned, accompanied by the other Dons and their bodyguards, who'd freshened up from their airsickness episode but still seemed shaky. Frank Falcone entered with a heavy-lidded stare, bovine in its blankness. It told the whole story. Molinari had, as planned, told him who Geraci was. Falcone pointed at the paintings of men in jodhpurs and pale stout women in tiaras. "People you know, Don Forlenza?"

"Came with the place. Anthony, Frank. Let me introduce you to an *amico nostro*." A friend of ours. A friend of *mine* was just an associate. A friend of *ours* was a made guy. "Fausto Dominick Geraci, Jr."

"Call me Nick," Geraci said to Falcone and Molinari.

"A good Cleveland boy," Forlenza said, "Ace, we used to call him, who now does business in New York. He is also, I am proud to say, my godson."

"We met," Falcone said. "More or less."

"Eh, Frank. I'm sure you can indulge a man's pride in his godson."

Falcone shrugged. "Of course."

"Gentlemen," Geraci said, "I bring you greetings from Don Corleone."

Forlenza looked at the guards and pointed to Geraci. "Go ahead, do your job."

Geraci presented himself to be frisked, though of course they'd done it to him back in Detroit, too. *One more time today and we'll be going steady,* he thought. This search was state of the art, complete with a hand inside his shirt and under the band of his underpants, looking for recording devices. As they finished, two white-haired waiters in bow ties brought out a crystal tray of *biscotti all'uovo,* small bowls of strawberries and orange wedges, and steaming glass mugs of cappuccino. They set a silver bell beside Forlenza and left.

"They came with the place, too." Forlenza took a sip of his cappuccino. "Before we get started," he said, "you must all understand that the decision to invite an emissary from Don Corleone was mine alone."

Geraci doubted this but had no way of knowing for certain.

"No offense, Vincent," said Falcone, "or, what's-your-face? Geraci. No offense, but I still can't get used to calling that little *pezzonovante* Michael *Don Corleone.*" Falcone had ties with the Barzini Family and also with a Hollywood union guy named Billy Goff whom the Corleones had supposedly clipped. On top of which, he had made his bones in Chicago, under Capone.

"Frank," said Molinari. "Please. This accomplishes nothing."

Forlenza asked them to sit, and they did. Narducci sat in a leather armchair a few feet away. The bodyguards took seats on a sofa against the far wall. As they all watched, the nurse, without a cue, turned and walked out of the room.

Falcone gave a low whistle. "It's that white uniform. You could put any dame in one of those, I'd want to bend her over a gurney, hike it up, and screw her silly. Every time I go to the hospital, my dick gets so hard and stays so hard they got to give me extra blood."

"Frank," said Molinari.

"What? Jokes are fucking wasted on *you,* my friend."

Forlenza asked Molinari and Falcone about the wedding of Joe Zaluchi's daughter and Pete Clemenza's son, who wasn't in the business per se (he built shopping centers). They also asked how it was that a Cleveland boy had come to fall in with the Corleones. Geraci said that after his boxing career didn't work out, he was stuck in New York with a wife and kids, and his godfather made some calls. Some expression returned to Falcone's face. Forlenza cleared his throat in a way everyone understood as a call to order, took a long drink of water, and began.

"*Sangu sciura sangu,*" he said. "Blood cries for blood. This has been the undoing of our tradition in Sicily. An endless spiral of vendettas has left our friends there less powerful than any time in a century. Yet here in America we are flourishing as never before. There is enough money, enough power, for everyone. We have legal operations in Cuba and, particularly in the case of the Families represented here, Nevada. The amount we can make from this is, if I may be honest, limited only by our imaginations *and*—" he held up one finger—"*and* by our unfortunate tradition of riding the runaway train of vendetta to oblivion."

Forlenza looked toward the high white ceiling and continued in Sicilian, which Geraci understood though couldn't really speak. "Perhaps there are men in this room who know who is responsible for the killings in New York." He gave Geraci, Falcone, and Molinari each a glance of precisely equivalent duration, then took a long, strategic sip of his cappuccino. "Emilio Barzini, a great man and one of my oldest, dearest friends, has been killed. Phillip Tattaglia is dead." Forlenza paused to eat one of the tiny *biscotti,* underscoring all that was implied in his lack of any encomium to describe the weak and whiny Don Tattaglia. "Michael Corleone's oldest, wisest *caporegime,* Tessio, was killed. Don Corleone's brother-in-law, the father of his baby godson, was killed. Five other *amici nostri,* dead. What happened? Maybe one of you knows. I for one do not. My sources tell me that Barzini and Tattaglia, frustrated by the weak protection their narcotics business got from the Corleones' judges and politicians, went after the Corleones and were killed in return. Perhaps. Others say Michael Corleone killed Barzini and Tattaglia so he could transfer his base of operation west and have it not seem to be a move made out of weakness. A possibility, no question. Could it be that we are witnessing revenge for the deaths seven years ago of the eldest sons of Vito Corleone and Phillip Tattaglia? Why not? In such matters, seven years can be but the flick of a fish's tail. Or"—and here he took another cookie and took his time munching it—"perhaps—who knows?—this is all a plot by Don Stracci and Don Cuneo, whose families have never had the power held by either the Barzinis or the Corleones, to seize control of New York. Their quick negotiations for peace have, in the minds of many people, added force to this speculation. Even the newspapers are adopting this wild guess and promulgating it to the stupid masses as fact."

This inspired knowing chuckles. The newspaper stories were plants. The Straccis' power base was New Jersey, and the Cuneos ran upstate New York (and the biggest milk company in the region, which was how Ottilio Cuneo had become "Leo the Milkman"). Neither was believed to be powerful or ambitious enough to make an attack on the three stronger families.

"Or maybe," Falcone said in English, "who knows? The Corleones killed 'em all."

Falcone, Geraci was fairly certain, would have been surprised to learn that his angry hyperbole was one hundred percent correct.

"Even their own men?" Molinari said. Though a friend of the Corleones, Molinari, too, almost certainly did not know what had really happened in New York. "C'mon, Frank."

Falcone shrugged. "I don't know. I'm like Vincent, I can't unravel this fuckin' thing. I hear people talkin', that's all. But a lot of what I hear is that even though Don Vito, may he rest in peace, pledged on his life that he would not avenge his son's death, what's-his-face—"

"Santino," Geraci said.

"Another country heard from." He raised his cappuccino cup in a mock toast. "Thanks, O'Malley. Yeah: Santino. He said he wouldn't avenge it or even look into it. The way *we* understood it was that his *Family* wouldn't do that, but, see, it was all a bunch of fucking double-talk. All he meant was that he personally wouldn't do it. Vito stepped down so that Michael could plot revenge and carry it out as soon as the old man died."

"Forgive me," Geraci said. "It's not double-talk. It didn't happen that way."

"Look, Vincent," Falcone said, "why are the Corleones the only New York Family represented here, huh? Why am I having a sit-down with you two and someone else's wet-behind-the-ears *soldato*? Even your *consigliere*'s not at the table."

"No one ever called it a sit-down," Molinari said. "It's just a few friends talking is all. The weather clears, maybe Don Forlenza will loan us some clubs, we can grab some golf—"

"Very comfortable chair," said Narducci, rubbing its arms.

"—or take a boat and go fishing," Molinari continued. "Maybe have a cocktail with your nurse friend and a lovely afternoon of buttfucking."

Falcone frowned. "I don't do that-there. *In culo?* Did somebody say I did that?"

"Hit a nerve, did I?" Molinari said.

Don Forlenza drained his cappuccino and set his mug down so hard it shattered. No one at the table reacted. At first no one made any attempt to pick up the mess.

A door opened. The bodyguards leapt to their feet and faced it. Two of Forlenza's men entered. Laughing Sal motioned for them to go. They went.

"We are not clever little policemen trying to solve crimes," Forlenza said. He said "solve crimes" as if it were a fresh cat turd in his mouth and switched back to Sicilian. "I have my own problems and so, I gather"—he motioned toward Falcone and Molinari—"do you. If I have trouble in Cleveland, this affects no one in New York. No one there is concerned.

The trouble is mine, as it should be. Yet if New York has problems, too often this, of no concern whatsoever to me, becomes my problem. The papers are filled with speculation. The police have questioned and harassed friends of ours far from the scenes of those crimes in New York—even our partners, people handling the money, running the businesses, fronting the investments. Some in Washington are pressuring the FBI to take agents away from their war on communism and send them after us and our interests. Senators are threatening to hold hearings. Even our legitimate businesses may be targeted by the IRS. I have grandchildren going to college, buying their first houses, and the complications I have had to endure simply to get my own money to them—"

He took a drink of water. They watched his hand as he set the glass down carefully.

"Well, you know. Millions of dollars of lost business, and it must be the same for you."

Falcone began making a little sculpture out of cookies, strawberries, orange rinds, and nearby shards of glass.

"Our concerns," said Forlenza, "are four." He thrust out his left hand to say this, ready to tick off those reasons. It was a pet gesture. Forlenza had four reasons for anything. Four reasons Jews were misunderstood. Four reasons why, all pride aside, Joe Louis would have knocked out Rocky Marciano. Four reasons veal was better than sirloin. If Don Forlenza had been born with two extra fingers, he would have had six reasons for everything.

"First," he said, returning to English, his right index finger bending back his left, "New York. Helping them understand that this thing of ours can stand up to anything but infighting, that we all win the uneasy peace we have achieved simply by observing it."

This met with nods of agreement all around, even from Geraci.

"Second"—middle finger—"Las Vegas. Seven years ago, we sat in a fancy bank building in New York City and agreed that Las Vegas would be open for business for us all. A city of the future, where any Family could operate. Yet now the Corleones have set up headquarters there—"

Geraci started to talk, but Forlenza wagged a finger at him.

"—and the Chicago outfit all of a sudden thinks it's in charge of enforcement there."

"Fuckface," muttered Narducci, a faraway look in his eyes.

"For your information," Falcone said, now adding strawberries and more glass to his pile, "he don't like to be called that." Luigi Russo, who ran things in Chicago, preferred to be called Louie. He'd gotten his more colorful nickname (which the newspapers were forced to shorten to "the Face") from a hooker who claimed the only sex he wanted was to stick his

big nose up her cunt. Her decapitated body washed up on the Michigan side of the lake; her head was never found.

"Speaking of which," Forlenza said, "third"—ring finger—"Chicago."

Geraci glanced at Falcone, whose operation was once just a branch of the Chicago outfit. No reaction. Every piece of glass that had been on the table was in front of him now.

"When we all met seven years ago, Chicago wasn't even invited," Forlenza said. "Can you imagine?"

Once, eager to direct Capone's growth away from them, the New York Families had agreed that everything west of Chicago belonged to Chicago. There was still enough Cleveland in Nick Geraci to recognize this as a plan that could have made sense only to a New Yorker. Capone fell; brutal chaos followed. L.A. and San Francisco split off. Moe Greene, from New York, had a dream that became Las Vegas, which was designated an open city with no say from Chicago. After Greene was killed, the Corleones took over his casino and built the Castle in the Sand, but the most powerful force in the city was a coalition of the midwestern Families, led by Detroit and Cleveland. Chicago had points in that coalition (as did the Corleone Family, but only a few), and Louie Russo had made noises about wanting more control of it. Chicago was unified again and getting stronger by the day. With New York in turmoil, many saw Russo as the most powerful figure in American organized crime.

Forlenza shook his head in disbelief. "The New York Families said they'd given up trying to civilize Chicago. Back then, people called them our black sheep. Our mad dogs."

"Our castrated chickens," said Molinari, referring to the literal translation of *Capone*.

"Bunch of animals," said Laughing Sal.

Falcone patted his pile on either side, shoring it up. It stood about two hands high. He leaned his face toward it as if he were trying to catch his reflection in the larger shards.

"And fourth"—pinkie—"drugs." At that word, Forlenza slumped back in his wheelchair. He looked exhausted.

"Drugs?" Molinari said.

"Oh, boy," said Narducci.

"Not this again," said Falcone.

Geraci tried not to react at all.

"An old riddle, yes," Forlenza said, "but one still unsolved. It is the biggest threat to our thing. Yes, if we don't control it, others will, and we may lose power, but if—"

"If we do," Falcone interrupted, "not that we aren't already, the cops supposedly won't look the other way like they do with gambling, women, unions, and so forth. C'mon, Vincent. Learn some new songs, huh? Look

around. This little booze smuggler's paradise"—a thunderclap boomed, in perfect synch with *paradise*—"that was your thing. You've done well, and *salu'*. But for men of my generation, it's narcotics. For the next one, who knows?"

Narducci muttered something that Geraci heard as "Martian hookers."

"Many of us," Forlenza said, "when we took our oaths swore—*swore*, on our Family's saint—that we would not be involved with narcotics." He pointed to Falcone's heap of cookies, fruit, and glass. "What are you doing?"

"Something to do is all," he said. "Look, Vincent, I love you like you was *my* godfather, I do, but you need to live in the present day. Out west, we got it all set up, foolproof, layers and layers of guys between all the suckers who use it—your niggers, your Mexicans, your artistic types, your hotshots—and the people who sell it to 'em and the people who sell it to *them*. And so forth. The way we do anything else, and it works fine. The cops or whatever, they can slow it down a bit, especially in troubled times like this here, but the number of things that'd have to go wrong for them to get any of *us* in legal problems? Forget it. Not a chance."

The Cleveland Family, Geraci knew, had some dealings in narcotics but contented itself with tributes and left most of the profits to the Negroes, the Irish, and the miscellaneous. After Prohibition, Cleveland had simply taken its next best things, gambling and unions, and expanded those. It wasn't an organization open to new ideas or even new men. Geraci's father said it had been more than ten years since Cleveland had initiated a new member.

Forlenza forged ahead, repeating himself: booze was different—cops drank and didn't really want to break that up—but drugs were something else.

As Falcone reached down, got a piece of glass from the floor, and held it up toward the chandelier, Molinari diplomatically pointed out that Forlenza might be slightly naive about the makeup of today's young street cop.

"That's it," Forlenza said. He stuck his fingers in his mouth and whistled. The waiters returned. He pointed at the glass and cookies. "Take that away."

"Did I *say* I wanted that taken away?" Falcone set down the shard and looked at the waiters. "Take it away and I'll blow your fucking head off."

Chicago, right there, Geraci thought. *Chicago in a fucking nutshell.*

The waiters stood still. The one on the right—a Slavic-looking man with thick gray hair—had gone as white as his shirt. The one on the left, a man with a fringe of white hair and a tire black moustache, faced Forlenza, his head slightly bowed.

"Take it away," Forlenza said.

"Just try it." Falcone took the last *biscotto* and placed it like a cherry atop his pile.

"I got a grandkid going to some expensive school," Narducci said. "Makes sculptures kind of like that. You two should meet."

"Oh yeah?" Falcone swiveled in his chair to look at him. "Where at?"

"Where you going to meet or where does he go to school?"

"School."

Narducci shrugged. "I just pay for it. To me, one kindergarten's the same as another."

Falcone leapt from his chair, and as he lunged toward the old *consigliere,* Geraci, still seated, hit Falcone squarely on the chin. His head snapped back. He staggered and fell.

The bodyguards rushed the table. Geraci stood. Time seemed to slow down. Amateurs had such bad footwork, he expected this to be over fast.

Molinari burst out laughing. Amazingly, a beat later, from the floor, so did Falcone. The bodyguards stopped. Geraci didn't move.

"Kindergarten," Molinari said. "That's pretty funny."

Falcone stood, rubbing his jaw. "Nice punch, O'Malley. Sittin' down. Wow."

"Instinct," Geraci said. Narducci didn't even say thank you. "Sorry. You all right?"

Falcone shrugged. "Forget about it."

"What were you going to do," Molinari said, "beat up an old man?"

"Wouldn't be the first time," Falcone said, and now everyone laughed. Geraci took his seat, and the bodyguards took theirs. "I don't give a fuck," said Falcone. "Take it."

The two visibly grateful waiters rushed to obey. The one with the dyed moustache even had the poise to return a moment later and refill everyone's water glass.

"Blow their head off with what, Frank?" Forlenza asked.

"Figure of speech," said Falcone, which got another big laugh.

Geraci had been looking for an opening, a chance to say what he'd come there to say, and this seemed like the time. He made eye contact with his godfather.

Forlenza nodded.

Again he cleared his throat as a call to order, and in the pause this created took a regally unhurried drink of water.

"Gentlemen," Forlenza said. "Our guest unfortunately needs to go." By which, everyone understood, he meant, *should leave before certain things are discussed,* not *has somewhere else to be.* "But he has come a long, long way, and before he leaves, he'd like to say a few words."

Geraci, in addressing his superiors, stood. He thanked Don Forlenza

and promised that his words would be few. "Though I am flattered to have been allowed at this table," Geraci said, "Don Falcone is correct. This is not my place. As you point out"—indicating Falcone and thinking of Tessio, who always stressed the natural advantages of being underestimated—"I'm just someone's wet-behind-the-ears *soldato*." A lie, but one Falcone had initiated.

Narducci's echolalia had grown so faint that this time Geraci couldn't guess at what he said.

"The Corleone organization," Geraci said, "is not, I assure you, a threat to any of you. Michael Corleone wants peace. He's determined that this cease-fire become permanent and has taken measures to achieve it. He never had any intention of running Las Vegas. After three or four years in this interim location, the Corleone Family will relocate to Lake Tahoe. Actually, it will cease to exist. Our New York operation will continue in some form, but everything in Lake Tahoe will be run by Michael Corleone like the affairs of any American business magnate—Carnegie, Ford, Hughes, whomever."

"Law school," Narducci said, presumably triggered by *whomever*.

"The Corleone Family," said Geraci, "will not in the future initiate any more members." Tonight, in other words, to be construed as the present. "Michael Corleone will retire from our way of life, and he will do so in a manner that will both be respectful of other organizations and, if anyone chooses, also provide a model for any of us who wishes to take a similar path." He pushed his chair in. "Gentlemen, unless you have any questions or concerns . . . ?"

He waited a moment. Falcone and Forlenza both looked at Molinari, who ever so slowly blinked. A known friend of the Corleones, he was prepared to elaborate and the more appropriate person to do so.

"In that case," Geraci said, "I'm going to go check on the weather, in case we—"

"Fuck the weather," Falcone said. He had a hundred grand on the fight. "When it's time to go, hotshot, we're going."

Narducci muttered something that sounded like "acts of God."

"Fuck God," Falcone said. "Don't take this wrong, Vincent, but I'm not getting stuck—"

"I'm sure it will be fine," Geraci said, and left.

Tom Hagen went back to his room to wait. He tossed his unused three-hundred-dollar tennis racquet onto the bed. He kept on his tennis shirt and changed from shorts into chinos, from sneakers into loafers. On the two different golf courses he could see from the air-conditioned splendor

of his room, foursomes of brightly dressed men laughed and drank cock-
tails on the vast expanse of green where a few decades earlier there had
been only cactus and sand, where anyone out there at midday would have
been roasting, starving, dying of thirst, gleeful buzzards circling overhead.
Instead, servants on golf carts bore cold beer and fresh towels. It reminded Hagen of the stories he'd read about ancient Rome, where the
emperors cooled their palaces in the summertime by having slaves haul untold tons of heavy, melting snow down from the mountaintops. More
slaves stood beside the mounds of snow night and day, drenched in sweat
and waving big papyrus fans. For a king, no corner of the earth is inhos-
pitable.

Hagen told the front desk to call him whenever a car came for him.
He left a wake-up call for 1:45.

It came. He awoke famished. Hagen hated late lunches. Two o'clock
came and went. Hagen called down and was told, "No, sir, there still
hasn't been anyone asking for you."

He hung up the phone and stared at it, willing it to ring. Like a stupid kid waiting for his sweetheart to call. He picked up the phone again
and had the operator connect him with Mike's office. No answer. He tried
Mike's home number. If the meeting with the Ambassador were about
anything of lesser stakes, Hagen would already have been on a plane
home. Kay's father answered. Michael and Kay had gone out for their anniversary lunch. Hagen had forgotten. He'd catch up with Mike later.
Then he called home to say he'd gotten in okay and everything was fine,
and Theresa was crying because Garbanzo, their arthritic dachshund, had
run away. The kids had made flyers and posted them in the neighborhood
and now were out looking for their pet. What if the dog wandered out
into the desert? Think of all the ways it could die then: coyotes, cougars,
snakes, thirst. There was an atomic bomb test tomorrow; think of that.
Hagen tried to calm her down. He reassured her that an arthritic dachshund probably couldn't have made it out of the subdivision, much less the
sixty-some miles to that test site.

Hagen looked at the racquet, available for twenty bucks at any hardware store and not nearly as good as the one he had at home. In his mind's
eye, he saw his brother Sonny, outraged at this show of disrespect, ordering everything on the room service menu, eating what he wanted and pissing over all the rest, then smashing up the racquet and the room, too,
sticking the Ambassador with the damages—*we don't take cash, you have to
sign for it*—and heading home. Hagen's stomach growled. He smiled. He
missed Sonny.

The phone rang. His driver was here.

Hagen went down, but there was no car there. He asked the parking

attendant. No cars for a while now, he said. Hagen's head pounded. He'd forgotten his sunglasses. Squinting was painful. Back in the lobby, he saw a Negro in a tuxedo. He'd pulled up on the other side of the building, in an optic-white-roofed, six-seater golf cart. It was after two-thirty.

"This may be the biggest golf cart I've ever seen." Hagen shielded his eyes from the glare off the vehicle's white skin.

"Thank you, sir," said the driver, clearly someone who'd been told in his training not to make eye contact with his employers or their associates except when spoken to.

The ride across the golf course, through a maze of tennis courts, and across another golf course took about fifteen minutes, during which each of them averted his eyes from the other.

When the Ambassador had first gone into business with Vito Corleone, his name had been Mickey Shea. Now he was known in the newspapers as M. Corbett Shea. No one called him Mickey. Close friends and family, even his wife, called him Corbett. To everyone else, he was the Ambassador. His father had left County Cork, settled in Baltimore, and opened a saloon across the street from the one Babe Ruth's dad owned. The oldest of six children, Mickey Shea grew up working hard—scrubbing floors, lugging boxes, shoveling manure from the street and snow from the alley. But his life, especially compared to other Irish kids' in the neighborhood, was a comfortable one. Soon, though, his parents began sampling too much of their own wares. They lost everything. His mother became the rare woman who chooses a gun to kill herself, opening wide to wrap her mouth around the barrels of a sawed-off shotgun taken from the shelf under the cash register. Mickey, snow shovel in hand, was the one who discovered her near-headless body in the alley behind the bar. His father just kept drinking until that, too, did the job.

Mickey joined the army at seventeen and soon became a supply sergeant. It was there, not (as legend had it) on the streets of Baltimore, that he learned that there were the rules and then there was what people do. The black market, lucrative in peacetime, proved to be a license to print money once the United States entered the war. The week after the armistice, Sergeant Shea rigged himself an honorable discharge. He was a millionaire, most of it in cash. He went to New York and opened a tavern in the Tenderloin district. Being both Irish and a fine negotiator, he quickly forged useful bonds with the police and, more important, Irish street gangs like the Marginals and the Gophers. He bought a few warehouses near the piers, a solid investment that helped him keep his import-export skills sharp. And that might have been that, if not for Prohibition. Shea was God's perfect bootlegger. He owned warehouses. He employed dockworkers. He knew how to move goods outside the law. He had

friends in two eastern cities and people in Canada, former supply sergeants from the RAF with whom he'd done business and remained friendly. And not only did he run a tavern, he ran one known as a cops' bar. Nearly overnight, that tavern became an ice cream parlor and its basement was gutted, remodeled, and reopened as a speakeasy. The cops, his former regulars, were now paid to drink there for free—money well spent, since the place got a word-of-mouth reputation as one safe from raids. Before Shea knew it, that basement was a who's who of Manhattan swells—opera divas and Broadway stars, newspaper publishers and their star columnists, flashy lawyers and florid aldermen, even presidents of banks and titans of Wall Street. Shea bought the building next door and tunneled through to its basement, almost tripling the size of the place. A full orchestra played there every night. It was as brazen an operation as existed anywhere in America.

But Mickey Shea was a man who had seen things. During the war, men like him could get rich, but there was a whole tier of rich and powerful people above that, people who hadn't had to get their hands dirty setting up a swap of morphine and girlie pictures for blood and generators, who'd never had to work the room slapping the backs of men they'd bribed. He'd used his connections with the cops in lower Manhattan to help keep the converted olive oil trucks from getting stopped on the way to his warehouses (and to keep those warehouses from getting raided), but what were those men in those trucks doing that he couldn't do? Why was he getting only the warehousing money and the money from the speakeasy when he could just as easily—*more* easily—bring the stuff down and sell it himself? So men in Canada set him up with a fleet of speedboats and retrofitted syrup trucks. Soon the men in the olive oil trucks were blowing up his boats and his trucks—often with Shea's men still inconveniently inside. Shea got cops to get other cops to get other cops to look out for his people, a corridor of sheriffs, judges, and beat cops all the way from Quebec to Manhattan, which helped but didn't solve things.

One day, Genco Abbandando—Hagen's predecessor as *consigliere* and the man Shea thought owned Genco Pura Olive Oil—contacted a police captain on Shea's payroll and set up a meeting between Mickey Shea and Vito Corleone. They met at the lunch counter of an Italian grocery store in Hell's Kitchen, only six blocks from Shea's warehouses but someplace he'd never been. He hated spicy food and refused to eat anything but bread and sauceless noodles. When the meal was finished, Don Corleone explained that the men running those converted trucks were only leasing them from Genco Pura, then let the implications of this sink in. He spoke of the wastefulness of free-market competition, and here, too, Mickey Shea was a quick study. Don Corleone told Mickey Shea that he

believed that someone with so many friends (he did not have to say in City Hall and on Wall Street and especially among the Irish-dominated ranks of law enforcement) must be a great man, someone it would be profitable to know. Mickey Shea's friends became friends of the Corleone Family. Shea was instrumental in building up Don Corleone's political and legal connections, ultimately his biggest source of power. Don Corleone was instrumental in amassing for Shea so much wealth—at such great reserve both from any bloodshed and from the overt display of muscle necessary to prevent it—that even before the death of that great cash cow Prohibition, Shea was able to sever all traceable ties to the sources of his wealth and reinvent himself in the public eye as a blue blood: M. Corbett Shea, president of a brokerage house, part owner of a baseball team, and much-photographed philanthropist (the country's many Corbett Halls, Corbett Auditoriums, and Corbett Public Libraries were funded by the Ambassador). His children went to Lawrenceville and then to Princeton. Their service in the war was packaged in national magazines as heroism. He served as the ambassador to Canada for the last six weeks of a lame-duck president's term—not long enough to move his family but long enough to get the title. His oldest daughter was married to a Rockefeller. His oldest son was now governor of the great state of New Jersey.

The Ambassador would have no way of knowing that it had been Tom Hagen, while Genco was still *consigliere*, who'd taken care of that wartime news coverage.

And even though the Ambassador thought he'd bought his ambassadorship—which was mostly true—it was Hagen who, behind the scenes, had secured it.

It was Vito Corleone who'd taught Hagen the power of staying silent about such matters.

Motorized iron gates glided open. The driver stopped the golf cart in front of a house made of stone blocks, designed like a half-scale replica of an English castle. A crew of Mexicans was laying sod and planting cactus. Shirtless, leather-skinned blond men on scaffolding were antiquing the stones with narrow brushes. Hagen thought his head would explode.

"This way, sir." The driver still made no eye contact.

Hagen, squinting, wondering if three hundred more bucks could get him four aspirin and a pair of shades, headed up the front walk.

"No, sir. This way."

Hagen looked up. The man was standing in the rocks of the unfinished yard. The driver took him around the side of the house to the pool, as if Hagen couldn't be trusted to go through the house. Hagen checked his watch. Almost three. He would have to catch a later plane home.

In the backyard, the pool was shaped like the letter *P*, a circle spliced

onto a single lane for lap swimming. Around the perimeter of the circular part were seven identical white marble angels. The Ambassador sat at a stone table, shouting into a white telephone. A platter of meats and cheeses was set out. In front of the Ambassador was a plate smeared with mustard and strewn with crumbs. This arrogant fuckjob had already eaten. Plus he was stark naked (which might have thrown Hagen except that the last meeting he'd had with the Ambassador had taken place in the steam room of the Princeton Club). His skin was the color of rare prime rib. His chest and back were hairless as a fetal pig's. He didn't have sunglasses on either.

"Hi ho!" he shouted at Hagen, though he was still on the phone.

Hagen nodded. "Mr. Ambassador."

The Ambassador motioned for Hagen to sit down, which he did, and to eat up, which he did not. "Already ate," Hagen mouthed, and he made a wincing gesture that indicated he was sorry for the misunderstanding.

The Ambassador lowered his voice but kept on talking, cryptically, but the conversation seemed personal, not business. At one point he put his hand over the receiver and asked Hagen if he'd brought trunks. Hagen shook his head. "Too bad," the Ambassador said.

Naturally. Only a *pezzonovante* could sit there in his fluorescent altogether. Not that Hagen would have stripped naked and gone for a dip. The point, of course, was Shea's rude semiassertion that he couldn't.

Finally, the Ambassador got off the phone.

"Hey hey! It's the Irish *consigliere.*" *Cahn-sig-lee-airy.*

Hagen wondered if the Ambassador really didn't know how to pronounce the word or if the mispronunciation was willful, a joke on the "Irish" part of it.

"German-Irish," Hagen corrected.

"Nobody's perfect," said the Ambassador.

"And I'm just a lawyer," Hagen said.

"Even worse," the Ambassador said—a strange thing to say, Hagen thought, for a man who'd sent four children to law school. "Drink?"

"Ice water," Hagen said. Said, not asked. In public, the Ambassador was a famously charming man. The lack of any apology had to be both on purpose and purposeful.

"Nothing stronger?"

"Ice water will be fine." As a chaser to a fistful of aspirin. "Heavy on the ice."

"I quit boozing, too," the Ambassador said, "other than a nip of Pernod from time to time." He raised an iced half-empty glass. "Prune juice. Want some?" When Hagen shook his head, the Ambassador shouted for water. "My father went the same way as yours, you know? Drink. Curse of our people."

A young Negro woman in a French maid costume brought out a silver pitcher of ice water and one small crystal class. Hagen downed his water and refilled the glass himself. "Sorry to have missed you on the court," he said, pantomiming a ground stroke. "I've been hearing for years you have quite a game."

The Ambassador looked at him as if he didn't know what he was talking about.

"From other people," Hagen said.

The Ambassador nodded, slapped together another sandwich, stood, waved for Hagen to follow him, walked to the side of the pool, and sat down on the top step of the shallow end of the circular part. His prick lolled in the water, half submerged before him. He tapped it, absently.

"I'm fine right here, sir," Hagen said. "In the shade. If you don't mind."

"You're missing out." He held the sandwich in his teeth and made a show of splash-sprinkling water on himself, then bit off a chunk. As if it could see this, Hagen's stomach growled. "Refreshing," the Ambassador said.

The Ambassador finished his sandwich. Hagen asked about his family. The Ambassador went on and on about them, especially Danny (Daniel Brendan Shea, former law clerk to a U.S. Supreme Court justice and now the assistant attorney general of the state of New York) and Danny's big brother, Jimmy (James Kavanaugh Shea, governor of New Jersey). Danny, whose wedding last year, to a direct descendant of Paul Revere, had been a highlight of the Newport social season, was screwing a TV star, the hostess of a puppet show Hagen's girls watched. And Jimmy. The governor. Though only in his first term, he was already inspiring talk about a run for the presidency. The Ambassador did not ask about Hagen's family.

The Ambassador went on to ask about several of the men's mutual associates and acquaintances. Hovering between and among their every chatty word were the recent events in New York. But neither man spoke the names of any of the dead—Tessio, Tattaglia, Barzini, nobody. Neither Hagen nor the Ambassador spoke specifically of those events, or had to.

The Ambassador stood, knee deep on a step of the pool, and stretched. He was a tall man, a giant by the standards of men of his generation. He'd claimed to have licked Babe Ruth in a fistfight when they were kids; this was a lie, but with the Babe dead for years now and the Ambassador standing there in his aging, ropy-penised glory, the story contained its own sort of truth. The Ambassador dove forward and began swimming laps. After ten he stopped.

"Fountain of youth, fella," he said, not as breathless as Hagen would have thought. "Swear to you. Swear to fucking God."

Had it not been for the beating sun, his headache, his irritation at

being trifled with by the Ambassador, and his need to get home tonight, Hagen might have let things drag out.

"So, Mr. Ambassador. Do we have a deal?"

"Ho ho! You get right to the point there, don't you?"

Hagen glanced at his watch. It was pushing four. "I'm like that."

The Ambassador got out of the pool. How the woman in the maid outfit knew to appear from out of nowhere with a towel and a thick robe, Hagen couldn't imagine. Hagen followed the Ambassador into a glassed-in porch, which was, thank God, both dark and air-conditioned.

"You flatter me. You and Mike do. Or rather you people flatter *Danny*." He paused for Hagen to catch his implication. "I can't really call off the investigation. You must know that. And Danny certainly can't. Even if he could, it's a local matter. New York City, not state."

All of which Hagen correctly understood to mean the opposite. What that little turn of phrase about Danny meant was that the Ambassador had rigged it so that nothing came directly from his office, nothing could be traced back to him.

"We wouldn't want anything called off," Hagen said. "It's important that justice be served. Moving forward, getting back to business without the disruption these false accusations have caused, that's in the best interest of all involved."

"Hard to argue with that," said the Ambassador, nodding. They had a deal, presuming Hagen had come through.

"And you, sir, flatter me," Hagen said. "Or rather, our business connections. As I'm sure you're aware, many people have a say in choosing a person to give the nominating speech at the national convention next year. We've spoken to people, it's true. The convention is set for Atlantic City. That's definite now."

"Definite?"

Hagen nodded.

The old man shot a fist into the air, an oddly boyish gesture. This was terrific news for him, of course. Now, even if the more delicate aspects of this deal fell through, Governor Shea would, at minimum, be able to take credit for bringing the convention—and the conventioneers and their money—to his state.

"The location is a helpful sign," Hagen agreed. "Having the governor of the host state deliver the nominating speech will strike a lot of people as a good idea. After that, who knows?"

After that, Hagen said, as if the speech were sure to happen, which the Ambassador now understood that it was.

"Theoretically speaking," the Ambassador said. "Once Jimmy gives the speech—"

Hagen nodded. The list of *if*s was long. "I'm a careful but optimistic man, sir. Let's just call it a long haul to 1960."

Haul being the operative word. If the most important *if*s went right, the labor unions the Corleones controlled would support James Kavanaugh Shea's bid for the White House.

"Rumor has it," said the Ambassador, escorting Hagen though the house now and to the waiting golf cart, "you have political aspirations yourself."

"You know how it is, sir," Hagen said. "This is America. Land of opportunity. Any boy can grow up to be president."

The Ambassador laughed like hell, handed him a cigar, and sent him on his way. "You'll go far," he shouted after him, as if Tom Hagen's life up to now had been nothing, nowhere.

Chapter 6

I<small>T WOULD BE YEARS</small> before anyone outside the Chicago outfit learned that Louie Russo had ordered a hit on Fredo Corleone. Russo had nothing against Fredo per se. It is a meaningless coincidence that the attempt to kill him came a few months after Russo's estranged son (and namesake) moved to Paris and began his life as an openly gay man. That said, Russo Jr. did live in Las Vegas for a year, and he was the indirect source of his father's intelligence on Fredo Corleone's occasional proclivities. The killers were supposed to wait until they found Fredo in bed with another man—ideally near dawn, so it would seem more incriminating—then make it look as if Fredo had shot the other guy and then himself. This sordid scene would humiliate and weaken Michael Corleone—who'd just named his brother *sotto capo*, to the dismay of many in his own organization—without Chicago getting blamed for anything or having to fear any reprisals. It wasn't only violent reprisals Russo was trying to avoid, either. He desperately wanted a seat on the Commission, La Cosa Nostra's ruling body—something that he'd never get if it became known that he'd killed a made member of another Family without first getting the Commission's approval. It might have all worked, too, if, after slipping the phony suicide note under the windshield wiper of Fredo's borrowed car, one of the killers hadn't had a violent colon spasm and been forced to stop at a filling station men's room.

Fredo Corleone would live another four years, though he never found out what happened. He might have figured it out if he hadn't turned on the windshield wipers and mangled the phony note. The ink had bled, and all that was legible was "Forgive me, Fredo." Fredo presumed the note had been from that desperate faggot salesman from last night, asking for forgiveness—which, in Fredo's experience, those sick people were always doing.

As for the cops, they took him inside the white A-frame building alongside the customs booths, gave him a handwriting test, which he took, and started asking a lot of questions, which he refused to answer without a lawyer present. He mentioned that though he was from out

of town, his good friend Mr. Joe Zaluchi could probably recommend an attorney. The handwriting didn't match, and a police captain on Zaluchi's payroll materialized and said he'd take everything from here. Everyone but the captain still thought they were dealing with an assistant trailer park manager from Nevada named Carl Frederick who was that rare drunk made more agile and articulate by a few stiff belts.

Fredo said he had to make a couple quick phone calls, and the captain told the other men they could go. Fredo took a seat behind a desk like he owned the place and called the airport to have them page his bodyguards, who would have expected him there an hour ago. The captain sat down at a desk across the room and started eating the confiscated oranges. There was a battered radio on the filing cabinet next to him, and he turned it on. A bouncy Perry Como song came blaring out and Fredo frowned and the captain turned it down and mouthed, "Sorry."

Fredo kept waiting, but neither Figaro, which is what he called the barber, or the goatherd came to the phone. He hung up and had the operator connect him with Joe Zaluchi. There was no listing, of course. The captain was sipping coffee and going at those oranges like crazy, averting his eyes, giving Fredo his privacy.

"Sir?" Fredo said. "You don't by any chance know how I can get in touch with Joe Z.?"

"No idea," the captain said, winking. He'd loved the *sir*. "What do you need?"

"I borrowed a car from him. I already missed one flight. If I take time to drop the car off back in Grosse Pointe, I'll never—"

The captain waved him off. "Leave it here. The airport's on my way to where I'm going. I'll give you a lift. I'll take care of things with the car later."

That would have been suspicious, except that the guy had been at the wedding yesterday.

"Thanks," Fredo said, and tried the airport once more. Again, nothing. He called the phone service in Las Vegas. "It's Mr. E.," he said— short for "Mister Entertainment." "Anybody asks, tell 'em I missed my plane but I'll be on the next one, guaranteed, all right?"

Fredo would certainly have figured everything out if he hadn't told the captain to turn down the radio. When the song finished, the news came on. Among the top stories: police were investigating a homicide at a motel in Windsor. A restaurant supply salesman from Dearborn claimed that the door to his room had been broken down by two armed intruders, both of whom he had shot with a Colt .45. One intruder had died; the other—Oscar Gionfriddo, age forty, a vending machine supplier from Joliet, Illinois—was in critical condition at Salvation Army Grace Hospital.

The dead man's identity had not yet been released. The shooter said that the gun belonged to a friend. "I never fired a gun before in my life," the man said. His voice cracked. "I can't believe my luck." He came off more like a winner of the Irish Sweepstakes than someone who'd just killed one, maybe two men.

The captain, of course, had no reason to think anything of it, and the radio was far too soft for Fredo to hear from across the room.

The phone rang. The captain answered. It was the bodyguard, the barber. Figaro. Fredo told him he'd be right there.

"All set," Fredo told the captain.

"You got everything? Well, except these." His mouth was full of orange. "You can't take these. A gun's easier to bring into the country than a piece of fruit, isn't that something?"

A gun.

Neri had said that the whole crate of Colt Peacemakers was untraceable. Still, it couldn't be good, leaving the gun behind. It made Fredo look like a fool. Worse, he was left without a gun. He considered asking the captain for one but didn't want to push his luck.

"I got everything," Fredo said, heading toward the door.

They got into the captain's unmarked car. The radio came on, full blast. *"And now, more music!"* The captain turned it down and again apologized. It was an old song: the big-band sound of Les Halley and His New Haven Ravens, featuring the vocal stylings of Johnny "Memory Lane" Fontane. One of their last sessions together, the deejay said, "before he left the world of platters for movieola matters."

"My wife," said the captain, pointing at the radio, "always used to love this record."

Fredo nodded. "Everyone's wife did. That's how a lot of 'em got to *be* someone's wife. Songs like this here."

"Hard to imagine how much pussy a guy like that must get."

"Oh, I can imagine," Fredo said. "It doesn't hurt that John's a hell of a great guy, either."

"You know Johnny Fontane?"

"Personal friends," Fredo said, shrugging.

They didn't say anything more until the song was over.

"Personal friends, huh?" asked the captain.

"Personal friends. Matter of fact, my dad was his godfather."

"No shit."

"No shit."

"Let me ask you something, then," said the captain. "Is it true he's got a dick the size of your arm?"

"How the fuck would I know a thing like that?"

"I don't know. Sauna or something. It's just a rumor I heard, and I figured—"

"What are you," Fredo asked, "a fruit?"

The captain rolled his eyes and turned on his siren. They drove the rest of the way to the airport like that, a hundred miles an hour and not talking.

Chapter 7

PHIL ORNSTEIN'S corner office on the forty-first floor was lined with gold records and pictures of Philly's frankly unattractive family but none of famous people, which was either an affectation or a reason to love the guy. He ushered Johnny Fontane behind his stainless steel desk. "Take as long as you'd like," he said, though he couldn't have meant that. Milner was getting the band squared away for the next number. Johnny dialed the number to his old house.

Halfway through, he stopped. Ginny and the girls had no idea he was in L.A. If he didn't call, they'd be none the wiser. He was calling to apologize for not seeing them while he was in town, but the only thing that made the call necessary was the call itself.

He took out the pep pills, considered the label, then took one out and swallowed it dry.

Shit. What was he, some schoolboy *segaiolo*, afraid to ask out the prom queen? He'd known Ginny, his ex, ever since they were ten. The literal girl next door. He redialed.

"It's me," he said.

"Hello, my life," Ginny said. She managed to say that in a way that was sweet and sarcastic at the same time. There's nothing like a Brooklyn girl. "Where are you?"

"God, it's great to hear your voice," Johnny said. "What are you doing?"

They'd just gotten back from May Company, she told him. His oldest daughter had purchased her first brassiere.

"You can't be serious," Johnny said.

"When's the last time you saw her?" Ginny said.

He'd had good-paying gigs in Atlantic City and at private clubs in the Jersey Palisades and the one Louie Russo had outside Chicago. He'd done a picture on location in New Orleans. The early scenes of it were shot here, on soundstages. Probably then. "Memorial Day?"

"Rhetorical question," she said. "So where are you now?"

"Remember that one Labor Day, I don't know what year," he said. "We rented that place at Cape May, and we all went to that clambake?"

"No," she said.

"You're kidding," he said. He could hear his girls in the background, arguing.

"Of course I'm kidding. Those were the times of my life. Back when I didn't exist."

Les Halley had insisted that Johnny pretend he was single so that the bobby-soxers would all keep screaming. "That was never my idea," he said.

"And you had your floozy across town so that every time you went out for cigarettes—"

"Remember when I burnt my hands trying to cook that corn and—"

"And then burnt them *again* on those firecrackers."

"True." He had to laugh.

"There's a block party tomorrow," she said. "We have to make pie. You want to come?"

"To the party?"

"You're in town, right? You sound so close."

He cradled the phone against his shoulder and covered his eyes with both hands. "No," he said. "I'm not. It's just a good connection."

"Oh," she said. "Your loss. I'm making chicken *scarpariello*, too. Same recipe your ma showed me. Actually, the girls are. If they don't kill each other first. They're at that age."

Johnny loved them, but as far as he could tell they'd always been at that age.

She asked if he wanted to talk to them. He said he did, but only his younger daughter would get on the phone. Philly came in, tapping his watch.

"Tell your mother," Johnny said, "that I'll do my best to make it to the party tomorrow."

"Okay," she said. She'd convey the message—she was that kind of kid—but there was a note in her voice that made it clear she knew he'd never show.

The green pills had been prescribed by Jules Segal, the same doctor who'd diagnosed the warts on Johnny's vocal cords and referred him to the specialist who shaved them off, an operation that made it possible for Johnny to get back into good voice and into the studio, a diagnosis two specialists had missed. Point being, there were a thousand Hollywood quacks whose interest in the human body had dwindled to the fleshy parts of their starlets *du jour* and the finer points of their own backswings, getting rich by handing out pills and taking care of girls in trouble, and then there was Segal, who had the same kind of rep but turned out to be a first-rate doctor, good enough to be chief of surgery at the new hospital the

Corleones were building in Las Vegas. So why was it that every time Johnny popped another of those pills—still in line with the dosage recommended on the side of the bottle, never more—he went off by himself?

Johnny shook it off, like a dog with an itch in its ear. He'd be fine, really. Both under control and not. Which was okay, which suited the task at hand. He was getting by on four pills, twenty cups of tea, a pot of coffee, a ham sandwich, and no sleep. In the space between his scalp and skull, microscopic ants danced some hepcat thing like the hucklebuck. The aching in the big muscles on top of his thighs, whatever they were called, sharpened almost by the minute. But Johnny stayed on his feet, too spent even to fall to the floor for a nap. At the same time, he had too much energy. He couldn't help but take each piece of barely perceptible direction he got from that brilliant lummox Milner and do his level best to put it in play.

He'd have given anything to stop.

He'd have given anything to make this feeling last forever.

He'd come here thinking he'd lay down half a long-playing record. A few minutes into the session, he realized he'd be doing well to finish one song to both his and Cy Milner's satisfaction. Yet, minutes before he'd have to catch a plane back to Vegas, he found himself doing the third song of the day so well he got to the end without stopping or being stopped.

As he finished, he opened his eyes and saw Jackie Ping-Pong and Gussie Cicero standing inside the far door to the studio. How long they'd been there, Johnny had no idea.

Milner had already whipped out a pad of paper. As a conductor, he was laconic and fluid, but he wrote charts the way a stray dog eats a pork chop. He was oblivious to anything else in the studio, even the intern standing next to him with a bottle of soda and a fistful of pencils.

Johnny sat on his stool and lit a cigarette. "Mo-o-om! Da-a-ad!" Johnny called, looking first to Milner and then Ornstein, then pointing at Ping-Pong and Gussie. "My ride's here. Don't wait up!" His legs felt impossibly heavy. Finally he looked up and waved Gussie and Ping-Pong over.

"My friend!" Jackie said, waddling toward him. He was a hugely fat man, just an acquaintance, really. "You're looking like a million bucks. You sound even better."

Johnny knew he looked like death on toast. "What's better than a million bucks?"

"A million bucks and a blow job," said Gussie Cicero, a pally from way back.

"Wrong," Johnny said. "If a chick knows you got a million, she'll blow you for free."

"Those free blow jobs are the most expensive kind."

That cracked Johnny up. He slapped Cicero on the back. "Well, if I look like a million bucks," Johnny said, "you two look like a shit I took this morning."

Johnny stood and let Ping-Pong and Cicero embrace him. For years Johnny had assumed that Jackie's nickname had come from his bulging eyes, but not long ago Frank Falcone told him Jackie's eyes hadn't done that until years after he got the nickname, which had actually come about because of his name, Ignazio Pignatelli. Gussie Cicero owned the swankiest supper club in L.A. Johnny hadn't played there since the time his voice went out onstage and *Variety* wrote it up like it was an occasion for the whole staff to break out the Crown Royal and dance on Johnny's fresh grave. Gussie and Johnny had remained friends, though.

"Frank Falcone sends his regards," Gussie said. Gussie was said to be a made guy in the L.A. organization, which was connected somehow with Chicago.

"He's not coming?" Johnny said.

"Mr. Falcone came down with something," Ping-Pong said. His meaty fist clutched a new-looking satchel. He was Falcone's underboss. Johnny couldn't have said just what an underboss did. Johnny tried not to know more about that kind of thing than he had to. "Other than his regards, he also sends this."

"Nice," said Johnny.

"I'll get you one," Ping-Pong said, "quick as I can get it made and shipped over from Sicily. I got a guy there, works like a dog and makes ten of these a year. Virgin leather, best there is. Want me to send it to the Castle in the Sand? Your home? Which?"

Fontane had been working on some kind of joke on the *virgin* part of *virgin leather*, but he was just too frazzled. Nothing clicked. "This one isn't mine?"

"I'll get you one."

"Kidding, Jack."

"I'm not offering, I'm *telling* you. All right? But this one here," he said, handing it to Johnny, "is for Mike Corleone, *capisc'?*"

Meaning: *Enough with the ragging* and *Whatever you do, kid, don't fucking open it.*

The bag, packed tight, was heavy as a bowling ball. Johnny gave it a little shake, like a kid at Christmas, then held it up to his ear, making a show of seeing if it was ticking.

"Funny guy." Ping-Pong narrowed his eyes in his fat face and just stood there, apparently until he was satisfied that Johnny had gotten the message. "I must express my regrets also," Ping-Pong finally said. "I have to see to some personal family matters."

"No sweat," Johnny said. *So I'm your fucking bagman now?* But he just stood there, absorbing the indignity like acid into cheap cement.

"It's our loss, not seeing you," Ping-Pong said. "You're sounding great, John."

Milner kept writing. The musicians filed out. Johnny said his good-byes and headed out with Gussie and Ping-Pong. A Rolls-Royce Silver Shadow was idling by the back door.

"Where's the queen?" Johnny said.

"Excuse me?" Ping-Pong frowned, as if he took it that he was being called a fag.

"He means *of England*," Gussie said. "He's joking."

Ping-Pong shook his head in a kids-today way that Johnny could have done without.

"The car's mine, Johnny," Gussie said.

A black Lincoln pulled up. Ping-Pong and his men got in and sped off.

As they did, Johnny caught a flash of metal out of the corner of his eye and jerked out of the way. He stumbled and fell against the side of the Rolls.

It hadn't been a bullet.

Johnny wasn't exactly sure why he'd thought it might be.

"Nice catch," Gussie said. "You all right?"

Johnny reached down to pick up Cicero's car keys. "Long day," Johnny said.

"All you had to say," Gussie said, "was no thanks."

"No thanks what?"

"No thanks you didn't want to drive my fucking Rolls-Royce."

Johnny tossed him his keys. "No thanks I don't want to drive your fucking Rolls-Royce."

"See? Is that so hard?"

"I didn't hear you, okay? I'm bushed, brother." The sun was about to set. Johnny couldn't have said how long it had been since he'd had an honest-to-God night's sleep.

Gussie gave Johnny a hug and said it had been a privilege to hear him sing. They got in and headed for the airport. Johnny started spinning the dial on Gussie's radio, checking out the competition. All around the dial were fads. Rock and roll. Fast-talking disc jockeys. Mambo: another fad. Weepy girl singers: yet another. Johnny never once came across his own voice. Maybe the other record companies were right. Maybe the kind of record Johnny Fontane was trying to make didn't have a Chinaman's chance. He kept spinning the dial. Gussie must have picked up on how jangled Johnny's nerves were and for most of the ride there had the de-

cency not to say anything until they were getting off the freeway for the airport.

"What's the difference," Gussie said, "between Margot Ashton and a Rolls-Royce?"

Margot had been Fontane's second wife, Gussie's first. Fontane had left Ginny for Margot. It wasn't enough that Margot stole his heart; she took everything, even his self-respect. One time, he showed up on the set of a movie she was doing and the director put him to work cooking spaghetti. Without a word of complaint Fontane tied on an apron and did it. Love. Fucking love. "Not everyone's been inside a Rolls-Royce," Johnny said.

"You heard that?"

"Everyone's heard that. You know, with different fancy cars and different sluts."

"Sluts don't come much more different," Gussie said, "than Margot Ashton."

"That's where you're wrong, pal-o'-mine. A slut's a slut."

Gussie made a wrong turn, toward the commercial flights.

"You made a wrong turn," Johnny said, pointing to the road to the private hangars.

Gussie shook his head. "Actually," he said, "I'm not going either. Frank didn't want you to be sore, but, you know, a whole airplane, just for one guy—"

He reached into his breast pocket, for a gun. But no, not a gun. Johnny was wrong. Gussie pulled out an envelope. "It's commercial, but it's first class."

Johnny took the plane ticket. His flight left in fifteen minutes. "You're really not going?"

"Actually," Gussie said, "I was never invited."

"Of course you're invited. I'm inviting you."

"It's okay," Gussie said. "Gina and I got plans." Gina was the girl he'd married after he'd been dumped by Margot Ashton. Ashton had married an Arab sheik after that and already divorced him, too. "Our fifth anniversary, if you can believe it," he said, stopping the car. Skycaps practically ran to help, seeing a Rolls, imagining big bags and bigger tips. "Next weekend, though, she and I got tickets to come up there and see you."

"You *bought* tickets?"

"A bargain at any price, if you sound half as good as today."

"I catch you on anything but a comp list for any show I ever do, it's your ass, pally."

There was a crowd, maybe twenty people, all different ages. He told the skycaps he didn't have any bags except just this little one here, but he

duked them anyway, twenty apiece. Two men in sky blue sport coats rushed to meet him and help him through the crowd, which caught everyone's attention, even in a place like L.A. The crowd snowballed, surging behind him all the way to the gate. Against his better judgment, Johnny handed the satchel to one of the airline guys so that he could sign quick, illegible autographs, including one some dame wanted right on her face. He duked the two airline guys fifty.

When he boarded the plane, there was applause. He waved and smiled but did not remove his sunglasses. He took his seat. He put the bag on the floor between his legs. Under different circumstances he'd have been after that redheaded stewardess with the big tits, but all he asked her for was a pillow, a bourbon rocks, and a hot tea with honey. He looked at the satchel. Another sort of guy would open it now. Johnny couldn't have given a shit.

It took her forever to bring the drinks. "We don't have honey," she said.

"No tea, either, looks like."

"I'm heating the water right now."

She turned around. He looked down at the satchel. He opened it.

It was jammed with cash, of course. On top was an unsigned, typewritten note that said, "Told you not to look." The *o*'s in *look* had dots inside; underneath was an upside-down smile.

Johnny wadded the note up. He saw the redhead coming with the tea and downed half his bourbon. He chewed ice as she set the tea down. He made his left hand into a pistol, pointed it at her, winked, and made a little clucking sound. She blushed.

By the time the redhead passed through the cabin getting everything squared away for takeoff, he'd finished the bourbon and the tea and was sound asleep.

Chapter 8

You WERE at the Tri Delt ice cream social, right?" said the honey-voiced blonde in line in front of Francesca Corleone as she took her food: cling peaches on cottage cheese and a wilted leaf of iceberg lettuce. This, plus sweet tea, was the entirety of the girl's dinner.

Behind Francesca, Suzy Kimball kept her eyes on her tray and hummed.

"That wasn't me," Francesca said. "I'm sorry."

"Oh." This was where a normal person would introduce herself. Instead, the girl turned around and went back to her chirpy giggling with the girls she'd come with.

There were many other girls in line at the dining hall who did not have Greek letters on their clothing, other girls who weren't whispering among themselves, who weren't cowering underneath their raincoats as upperclassmen came in. These girls existed, but Francesca didn't see them. What she noticed was Suzy, the quiet dark-skinned girl behind her, choosing the food Francesca chose, following Francesca to a table by the window.

"You know," said a deep voice behind Francesca, "this *used* to be a girls' school."

Francesca turned around. At the next table was a tanned young man in a seersucker suit. He clutched a wooden replica of a rocket ship. Pushed up in his curly blond hair was a pair of sunglasses, the kind pilots wore.

"Excuse me?" she said.

"Florida College for Women." His white teeth revealed a crooked smile. "Until right after the war. Sorry for eavesdropping. I was just there helping my little brother move in. It's good that your mother's protective. She really loves you. You're lucky."

His own mother couldn't *wait* to get him and his brother out of the house, he said. He finally set the rocket ship down.

Francesca felt dizzy, awash in the smell of blooming tea olive bushes.

He'd turned away from a group of people—upperclassmen, from the looks of them, including the blonde with the peaches—to talk to her. There was something about this boy, both awkward and smooth, in the way he couldn't stop talking. Finally he apologized for not introducing himself. "I'm Billy Van Arsdale." He extended his hand.

This was her big chance. *Fran Collins. Franny Taylor. Frances Wilson. Francie Roberts.* As she reached out her hand, she realized her palms were sweaty. Not just sweaty: drenched. But she was committed. No stopping now. In a panic, she took Billy's hand in her somewhat less damp fingertips, turned it, and kissed it on the knuckles.

Billy's dinner companions broke out laughing.

"Francesca Corleone," she said, barely in a whisper and, despite herself, pronouncing all four syllables of her last name, in her best Italian. She tried to smile, as if she'd meant the kiss as a joke. "So, um. What's the story with the spaceship?"

"That," Billy said, "is a really lovely name."

"She's Italian," blurted Suzy Kimball, bright-eyed, as if she were in class and it was the first time all term she'd known the right answer. She was saying it to Billy's whole table. "They're big kissers, the Italian people. I thought it was Corle-*own*, not Corle-*oney*. Which is it?"

Francesca couldn't bear to say anything, couldn't take her eyes off Billy.

Someone at the other table said, "Mamma mia, where's-a da mozzarella?" which inspired more laughter. Billy ignored them. "Welcome to FSU. If I can ever do anything—"

"Here it goes," said one of the men at his table.

"Honey," said the girl with the cling peaches, "you are in*cor*rigible."

"—don't hesitate to ask."

"Corleone, huh?" said the mozzarella boy. He held up an invisible tommy gun and made *ack-ack* sounds. "You any relation?" someone said.

"You guys are jerks," Billy said. "Don't be ridiculous. They're jerks," Billy said to Francesca. "Anyway, I have to run, but if you need anything, I'm in the book. Under 'W.B.' "

"Yes, dahling," Cling Peaches said, "William Brewster Van Ahhhsdale the Third."

Billy rolled his eyes, gave Francesca's shoulder a gentle squeeze, grabbed his wooden rocket, flicked his sunglasses into place, and left. Francesca expected the people at the other table to keep needling her, but they lost interest and went back to talking to one another.

"I'm sorry," Suzy mumbled. She was quivering like an abused house pet.

What could Francesca say? "You're right. I am." Italian. "We are." Big kissers. There were worse things to be, no? "Forget it. Say my name any way you want."

Suzy looked up, then covered her mouth. "You should see yourself."

"See myself why?" Francesca said.

A thunderclap sounded.

Suzy shook her head, but Francesca knew. She could still feel Billy's touch.

After dinner, they worked on their room. Suzy's clothes were more like uniforms: nearly identical skirts and blouses, utterly identical bras, socks, and underpants. They agreed to make more room by bunking their beds, and Francesca said Suzy could pick. She picked the bottom. Who *picks* the bottom? The rain stopped. The dorm mother herded everyone out, handed them small white candles, and marched them across campus to freshman convocation. The marching band played as they entered the football stadium. A misty rain began. There were rows and rows of white wooden folding chairs. Suzy and Francesca sat near the back. *The swarthy ones.* She had to find a way to distance herself from this girl and not be a bad person.

On a platform at the fifty-yard line, some dean welcomed them. Then he introduced the university president, a lugubrious man in a black robe. The dean sat down, and only then did Francesca notice, in the seat beside the dean, that blue seersucker suit, that blond hair, and even from across the field those white teeth. For a moment, she thought it must be a delusion. The heat. Then Suzy dug her elbow into Francesca's side and pointed.

"It's William Brewster Van Arsdale the Third!" she said.

"That was a joke," Francesca said.

"You have that look on your face again," Suzy said.

Francesca tried to cock her eyebrow the way Deanna Dunn had in that movie a few years back where she played a killer.

Billy spent the duration of the president's remarks making notes on index cards. Francesca spent it telling herself that in a world of stupid crushes, this was plainly the stupidest.

The president tugged at his sashes. He told them to look right and look left and that one of those people wouldn't make it to graduation and to make sure that one person wasn't you, then he directed jumper-clad Spirit Leaders at the ends of the aisles to start lighting everyone's candles. Thunder sounded. He said it was now his pleasure to introduce the student body president. "Of course, anyone out there who ever ate any fresh Florida fruit is already a faithful friend of his family." The president paused to chuckle and call attention to how pleased he was at his own alliteration. "Ladies and gentlemen, Mr. William Brewster Van Arsdale."

"I thought you said that was a joke?" Suzy said.

Francesca shrugged. Van Arsdale *Citrus*?

Billy came to the podium, waving. He pulled out the rocket ship from inside his jacket. As he did, the rain began to fall harder. Billy forged on. The rocket was a prop for him to talk about the coming space age in which

the students here would live their exciting lives. Candles flickered out. People started to leave. Abruptly, in that Florida way, the skies opened. Francesca buttoned her raincoat. The band ran for cover. Moments later, water filled the track around the field. Billy tucked the rocket back into his jacket and whipped his index cards into the wind. "Our formal education," he shouted, "should stay in balance with the important things we've already learned. Love. Family. Common sense. C'mon, everybody, let's have enough sense to come in out of the rain!"

By the time he said it, most everyone had. Except Francesca, who just sat there.

She was kidding herself. It was ridiculous. It was obvious to her now that, in the dining hall, he'd been up to one of two things. Either he was trying to be a do-gooder, reaching out to the two weird-looking ethnic girls. Or else he'd been making fun of her.

She watched him jog alongside the dean and the robed president, sharing a golf umbrella.

Of *course* he was the sort of person for whom a big umbrella would just materialize.

Francesca, the last person sitting, cast off her wet candle and put her head in her hands.

She should go home. Not her dorm. *Home* home.

As she always did in her darkest moments, she tried to picture the face of her father. Every time, it got just a little bit more difficult. He struck the poses and smiled the smiles he had in photographs. Was it really Daddy she saw now, or was it just that picture of him at Aunt Connie's wedding, where it seemed like he'd managed to drape his arms over every adult in the family, where he was happy and in love with Ma and looking out for everyone? Francesca and Kathy had been off to the side, dancing with Johnny Fontane, a character who now seemed as unreal to her as Mickey Mouse. For that moment anyway, things had worked.

She bent over and let the rain pelt her. Francesca knew in her heart she no longer really remembered the sound of her father's voice. And, really, on this count too, she was kidding herself: reading much too much into the old-fashioned haircuts, the tuxedos and the dresses and Uncle Mike's wonderful Marine Corps uniform and its ill-fitting cap, tricked like some dumb girl by the natural-seeming smiles on the faces of dead people, by skillful photography, by some freak accident of misleading light. Things had *never* worked. Who doesn't know that? There were other family photographs, ones Francesca usually chose not to think about. The one of her Uncle Fredo sitting on the curb, sobbing. The one of Grandpa Vito hiding his face from the photographer that *The New York Times* had used for his obituary. The Polaroid of her mother, sitting with her shirt off in Stan

the Liquor Man's Naugahyde office chair, which Kathy had found hidden next to a huge rubber penis in a hollowed-out corner of their mother's box spring. The scalloped-edged one, where her father was clubbing a tuna to death somewhere off the coast of Sicily, smiling like a boy on Christmas morning.

Are you any relation? What *would* Francesca have said if Billy hadn't told his friends not to be ridiculous? She had no idea.

There were so many reasons to love storms. Francesca Corleone might or might not have been crying. She had no intention of leaving the field until the last fat drop fell.

Chapter 9

ANYONE WATCHING Michael Corleone land the plane on Lake Mead—the drivers of those two Cadillacs, for example, standing at the end of the dock and holding ropes—might have thought he'd done this hundreds of times instead of maybe twenty. Kay, asleep in the seat beside him, didn't even stir—not until Tommy Neri and the two young guys squeezed into the back with him broke out in applause.

Kay sat bolt upright, eyes wide in panic. "My babies!"

Michael laughed. A beat later, he regretted it. It had struck him funny, her needless panic, and kind of touching, too. With anyone else, he wouldn't have reacted without thinking. Kay was the only person in the world who could make him act against his own nature.

"Sorry, Mrs. C.," Tommy said. "Should've seen it, though. Your husband's a natural. I'll admit it now, I was a little edgy about it. I didn't go on a *regular* airplane until last year."

Kay rubbed her eyes.

"I wasn't laughing at you," Michael said. "You okay?"

"They *do* float," Kay said to Tommy. "Floatplanes. Though sometimes they also flip."

"Yes, ma'am."

"What were you dreaming about?" Michael said.

She put her hand to her chest, as if to still a racing heart. "I'm fine. We're home?"

"Well, we're back at Lake Mead."

"That's what I meant. What do you think I meant, the mall back in Long Beach?"

Michael hated it that the notion of *home* had any shred of ambiguity. He also hated having even a tiny quarrel in front of people who weren't that close to him. He didn't answer her until he got the plane to the dock. "No," he said. "That's not what I thought you meant."

Kay unbuckled her seat belt and elbowed past the men. She'd been sore since Michael had swung back by their property to pick up the men for the ride back. She got into the back of their car, the yellow one with the black roof.

Michael told the men to give his regards to Fredo and Pete Clemenza—the red Cadillac was Fredo's; it was supposed to go meet their respective planes—and that he'd be at the Castle in the Sand no later than six-thirty.

He got in back beside Kay.

"A date," she said. "Like old times. All day until late tonight. That was what you said."

"I needed to get them back here somehow. You slept through it all anyway."

She shrugged. It was not a conciliatory shrug. There were two kinds of wives in this way of life. Once, he'd been married to the other kind. In the end, a wife like Apollonia, which is also to say a wife like his mother, a Sicilian girl who went along with every word her husband said, wouldn't have suited him and certainly not his children, not in America.

Still, he couldn't stand for this, not in front of others. Even his most loyal men should not see the head of their Family commit any weakness, however petty.

"Business," Michael said. Code, in their marriage, for *this is not up for discussion.*

"You're right," she said. "Of course."

They rode home with cowboy songs on the radio.

Kay's parents had parked in the driveway. Across the street, in front of the construction site that was supposed to be Michael's sister Connie's house, was a gray Plymouth. Some kind of cop—both because of the kind of car it was and because if it had been anyone but a cop, Al Neri's crew would have already taken care of it.

From inside his house came the sound, the *noise,* of some keening opera, Michael couldn't have said which one. Unlike the old Moustache Petes, Michael had never felt the need to affect an interest in opera. The music in the house was all Kay's.

Kay winced and then rolled her eyes. "It's Dad," she said.

Her chilly relationship with her parents baffled Michael. They'd been in her corner for everything she'd wanted to do. Federal agents had once come into the same study where her father wrote his sermons to call Michael a gangster and a murderer, yet when she decided to marry him, they hadn't hesitated to give their blessing. He was about to say something—tilting, as married people do, at the windmills of the immutable—when it occurred to him: the record player they'd brought with them from New York couldn't possibly have been this loud. The sound was coming from the hi-fi in Michael's den.

"He's in my den," Michael said.

"He's losing his hearing, among other things," Kay said. "Be nice."

"He's in my den," Michael repeated.

She straightened her skirt and pointed to the backyard, where her mother was pushing Mary on the swing set. Michael nodded and went inside.

He climbed the stairs and crossed through his bedroom. The den was a nightmare of orange and brown, with molded plastic chairs and pole lamps with bulbs spraying inefficient light. Two redheaded children he'd never seen before were playing on the carpet with Tonka dump trucks. Thornton Adams sat behind Michael's blond Danish modern desk. Anthony sat on his lap. Each had his eyes closed and his head back like some beatific stained-glass Jesus. Michael crossed the room and flicked the knob on the wall-mounted reel-to-reel tape deck.

Anthony's startled look was so much like Kay's had been a few minutes before that Michael's heart hurt. The kids on the carpet stood and ran away.

"Thornton," Michael said.

"I took the liberty of—"

"Forget it," he said. "It's fine."

"Are we in lots and lots of trouble?" Anthony said.

The boy's upper lip trembled, and his eyes were wide. Michael had spanked the boy maybe three times ever. Anyone who thinks he can explain everything human beings do can wise up simply by having a kid or two. "No, sport," Michael said. "You're not in trouble." He picked Anthony up and gave him a hug. "You like that? That music?"

"I told Grandpa that we weren't supposed—"

"It's all right," Michael said. "What was it you were listening to?"

"Tell him, Tony," Thornton said, putting his thick black-rimmed glasses back on.

"It's Puccini."

"He's an Italian," Thornton said. "Or was one." He chuckled. "Quite dead, of course."

"I'm aware of that," Michael said.

"Say again?"

Michael raised his voice. "Puccini's dead. You eat? Want me to make you something?"

"Agnes has a casserole going," Thornton said. "It involves beans."

Michael smelled nothing. What could be baking that smelled like nothing?

"Puccini's dead?" Anthony said, ashen.

Michael tousled his son's hair. "He had a good life, Puccini," Michael said, though he didn't know a thing about Puccini's life. He could feel his son relax. "Who are the other kids?"

"Your neighbors," Thornton said. "Their backyard and yours touch. They seemed like they were already friends with Tony and Mary. C'mon, Tony. We should go. Sorry if I—"

Michael just gave his father-in-law a look, which proved to be more than enough. He set his son down, closed the door, and was alone.

The shower in the next room started. Kay. Michael got his tux. It was the one he'd been married in (he'd worn his other one last night), though the pants could stand to be let out. He sneaked a peek at Kay through the glass shower door and went back into his den to change.

Fredo had meant well, which probably someday ought to be his brother's epitaph. That car, for example. It was a truly great car, with a golden grille and sabre-spoke wheels. Michael still thought Fredo was a bungler for buying such flashy cars, but look around: out West, would a plain black sedan have blended in better than the lovely, finned thing down in Michael's driveway? Or this hi-fi rig. The same kind they used in recording studios, Fredo claimed. Took up a whole wall. Who needed this in his home? For all Michael knew it really was the coming thing, but he'd never been one to waste time listening to recorded music.

He sat down at his desk, fully aware of how exhausted he was. Two days in New York, a day in Detroit, then the time difference and the concentration for the flight to Lake Mead and back. And he still had what promised to be a long night in front of him: meetings at the Castle in the Sand, the impending news from Rattlesnake Island, an appearance at the Fontane show, and the thing after that. The ceremony. Michael ran a finger absently around the perimeter of that big ceramic ashtray with a mermaid on a ridged island in the middle. It had belonged to Pop. The crack where the ashtray had been glued back together was still visible. Michael lit a cigarette with his big table lighter, six inches tall and shaped like a lion. He drummed his fingers on that hideous blond desk and thought of golf. Golf was a brilliant idea, both a sport and a pastime, both a way to relax and a means of doing business. Custom clubs. Perfect.

He fell asleep so soundly he could have stayed like that, hunched over and dead to the world, for the rest of the night.

He snapped awake. "I'm not asleep," he said.

It had been Kay's hand on his shoulder. "I saw you peeking," she said. "Sorry."

"Don't be. It's when you stop peeking that I'll worry."

"So why'd you change? Where are you going?"

She frowned. "To see Johnny Fontane, of course. C'mon. Let's go."

"To see Fontane?"

"It's like when you live in New York and can go up in the Statue of Liberty but never do. Johnny Fontane's been singing at your casino—"

"We're just partners in it."

"—for weeks now. We could go anytime but we never do. Do you realize it's been ten years since I heard him sing at your sister's wedding?
That was the first, last, and only time."

Then she laughed.

"You should see your face," she said. "Right, right, business, you have
business. Go on, go. Go. I'm taking Mom and Dad and the kids to dinner
at this steak place that just opened."

"I thought your mother had a casserole going."

"Have you *tasted* my mother's casseroles?"

Michael kissed her. He thanked her for a great day and a great life,
too. "Don't wait up," he said. "I'll be late."

"You always are." Kay smiled as she said it, but they both knew it
wasn't a joke.

"Good fwight?" asked Hal Mitchell, dressed in golf clothes. *Flight.* The
sarge had trouble with his *l*'s and *r*'s. He'd been razzed about it during
the war, since most of the passwords had had *l*'s in them to trip up the
Japs. The men loved him, though. No one ever called him Sergeant Fudd
to his face.

"Uneventful," Michael said, hugging his old brother in arms. "The
best kind."

Behind Mitchell, already there of course, was Tom Hagen. Hagen and
the white-haired cowboy stood. The bald man in the wheelchair extended
his hand to be shaken. Michael was the only one wearing a tux. It wasn't
sundown yet, but there'd be no real chance to change.

Mitchell's office walls were covered with photos of celebrities, save a
twelve-year-old snapshot of Sergeant Mitchell, PFC Corleone, and several
Marines who never made it home, posing in front of a burned-out Jap
tank on the beach at Guadalcanal. The office overlooked the main entrance to the Castle in the Sand. The marquee said WELCOME AMERICAN
LABOR!; Fontane's name would go back up tomorrow. On the stone plaza
below, union officials arrived steadily for the convention that would start
tomorrow, as did other friends of the Corleone Family.

Mitchell offered Michael the seat behind his desk, though Michael
would have none of it. The man in the wheelchair was the president of a
Las Vegas bank. The white-haired man in the cowboy hat was a lawyer, in
private practice now after a term as state attorney general and then many
years as the chairman of the Nevada Republican Party. On paper, these
two men, Mitchell, and a real estate holding company controlled by Tom
Hagen were the casino's four biggest stockholders. Michael's construction
company was, on paper, sixth, behind his brother, Fredo, who—in a risk

that had inspired much debate within the Corleone Family and the Nevada Gaming Commission alike—had used his own name. Fredo was also supposed to be here.

"Fredo Corleone sends his regrets," Hagen said. "His flight was unavoidably delayed."

Michael only nodded. There was nothing more to say, not in the presence of people outside the Family and most certainly not in this room, which was bugged.

The meeting lasted about an hour. It was not purely theater—neither the bank president nor the cowboy lawyer had any idea that law enforcement officials were listening in—and it didn't differ in kind from any meeting of the top shareholders of any privately held corporation: purchasing matters, personnel matters, assessments of the effectiveness of current marketing and advertising efforts. There was discussion of Mitchell's idea to hold A-bomb picnics on the roof. Privately, Michael wondered what kind of idiot would go up to the roof at some ungodly hour and pay ten bucks to hear a lounge act that was free downstairs, all to view a puff of smoke they could easily see from their rooms. But he didn't say anything. His mind was on the next two meetings. The most spirited debate in this one concerned what to call the new casino in Lake Tahoe. Hal's idea—Hal Mitchell's Castle in the Clouds—emerged as the consensus choice.

When they finished, Mitchell said he hoped he'd see everyone and their wives at the Fontane VIP show. Johnny was their new partner, after all, with a ten percent share in the Castle in the Clouds. The other men said they wouldn't miss it for the world.

Hagen waited for them to leave and then made a quick phone call to Louie Russo.

"Don Russo is on his way to the Chuckwagon now," Hagen said to Michael.

They started down the back stairs.

"What's the deal with Fredo?" Michael said.

"He'll get in early tomorrow," Hagen said. "He's fine. There's two good men with him."

"You mean to tell me that barber and that kid off the boat, the goat farmer—"

"Right."

Michael shook his head. The barber was supposed to get straightened out tonight, after the Fontane show. It was to be a surprise—that's how initiations were done—but he was on tap. "So why'd Fredo miss the plane, huh?"

"I don't know. People miss planes, I guess."

"You don't."

"I actually did," he said. "Today, in fact."

"Yet here you are, on time."

Hagen didn't say anything. He'd always been soft on Fredo.

"So how'd that go?" Michael said. "Palm Springs."

"Just what you and I discussed. We're on target there."

They crossed the lobby to a café, the Chuckwagon, that was open only for breakfast. Michael had a key. He and Hagen took a seat at a table in the corner. Moments later, one of Hal Mitchell's assistants let Russo and two of his men into the café and relocked the door behind them. Russo was a pale man with a bad rug, gigantic sunglasses, and tiny hands. He made a beeline to the wall switches and turned off all the lights. His men closed the curtains.

"Hey, you brought your Mick *consigliere*." He had a high, girlish voice. "That's cute."

"Welcome to the Castle in the Sand, Don Russo." Hagen stood, his overly wide smile the only trace of his insincerity.

Michael didn't say anything until Russo's men retreated across the room and sat down on stools at the counter.

"I assure you, Don Russo," Michael said, pointing at the light fixture above him, "we've paid our electric bill."

"The dark's better," Russo said, tapping his sunglasses, the size of which made his nose seem even more like a penis than it might have otherwise. "Some punk tried to shoot me through the window of a candy store. The glass cut my eyes. I can see good, but most of the time, the light's still painful."

"Of course," Michael said. "We only want you to be comfortable."

"I can tell it bothers you," Russo said, taking a seat at the table, "that I turned all the lights off and closed the curtains without sayin' nothin'. Right? So now you know how it feels."

"How what feels?" Hagen said.

"C'mon, Irish. You know what I mean, and your boss does, too. You New Yorkers are all alike. You people made a deal. Everything west of Chicago is Chicago. Soon as you realize there *is* anything west of Chicago, you backpedal. Capone gets what's coming to him, and you think that syphilitic Neapolitan shitweasel *is* Chicago. The rest of us? We're nothing. You put together that Commission, and are we a part of it? No. Moe Greene takes all that New York money and builds up Las Vegas. We're not consulted. You just up and call this an open city. Which you know what I think? I think great. Open works in Miami. Works in Havana, and I hope to God it stays that way. And it's workin' maybe best of all here. But why does it have to be so disrespectful? We weren't so much as *asked*. That's my point. Yet we went along with it. We weren't in no position to argue. We had a few years where, forget about it, nothin' was organized good. What

happened was—I don't want to say you took advantage, but we lost out. *Fine.* Vegas is working out perfect as is. In Chicago, everything's under control. In New York, for a while you had blood running in the streets and all that bit, but from what I hear you got peace again. I pray that's true. My point is this. During your troubles, did I think, *Hey, time to take advantage of my friends in New York?* No. I stayed out of it. I don't want you to hold a parade for me or nothin', but *Christ.* What do I get for the respect I gave you during your hour of need? You move the headquarters of your whole thing *here.* Here! Which is supposed to be open and, if you want to be technical about it, is rightly ours. I'm not *stupid,* all right? But I'm not a lawyer like Irish here, and I didn't go to no fucking Ivy League school neither. So help me out. Tell me why I should stand for this."

Louie Russo supposedly had an IQ of 90, but he was a genius at reading people. The glasses made it difficult to read him in return.

"I appreciate your candor, Don Russo," Michael said. "There's nothing I appreciate more than an honest man."

Russo grunted.

"I don't know where you're getting your information," Michael said, "but it's not true. We have no plans to run Las Vegas. We're only here temporarily. I have land on Lake Tahoe, and once we complete some construction there, that's where we'll go, permanently."

"Last I checked," Russo said, "Tahoe's west of Chicago, too."

Michael shrugged. "When the time comes, that won't be of any concern to you."

"It's of concern to me now."

"It doesn't need to be," Michael said. "In the future, we won't be initiating any more members. I'm gradually splitting off from everything we had in New York. The businesses I'll be running here will be legal. I look forward to your cooperation—or at least your lack of interference—as we get things to that point. As you know—you mention my time at Dartmouth—I never planned to take part in my father's business. It's not what he wanted either. As I say, it's only temporary. We'll be opening a new casino in Lake Tahoe, and we're planning on running it so clean that an army of cops, IRS agents, and Gaming Commission men could live there night and day."

Russo laughed. "Good fucking luck!"

"I'll have to take that as sincerity," Michael said, standing, "because we need to go. My apologies. It's our pleasure to have you as our guests. We look forward to seeing you tonight."

Tom Hagen opened the door to the basement office of Enzo Aguello, an old friend of the Corleone Family and now the casino's head pastry chef.

All three men inside—the two established *capo*s, Rocco Lampone and Pete Clemenza, as well as the head of protection, Al Neri—had been together yesterday in Detroit, at Pete's son's wedding. Every eye in the room was bloodshot. Lampone was only thirty but looked ten years older. He'd used a cane ever since he'd been shipped home from North Africa with a Purple Heart and no left kneecap. Clemenza gasped from the effort of getting out of his chair. Hagen always thought of him as one of those ageless fat men, but now he just looked old. He must have been about seventy.

They could have met in a suite upstairs, but Enzo's office had the advantages of being humble, close to the food, and one hundred percent secure—a cinder-block bunker that, with the best equipment money could buy, Neri had swept for bugs. Neri took his place in the hall, closing the door behind him.

"Where's Fredo?" Clemenza said.

Mike shook his head.

"He's fine," Hagen said. "His plane's late. Storms in Detroit. He'll be in tomorrow."

Clemenza and Lampone looked at each other. They sat down on hard metal folding chairs around Enzo's gunmetal gray desk.

"I wasn't gonna say nothin'," Clemenza said, "but I hear weird fucking things about Fredo, I hate to say." Fredo's new bodyguards had come from Clemenza's *regime*.

"What do you mean?" Mike said.

Clemenza waved him off. "Believe me, it's too flaky and ridiculous to talk about, and from what I hear it comes from junkies and niggers, so you can ignore ninety-nine percent of it right there. But the thing is, we all know he's—" Clemenza grimaced, as if he were enduring a gas pang. "Well, I ain't one to preach the abstemious life, but he's got a problem with the juice."

"*Abstemious?*" Mike arched his eyebrows. "Where'd you learn *that* word?"

"I sent my fucking kid to that same fancy school you went to, Mike, that was how I heard about it." He winked. "Only unlike *you* he finished it up."

"He says *abstemious?* Out loud?"

"How else you say things? You know what else I learned about that word? It's one of just two words in the whole English language that uses all five vowels and in order."

"What's the other one?"

"How the fuck should I know what the other one is? A minute ago, you thought I was too fucking dumb to know how to use even one of them."

Everyone laughed, and the men got to work.

The little time Hagen had spent as a corporate lawyer, for a meeting half this important and ten percent as detailed, there would have been a squadron of secretaries, scribbling like mad, and still half of what was said would have been lost or distorted. These men of course wrote down nothing and, as tired as they were, could be counted upon to remember everything. They spent three hours chewing through old business, new business, grilled calamari, and *pasta e fagioli*.

They discussed the toll the war with the Barzinis and Tattaglias had taken on the Family's business interests. They discussed the accommodations made for the wife and family of Tessio, that saddest and unlikeliest of traitors, friend and partner of Vito Corleone since their youth, and the medical, funeral, and family financial needs of the organization's other casualties. They discussed the triumph of the erroneous but widely held opinion—among the NYPD and the newspapers, among other crime families, among nearly everyone outside the Corleone Family—that both Tessio and the wife-beating brute Carlo, Mike's brother-in-law and the de facto murderer of his brother Sonny, had been killed by men dispatched by Barzini or Tattaglia. On top of this, the Corleone Family's man in the New York D.A.'s office (a classmate of Mike's at Dartmouth) planned to bring a series of indictments this week charging members of the Tattaglia Family with the murder of Emilio Barzini and charging members of the Barzini Family with the murder of Phillip Tattaglia. Even if, as was likely, these arrests didn't result in convictions, the FBI would consider the matter closed and stay out of it. Local cops—hundreds of whom had suffered from the lost income as much as any shylock—were happiest with business as usual. The short attention span of the public would soon swerve back, as it reliably does, to bread and circuses. All in all, the current cease-fire stood to be a genuine peace.

"Every ten years," Clemenza said, shrugging. "We have these things and then we get back to work." He'd found a whole box of toothpicks in Enzo's desk and was chewing up a new one every couple minutes. The other men all had cigars or cigarettes going. Clemenza's doctor had told him to stop smoking. He was trying. "Like clockwork. This one's my fourth."

Everyone had, over the years, heard this theory of Clemenza's. No one said anything.

"So," Clemenza said. "You think that's what we got, Mike? Peace?" He even brandished the toothpick like a cigar. "Do we need to call for a meeting of the Commission?"

Michael nodded, more in concentration than assertion. Hagen knew that Michael had failed to present the Commission with a list of the men

being initiated tonight. Probably the last thing he'd have wanted was for the Commission to meet. But his face registered nothing. "Rocco?" he said, bowing his head, extending his palm: *after you*.

That long pause—Hagen noted, impressed—made it look as if Michael were giving the question serious thought and then consulting with a trusted aide. If Sonny had lived and been in charge now, he'd have just blurted out what he thought and been proud of his decisiveness. Michael had inherited and honed his father's ability to create consensus.

Rocco Lampone took a long puff on his cigar. "That's the sixty-four-thousand-dollar question, ain't it? How do we know the war's over unless someone comes out and says it, huh?"

Michael knitted his fingers together and said nothing, his face utterly blank. The Commission functioned as an executive committee for America's twenty-four crime families, with the heads of the top seven or eight Families approving the names of new members, new *capo*s, and new bosses (these were nearly always approved) and arbitrating only the most intractable conflicts. It met as infrequently as possible.

"I'd say yeah," Lampone finally said, "we got a peace. We got the word of, what? Joe Zaluchi, that's a given. Molinari, Leo the Milkman, Black Tony Stracci. All but Molinari are on the Commission, right? Forlenza's leaning our way, right? Any word yet from the Ace?"

"Not yet," Hagen said. "Geraci's supposed to call in after they get to that fight."

"That's a sure thing," Rocco said. "Geraci, not the fight. The fight, I like that half-breed nigger lefty, what a sweet cross he's got. Ain't even human how fast and smooth it is."

Clemenza slapped the top of the metal desk four times and arched his eyebrows.

"Anyway, Forlenza makes five," Rocco said. "We still think Paulie Fortunato's the new Don of the Barzinis?"

"We do," Hagen said.

"Then six. He's a reasonable man, and in addition to that he's closer to Cleveland than Barzini was. In other words, he'll do what the Jew does. So that just leaves the other ones." In lieu of pronouncing the name Tattaglia, Rocco made a filthy Sicilian gesture. His differences with the Tattaglias were personal, visceral, complicated, and many. He'd been the one who burst in on Phillip Tattaglia, surprising him in a bungalow off Sunrise Highway, out on Long Island. Tattaglia was standing there naked except for his gartered silk socks, a hairy man in his seventies, with this teenage prostitute spread out on the bed in front of him, squeezing back tears while he tried to jack off into her open mouth. Lampone put four rounds into the man's soft gut. The Tattaglias' organization was in sham-

bles, and the man who'd taken over, Phillip Tattaglia's brother Rico, had come out of a comfortable retirement in Miami. It seemed unlikely a man like that would have the stomach for more vendettas, but a Tattaglia was still a Tattaglia.

When Mike said nothing, Lampone frowned like a determined schoolkid working to please the teacher. Mike was the youngest man in the room, the youngest Don in America, yet all the others were straining to prove themselves to him. He stood and walked to the place on the wall where a window would have been if there had been a window. "What do you think, Tom?"

"No Commission meeting," Hagen said, "not if we can avoid it." Hagen, as Vito's *consigliere,* was the only one of them ever to attend such a meeting. He was also the only one ever to attend an even more rare meeting of all the Families, which is what a call for a meeting of the Commission would snowball into. "Reason being, three Commission members have died this year. With that many new men, if they meet, they'll have to figure out whether to add Louie Russo. No matter what anyone thinks of him personally, with Chicago what it is, they have to say yes. They don't meet, they can keep him on the hook and say they'll get to it next time they do meet. Once they meet, Russo's got to be a part of it, which means a lot of different things could happen. Unpredictable things."

"Older that guy gets," Clemenza said, "the more his nose looks like a pecker."

This made Mike smile. Clemenza had had the same knack with Vito, though, truth be told, it had been a hell of a lot easier to get a smile out of Vito than it was Mike.

"When he got the nickname, his nose was just big," Clemenza said, inserting toothpick number nine into his little round mouth. "Now the end's red and shaped exactly like a dickhead. And those eyebrows? Pubic hair. Am I right? All he needs is a vein to stand out on the side of his nose, and Fuckface'll get thrown in the joint for indecent exposure. Shit, they got Capone for tax evasion." He shook his head. "Pantywaist arrests"— and here Clemenza grabbed his balls and put on a good Chicago accent— "it's da Chiacahgo way."

Everyone laughed, even Hagen, though he privately believed that the reason Irish and Jewish gangsters had managed to move from most-wanted lists to ambassadorships was that they (like Hagen himself) paid their taxes, to a point anyway. It was understandable that many Sicilians, whose distrust of a central government had run through their veins for centuries, did not. And it was also true that theirs was a cash business with nothing of importance written down. A hundred IRS agents working around the clock for a hundred years couldn't figure out one percent of

what went on. Still: Governments were no different from anyone or anything wielding great power. They wanted what was theirs. You had to wet their beak. Or kill them.

They discussed a host of practical matters that had to be addressed so that the Family and its interests could again become fully operational. Only near the end did Michael discuss the ambitious long-term plans that he and his father, in the months Vito had spent as Michael's *consigliere*, had envisioned. Hagen let everyone know about his discussions with the Ambassador and the Family's role in James Kavanaugh Shea's plan for the White House in 1960. They already knew about Hagen's own, not-unrelated plan: to run for the Senate next year and lose (that senator was in the Corleones' pocket anyway), then use the legitimacy garnered by a respectable loss to make it easy for the governor to appoint him to a cabinet position. By 1960, Hagen could run for governor and win. Which brought Michael to the last order of business.

"Before we take care of our shorthandedness in other areas, we need to fix it at the top. First, there's the matter of Tessio's old *regime*. Any thoughts before I make my choice?"

They shook their heads. The choice was obvious: Geraci would be a popular pick, especially among those who resented what had happened with Tessio. True, there had been grumbling about him from some of the older men in New York. He was Tessio's protégé, but Tessio had betrayed the Family. There was the issue of a narcotics operation Geraci had been allowed to have (though it was still only a rumor). There was his age (though he was older than Michael). He was from Cleveland. He had a college degree and a few law school classes. Hagen had first heard of him when Paulie Gatto had him beat up the punks who'd assaulted Amerigo Bonasera's daughter. Three years later, after Gatto was killed, Geraci had been Pete's second choice to take over as top button man, after Rocco. Rocco had made the most of that opportunity and was now a *capo*, but Geraci was Michael's type of guy. He was also one of the best earners the family had ever had. There were other options, older guys like the DiMiceli brothers, or maybe Eddie Paradise. Solid, loyal men, but not in the same league with the Ace.

"My only words of wisdom on this subject," Pete said, "are that if Christ himself was ready to get promoted to *capo*, you'd hear complaints. I been around a long time, and I never seen a guy who can earn like this Geraci. Kid can swallow a nickel and shit a banded stack of Clevelands. I don't know him in and out, but what I do know is good. He's impressed me."

Michael nodded. "Anything else?"

"Quick thing on Eddie Paradise," Rocco said.

"Yes?" Michael said.

Rocco shrugged. "He's a good man. Paid his dues. People know him."

"All right," Michael said. "Any other words on the subject?"

"Eddie's my wife's cousin is all," Rocco said. "When she asks me if I vouched for him, well—you're all married, you all got families. Nah, no other words."

"Vouching duly noted," Michael said. "All right. My choice is Fausto Geraci."

This was greeted with hearty approval. Hagen had never heard anyone else call Geraci *Fausto,* but Michael rarely called anyone by his street name, a quirk he'd picked up from the old man. Sonny had been the opposite. He'd know someone for years, pull jobs with him, eat dinner in his home, and most of the time he didn't know the guy's last name until he saw it printed in the bulletin at a wedding or a funeral.

"Which brings me to you, Tom," Michael said. "Your job, that is."

Hagen nodded.

Michael looked to Pete and Rocco. "With Tom involved more in politics, we need to move him out of certain things. Since stepping down as *consigliere*—"

Hagen had not been consulted and had not sought change.

"—Tom has remained a trusted adviser, as anyone's legal counsel should be. That's how it's going to stay. But it leaves a void as *consigliere.* Tom has done an excellent job, and my father—" Michael turned up the palm of his hand. Words couldn't do justice to the late Don's greatness. "I don't see a clear successor. For the next year or so, I'll be spreading the responsibilities of *consigliere* to all the capos and also you, Tom, when it's appropriate."

The failure to mention Fredo was no accident, Hagen thought.

"However," Michael said. He let the pause linger. "There are situations where I need to be represented along with my *consigliere*—Commission meetings and the like. There's no one I'd rather have at my side on such occasions than my father's oldest friend, Pete Clemenza."

Hagen applauded and slapped Pete on the back. Clemenza said he'd be honored. Rocco gave him a bear hug. Clemenza called out for Neri to have Enzo grab some strega for a toast. Hagen smiled. That was another thing: once men like Clemenza were gone, the important toasts would no longer be made with strega or homemade grappa. It would be Jack Daniel's or Johnnie Walker. Before long they'd be in boardrooms clanking mugs of weak coffee.

Enzo, it turned out, had a bottle of strega in his desk drawer. He joined them for the toast. "May we live our lives so that when we die we are smiling," Clemenza said, "and everyone else is crying like a fucking baby."

They were about to leave when there was a knock on the door.

"Sorry, fellas," Neri said, opening the door. "Seemed like you was wrapping up and—"

Johnny Fontane, carrying a fancy leather satchel, elbowed past him and, in a voice barely above a whisper, said something that sounded like "How're your birds, fellas?" Neri scowled. He wasn't the sort of man one elbowed past, not even a *pezzonovante* pretty boy like Fontane.

"We was just talking about you," Clemenza said. "That statue you busted, up in your room there, you know that thing cost three grand?"

"You got a good deal on it," Fontane said. "I'd have guessed five."

He'd never been close to Michael, but he presumed to cross the room and, with his free arm, embrace him. Michael did not react. He said nothing.

Hagen had no use for show business people.

Hal Mitchell appeared in the doorway, now in his tux, too, breathless and apologizing. "It's just that the opening act's already on and—"

"First thing." Fontane lifted the satchel as high as he could reach. "Here's this." He dropped it. It landed hard on the desk in front of Michael. It sounded like money. "Airmail from Frank Falcone. He sends his regrets, and so does Mr. Pignatelli."

Presumably it was a "loan" from the pension fund of the Hollywood unions Falcone controlled—an investment in the Castle in the Clouds.

Michael remained seated. He looked at the satchel. Other than that, he was motionless. His expression couldn't have been more blank if he'd spent all afternoon dead.

A vein in the singer's temple began to twitch.

Michael ran his finger around the rim of his empty glass.

The other men kept still, letting Fontane and Mike stare each other down and waiting for Fontane to say what the second thing was. It seemed unthinkable that this, such a small favor in return for all that had been done on his behalf, would have provoked such a childish outburst.

Hagen would never understand Fontane's lack of gratitude. Ten years ago, on Connie's wedding day, Hagen had walked away with two favors to carry out: getting Enzo Aguello his American citizenship and getting Johnny the part in that war movie. Since then, Enzo had been a faithful friend, even standing unarmed at the hospital alongside Michael when two cars full of men had come to kill Vito, an act of bravery that probably saved the Don's life. What had Johnny Fontane ever given back to the Corleones?

No one had put a gun to Johnny's head to sign a contract with the Les Halley Orchestra, yet Vito Corleone had to send a man to put a gun to Halley's to get him out of it. The Corleones had gotten Jack Woltz to cast him in that war picture, which Johnny would have had in the first place if

he hadn't sport-fucked a starlet Woltz was in love with. Hagen shuddered. After the murders of so many people, how was it possible that what stayed with him in his nightmares was Luca taking a machete and hacking off the head of Woltz's racehorse? Something Hagen hadn't even seen. And something Johnny didn't even know about, since Woltz, as expected, had hushed it up. Another gift from the Corleones: the blessings of ignorance. The Corleones had even bought Fontane an Academy Award. All those favors, and this was how he acted?

The silence in the room thickened.

Fontane shifted his weight from foot to foot. Did he really think he could win a battle of nerves with Michael Corleone?

Finally, Fontane let out a deep breath. "All right, but here's the second thing." He pointed to his throat. "I'm sorry as hell, but I don't think it's a good idea for me to go on."

All Michael said was "Is that right?"

Clemenza pursed his lips and flicked a softened toothpick past Fontane's ear. "I thought Fredo's doctor friend fixed that. Your throat. The Jew surgeon, what's-his-face. Jules Stein."

"Segal," Johnny corrected. "He did." He looked around the room. "Which reminds me. You guys seen Fredo? I got something for him. A present. A present from me."

"His plane was delayed," Hagen said.

Fontane shrugged. "It'll wait, I guess," he said. "Look, fellas, you know me. I'm a pro." The stage whisper made him seem like one of those women who do it to make men come closer. "My voice is good, but my throat?" He shook his head. "Not a hundred percent. Even so, I been doing these shows here, filling up the joint. Today I had a terrific recording session in L.A. Sometimes you just know. Here's the rub. On the plane back here, I fell asleep. When I woke up, my throat? Awful sore. So I was thinking—"

"Your first mistake right there," Clemenza said.

"—I should gargle some salt water and hit the hay. I'm no good like this. Numbnuts could go long." Morrie "Numbnuts" Streator was Fontane's long-suffering opening act, a comic he'd rescued from the Catskills. "He's on now. He's killin' 'em. Ask the sarge."

No one did. The issue here wasn't how much the guests were enjoying the blue jokes.

"I took the liberty," Fontane said, "of calling Buzz Fratello. He and Dotty don't have a show tonight. They could do it. Step in for me. In fact, they're on their way over right now."

"Yeah?" said Clemenza, impressed. "The more I see that Buzz, the more I like him."

"No can do, Johnny," Hal said. He had not been invited to come in the room and, like Neri, had remained just outside the doorway. "Buzz Fratello and Dotty Ames are under contract across the way." Meaning the Kasbah, which the Chicago outfit controlled. "Exclusively."

"They don't start there until next weekend. This thing's just a private show, right? A party. It's no different than someone singing in one of the lounges afterward. We all do that."

Michael remained still, his eyes on Fontane. After a very long time, Michael reached up and flicked his fingertips backhanded against his own jawbone, a gesture so identical to the late Don's it gave Hagen chills.

"Mike," Fontane said. "Michael." He was getting nowhere. You had to hand it to the guy, though. A different sort of person would have turned around and looked at the other people in the room, trying to read anything he could from the less inscrutable faces. He might even have made a wisecrack—Fontane's nature, most of the time. But Johnny held his spot. "Don Corleone. I have the greatest respect for you. I mean that. But this? This is just one show."

Michael folded his hands on the desk. He didn't even blink. Finally he cleared his throat. After the long stillness, it had the effect of a gunshot.

"What you do," Michael said, "is of no concern to me. Get out."

Chapter 10

FRANK FALCONE had a hundred grand on that fight at the Cleveland Armory. He was going to be ringside, he told Nick Geraci, even if it meant Geraci swimming to shore with Falcone lashed to his back. Don Forlenza offered the services of one of his boats. Laughing Sal Narducci pointed out that the bigger ones were already at the fight. There was nothing left but fishing boats unfit to go that far in open water during a storm.

It was not a long flight: maybe fifteen minutes. Geraci told them not to worry, he'd flown in conditions a hundred times worse than this—which of course he had not—and he went to ready the plane. He radioed the tower at Burke Lakefront Airport, which issued a staunch warning not to take off. He pretended not to hear.

The twin-engine airplane carrying Tony Molinari, Frank Falcone, Richard "the Ape" Aspromonte, Lefty Mancuso, and their pilot, officially listed as Gerald O'Malley, lifted off from Rattlesnake Island and into the dark sky. From the moment they were airborne, the flight was a struggle. He was so preoccupied with the challenges the storm threw his way that he wasn't at all sure if there was anything wrong with the fuel. Probably there wasn't. He'd checked both tanks before takeoff. He switched to the other tank not so much as a precaution but because he needed to focus on other things. As he strained though the soupy sky to see the lights of Cleveland, he thought he heard the engine sputtering, and without thinking he switched the tanks again and blurted something to the tower about sabotage, which, under these conditions, would have been difficult to assess for a pilot ten times more experienced than Nick Geraci.

The plane made its hapless approach toward Cleveland. The pilot's last words to the tower were "*Sono fottuto.*" Translation: "I'm fucked."

Then, a mile from shore, the plane plowed into the frothy brown chop of Lake Erie.

Geraci had been hit hard playing football in school, much harder in the ring. Once, at Lake Havasu, he'd been in a speedboat driven by his father and slammed into an aluminum dock. The hardest tackle, the most brutal punch, and that speedboat crash he'd somehow survived *combined* would have felt about half as bad as smacking into Lake Erie in an airplane.

The plane flipped. What felt like a moment later, Geraci was underwater. His door was jammed. He worked his legs free and started stomping a bigger hole in the glass of the windshield. The water was completely black. As he tried to get through the hole, a hand grabbed his arm. It was too dark to know whose hand it was. He tried to pull the man with him, through the hole in the windshield, to safety. The man was stuck. If Geraci hung on, they'd both die. He was about out of breath. The grip was strong, digging deep into the flesh of his arm. Geraci pried off the fingers, feeling and hearing the bones actually break.

Geraci swam free of the sinking wreck. He used the sound of the pounding rain to find the surface. His lungs spasmed and his Adam's apple bucked. A tingling feeling shot down his arms. He felt a twinge, almost a draining feeling, at the top of his skull. He'd never make it to the top. He was going to breathe water. This was it. *Have a good last thought, something worthy,* but all he could think of was this filthy water, near home, and how this was where he was going to die. He kept swimming. His mother had loved to swim. His mother! Ah. That was a good last thought. He loved her. She was a good mother, a good woman. He could see her. She was younger than when he'd last seen her. Now she was sipping a martini and reading a movie magazine beside the public pool in his old neighborhood. She was dead, too.

Johnny Fontane, along with his very special guests Buzz Fratello and the lovely and talented Miss Dotty Ames, finished their boffo show at the Beautiful Oasis Room at the Castle in the Sand with a lengthy and hilarious medley of songs about booze, performed for a crowd that didn't yet know thing one about the crash. It was a crowd, invitation only, largely made up of Teamsters officials from all over America, along with their wives (or more youthful simulacra). Michael Corleone had also, as an olive branch, invited a few select others—food, lodging, and a thousand dollars worth of chips, all on the house. Because it was a private party, even those who were ordinarily unable to set foot in Las Vegas were able to attend. For example: right by the stage was Don Molinari's brother Butchie (who'd done time for hijacking and extortion) and several other top men from San Francisco. In the men's room, trying to urinate and cursing inventively at his prick in Italian, was Carlo Tramonti (manslaughter; grand theft; arson; insurance fraud), the boss of New Orleans and a rising power in Havana. There was at least one member representing each of the other New York Families, each accompanied by women and bodyguards. The pale man in the gigantic sunglasses in the booth all the way in the back was Chicago's Louie "the Face" Russo (possession of stolen goods; aggravated

assault; bribing a federal agent), believed by some members of the FBI to be "in line for the still vacant position of '*capo di tutti i capi*' of the entire so-called La Cosa Nostra." Together, the appearance of all these people had provided enough cover to fly in several of the Corleones' own associates from New York without arousing suspicion. Also noteworthy—particularly since they were right by the stage and had come in for so much good-hearted innuendo-laden needling—were those blushing, happy honeymooners, the former Miss Susan Zaluchi and her new husband, Ray Clemenza. C'mon, folks: Put your hands together. Let's hear it for 'em.

In his own black velvet booth, Michael Corleone leaned back and took a long drag of his cigarette. He looked at his watch. It was Swiss, more than fifty years old. It had once belonged to a marine named Vogelsong, who'd used his dying breath to say he wanted Michael to have it.

By now, if everything had gone right, everyone on that airplane should be dead.

Michael had seen planes crash. Up close. It was all too easy for him to picture the terror on the men's faces as the plane went down. He shook his head. He didn't want to think about it.

Instead, he'd think about this: His plan had worked. He'd had setbacks, collateral damage, and midcourse corrections, but in the end, all had worked.

Now the Commission could meet. Hagen was wrong: no agreement would last unless it involved Chicago, but no peace involving Chicago would be in the Corleones' best interest unless Louie Russo came to the table motivated. This crash should motivate him plenty.

Michael had probably never smoked a whole cigarette so fast or enjoyed one more. He lit another and inhaled deeply.

He'd done what he needed to do. Period. Because of that, he'd sleep just fine. After all this was wrapped up in a month or so, he'd take a vacation and sleep twelve hours a day. Had he *ever*, as an adult, taken a vacation? Those years he'd spent hiding in Sicily were a lot of things, but a vacation? No. During the war, he'd taken liberty—Hawaii, New Zealand. But a family vacation? Never. He and Kay and the kids should go to Acapulco. Maybe see Hawaii again, at peace. Why not? Clown around with Anthony and Mary the way Pop always made time to do, get buried in the sand, rub oil on Kay's sexy back, maybe see if he could get her pregnant again. He'd wear flowery shirts and dance the mambo.

Michael lifted his half-full water glass. *We did it, Pop,* he thought. *We won.*

"God almighty," Clemenza said, red-faced from laughter and pointing a fat thumb at Fratello, who was racing around the stage like some frantic pillhead. "He's something, eh?"

"Something," Michael said.

Fontane had held back, doing quiet numbers and joking around in the ones that would have made him push his voice, but the brilliance he exuded even when he wasn't trying—maybe especially then—was a thing of beauty. He was a punk, but he was an artist, too. Michael couldn't be talked to the way Fontane had this afternoon, but by the same token he couldn't stay mad at the guy.

Fratello? An embarrassment. Here was a guy who'd knocked around for years as "the *cafone* on the saxophone." Then he'd put down the sax, started singing like a Negro but with a mamma-mia Italian accent, married a leggy blonde half his age, and bam: Buzz Fratello and Dotty Ames, stars of *The Starbright Soap Variety Hour.*

Fratello finished the set by sprinting across the stage, diving to the floor, sliding ten feet or so through Dotty's legs, coming to a stop perfectly timed so he could roll over, look up at her crotch, and rub his eyes in comic disbelief. Fontane cracked up. Dotty helped Buzz up, and they all took a bow. The crowd rose to its feet. The singers left the stage. The ovation continued. The orchestra members kept the fanfare going; clearly, there would be an encore.

Michael felt a hand on his shoulder.

"Phone," Hal Mitchell whispered. "It's Tom."

Michael nodded and put out his cigarette. *Showtime.* He glanced at Louie Russo's table. Someone was whispering something in his ear, too, and when Michael made eye contact with the whisperer, the man looked away. Michael reached over and tapped Clemenza.

Seconds later—as the orchestra launched into a vampy take on "Mala Femmina" and Buzz, Dotty, and Fontane locked arms and gamboled back onstage for their encore—some of the implications of what may or may not have happened on Lake Erie, sketchy as the details were, must have dawned on Louie Russo. But by the time he peered over his sunglasses at the black velvet booth in the corner, it was empty. Even the candle had been blown out.

Nick Geraci's head broke the surface. He gasped for air, and it surged down his arms and legs, and then he screamed. It was the first time he felt the excruciating pain from his cracked ribs and broken leg.

About a hundred yards away, a flaming oil slick marked the spot where the plane had smashed into Lake Erie. Bobbing in the middle of it were one of the wings, a big chunk of the side of the fuselage with the painted lion logo on it, and the upper half of what turned out to be Frank Falcone's corpse.

Geraci wasn't sure what had happened or whose fault it had been, though the pain and adrenaline made it hard to think clearly. He was tethered to reason only by his conviction that if everyone back there was dead, he might as well be. Rescue could mean death.

Through the rain he could see the haze of the Cleveland skyline. He swam away from it. North. Back to Rattlesnake Island, to Canada, a passing boat. Someplace where he could buy himself some time to work things out. Someplace where he'd have a shot at controlling his own fate. His leg felt like it was on fire with pain and his cracked ribs made it almost impossible to breathe, yet by the time the Coast Guard speedboat spotted him, Geraci was about a quarter mile from the crash site, in extreme shock, unconscious, his lungs filling with water, going down.

Concealed behind the parapets of the highest of the Castle in the Sand's three Moorish towers and encased in a spire of mirrored glass was an unnamed, revolving ballroom where the ceremony would be held.

"I bet you're smelling printer's ink right now," said Clemenza, giving Michael a gentle elbow. "You can about taste it, am I right? In the back of your throat, eh? Like oil, but worse."

The reflection of Michael in the shiny brass elevator doors was sipping a crystal goblet of ice water. He looked like a put-together, invulnerable, slick-haired man of respect, with the wind at his back and the world by the balls.

"I'm tellin' you," Clemenza said. "I don't think I ever seen your old man so—"

Michael nodded.

"Waterworks," Clemenza said. "Only time in all the years I ever saw him like that."

Clemenza had been the one who'd brought Michael to be straightened out, a few weeks after he returned to America from his exile in Sicily. The killings of Sollozzo and McCluskey, which had served to make his bones, had happened three years earlier. Clemenza had had tickets to a Dodgers game he'd gotten from a friend he had with the team. Second row, right behind the plate. It was the first game Michael had seen since they started letting Negroes play. He'd had no idea that this had happened, or when. He'd spent seven of the last eight years away from America, fighting and killing and in constant danger of being killed. He'd missed things. He hadn't even been to his brother's funeral. The Dodgers beat Chicago, 4–1.

On the way home, they stopped at what, when Michael left the country, had been the offices of a daily newspaper. One of Clemenza's shylocks

had, for the usual reasons, found himself in possession of the building. Clemenza said he needed to take a look at the place to figure out whether to rent it, sell it, or torch it. All of which was true.

When they entered the huge empty room where the printing press had been, there, in the pale late-summer light, sitting behind a long table, its blue paint peeling, were Tessio and Michael's father. On the table were a tapered candle, a holy card, a pistol, and a knife. Michael knew what was coming: they were initiating him into the Family. After all that had happened, this was just a formality. It had been Michael's own idea to kill those men—the man who'd arranged the hit on Vito Corleone and the crooked cop who, when he came to the hospital to finish the job, had had to settle for smashing Michael's face. It had been his brother Sonny's job, as acting Don, to okay those killings (Tessio had objected, saying it would be like "bringing a guy up from the minors to pitch in the World Series"). Later, Vito claimed he'd never wanted this life for Michael, but it had always been obvious he thought no one else could ever be good enough. At Michael's initiation, his father mumbled a few unintelligible words before his shoulders started heaving. He began to sob. Clemenza followed suit. Tessio finished the job, in a combination of Sicilian and English, with saturnine eloquence. Afterward, they killed two bottles of Chianti. Vito couldn't stop weeping. The smell of ink and grease registered on Michael, but somehow not the intensity of it. The next day, his clothes stank so badly they had to go in the trash. A week later, the building burned to the ground. Lightning, ruled the fire marshal. A month after that, the guy quit the fire department and moved to Florida. Now he fronted money-laundering operations down there—liquor stores, vending machines, real estate—and was engaged to Sonny's widow, Sandra.

The elevator doors opened. Michael and Pete boarded it and rode it together to the top.

"Forlenza'd never clip his own godson." Clemenza—who, on Michael's orders, had killed Carlo Rizzi, the father of Michael's own godson—sucked three olives off his toothpick and kept the pick in the corner of his mouth. "I also don't think it's possible a guy from another outfit could set foot on that fucking island without the Jew knowing about it," Clemenza said. "I say accident."

The best information Hagen had been able to get was that there had been one survivor. This had not been confirmed. If the survivor was one of the two Dons or one of their men, it would look better. If it was Geraci, what would happen next was hard to figure. It might or might not be possible to pass him off as some private pilot named O'Malley with no connection to the Corleone Family. Also, it was going to be nearly impossible to learn what he knew or had been able to figure out. And then there was

the matter of the thunderstorm. The storm might take the blame for everything, which would keep the crash from having its full effect. But Michael was already plotting how he might use any uncertainty over the cause of the crash to his advantage. "Accidents don't happen," Michael said, "to people who take accidents as a personal insult."

"So sabotage?"

"I don't know. I agree, Don Forlenza wouldn't kill his own godson, even if he had a reason to. As far as we know, he didn't have a reason. But I'm not so sure it's impossible to sneak onto that island somehow."

"If not Forlenza—"

Michael shrugged and arched an eyebrow and kept his eyes fixed on Pete's.

"*La testa di cazzo.*" Clemenza pulled out the elevator's emergency stop knob with one hand, pounding the wall with the other. "Russo."

Michael nodded, as if in thought. "One airplane," he said, "and who gets hurt? They hit us, they hit Molinari, they hit their own guy Falcone, a reckless man who maybe they thought had stepped too far out on his own, and it all *looks* like Forlenza ordered it. Their four biggest competitors not just here, in Las Vegas, but in the western half of the country."

" 'Everything west of Chicago is Chicago,' " Clemenza said, mocking. "*Quello stronzo.*"

"If you're right," Michael said, "*turd* only scratches the surface of what that guy is." He shook his head in a way he was sure looked sincerely rueful.

Clemenza filled his fat cheeks with air, exhaled slowly, then pushed the button in. When the elevator doors opened, a few dozen people were already there, scattered throughout the ballroom. Clemenza patted Michael on the back. "Don't let that shit ruin this thing here," he whispered. "Enjoy it, okay? You went to all that trouble to have your face fixed where that cop fucked it up. Show it off a little. Smile."

Michael had lied.

Not lied exactly. More like: he'd led a horse to water, and Pete Clemenza had bent over and drunk. If Pete blamed Russo that fast, he wouldn't be alone.

The truth was that Michael Corleone had sought to hurt all four of *his* biggest rivals in the West. That was the *easy* part. The hard part had been to do it without taking the blame. By orchestrating the incident so that not another living soul knew all of what he'd done (not Hagen, not Pete, nobody), he might have done that, too.

Frank Falcone was a menace. Ever since Michael had had Moe Greene

killed, Falcone had been the biggest roadblock to the Corleones' expansion into Las Vegas. Pignatelli would be more obedient to Chicago than Falcone was, yet because of his business relationship with the Corleones—both his involvement in the Castle in the Clouds and the satchel of cash he'd had Johnny Fontane deliver as a tribute for killing Falcone—he posed no threat.

Tony Molinari was a longtime ally, true, but his increasing wariness about Michael's setting up a base of operations in Lake Tahoe, a couple hundred miles from San Francisco, was a problem destined to escalate. Unfortunately, he'd become a cancer best removed now.

Forlenza was an old man. Disgracing him while he was still alive was better than killing him. He'd been bragging to the other Dons for years about his little island fortress. He'd get all or part of the blame for the crash. Even if no one came after him for revenge, there would be pressure from his own men for him to step down. Sal Narducci—who'd struck a deal with Michael Corleone and overseen the sabotage of the plane—would become Don. After waiting for the job for twenty years, he was a good bet to keep his mouth shut about how he finally got it. Installing Narducci as Don would also sever Cleveland's ties to the Barzinis.

The best part of the plan was what it would do to Chicago. It would be impossible to prove that Russo had been behind it and equally impossible to disprove it. But once Michael let the members of the Commission know that the dead pilot O'Malley had really been his new *capo*, all the right people would consider who'd had the most to gain.

Would Forlenza kill his own godson? No.

Would Michael Corleone kill his new hotshot *capo*? Who could imagine?

That left Chicago.

Michael had managed to hit Chicago without killing a single one of Russo's men. Michael would thus not have to worry about Russo seeking revenge. The only tangible loss Russo would suffer was that now he'd come to the peace table dealing from a position of weakness. But that was all Michael needed.

The most difficult decision Michael had made was to kill Geraci.

Without question, Geraci had done a brilliant job with the drug business, but his aggressiveness was an issue. His ambition was boundless, larger than even he himself understood. Though he'd been unswervingly loyal, his connection to Forlenza would always be a concern. He'd always be sore about Tessio. And when Michael had made Fredo *sotto capo*, Geraci had asked him, in public, if he'd lost his mind. They'd been at dinner at Patsy's. No one else had been at the table. No one else had heard. Geraci had apologized. But few Dons would tolerate such disrespect. It

might have seemed petty, but it convinced Michael Corleone that all the smaller concerns about him were well founded and destined to grow more severe.

Still, only the last justified having Geraci killed. Even that might have been forgiven. There had been no betrayal. Geraci's assets easily outweighed his liabilities. Michael liked him.

Sacrificing Fausto Geraci, Jr., was not what Vito Corleone would have done.

It was, rather, the act of a marine who'd seen at least a thousand good men die, seemingly at random: a necessary evil swapped for the chance to achieve a greater good.

It was a perfect plan, unless it was true that one of the men had survived.

Clemenza had lied, too.

Michael's initiation was not the only time he'd seen the Don like that. Still frail from his own gunshot wounds, Vito had returned home from burying Santino so wracked with grief it haunted everyone who'd seen it. Michael hadn't seen it. The people who had—Michael's mother, his sister and her husband, his brothers, Tom and Fredo, and Pete Clemenza, who, soon after the sobbing started, embraced his friend and went home, leaving the family to themselves—carried with them the image of that broken man and the sounds of his horrible wails. They had never spoken of it, not to one another and certainly not to anyone who hadn't been there, not even Michael.

Several people who'd been at the Fontane show made an appearance in the rotating ballroom. A reception, that's all it seemed to be. There was no discernible mass exodus of the union officials, orchestra members, or women. As far as any of the thirteen new men might have been able to tell, one moment those other people were there. The next, made members of the Corleone Family were carrying two long tables, already covered with white linen tablecloths, to the center of the parquet dance floor, and every single one of the outsiders was gone.

Someone hit the lights.

Throughout the room, men put hands on the shoulders of the inductees and in hoarse whispers congratulated them (there would have been fourteen if Fredo hadn't made Figaro miss his plane). These were men the new guys had looked up to for years—running their neighborhoods, dressed in tailored suits and holding forth in barbershops and at

lunch counters and on empty peach crates in front of certain garages, driving fancy cars and fucking fancier women, dispensing favors and looking out for their own, running a court of last resort for a maligned people who needed one, operating in a world that, back then, had seemed mysterious, powerful, and unattainable. Outside the dark ballroom, oblivious tourists swam in the rooftop pool.

When the ballroom lights came back up, the table was set: thirteen place settings, each with a votive candle, a holy card, a dagger, and—in a gesture meant to denote the Family's expansion into the Wild West (Fredo's idea, in other words)—a gleaming, unloaded Colt .45.

The thirteen new men were shown to their places. The others—fifty-two of them were able to make it, some who'd been at the show, some who'd slipped into town and into the Castle in the Sand just for this—sat in the chairs around the circle.

Michael Corleone sat with the rest of his men. He milked the silence. He was not a superstitious man, but he worked with superstitious men and he knew that they were counting and recounting the number of men in the middle and not liking it that the number kept being thirteen. But the risk of letting them dwell on that pointless coincidence seemed worth the reward of letting the men at the tables stew in their barely concealed anxiety. To a person, they were transparently trying, and failing, to look as if this were just another moment in their lives. They knew who he was and that he was in charge of this, and so it was comical to watch them try not to look at him. He could hear the voice of Sergeant Bradshaw, his old DI: *Your fool deniiiies fear. A maRINE is unafraid to admit fear. Your fool scoffs at danger. Your fool ignorrrrres danger. In the face of danger, a . . . MARINE . . . IGNORES . . . NOTHING.*

At last Michael stood.

"Let me tell you the story of a boy," he said, approaching the tables. "He was born one thousand, one hundred and forty years ago in the Sicilian countryside, near the town of Corleone. His childhood was one of wealth and happiness, until, at the age of twelve, the Arab hordes, on their way north through the mountains, slaughtered the boy's parents. The boy, hiding in a clay pot, peeked out and saw the blade of a scimitar decapitate his mother, and from the dead lips of her severed head she shouted words of love to her only son. These murders were acts of savagery. The Arabs were protecting nothing, avenging nothing. They did not so much as pick a tomato from the vine, a grape from the field, or an olive from the grove. They killed for the sake of killing and proceeded north toward their objective, Palermo."

Michael took a cigar from the breast pocket of his tuxedo jacket. More than one of the men at the tables rubbed their damp palms against the sides of their thighs.

"The boy's name," said Michael, "was Leolucas." Michael paused to light the cigar and let the importance of the name sink in. "Though only twelve years old, he managed not only to run his family's estate but also to work the land as long and as hard as someone twice his age. But as the years passed, he heard, in the solitude of the fields, a summons to his one true destiny. He sold his assets, gave his money to the poor, and became a monk. After many years, he returned to the village of his youth, where he performed countless selfless acts and was beloved by all who knew him. He died peacefully in his bed at the age of one hundred."

"*Cent'anni!*" shouted Clemenza. Every man who had a drink knocked it back.

"Five hundred years later," Michael said, circling the men at the tables, "the intercession of Leolucas protected the town of Corleone from an outbreak of the Black Plague. And in 1860, more than a thousand years after his death, Leolucas avenged the murders of his parents by appearing as a tower of white flame before the occupying army of the Bourbon French, spooking them from Corleone and into the hands of Garibaldi, who drove them from Sicily altogether. These miracles, and many others at the site of his tomb, were affirmed by the Holy Father in Rome. Leolucas is now and forever—" Michael took a regal puff of his cigar, strode to one of the tables, and took the holy card from in front of Tommy Neri, who was one of the thirteen. He kissed the card and set it back down. "—the patron saint of Corleone. Gentlemen?"

He made a sweeping motion with his hand. Each of the thirteen kissed the pasteboard image of St. Leolucas.

"Only a few years after the terrifying appearance of Saint Leolucas in the tower of flame," Michael said, "in a cottage adjoining the fields once owned and tilled by the sainted Leolucas, another boy was born. His childhood was also happy, until, also at the age of twelve, men came to kill his father. The murder was accomplished with three blasts from a *lupara*. His mother was stabbed. Gutted, like an animal. Mortally wounded, she, too, managed to shout words of love to her son. The boy escaped. The murderers came after him, knowing that someday he would try to kill them. That man's name—" Michael took another long draw off the cigar. He felt his own destiny flow through him. "—was Vito Andolini. He immigrated, alone, to the cold shores of America, where, to keep the murderers from finding him, he changed his surname, adopting the name of his hometown. It was one of the few sentimental gestures he ever made, all having to do in some way with *la famiglia*"—and here he smacked his chest with his fist—"with his beloved *figliolanza*"—and here he touched his chin. "He worked hard, helped his friends, built an empire, and never harbored an immodest thought. One day he did indeed return to Sicily and avenge the death of his parents. Vito Corleone, who earlier this year

died peacefully in his beloved garden, was my father. I, Michael Corleone, am his son. But"—and he indicated the men in the outer circle—"these men of honor, too, are *la famiglia Corleone*. If you wish to be with us, we invite you to be reborn as such."

Michael took his seat. Fredo had been meant to perform the next part. Despite what people like Nick Geraci thought, Michael's installation of his older brother as *sotto capo* had been more a means of encouragement than a job. Fredo had been given a few narrowly defined responsibilities, a small crew of reliable but mediocre men, a whorehouse in the desert, and some symbolic responsibilities, which he was discharging with his usual inconsistency. Michael was resigned to this. No matter how hard you beat a donkey, it will never become a racehorse.

Clemenza planted his cane on the floor, grunted loudly, and stood.

Undoubtedly, each of the thirteen already understood the formalities of this arrangement. But there were conventions to observe. Clemenza began by explaining the structure of the Family. Michael Corleone was the Godfather, whose authority is absolute. Frederico Corleone was the *sotto capo*. Rocco Lampone and himself, Pete Clemenza, were the *caporegime*s. Clemenza made no mention of the role of *consigliere*. This had been the case since the death of Genco Abbandando, first because Hagen, who was not Sicilian, could never participate in, observe, or even be mentioned in these ceremonies, then because during Vito's brief stint as *consigliere,* the books had remained closed. Clemenza made no mention of Nick Geraci at all.

"Before you join us," Clemenza said, "you gotta be clear on some things." He switched to Sicilian and continued, hobbling around the perimeter of the thirteen. "This thing we have is not a thing of business. It is a thing of honor. If you agree to join, this thing of ours must come before country. It must come before God. It must come before your own wife, your own mother, your own children. If you are summoned and your mother is on her deathbed, you will kiss her fevered brow and leave to do the bidding of your superiors."

He stopped in front of the chair where he'd started. He leaned forward on his cane, so far it seemed he might topple over. "Do you understand? Do you agree?"

The men unhesitatingly gave their assent.

In return, Clemenza nodded slowly and sat.

Michael again stood and, as if to compensate for Clemenza's frailty, approached the tables with great, vigorous strides. He'd had too much to eat, too much to drink, too much to do, and too little sleep. Acid rose in his throat.

"There are," he said, "two laws you must obey without question. You must never betray the secrets of this society, observing the ancient tradi-

tion of *omertà*. The penalty for violating this law is death. You must never violate the wife or children of another member. The penalty for violating this law is death. Do you vow, with your very life, to keep these laws?"

They did.

The older men would have noted the absence of a third law, sworn in every initiation Vito Corleone had performed: *You must never get involved in the narcotics trade.* No one said anything about this, not even a murmur.

"You come in alive," Michael said, "and you go out dead."

The day I asked you to marry me, Kay, I said our businesses would be legitimate in five years.

Michael approached Tommy Neri. "The instruments by which you live and die are the gun"—here Michael bit down on the cigar and picked up the Colt with one hand—"and the knife." He picked up the dagger with the other. He set the weapons back down in front of Tommy, crossed over each other.

"Do you agree," Michael said, "that, when called upon, you will use the gun and the knife to help this Family?"

"Yes, Godfather."

Michael took a puff on his cigar and used it to light Tommy Neri's votive candle. Then he pointed to Tommy's right hand. Tommy extended it. Michael picked up the dagger, pricked Tommy's trigger finger, folded it into his palm, and squeezed his fist hard, careful to apply the pressure away from the wound and thus increase the amount of blood.

One by one, the other twelve men gave the same answer and submitted to the same ritual.

Michael returned to the end of the table. He tapped Tommy's closed fist. Tommy opened it, then brought both hands together, the bloody right and the clean left, turned his palms up and cupped them. Michael picked up the holy card of Saint Leolucas, lit it with the votive candle, and dropped it into Tommy Neri's hands. "Back and forth," he whispered.

Tommy juggled the flaming saint from hand to hand.

"If you *ever* betray your friends," Michael said, "you will burn." He blew a small puff of cigar smoke into Tommy's unflinching face. "Like the picture of our beloved patron saint now burns your bloodied palm. Do you agree to this?"

"Yes, Godfather."

Michael watched the card turn fully to ash. Then, tenderly as a lover, he rubbed the ash into Tommy's palms, then kissed him, softly, on each cheek.

One by one, the other twelve men submitted to the same ritual and gave the same answer.

"You are now qualified men," Michael finally said, "*Gli uomini qual-ificati*. Gentlemen, please introduce yourself to your brothers."

The room exploded in a cacophony of congratulations, popping champagne corks, Italian toasts and benedictions. The men in the outer circle maintained their positions to ensure that the new members did in fact dutifully go around the room introducing themselves, kissing the cheeks of every man in the outer circle, missing no one. Michael had already kissed them. He ducked out the back door and down the stairs. He knew that what might greet him at home was news of the escalation of his troubles. But there was a chance his day was over. There was a chance he could get some rest and fight his fights with a clear head tomorrow. Already, he felt better, getting out of that room, away from the smoke and the liquor fumes. The only kisses he wanted were from his wife, his son, his daughter.

You go out dead.

He made it to the car. While he waited for Al Neri to collect the empty pistols and catch up to him, Michael felt his stomach lurch. For a moment he fought it. Then he dropped to his knees and vomited. It all came up—the strega, the whiskey, the food Enzo had prepared so lovingly, everything from the picnic, and what looked like every last kernel of the movie popcorn.

"You okay, boss?" The pistols clanked against one another in the pillowcase Neri was using to carry them, like Jacob Marley's chains in the production of *A Christmas Carol* Michael had been in as a kid. Neri was the chief of security here, but humping down fifteen flights of stairs and through various lobbies and hallways with a pillowcase full of thirteen pistols? Christ.

"Oh, yeah," Michael said. He was drenched in sweat. He managed, however unsteadily, to stand up. He'd ripped the knee of his tux pants. "I'm perfect. Let's go."

The daggers that had been used to cut the men's trigger fingers were theirs to keep. They were dazzling, jewel-handled things that had cost the Family nothing. Nick Geraci had a guy.

Chapter 11

Fᴀᴇᴅᴏ Cᴏʀʟᴇᴏɴᴇ whipped his rented Chevrolet up the drive and slammed on the brakes under the valet parking overhang. In back, Figaro woke up cursing in English, Capra in Sicilian. "See you up there, fellas," Fredo said, hopping out. He peeled off a twenty for the valet, then saw that he was a regular and paused. "Just curious. What's the biggest tip you ever got?"

The man looked at him funny. "A hundred," he said. "Once."

Fontane, Fredo thought. He just knew it. He peeled off two hundred. "Find me a good spot, okay, and get those bums out of the back first. So whose record did I break?"

"Yours, sir," the valet said. "Just last week."

Fredo laughed, went inside, and broke into a jog. Three in the morning, but inside the Castle in the Sand about the only way a person would know it wasn't a more decent hour was the presence of hypnotized women in housecoats and curlers, cigarettes dangling from the corners of their grim, unmade mouths, feeding coins into the slot machines as if it were a part of making supper for an ungrateful family. Not a lot of people run through casinos, but none of those dames, and no one at the blackjack tables either, so much as looked up. The pit bosses looked, of course, and so did the eye in the sky if there was anyone up there, but these were men who'd seen Fredo Corleone hurry past them before, which is another way of saying that if anyone not associated with the security cameras or the Nevada Gaming Commission asked them if they'd seen Mr. Corleone go by, they'd have frowned and said "Who?"

He lived in a suite on the third floor—five rooms, including a den with a bar and a tournament-sized pool table. He'd been gone for two weeks, attending to business in New York and trying to help his mother get squared away for the move west. As soon as he opened the door, he knew in his gut that something was wrong. The first concrete thing he noticed was that the curtains were drawn and the place was inky dark. Fredo never closed his curtains, and he never turned off his television set, even when it went to the test pattern, even when he left town. When he slept during the day, he used one of those masks. He jumped back into the hall, out of the line of fire, and reached into his jacket for his gun.

No gun. That gorgeous Colt Peacemaker, the gun that had brought down ten thousand desperadoes in a thousand dusty movies, lost somewhere in the wilds of greater Detroit.

At the other end of the hall a door opened and some old frump in a hairnet and a housecoat came out, carrying a tin cup full of coins and an actual horseshoe. Behind her trailed some milquetoast in an undershirt, Bermuda shorts, and a shiny white cowboy hat he must have bought earlier that day. Fredo froze. There was no noise at all from his room. The frump must have seen Fredo crouching outside a door down the hall, but she kept her head down and headed straight for the stairs. The husband waved, his face contorted into a desperate rictus.

The stairwell door closed.

Fredo counted to ten. "Hello?" he called. "Who's in there?"

He should have gone and gotten security. But he was exhausted and not thinking straight. He just wanted to grab a quick shower and get up to the ballroom. He did not want to be the candyass who called hotel security because some new maid hadn't been told never to shut Mr. Corleone's curtains or turn off his television set.

There was no noise at all. That had to be it, he thought: a new maid. As he walked in and reached for the light, the thought struck him that this was exactly the moment when guys got a slug right between the eyes, when they let down their guard and thought, *Ah, fuck it, it's nothing.*

The instant he flicked the switch, the toilet flushed. His heart nearly knocked the meat from his ribs, but before he had a chance to run or duck or even shout "Who's there?," out of the open door of the bathroom came a naked woman, platinum blond. She screamed.

"My *God,*" she said. "You scared the *crap* out of me!"

Zee crap. Thick French accent. It sounded real. Fredo closed the hallway door behind him and felt his heart slow down a little. "Do I *know* you?"

She walked toward him and smiled. Her bush was jet black, though her eyebrows were also blond. "I've been waiting for you do you know how long?"

"Seriously, sweetheart. Who are you? What the hell is going on here? Who let you in?"

"Since five o'clock in the afternoon," she said. She pointed to the champagne bucket next to his bed. "The ice, it finished melting hours ago." She shrugged, which made her little tits bounce. She had dull red nipples so big around they practically covered the whole business. "I'm sorry, but the bottle, it is empty now, too."

The accent was real. She was also slurring her words.

"Honey," he said. "I don't think you know who you're dealing with, okay?"

"I think I might." *I sink.* She jutted one of her hips and stuck out a pouty lower lip. "You're Fredo Corleone, yes?" *Fraid.*

"Why don't you start by telling me who you are?"

She extended her hand and giggled. "My name is Rita. Marguerite. But"—she dipped a naked shoulder, shy now—"I use Rita now."

Fredo didn't shake her hand. "Hello, Rita. The reason I shouldn't have you thrown in jail for breaking and entering is what?"

"It's not enough that a naked woman is waiting in your room to make love to you, huh?"

"I'm losing my patience with you, doll."

"Ah!" She threw back her head, exasperated. "You are no fun. Johnny Fontane sent me, all right? I am"—she laughed, as if at a rueful private joke—"I am a present for you, no? Johnny said, you know, that I was to be naked and in your bed, waiting." She blushed. "But a girl, she drinks the champagne, she's going to have to tee-tee."

Tee-tee? "That was real nice of Mr. Fontane, but it's awful late, you're awful drunk, and I'm awful tired, on top of which I still got one more thing to do tonight. This morning. Whatever. You should go, hon. If you need a cab or something, I got it."

She nodded, turned around, and went to get her clothes, which she'd folded so neatly on the nightstand it broke his heart. She had nice muscular legs. First he'd noticed it.

He went into his closet to grab his own change of clothes. When he came back the only thing she'd managed to put on was a flowery cotton bra. He'd never understand that. You'd think they'd always cover up their snatch first, since that's usually what came off last, but leave a woman alone to get dressed, and most of them start with the bra. She had her head in her hands, and she was sitting on the edge of the bed, crying.

Drunk broads, he thought, shaking his head.

"I'm so sorry," she said.

"Sorry, nothin'," Fredo said. "Look, it's not any sort of, I don't know—" He put his hand on her cheek. She looked up at him. Real tears, and she was fighting them. She looked mad at herself. "You're a beautiful girl, okay? It's just that it's late, and I got someplace to be. It's business. I mean, I guess if you really want to wait here, I—"

She shook her head. "You do not understand." She wiped her face with her underpants. They matched the bra. He caught a glimpse of the label: Sears. "I don't do this. I mean—" She rolled her eyes and looked at the ceiling. "I mean, I do *this,* just not—" She let out a deep breath. "I'm a dancer, okay? I'm in a show, now, a tasteful one, too. Not even topless. This was supposed to be—a lark. That's the word, yes? A dare I made to myself. I'm not a—"

Fredo got her a handkerchief. He'd been with a lot of broads since he'd moved to Las Vegas, and the one thing he'd learned about their crying is that it was always better to shut up and give them a nice handkerchief than to tell them everything would be okay.

He sat down next to her. He needed to get going. He ran his hand over her back. The little bit of her round ass he could see had skin tighter and smoother than most women, even really young ones, managed to have on their faces. Got to hand it to dancers, their bottom halves were something else. Finally, he just couldn't take any more time for this. Johnny was just trying to be a good guy, but it was probably true he'd done her first and turned her head all around and gotten her to agree to do something that she wouldn't have done in a million years back in whatever village in France she came from. "I got an idea," he said.

She looked up at him. It looked like she'd gotten the tears under control.

"How much did Johnny pay you to come up here?"

"A thousand dollars."

"Wait right here."

Fredo went into the den, pulled back the hinged oil painting replica of the *Mona Lisa*, opened his safe, and got out two thousand-dollar bills. She'd probably never seen one of these before in her life, much less two. The government had hardly bothered to design it. The back just said ONE THOUSAND DOLLARS. And Cleveland on the front? What the fuck had Cleveland ever done? He folded the bills in half, came back out, and pressed them into her hand.

"Keep the thousand you already got," he said, "and keep these, too. You don't gotta feel bad you're a whore, right, because how can you be a whore if we don't, you know?"

"Fuck?" she said.

There was a hopeful tone in her voice that confused Fredo, as if fucking would cheer her up or something. He'd been trying not to even say *fuck,* since she was all bent out of shape about maybe being a fucking hooker. "Sure," he said. "If we don't fuck. Just one catch."

She nodded, taking the money and slipping it into a pocket in the red dress beside her.

"All you have to do is go back to Johnny and, when he asks you how it was"—and he would, Fredo knew, that was just how Johnny was—"you got to promise to tell him"—Fredo paused to wink and flash her a grin—"that I was hands down the best you ever had."

"Hands down," she repeated, slipping on her underpants now. She seemed sad about it. "All right."

"Attagirl," he said.

The phone rang. It was Figaro, which is what he'd been calling the new bodyguard, whose name it embarrassed him not to be able to keep straight. Yes, Fredo said. He was fine.

As he watched her get dressed, he took off his shoes and socks and shirt.

He'd be up in no time, he said. Figaro said there were still guys up there. Fredo said that was good. Was Michael still there? He wasn't. "Too bad." Relieved, Fredo hung up.

He had stopped wearing undershirts a long time ago, after that one movie. After that, a guy wears an undershirt and these modern girls think he's just off the boat. Only after he was standing there bare-chested in just his pants did it occur to him that if he was half the gentleman he was pretending to be, he'd either have waited for her to go or else himself gone into another room. Her dress was red satin. Somehow, with it on, seeing her like that and knowing about the cheap underwear underneath, he felt differently about her. He felt something.

"That's a nice painting," she said. She pointed to the Madonna in the small pine frame over his bed. The painting that had come with the room was a huge thing with an Indian on a white horse, slumped in the saddle, watching the sun set. "Did you paint it?"

"What? No."

"Do you know the artist?"

"It's just a painting, okay?"

"I had a long time to look at it. That model, she has no vanity. It's a good piece."

"A good piece?"

"I studied art." She looked down. Her toenail polish was chipped. "A long time ago."

"It is a good piece," he said.

"Okay," she said, grabbing her purse.

"Okay," he said, walking her to the door.

She pulled out a cigarette. He reached in his pocket. "Shit," he said. "I lost my lighter."

"You're sweet," she said, tucking the cigarette behind his ear.

"Not really," he said. He gave her back the cigarette. "Not my brand, honey."

She leaned toward him. It had all the makings of a peck on the cheek, but something else Fredo had learned about these girls on the make in the west, a lot of things at three in the morning that have the look of something that would make sense by the rules of three in the afternoon turn into things the men asleep in their beds on Long Island would never believe. Her lips parted. His tongue obeyed, driving into her little wet

mouth, sliding his hands through her coarse platinum hair. A tiny gasp came out of her that seemed to startle them both.

They looked into each other's eyes. Hers grew wide, as if she'd just found an earring she'd lost. She was right, she wasn't a pro. They don't look at you like that.

"My life," she said, "it is so fucking complicated."

"Everybody thinks that," Fredo said. "Probably you're right, though. About you."

This Rita had a crooked grin.

"Oh?" she said. "And what about you, eh?"

"I can't complain," he said. "Though I still do. I guess I got it all under control, though."

"You think so?" With her index finger she touched his bare rib cage and did a little screwdriver thing.

They kissed again. Her mouth was sour from all that champagne, but he stayed with it.

"Fray-die Cor-le-o-ne," she said.

If this hadn't been three in the morning, it would have occurred to him right away that it was stupid to run the risk that someday this girl would blab about how she was bare-ass naked in front of Fredo Corleone and he paid her two grand *not* to fuck her. Why was he in any hurry to get upstairs? Anything worth being there for was over. "At your service," he said.

"You dirty rat," she said. She said it weird.

"Say what?"

"Nothing," she said. She sighed heavily and reached for the door-knob. "See you in the funny papers, okay?"

Oh, right. She'd been doing an impression of some movie gangster. He put his hand on her hand. "Stay," he said.

She screwed up that funny lopsided mouth. "I don't know," she said. "Will you take your money back?"

"I never paid you for that," he said. "I paid you to give Johnny Fontane nightmares."

She seemed deep in thought about this. "So I could just give him his money back, yes?"

Fredo smiled. "Perfect," he said. "Tell him, you know, the thing I paid you to tell him. You want me to write it down or you got it?"

"Hands down," she said. "Best I ever had. Got it."

"And then tell him to take his money back," he said, "it was that good."

"I'm not sure about this," she said. "Maybe—tomorrow? We could start over. A date or something?"

"Today's tomorrow, baby."

She still looked deep in thought. She put her finger in her mouth and sucked on it and ran it slowly down Fredo's bare chest from his neck to his belt buckle. She kept her hand there.

"I love sex." She said it like an admission of defeat. Her voice was small, too, not the husky voices people always talk about with French girls. She was still slurring her words. "It's bad, you know, but like a man I love it."

For a moment, the line—*like a man I love it*—went through Fredo like an electric shock. Though of course she didn't mean it the way, for a split second, he was afraid she did. Then he snapped out of it and grabbed onto those little tits with both hands.

She moaned, but now she did sound like a pro. Trying too hard. It couldn't feel that good, her tits.

They moved to the bed, and she undid his belt and yanked at his pants and his underwear. Fredo fell back on the bed. She stood over him and reached back to unzip her dress.

"Don't," he said.

She turned around for him to do it.

"Keep it on," he said. "It's dynamite."

She shrugged and sat down beside him on the bed. They kissed for a while and she put her hand on his cock. He could have blamed it on all the drinking he'd done today—this morning and who knows how much he had waiting at the Detroit airport, though nothing since then. And also how tired he was, the jet lag. He didn't, didn't, didn't want to think about the other thing. That never happened. And anyway he'd knocked up better showgirls than this here, in his sleep. Now that he was thinking about it, of course, he was doomed. *So, okay, don't think about my cock,* he thought. He thought about her, kissing her and grabbing her tits and how great it would be to fuck her with that shiny dress on, which could happen in like ten seconds if he could just stop thinking about all the things he was thinking about. If he could just stop thinking at all. He really needed to go easier on the booze.

She dropped to her knees and took him in her mouth so fast he couldn't say no. A terrible shiver went through him. "No," he said, tugging her up to him by her armpits.

She looked hurt.

"I don't do that," he said. "Don't be sore, okay? Come on and kiss me."

She obeyed. He did keep her hand on him and tugged her flowered Séars underpants down and did the same for her. They kissed some more.

"How about you get on your knees?"

She sighed. She looked like she was losing her patience. She looked like a girl at work.

"*No*," he said. "Like I said." Then he tried to sound more tender. It wasn't anything she'd done wrong. She seemed like a good egg who'd been willing to fuck him for nothing, probably because she'd heard rumors he was a dangerous gangster, but also because he'd been nice to her when he maybe didn't have to. He positioned her on her knees and hiked up her red dress and grabbed himself and with the other hand groped for her cunt. She reached back to help him. Something about the vulnerability of that gesture made him go rock hard in her hand, and he was in, and he was going for it from thrust number one. He had to act and not think. He grabbed onto her hips, curling his fingers in by the bones. He told her to beg him for it. She started chanting about how badly she wanted it and not to stop and then just, over and over, *big man, big man, big man,* and he closed his eyes and sped up, as fast as he had the strength to go.

His body tensed and he cried out.

"Pull out," she said, panting. "Big man. Pull out." In that squeaky voice. "Big man."

He didn't. He ground his hips in a twitchy circle against her muscular dancer's ass, oozing what little he had left into her. After that, his prick was so sensitive it hurt and he had to pull it out. It would have been sexy, dribbling little wet pearls onto her ass and that red dress. What could be better than that? He couldn't have said why he didn't do it.

That's not true. He knew. He liked knocking them up. He couldn't have said why.

Though that wasn't the whole truth either.

He flopped on his back. He closed his eyes and hit his head with the heel of his hand, a half-dozen little staccato blows. With every fiber of his being, he hated himself.

Rita rolled onto her side and into a ball. Naturally, she started crying again.

He got up and went to the windows and threw the curtains open.

Better. He did love that neon light. It wouldn't be dark much longer.

The phone rang again. He took it in the den. He told Figaro to keep his pants on, he'd be right up. Figaro said it was good they'd decided to drive up and not stay in L.A. because there was some news Fredo would probably want to hear about in person, and Fredo asked Figaro if he was deaf. He said he'd be right up, okay?

Fredo got another clean linen handkerchief, the best money could buy, and lay back down on the bed beside Rita. "Hey, darlin'," he said. Like a cowboy. "Hey, beautiful."

She blew her nose and was spooky quiet.

"I'll be right back," he said. He checked his watch—a habit he'd gotten into as a kid—and managed to shower and shave in less than five minutes. He put on a robe so thick it always felt to him like football shoulder pads and came back out, and she was still there.

"I'm sorry," she said.

He could have done without that. He wanted her to leave, yes, and right away, but he didn't want to feel like a shit about it. She wasn't crying, though, which was something.

"That was sure fast," she said. "The shower."

"I know where everything is by now." It was what he always said when people said that.

"I should go. I'm sorry. I know I should go."

"Stay as long as you want," he said. "I'm sorry as hell, but I've—"

"Got business," she said. "I know. I'm sorry." She dabbed her eyes and pointed to the bathroom. "I'll hurry."

She did not, at least, say *tee-tee*. While she was in there he threw on some clothes and called downstairs to arrange and pay for her cab.

Twelve excruciating minutes later she came out with her hair combed and her face pink from being scrubbed and her lipstick on and smelling of some kind of perfume that she must have had on when she got here. She wore it thick. There weren't a lot of things he found more disgusting than thick perfume. He turned on the television and herded her into the hall.

"We got a deal, right?" he said as he pushed the button for the elevator.

"We do." She held up her right palm. "I am," she said grimly, "a girl of my word." She forced a smile. "You're presuming I wouldn't say that anyway. Hands down."

What the fuck was there to say about that? He thought he should probably ask her for her number, but usually that only made things worse.

The elevator showed up and put him out of the misery of his silence. He patted her back as she stepped on.

"Good luck," she said, "with your business." She blew him a kiss. "Cor-le-on-e."

He watched the doors close. He looked at himself in the distortion of the buffed brass doors. There wasn't much to see. He hit the button for the sixth floor, planted his hands against the cool of the metal, and hung his weary head. Who said life was easy? Yet here he stood. He'd made his mistakes, like anybody, and lived to tell about it, unlike a lot of people he knew.

The doors opened and he got in.

People thought of him as a nice enough guy who was also weak and a fuckup, he knew that. But how many guys could have withstood a day like

today and held up any better than Frederico Corleone, eh? He'd woken up in the middle of a really bad decision he couldn't let himself think any more about, not even knowing where he was, not even what fucking *country*. Yet he still managed by dawn's early light to haul ass out of there, and by some miraculous instinct in the right direction, too. Okay, he left his gun behind, but in another country, so you had to think that was the end of that. He maybe fucked up a little bit at customs, but for Christ's sake the oranges weren't even his, and the drink he'd had was just an eye-opener, and dropping Joe Zaluchi's name had been a calculated risk. Just as easily, it could have gotten Fredo waved through. But, okay, it hadn't. That said, how many guys could have stayed as cool as he had after the pinch? He walked that white line like a champ. The rubes in customs were in awe of him. Two encores, perfect every time. He didn't say anything he didn't have to say, didn't even call in some lawyer. Dumb clucks let him go still thinking he was Carl Frederick, assistant manager of the Castle in the Sand Trailer Park (which, on paper, he was; he'd driven by it but never been there).

In the end, the only reason people thought Mike was so brilliant and Fredo was such a fuckup was that Mike wanted to build some big empire and all Fredo wanted was to have a good time and to have a little piece of the business that was his alone. Something bigger than a trailer park but smaller than General Motors. What the hell was wrong with that, huh? Yet even *that* was more than Mike would give him. Instead, he gave Fredo a fucking *title*. Underboss. *Sotto capo*. Might as well have made him Court Jester. Tit on a Mule. Vice President.

He got off on the sixth floor and used his passkey to enter the dummy room. This whole arrangement here? Fredo's idea. People loved it, and other people claimed to have thought of it. He'd heard that other casinos were copying it. Big deal. Who needs credit for shit? But still.

"A drink, sir?" asked the bartender on the secret landing.

"Nah," Fredo said. "Just a cold beer, okay?"

Probably he should take the stairs. Chance to get the blood flowing. But he was beat and the beer felt good and cold in his hand and so he waited for this elevator to come, too.

When it did, Figaro and Capra and two of the new New York guys came rolling out. They did not look like men who had come from the happy event they'd come from. This couldn't be attributed to Figaro learning that he'd missed out on his big night. This was the first one ever outside New York, so he'd have never guessed and nobody would have told him.

"Goddamn," Figaro said. "We were about to send a search party. Actually, we *are* the search party. Where you been?"

"You call me in my room twenty times, you fucking want to know where I been?"

"No, I mean, what took so long? There were only a few people left when we got there, but now there's nobody. Excepting Rocco. He's waiting for you."

The news Fredo was supposed to hear in person.

"My family?" Fredo said.

Figaro shook his head. "Nothin' like that. You should really just go up and see Rocco."

"Nobody nobody up there?" Fredo asked. "Or just not-so-many-guys nobody up there? Other than Rocco, I mean."

Capra—whose real name was Gaetano Paternostro, which was too much of a mouthful and also too regal for this baby-faced country boy—stopped Figaro before he could answer and asked him what Fredo just said, which Fredo had had it up to here with. Fredo was fluent, and this fucking barber might as well have been some mayo-slurping yutz from Ohio. As a bookie, the barber might have been a good earner, but so far it was hard for Fredo to see what beyond that Mike saw in the guy.

"I asked our friend the barber of epic flatulence," Fredo said in Sicilian dialect, "how many of our other friends remained upstairs in the banquet hall."

Capra laughed. *"Non lo so. Cinque o forse sei."*

Fredo nodded. He'd stop up anyway. What was the point of driving up tonight instead of flying up tomorrow if he didn't even make an appearance? "Look," he said to Figaro. "Why you *think* it took me so long?"

"You think if I knew I'd fucking ask? C'mon, Fredo. I'm given a job, I do a job. With all due respect, please, *non rompermi i coglioni,* eh?"

Capra and the other two men had gone to the bar. Coffee all around.

"I'm not busting your balls." Fredo arched an eyebrow. "You mean you didn't hear her? In the background there?"

"You gotta be kiddin' me." Since it had been the gist of his excuse this morning, too.

"French girl. Dancer, I forgot to ask where. I ran into her on the way up, one thing led to another, you know how it goes. *Che fica.*"

Figaro was bald, ten years older than Fredo, and probably did not, hookers aside, know how it goes. He shook his head. "You fuckin' guy. You goin' for some kind of record?"

Someone had shut off the motor that made the ballroom rotate. The air was thick with smoke and spilled booze. At a table covered with a dirty white tablecloth sat four old guys from what had used to be Tessio's *regime,* playing dominos. Two of them were the DiMiceli brothers, one of whom (Fredo couldn't keep them straight) had a boy, Eddie, who had

gotten initiated that night. He didn't know the other two. Fredo wasn't real good on the Brooklyn guys.

Slumped alone in an aquamarine armchair was Rocco Lampone, staring out the window and muttering something to himself. Décor aside, it was as if Fredo had walked into one of those joints in Gowanus where the regulars show up first thing in the morning for a chipped mug full of brandy-laced coffee and either sit there in silent misery or else pick petty fights about what's on the jukebox or what the world's coming to.

"Hey-hey!" shouted one of the DiMicelis. "If it ain't our underboss."

Fredo waited for someone to make more of a joke about this. He hadn't asked for the title. He knew men thought he was weak. He knew they weren't clear on his responsibilities or Michael's reasons for creating the job. Missing the thing tonight wouldn't help matters. But the men at the table only nodded and grunted their hellos.

Rocco motioned Fredo over. Next to him by the window was an empty metal chair. Outside, a brassy jazz combo on a makeshift stage on the rooftop below played a tune from that famous musical about Negroes. The whole rooftop swarmed with people, though there was no one in the swimming pool. A couple dozen slot machines, four blackjack tables, and two craps tables had been carted up here. There were several full bars and a breakfast buffet.

"What the fuck?" asked Fredo, pointing.

"Where you been?"

"Detroit. Los Angeles. Missed my plane. Long story."

"It's one I heard. Where you been since you got back here? To the hotel? And made me wait here like I'm—" Rocco rubbed his ruined knee. "And made me wait. Here. For you."

One of the men playing dominos cackled. Fredo looked over his shoulder. The cackling guy rubbed the bald head of an unamused guy, who sat still and took it.

"Seriously," Fredo said, "what's going on down there?"

"Sit down. Please." Rocco had never been much of a talker. It was clear from the look on his face that he hadn't figured out either what he had to say or how he was going to say it.

Fredo sat. "Is it Ma?" he blurted.

"No." Rocco shook his head. "There was an accident," he said. "Friends of ours. It looks I would say bad."

On the rickety stage, the mayor of Las Vegas—a former Ziegfield dancer herself, a terrific old broad, Fredo thought, who still had some of her looks—adjusted the fluorescent orange sash over the huge, impractical tits

of the laughing brunette Hal Mitchell had, apparently after no competition at all, named Miss Atomic Bomb. The tiara was an even tougher fit.
Miss Atomic Bomb had done her hair up in some great shellacked mass
vaguely in the shape of a mushroom cloud. The mayor tried to put it on
her from the front, which was impossible without leaning into her tits, so
she tried it from behind and kept dropping it. The mayor stopped and
handed the brunette her tiara. Miss Atomic Bomb had to crown herself.
She was undaunted. This was a very happy young woman. Her bathing
suit was cut so low you could just about see her belly button. The trom-
bonist struck up the band. Miss Atomic Bomb stepped to the microphone
and started singing "Praise the Lord and Pass the Ammunition."

The gaming tables were packed. Every slot machine was in use. Scattered everywhere were people on chaise lounges and at picnic tables,
working on paper plates heaped with eggs.

Fredo had gotten all the way down here—entourage in tow, even in
his own hotel: Figaro and Capra plus those two guys from New York, his
shadows until whatever happened because of those deaths in Cleveland
happened—before he had any idea what was going on.

Miss Atomic Bomb, who bounced as she sang and was smiling so wide
and with such apparent sincerity that any reasonable person would have
wanted to slap her or break her heart, started singing "Take the A Train,"
only with new lyrics. "Drop the A-Bomb."

Fredo was all for coaxing pigeons out of their rooms early and often,
but he'd seen enough. He cocked his head toward the exit, and his bone-
tired bodyguards looked at him like he was Jesus bearing chocolates.

Just then, for no perceptible reason, everything got quiet. The band
stopped, the drone of the guests' babble seemed to be sucked inside their
throats, and the faint sounds of traffic from the street below made themselves known by ceasing to be. Fredo looked up, and there it was: a puff-
ball of white smoke in the northeastern sky.

And then sound returned.

That was *it*?

Everywhere on the roof, people lounged and gambled. Slot machine
zombies kept their eyes steadfastly on the spinning fruit decals. The beauty
queen seemed to be the only person applauding. And then:

A blast of heat that felt like standing inside a raging dryer vent lined
with sunlamps snapped his head back. Fredo shielded his eyes with both
hands.

Seconds earlier, on a salt flat sixty-five miles away, there had been a
place called Doomtown—a cluster of ordinary but variously constructed
American homes (no two alike), each filled with the aroma of one of the
various, ordinary American meals (no two alike) cooling on the dining

room table, each table surrounded by human figures dressed variously in brand-new JC Penney clothing. In and around Doomtown, at various distances from the fifty-foot tower that was the town's epicenter, were dozens of individually penned and oddly quiet pigs. As two hundred American soldiers watched, crouched in trenches they'd dug themselves a mile from the outskirts of Doomtown, the U.S. government detonated a twenty-nine-kiloton bomb. In the first second after that, the houses, mannequins, food, and pigs nearest the tower became flame, wind, and dust. Farther away, as government cameras whirred, siding ignited and debris pulverized lawn jockeys and decapitated mannequins of smiling babies in disintegrating high chairs. Flaming pigs ran screaming in irregular paths and exploded. Another half second passed, and that was all dust, too. In the half second after that, a hot wind worse than twenty harnessed hurricanes leveled most of the rest of the town. Grit—it could have been anything: sand, salt, glass, particles of steel or wood or uranium, bonemeal from pigs killed only because their skin superficially resembled that of the humans so eager to study what remained of it—shot with supersonic speed through Thanksgiving dinner, shiny automobiles, plastic fathers with real tobacco in their pipes, solid-state monitoring equipment, brick walls, everything.

The trenches collapsed. The soldiers were buried alive, but all survived—for now.

Most of the pigs farther than a thousand yards from the tower survived but were so badly burned men shot them long before anyone got around to whipping out the Geiger counters.

The Hagens would never find their arthritic dachshund, Garbanzo. Just as well.

The main stage was really Doomtown: officially classified and yet—because those houses (built by a certain Las Vegas contractor) and even that food (flown in fresh from a certain San Francisco food wholesaler) had to come from someplace—something more than a rumor and less than an open secret.

The rooftop of Hal Mitchell's Castle in the Sand was just the lounge act. In the time it took Fredo Corleone to think to cover his eyes with both hands until the time his hands met his face, the intense heat waned. After that, some kind of dust fell, too small to see and barely big enough to feel. It was roundly ignored. People kept gambling and barely moved.

"This can't be good," Fredo said.

"This shit here, you mean?" said the barber, motioning to the dust, to the very air.

The young goatherd had his tongue out, almost as if he were catching snowflakes.

"The Reds want you to think this shit's something," the barber said, "but that's just a conspiracy to make the U.S. stop all this testing so that the Russians can catch up to us. Believe me. This is nothing. Dust. Less than nothing. 'S go."

"Nothing," murmured Fredo, whisking the invisible dust from his shirtsleeves.

Directly above, two of the huge mirrored windows in the ballroom concealed by the casino's top parapet were gone. The old domino players from the Patrick Henry Social Club stood there in full view and jowly disbelief. Fredo didn't look up. Why would he? The windows had imploded. Every shard of broken glass had been sucked inward.

BOOK III

Fall–Christmas
1955

Chapter 12

THE DEATHS OF Tony Molinari and Frank Falcone—coming as they had on the threshold of what had looked like a lasting peace—sent shock waves through the underworld of the nation. Out of context, anyone would have presumed the crash was an accident: severe thunderstorm, lake-effect air pockets, case closed. The unsolved disappearance of Gerald O'Malley, the crash's lone survivor, aroused suspicion, as did his garbled words to the tower in Cleveland, in which he had apparently wondered if the plane had been sabotaged. Despite this, his voice had remained calm until right before impact, when he shouted, "*Sono fottuto,*" which the FAA report translated from the Italian as "I'm a goner." Investigators found no clear evidence of sabotage. They attributed the pilot's assertion to his inexperience. They ruled the crash an accident. Pilot error.

It was, by any measure, a meaningless coincidence that the last funeral the four dead men had attended together was that of Vito Corleone. But from the Mafia's murky, contested origins in nineteenth-century Sicily to the present day, every human act—benevolent or violent, willful or inadvertent, whether born of aggression or self-preservation, of passion or ice-cold *ragione*—becomes part of one vast gossamer web, where no quiver or throb is too small to be felt everywhere. For a Sicilian, whose mother tongue is the only one in the Western world that lacks a future tense, the past and the present are as one. For a Sicilian, whose blood has endured six thousand years of invasion and occupation, an accident or a coincidence is no more meaningless, or meaningful, than an act of will. Each may be indistinguishable from the other. For a Sicilian, nothing happens out of context.

The Coast Guard rescuers had lashed "O'Malley" to a body board and raced him to a nearby hospital, where the admitting nurse—referring to the man's Nevada driver's license, which formed the core of the fat wad of bills in his front pocket—logged him in at 10:25 P.M. as "Gerald O'Malley, male Caucasian, age 38." His broken leg was set and put in traction, his broken ribs taped, his other wounds sewn shut. He did not appear to have any serious internal injuries, but there were still tests to run. He remained unconscious, but the long-term prognosis appeared excellent. His

condition was upgraded from critical to serious. According to his chart, the doctors finished with him at 4:18 A.M. The final notation on the chart came at 4:30 A.M.—though that one seemed likely to have been a fake. Nothing was noted but the time and some illegible initials no one at the hospital could identify.

By that time, irregularities in both the flight and the other four bodies, or at least parts of them, had either surfaced on their own or been lifted into the gray light of day by human hands.

The bodies had not yet been identified, and the riot of reporters and law enforcement officials that those identifications would trigger was not yet unleashed. The flight plan in Detroit was shown as having been filed, but no one could find it. The plane had left Detroit in the morning and so had to have stopped somewhere else in the twelve ensuing hours, but when the pilot made radio contact with the tower at Burke Lakefront Airport, he indicated he was coming directly from Detroit. The tower tried to get a clarification, but the plane's radio transmissions—probably because of all the lightning—were a roar of static. When it became clear the plane was in distress, attention turned exclusively to bringing it down safely.

The meatpacking company whose logo was on the side of the plane was located outside Buffalo, New York. The president of the company, groggy with sleep, at first told the investigator he had the wrong number, that his company had no plane, though when the investigator asked if he was sure about that, the president paused and then said, "Ri-i-ight, our plane," and hung up. By the time other calls were made and the state cops sped out to his lakefront home to bring him in for questioning, he was freshly shaved and showered, dressed in a suit, waiting in his living room, flanked by a lawyer who had once been the state's attorney general. On behalf of his client, the lawyer informed the officers that a week's unlimited use of the aircraft in question had been a gift from his client to his friend Joseph Zaluchi—two-time winner of the prestigious Michigan Philanthropist of the Year Award and a board member since 1953 of Detroit, Hooray!—to aid the transportation of guests to and from his daughter's lovely wedding this past weekend in Detroit, which, owing to a prior commitment, his client had been unable to attend. The client knew nothing about the men and/or women on board, or any details about the flight other than what had become public knowledge. The lawyer asked the cops if they had any warrants, for either search or arrest, then thanked them for their time and for leaving his client alone so he could begin to mourn this unfortunate tragedy.

An attorney for Joseph Zaluchi said that Mr. Zaluchi knew nothing about the man who had crashed the plane, other than that he was a licensed commercial pilot who worked for a reputable charter company in

New York. He'd been hired over the telephone by an associate of Mr. Za-luchi. Mr. Zaluchi expressed his deep sympathy for the victims and to their families.

"Gerald O'Malley" disappeared from the hospital sometime between the 4:18 notation on the chart and about five, when an orderly walked into the room and found the bed empty and tubes dangling from the de-vices that had been connected to the patient's arms. The pulley that had been attached to his broken leg was also gone, as were the patient's per-sonal effects.

Nick Geraci had been arrested several times (though never convicted), so his fingerprints were on file. But when he arrived at the hospital, there had been no reason to fingerprint him. His room had been wiped clean.

The two attending nurses whose responsibility it might have been to check frequently on the man admitted as Gerald O'Malley each claimed she was certain he'd been assigned to the other. The head nurse would later take full responsibility for the mistake and resign in disgrace. She moved to Florida and got what was presumably a lower-paying job for a company providing in-home nursing care. Many years later she died peacefully in her sleep. When her will was read, her newly rich children marveled at the savings habits of that generation of Americans forged by the Great Depression.

Several law enforcement agencies and countless reporters tried for months to solve the mystery of the missing pilot. All failed. Members of the U.S. Senate, capitalizing on the public's fascination with the case, began to discuss holding hearings on this and other matters related to the growing and perhaps Communist menace of organized crime syndicates in America, variously calling such proceedings "long overdue," "perhaps in-evitable," and "something we owe to our women and children and, indeed, our way of life."

The driver's license wasn't a forgery, but the birth certificate the State of Nevada had on record actually belonged to an infant buried in a New Hampshire cemetery.

The information the feds had for O'Malley on his pilot's license led of course to that same New Hampshire cemetery.

(Only God and Tom Hagen knew the rest. The cemetery lay beside a road that, many miles north, became the main drag of the town where Kay Adams Corleone had grown up. Soon after Michael killed his sister's hus-band and lied to Kay about it, she left him. She took the kids and went to her parents' house. Michael called her only once. A week passed. One morning, Hagen showed up in a limousine. Tom and Kay took a long walk in the woods. Mike wanted her to know that she could have anything she wanted and do whatever she wanted as long as she took good care of the

kids, but that he loved her and—in a characteristically labored joke—that she was his Don. Hagen relayed this message only after confiding in her about some of the things Mike had done—an act of defiance that might have gotten Hagen killed. But it worked; Kay eventually came home. On Hagen's way back to New York, he stopped at a random public library, leafed through an old volume of the local newspaper, and learned of the sad story of Gerald O'Malley, stricken by diphtheria and taken by the Lord at the age of eleven months. Hagen kept the limo idling out of sight and walked to the courthouse. He was a nondescript man who knew how to behave in a library or courthouse so that people would forget him the moment he left. His various travels had allowed him to collect notarized copies of birth certificates from all over the country, never the same courthouse twice. He had a stack as thick as a Sears catalog. When Geraci asked for one with an Irish name, poor O'Malley's was right on top.)

Once the identities of the dead were confirmed and then made public, anyone who knew or suspected what Vincent Forlenza was and what sort of situation he had on Rattlesnake Island immediately presumed that the plane had spent the afternoon there—this, with no inkling that the pilot was Forlenza's actual godson. The authorities, of course, could prove nothing. Forlenza, questioned two days after the accident, also in the presence of distinguished legal counsel, wondered if the good men of the law might not be watching too much television. *Gangsters?* On his beloved island sanctuary? Now he'd heard everything. In any case, he'd been home all weekend, except for Sunday afternoon, when these so-called gangsters supposedly landed on Rattlesnake Island to have some kind of—what? Summit? Powwow? No matter. Forlenza said he'd spent the day in question as a guest at a Labor Day clambake sponsored by one of the union locals, huddled under a big-top tent, sipping ice-cold union-made beer and refusing to let the downpour spoil his celebration of an important national holiday, a story corroborated by any number of office-holding Cleveland Teamsters.

The physical description of O'Malley the police cobbled together from their interviews with rescue and medical personnel held little promise. They'd seen the man's injuries but not the man. They were more fixated on the patient's vital signs than the size of his ears, the shape of his (closed) eyes, or the subtleties of the jagged ridge of his much-broken nose, which had at any rate been broken again and was too purple and swollen to look much like the way it had.

No one outside the Corleone and Forlenza organizations could have guessed that Gerald O'Malley was the same guy as Nick Geraci. No one outside those Families knew much about who Geraci was or what he did. His seven years in the ring, even with all the fixed fights, had rearranged

his face enough that boyhood friends would be unlikely to recognize him. He'd fought under more fake names than he himself could remember. Boxers become muscle guys every day, and any loyal muscle guy with half a brain can become a button man. But those guys don't turn into big earners so often, much less into big earners a few courses shy of their law degree. He was known in New York as a guy who'd been under the wing of Sally Tessio, but all the different things he'd done would have made it nearly impossible for anyone to put all the pieces together. The more exceptional a person becomes, the more his place in the world seeks a similar extreme. It becomes more likely that he will be known either by everyone or by no one. He will either stand out, even though most people will never see him in the flesh, or he will vanish, even if he's sitting right next to you at a lunch counter in Tucson, humming the bridge from that new Johnny Fontane record and tapping a dime on the Formica, waiting to use the pay phone.

It's a crazy goddamned world. For months, Nick Geraci or what was left of him was out there in it, somewhere. Hardly anyone knew where. Hardly anyone was even looking for him.

Richard "the Ape" Aspromonte, who was asked only once, by a blind woman, how he got that nickname, was buried in Los Angeles, followed by a reception afterward at Gussie Cicero's supper club. When the time came to make toasts, all four of Aspromonte's brothers looked to Jackie Ping-Pong, who hardly knew the Ape, but whose words proved eloquent, moving, and a comfort to the dead man's grieving mother. In San Francisco, Lefty Mancuso's parents tried to keep his funeral small. The only celebrity there was a lesser DiMaggio brother, a high school classmate of Lefty's. The only member of the Molinari Family was Tony Molinari's younger brother Nicodemo. Out of respect, even his bodyguards stayed on the periphery, just in front of the small cadre of the cops and the curious.

Ordinarily, a Don would attend a funeral of such men only if they were close personal friends. But these were not ordinary times. And so it became known beyond their own small circles and throughout the underworld that, as expected, Jackie Ping-Pong and Nicodemo "Butchie" Molinari had each, apparently peacefully, assumed control of his organization.

Aspromonte's and Mancuso's bosses, Frank Falcone and Tony Molinari, were buried the next day. They'd had many common friends, but no one could attend both funerals.

A choice had to be made. These choices would be watched.

On a walk back and forth past the unfinished houses on Tom Hagen's

cul-de-sac, with Al Neri and two others in the car, parked so it blocked off the whole street, Michael Corleone, smoking cigarettes, told Hagen, who was smoking a cigar, only that he should start amassing untraceable cash, in case there was a ransom to be paid. Michael wanted to be protected from knowing exactly where the money came from, and otherwise he needed to protect Hagen from this entire matter. Hagen stopped at the end of the cul-de-sac. At the far end of the street, his boy Andrew, the thirteen-year-old, ran out the front door with a football under his arm, then apparently saw Neri's car, dropped his head in lolling teenaged exasperation, and went back inside. Hagen looked past Michael to some vague spot on the saw-toothed horizon, and for a very long time he said nothing. Michael lit another cigarette and said that was just how it had to be. "You wouldn't pay the ransom, though, would you?" Hagen asked. Michael looked at him with obvious disappointment but only shrugged. Hagen stayed silent for a while longer, then whipped his half-finished cigar across the bright white cement and said, "Protect me," in a way that was neither a plea nor an incredulity, just a statement. Michael nodded. Nothing more was said.

Michael summoned Rocco, Clemenza, and Fredo to his home. They huffed upstairs and sat in front of his blond desk in those orange plastic chairs. He asked point-blank if any of them had any idea what happened to Geraci. Each said no with equal vehemence. "It wasn't you?" Rocco asked and Michael shook his head, and they all seemed surprised. An accident was bad enough, but eventually the people who mattered would learn that the pilot had been Geraci. "Which is when the fan'll hit the shit," Clemenza said.

Michael nodded. The only way to fix this mess, he said, was to call a meeting of all the Families, the first since the one his father had convened right after Sonny was killed. Admit that this was a dumb decision, trying to go see a boxing match, even if Falcone did have a big bet on it and pressured him to go. Restitution could be made, all the Dons would give their word that the matter was finished, and it would all be a blessing in disguise because they could go right from that to formalizing a larger peace agreement. Everyone would benefit. Yes, such a meeting would mean that there would be a vote about putting Russo on the Commission, but at this point the definitive end to this war would be worth even that. It was going to happen sooner or later anyway. "But the problem we have now," Michael said, "is that whatever happened—cover-up, kidnapping, maybe even the government—makes that kind of a summit impossible."

Clemenza snorted and said he smelled something rotten in Cleveland, and Michael cocked his head. "I seen Hamlet with that fruit, what's-his-face. The famous one. Not half bad, once you got past the tights." He

looked at Fredo and Fredo said "What?" and Clemenza shrugged and asked Mike if he figured Forlenza's men sabotaged the plane or if they were trying to keep Geraci's identity secret so that people wouldn't *think* they'd sabotaged the plane? Since the best way out of this mess would be to point out that the Jew certainly wouldn't sabotage a plane flown by his own godson, which would open up a whole other can of worms. Maybe it was all just a misguided attempt by Forlenza to protect his godson? Maybe even from us?

Downstairs, Michael's half-deaf father-in-law had the TV blasting. In a piercing falsetto, little Anthony Corleone sang along to the theme song for a cowboy show.

"Jesus, what a *giambott'*," Fredo said. "Makes my head hurt, how many different ways this thing could go."

Michael nodded, so slowly it was clearly a theatrical pause for thought, not agreement. A necessary pause. He was not, so soon after his brother's elevation to *sotto capo,* going to disagree with him forcefully, even in front of men as trusted as Clemenza and Lampone.

"None of this," Michael said, "brings us closer to finding out what happened to Geraci."

He leaned across his Danish modern desk. It was time to stop speculating. Time to get down to business.

The next day, Clemenza returned to New York with orders to run his operation as if peace were assured and the crash never happened. His men were to do the same. The day after that, Rocco, who knew the men in Geraci's crew, also went to New York, where he would remain and oversee those operations until further notice. Fredo, as underboss, would temporarily be in charge of Rocco's men in Nevada.

The Corleones had long been close to Tony Molinari, who'd protected Fredo in the aftermath of the assassination attempt on his father and whose cooperation had helped make it possible for the Corleones to establish themselves in Las Vegas and now in Tahoe and Reno. Neither Vito nor now Michael had ever regarded Frank Falcone as a serious person. Neither believed that his flashy, second-rate operation possessed either the means or the will to come out from under Chicago's apron skirts. Michael might have opted to be represented at neither funeral. Many expected him to make just that decision, and, on the face of it, this might have seemed the more cautious and more prudent of choices. But these are only words—*caution, prudence*—and they are words that can easily be replaced by other words—*hubris, fear, weakness.* A man *is* his actions, public and private, both when watched and when alone.

Fredo, who after all had been the closest of anyone in the organization to Tony Molinari, was dispatched to San Francisco. Michael, accompanied

by Tommy Neri and the same two others who'd been hiding in the woods in Lake Tahoe, went to Chicago: the city where Frank Falcone was born, the city where he'd made his bones, was where his own bones, or what remained of them, would be buried. Those who'd known Vito Corleone recognized the logic in Michael's decision. *Keep your friends close,* the great Don had said, *and your enemies closer.*

The ceremony was held in a tiny white clapboard church on the near west side of the city, in the Italian neighborhood known as the Patch, where Falcone had been raised and where his parents had once run a corner grocery. Hot for Chicago in September. The Chicago police had blocked off traffic for two blocks in every direction. Several of the dignitaries—including the lieutenant governor of California, the heavyweight champion of the world, and several movie stars, including Johnny Fontane—received a motorcycle escort right to the back steps. Others, including Michael Corleone, came early enough to take their seats without such ostentation. Out front, the street was packed. Falcone's origins were the stuff of local legend, and although the mourners inside observed a respectful silence, no one among the buzzing horde in the street could have failed to hear someone tell the dead man's story. When Frank was only a boy of fifteen, his father had closed the store and his older sister was counting the day's receipts when they were both killed in a stickup, a crime investigated so halfheartedly by the police—"ain't nothin' but dagos killing dagos in Dagotown," a detective said, laughing, within earshot of Frank and, worse, of Frank's mother—that the boy vowed to get revenge. It didn't take long. Somehow, the kid's passion got him an audience with Al Capone. The thief's corpse was found on the front steps of the precinct station, stabbed, as legend has it, sixty-four times (Frank's father was forty-five years old; his sister was nineteen). The detective and his partner went on a fishing trip to the Wisconsin Dells and were never seen again. For a time, Frank and his mother ran the store, but the memories were too much. From nowhere (Trapani, actually), a buyer emerged and paid a fair price. Frank's mother took that money and the money from selling her house and moved in next door with her brother's family. Frank found employment with Mr. Capone. After Mr. Capone had his problems, Frank pursued other opportunities in Los Angeles. At first, he managed to remain in everyone's good graces by doing well, remembering where he came from, and repaying the men who'd helped him get where he was. These men had enough problems without worrying about everything west of here that was supposed to be Chicago's, too, and Falcone was their boy anyhow, always would be. It's hard to say when it happened, but it

came to seem as though Falcone had always been the guy out there—his own outfit. Never did get his mother to move, even though he built her a house in the Hollywood Hills—swimming pool, the works.

Twenty policemen on horseback (every horse in blinders, because of the incessant flashbulbs) cleared a path through the crowd, and the funeral procession, many of the cars sporting large campaign signs for the politicians and judges inside, made its way to Mt. Carmel Cemetery. Thousands of people followed it on foot. Just inside the main entrance, the procession passed the final resting place of the rotting, syphilitic remains of Al Capone, who died sixteen years after the IRS killed him, and whose own anticlimactic funeral had been attended by a fraction of the people here for Falcone's. Vito Corleone had sent nothing but flowers.

The Falcone mausoleum was made of black granite and topped with a statue of an angel with a falcon tethered to its right arm. The falcon was taking off, its wings spread wide enough to provide welcome shade for several sweaty bystanders. Falcone's father and sister had not been buried here, but brass plaques on two of the doors bore their names.

Falcone's mother and his wife and kids sat beside the coffin. The only other person in the front row was Louie Russo, sporting those gigantic sunglasses. The rest of Falcone's blood family sat in the second row, along with Jackie Ping-Pong and Johnny Fontane, who was listed in the bulletin as an honorary pallbearer. Fontane cried like a woman.

The other forty-nine honorary pallbearers—politicians, police captains, judges, businessmen, athletes, and entertainers; no one from the Chicago Outfit or any other organization—were all shown seats near the front as well.

Certainly there were people watching Michael Corleone, but, especially in the context of this circus, not many. He was not a famous man, certainly not in comparison with Fontane, the heavyweight champion of the world, the lieutenant governor of California, or even philanthropist and former ambassador to Canada M. Corbett Shea (row six, next to Mae West). Michael Corleone was not the target of the photographers' flashes, and only a few of the men from law enforcement knew more about him than the public did, which was not much. He'd been a war hero, but a lot of men had been war heroes. His name had been in the papers during the troubles in New York in the spring, but the pictures of him were blurry, shot at a distance, and the public's memory is shorter than a senile dog's. In his world, Michael Corleone was known by all, but many of those men knew him only by reputation and couldn't have easily connected the name to the face. He knew several of the people here well, but he did not approach them. Somber nods sufficed. Fontane didn't appear even to notice him. Michael watched the proceedings in silence. Afterward, he stood pa-

tiently in line to offer his condolences to Falcone's widow and mother, the only words he said in public all day, then disappeared into the frosty backseat of the humble black Dodge that had brought him.

Inside, for the first time, Michael Corleone wept for his dead father.

Don Molinari's funeral procession rolled through the fog, a line of more than a hundred cars in long, snarling traffic, winding southbound and out of San Francisco. Frederico Corleone rode in the fourth car behind the hearse, in a two-tone Cadillac—black and white—that Tony Molinari used to like to drive himself. Fredo had come alone. He'd told Michael that bringing along Capra and Figaro, after all the protection the Molinaris had provided Fredo over the years, would look like disrespect—or worse, like the Corleones had something to fear in San Francisco—and was shocked when his brother had agreed. The driver was a Molinari *soldato* whose name Fredo was trying to remember. Also up front was Tony's little brother Dino's wife. Her two girls rode in back beside Fredo.

It was the longest ride to a graveyard that Fredo could remember ever taking, made longer by the crying kids and his clumsy attempts to console them. He'd had the foresight to bring two handkerchiefs, soft silk monogrammed ones that floated from kid to kid until one of them blew her nose so hard she got a nosebleed and had to use both of them to help stop it.

"Where *is* this place?" Fredo asked, reaching for the prayer card that had the name of the cemetery on it: THE ITALIAN CEMETERY.

"Colma," said the driver. "They're all in Colma."

"Who's all in Colma? Where the h—" He stopped himself. "Where's Colma?"

"Cemeteries. They're illegal in San Francisco. Gotta go to Colma, which we're almost to now. Back in the gold rush days, you buried your people wherever they fell. The garden, backyard, some alley, whatever. There were some cemeteries, mostly for the rich ones. But those got moved to Colma, the bodies. They had to do it. My *nonna*, she still talks about how during the earthquakes all over the city, dead bodies would heave to the surface and come shooting—"

"*Enough*," said Dino's wife. "Talk," she said in Italian, "when the chickens piss." Meaning *Shut your damn mouth*. Her children didn't seem to understand Italian.

The driver didn't say another word.

Fredo supposed that the driver's story wasn't the kind of thing to tell the kids, but they'd both stopped crying and looked pretty interested.

Outside, the houses and neighborhoods just stopped, superseded in

every direction by undulating plains covered with gravestones, vaults, statues, crosses, and palm trees, a vast, unyielding city of the dead, and for some reason he thought of what his brother Sonny had said when he'd effectively banished Fredo from the family: *Las Vegas is a city of the future.* No, Sonny. This, Colma, is a city of the future. *The* city of the future. City of the dead. Dead, like Sonny. Fredo felt a nervous laugh, the crazy kind, rising in him, and he stifled it.

The Italian Cemetery stretched for miles along both sides of the road. The procession entered a path on the south side, past a monument that had dozens of green metal hands sticking out, grasping a long black chain.

Fredo shook his head in wonder. *This is the greatest racket I ever saw. Of course there's a cemetery here just for Italians.* Before any of this was here, back when you could still plant the dead under your rosebushes, Fredo would bet that this whole place had been bought up quietly by Italians. Land that looks like the Sicilian countryside, where poor farmers struggled to grow grapes and olives until someone came up with the idea for a better crop. You get the papers to run sob stories from doctors talking about health risks, you get an ordinance passed, presto! you're getting paid twice to bury a hundred years' worth of people who'd already been buried. Get paid once to dig and move, again for the grave site in Colma. Give jobs to a hundred Italian stonecutters who now owe you a favor. Same goes for anyone, really, who needs work and can handle a shovel. Then, for good measure, you buy up the land in San Francisco where the cemeteries were, prime real estate that comes cheap because it used to be full of corpses. But this is America. No history, no memory. You develop the land, and people line up to buy it. On the back end, you get a piece of everything it takes to keep hauling stiffs down here—plots, stones, caskets, flowers, limos. All this plus the traditional benefit of being a silent partner in the graveyard business (if that cemetery in Brooklyn that Amerigo Bonasera ran ever got dug up, it'd be kind of like Cracker Jack, a surprise under every box).

Colma. Even sounds Italian.

A chill went through him. His solar plexus contracted. He closed his eyes. He could *see* it: the marshes of New Jersey stretched before him like ten Colmas. The Corleones had the political clout in New York to get the ordinance passed. The turf battle in Jersey with the Straccis, that could be worked out. He could practically hear Pop's voice: *Every man has but one destiny.*

"You all right?" asked Dino's wife.

Fredo opened his eyes. Against the tide of his own elation, Fredo summoned what he hoped was a sorrowful nod. She and the kids piled out of the car. Fredo drained the rest of the whiskey in his flask and hurried to take his place beside the other pallbearers.

After the service, everyone drove all the way back to the city and through it, to Fisherman's Wharf, where Molinari's, the best restaurant in the city, had been closed to the public since the employees had heard the news of their boss's death. The moment Fredo stepped out of the car, though, one whiff and it was clear that the staff had not spent the week at home curled on their davenports, weeping. The sea breeze throbbed with the aromas of drawn butter and soft-shell crab and bluefish and broiled lobster, tubs of boiling marinara sauce, newly built oak-fired grills crowded with filet mignon that the best meat cutters on the West Coast had competed to donate. Children, dozens of them, sprinted from cars to the back of the restaurant, where a prep chef waited not with scraps, as they must have ordinarily received, but gleaming steel buckets crammed with fresh sardines for the kids to drag out to the end of the pier and whip into the air fish by fish, detonating an explosion of beating wings, a roiling blur of gulls and pelicans. As Fredo lingered outside, watching, the birds swarmed over the unsupervised children like a shrieking biblical plague. This would have terrified Fredo as a child. His sister, Connie? Forget it. She'd still be screaming. Mike would have sat on one of the pilings, watching the squandering of good sardines in silent condemnation, his hands clamped over his ears. Sonny? Chucking rocks, not sardines, unless he'd somehow found a gun, which he would have. Hagen would have been dying to shoot the birds, too, but he'd never have risked Pop's disapproval and would have watched the whole thing through the car window. But these kids just jumped around on the pier laughing, their faces lit up as though they'd been handed the keys to Coney Island. Even when some of the gulls started dive-bombing the buckets, the kids just found it hilarious. It wouldn't be long before some adult ruined things, told them to simmer down and show some respect for poor Uncle Tony. Sure enough, a moment later, someone's stout and scowling *zia* came bustling toward them. Fredo couldn't bear to watch and turned to face the black ribbons on the restaurant door. It was at any rate time for him to do what he'd come here to do. He'd have rather gone back to his hotel room and thought about how to present his Colma East plan to Mike. If he were honest with himself, which he was not quite drunk enough to be, he might have allowed himself to think of other places the day and the night might take him, but he would not let himself think of that. Instead, he took a deep breath and went inside.

Under any circumstances, Molinari's was a dark restaurant, with black cypress-plank walls, black leather booths, and red-curtained windows, drawn on every side but the one that faced the bay, where often the only light was a fog-defeated pallor. Today, even those curtains were closed. The usually dim lighting was even lower, the candles were smaller,

and the room was filled shoulder to shoulder with dark-haired, olive-skinned people dressed in black. The brightest things in the room were the tablecloths, starched so impossibly white that Fredo found himself squinting. Standing in the middle of the restaurant's famous marble fountain was a life-sized ice sculpture of Tony Molinari, its hand extended toward the bar. People kept reaching across the water and touching its forehead.

The crowd was bigger than the one at the cemetery—something that anyone who took a bite of anything could have explained. Fredo made his rounds, embracing people and shaking his head about the tragedy and the terrible waste of it all. A few people made cryptic allusions to his promotion to underboss, and Fredo thanked them and said, you know, a man's got to eat, and then ate. He drank beer so he wouldn't get drunk. He lacked the charisma his father and brothers had, but as he'd grown older, he'd realized that for that very reason he was better at this kind of thing than they were. He intimidated no one. He was so frankly awkward that women wanted to mother him. Men would see him hovering at the edge of their conversation, hand him a drink, and bring him up to speed on the story they'd been telling. He'd reciprocate; drink with him once, and until the end of time Fredo Corleone would remember your poison. He'd thrived during his years of exile on the hotel side of the casino business because he genuinely liked to see people enjoying themselves, not just because then they'd owe him a favor.

Around the other Corleone men, people behaved like robots, silently rehearsing each word before they dared to speak. Around Fredo, they could be themselves. People liked him. He knew people saw this as a weakness, but that's where they were wrong. *There is no greater natural advantage in life than having your enemy overestimate your faults,* Pop had said. Not to *him,* true. To Sonny. Pop had given Sonny lessons, a lot of times with Fredo sitting right in the room, totally ignored. Sonny heard. Fredo listened.

The room buzzed with speculation about the missing charter pilot known as O'Malley, and people opened up to Fredo about it as they never would have to Mike. He heard every theory under the sun, the most frequent being either that O'Malley was some kind of undercover cop or else that he was somehow connected to the Cleveland family. Both, maybe. But the higher-ranking men had other ideas. Butchie Molinari, for example, as he released Fredo from his embrace, merely whispered, "It's Fuckface, no?" As he had all day, Fredo said he had no idea whatsoever, which was also something Mike could never have pulled off.

Why did he *do* this to himself? This endless comparison with his brothers. Fredo stood in front of the gilded mirror in the men's room.

He stood up straight and sucked in his gut. His eyes looked like, how did that song go? Two cherries in a glass of buttermilk. His brothers, he was sure, didn't waste time comparing themselves with each other, and certainly not with him. He ran his hand through his thinning hair. He'd had enough to drink, that was for sure. He looked at his round face and tried not to see in it the traits he'd inherited from his parents, the stronger version of his jawline that Sonny had, the eyes that were just like Mike's only closer together. He picked up the glass jar full of combs and tonic and smashed it against his own reflection. Green liquid rained everywhere. The mirror only cracked. Fredo handed C-notes to the man at the sink next to him and to the Negro attendant, who said he understood, we all loved Mr. Tony. Fredo headed through the nearly empty restaurant, past the ice sculpture of Tony Molinari, its forehead gruesomely melted, as if it had taken a hollow-point slug instead of a thousand loving caresses, and out the door into the cool dark, determined to be nobody at all, not even himself.

He ignored the men at the cab stand and, head down, continued down the wharf. It wouldn't be long, he knew, before the neighborhood turned rough, before he got to the bars full of stevedores and sailors and the back-alley bars that only the most depraved of those men knew about.

He stopped himself. No. Not again.

Ahead was Powell Street. A straight shot to his hotel. A long walk, but it'd do him good. Clear his head. He looked toward the gloomy distant lights of those bars, then up Powell Street. He was pretty sure it went by that old Italian neighborhood, North Beach. He could stop there, take a break, have a coffee, think this Colma thing through. It'd be nice, just the ticket.

The second he turned up Powell he felt a wave of self-congratulatory relief.

By the time he climbed the first big hill, though, he was sweating and having second thoughts. He was too winded to think about his plan or anything else except that he didn't want a coffee anymore, he wanted something cold, even a beer, what could it hurt?

The street leveled out. The businesses started to have Italian names, but something was wrong. The streets were full of dirty-looking kids in sweaters and dungarees, some of them Negroes, hardly any of them looking especially Italian. He tried to remember when the last time was he'd been down here—'47? '48? He looked down Vallejo and saw the coffee shop he was thinking of, smelled it a block away, and it still had the same name, Caffè Trieste, which he took as a sign—*have the coffee, not a drink*—but when he opened the door he caught sight of a redheaded white kid playing the bongos while a Negro in a black sweater stood next

to him shouting who the fuck knew what—it was hard to make out over the shouting and finger snapping of the people at the tables. *Mulberry-eyed girls,* the man might have said. *Mint jelly. Turtleneck angel guys.*

Fucking Bohemians. He left. Somewhere in this city was a very tall whiskey and water with Fredo Corleone's name on it.

He stopped in at another Italian place he remembered, Enrico's, which looked about the same except for the sign outside saying LIVE JAZZ TONIGHT! Bohemians here, too, but the music sounded better, so fuck it. He paid his three bucks and took a seat at the bar. Piano, soprano sax, and a drummer with brushes. Crazy stuff, but Fredo got his drink and bobbed his head along with the syncopated beat. He was the only one in the room in a suit, which for some reason seemed to provoke people into coming up to him and talking to him about the "scene" and telling him about the wonders of reefer. He resisted the impulse to tell them he'd just come from the funeral of the guy who'd made most of the profit off their precious reefer. After another drink he started thinking this combo was about the best goddamned thing he'd ever heard. Before long he was at a table with a big group of people, men and women, even smoking some reefer when it came his way. The band took a break, and a fat Norwegian in a fez took the stage and said that after the intermission he'd read his haikus and the combo would jam along. Fredo felt a hand on his arm. It was a long-faced man with long sideburns, about thirty, in a sweater and taped-together eyeglasses. "I hear you're with a record label," the man said, practically blushing.

"That's what you hear, huh?" Fredo dimly remembered having told this lie when he'd first sat down at the table.

"I got a band that plays here tomorrow," the man said, and started describing his music in what was probably English. More gibberish. *Turtleneck angel guy,* Fredo thought. He looked him up and down. A fag, no question.

"I'm Dean," the man said. "I like your suit."

"Pleasure, Dean," said Fredo. "Sit down, huh? The name's Troy."

The search for the missing pilot ended several weeks later, when a body was found at the bottom of a ravine by the Cuyahoga River, not far from the hospital, wedged in a sewer grate. Sewage and rushing water had accelerated decomposition. What remained had been feasted upon by river rats. The face and eyes were completely gone, and when the body was first lifted, live rats slithered out of its mouth and rectum. The admitting bracelet (GERALD O'MALLEY, MALE CAUCASIAN, AGE 38) and what was left of the gown were deemed authentic. The coroner ruled that the body's in-

juries were consistent with the ones the pilot had suffered, right down to the distinct stitching style of his ER surgeon. Dental records might have been helpful, but the authorities had no idea who Gerald O'Malley had really been. Whoever he was, however he got from the ICU to the bottom of that ravine, the poor fellow was really most sincerely dead.

Chapter 13

THE PLAN HAD BEEN for Billy Van Arsdale and Francesca Corleone to fly from Florida to New York along with Francesca's brothers, her mother, and her mother's perpetual fiancé, Stan the Liquor Man, but Billy's parents gave him his Christmas present early: a two-tone Thunderbird, waiting for him the day he came home from school in his yellow Joe College jalopy, an old Jeepster that Billy loved partially because it mortified his parents but that, in truth, had done well to make it back to Palm Beach from Tallahassee. The chance to hit the road for a long trip in a car like that Thunderbird, he told Francesca on the phone, was too much to pass up. She thought she knew what he was also saying, but she said nothing about it and neither did he. The plane tickets had been bought, but Billy's parents, who were going skiing in Austria, called their travel agent and had him take care of the refunds.

The night before the trip, Billy drove down to Hollywood. He'd been there once before, at Thanksgiving, a month after he and Francesca had started dating, and seemed to have made a good impression on everyone but Kathy, who was cold to him the whole time and then wrote Francesca the next week to say she was disappointed that Francesca's self-hatred ran so deep. Francesca's translation: Kathy was so jealous she could die.

Without Kathy around, though, everyone else in the family apparently took it on themselves to make Billy uncomfortable. Before he even had a chance to give Francesca a hug, Poppa Francaviglia had dragooned him to go next door and help put in a new toilet. In the middle of that, Nonna came in carrying a plate with slices of the oranges she'd grown herself on one side and ones that had come from his family's company on the other, asking him to taste and see if he could tell which was which. They all went to dinner at a tacky steak joint just because Frankie's football coach's cousin owned it. Frankie asked Billy why he'd been a swimmer instead of a football player, had he been cut from the football team? Francesca was about to kick her brother under the table, but Billy said that was exactly what had happened and told a funny story about it. Chip spilled his Coke on Billy. Twice. Is it really possible for a ten-year-old to spill his drink *twice*, on the same person, accidentally? Everyone but Francesca seemed to think so.

Sandra supervised Billy's loading of the Christmas presents into the trunk and backseat of his car (the hauling of same being a key to getting Sandra to go along with this trip), then escorted Billy and Francesca next door to her parents' house, where Billy was being exiled as a deterrent to intimacy. It was only nine-thirty, but they had a long day tomorrow. The only reason Billy was spending the night—he only lived an hour away—was so that they could leave at dawn and abide by their pledge to drive all day and night, twenty-four hours straight through to New York without stopping at any hotel. "And if you *do* have to stop," Sandra said now, yet again, "for some, God forbid, act of God, you'll what?"

"Get separate rooms, Ma," Francesca intoned. "Call to let you know we're okay."

"Call when?"

"Immediately, Ma. C'mon. Stop it."

"And the receipts for those separate rooms?"

"We'll show them to you to prove it." As if that would prove a thing. "Ma, this is crazy."

Sandra made Billy repeat the same litany. He complied. Sandra nodded and said that was good, she trusted them, and she hated to think what would happen if they ever betrayed that. "I know you want to enjoy a nice kiss goodnight," she said, "so I'll leave you alone now, eh?"

Hypocrite, Francesca thought. When her mother was her age, she was already pregnant.

"I love you," Billy whispered, leaning slowly toward her, and she whispered it back, her lips still moving with the words when he kissed her. As if so triggered, the porch light went on.

"I love your family," Billy said.

"You're nuts."

"You wish they'd get off your back, but everyone who doesn't have what you have wishes they had it."

It was not the first time she was afraid Billy was with her only because she was different, exotic, *the Italian girl,* a means of shocking his parents but less extreme than going out with a Negro. Or an Indian, like her roommate Suzy. But it was the first time she summoned the courage to say something about it. "You sure you don't just love me for my family?"

He shook his head and looked away. Immediately she wished she hadn't said it. He must have said or thought this about every girl he ever dated, including Francesca herself. As she started to apologize, he leaned toward her and kissed her again, touching her with nothing but his warm lips, and held it. When she opened her eyes, his were already open.

Before noon the next day, they had registered as man and wife at a small beachfront hotel north of Jacksonville. Francesca was afraid the desk clerk would object—neither of them wore a wedding ring—but Billy tipped the

clerk as he registered. "You'd be surprised," he said as they walked to their room, "how much discretion you can buy for twenty bucks."

Now Francesca stood in the bathroom and took out the pale green negligee that—knowing her mother would go through her luggage—she'd rolled up and hidden in her purse.

Okay, she thought. *Here goes.* She watched herself undress, as if it were someone else, there in the mirror. *A girl—a woman—in the last moments of her virginity.* Unbuttoning, unfastening, pulling off, stepping out. Folding each piece of clothing, placing it gingerly on the marble countertop, as if she is afraid it will explode. Patting her stomach. Rubbing her hands over the small dents in her flesh where her fat bra strap had been, trying to make them go away. Twisting around, craning her neck to see what she must look like from behind. She touches her hair, and it doesn't move. She brushes out the hair spray—long, even strokes—then looks up and tosses her head to watch which way her hair falls, what it looks like after it does. She dabs perfume onto her fingertips, applies it to all the places any woman at a makeup counter would advise, then bends her head and slowly reaches for the flame of black hair between her legs and dabs it, too. The woman's breasts are large but (*Francesca noticed, sighing*) cumbersome, asymmetrical: the bosom of a peasant girl in a painting of a half-harvested field (*or like Ma's, the last person on earth Francesca wanted to be thinking about now*). The woman takes in a deep breath, deeper now; her breasts rise, assuming shapes somewhat more like the ones in those magazines. Almost imperceptibly, she reddens. She grabs an obviously expensive silk negligee from atop her scuffed brown purse and holds it in front of her by the delicate ribbonry of its shoulder straps. She juts one hip, then the other. She frowns. The negligee is undeniably beautiful, but, somehow all wrong for this woman, at this moment. She holds it at arm's length and lets go. It falls, a pool of fabric atop her neat pile of clothes. She stands naked, breathing not so much deeply now as heavily. Naked. Nude. But nothing like a painting. A real woman, young and scared, shaved and powdered, covered with goose bumps and shivering despite the tiny beads of sweat on her brow and under her breasts, her chest covered with a faint, splotchy blush. The woman shakes her head and chuckles silently, then smiles in a way she must hope is wicked, or at least brave. She opens the door. She faces the doorway. "Okay," she says (*Is that me?* Francesca thought, *that chirpy girl's voice?*), "close your eyes." She crosses her arms over her breasts, hugging herself, closes her own eyes, and emerges into the uncertainty, the inevitability of the next room.

They planned their stops miles in advance, looking for filling stations where they wouldn't have to wait for an attendant. To cut down on stops,

they drank as little as possible. They ate nothing but the sandwiches, fruits, and little *strufoli* cookies from the picnic basket that Nonna had sent, even though Francesca warned Billy he'd be sorry he was eating even that much. They were each supposed to sleep as much as possible while the other drove, and Francesca did try, but between the replaying of those four hours in the Sand Dollar Inn and the bracing speed at which Billy drove that T-Bird, trying to make up for those four hours, blowing past tractor-trailers and decent families motoring unhurriedly along in their dull Chryslers—not to mention Billy's habit of turning up the radio all the way whenever he found a rhythm-and-blues song or a song off that amazing new Johnny Fontane long-player—the best she could do was close her eyes.

A state trooper pulled them over. Billy showed the man his license, registration, and another piece of paper, mumbling something about "courtesy." Moments later, they were back on the road, uncited, going just as fast. His father's massive donations to the Fraternal Order of Police, paying off once more. "My Get-Out-of-Jail-Free card," Billy said. He blushed.

What an upside-down world, Francesca thought, the Carolina pines rushing by her window in a liquid blur. Billy, this older boy she'd once hated herself for being stupid enough to believe she might have, this big man on campus, this rich boy, reduced before her eyes to a boyfriend, her excellent boyfriend, eager to please, calling in favors on her behalf, crazy about her. It all started the day her sister left. That was the same day Francesca met Billy, but Billy's falling in love with her, as much as he meant to her now, was a lucky by-product.

Growing up, Kathy had always been the smart twin. Francesca was the pretty one, or at least the one more interested in being pretty; the girly one. Kathy was the bohemian who loved wild jazz music and sneaked cigarettes. Francesca was the good Catholic girl. Francesca was a cheerleader and an attendant on the Homecoming Court. Francesca did her homework, or pretended to, in a malt shop. Francesca owned not one but two poodle skirts. But without Kathy around, Francesca—unconsciously—filled up the empty part of her where her sister had been by somehow *becoming* Kathy. At the time, she told herself that all the clothes shopping she'd done the first few weeks of the term was for her roommate, Suzy's, benefit, something they could do together and a means of getting Suzy to stop wearing the terrible little-girl jumpers and dresses she'd shown up with. Only after she'd done it did Francesca notice she'd remade her wardrobe into Kathy's, blacks and reds, turtlenecks and slacks. Likewise, Francesca couldn't remember making a decision to start smoking, her sister's brand, no less, but open her purse and that's what was there. The

smoking was probably a consequence of the studying. She never made a conscious decision to study more, but for no reason she understood, suddenly in class she was one of the smart kids, her judiciously raised hand sought by her beleaguered professors when they wanted to move things along. Which came first, the chicken of how good it felt in class to be one of those kids or the egg of long nights bent over her desk, smoke curling in the languorous haze of her study lamp?

Several times, she'd seen Billy Van Arsdale in the library studying next to a girl or coming out of a movie theater with a different girl, out of one of the bars on Tennessee Street with a different girl yet. Sometimes, Francesca, too, would be on a date (freshmen, no one special) or in a study group. Always Billy would nod hello, often he would make eye contact, occasionally he'd even pause and exchange pleasantries. She despised him for mocking her like this. She was cool toward him but polite, afraid that if she tried to ignore him or, worse, told him off, he'd embarrass her even worse. She had not for a moment believed she was deploying Kathy's favorite tactic—indeed, her only tactic—in getting boys to like her. Francesca might never have known that was exactly what she was doing—however inadvertently—if it hadn't been for Suzy, who was in Glee Club with Billy's heavyset little brother George. One day, studying for midterms, Suzy told Francesca that if she wasn't careful her playing-hard-to-get act was going to make it so that Billy Van Arsdale never worked up the courage to ask her out.

Playing hard to get? Ridiculous. Francesca was too nice, too eager to please, lacking the nerve it took to try to get what she wanted by rebuffing it. Francesca told Suzy she was out of her mind, but Suzy cited George, who cited a conversation he'd had with his brother about whether he had any classes with this girl Francesca Corleone. Why do you ask? George had asked. No reason, Billy had said. What, do you like her? George asked. Shut up, dickhead, Billy said, are you in her class or not? I thought you told me to shut up, George said. You're an asshole, Billy said, and punched him in the arm and said forget it. And George said he wasn't in any classes with Francesca but he was friends with her roommate. How do you know they said all that? Francesca had asked her, and Suzy said she didn't know, though why would George lie? Francesca had thought about the way her brothers talked to each other and decided that Suzy, an only child, couldn't have made something like that up. The next time Francesca ran into Billy she did nothing more than just hold his eye contact a few beats too long, but of course that did it. Seconds later, he was asking her out. He knew this great juke joint out in the country. H-Bomb Ferguson was playing; his hit was called "She's Been Gone," had she heard it? Can't say as I've had the pleasure, Francesca said, trying, and failing, to restrain

her smile, to stop blushing. The next day, the dorm mother knocked on her door and handed Francesca a single red rose and an envelope containing an H-Bomb Ferguson 45. Two days later, they had their first date. Two months later, here they were. Racing north.

Watching him now, and pretending not to, she could see—now that she'd seen all of him there was to see, now that they'd gone to bed together and even though he'd probably been with a hundred girls, he'd turned out to be the straitlaced one and she the curious one, pointing, asking, trying things out (yes, it hurt, some; yes, four times in four hours had left her tender enough that it now seemed slightly greedy), now that she was convinced they were in every adult way *in love*—that Billy Van Arsdale was not what she'd thought he was, that first day of school. He was a little short, with hound-dog eyes and a crooked smile that she thought was cute but certainly wouldn't make it in the movies. His blond hair was always disheveled. He had the wardrobe of a small-town southern lawyer—brogans, seersucker and linen suits, pocket watch on a fob (it had belonged to his great-uncle, who'd been chief justice of the Florida Supreme Court), tailored Egyptian cotton shirts rendered unpretentious by their frayed cuffs—and somehow only moments after he got dressed, no matter what he was wearing, his clothes were shot through with wrinkles. He was a frankly awful dancer and seemed unaware of it. He sang along loudly to songs he barely knew. He laughed through his teeth, like a cartoon character. His parents hated each other and had neglected him and his brother. The beloved Negro woman who raised him had killed herself after her grown son was murdered in Mississippi by the Ku Klux Klan, and Billy had been the one who found her, crumpled on the bathroom floor with a cabinet full of pills in her stomach. He went to a psychiatrist once a week and spoke of it as if it were nothing to be ashamed of. All of which is to say that it was not his undeniable good looks, his multitude of talents, or his perfect storybook life that had gotten him all those other girls and the student body presidency as well. He was a born politician: one part the Van Arsdale name and what that meant in Florida, one part his own exquisite manners and social nature, and a third part that was hard to define. More than charisma, Francesca thought. Just shy of magnetism.

Except for a stretch of Virginia, Billy drove the whole way. Francesca did eventually get some sleep, too, before she felt Billy's hand on her shoulder and awoke, disoriented, to the harsh glare of winter light off fallen snow.

"Thought you'd want to see this." He pointed at the New York skyline. "Your hometown."

She sat up and rubbed her eyes. Billy was so obviously proud of his accomplishment, of providing this miraculous view for her. She wasn't sure

she'd ever seen the city from the Jersey side before. It was a stunning view, but nothing about it looked like home. "Pretty."

"Aren't you excited?" he said.

"Are you okay? You sleepy? Have you ever driven in snow before? What time is it?"

Yes. No. Often, on ski vacations. Right on schedule. They'd made up all four hours.

"I love you," she said, leaning over to kiss his stubbly cheek.

"Name's Junior Johnson, ma'am," he said, affecting a southern drawl. "At your service."

"Who's Junior Johnson?"

A race car driver who'd first developed his skills evading federal agents during bootlegging days. She'd never heard of *Junior Johnson*? A distant cousin, it turned out, of Billy's mother.

"Ah," said Francesca. "So *that's* where the Van Arsdale fortune originated."

Billy started to say something and stopped himself.

"It's okay," she said. "Get it out of your system now."

"No need," he said.

"You sure?" They'd discussed it before. She'd told him that her father had rebelled against all that, that he was a legitimate businessman. His import-export company was called The Brothers Corleone, but only out of respect for his father's wishes. He'd been the only brother involved. "Because this isn't discussed, okay? Anything you want to ask about all that, you ask it right now, but whatever you do, don't embarrass me in front of my family."

He turned toward her, his mouth open. "I don't believe you think I would—"

"I don't," she said. "You wouldn't. We're just tired. I'm sorry. Just drive."

Christmas Eve, yet still the morning traffic was awful. By the time they made it to Long Beach, they'd lost one of the hours they'd regained.

Two squatty men in long overcoats came out of the stone gatehouse at the entrance to the semicircle mall of houses her family owned. Billy rolled down the window. Francesca could smell the food cooking from inside her grandmother's house, a good fifty yards away. She leaned over Billy's lap so the guards could see her.

One of the men called her Kathy and said he was sorry, he hadn't recognized the car, hadn't recognized her at first either, without her glasses.

Glasses? "I'm Francesca, actually," she said.

The man nodded. "We were told Silver Hawk, not Thunderbird. Your ma don't know cars too well, I guess. Better get a move on. She's been callin' down here for hours." The outside of her grandparents' house—the

smallest and least ostentatious on the half-circle mall, all eight of them owned by her family—was entirely undecorated. Her grandmother was still in mourning. With no lights or wreaths, the house seemed smaller. Diminished. Across the street, the bungalow where she and her family had once lived stood dark and empty. Someone had built a snowman in the front yard and hung a wreath the size of a truck tire on the door.

Before Billy could even turn into the driveway, Francesca's family started pouring out of her grandmother's house, led—of all people—by her twin sister, the languid bohemian one, wearing big black eyeglasses and bounding across the snowy lawn like, yes, a cheerleader.

"Hungry?" Francesca asked Billy.

"Starving," Billy said.

"Pace yourself," Francesca said, "but not too much, or they'll think you don't like them."

She opened her door, blasted first by the shock of the cold—*how could she have ever lived here, in this icebox?*—and then by Kathy, whose embrace slammed her against the side of the car. They jumped up and down and squealed, none of which had been Kathy's style for years. Though at Thanksgiving their reunion had been similar. Only when they separated to look at each other and Francesca felt the cold wind in her face did she realize she'd been crying. "You got glasses," Francesca said.

"You're pregnant," Kathy said, then stepped back as the rest of the family descended.

Francesca, stunned, was enveloped in their hugs and kisses. Kathy rocked on her heels, smiling, and gave a little innocent-seeming wave, though the glasses made her expression hard to read. Francesca knew a person could get pregnant the first time, and she knew that what Billy had done wasn't safe—pulling out of her, grabbing her hand and clutching it over him. But it was hardly a dangerous time of the month. And anyway, twins or not, *how could Kathy know?*

Billy hoisted a huge mesh bag of Van Arsdale oranges onto one shoulder, grapefruit onto the other. "The tree's where?" Billy said.

"What tree?" Kathy said. She scooped up Mary, Aunt Kay's adorable little girl, holding her against her hip, like somebody's mom. "Wha 'twee?" Mary parroted.

"The Christmas tree," Billy said. "To put the presents under."

"We're Italian, Billy-Boy," she said. "There is no Christmas tree."

"We *Italian,* Bee-Boy!" Mary shouted.

At least this was the Kathy of old. "For God's sake," Francesca said, "we have a Christmas tree at home. Grandma doesn't have a Christmas tree, is all. Put it by the *presepe.*"

Her grandmother clucked at the *for God's sake.* Billy cocked his head.

"A whaddyacallit," Francesca said. "A nativity scene, I guess." She stopped herself and looked at Kathy, who understood the unspoken question and nodded: yes, the *presepe* was holy enough to be in keeping with Grandma Carmela's mourning. "In the living room. You'll see it."

Francesca's mother arched an eyebrow, raised her left arm, looked at her wristwatch.

"The snow," Francesca said. "It slowed us down."

"All the way it snowed?" her mother said.

"From D.C. on," Francesca said, just guessing. She'd been asleep.

"No, you made real good time," blurted a bald guy, who'd introduced himself as "Ed Federici, friend of your auntie's." Kathy had mentioned him in a letter; he and Aunt Connie were engaged, even though her annulment hadn't come through yet. "I'd say. With that much snow."

Stan Jablonsky agreed. "Don't mind her," he said, winking at Sandra, which Francesca always found creepy. "She's been up since dawn, your ma, looking out the curtains for you."

The two fiancés loaded themselves up with the rest of the packages and on the way inside began interrogating Billy about the routes he'd taken, the bridges, the shortcuts, the gas mileage.

How is it possible, a family Christmas, and *those two outsiders* were the only other men? Stan, who'd been engaged to her mother for three years with no date set, and the accountant who did her family's taxes, engaged to a woman who was still married? The manliest of them all, Francesca's father, Santino, was dead. Her grandfather, always the laughing, doting epicenter of any family gathering, was dead, too. Uncle Mike wasn't coming (he was in either Cuba or Sicily on business—she'd heard both, maybe it was both, but *for Christmas*? Grandpa Vito must be rolling over in his grave). The Hagens had moved to Las Vegas and weren't coming either. Uncle Fredo was supposed to have been here yesterday but apparently had called and said he might not make it at all. Uncle Carlo had apparently disappeared from the face of the earth.

Just the two sorry fiancés. And Billy. *Her Billy.*

Francesca watched him go, eager to save him from an afternoon of cards, televised football, and endlessly proffered snacks, suddenly weak in the knees with desire for him—had that even *happened*, back in Jacksonville? But she was pulled away from him, powerless against the tide of women who swept her, as if in a dream, into her grandmother's hot, pungent kitchen: a fortress of enduring love that time had somehow never touched.

Clouds of steam, a mist of flour, tubs of boiling oil, counters spread with sheets of dough, waxed paper covered with slabs of fresh, seasoned fish. That hulking white stove, a museum piece that would probably out-

live them all. In the next room, the spindle of the record player was crammed with the same Christmas 45s that had been wafting into this kitchen for Francesca's whole life: Caruso, Lanza, Fontane, you name it. Children ran in and out, always underfoot, nibbling sweet scraps. Aunt Kay stood at the sink, washing dishes until it came time to make the handful of things she knew how to make. Her mother, Sandra, sturdy and earthy, and Aunt Connie, shrill and bitter, had never liked each other, but in this kitchen they anticipated one another's moves and needs as if they were Fred Astaire and Ginger Rogers. Angelina—her grandmother's Palermitan aunt, who must be a hundred years old now and still without a word of English—sat in the corner behind a card table, assembling ingredients that came her way. And of course Grandma Carmela oversaw everything, barking out instructions, stepping in to execute the most tricky tasks, all with an abiding love always felt but never stated.

Kathy pointed to a pyramid of milky-white eggplant, then handed Francesca a chef's knife and a freshly uncapped bottle of black cherry Brookdale soda, chilled in a snowbank outside. One look at the bottle—they couldn't get it in Florida, of course—and Francesca broke into tears again. Where had the tough girl gone? Where was the part of her that had been Kathy?

"Ah, the sweet tears of joy," her grandmother said in Italian. She raised her chipped coffee mug, the same one she'd used for as long as Francesca could remember, its faded image of the Hawaiian Islands now crusted on the outside with the remnants of a dozen doughs and batters. "For a proper *cena de Natale,* this is the ingredient most crucial of all!"

Who could help but be moved by this affirmation, from the lips of a woman widowed less than a year? Each of the other women scrambled to find her own cup, mug, or bottle and raised it high.

Against the nape of her neck, Francesca felt Kathy's face, the temple of those eyeglasses. "You're just a big sap," Kathy whispered, and together, identically, the twins laughed.

At Mass, Francesca had to keep whispering instructions to Billy, who'd never set foot in a Catholic church before. He was as endearingly clumsy with the kneeling and the crossing as he was on the dance floor. But she could feel Kathy's eyes on Billy, even if Billy couldn't. She could hear Kathy saying that this was just the kind of thing that's lovable now and makes you crazy later, even if Kathy—seated at the far end of the pew, steadying poor Zia Angelina—uttered nothing but hymn and litany.

When the church bell tolled for repentance, Francesca made a fist and struck her breast softly four times, one for each hour in the Sand Dollar

Inn. At the altar rail, she did it again, one for each time that they'd made love. Walking back to the pew, she kept her eyes down, penitent, away from Billy's, but once she kneeled and finished her prayer, she sat back and took his hand. Only then did she realize that Aunt Kay—next to her, still on her knees, her lips moving in silent prayer—had taken Communion, too.

"She converted," Kathy said on the ride home.

"I figured that, but after all these years?" Francesca said. "For the kids, I guess?"

They were in Billy's T-Bird.

Kathy raised an eyebrow. Even with the glasses, she bore a disconcerting resemblance to their mother. *"Per l'anima mortale di suo marito."* For her husband's mortal soul.

Her husband's mortal soul? Francesca frowned at her sister.

"She goes every day," Kathy said. "Just like Grandma. And for the same reason."

"Everybody goes for the same reason." Francesca still hadn't been able to pull her sister aside and ask what she'd meant when she'd said, *You're pregnant.* "More or less."

Kathy's eyes widened, exasperated.

Despite or more likely because of the heavy absences felt by nearly everyone around the table, the Corleone family's traditional Christmas Eve feast of the seven fishes was as loud and raucous as ever. The wine flowed freely, the women making up for what, in years past, would have been drunk by men. During the early courses, the children's Christmas letters, expressing their plainspoken love for their parents, were read one by one, youngest to the oldest. The poignant and disturbing notes receded as the writers got older, but every letter was received with strident good cheer, culminating in the letter from Aunt Connie. It was the first time in more than thirty years that Carmela Corleone had received only one declaration of filial love—a delicate moment that Connie, to the astonishment of more than a few, lightened with a letter so hilarious that it was still being passed around courses later.

Likewise, all hearts were warmed by the story of Vito Corleone's lone intrusion into the romantic lives of his children—the blind date he'd arranged many years before for Connie, soon after she'd begun dating Carlo Rizzi, with a nice boy who'd just graduated from college with a business degree. Ed Federici's lively, self-deprecating version of the disastrous date inspired Mama Corleone to slip a champagne toast to the happy *fidanzati* in between courses.

And what courses they were: Crab legs and shrimp cocktail. Fried *baccala* and stuffed calamari. Steamed clams in a marinara sauce, over fresh angel-hair pasta. And finally—at least until the break before dessert— flounder stuffed with spinach, sun-dried tomatoes, mozzarella cheese, and several secret ingredients Zia Angelina had inserted when no one was watching.

"The risk of heart attack," said Ed Federici, palms on the table, dazed as a man looking at the empty space where his stolen car used to be, "triples in the first hour after a heavy meal."

Stan had given up halfway through the last course and was asleep in the next room, bathed in the flickering glow of an unwatched football game. Only two people were still eating: Frankie, forking it in like a champ, and Billy, who was poking at his flounder like a man who'd found gold and was trying to recall why it was valuable.

Connie shushed Ed and slapped him on top of his florid, prematurely bald head. "Mamma hears that, she'll be the one who has the heart attack." She'd been drinking wine at the same pace all day and had just opened a new bottle of Marsala. Her slap, theoretically playful, was loud enough that those watching it flinched. Several people in other rooms stuck their head around the corner to investigate. The slap had immediately left a hand-shaped mark.

Francesca led Billy from the table, taking him into her grandfather's old office just as Aunt Kay finished folding up the kids' table. "You get enough to eat, Billy?" Kay asked.

"Yes, ma'am." He sat down heavily on the leather couch against the wall.

"Save room for dessert," Kay said, smirking. "Hey, either of you seen Anthony?"

"He's outside, I think," Billy said. "With Chip and a bunch of the Clemenza kids." They were the children of kids Francesca used to play with when she was Chip's age. Now those playmates had families of their own and lived in houses down the street.

They were alone now. "You did good, baby. They like you, I can tell."

"Why are you grinning like that?" he asked, lying across the couch, clutching his stomach.

She knelt on the floor beside him. "No such thing as a free lunch," she whispered. "So pay up, buster. Kiss me."

He obeyed. It lingered, not the sort of kiss Francesca had meant to have in this house. When she opened her eyes, the lights were flashing off and on.

"Don't make me dump cold water on you," Kathy said. "C'mon. Dishes. March. I'll wash, you dry."

Billy lay back, the same sated look on his face he'd had in the hotel, and finger-waved.

The women had of course been doing dishes all day. Francesca was looking at ten minutes' worth of plates, knives, stemware, serving bowls, and baby bottles. A jazz station played on a small console radio Kathy had found somewhere. On a creaking wooden chair in the corner, Zia Angelina snored. The twins were otherwise alone together. "Where's Grandma?" Francesca said.

"Mass. She and Aunt Kay just left."

"Twice? You're kidding me."

"Go look. Car's gone." Kathy bent her head toward Angelina. "Thank God she snores," Kathy said. "Otherwise we'd have to be checking her all the time to see if she was dead. Don't look at me like that. She's deaf on top of her no English."

"How much you want to bet she can understand more than she lets on?"

"Oh, you mean like Bee-Boy?"

"What are you talking about?"

"You think everyone else is so blind—"

"I don't think everyone is so anything."

"—but you're the blind one. That snotty little good ol' boy in there, *asleep in Grandpa's office*—that's some nerve, don't you think? Can't you see he's just using you?"

"*Using me?*" Francesca said. "What are you, back in high school? I took him in there."

"What are *you*, the Slut Princess of Tallahassee?" Her glasses were half fogged from the steam from the tap, but she kept them on.

"You've lost your mind. It's sad, actually. I feel sorry for you." Francesca held up a fish-shaped porcelain platter and arched her eyebrows.

"No idea," Kathy said, "just stack it with that stuff under the phone there. Can't you see Billy's just here to experience a gen-u-ine Mafia Christmas? To him, we're a bunch of dirty Guineas. Something for him to laugh about over highballs at the yacht club with Skip and Miffie, the year he saw real dago gangsters with tommy guns in their violin cases."

Anthony Corleone had brought his violin all the way from Nevada just to play "Silent Night" for them—not well, but it was sweet. "I'm not even going to dignify that with a reply."

Kathy clanked a wineglass against the faucet, and it shattered. She didn't even curse. She was cut. It bled like mad at first but was really nothing. They cleaned it up, together, without saying a word. Francesca got her a bandage.

Kathy heaved a sigh, met her sister's eyes, and said something in a

voice so small Francesca had to ask her to repeat it. "I said," Kathy whispered, "that it's all true."

"What's all true?"

Kathy rinsed the scum from the sink and told Francesca to get her coat. They walked to the farthest corner of the yard, concealed behind a floodlight, and Kathy—an old joke they'd each done dozens of times—lit two cigarettes at once, in the manner of a Hollywood tough-guy leading man, and handed one to her sister. "You and Billy? That was probably the first kiss anyone ever had in that room that didn't lead directly to—" She looked up into the snow, as if the right word might land on her.

"To what?"

Kathy stood with her hand on her hip and blew a stream of smoke away from the light. "Do you know how long it takes to have someone declared legally dead? Do you know how long it takes to get an annulment from the church?"

"A couple months, I guess."

"You guess wrong, little sister." Kathy was four minutes older. "Longer. That's how it started." When Aunt Connie had announced her engagement and set the date for December, Kathy had been as shocked as everyone else. She'd presumed that Connie was pregnant, but a chance discovery in Connie's bathroom ruled that out. Kathy, being Kathy, had gone to the library and made some phone calls. It takes a full year before the state declares a person legally dead, and it's complicated. Most annulments, even for a woman abandoned, take just as long.

"Oh, come on," Francesca said. "Is that all? A donation to some judge's campaign fund, another to the Knights of Columbus, and everything gets sped up. It's the way of the world."

Kathy shook her head. She looked away from her sister, into the darkness. "You don't get it. She's not *getting* an annulment. It's a lie. She doesn't need one. They lied to us. They hushed it up. Uncle Carlo didn't disappear. He was murdered."

"Who's 'they'?"

"Uncle Mike and everyone he controls."

"You're a retard," Francesca said. "There was never even a funeral for Uncle Carlo."

"There's a death certificate on file," Kathy said. "I went to the courthouse and found it."

"I bet the New York phone book has a dozen people named Carlo Rizzi."

Kathy stood in the darkness, smoking, shaking her head. "The human eye is utterly passive," she said, obviously quoting some professor or textbook. "Only the brain can see."

"What's that supposed to mean?"

Kathy didn't answer. She finished her cigarette, lit two more, and started again. One Sunday, she'd met Aunt Connie in the city, for lunch at the Waldorf. Connie showed up drunk, with a man who wasn't Ed Federici, kissed the man good-bye, took her seat, and when Kathy confronted her by asking how it was going with the annulment, Connie blurted it out: Carlo didn't disappear, she said. Mike killed him. Connie held up her hand and told Kathy not to speak. She was drunk, but her voice was steady. Mike killed him, Connie said, or had him killed, because Carlo killed your father. Carlo killed Sonny.

Francesca burst out laughing.

Kathy's eyes looked lifeless. "Connie said that Carlo beat her up, knowing that Pop would come to her rescue. When she called him, Pop did just that, or tried to. Men with machine guns killed him when he was stopped at a tollbooth on the Jones Beach Causeway."

"Aunt Connie is out of her mind," Francesca said, "and so are you if you believe that."

"Just listen," Kathy said. "Okay?"

Francesca didn't answer.

"Pop's bodyguards were on the scene right after he was killed, and they took his body to an undertaker who owed a favor to Grandpa Vito. Nothing about it ever got into the newspapers. Some cops took bribes to write the whole thing up as an accident."

"Pop didn't have bodyguards. No one—" She was going to say *killed Pop* but couldn't.

Kathy tossed away her cigarette butt. "Come on. You don't remember the bodyguards?"

"I know what you're thinking about, but those were guys from his company. Importers."

Kathy bit her lower lip. "Do you honestly think I'd *joke* about this?"

"I don't think you're joking. I just think you're wrong."

"This is hard," Kathy said. "Just hear me out."

Francesca, frowning, gave her an after-you gesture.

"All right," Kathy said. "So then Aunt Connie says that the men who . . . Well, the men at the tollbooth, those men, it turns out, were working for the same men who paid Uncle Carlo to beat her. She was crying her eyes out at this point, and if you'd seen it, believe me, you'd have believed her. Her own husband took money to beat her, and he did it, and the *reason* he did it was so that those men could kill *her brother,*" Kathy hissed, "so they could kill *Pop*—"

"Stop it."

"—and she stayed with him for another *seven years.* She *fucked him* for another—"

"That's enough."

"—seven years, and she had *babies* with that monster. But it's so, so, so much bigger than even that. Connie says that the same men who did all that are also the ones who shot Grandpa Vito *and* they're the same people who killed Uncle Mike's wife."

"First of all," Francesca said, "Aunt Kay's not—"

Again, the hand. Not Kay, Kathy said. The other one, Apollonia, his first wife, in Sicily, about whom Kay knows nothing. She was blown to kingdom come with a car bomb.

Apollonia? Francesca thought. *Car bomb?* Kathy had enough imagination to invent things that wild, but Aunt Connie certainly didn't. If Connie had really said that, she'd either fallen for someone else's lie or was telling the truth.

Kathy kept talking faster, the stories Connie told piling onto the things Kathy had been able to confirm later. Moment by moment Kathy's voice sounded colder. She might have talked for five minutes or five hours, Francesca had no idea. Francesca couldn't stand there anymore and couldn't move. She concentrated on the popping of the firecrackers in the front yard, the sound of children's laughter. Later, she noticed those sounds were gone, but she hadn't heard them stop. For a while she concentrated on how it felt to have snow melting in her hair. She tried to look at her sister and also past her, to the wintertime remnants of her grandfather's beloved garden, where he died, happy, at peace.

". . . and that's why Aunt Kay became Catholic and why she goes to Mass every day and sometimes twice. They're on their knees trying to pray their evil murdering husbands' souls out of hell, just like Ma ought to do for—"

And then just like that Francesca was looking down at her sister, crumpled in the snow, bleeding again, this time from her nose. Her cigarette was still in her mouth. Her glasses had flown off her face and landed a few feet away. Francesca's right hand was still balled into a fist, and it hurt. Kathy stirred. "Lunatic," she muttered.

A tide of rage roared in Francesca's ears. She kicked Kathy in the ribs. It wasn't a direct hit, but it was enough to make Kathy grunt in pain.

Francesca turned and ran.

Francesca lay on her side on the edge of a double bed, in a darkened room that had once belonged to Uncle Fredo, who'd lived here with his parents until he was thirty. He'd been in Las Vegas for ten years, but the décor— dark drapes and wood paneling, a faded map of Sicily, and a fly-fishing painting that looked like it came from Sears—seemed unaltered, as if Grandma Carmela expected him to move back in any day.

After what might have been hours or minutes, Francesca heard someone in the bathroom across the hall, banging and running water in a rhythm that was unmistakably Kathy's. Francesca heard Kathy's footsteps, heard her get into the other side of the bed. She did not have to look to know that Kathy was facing the other wall, lying on her side, a mirror image of Francesca except for the pajamas. Francesca wore nightgowns.

For a long time they lay there. If Francesca hadn't spent thousands of nights in the same bedroom as Kathy, she'd have had every reason to presume she was asleep. "Why did you say I was pregnant?" Francesca said.

"What are you talking about?"

"When we first got here. When you ran to the car like you were actually glad to see me."

Again, anyone else might have thought Kathy had fallen asleep. "Ohhhhh," she finally said. "That. Don't you remember? When we dropped you off at school, the last thing you said to me was to not wreck my eyes reading. I said don't get pregnant. You got here and the first thing you do, with your remarkable grasp of the self-evident, is tell me I have glasses. So I—"

"Other way around. You said don't get pregnant and I said don't wreck your eyes."

"I stand corrected. So are you?"

"No," Francesca finally said. "Of course not."

"You haven't? At all?"

"Why? Have you?"

"No," Kathy said, so quickly Francesca figured the answer was yes.

They did not talk about what had happened behind the floodlights— the stories or the punch or even the fate of Kathy's eyeglasses. They stayed on opposite hips on opposite sides of the bed. They stayed awake long enough to hear their grandmother downstairs, beginning to fry sausage, which meant that it was probably about four-thirty. Eventually, they did fall asleep. Eventually, as sleeping people will, they moved. Inexorably, each was drawn toward the center of the bed. They entwined their arms and legs. Their long hair seemed blended together. They even breathed as one, each exhaling on the neck of the other.

"Oh, honey," Francesca whispered in the darkness, presuming her sister was asleep. "I can't believe what I did. What I did to you."

"Maybe I *am* you," Kathy murmured, and they, as one, went back to sleep.

Francesca awoke to the piercing shrieks of children and the murmurs of herding adults. She sat up. Snow was falling. Downstairs, the pitch of the

din grew higher. Over it all rose Grandma Carmela's deep call of *Buon Natale!* Someone had arrived. Francesca hurried down the narrow back stairs. The kitchen was full of food but empty. She heard two sets of feet coming her way and stopped so she wouldn't get smacked in the face with the kitchen door. The door flew open. Kathy and Billy were both showered and dressed, grinning like they'd just caught Santa Claus red-handed and commandeered the sleigh. Billy was decked out in a red blazer, a green tie, and a shirt so white it put snow to shame. Unfrayed cuffs. The white of divinity fudge.

"You'll never *guess* who just drove up with your uncle," Billy said.

"Which uncle?" She smoothed her ratty hair. She hadn't even brushed her teeth.

"Which one do you think?" Kathy said.

"Mike." *They both came to get me because they were competing to tell me this news.*

"Oh, please." Kathy rolled her eyes. "Uncle Fredo." She wasn't wearing the glasses. She had a black eye, but not much of one. A person would have to be looking for it.

"C'mon, guess," Billy said.

"I give up," Francesca said. "Santa Claus."

"Weirder," Kathy said.

"Who's weirder than Santa Claus?"

"Deanna *Dunn,*" Billy said.

Francesca rolled her eyes. On their last date, they'd gone to see that Deanna Dunn picture where she has a deaf baby and her husband dies at the end fighting the Great Chicago Fire. "Just tell me."

"I'm serious as a judge." He held up his hand, ready to be sworn in. Even at twenty-two, dressed in a red blazer on Christmas morning, Billy was easy to picture as a judge.

"He's not kidding," Kathy said. "It's Deanna Dunn. Cross my heart." Which she actually did. "I'd actually heard a rumor that she and Uncle Fredo were dating, but I didn't—"

Just then the kitchen door swung open, and trailing in Grandma Carmela's wake came Uncle Fredo and Deanna Dunn. In person, Deanna Dunn's head seemed gigantic. She was very tall and more beautiful than pretty. On her left hand was a diamond ring as proportionately absurd as her head.

"Miss Dunn!" Francesca said.

"What'd I tell you?" Kathy said, even though it had been Billy who'd told her. Kathy liked foreign movies. Deanna Dunn was someone she made fun of. But the way Kathy was looking at her now, she could have been the secretary of the Deanna Dunn Fan Club.

"Please, darling. Call me Deanna." Her accent was neither American nor British and in person sounded remarkably unlike human speech.

She took Francesca's hand.

Deanna Dunn, so magnetic Francesca felt dizzy. Yesterday in Jacksonville had only in the most indirect way unleashed last night's exchange with Kathy. It had nothing to do with the surreal sight of *Deanna Dunn* in this old, familiar kitchen. Francesca's life had been seized by dream-and-nightmare logic.

The rich boy Francesca loved calmly served black coffee to a two-time Oscar-winning actress. Francesca's grandmother sang a Christmas carol— not a hymn, but one about *Santa Claus.* Francesca's dead father had been both a murderer and murdered. Uncle Fredo slouched against the doorframe, staring at his shoes. He looked like he'd eaten some bad clams. Behind him, as if someone had given a signal, came an explosion of flashbulbs. Francesca expected to see men with visors and big cameras jostling for position, shooting them as if from the edge of the red carpet. Fredo didn't even look up.

From the next room, over shouted thank-yous and the shredding of gift wrap, came the voice of her mother—the voice that had been lying to Francesca all her life.

"If you people don't hurry up," Sandra called, "you're going to miss Christmas."

"Christmas!" cried Deanna Dunn, hurrying past Uncle Fredo. Deanna Dunn was not tall. She'd only come off that way standing next to Uncle Fredo, who was short, and because she had a tall woman's walk and also a colossal head. The eye is passive. Only the brain can see. "How *marvelous!*"

BOOK IV

1956–1957

Chapter 14

THAT SPRING, after months of negotiation, the Commission finally agreed to meet. Its first order of business would be to add Chicago's Louie Russo as its eighth member. Next would be the formal approval of the peace agreement. The heads of all twenty-four Families were invited. Every effort would be made to ensure that this time, peace would last.

Michael Corleone flew to New York on the red-eye, accompanied only by three bodyguards. Hagen, a declared candidate for the U.S. Senate, could not be a part of this. Since every important item of business had already been decided, for today, what Michael needed at his side was not a brilliant strategist but rather a man whose very presence suggested stability and respect for tradition. Clemenza was the perfect *consigliere* for such an occasion.

Michael had no intention of ever choosing a permanent *consigliere*. The job required an elusive set of contradictory skills. A schemer who's also loyal. A Machiavellian negotiator who's also guileless. A driven man with no personal ambition. The plan had been for Vito to be the last to hold the job. A CEO has a board and a battalion of lawyers. The president has a staff, a cabinet, judges whose places on the bench they owe to him, and the control of the world's mightiest army. The Corleone organization would develop in the open and along such lines.

Clemenza picked them up at the airport himself. The very sight of the fat man was reassuring. He'd quit chewing toothpicks and gone back to cigars. All that had changed about him since Michael was a boy was that now he walked with a cane.

They drove into Manhattan, stopping at a bakery on Mulberry for a box of pastries, then on to the apartment on West Ninety-third where the Corleones were holding a Bocchicchio hostage—some baby-faced third cousin who'd gotten in from Sicily yesterday. He was playing dominos with Frankie Pants, Little Joe Bono, and Richie "Two Guns" Nobilio—Clemenza's men. Kid couldn't have been more than fifteen. They stood. Michael and Pete embraced and kissed each in turn. In halting English, the kid, whose name was Carmine Marino, addressed Michael as "Don Corleone" and thanked him for the chance to see America. The only win-

dow in the apartment was blackened with what looked like tar. *"Prego,"* Michael said. *"Fa niente."*

"You didn't bring coffee?" said Richie Two Guns, opening the box.

"Make coffee, you lazy fuck," Clemenza said. "Or go downstairs to some deli. Good bakery can be hard to find, but you can get coffee anyplace. What, I'm supposed to slosh coffee all over my clean car while I drive it up here and deliver it to you, half spilled and cold?"

Clemenza winked, gave Frankie's shoulders a quick rub, set out the pastries, and, like a tour guide, pointed out some of their finer points.

The peace talks started at two. By now, each Family coming to the table was holding a Bocchicchio hostage. The hostages went willingly. It was how the Bocchicchios made their money. If, for example, anything happened to Michael or Clemenza, one of their men would kill this boy. No Bocchicchio would rest until the boy's murder was avenged—not on his killer but rather on those who'd harmed the killer's associates. The Bocchicchios were the most single-mindedly vengeful clan Sicily had ever seen, wholly undeterred by prison or death. There was no defense against them. Bocchicchio insurance was better than a hundred bodyguards. The men who came to the table would do so with just their *consiglieres.*

Back in the car, Michael asked Clemenza how old he thought that baby-faced Bocchicchio kid was.

"Carmine?" The fat man considered this for a long time. "I'm not so good at this no more. All of a sudden everybody seems like a kid to me."

"He looked like he was all of fifteen."

"I hear there ain't a whole lot of Bocchicchios left," Clemenza said. "On the other hand, at my age, sometimes *you* look like you're only fifteen. No disrespect or nothin'."

"Of course." Fifteen. When Michael was fifteen, he'd stood up at the dinner table, looked his father in the eye, and said he'd rather die than grow up to be a man like him. What happened after that still gave Michael chills, all these years later. Without that moment of stupid, boyish pride, Michael wondered, would he himself even be in this business? "I wouldn't have thought," Michael said, "that a kid that young would even be allowed to fly here alone."

"I don't know about that," Clemenza said, "but he didn't fly. He came over on a boat, along with most of the other hostages. In steerage. They still have that on boats? Whatever the cheapest one's called. I doubt if the Bocchicchios are even paying him. Lot of times, they just send over shoestring relatives who want to come live in America. We're paying a king's ransom for this, y'know, but how they spread the wealth? Forget about it."

Clemenza shook his big, sad head. They crossed the Tappan Zee Bridge and headed north.

"So tell me," Michael said after a long silence. "What *were* those rumors you heard about Fredo?"

"What rumors?" Pete said.

Michael stared straight ahead at the road.

"I told you," Pete said. "Drinking too much, and the rest of it comes from bad sources."

Michael took a deep breath. "Did you hear that he's a homosexual?"

"What's wrong with you? You think that's what I heard?"

"The man he beat up in San Francisco was a homosexual."

"Don't mean he wasn't also a robber. A guy can be a robber and a queer both. If everybody who killed a queer turned queer, there'd be a lot of queers out there."

Fredo's story was that he'd been out for a walk to clear his head after Molinari's funeral and stopped for a drink. A kid from the bar followed him to his hotel and later broke into his room to rob him. Fredo beat the kid up and he died. It was a ridiculous story—why, for example, didn't the kid just rob Fredo on the street? Why wait until it was necessary to pick the lock on the door to Fredo's room? On top of that, the kid's parents had recently died and left him almost thirty thousand dollars—no fortune, but why was he robbing anyone? Hagen—acting strictly as a lawyer—had managed to keep the matter out of the newspapers and see to it that no charges were filed, but he'd returned from San Francisco with several matters of concern.

"So you're sure you never heard that?" Michael said.

"I never said I never heard it. I said it came from bad sources. If I was to start believing everything I hear from bad sources, I'd never—" he said. "Jesus Christ, Mikey. This is your *brother*. He may have done some stupid shit and beat up a fag and all, but I can't believe you think he maybe is one. This *is* Fredo we're talking about, right? Curly hair, yay tall? Spends all his money on abortions and jewels, married to a fucking *movie star*—is *that* the guy you mean? I tell you what I got from a *good* source. That doctor you guys have out there? Segal? He told me that even *after* Fredo started up with Deanna Dunn, he knocked up a showgirl. Marguerite something. *French*, as in va-va-voom. Does that sound like fag behavior to you?"

Michael remained blank.

He'd given Fredo a chance to distinguish himself, and what happened? More boozing. More knocked-up showgirls. Michael wasn't sure what Fredo was trying to prove by running off and marrying that Hollywood *puttana*. Though if anything can make a man more of a man, it's marriage. Also, there's a certain public image value right now to having a Corleone married to a movie star, even one whose best screen years were behind her. So he had to give Fredo that.

"Want to know something?" Pete said. "I'm going to tell you something whether you like it or not. It was *you* your pop worried about. In that way. For a while there."

Michael leaned over and turned on the radio. Clemenza wasn't telling him anything that Michael hadn't heard directly from his father. For miles, neither Michael nor Clemenza spoke.

"Bocchicchios," Clemenza finally said.

"What?" Michael said. They'd been silent long enough that Michael had progressed through several dozen other topics. "What about them?"

"What a fucking thing they got going, that's all. How would a person—especially guys as dumb as your typical Bocchicchio—ever even think up a service like that?"

"If something's your destiny, maybe you don't need to think," Michael said. "You just need to listen."

"Listen how do you mean?"

"If anyone I know ever found his destiny, it's you, Pete."

Clemenza furrowed his brow and considered this. Then his face broke into a grin. "Hark!" he said. "I think I hear destiny calling!" He arched his eyebrows in mock surprise and cupped his hand around his left ear, as if straining to hear some noise coming from the woods. "*Pete,*" he said in a stage whisper. "*Pull over and take a leak.*"

Nick Geraci remembered the crash and everything up to the point where he'd gone into shock and passed out in the water. There was probably a way of finding out now whose fingers he'd pried off and broken, but he hoped he'd never know.

He'd been unconscious the whole time he'd been in the hospital and for several days after that. When he finally woke up, he found himself in a lemon yellow room so tiny the twin bed he was in nearly filled it. His leg was in a cast and rigged to a pulley screwed to a beam in the ceiling. Light streamed in from a pair of French doors, beyond which there seemed to be a balcony. This was no hospital, but he was hooked up to all kinds of hospital equipment. He stared at the ceiling, trying to reconstruct the events that had brought him here. Wherever *here* was.

Many, many doctors are Jewish, of course, but when the first person Geraci saw after he woke up in that room was an obviously Jewish-looking old man with a stethoscope, Geraci assumed—ridiculously, he knew even at the time, but also, as it turned out, correctly—that wherever he was, it was by the grace of his godfather, Vincent "the Jew" Forlenza.

"He's awake, geniuses," the doctor called back over his shoulder. From the next room came the sound of chairs sliding back from a table and someone dialing a phone.

"Who are you?" Geraci muttered. "Where am I?"

"I'm nobody," the doctor said. "I'm not even here, and, if I were to venture a guess, neither are you."

"How long have I been here?"

The doctor sighed and gave Geraci a series of quick tests and a run-down on his injuries. Geraci, reading between the lines, guessed (once again correctly) that he'd been in this room for less than a week. What hurt the most was Geraci's ribs, but he'd broken them enough times to know it was nothing. Same with the nose. The doctor took Geraci's leg out of traction. "The only thing I'm worried about long term," the doctor said, "is that concussion. Not your first, was it?"

"I boxed," Geraci said.

"So you did," said the doctor. "And, if you'll forgive me for saying so, not that well."

"You saw me fight?"

"I never saw you before in my life," the doctor said. "Whoever you are, you've had about the last concussion you're going to be able to take and not become a drooling moron."

"So you're saying I'm not a drooling moron now? That's great news, Doc."

"I'm not saying anything," the doctor said. "Though I will say, your ability to heal borders on the extraordinary."

"Runs in the family," Geraci said. "My dad was given last rites after a speedboat wreck, and a month later he came one ball short of bowling a 300."

"Not to mention the time he got shot in the gut on a Friday and he was back driving his truck that Monday."

"You know about that?"

"I don't know about anything." He shrugged in concession. "Don't worry." He tapped Geraci's cast with the capped tip of a fountain pen. "Medicine, I know."

He told Geraci not to move and left.

Geraci smelled doughnuts. Presti's. Another ridiculous assumption; who can tell the aroma of one doughnut shop from another? Even if he was in Cleveland someplace, the last place he'd have expected to be was Little Italy. Too obvious. But minutes later, Geraci heard the sound of a man laboring up a staircase. The door opened, and into Geraci's little room limped Laughing Sal Narducci, arm extended, clutching a big bag from Presti's. "Taste of home?" he asked. "C'mon. Take two."

Nick Geraci obeyed.

The men in the other room slid a chair behind Laughing Sal and he sat. He explained things. Geraci had been taken to a third-floor apartment in Cleveland's Little Italy, only a few blocks from the narrow house where

he'd grown up. No one outside Don Forlenza's most trusted men knew Geraci was here. The idea had been entirely Don Forlenza's, a snap decision he'd made out of concern that even if the crash was nobody's fault, either his organization or his godson might take the blame. "I don't gotta tell you," Narducci told him, "a lot of men in our tradition, if one of their friends has a heart attack they start plotting revenge against God."

"You were there, Sal. You know how Frank . . . how Don Falcone was about that fight."

"How he was," Narducci said. "True! Hell of a punch by a man sitting down."

You're welcome, Geraci thought. "No, I mean the boxing match. He *insisted—*"

"His guy won, you know that? His fighter paid five to one. Frank hadn't of died, would've been his lucky day."

"My family," Nick said. "My wife and—"

"Charlotte and your girls are fine," Sal said. "Your old man's still . . . y'know. Your old man. Piss and vinegar, right? He don't talk so much, but far as we know, he's fine, too."

"Do they know I'm fine?"

"Fine," Narducci repeated. "I don't know. *Are* you fine?"

"I will be soon," Geraci said. "A man who was probably a doctor said that in his professional opinion I'm not a drooling moron."

"Moron," Narducci said. "What do doctors know? So look. Tell me. What happened up there that made you say *sabotage?*"

"I never said that."

Narducci winced. "I sort of think you maybe did."

"Huh," Geraci said. "I have no memory of that. None at all."

"None at all. On your radio you never did? To the control tower? This ring a bell?"

"No," Geraci lied.

"No? Think hard."

Geraci had a pretty good idea why Narducci was making such an issue of this. If it *had* been sabotage, it would mean that somehow someone got onto that island and did it. Even if it came out later who that was, who'd been behind it, Don Forlenza would still take the blame.

Had it been sabotage? So much had gone wrong in those last few moments. Geraci thought he remembered everything, and still he had no real idea what had happened. It was not unlikely that the fault had been entirely his. Knowing the plane was about to go down had made him say and do stupid things. He'd blurted it out. *Sabotage.* The tower had said, *Say again,* and he hadn't. It had been *wrong* to think of Charlotte and his girls, their sweet faces contorted in pain when they got the news that he'd

died. That couldn't have taken more than a couple seconds, but who knows? Might have been a couple seconds he didn't have. He couldn't see the runway, but he'd known he wasn't far from shore. There was a problem with the artificial horizon, yes, but a lot of things might have caused that. His instruments had told him conflicting things, and he'd gone with what felt right. *If you indulge your feelings,* his flight instructor had said, *they will kill you.* The instructor was a former test pilot. *Reality,* he preached, *is absolute.* A good pilot never loses sight of this. Geraci was afraid he might have.

"Things went wrong," Geraci said. "It happened fast."

Narducci waited. He didn't move.

"If I said something about sabotage—which I don't recall, but if I did—I was just thinking out loud. Ruling it out." Geraci thought he'd finished both doughnuts and was surprised to see one last big bite left. He ate it. "What happened was terrible, but it was nobody's fault."

"Nobody's fault." Narducci repeated it several more times, blankly. "Well," he finally said, "that's good. I got one more question right now."

"All ears."

"Tell me about O'Malley. Who knows he's you? Or could figure it out? Lot of lucky guessers in the world, don't forget. Lot of guys smarter than you think. Again, take your time. I'm in no hurry. Just the *thought* of going back down all them stairs . . ." He shuddered.

It was a short list. It included no one but Narducci, Forlenza, and the top people in the Corleone Family. There was no reason not to recite it. If all Don Forlenza had wanted to do was cover his tracks, Geraci would have been dead already. If Forlenza and his men were going to help Geraci talk his way out of this mess, they'd need some information.

On a narrow road in upstate New York more commonly traveled by tractors and pickup trucks, there came an irregular but persistent stream of Cadillacs and Lincolns. Uniformed police officers directed Clemenza's car to a pasture behind a white clapboard farmhouse. Judging from the long row of big and precisely parked cars, they were among the last to arrive. If Hagen were still *consigliere,* Michael would have had to hear that Vito Corleone would have been among the first. That was one way of doing things; Michael's was another. Even his father had, during his final months, stressed that Michael needed to do things his own way. Clemenza whistled an old folk song and questioned nothing, not even how far he had to walk.

They got out. Behind the house was a catering tent. Next to it, hissing over a pit of coals and rotating on a spit, was a pig large enough to pass for an immature hippo.

Neither Michael nor Clemenza had ever been to one of these, but they approached the house like men who knew what to expect. Michael was fairly sure he did. But he'd also been fairly sure he knew what to expect when he was crouching in that amphibious tractor off the shore of Peleliu, ready to take the beach.

This was not the same thing, he told himself. War was at his back. Peace lay before him.

"Every ten years, eh?" Clemenza tapped his wristwatch. The gesture was a good excuse for him to stop for a moment and catch his wheezing breath. "Like clockwork."

"Actually," Michael said, "it's only been eight." Despite the Bocchicchio insurance, he scanned the woods for snipers or anyone else who shouldn't have been there. Habit.

"So next time, it'll be twelve. Average it out. Hey, get a load of that big fuckin' pig."

Michael laughed. "You sure you don't want to do this permanently?"

Clemenza shook his head and began walking again. *"A chi consiglia non vuole il capo."* He who advises doesn't want to be boss; an old saying. "Nothing against Hagen or Genco, any of them," he said, "but I'm a guy who helps."

The rear door opened. They were met by a chorus of greetings, as if from friends at a party. With a quick glance back at the roasting pig, Clemenza clapped his hand on Michael's shoulder and followed him inside.

Nick Geraci spent weeks in that lemon yellow apartment, waking each morning to the aroma of doughnuts and the sound of women in slippers muttering in Italian and sweeping their stoops. Charlotte and the girls were still doing fine, he was assured, and knew he was recuperating nicely. He was told that Vincent Forlenza and Michael Corleone were doing everything they could to negotiate a deal to bring him home safely. Hardly a day went by without someone telling him how lucky he was to have two godfathers, both of whom loved him.

In all that time Geraci never learned the name of that old doctor or how the man had become beholden to Don Forlenza. It must have been something big. To prepare the body that would be discovered in the ravine down by the river, the doctor had stood by, holding a clipboard with several diagrams, and advised Forlenza's men as they took some corpse about Geraci's size and gave it injuries nearly identical to the ones Geraci had. The doctor sewed the contrived wounds himself, imitating the stitch work of the emergency room hacks. Geraci never found out where

the corpse had come from. The only question he asked, the day they got him out of there and sent him to Arizona to meet his family, was if they knew the rats would eat that much of the body and if so, *how* they knew. The face had helpfully been destroyed, he'd heard, and rats were living inside the rotting corpse. Was that just what happened naturally when you hid a body near the river? Or had they done things to make sure?

"What difference does it make?" asked Laughing Sal, beside him in the hearse they were using to take him to the train station.

Geraci shrugged. "Knowledge for knowledge's sake."

"There you go!" Narducci said, nodding. "That college-boy angle you play."

"Something like that."

"I bet there are some people who aren't all that crazy about it, that angle."

"People," Geraci agreed. "I bet."

He'd studied the way Narducci used echolalia and silence. He copied it now. People never recognize themselves. Even in a boxing ring, you can knock men out this way.

"Odds are," Narducci finally said, "nature would have taken its course. But like a lot of things where the odds are in a man's favor, you still want to make sure."

Despite how far it was to Arizona, Geraci had refused to fly, not even in a luxurious medical plane that came complete with a hi-fi system and a pretty nurse. No more planes, ever. And so they sent him there in a casket, shipped in a freight car to the same funeral home he'd gone to that summer, after his mother died.

The only part of the trip Geraci had to spend actually inside the casket was the loading and unloading. Onboard, in a car with four other caskets and a crated-up piano, he was able to get out, read, relax, play cards with the two men watching him, and take them for everything they had. He felt sorry for them. He had a place to sleep and they didn't. He suggested they take the dead people out of some of the other caskets, but they wouldn't. As a gesture of goodwill, he offered them their money back, and of course they refused. Good Cleveland guys, all the way around.

As the train pulled into Tucson, he told the men good-bye and shut the lid on himself. Two days sleeping in this thing, and the velvet pillow stank. The next face he'd see would either be Charlotte's, as he'd been told, or that of some ugly fucker who was about to kill him.

He lay in the dark, utterly still. Soon he heard men speaking Spanish and felt hands grasping the handles and lifting. There was a lot of jostling

and banging into walls until Geraci heard someone say "Look out" in English and a moment later he hit the ground, hard. It knocked the wind out of him. The Mexicans exploded in laughter. Geraci put his hands over his mouth and tried to control the little wheezing squeals his lungs made as they fought with his spasmed muscles to fill. So maybe the next face he saw wouldn't be Charlotte's or a killer's.

The men kept laughing and cussed at one another in a mix of English and Spanish. They picked up the casket. Geraci's breathing returned to something close to normal. He'd banged his head, too, he only then realized. Soon they slid him into what was probably another hearse.

Michael Corleone had sent word that he didn't blame Geraci for the crash and that after all of Geraci's hard work these past months, he'd more than earned a few quiet months in the desert with his family. He'd been assured that things were going well, that no one was coming after him. No one was looking for him. Smuggling him out of Cleveland like this had just been a precaution, something to ward off cops and lucky guessers.

Probably all that was true. But it was also just the kind of reassurance a guy heard right before he got clipped.

Still, though Geraci would probably never *like* Michael Corleone, he did admire him. He had faith in him. Michael would save Nick Geraci, if for no other reason than that he *needed* him. He needed his loyalty, his ability to make money, his *smarts*. Michael wanted to transform an organization made up of violent peasant-criminals into a corporation that could take its place in the greatest legal gambling scam ever invented—the New York Stock Exchange. If he was going to succeed, he certainly couldn't afford to lose a man like Geraci. In the scheme of things, Geraci knew, he was just some mook from Cleveland, a striver who took his lumps, worked hard, went to night school, and had a little success as a small-time attorney and businessman. But compared to most of the guys in this business, Nick Geraci was Albert Einstein.

Even so, Geraci *had* made mistakes. He should have stood up to Falcone and refused to fly in such weather. He shouldn't have said he thought the plane had been sabotaged when he'd really had no idea. Crashing: also bad. He certainly shouldn't have swum away from the wreck as if he were guilty of something. His mistakes had narrowed his options. He had no choice but to play out this hand.

This would be a very elaborate way to kill him, though that hardly ruled it out. He'd heard of more elaborate. He'd *participated* in more elaborate.

When he'd been forced to kill Tessio, Geraci couldn't have been more angry at Michael Corleone. But from the moment he'd walked away from Tessio's open grave site until that trip from the train to wherever he was really going, Geraci truly hadn't given it another thought.

The hearse stopped. He was unloaded by men who didn't say a word, which did not seem like a good sign.

Geraci's head throbbed. He could hardly breathe. It's not as if caskets have airholes. On the way here, he'd spent maybe one tenth this much time with the lid down. He was going to die choking on his own funk. They'd come to whack him, and he'd already have suffocated. Still, he'd do as he was told. He'd stay inside with the lid closed until Charlotte came to get him.

The men walked him across a cement floor and set him down on something. Definitely cement. This could very well be the back room of the Di Nardo Brothers Funeral Parlor. The night he killed Tessio, that crematory where they took the heads, it had a cement floor, didn't it?

This could also be a warehouse. A meat locker. Somebody's two-car garage. Anything.

He heard a door open. A person's rubber-soled shoes squeaked as they drew near him. A *polished* cement floor. He held what was left of his breath.

The lid came open.

It was Charlotte.

He sat up and felt oxygen surge through him, tingling as it reached his hands and feet. He could feel air spread up his back and wash over his scalp. Charlotte looked tanned and happy. "You look so good!" she said. She seemed sincere. She did not react at all to his gasping. It slowed. Only then did he notice Barb and Bev standing together against the paneled back wall, obviously frightened, holding a pair of crutches waist high, parallel to the floor.

Charlotte gave him a quick kiss on the lips. It was like she was high on something. Geraci didn't smell liquor. "Welcome home."

"Thanks," he said. Well, not home, but he knew what she meant. Upstairs, a funeral was going on. Muffled chanting. Some prayer or creed. "It's good to be . . . back. How are you?"

Geraci held out his arms toward his daughters. They nodded at him but stayed put.

"Busy," Charlotte said. "But fine." Softly, she touched the knot on his head where he'd banged it.

Barb was eleven; Bev had just turned nine. Barb was a little blond replica of Charlotte, right down to the new suntan. Bev was a pale, hulking, dark-haired girl, tallest in her class (including the boys) and a full two inches taller than her big sister, who was also tall.

"They got to see a movie getting made out in the desert, and they've been talking about it ever since," Charlotte said, waving the girls toward the casket. "C'mon, girls. Tell him."

Bev let go of the crutches with one hand so she could point at him. "See?" she said to her sister. "You see? I *told* you Daddy's not dead."

"Not yet, maybe," Barb said. "But he will be."

Geraci motioned for Charlotte to help him climb out, but she was oblivious.

"Daddy won't *ever* die," Bev said.

"You're stupid," Barb said. "Everybody dies someday."

"Now, girls," Charlotte said. "Be nice."

It was as if she didn't see the first thing strange about this scene, being brought two thousand miles to the back of a funeral home to retrieve her missing husband from a casket. Upstairs, an organ, God knows why, started playing "Yes, Sir, That's My Baby."

"He will too die," Barb said. "Everybody does."

"Not Daddy," Bev said. "He promised. Didn't you, Daddy?"

Actually, he had, once. His father had always said that a promise is a debt. *Ogni promessa è un debito.* It had taken being a father himself—even more than his treacherous professional life—to drive the lesson home.

"Now you see what *my* days are like," Charlotte said. She said it cheerfully, though. She didn't sound like she was trying too hard. She smiled and took his bruised face in her hands and kissed it. Nothing needy or passionate, just an ordinary, slightly lingering marital kiss, the kind a man might enjoy one morning at the breakfast table. It was not the sort of kiss Geraci would ever have expected to receive while sitting in a casket with bandaged ribs and a broken leg—and, who knows, maybe a fresh concussion, too—while a chorus of muffled voices in the room upstairs sang an old Tin Pan Alley song at some poor stiff's funeral. Though in fairness to Charlotte, perhaps there was no right sort of kiss for an occasion like this.

"Can you give me a hand?" he said. "Getting out?"

"Your dad's waiting in the car," she said. "Should I go get him?"

"No." Naturally, his father couldn't be bothered to come in and greet him. "I really just need a hand. We can do it."

They did. The girls came forward, perfectly in step. They'd rehearsed this. They presented him with his crutches as if they were peasants bestowing a humble gift to the king.

Then they cracked up, and for a long time he didn't do anything much but hold the girls' embrace. At some point Bev whispered, "You did promise," and he whispered, "So far, so good."

"It's nice to have you back," Charlotte said.

Outside, the funeral home's pebbled parking lot would have been big enough for a shopping center. Maybe fifty cars, but his father, Fausto, of course, had the best space, closest to the door. He'd probably come by yesterday, sized up the parking situation, then gotten here hours ago to make sure he got that space. He sat behind the wheel of his idling Oldsmobile, looking straight ahead and listening to Mexican music on the

radio. He had the air-conditioner going full blast, probably for no other reason than to create a need for him to wear the old quilted jacket with his union local's logo on the back. He waited for Nick to finish struggling with the crutches and get situated in the passenger seat even to turn to face him.

"Well, well, well," said Fausto Geraci, "if it ain't Eddie Rickenbacker."

A team of local carpenters had been hired to make long maple tables especially for the peace talks. The tables were arranged in a big rectangle inside a ballroom that had once been the stable. The stain on the tables was dry but so fresh it still smelled. The odor wasn't too bad until the room also filled with cigar and cigarette smoke. They opened all the windows, but the *consigliere* from Philly, who had emphysema, and Don Forlenza from Cleveland, who had just about every affliction under the sun, both had to listen from the next room. The temperature outside was forty. Other than Louie Russo, who must have been trying to prove something, the men conducted the entire meeting in their scarves and overcoats.

What everyone at the table agreed to believe for the sake of peace was this: The plane crash in Lake Erie was nobody's fault. Frank Falcone did in fact bet a hundred grand on that fight at the Cleveland Armory, and he'd insisted on going to see it no matter how bad the storm was. As the plane went down, someone in the tower heard Geraci say the word *sabotage*, but Geraci was merely thinking aloud in a time of great stress and *ruling out* sabotage. The thunder and lightning made the radio transmissions difficult to hear. The plane crashed and everyone died on impact except Geraci, who almost did. Don Forlenza learned about the terrible deaths of his recent guests, and he learned that the authorities thought the crash might have been the result of sabotage. Immediately, Don Forlenza made certain that no one in his organization had sabotaged the plane. Then he rescued his injured godson from the hospital. What else was there to do? Had Don Falcone and Don Molinari been killed as a result of sabotage, there was the chance this might be blamed on the Cleveland organization. There was a chance it might be blamed on his godson, who was unconscious—unable to protect himself, unable to answer for himself. Who in this room would not have done the same for his own godson? Also, because Geraci was a member of the Corleone Family, Don Forlenza was concerned that his godson may have been the target of violence by one of the other New York Families. Geraci had regained consciousness. The federal authorities had ruled out sabotage. The crash had been an act of God. Don Corleone had let the other members of the Commission know that the missing pilot was Geraci. As Don Corleone had said then and re-

asserted now, the fake name on Geraci's pilot's license was intended to be a deception to no one but law enforcement officials, no different in kind than the driver's licenses many of them were carrying now. In this case, the alias had done its job. While every man in this room had known for months that Gerald O'Malley was in fact Fausto Geraci, Jr., the authorities had presumed that O'Malley was the rat-gnawed corpse in that ravine.

What a fitting monument to the four men who died that the discussions initiated to help understand the crash soon expanded themselves to other issues. Soon an agreement for a lasting peace had been struck—an agreement they'd had all come here to ratify.

Much of the official story was true, but no one in that farmhouse believed every word of it.

Though no proof had come to light, there seemed to be little doubt that Louie Russo's men had penetrated Vincent Forlenza's little island fortress and sabotaged the plane. After all, the men in that plane *did* represent all four of Chicago's biggest rivals in Las Vegas and the West. The crash had succeeded in making Don Forlenza look like an old fool. The struggles in New York had given Russo an opening, and he'd seized it. He'd forged allegiances with several other Dons—Carlo Tramonti in New Orleans, Bunny Coniglio in Milwaukee, Sammy Drago in Tampa, and the new boss in L.A., Jackie Ping-Pong. When Russo went to Cuba, he stayed in the presidential palace. No one but Russo's allies relished Chicago's return to power, but the consensus was that Russo posed less of a threat with a seat on the Commission than he had as a turf-grabbing outsider. To most of the men at those tables, trying to prove Russo responsible for that crash was unimportant. What mattered was returning their full attention to their own business. Even Butchie Molinari had been persuaded (by Michael Corleone, in fact) to declare publicly that he accepted the official version of the crash and to vow not to seek revenge.

Louie Russo and also his *consigliere* were not about to deny an accusation that no one had openly made, even if they knew it was false. Russo hadn't ordered a hit on the men in that plane. If he had his theories about who if anyone had, he wasn't letting on.

Russo, naturally, knew some things. Jackie Ping-Pong knew some things. Sal Narducci—who because of Forlenza's health problems sat alone at the head table, as if he were already running Cleveland—knew some other things.

The man Narducci hired to sabotage the plane went on vacation in Las Vegas a few days later and hadn't been seen since.

(Or, rather, he hadn't been seen since Al Neri, a man who didn't know or care about who he killed or why, shot him and buried him in the desert.)

Clemenza knew a lot, but not everything.

Michael Corleone was fairly certain that he'd covered his tracks well enough that no one—neither friend nor enemy, cop nor *capo*—would ever put it all together.

Who would *possibly* surmise that not only did Michael order the deaths of Barzini, of Tattaglia, of his own top *caporegime* Tessio, *and* of his own sister's husband—not to mention all the collateral killings those killings unleashed—but that he then negotiated a cease-fire and used that uneasy truce to orchestrate a hit on the men in the airplane, including Nick Geraci, whom he'd recently promoted to *capo,* and Tony Molinari, a steadfast ally? There were no rumors that either man had betrayed him—largely, of course, because they had not.

Who'd ever figure out what that satchel Fontane delivered was really for? Even Hagen had unquestioningly presumed that it was an investment in the new casino at Lake Tahoe.

From where Michael Corleone sat, tapping that old Swiss watch given to him by Corporal Hank Vogelsong, how could anyone—even someone who'd only *read* about Jap planes exploding into fireballs, cutting troop-ships in half—think that a man who'd seen what Michael had seen in the Pacific would kill *anyone* by ordering a plane crash?

Every morning, Fausto Geraci—it's *Jair-AH-chee*, but, what the hell, people'll say it how they want—was always the first one up. He'd make coffee and go out on the back patio of his little stucco house in his boxer shorts and an undershirt, where he'd sit on an aluminum lawn chair, reading the morning paper and chain-smoking Chesterfield Kings. Once he finished the paper, he'd stare out at his empty swimming pool. Even having his granddaughters in the house for the better part of a school year had had little visible effect on his mood.

Fausto Geraci's heart was pickled in a bitterness more corrosive than battery acid. He was a man convinced that the world had fucked him over. Years and years of dragging himself out of bed and climbing into the freezing cab of some truck and hauling anything a person could imagine and a lot of things a person wouldn't *want* to imagine. Loading and unloading his own trucks, hard work that was taken for granted by everyone who wound up with any goddamned thing he'd ever hauled. Driving what maybe were getaway cars; he wouldn't know. But he did it. He spent a lifetime standing firm against everyone who was against the Italians, and he stayed loyal to that prick Vinnie Forlenza and his organization. He went to *prison* for those people. Did he complain, say a word about it? No. To them he was just Fausto the Driver, some quiet ox who worked hard and

followed orders. He did all that work for them, jobs that doomed his soul to Hell so long ago even his own wife told him she stopped praying for it, but did they cut him in as an equal? No. He got some money, sure, but they gave Jews and niggers more of a break than they ever gave Fausto Geraci. He was supposed to be grateful for how they set him up in the union. Ha. He was still their puppet. The pay was good but not enough to make up for having to sit at a desk all day and listen to petty complaints from lazy people. Still, he listened, said almost nothing, and did his job. He spent years solving other people's problems, but who ever gave two shits about Fausto Geraci's problems, huh? Then after all those years of loyalty, one day: *pow.* He's out. They gave his job to someone else (Fausto knew better than to ask why), and they gave Fausto the Driver "early retirement." Hush money. Go-away money. What did he do? He went away. Loyal to the end. Loyal *past* the end. Good old Fausto.

And, Jesus Christ, don't get him started on kids. His daughter was a dried-up old maid schoolteacher who moved from Youngstown to Tucson just to make his life miserable—every night after school she comes by and it's *eat this, don't eat that, how many cigarettes is that today, Poppa?* On and on. And the boy, his *namesake?* He thought he was better than everybody else. His mother encouraged it, too. Everything came easy for that kid. Married a blonde with tits out to here. Went not just to college but to fucking law school. And that business with the flying? Just another way of showing the world he wasn't his old man—a hotshot private pilot, see, not some broken-down truck driver. Every breath that ungrateful shit drew was an affront. Even says his *name* wrong. Ace Geraci. Goddamn. Who'd he think paved his way? Vinnie Forlenza, that's what he probably thinks. Or those cocksuckers in New York.

When the others started waking up, before they could start bothering him, Fausto got up from his lawn chair and went to the garage. He kept a robe and slippers in there. He'd put them on and work up a sweat doing yard work. On their way to school, Barb and Bev, bless their hearts, would come out and give him a kiss. He wanted to protect those sweet kids from a world that was going to disappoint and then destroy them, but instead he'd just stand there in his robe, holding a hose or a rake, smiling like a happy peasant and waving good-bye.

Then he'd go in and clean himself up and drive across town to Conchita Cruz's house trailer. She barely spoke English, and he barely spoke, but somehow they'd met in a bar not long after he'd moved here and come to this arrangement. He couldn't remember how, that's how relaxed this thing he had with her was. *Hair-AH-see,* she pronounced his name, which was a fuckload closer than how his own son said it. Sometimes they'd fuck, but more often they'd spend an hour together not asking

questions. Just existing. Television's good for that. Other times there'd be cards, dominos, maybe a foot massage. They'd eat lunch, there or at the diner on the corner, and then he'd kiss her on the forehead. They'd declare no love and make no promises, and she'd go to her second-shift job at the cannery and he'd go for a short drive in the desert. Every day but Sunday, on the same straight stretch of road, he'd stomp on the gas and blow the carbon off his engine—and his heart, too, or so it felt once he buried that speedometer needle in the black space beyond 120. Once he did, he'd ease off the gas, letting his speed and pulse and spirits drop. Then he'd go home, where his sorry-ass namesake and that goddamned Swedish wife would be bickering. When they'd first gotten there, Charlotte had been a model wife, and Nick was humbled by having just fucked up so bad. But a few weeks later, about the time he got that cast off his leg, the bickering started. Even the turning on of the television would touch off some stupid argument. Especially that. Day by day, they behaved more and more like Fausto had with his late wife, another way the boy seemed determined to mock him.

They had nothing to do. Nothing. The amount of time they wasted made Fausto Geraci sick. Charlotte went out and spent Nick's money on things she didn't need. Sometimes Nick drove around in a rented car making calls from random pay phones and stopping by this rathole bar and grill he'd muscled into, but most of the time he sat around reading books and talking to the men who came by to give him messages.

One day, Fausto came home and Nick was filling the fucking swimming pool. All it took was a little frown from Fausto, and he went on some long explanation that even though his ma had died in that pool when her cancer-weakened heart gave out, she'd died doing what she loved. She'd never have wanted him to drain the pool. What did that boy know of such things? He wasn't the one who fished her dead body out of there. Selfish punk. Her wishes, Fausto Geraci's ass. Nick only wanted to fill the pool so he could use it himself. Sure enough, next day, Fausto came home and not only was the boy floating on an inflatable raft, he was reading some book about Eddie Rickenbacker. More mocking! For weeks he wouldn't stop with the flying ace stories, the race car driver stories, the lost-at-sea stories, the airline magnate stories. A remarkable man, Fausto Geraci couldn't deny it: American hero, all that good shit. But you know what? Fuck Eddie Rickenbacker.

Nick treated both his daughters like boys, especially poor Bev, who worshiped her father and would probably grow up to be an old maid gym teacher just like her dried-up shrew of an aunt. He and Charlotte took those kids to everything under the sun: the zoo, the circus, concerts, ball games, movies—like they were trying to make something up to them.

Still and all, those little girls had adapted to their move out here like champs. They'd made friends in the neighborhood, they did good in school, the works. They were happy just being children, but their parents couldn't see it.

When out of the blue it came time for them to go back to Long Island, it was Charlotte who told him. Apparently his hotshot son couldn't be bothered with anything having to do with his old man's feelings. Fausto Geraci snapped. He wasn't proud of it, but for once he'd spoken his mind. Those girls had transferred schools in the middle of a school year and come here and done just great, and now what? They want those poor kids to transfer *back,* two months before the school year was even over? What a selfish load of shit! Don't they know *anything* about how hard it is for kids to fit in? He wouldn't stand for it. Let Nick go back. Charlotte, too. God knows, there were more places to blow money in New York than out here. But the girls were staying. Did she think Fausto Geraci, after a life full of taking care of other people's problems, couldn't take care of those two little angels for a couple months? Was she really such a stupid cunt that she thought she'd do a better job than he would?

While he was telling her off, he did, yes, break some things, but they were his things. The tears he shed were tears of rage. Now his goddamned kids wanted him to go see a doctor.

That's what a man gets for speaking the truth. Nothing. Fausto Geraci was a man with nothing good in his life except for his two granddaughters and a Mexican woman who lived in a trailer and barely knew a thing about him. And now the girls were gone. He drove them to the train station himself and saw them off with a big wave and cheerful good-bye. His son and that woman didn't even look back, and neither did the older girl. But Bev turned around, unhunched her shoulders, and blew him a kiss. What a smile! She should smile more, that Bev.

The trip to the train station had made him miss his lunch with Conchita. He didn't feel like taking his drive either. He went home to his empty house. He could have been alone anywhere, but he was used to that patio. It was only a matter of time, he thought, before Conchita vanished, too. Fausto Geraci looked out at his pool. One more Chesterfield King, maybe two—three at the most—and then he'd drain that goddamned thing for good.

Historians and biographers have often noted that every bold decision of Michael Corleone's formative years was made in opposition to his father. Joining the Marines. Marrying a woman like Kay Adams. Joining the family business while Vito Corleone was in a coma and helpless to prevent it.

Entering the narcotics trade. Some sources have even suggested that Michael Corleone used his father's death as an excuse to go to war with the Barzinis and the Tattaglias sooner than Vito Corleone had thought prudent.

The first breach in this pattern may have been Michael's decision to keep Nick Geraci alive. Whatever one might say about the consequences of that decision, it was exactly what his father would have done, for four reasons.

First, naming Geraci the *capo* of Tessio's old *regime* had, as Michael expected, put to rest any lingering resentment over Tessio's unfortunately necessary execution. He was popular with the men on the street, who had no idea he was O'Malley, who merely thought he'd been in Tucson opening up new business ventures, which Geraci in fact had done. The Corleones had a few shylocks up and running, owned a bar and grill and a police captain, and had tapped into a source for marijuana that was protected by a former president of Mexico.

Second, every reason to be wary of Geraci had been tempered or eliminated. Even if Chicago, Los Angeles, or San Francisco never sent someone to kill him, he'd be worried about it, which would rein in his aggressiveness. He seemed deeply, sincerely grateful to Michael for ensuring his protection after Forlenza's ridiculous kidnapping stunt, setting him up in Tucson, and engineering his return to New York. And now that Narducci was poised to take over in Cleveland, Geraci's ties to Forlenza were of little concern.

Third, Geraci was a great earner. His every human transaction leaked gold.

Fourth, Michael Corleone needed peace. His organization was not the U.S. Marine Corps. He had neither enough nor good enough personnel to wage war indefinitely. Keeping Geraci alive helped Michael cement the perception that Louie Russo was to blame for that crash, a key component of the peace agreement formalized at that first summit meeting in upstate New York.

So why the need for a *second* meeting? Why the need to hold such meetings annually? And why hold them in the same location?

The men who assembled for the first time in that white clapboard farmhouse certainly had no compelling reason to agree to reconvene there the following year (and, indeed, the 1957 meeting, by all accounts, was a routine affair, almost certainly unnecessary, a historical footnote to the 1956 meeting and the fateful one in the spring of 1958). The issues they had come to discuss and resolve had been discussed and resolved. The peace struck that day was historic and enduring; to this day, there has not been an outbreak of violence between Families comparable to the

1955–1956 war (or to the two that preceded it, either, the Five Families War of the 1940s and the Castellammarese War of 1933). There was no precedent for scheduling such a meeting; all previous summit meetings had been convened only in direct response to existing problems.

The decision to hold these meetings annually was made *not* at the 1956 meeting but soon thereafter. None of it would have happened if it weren't for the sudden turn in the weather and, more so, that gargantuan pig.

Michael had intended to leave immediately after all the business had been transacted. But for hours, the windows had been open. For hours, the aroma of that roasting pig had wafted in, working its succulent magic. Clemenza—like most everyone else there—was hardly the sort of man who'd leave on a long drive without having a slice or six. The garlic bread was good enough to make grown men weep, if not these particular grown men. Still: great bread. Also there was pie. A humble but inviting feast on what, propitiously, turned out to be the first warm day of spring. Men lingered. To have done otherwise would have been an *infamità*.

Michael Corleone felt an icy hand on the back of his neck. "I can't eat pork," Russo said. His voice was barely lower than Michael's three-year-old daughter's. "Breaks my heart. But if I eat it," he tapped his chest, "it'll break it worse. A word with you before I go?"

They went for a walk together across the lawn as the other men dug in. Russo's *consigliere* went to get the car.

"I didn't want to say this back there. I'm new. The new man should shut up and listen."

Michael nodded. Russo had actually talked plenty at the meeting.

"I'm not an educated man such as yourself," he said in that odd, high voice, "but I'm confused about something. When you were talking at the end there about *change*, you lost me."

"I have no interest in telling others how to run their business. But there will come a time when others will take control of street crime, the way Italians took over from the Irish and the Jews. Just look at the Negroes, who in some cities are gaining more power every day."

"Not Chicago."

"In any case, I see no point in our amassing greater power and prosperity if we don't use it to move out of the shadows and into the light. And that's what I intend to do."

Laughter echoed in the dusk. Sitting on a big rock beside the tent, Pete Clemenza and Joe Zaluchi, related through the marriage of their children, were holding court and telling stories.

"You're losing me again with the shadows and light."

Michael started to explain.

"No, no, no," Russo said. "Don't talk to me like I'm *stupid*."

Michael did not apologize or acknowledge the petty outburst, which was shocking in a Don, even one from Chicago.

"I'll put it to you like this," Russo said. "You talk about how one day our kids can be congressmen, senators, even president, yet we got fellas like that on *our* payrolls."

"Never a president," Michael said, thinking of the Ambassador, and thinking *not yet*.

"Not yet," Russo said. "Don't look at me like that. I know you talked to Mickey Shea. You think you're the only one he's making deals with?"

Several Dons were looking their way. The last thing Michael needed was to have anyone think he was plotting something. "We should get back," he said.

"I'm not *getting* back, remember?" Russo said. "I'm going. Look, all I'm trying to say is that, at least in Chicago, we elect who we want, and once they're in office we get out of them what we want to get out of them. Even the ones *we* don't control are controlled by *someone*."

Don't talk to me like I'm stupid, Michael Corleone thought but did not say.

"Why, then," said Russo, "would we wish this on our children? Why would we want for them to be puppets? We ain't naive, you know, none of us, yet some of us got this big naive dream. I don't understand it. I don't understand it one bit."

The men under the tent were calling for them.

Michael smiled. "No man is beyond the control of others, Don Russo. Not even us."

"Just wanted to say my piece," Russo said. "Oh, and also—"

"Hey, Mike!" Clemenza called. "When you get a chance, we need you for something."

"Yes?" Michael said to Russo.

"Real quick," Russo said. "I want to clear the air and be done with it. I'm sure you know that Capone sent my brother Willie and another guy to help Maranzano out, back when him and your father were havin' it out."

So *this* was what the walk had really been about.

"So I've been told," Michael said. The *help* had been a contract on Vito Corleone. The only part of Willie "the Icepick" Russo that had made it back to Chicago was his severed head.

"I blame Capone. I want you to know that. It wasn't none of his business, the problems in New York." Russo extended his soft and tiny hand. "Your father just did what he had to do."

Michael accepted the handshake, which became an embrace, sealed with a kiss, and Don Russo got into his idling car.

"Where'd Don Russo go?" Clemenza asked when Michael got back to the tent. It must have almost killed Pete not to be able to call him "Fuck-face" to the other Dons.

"He can't eat pork," Michael said.

"I thought Vinnie Forlenza was our token Jew," Zaluchi said.

"Enough!" Forlenza said from his wheelchair. "If it wasn't for the Jews I sent to Las Vegas, most of you bums wouldn't have a pot to piss in."

"We'd have even more money than they made us," said Sammy Drago, the Don of Tampa, "if we had a dime for every time we hadda hear you tell us about 'em."

Forlenza waved him off in disgust. "Hey, Joe. You called for a vote, let's vote."

Blissed out on barbecue and good company, Pete had said they ought to hold these things every year, and Joe Zaluchi had raised a glass in assent and pushed for a postmeeting vote. All but one of the Commission members were still there. The vote was unanimous.

Not long before he returned to New York, Nick Geraci met Fredo Corleone in a saloon on the set of *Ambush at Durango*. It looked real enough if you didn't look up at the cables and catwalks. Fredo had a part in the movie ("Card Sharp #2") but wasn't yet in costume. They sat at a table near the swinging doors. They were the only ones there. Outside, the director, a German with a monocle, yelled at someone because he disliked the color and texture of the mud.

"You see this shit?" Fredo said, throwing the morning paper on the table. MOVIE QUEEN HONEYMOONS HERE WITH HOODLUM HUSBAND, the headline read. The first two paragraphs had innocuous quotes from Deanna Dunn. The third mentioned that Fredo was in the movie, too, "making his screen debut as a bad guy." After that, the story was a clip job, full of old news that had, over the years, already appeared in papers in New York and was peppered with the word *allegedly*. There were pictures, though. Fredo was furious they'd dredged up the shot of him sitting on the curb right after Vito had been shot, bawling his eyes out instead of trying to save the old man's life. "I don't play the *bad guy*," Fredo said. "I catch the bad guy *cheating*."

"What's the point?" Geraci said. "If you call the paper or go down there, then they'll really have a story. It'll make things worse. That's a nice suit, by the way. You have a guy?"

"You said *worse*? Right? So you *agree*. This *is* bad. You don't get to *worse* from *good* or *just fine*. Not unless you're already at *bad*."

"What do you care?" Geraci said. "It's the fucking Tucson newspaper."

"They got all *kinds* of facts wrong."

Like the fact that Deanna Dunn qualified as a movie "queen" anymore. She was a lush, and her looks and her career were suffering for it. Geraci figured she'd married Fredo only so she could keep living the high life even when her roles dried up completely.

Outside, the director yelled "Action!" A buckboard wagon hurtled down the dusty street, and Deanna Dunn began screaming.

"That's in the script," Fredo said. "Fontane dies and Dee Dee screams." She was playing the sheriff's widow. Johnny Fontane was the gunslinging priest.

"You want facts," Geraci said, "there are better places to go than a newspaper."

"We got married a *month* ago. It wasn't a secret, like it says, and we already took a honeymoon. Weekend in Acapulco at that place with the pink Jeeps that go down to the beach."

"Short honeymoon."

"We're busy people."

"Hit a nerve, did I?"

"Hey, who wouldn't want to spend more time on his honeymoon, y'know?"

Geraci wouldn't, not if he had to be stuck in a hotel room with a woman as militantly self-absorbed as Deanna Dunn. Unless maybe you could make her scream like that in the sack. The director called action on another take. Deanna's screams sounded even better. "I've never been to Acapulco," Geraci said. "Nice?"

"I don't know. Sure. It's like a lot of places, I guess." Fredo pounded his fist on the table, right on the photo of him getting into a limo at the airport. "Explain this to me, huh? She's been here three weeks solid, me off and on, now all of a sudden this shit's news?"

"You married a movie star, Fredo. What did you expect?"

"I married a movie star a *month* ago."

"You're a movie star now yourself, for God's sake."

"Aw, that's just for shits and giggles, the acting. I got like two lines."

"Still."

"So why don't they talk about me as someone with a background in entertainment who's trying to branch out, huh?"

Geraci recognized Michael Corleone's words in his brother's mouth. Michael had gone along with Fredo's more public image as something useful in helping to make the Corleones legitimate, or at least ostensibly so.

"Look," Geraci said. "I been reading that paper for months. Trust me, nobody reads it."

Fredo laughed. A moment later the smile drained from his face. "You meant that as a joke, right?"

Geraci shrugged, but then smiled.

"*Coglionatore*," Fredo said, smiling too, punching Geraci's shoulder affectionately.

Until three weeks ago, when the filming on this movie started, Geraci had barely ever spoken to Fredo. He'd turned out to be a thoroughly likable guy.

"You think all that whiskey's real?" Fredo said, pointing to the clear, unlabeled bottles behind the rough-hewn bar.

"How would I know? Why don't you go look?"

Fredo dismissed the notion with a frown and a wave. "Last thing I need."

Geraci nodded. "Aspirin?"

"Had some."

"That was some night."

"I'll tell you what," Fredo said, shaking his head and suddenly looking both rueful and amazed. "Anymore, every night is some night."

Last night, they'd taken their wives and gone out on the town, such as it was. On a whim, they'd headed to Mexico. When they'd gotten there, Deanna Dunn insisted on going to see a donkey show. Charlotte, at least as of this morning, still wasn't speaking to him. Though she might have been angry because all night, no matter what anyone said about anything, Deanna Dunn brought the conversation back to Deanna Dunn. Geraci started changing the subject arbitrarily, but no matter how ridiculous the changes were, she took it as a cue to tell another Deanna Dunn story. After they got home, Char had accused him of flirting. He'd let it roll off his back. She couldn't help but be disappointed that the Movie Queen she'd been so excited about hobnobbing with turned out to be a large-headed loudmouth who joked about how her husband didn't like blow jobs—with Fredo sitting right there, like a man trying to smile through bowel cramps—and who thought that watching a donkey fuck a teenage Indian girl was a hoot. Give Charlotte time, though, and she'd be telling all the hens back in East Islip about her wild night, making herself sound like some jet-setter.

From down the street came a horrible splintering crash. The buckboard.

"Don't worry," Fredo said. "That's in the script, too."

"Yeah, well," Geraci said. "Forgive me if I'm a little jumpy about crashes."

"I don't have that kind of power," Fredo said. "You want forgiveness, it's Mike's department."

Geraci tried not to look surprised. He'd never heard Fredo voice any sort of resentment toward his brother. "So Fontane's here?"

Fredo shook his head. "They flew in some writer to write him out of the picture, can you believe that? It's his stand-in that's out there dying."

Fontane's inattention to his own production company was getting to be a bigger and bigger problem, but this was the first time he'd ever skipped out on a movie in the middle of shooting. "So that's all?" Geraci said. "He's going to get away with that?"

"I don't want to get into it," Fredo said. "I got Dee Dee in one ear, my brother in the other, fucking Hagen in the other."

"You have three ears?"

"Feels like it," Fredo said. "It ain't a feeling I'd recommend."

They got down to business. Geraci had expected Fredo—as he had done other times they'd sat down to meet—to relay messages about Geraci's operation back in New York. Instead, Fredo gave him the news about the peace talks the day before. It was all set: Geraci was going home.

This, too, was the sort of thing a guy might hear right before he got clipped. But if that's what was going to happen, why had Mike sent Fredo?

"You okay?" Fredo said. "Your hearing going or something? I'd've thought a guy gets news like this he'd be on cloud nine."

Men from the lighting crew had come in and started to set up a shot. Prop guys scattered sawdust on the floor and set out playing cards, poker chips, dirty glasses, and sheet music for the presumably doomed piano player. "It's just going to be complicated, that's all," Geraci said. "Going home."

Fredo lowered his voice. "Hey, how are you with the Straccis? I mean, you know, how were you? Before all this down here. I got a reason for asking."

"I've got guys there I work with." Without the tributes he paid to Black Tony Stracci, the drugs could never land in Jersey and get to New York so smoothly. "What's your reason?"

"I've got this idea. There might be something in it for you. New source of income. Could be one of the best things we ever had. When I talked to Mike, he said no dice, but the more I get to know you, the more I think you and me together can make him come around."

"I don't know, Fredo." Geraci hoped he didn't show it, but he was shocked. Fredo hardly knew him yet was enlisting him to defy Michael Corleone. "If the Don turned it down—"

"Don't worry about that. I'll take care of that. I know him like nobody knows him."

"I'm sure that's true," Geraci said. This sort of open disloyalty would have been outrageous coming from some neighborhood punk. But from the *sotto copo*? From the brother of the Don? "I have to be straight with you, though, Fredo. I'm not going to—"

"I appreciate what you're saying, but hear me out, okay? Okay. So here it is. You're a lawyer, right? Did you know it's against the law to bury people in San Francisco?"

Wrong, he wasn't a lawyer, but Geraci didn't bother to correct him. Just then, Deanna Dunn burst through the swinging doors.

"Barkeep," she growled, "gimme a shot of your best red-eye."

"That's pretty good," Geraci said, because it was. She sounded exactly like the actor who played the villain in this movie, a grizzled lout who'd also started out as a boxer.

"Those aren't real bottles of whiskey," Fredo said.

"This attachment you have to the real," she said, "is very cute. Knock it off, will ya?"

"Oh, and yeah," Fredo said, ignoring his wife and addressing Geraci. "I almost forgot." He grabbed the lapels of his own suit. "I do have a guy. He's out in Beverly Hills, but I fly him to Vegas for fittings. He's Fontane's guy out there, too, which is how I heard about him."

"Unlike you," said Deanna Dunn, "Johnny *has* to have his pants made special. Otherwise they wouldn't fit right because his dick's—"

Fredo smiled wanly. "It's true."

"Big one, huh?" Geraci couldn't believe Fredo was going to let her get away with that.

"That's what they say," Fredo said.

"Who's they?"

"Oh, *darling*." Deanna Dunn turned a chair around and straddled it. "Who *isn't* they?" She waggled her eyebrows.

Geraci could see in Fredo's eyes that he was mad, but the smile lingered gruesomely on his face of the underboss.

"I did a picture with Margot Ashton," said Deanna Dunn, "while she was still married to Johnny. The director—Flynn, that fat Mick slob—was razzing her about being married to a skinny ninety-eight-pound weakling like Johnny Fontane. This was awhile back, you know. So in front of *ev-v-v-v-v-verybody*, Margot says, *real loud*, 'He may be skinny, but his proportions are perfect. Eight pounds Johnny and ninety pounds of cock.'"

Fredo exploded in shrill laughter.

"Lovely woman, Miss Ashton," Geraci said. *And you, Miss Dunn, are eight pounds Deanna and ninety pounds of gigantic head.*

"Naturally," Deanna said, "after she said that, I made it my business to see if she'd been exaggerating."

The only people Geraci had ever seen whose faces could go from joy to despair as swiftly as Fredo Corleone's were his beautiful daughters', but only when they were still babies.

"And so it is with great pleasure, in front of all you good people, that I can reveal, at long last, and I do mean long—"

"I should go home," Geraci said, and he did. He'd hear about the stiffs in San Francisco some other time.

One thing kept bothering Pete Clemenza.

That night at the Castle in the Sand? When they were watching Fontane and Buzz Fratello and Dotty Ames, until Mike got the phone call from Hagen with the news about the plane crash? Why did Mike tap Clemenza on the shoulder to get his attention to leave *before* he even started talking to Hagen? How did he know they'd be getting up and going?

Not that Clemenza would ever say anything.

But it's the kind of little thing a guy thinks about a lot. Kind of thing that can make a guy go outside at two in the morning in his silk pajamas, light a good cigar, flip on the floodlights, and wax the living shit out of his Cadillac.

Chapter 15

THE CONGRESSMAN—a former state attorney general, a vigilant opponent of the incursion of the Cosa Nostra into his beloved Silver State, and also, for what it's worth, a rancher whose property lay downwind of Doomtown—first received his grim diagnosis in the hospital's newly completed Vito Corleone Wing. When he went back to Washington, he got a second opinion from a specialist. The news was the same: the Big C; lymphatic, inoperable; six months to live. He chose to keep his illness a secret and fight it. If anyone was tough enough to lick the Big C, it was that big ox. A year later and eighty-eight pounds lighter, he died. As so often happens, the person whose constitutional responsibility it was to appoint a successor was a political rival of the deceased. The governor asked Thomas F. Hagen, a prominent Las Vegas attorney and financier, to abandon his long-shot bid for his party's Senate nomination and accept the appointment to Congress. Mr. Hagen graciously agreed to put aside his plans for the chance to serve the good people of the State of Nevada.

The appointment was unpopular. The issue was less Hagen's associates—he was hardly the only politician in that era with such associates—than his brief tenure as a Nevada resident. Also, he was a political novice with no record of public service. Every newspaper in the state, without exception, criticized the choice and gave the controversy prominent coverage. The primary added further complications. The late congressman had been running unopposed. Lawsuits abounded, but the November general election was shaping up as a contest between Tom Hagen and a dead man.

To build power, sometimes one must control those who seem the least powerful. This was the secret of the Corleones' ability to control judges. Though corruption and venality thrive in all classes of men, the normative judge—the public might be relieved to know—is more honest than the normative human being. In practice, judges are difficult and expensive to control. However. Cases are typically assigned "randomly" by a clerk of court who's paid no more than, say, a normative Spanish teacher. A person who controls ten percent of such people and a majority of the judges is vastly less powerful than one who's sewn up most of the clerks and a few strategically placed judges afflicted by cynical natures, bad habits, or dark secrets.

Newspapers work the opposite way. Some reporters can be swayed by a free lunch, a forgiven gambling debt, even a glass of ice-cold beer. But most have a crusading streak and a fixation on whatever strikes them as news that overrides their loyalty to anything. Happily, they are also excitable, eager for newer news, toward which they follow one another like lemmings. To control the news, one needs influence at the top. The public has a short memory. If a story goes away after a few days and is replaced by something new, the public wants not closure to the old but newer details about the new. Or something newer still. Control those who control those who decide how long to cover a story and where it goes in the paper, and you control the news.

After a few days, a magnetic, strange-looking man in black leather and blacker sideburns—a popular music sensation from Mississippi, a white boy screaming Negro songs—came to Las Vegas for the first time. Hagen was supplanted on the front page and in the public's imagination by gleeful news of the hillbilly sensation's poor performance and speculation about whether this signaled an end not just to the young hick's career but also to the whole vulgar, allegedly Communistic fad known as "rock and roll." The day Hagen was sworn in and flew to Washington to assume his duties, the only mention of him in any Nevada paper was a story by one dogged reporter from Carson City, who, from the wilderness of an inside page, tried to sort out the legal battle over the congressional contest. The late congressman's party was beset by infighting and injunctions and seemed increasingly unlikely to be able both to pick a candidate and to get that candidate onto the ballot in time. Congressman Hagen was faring better. Though he'd been appointed to office well after the filing deadline for the November ballot, he'd submitted all the necessary petitions and paperwork within a week of the announcement of his appointment. The clerk of the court was quoted as saying that, under the circumstances, the request by Hagen's lawyers to grant him the necessary extension promised to be "a routine matter."

The Dons and their top men were acting more and more like the top men in corporations or governments. This, Hagen knew, was what Michael thought he wanted: to be *legitimate*. Michael was continuing down this road without Hagen's advice. Until it was sought, Hagen would keep his reservations to himself.

Unlike Hagen, Michael had never worked for a corporation. In *this* business, who gets hurt who hasn't brought it on himself? It's rare. But in "legitimate" businesses? Before Hagen had quit to go to work for Vito Corleone, he'd spent his final months as a corporate lawyer working on "acceptable death rates": How many innocent people would have to die

various ways in various crashes of cars manufactured by the firm's client before the fully expected lawsuits justified the cost of installing safer, more expensive parts. Babies, high school kids, pregnant women, brilliant young white men with high salaries: all researched, all calculated, all written down in the report he filed the day he quit. What did *those* people do to bring on their deaths?

The government was worse, which Hagen knew long before he took office himself. Remember "Remember the Maine"? All a big lie concocted so the United States could go to war under false pretenses and the men in charge could make their rich friends richer (including the newspaper moguls who self-servingly spread the lie in the first place). More people died in that trumped-up war than in every Mafia conflict put together. It's only the negative stereotypes about Italians that make people think they're a threat to the average Joe. The government, on the other hand, wages nonstop war on the average Joe, and the suckers just eat their bread, go to their circuses, and keep on pretending they live in a democracy—a lie so cherished they can't grasp the self-evident, that America is run entirely via backroom deals involving the rich. In almost every election, the richer candidate defeats the poorer candidate. When the poorer candidate wins, it's usually because he's agreed to be a stooge for people richer than the ones who backed his opponent. Go ahead, try voting the bastards out. See what happens. More to the point: see what doesn't. That ought to be his slogan: *Hagen for Congress. See What Doesn't Happen.*

Hagen doubted that the world had ever seen a better racket than the American government. It's hard to sue the government, for example, and even if you win, so what? Here's a million bucks. Then they raise taxes two million. Plus, with businesses, someone somewhere has to buy their crummy product. What are people supposed to do about the government? It's yours, it's *you,* you're stuck with it, end of story.

For years, Hagen had been working out deals with politicians, looking into their dead eyes and seeing what soulless opportunists those men had become, long before Hagen ever set foot in their offices to explain whatever mutually beneficial arrangement they would have little choice but to accept. These men—and, very occasionally, women—accepted without objection, thanked Hagen, shook his hand, smiled those public-servant smiles, and told him to come back anytime. If Hagen ever looked in the mirror and saw that look in his own eyes, he might just have to put a bullet between them.

He'd never expected to hold elected office outside the state of Nevada (and was reluctant even to do that), and he never would have if not for the unforeseen opportunity provided by his predecessor's death. The people of Nevada seemed as alarmed to find Tom Hagen in Congress as he was to

be there—though less alarmed than his wife, Theresa. The criticism of his appointment, even after it had died down, was too much for her. She was concerned about the effect it would have on the kids. And the idea of being a Washington wife gave her the creeps. "You always seem to get what you want," she'd told him, "and I know you well enough to know you never wanted this." He tried to deny it, and she saw through him. She needed time to think about all this. She took the kids and went to spend the summer with her folks at the Jersey shore.

Perhaps it was precisely because Tom Hagen had gone into this so grudgingly that his arrival in Washington was such a shock to his system. As his taxicab crossed the Potomac, it hit him, really, where he was, who he was. As realistic as Hagen was about what went on in that city, the sight of the Lincoln Memorial put a lump in his throat.

That first night in his hotel, when he couldn't sleep, he initially blamed it on jet lag and coffee, but he flew all the time and drank coffee by the gallon and ordinarily could go to sleep anytime he allowed himself to do so. He pulled back the curtain and saw the lights of the Mall, and felt goose bumps.

He was a millionaire. He was a *United States congressman*. He started laughing.

Then he got dressed.

The impulse had come from the heart, and he was in the elevator before he thought about what an indefensibly sentimental thing he was about to do.

He knew even as it was happening that this was not a story he could ever tell to anyone.

He crossed Constitution Avenue and stood at the west end of the Reflecting Pool, which smelled like rotten eggs. Lights shone on the water. A couple opposite him held hands and kissed. What tremendous beauty.

He was an *orphan,* that's what he was. When he was ten, his mother went blind and then died and his father drank himself to death, and Hagen got stuck in an orphanage and ran away and lived on the street for more than a year before he made friends with Sonny Corleone and Sonny brought him home like a stray puppy. At the time, it had made no sense that Sonny's father had gone along with this, but Hagen had been too grateful to question anything. After that, it became something Hagen didn't think about. His mother died of a venereal disease and his father was a violent, rampaging, death-courting drunk. Hagen was an expert about not talking about things or thinking about them a long time before Vito Corleone honed and harnessed those skills.

But that night it suddenly hit him. *Vito* had been an orphan, too, taken in by the Abbandandos at about the same age as Hagen was taken in by the Corleones. Vito grew up in the same house as the man who would become his *consigliere*. Vito had re-created a mirror image of that dynamic in his own house, as first Sonny and then Michael used Hagen in that role.

Hagen turned around slowly, arms out, taking it all in, the Lincoln Memorial, the Jefferson Memorial, the Washington Monument. The Capitol and, above it, the seemingly random stars that had somehow aligned for that to be his new place of business. Hagen stayed where he was, at the west end of the pool, both reflected and reflecting, and kept turning around. He didn't believe in God, an afterlife, or anything mystical, but at that moment he did, without a doubt, feel the presence of the dead, heavy and literal as a block of ice. Washington, Jefferson, and Lincoln. The late congressman. Sonny and Vito Corleone. Bridget and Marty Hagen. Those untold thousands of men who'd taken bullets in the head and heart for something bigger than their own immediate families and interests. All the people whose lives had been laid down so that he could have his—so that, for however long, he would find himself here, transformed into some excellent gray-haired stranger named Congressman Thomas F. Hagen.

During his time in Congress, he'd often think back to this moment and the euphoria he'd felt—usually at one of the surprisingly many times people seemed legitimately and even selflessly interested in improving the lives of strangers. Unlike those whose early days in Washington were spent watching their naive idealism swiftly ground to dust, pulverized by the realities of politics and money, Hagen had no ideals to crush. When congressmen he'd last seen when he'd come to bribe them saw him inside the Capitol and introduced themselves, pretending never to have met him, Hagen was only mildly amused. He'd spent his life sitting in an office while people paraded in one by one, asking for favors, so their piggishness barely registered on him, either. On the other hand, while virtue and altruism are in short supply on Capitol Hill, for a man incapable of disillusionment, they're everywhere.

That first night in Washington, though, his euphoria was finally interrupted when, as he was staring up at the night sky, he felt the barrel of a gun against his ribs. It was a Negro in a white cowboy hat with a bandanna over his face. He wore crepe-soled shoes. Hagen hadn't heard him coming.

"Hope that watch doesn't have sentimental value," the man said.

"It doesn't," Hagen said, though it had been an anniversary present from Theresa. Not a milestone anniversary, but he did like the watch. "It's just a watch."

"It's a hell of a *nice* watch."

"Thanks. Be sure to point that out to your fence. I like the hat, by the way."

"Thanks. You're rich, huh?" he said, handing back Hagen's emptied wallet.

"Less so now," Hagen said. He'd only had a couple hundred dollars on him.

"Sorry about that," the man said, turning away. "It's just business, you know?"

"I understand completely," Hagen called after him. Had the city ever seen a more cheerful mugging victim? "Good luck to you, friend."

Hagen, being Hagen, had left plenty of time for the drive from Theresa's parents' house in Asbury Park down the shore to his party's national convention in Atlantic City, and it was only after he hit Atlantic City and the traffic was rerouted and snarled that he had any reason to check his watch. He'd replaced the one that had been stolen with a replica of it so he wouldn't have to say anything to Theresa. But he'd left it on the nightstand. He could picture it. It was right next to his convention credentials. He slammed the steering wheel with the palm of his hand.

It had been ridiculous not to get a hotel in Atlantic City, but he'd been trying to bring Theresa around, and it had been great to see the kids. Even the boys had been glad to see him, shooting baskets in the driveway and talking about girls and cars and even that barbaric, tuneless music they loved. It had all worked out great. Theresa was coming home at the end of the summer—Hagen hadn't been sure she would—and had even said she would consider showing up at various campaign events, so long as Tom wrangled her an appointment to the board for the proposed new museum of modern art. But he'd underestimated how much the drives back and forth would take out of him, and of course *naturally* the day the traffic was the worst was the only day he really had to be there, and it also just figured that, spread so thin, he'd forget things. If he hadn't tried to do so much in such a little time, he'd have traveled with his chief of staff—an unlikable but witheringly efficient young Harvard-educated twit recommended to him by the governor—and Ralph would have made sure he had everything, no matter how distracted his boss had been by running out to the beach for a last-minute swim with his daughter.

Hagen had no idea how long he'd been beating the steering wheel when he caught sight of himself, red-faced and sweating, a heart attack waiting to happen. He took a deep breath. He pulled out a comb and put himself together.

With no parking pass, he took a spot far up the boardwalk from Convention Hall. By the time he got there, he was soaked with sweat, so disheveled that, despite several inventive tactics with different gatekeepers, he failed to talk his way into the hall in time to see Governor James Kavanaugh Shea's nominating speech. From the roar of the crowd, it seemed to be going well.

For the first time, Hagen noticed the words carved into the hall's limestone facade: CONSILIO ET PRUDENTIA. Latin. "Counsel and prudence." *Consiglio. Prudenza.*

The way things were going, it wouldn't surprise Hagen if someday the Mob rented an arena like this for its own business. Shock, yes, but not surprise. If Hagen were still *consigliere,* his first words of counsel would be that the gatherings of men from various Families—weddings, funerals, title fights, one nightclub's secret owners trying to impress another's with the biggest shows, the biggest names—had become too frequent, too public, too *glamorous,* even the funerals. He'd heard that the meeting in New York had led to an agreement that they'd meet annually. What next? Printed stock certificates? Live television coverage?

From inside, more cheers.

Hagen heaved a sigh, walked across the boardwalk, and took a seat on the bench.

A few hundred yards away, crews scrambled to finish the temporary stage for Johnny Fontane's outdoor concert later tonight. A film crew set up, too—on the payroll of Fontane's production company, even though there were no plans to release the footage or to show it anywhere outside Fontane's house in Beverly Hills. Men unloaded trucks bearing risers and chairs—concessions controlled by the Stracci Family.

What difference did it make if Hagen didn't actually hear the speech? Who'd even know he'd missed it? What difference did it make that if it weren't for Tom Hagen and his negotiating skills, this convention would probably have been held in Chicago? Other people got the credit, and, in the end, that was how Hagen liked it. It was against his nature to take credit for things, the way a man has to do if he wants the saps who think we live in a democracy to vote for him.

He mopped his brow, wrung his handkerchief, and mopped it again. Hagen had done the negotiations, but the plan had been Michael Corleone's, and this—holding the convention in Atlantic City—had been its master stroke. It brought everything together. The Straccis controlled the party machine in this state. But Black Tony (who'd been dying his hair jet black since he was a kid) lacked connections outside New Jersey and had been most grateful for the full cooperation of the Corleone-controlled politicians. The Straccis further benefited because they controlled the

linen services and the waste removal in Atlantic City, as well as the illegal casinos in the Jersey Palisades. This had cemented a friendship between the Corleones and Don Stracci, enabling Ace Geraci's *regime* to use the Stracci docks for the smuggling operation that had bankrolled so much of what came thereafter.

Governor Jimmy Shea got credit for bringing the convention and all its economic benefits to New Jersey. He got to make a big speech live on all three networks, prime-time TV, without having to go to the expense of being also-ran in the primaries. In return for these favors, his brother Danny (who didn't know on whose behalf his father was intervening) helped curtail the prosecution of any of the Families in the recent killings. And (again via the Ambassador) Jimmy Shea agreed not to oppose a measure that would legalize gambling in Atlantic City. Now, with a good speech, Jimmy Shea had the chance to lay the groundwork for becoming—whether he knew it or not—the first American president ever to owe his election to the Cosa Nostra.

He'd know it eventually, that was for certain.

From inside the hall came an eruption of applause. A muffled brass band played "Into the Wild Blue Yonder."

This evening was the valedictory to the peace. Hagen had been the point man for it all, but at its culminating moment, where did he find himself? On a bench, across the boardwalk, outside looking in. He'd never even set foot inside Convention Hall. It housed the world's largest pipe organ, he'd been told. Every year, it hosted the Miss America pageant, which Hagen had seen, on TV. No doubt the only difference between Miss Alabama's positions on opportunity (it's knocking!), children (they're the future!), education (for it!), the keys to a good life (hard work! churchgoing! family!), and world peace (possible in our lifetime!) and those of Governor Shea was that Shea didn't have to say it in high heels and a bathing suit.

What the hell. Why should Hagen care?

Hagen walked to the hotel where the Ambassador had rented the main ballroom, figuring that he'd be early but with any luck he'd be able to grab a drink. A blue velvet banner with a union logo on it welcomed the delegates, but the Ambassador had quietly paid for everything. The place was already surprisingly crowded. Jimmy Shea had finished his speech, and a steadily increasing tide of people swept into the room, raving about how inspirational the governor had been, lamenting that it was too bad he'd been giving the nominating speech instead of the acceptance, that maybe Shea—young, attractive, a war hero—would stand a chance in November, unlike that dull scold from Ohio that the party was running as a sacrificial lamb.

Hagen knew that some of these people were plants, paid to talk up Shea's speech, no matter how he'd done. He also knew that Shea's war heroism, while genuine, had been exaggerated in the public's mind by the amount and nature of the news coverage it had received at the time, coverage Hagen had personally orchestrated. And he also knew, even in his brief time in Washington, that the "dull scold from Ohio" was an honorable and formidable man. What being young and attractive had to do with being president, Hagen had no idea. Hagen got a double scotch and water and scanned the room for people whose hand it was prudent for him to go shake. Just then there was a commotion at the door, including gleeful screams. Hagen turned, and as he did a hand pounded him on the shoulder.

"My congressman!" said Fredo Corleone, wearing a white dinner jacket. "Hey, fella, if I promise to vote for you, can I have your autograph?"

Hagen put his mouth by Fredo's ear. "What are you doing here? How's Ma?"

Fredo was drunk. He jerked a thumb toward the doors.

It had not been Shea who entered, as Hagen had presumed, but Johnny Fontane, complete with a sizable entourage.

"I came with Johnny," Fredo said.

"And Ma?" Two weeks ago Carmela Corleone had been rushed to the hospital for what had turned out to be a blood clot in her brain. At first, she hadn't been expected to make it, but she'd rallied. The last time Hagen had been there, Fredo had assured him he'd stay in New York and oversee things, but here he was: here.

"She's fine," Fredo said. "She's home."

"I know she's home. Why aren't you home with her?"

"Believe me, I'm just in the way up there."

Hagen doubted that. Connie Corleone had left Ed Federici and jetted off to Europe with some drunken playboy and had only sent a telegram and flowers. Carmela's aunt had died earlier that year. Mike and Kay had been there for a while but had had to go back to Nevada. They'd hired a nurse. The only family Carmela had up there was Sonny's daughter Kathy, who lived in a dormitory at Barnard.

Hagen nodded toward the back of Fontane's entourage—Gussie Cicero, a club owner in L.A. and an associate of Jackie Ping-Pong, and two men from the Chicago outfit. "So what are *they* doing here?"

"They came with Johnny, too."

"Come again?"

"Gussie was married to Margot Ashton before Johnny was married to her, remember? And now they're friends of mine. Relax, Tommy. It's a party, y'know. Christ almighty, did you see that speech?"

Fredo had credentials to the convention? "You saw it?"

"On TV. We were up in the penthouse where Gussie and Johnny are staying. Jimmy and Danny were up there last night, too. *Wild*. Hoo boy. You should have come by."

He hadn't been invited, hadn't had any idea. "Jimmy and Danny Shea?"

"Who we talking about? Of course Jimmy and Danny Shea."

Hagen knew he should have this conversation later. After all the bad publicity right after his appointment, being seen in public, here, saying anything more than hello, couldn't be good.

"Where are you staying?"

"So are those the biggest you've ever seen, or what?" Fredo nodded toward Annie McGowan and her famously enormous breasts. She was the blonde walking right behind Fontane, next to the comic Fontane called Numbnuts, whom she'd replaced as Johnny's opening act but who was somehow still a part of Fontane's entourage. Annie McGowan had superseded the aging Mae West as the person whose name people used in big-breasted-woman jokes.

"I should go, Fredo."

"You ever meet her?"

"Once," Hagen said. "She wouldn't remember me."

Finally Jimmy Shea made his entrance, flanked by his father and brother. The room exploded in applause and a recorded version of "Into the Wild Blue Yonder."

"Shea and Hagen in 1960!" Fredo yelled.

As far as Hagen could tell, Fredo was drowned out.

Hagen slipped away. By now the room was packed. He tried to shake hands with the right people, but it was tough. He did what he could, but there were more than a few times he extended his hand toward someone he thought he recognized as a senator or congressman or top aide and got a blank stare in return. He tried to find members of the Nevada delegation—the only people, presumably, who'd have noticed he wasn't there. The only one he saw was a schoolteacher from Beatty, wherever that was.

"Gateway to Death Valley," she said, shouting over the din.

"Oh, right," he said. *They brag about that in Beatty?*

"Mines," she said, "that's what we have there. Though several have closed."

"That's why we need to vote the bastards out," Hagen blurted out.

She frowned. Maybe it was the word *bastards*, maybe because he was one of the bastards she'd like to vote out, but before he could apologize, her face brightened. "You're wonderful!" she screamed in obvious delight.

It took Hagen a second to realize that behind him Governor Shea was drawing near, using his big smile like a snowplow. Shea directed the smile

at the teacher, gave her a thumbs-up, said, "Thank you, good to see you," and patted her on the shoulder. Then the governor shook Hagen's hand—they'd never met—and before his grip even eased he was moving his eyes to the next person in the crowd. That was it. But the postcoital look on the schoolteacher's face gave Hagen an immediate lesson about politics. Being young and attractive had nothing to do with being president but a lot to do with getting elected.

Hagen leaned toward her ear. "So I take it you saw Governor Shea's speech?"

"One *hears* a speech," she said, frowning again.

"Right," he said.

She put her mouth next to Hagen's ear. "Allow me to save you some time, sir," she said. "I've never crossed party lines in my life, but I'm doing so in November, to vote against you."

She pulled back from him, batting her eyes to underscore the sarcasm.

What was he supposed to say, *Lady, my opponent's dead*? "Well, okay," he said, patting her on the shoulder, unconsciously mimicking Shea. "Good to see you."

Hagen slithered through the crowd. Packed as the ballroom was, there was hardly anyone in line at the bar. Nearly everyone was gawking at the many celebrities.

Fontane, Shea, and Annie McGowan had climbed up on a table. Fontane and Shea were arm in arm and Annie was off to the side, her hands clasped in front of her, fig-leaf style. The Ambassador, standing on the floor beside them, stuck his fingers in his mouth and whistled. It was hard for Hagen to look at him and not think of him standing naked and sunburned in his swimming pool. Fontane asked everyone to please join in as they sang "America the Beautiful."

A few years ago, Hagen had taken Andrew to FAO Schwartz to see Annie McGowan, back when Andrew was still little and her puppet show, *Jojo, Mrs. Cheese & Annie,* was just starting. Last year, about the time Annie left Danny Shea (who was married anyway) and she and Johnny Fontane became an item, she'd quit her TV show to become a singer.

Shea climbed down from the table, waving. Fontane and Annie stayed, belting out a show tune that originally had celebrated another state and now sported lyrics extolling the virtues of New Jersey.

Hagen pulled out the index card on which his chief of staff had—in tiny, perfect handwriting—listed what parties to attend tonight, including meticulous directions, names of people to see, even conversational prompts. Screw it. He'd seen enough, had enough. Hagen was going back to Asbury Park to see his family.

On his way out, he saw Fredo sitting in the lobby, talking with the two

Chicago guys and a man in a plaid coat, Morty Whiteshoes, who worked mostly in Miami.

"You leaving, Tom?" Fredo called out.

Tom motioned for him to stay seated. "Catch you later tonight."

"No, hold on," Fredo said, excusing himself. "I'll walk with you. Be right back, guys."

Fredo fell in beside him on the crowded boardwalk. Hagen walked faster than he would have needed to.

"I need to ask you something."

"It's taken care of," Hagen said, presuming this was about the mess last year in San Francisco. "Forgotten, okay? So forget it."

"Look, did Mike ever say anything to you about this idea I had?" Fredo said. "This vision really, where we'd get a law passed so you couldn't bury nobody in New York—any of the boroughs and Long Island, too?"

"Keep it down." Instinctively Hagen looked around.

"I don't mean *that* kind of body burying," Fredo said. "I'm talking about regular, you know? Everybody. You get a zoning thing passed so that—"

"No," Hagen said. "You know I'm out of that end of things. Listen, I really have to go." He cut in front of Fredo and walked backward, hoping to put an end to this. "Tell Deanna I said hello, all right?"

Fredo stopped and looked puzzled. Though it might have been the sunglasses. Hagen couldn't see his eyes.

"Deanna," Hagen said. "Your wife. Ring any bells?"

Fredo nodded. "Tell Theresa and the kids I love them," he said. "Don't forget, okay?"

There was something about the way he said it that Hagen didn't like. He pulled him aside, into an alley. "You okay, Fredo?"

Fredo looked down and shrugged, like one of Hagen's sulky teenage boys.

"Do you want to tell me more about what happened in San Francisco?"

Fredo looked up and took off his sunglasses. "Fuck you, okay? I'm not answerable to you, Tommy."

"What sort of twisted Hollywood bullshit have you gotten yourself into, Fredo?"

"What did I just say? I don't have to answer to you, all right?"

"Why the hell are all of Fontane's friends either sleeping with women he used to sleep with or else used to sleep with the women he's sleeping with?"

"Say what now?"

Hagen repeated himself.

"That's low, Tommy."

It was. "Forget it," Hagen said.

"No, I know you," Fredo said, closing in on Hagen, backing him against the wall of the alley. "You don't forget jack shit. You'll keep turning it over in your mind until you think you got a solution, even if there *is* no solution, or the solution's so simple you couldn't stand it because then you wouldn't get to think about it over"—and here he jabbed Hagen in the breastbone—"and over"—again—"and over"—and again—"and over again."

Hagen had his back against a sooty brick wall. Fredo had been a violent little kid for a while, and then that part of him just disappeared. Until he beat up that queer in San Francisco.

"I should go," Hagen said. "All right? I need to go."

"You think you're so fucking smart." He gave Hagan's chest a little shove. "Don't you?"

"C'mon, Fredo. Easy, huh?"

"Answer me."

"Do you have a gun, Fredo?"

"What's wrong, you afraid of me?"

"Always have been," Hagen said.

Fredo laughed, low and mirthless. He reached up, open-handed, and gave Hagen's cheek something harder than a pat and softer than a slap. "Look, Tommy," Fredo said. "It's not complicated."

What isn't? Hagen pursed his lips and nodded. "It's not, huh?"

"It's not." Fredo had onions and red wine on his breath. He'd missed a spot on his neck, shaving. "See, when you're a pussy hound like Johnny? And all your friends are pussy hounds, too? It's *bound* to happen. Believe me. There's only so much quality pussy on Earth, and eventually the numbers catch up with a guy. You know?"

"In theory," Hagen said, "yeah. Sure. I know."

Fredo stepped backward and put his sunglasses back on. "Next time you talk to Mike," he said, "tell him I got a few more of the details worked out on my idea, all right?"

"C'mon, Fredo. Like I said, I'm out—"

"Just *go,* goddamn it." Fredo pointed vaguely toward the ocean. "You need to go, go."

That night, when Tom Hagen got back to Theresa's parents' house in Asbury Park, his sons were rolling around on the tiny front yard, fighting.

He got out of the car. The fight was, apparently, about a girl, some-

one Andrew had liked first and Frank had kissed. Hagen let it go on for a while, but when he saw Theresa coming through the front door onto the porch he stuck his fingers in his mouth, whistled, then walked into the middle of the fight and separated them. He ordered them to get in the car and then went inside and got his watch. Gianna was watching a TV Western with her grandparents. He picked her up and piled everyone into the car to go get ice cream. "Mom and Dad have ice cream here," Theresa said, but Tom shot her a look and she went along.

They got to the Dairy Duchess out by the highway just as it closed. Tom Hagen went around to the back door and slipped the owner a fifty, and a few moments later the Hagen family was sitting together at a sticky green picnic table under a yellow vapor light: a family. Gianna—nothing if not her father's daughter—ate her cone as fastidiously as a charm-school headmistress, not spilling so much as a sprinkle. Theresa's sundae melted as she dabbed at Andrew's puffy face with a spit-dampened paper napkin. Andrew had something with a brownie inside. Frank wolfed down a banana split in a red plastic boat-shaped dish. Tom just had coffee.

When everyone had finished, Tom Hagen rose and stood at the head of the table and told them they were going to spend the rest of the summer in Washington, as a family. Before school started, they'd all drive back to Nevada together, as a family. When he lost the election to a dead man, as he felt fairly certain he would, they would confront that, too, and how?

Gianna's hand shot up. "As a family!"

"Attagirl," he said, kissing her on top of her red head. "I know this hasn't been easy on any of you. I know that the papers have said some crazy things, and I know people have said things to your face that are worse. But we're in this together. For now, I am a United States congressman. It's an honor, a privilege, a miracle, really. An experience I want you all to remember for the rest of your lives. Our lives."

His children turned to look at Theresa. She took a deep breath and nodded. "You're right," she said. "And I'm sorry I haven't been—"

"No need," Tom said, waving her off. "I understand completely."

He didn't so much forget to tell Theresa and the kids that Fredo loved them as he never found the right moment to do it.

The next day, they got in the car together and drove to D.C. By the time they got there, Ralph had moved Hagen's things into a bigger suite and drafted an intern to act as a tour guide. They saw every monument, got behind-the-scenes tours of the Supreme Court and the Library of Congress. They went to every museum, and Theresa, who had an art history degree from Syracuse, seemed happier than she'd been in years. Tom and the boys played basketball at the congressional gym and got haircuts from the congressional barber.

Ralph even arranged a visit to the Oval Office, as a family, to meet the president. Better yet, Princess, the president's collie and a relative of the dog who played Lassie on TV, had given birth to a litter of puppies and the Hagens were going to get one. They walked from their hotel together and were caught without umbrellas in a downpour. In the picture taken by the official White House photographer, the Hagens, as diminished-looking as a family of dripping wet cats, stand flanking the president, who looks like a man trying to smile through an untimely bowel spasm. Little Gianna holds up the puppy—Elvis, they ended up calling it—grimacing, her eyes on the airborne green bean–sized puppy turd that seems destined for the president's coffee cup.

Tom ordered the biggest print of the photo he could get. The whole family thought it was hilarious. When they went back to Las Vegas, he hung it over the mantelpiece, superseding the Picasso lithograph Theresa had paid a mint for, which looked better in the dining room anyway.

Hagen's defeat was one of the most lopsided in the history of the state of Nevada—by far the most decisive victory the dead had ever exacted from the living, at least at the polls.

Again and again—whether at meetings of the Kiwanis, Rotary International, the United Mineworkers, the teachers union, or the Cattlemen's Association of Nevada—Hagen had proven to be a stiff, humorless, and unpopular speaker. He was an observant Irish-Catholic lawyer in a state run by Baptists and agnostic cowboys. The first time Hagen had really seen his new home state was when he began campaigning in it. There were transients in flea-bitten rescue missions who'd spent more time in Nevada than Tom Hagen. His debate with the congressman's fierce and tiny widow had been a hideous mistake but one Hagen had made out of desperation, a last-ditch effort, since all indications, even at that point, pointed to him as a hopeless long shot. The same poker-faced persuasiveness Hagen had deployed so effectively in delivering hundreds of unrefusable offers came across on TV as frankly reptilian. Nevada has more species of lizards than any state in America. It's a place that knows reptilian when it sees it.

Days before the election, a Las Vegas newspaper reported that Congressman Hagen had not only been the attorney for reputed mobster Vito "the Godfather" Corleone, as was widely known, but also his unofficial ward, which was not. According to the story, Vito's surviving children sometimes even called Hagen their "brother." Hagen denied nothing. He cited himself as one of the thousands of charitable efforts made by members of the Corleone family, along with the largest wing of the biggest hos-

pital in Nevada and the upcoming art museum, which would soon be the best in the country west of the Rockies and east of California. He showed the reporter a copy of the *Saturday Evening Post* article in which the Vito Corleone Foundation was called one of the best new philanthropies of the 1950s and a spread in *Life* that featured Michael Corleone's heroism during World War II. Hagen pointed out that the Corleones, whom the reporter seemed to regard as criminals, had never, to a person, been convicted of a crime of any sort, not even jaywalking. She asked him about the several times they'd been charged with crimes, especially the late Santino Corleone. Hagen handed her a copy of the U.S. Constitution and recommended that she read the part about being presumed innocent until proven guilty. The story pointed out that this turn of phrase appears nowhere in that document.

It was unclear if the reporter or her editor had gotten a tip about Hagen's origins. If they had, it could have come from several different people. Friends and neighbors Hagen had known growing up. Fontane, who'd never liked Hagen. The Chicago outfit, who'd been furious about Hagen's appointment. Maybe even—given the crazy way he'd been acting lately—Fredo. It was not inconceivable that the reporter might have figured it out for herself. However it had happened, neither Hagen nor Michael chose to waste any time trying to figure out such a puzzle, at least for now. What was the point? Even without that article, Hagen had been destined to lose the election, and badly.

Soon afterward, though, back in Washington, a different small puzzle was solved, a more trivial injustice redressed. The culmination of several weeks of the right people asking the right questions came when a red-and-black Cadillac with New York plates pulled up in front of a tenement building near the Anacostia River. Snow fell. Two white men got out of the car, a short one in a shiny suit and a tall one in a gray duster. They went straight to the front door, and almost without breaking stride the man in the duster kicked it open. A moment later, there came a gunshot. This was a neighborhood where gunshots were as common as lizards in Nevada. The man in the shiny suit came out of the building first, carrying a white ten-gallon hat under his arm like a football. Behind him, with Hagen's old wristwatch balled into his fist, came the man in the duster. Upstairs, the mugger—who'd liked the watch too much to sell it—was splayed unconscious on his cold linoleum floor. He'd been brutally kayoed by the tall man, a journeyman heavyweight boxer named Elwood Cusik, whose married girlfriend's abortion had been arranged—in a sterile New York hospital, no less—by a man with various reasons to be loyal to Ace Geraci. The short man—Cosimo "Momo the Roach" Barone, Sally Tessio's nephew— had fired a .38 into the Negro's thieving hand, as a lesson. The thief

hadn't woken up. Cusik, who'd never done a job like this before, lifted the thief's unmaimed hand and checked his pulse. Seemed normal. Same with his breathing. The thief's injuries were the sort that could have been easily avoided by anyone who never robbed anyone. Presuming the man regained consciousness before he bled to death, and unless he had any plans to take up typing or the piano, he'd be fine.

"So who's the wristwatch belong to?" asked Cusik, trying it on in the car.

Momo the Roach didn't answer. He flipped down the visor and checked his exoskeleton-hard shellacked hair in the mirror. They were out of the city before the boxer said anything else.

"The hat belongs to the same guy as the watch or someone else?"

"Try that on, too, why don't you?" the Roach said.

Cusik shrugged and obeyed. The hat fit perfectly. "What do you think?" he said.

The Roach shook his head. "It's you," he said. "Listen, Tex, do me a favor, see if you can shut up as good as you throw a punch."

Again Cusik shrugged and obeyed.

The thief—crumpled on the floor of a tiny room in a part of the world where people were slow to call the police and the police were even slower to respond—did in fact bleed to death. Call it business. Call it destiny. Call it the law of unintended consequences. Whichever. Why should Tom Hagen care? A man does things, and it sets other things in motion. A dead man doesn't have to mean anything. Few do.

Chapter 16

THE MOMENT she first glimpsed the island of Sicily, Kay Corleone gasped.

Michael looked up from the book he was reading—*Peyton Place,* which Kay had bought after her mother, Deanna Dunn, and several women from the Las Vegas Junior League had all recommended it, though she'd finished it hours ago and thought it was lousy. "What's wrong?"

"Nothing's wrong," Kay said. "My God. You never told me how beautiful it is."

He set the book down and leaned across Kay, toward the window. "It is beautiful."

A ridge of snowcapped mountains ringed the walled city of Palermo, visible from the air as a bounty of spires and carved stone and scrolled balconies. It was February, but the Mediterranean was impossibly blue and crested with the gold of the sun, the smoothness of the surface of the water marred only by what seemed the tiniest of vibration, like that of a glass of wine atop a softly playing radio. The runway was on a spit of land northwest of the city. Among the countless things Michael had said to dissuade Kay from coming here on their vacation was that, statistically, this was one of the most dangerous airports in the world. Most of the time, he himself flew into Rome and took a train and ferry here. As the plane banked low, over the water, so close to a small gray fishing boat she could see the men's unshaven faces, Kay—who'd been to Europe before, but always by sea—was thrilled she'd insisted they fly all the way here.

Only when the plane's shadow appeared on the boulders of the coastline did a hot pang of panic shoot through her—*my babies!*—but a pang was all it was. Seconds later, they touched down, a little harder than a person might like but an essentially uneventful landing.

"After all these years," Kay marveled, "here I am in Sicily for the first time."

"Birthplace of Venus," Michael said, rubbing her thigh. "Goddess of love."

For Kay's whole adult life, she'd been hearing about all the things that

were and weren't Sicilian, all the things she could never understand because she wasn't Sicilian. Michael had been here numerous times on business and had even, *for three years,* lived here. The least he could do was show her the place: a week's worth of sightseeing and a second week holed up in a romantic resort carved into a mountainside near Taormina. He owed her that much. At *least* that much.

As the plane taxied toward the terminal, Kay noticed a precisely parked row of tiny Italian cars in the grass infield. Beside the cars, thirty or so people, many with bread or flowers tucked under their arms, stood behind a waist-high rope, smiling and waving at the arriving plane. In front of the rope were four uniformed carabinieri, two with gleaming silver swords on their shoulders, two with their swords sheathed and machine guns held across their chests.

"People you know?" Kay said.

She'd been joking, but Michael nodded. "Friends," he said. "Friends of friends, really. There's supposed to be a surprise party at a restaurant on the beach at Mondello."

She gave him a look.

"I know," he said.

"I thought we had an understanding."

"We do. *I'm* not the one surprising you. No more surprises from *me,* that's the deal. As far as the portion of the world I don't control, you're going to have to take it up with God."

"What's that supposed to mean?" Was he making a crack about her becoming Catholic?

"Nothing," he said. "Look, I wasn't sure it was going to happen. I let you know about it as soon as I saw that it was. It would have been just as much a surprise if the surprise party I told you about ended up not happening, right?"

She shook her head and patted his knee. He *did* need a vacation. Her, too. She put her hand on his thigh. "We can't even check into the hotel and take a shower first?"

"If that's what you really want," he said, which was a way he had of saying *no.* "Try to look surprised, at any rate. For their benefit."

When the plane stopped, the carabinieri without machine guns sheathed their swords, too, and hurried across the tarmac. A stewardess told the passengers to keep their seats.

"What's going on?" Kay whispered.

"No idea." Michael swiveled his head, almost imperceptibly but enough to make eye contact with Al Neri, two rows behind them. That Michael had agreed to go on this vacation with only one bodyguard (albeit his best and most trusted one) seemed to be a clear sign that things had gotten better. And, true to Michael's word, they'd been on airplanes

or in airports for almost two whole days, and it really had been as if Neri weren't there.

The hatch opened. The steps came down. The head stewardess and the carabinieri had a conversation that, though she'd like to think she understood Italian, Kay couldn't quite make out.

The stewardess turned and faced the passengers. "May I have your attention?" she said in perfect English. "Would Mr. and Mrs. Michael Corleone please identify yourselves?"

She had less of an accent than most of Michael's employees. She'd even Americanized the pronunciation of *Corleone*.

Neri stood and walked toward the front of the plane. The stewardess asked if he was Mr. Corleone, and Neri didn't say anything.

Only after he passed Michael and Kay did Michael raise his hand. Kay followed suit.

Kay kept her lips still. "Surprise," she muttered.

"I'm sure it's nothing," Michael said. "Just logistics."

Neri started speaking with the stewardess in Italian—something about protection and about how Michael Corleone was an important man in America and something about rudeness and hospitality, all in hushed enough voices that Kay still couldn't figure out what was going on. Then Neri turned toward Michael and Kay and made a patting gesture—*there, there*. Michael nodded. The stewardess asked that Mr. and Mrs. Corleone remain seated until the other passengers disembarked. Neri took an empty seat toward the front of the plane and stayed there.

"What's going on?" Kay whispered.

"It's going to be fine," Michael said.

"That wasn't what I asked you."

When everyone else had left the plane, the two carabinieri came on board. Neri intercepted them. They had a quick whispered conversation, then proceeded down the aisle and stood next to Michael and Kay.

In Italian, Michael welcomed them. One of the men seemed to know him. Michael gestured for them to have a seat. They remained standing. They explained that reliable sources had indicated that the welcoming party in Mondello was not certainly but quite possibly a trap, that it would be inadvisable for him and his wife to set foot on Sicilian soil at this time.

" 'Reliable sources'?" Michael repeated, in Italian.

The men's faces were implacable. "Yes," the one who seemed to know him said in English.

Michael glanced at Neri, who mouthed the word *Chicago*. What could he possibly have meant by that? Maybe he'd mouthed something else, someone's name.

Michael got up and nodded toward the front of the plane. The carabinieri followed him, and they resumed their discussion there, in whispers,

out of her earshot. Kay didn't know whether to be terrified or furious. Outside, the waving people milled around, gesturing toward the airplane in various demonstrative ways. Several got into their cars and drove away. Kay pulled down her window shade. Finally, Michael clapped the two carabinieri on their backs. "*Bene,*" he said, no longer whispering. "*A che ora è il prossimo volo per Roma?*"

The carabinieri who'd seemed to know him beamed. "We are pleasurable to report," said one, again in English, "that you are upon it." And with that, the men left.

Not only were Michael and Kay and Neri already on the next flight to Rome, it turned out to be a private flight, too. The stewardesses claimed it had been supposed to happen anyway, though they struggled to explain why.

"Deadhead," Michael said. "That's the word you're looking for."

"I beg your pardon?" said the stewardess with the perfect English.

"*Nell 'inglese la parole è* deadhead."

"Deadhead," she said. "Why, thank you." She seemed offended that he'd resorted to Italian. She and the other stewardesses cleaned the cabin and left.

"This is *so* like you," Kay said to Michael. "You *never* wanted to go to Sicily, and now you're getting your way."

"Kay," he said, "you can't be serious."

"Think of your mother," she said, thinking of the trunk full of gifts sitting somewhere in the airplane. Preparing it had been her reason to live for months, the reason—everyone agreed, even the doctors—that she'd recovered so well from her brush with death.

"I'll have it unloaded," he said. "I know people who can get it all to the right people."

"Of course you do."

"Kay."

"I feel awful, flying all the way here and leaving the kids. For what? For nothing."

Michael didn't say anything. He didn't have to. He'd wanted to go someplace and take the kids. That kind of vacation would have been a vacation for him. The hardest thing he'd have had to do was sit still to be buried in the sand. Kay'd have spent her time tending to Anthony and Mary, which she loved doing but was not a vacation. For two years she'd selflessly done what Michael needed her to do. She'd had to raise the kids almost as if she were a widow (including holding them though hours of inconsolable crying the year he'd been so caught up in whatever he was trying to do in Cuba that he never even came home for Christmas). She still hadn't gone back to teaching and was starting to fear she never would. On her own, she'd coordinated the move to Las Vegas. Then she'd taken on

the even bigger job of designing and overseeing the construction of the whole complex in Lake Tahoe: their house, a bandstand for entertaining, and preliminary architecturally harmonious plans for houses for the Hagens, for Connie and Ed Federici, for Fredo and Deanna Dunn, for Al Neri, even a little bungalow for guests. Kay had been surprised by how much she'd enjoyed building a house, actually: the countless details and decisions, the chance to undertake the ultimate shopping spree, all for the greater good of her whole family. Still, it was work. She'd asked almost nothing from Michael except to go where she'd wanted to go on vacation, just the two of them.

"What are we going to do now," Kay said, "turn around and go home?"

"We don't have to go home. This kind of thing, if you'll recall, was a part of why I didn't want to go with you to Sicily."

"For God's sake, Michael. This is a murder threat we're running away from."

"We're not running."

"Right. We're flying."

"That's not what I mean. And it's not so much a threat as a precaution. Look, Kay, if there's one thing I've been completely . . . what's the word I'm looking for? Steadfast. Right. If there's one thing I've been steadfast about, it's been protecting my family."

Kay looked away and didn't say anything. He was steadfast about everything, actually. His good traits and his bad. It was the best and the worst thing about him.

"Those men," he said, "the carabinieri? One of them is Calogero Tommasino, the son of an old friend of my father's. I've had dealings with his father and with him, too. I trust him. We're certainly in no danger now and probably wouldn't have been at all. Again, just a precaution. Please understand. And you at any rate would *never* have been in any danger, obviously. It's the code not to—" He stopped himself.

"Harm the wives or children," she said, rolling her eyes. "Which no doubt goes double in Sicily, which I can't of course *hope* to understand, can I, because I'm not Sicilian?"

Michael didn't answer her. He looked like hell. Maybe it was just the flight. She couldn't admit it now, but if she'd really understood the ordeal involved in flying from Las Vegas to Palermo, she'd have probably gone along with going to Hawaii or Acapulco.

The pilots got back on board. Neri went up to the cabin to talk to them. Moments later he took a seat, far away from Kay and Michael. The cars and people were gone from the tarmac. The plane took off.

"You actually wouldn't understand," Michael finally said. "How could you?"

"Oh, Christ," Kay said. She got up and sat far away from Michael. Twice in a matter of moments he'd provoked her to use the Lord's name in vain.

He let her go.

But she knew it would work, eventually, her silence. Just because he so expertly wielded silence as a weapon didn't mean that he was invulnerable to it himself, especially from her. She sat on the right side of the plane and patiently watched the Italian coast ease by.

After about an hour he came to her. "Is this seat taken?" he said.

"So'd you finish your book?"

"I did," he said. "I thought it was good, actually. A nice escape."

"If you say so." The book he'd taken to read was Edwin O'Connor's *The Last Hurrah*, which Kay had given him for Christmas. He kept nodding off. Not long after she'd finished her book, he'd picked it up, and she'd taken his. Kay thought *The Last Hurrah* was the best thing she'd ever read about city politics. She was appalled he hadn't loved it. "And, yes, the seat's taken."

"Kay," he said. "The reason you wouldn't understand is because I didn't—" He closed his eyes. Maybe this, too, his struggling for words, had to do with the long flight, but there was something about him now that seemed more shaken up than exhausted. "Because," he said, "it's true that . . . that I haven't been entirely, you know . . ." He let out what started as a frustrated sigh and finished as a soft, agonized moan.

"Michael," she said.

"I want to tell you some things," he said. "I *have* to tell you some things."

Most of the time, she looked at him and hardly recognized the man she'd fallen in love with. He'd had his face smashed, then fixed. His hair was shot through with gray, and—though she told herself it was her imagination—he'd become a dead ringer for his father. But there was the same look in his eyes now as he'd had years ago, on a New Hampshire golf course on a warm starry night, when he told her what he'd done during the war, things he'd never told anyone, and he'd sobbed in her arms. Angry as she'd been, suddenly she just melted.

"I'd like that," she said, her voice quavering. "Thank you." She patted the seat beside her.

He sat. "I'm sorry," he said.

"Don't be," she said, taking his hand. "No apologies. Just talk to me."

They stayed in Rome only long enough to sleep off the jet lag and have a magnificent meal at a restaurant Kay had been to years before with her par-

ents. The next day, with Michael still asleep upstairs, she spoke to the hotel concierge herself and arranged a reservation at a resort in the Swiss Alps. He helped her rent a plane, too, for Michael to fly them there, which she knew he'd love. She'd never been to the Alps, but when they'd flown over them on the way here, she'd promised herself she'd go someday. Turned out, someday would be tomorrow.

When she finished, she turned and saw Al Neri, sitting in a leather chair across the lobby, smoking and chomping a sweet roll. She shook her head and he nodded. She told the concierge she'd been mistaken. She needed two rooms. Preferably not adjoining. He sighed and made an exasperated gesture but dialed the phone and was able to change the reservation.

Kay got an espresso from the hotel bar. The hotel had a glassed-in courtyard, and on her way to get a table, a man about her age whistled at her. A younger man next to him raised an eyebrow and called her beautiful. She tried not to react, but she was a happy woman and in truth they'd made her happier. She was only thirty-two years old. Yes, they were Italian, but it was still nice to think of herself as a woman able to summon blurted compliments from strange men.

She took a seat by herself, bathed in that pink-yellow light so distinct to Rome.

The day Michael had proposed to her, he'd warned Kay that they couldn't be equal partners. Kay had protested; clearly Michael's father confided in his mother, no? True, Michael had said, but his mother's first loyalty had always been to his father, for *forty years*. If things worked out as well with them, Michael had said, maybe someday he'd tell her a few things she didn't really want to hear. Turned out, *that* someday had been yesterday.

Kay should probably be furious, frightened, or at least unmoored. She wasn't. Despite or maybe even because of the things Michael had told her, Kay couldn't remember the last time she'd felt this happy. It was irrational as hell, but then again all happiness was irrational.

Her husband was a murderer. He'd fled to Sicily not because he had been unjustly accused of murdering those two men—the police captain and the dope kingpin—but because he'd shot them, one in the head, the other in the heart and throat. Three years after those killings, Michael came back to America. When he and Kay got together, he confessed that he'd been with a woman, yes, while he was gone, but only because he never thought he'd see Kay again, and at any rate not for six months. What he'd failed to mention until yesterday was that the woman, a teenage peasant girl named Apollonia, had been his wife. The reason it had been six months was because six months earlier she'd been blown sky high in a booby-trapped Alfa Romeo.

His brother Sonny did not die in a car wreck. He'd been shot to hamburger at a tollbooth.

Everything that Tom Hagen had told her two years ago—that Michael had ordered the deaths of Carlo, Tessio, Barzini, Tattaglia, and a host of related others—was true. The day Hagen had told her those things—and told her that if Michael ever found out about it Hagen would be a dead man—had felt like the worst day of her life.

Yesterday, when Michael had trusted her enough to tell her those things himself, had hardly been a good day. But it hadn't been the worst day of her life. No one could have been happy to have heard that those things had happened, but she was, she realized, elated that he'd told her about them. Kay was shocked but not surprised. A wife knows things. Kay knew who Michael was. From the time they'd first met, he'd been the perfect mix of good boy and bad boy. At Connie's wedding, Kay had blamed the strong red wine for her euphoric light-headedness, but what had really done it was Michael's deadpan explanation of his family's business. Afterward, when he dragged her into a family photo—*six years* before they got married—Kay felt like she'd been yanked into the cast of a Shakespeare play. She'd acted reluctant, but it was acting. She'd loved it.

If she was honest, she had to admit that she had her own secrets, ones she still hadn't confessed to Michael. During his years in hiding she'd had a long affair with her history professor at Mount Holyoke (she'd never thought she'd see Michael again, either) that Michael still didn't know about. Deanna Dunn had told her things about Fredo that Kay would never *dare* mention to Michael. And Kay never had let on that Hagen had told her anything.

Kay had fallen in love with Michael the night he'd told her about the horror of those Pacific islands—buddies decapitated, incinerated, rotting in hot mud. He'd told her about the men he'd killed. The raw male violence of it—and the strength this man had shown, not just to survive that but, in her arms, to allow himself to confide in her—had frankly excited her. He'd murdered men there, too, and it had *excited* her. If Kay had been able to fall in love with a man who'd killed men for his country (to fall in love with him, Kay knew, not in spite of this but because of it), how shocked could she be that he'd killed and had men killed in defense of his own blood?

Kay was older now, of course. She was a mother. That changed everything—everything but the way she felt now. She finished her coffee. Her heart raced.

She went back upstairs (she heard Neri following but didn't turn to watch), chained the door behind her, drew open the curtains, and flooded the room with light. Michael stirred but didn't wake. Kay got undressed and burrowed under the covers next to him.

"We're going to the Alps," she whispered. Her heart was going even faster.

"I don't ski," he said.

"We're not going skiing," she said. "I'm not sure we'll even leave the room."

"Except for Mass, obviously."

He wasn't mocking her. "Not even that," she said. "I don't have to go every day." Only as she said it did she realize she suddenly didn't feel the need to go every day, either.

She gave him the details. They'd take a little plane he'd fly himself. They'd stay a week, then go home early, get the kids, and go to Disneyland. She'd cabled a travel agent she knew in New York, and arrangements had been made for that trip, too. He seemed amazed she'd salvaged their vacation so fast.

"You underestimate me," she said. "Do you have any idea how far ahead of schedule we are on things at Lake Tahoe?"

"I'm really going to fly over the Alps?"

"I thought you'd love it," she said. "If it's too challenging or—"

"I do," he said. "I love it." He squeezed her hip. She squirmed in warm, carnal assent.

This was always where things had been the best for them, in bed. It was not at all unlikely he'd get her pregnant. The way she felt now, for the first time in a long time, that wouldn't have been unwelcome. Lately, in the rare times they'd made love at all, Michael had been on top or she had, and they'd stayed in the position where they'd started, executing the act like some grim household errand. This time, as they had when they arrived, too, they did it the way Kay liked best, switching positions often, him on top, then her, then she turned around and faced away from him, her eyes clenched closed, grinding into him, happy enough that it might have been enough, just that. But he surprised her by not coming. He rose from the bed and lifted her onto the marble sink. The cold stone sent jagged shivers through her, and she looped her arms around his neck. She threw back her head. Michael's hands slid over the curves of her breasts and trailed lightly across her ribs and she shivered again, harder this time. *Perfect* height. When she could feel how close he was, she put her fingertips gently to his sweat-slicked chest. She didn't have to say anything. He knew to stop and pull out, and she hurried to the bed and got on all fours. As Michael entered her, she heard a growl escape from her throat. The sun on her skin seemed baking, burning, scorching. The sheets had come loose from the corners, revealing the bare striped mattress beneath. Kay's arms gave out, and her face fell against the wadded sheets. The next thing she knew, so fast she was barely aware of how it happened, she was on top of him again. He was pulling her hard into him, and the look on his face,

his openness, his vulnerability, his ardor and attention to *her*, to what she liked and how she liked it, *that* was what did it for her. It was painful, more like electroshock than orgasm, and she felt like she was giving off sunlight—like it was radiating off of her, a haze of undulating waves. Somewhere in the trembling rills of aftershocks she felt his spasms below her, far below her. And at some other point—it could have been ten seconds or ten years—Kay felt herself tumbling exhausted onto the sodden mattress.

It hadn't been painful at all, of course.

Michael blew gently on her dripping back. He touched her, lightly, a single finger. He traced the words *I love you*. Over and over. Her breathing and her beating heart finally slowed. Suddenly, a torrent of words came out of her, a long and grateful expression of love. Only when she stopped did she realize she'd said it all in Italian.

"Where the hell did you learn all that?" Michael said, laughing in amazement.

"No idea whatsoever," she said in English, rolling over and kissing him. "That was—"

He put a finger to her lips. They smiled. He was right. No need for words.

Mary wore her new Mickey Mouse ears, Cinderella dress, and Davy Crockett moccasins everywhere, every day. She was three years old and thought the bear she'd danced with was real. Anthony went around belting out note-perfect renditions of the songs that had been featured at various rides and attractions. He had the spooky ability to hear a song once and perform it. This had caused him no small amount of trouble at his kindergarten, but Kay was sure this skill would bode well for the boy in the long run. In fact her father, an opera buff, planned to hire someone to give Anthony singing lessons for his next birthday. They were lucky kids, Kay supposed, but she felt even luckier to have them.

Could Michael possibly know how much he was missing by being gone so much? But he loved them, too. He'd taken an obvious, visceral delight taking them to Disneyland. Anytime Michael was home, he absolutely doted on Mary. Anthony was harder for him, but it was unabashed love for Anthony that made Michael's befuddled regard of his son so heartbreaking. Several days after their vacation, Michael had to go to New York, both for business and to see how his mother—who'd had a few complications but was back home again—was getting along. As he was packing, he called Kay to their bedroom window. Anthony had dug a big hole behind the swing set and was standing over it, alone, head down, praying.

"It's a funeral for his coonskin cap," Kay explained.

"You're kidding."

"Don't be angry," she said.

"I'm not angry. I'm—" He couldn't seem to come up with a word for what he was.

"I think it's sort of sweet."

"That cap cost four dollars."

"Unless there's something more you're not telling me, we can afford four dollars."

He paused. Obviously there were other things he wasn't able to tell her. They both knew that. "That's not the point. The four dollars. Obviously."

"Oh, really? So what is your point?"

Anthony was burying the cap, Kay knew, less out of sympathy for a dead raccoon than because several months ago on TV he'd seen a senator from Tennessee wearing such a hat, campaigning for president and denouncing Michael Corleone, among others, by name. Buying the cap had been Michael's idea, not Anthony's. Anthony rarely seemed able to tell his father what he did or didn't want, and Michael meant well but was oblivious. This whole matter wasn't something Kay wanted to get into with Michael, not right now.

Michael sighed, resigned. "Think that's real raccoon fur he's burying?" he asked. "Or rabbit?" She kissed the top of his head. He forced a chuckle and went outside and joined Anthony. Kay watched. They stood on opposite sides of the hole from each other. Anthony looked down and didn't seem to be saying anything. At a certain point, he broke into "Ave Maria." Michael heard him out. He could have hardly looked more uncomfortable if he'd learned his son was actually a little green man from Mars.

It was while Michael was on that trip to New York that their half-finished house at Lake Tahoe burned down. Tom Hagen, who was back working as the family lawyer, walked over to give her the news. There had been a lightning storm. The insurance should cover everything, he assured her. There had been no damage to the foundation. Kay had done such a good job of making all the decisions that they could simply hire a few extra crews and rebuild in no time. Also, there was a mansion in Reno, a castle really, that used to belong to a railroad baron; it was being torn down to make way for a modern hotel, and Kay could have any of the fixtures she wanted. Once Kay saw this place, Hagen said, she'd end up thinking the fire was a blessing in disguise. Hagen knew she'd been hoping to move this summer, so he'd talked to the head contractor, who seemed to think it was still possible to be done by Labor Day.

"*You* talked to him? Before he talked to me? Or you talked to me?"

"He's our contractor, too. For our house up there, too."

"Does Michael know?"

"He does."

She frowned and put her hands on her hips and stood in the doorway and did not invite him in. As of today, she'd realized she wasn't pregnant. As of this moment, it was happy news.

"I didn't actually talk to him," Hagen said. "I left a message."

"With *Carmela*?"

"Of course not." He left it at that. "I know what you're thinking," he said.

"Don't bet on it."

"We're looking into things, okay?" he said. "But, you know, rigging up a lightning storm, you have to admit, that's pretty much God's territory."

"And we know it was lightning?"

"We know it was lightning."

"And how do we know it was lightning? Did anyone see it?"

"I know you're upset, Kay. I'd be upset, too. I *am* upset, and so is everyone up there."

"Did anyone see it?"

Behind her, Mary started crying. Anthony dropped to his knees, threw out his arms, and burst into a song first introduced to the world by a melancholy cartoon jalopy named Dudley.

BOOK V

1957–1959

Chapter 17

So was Kay sore," Fredo asked, leaning across an empty seat, whispering into his brother's ear, "when she found out about the bugs?"

Michael lit a cigarette. Kay and Deanna were across the banquet hall by now, on their way to the ladies' room. Sonny's daughter Francesca and that rich WASP asshole she'd just married were on the dance floor (the kid had broken his leg skiing or some other rich-boy thing and was hobbling around out there on his wedding day in a cast). Most of the other guests were dancing, too, including, amazingly enough, Carmela, who'd been at death's door a couple months ago. She was twirling around with Sonny's kid Frankie, the football star. Michael and Fredo were alone at their table. Fredo couldn't remember the last time he'd had a moment alone with his brother, even one like this, in plain sight.

"She doesn't know," Michael finally said.

"Kay's smarter than you think. She'll figure it out."

Michael exhaled. He smoked with the studied cool of someone who'd cultivated the habit from watching people smoke in the movies. He'd smoked this way from the time he'd started. Sonny used to give him the business about it, and in truth, at first he'd looked ridiculous, like a little boy playing dress-up. Somewhere along the line he'd grown into it.

"Fredo," Michael said, "*you,* of all people, should not be second-guessing me about how I handle things with my own wife."

This was a crack about Deanna, of course, but Fredo let it go. "The bug situation," Fredo said, meaning the listening devices someone had managed to embed in the very beams of Michael's new house in Tahoe. Neri had used his gizmos to find them, and apparently Michael's house was the only one of the buildings affected. "Is it—whaddayacallit with bugs? Fumigated. Is it fumigated? Do we—" He hesitated. What he wanted to know was who planted them. "Do we know what species of bugs they were?"

Michael narrowed his eyes.

"So the exterminator got called in, right?" Meaning, *Did Neri take care of things?*

"Clever doesn't especially suit you, Fredo."

"What's that supposed to mean?"

"How much have you had to drink?"

"What kind of question is that?"

"Why don't you go dance?" Michael said. "She'd probably like that."

Okay, so Mike didn't want to be talking about this in public. Though it was mostly family and thus not *really* public. And anyway, it wasn't something anyone listening in could have figured out. Bugs. People get bugs. They fumigate. They exterminate. Especially in Florida. The vermin a person sees down here, even in nice hotels? Forget about it. So who's going to think twice about hearing a conversation about bugs in Miami Beach? C'mon.

"I'm sorry," Fredo murmured.

Michael shook his head. "Ah, Fredo."

"Don't 'Ah, Fredo' me, all right? Whatever you do, don't do that."

"The situation is under control," Michael said.

Fredo held out his hands, shaking them in frustration. *Meaning what? Talk to me.*

"You're leaving when?" Michael said. "I have an early flight to Havana, but maybe we can have breakfast someplace. Just you and me. Or at least take a walk out by the beach."

"God, that'd be great, Mikey. Really great. Our flight's in the afternoon, I forget when." Fredo had been trying to get in to see his own brother for months. Because of Deanna, Fredo spent half his time in L.A. Mike was gone half the time. Even when they were in the same town together, they never found time just to be brothers—to see a ball game, have a beer, go fishing. They hadn't done any of that since before the war. And that wasn't to mention business. Fredo needed to talk to Mike again about setting up a cemetery business in New Jersey, one like out in Colma. Fredo had looked into it some more. Nick Geraci had been a big help. Fredo was convinced he could make Mike reconsider.

"Kay's not going to Havana with you?" Fredo said.

"I'm going on business, Fredo. You know that."

"Right." Fredo banged the heel of his hand against his head. "Sorry. How's that going?" Fredo said. "Havana, Hyman Roth, all that?"

Michael frowned. "Tomorrow," he said. "At breakfast."

Fredo's vagueness was born of ignorance, not discretion. Roth had been an associate of Vito Corleone's during Prohibition. Now he was the most powerful Jewish Mob boss in New York—and, by extension, Las Vegas and Havana, too. Fredo had no clear idea what Michael and Roth were cooking up in Cuba, only that Michael had been working on it for a long time and that it was big. "Breakfast's great," Fredo said. He'd waited this long to learn what was going on, he could wait until tomorrow morning, too. "Most important meal of the day."

"When's your television show start?" Michael asked.

"September. I got Fontane booked for the first one." All the favors they'd done for Johnny Fontane, this was the least he could do. He'd said yes right away.

"That was a good idea," Michael said.

"What—Fontane? Or the show?"

"Both, I guess. The show was what I meant."

"Really?"

"We need to change people's perceptions. For our businesses to grow the way we want them to, it's valuable to show the public the Corleones are"—he gestured toward the groom's side of the ballroom—"no different, in the end, than people like the Van Arsdales."

"Thanks," Fredo said.

They made arrangements to meet in the hotel lobby at six the next morning.

"You know, I never could tell them apart." Michael nodded toward Francesca and Kathy.

"Francesca's the one in the wedding dress."

Michael laughed. "You don't say?"

Fredo embraced his brother. They held it longer than Fredo could remember ever doing before, then pulled each other even closer. It was Sonny they were thinking about, which they both seemed to know without saying anything. His spirit had been there all day, more present than any live guest. Both Fredo and Mike had been on the edge of breaking down when they'd stood in line to hand Francesca their envelopes. Now, when they let go, the brothers' faces were slick with unashamed tears. They patted each other on the shoulders and said no more.

It was a rough thing to handle, though. Who could blame a guy for wanting to drown his sorrows? Fredo knew even as it was happening that he was drinking too much, but under the circumstances it didn't seem like a federal offense. Also, there was the matter of that priest at the ceremony—a dead ringer for Father Stefano, the priest who'd made Fredo want to be a priest: same lopsided smile, a plume of black hair combed just the same way, same slim-hipped build, like a long-distance runner's. Fredo tried not to think about Father Stefano, and most of the time he succeeded—months passed without so much as a momentary image—but at those rare times he did think of him, Fredo wound up drinking too much.

If people everywhere didn't drink to forget, half the songs on the radio and three fourths of the world's distilleries would disappear. Fredo stayed at the wedding and didn't make a scene and didn't go out anywhere afterward. He and Deanna started dancing together to every song, and she did seem happy, though they were both too drunk for any emotion to be above suspicion.

Back in the room, he gave it to her in the ass, something he'd have never done sober, and she didn't complain, which was also the doing of all that booze.

When he woke up the next morning, Fredo had no memory of how he'd gotten to his room. He lifted Deanna's limp arm to look at her Cartier watch. His head pounded. He struggled to get his bleary eyes to focus. It was almost eleven. In a panic, Fredo called Michael's room. "I'm sorry, sir," said the operator. "Mr. Corleone and his entire family checked out hours ago."

(*The Fred Corleone Show aired irregularly, usually on Monday nights on a UHF station in Las Vegas, from 1957 until its host's disappearance in 1959. It was broadcast from the lounge at the Castle in the Sand on a minimal set: a low round table flanked by the host and a guest on leopard-print chairs. On a board behind them, white lights spelled out "FRED!" Behind the board was a dark curtain. The following is from the show's debut on September 30, 1957 [transcript courtesy of the Nevada Museum of Radio and Television].*)

FRED CORLEONE: This first show, I expect it to be real mothery. If you don't know what that means, I guess call it a gasser. I see these other shows with everything—girls, jokes, little skits, whatnot. Music. So on and so forth. Sometimes these guys got so many guest stars they need a traffic cop in the wings, y'know? The fellas who do those shows are good men, but, personally, I think maybe they're not sure they can grab you, so they keep throwing acts at you. More guests than they got folks at home watching. Tonight we're takin' a different road, and I hope you'll sit back and join us. One guest, that's it, but he's a major leaguer: a star of stage and screen and of course a singer like none other, not to mention being a fellow *paesano*. Ladies and gents, Mr. John Fontane.

(*Corleone stands and applauds. Fontane nods toward the audience. The men sit, and both take their time lighting cigarettes and getting started.*)

FRED CORLEONE: They tell me *Groovesville* could wind up being the biggest long-player in history. The rock-and-roll fad is dying, and you're on top, number one across the land.

JOHNNY FONTANE: Thank you. My recording career had a bad case of pavement rash for a while there, but I picked myself up and caught a few breaks. In all modesty, the records I've been fortunate enough to make with the genius Cy Milner—not just *Groovesville* but also *The Last Lonely Midnight, Johnny Sings Hoagy,* and starting with *Fontane Blue*—those may very well be the best records I've ever done.

FRED CORLEONE: Those are maybe the best sides anyone ever did.

JOHNNY FONTANE: You should have Cy on your show. He's doing my next

record, too, which is sort of a dream project for me, a duets record with Miss Ella Fitzgerald.

FRED CORLEONE: I'll do that. *(Looks offstage.)* Somebody write that down. Cy Milner, genius, and, um, y'know. Book him on the show I guess is the good word.

JOHNNY FONTANE: You should have Ella on, also. Like the song says, she's the top.

FRED CORLEONE: Sure.

JOHNNY FONTANE: I don't use the word *genius* lightly.

FRED CORLEONE: The way Hollywood phonies do. I know. You don't.

JOHNNY FONTANE: Any singer who works with Milner will tell you he's a genius, for the simple reason that during his years as a 'bone man with the Les Halley Band, he—

FRED CORLEONE: That would be the trombone, folks.

JOHNNY FONTANE: —played it so much like the human voice that he knows how to take a singer into the studio and make him or her feel better than the proverbial million bucks.

FRED CORLEONE: What's better than a million bucks?

JOHNNY FONTANE: A million bucks and . . . (*Takes a long drag from his cigarette. Shrugs.*)

FRED CORLEONE: Your records make millions, though. And not proverbial.

JOHNNY FONTANE: What I've learned, in all my years in this business we call show, is that whatever amount of success I've had—

FRED CORLEONE: Lots of success.

JOHNNY FONTANE: —I owe to the people. *(Acknowledges applause.)* Thank you. It's true.

FRED CORLEONE: Am I right that this rock and roll has gone about as far as it can go? To me it ain't . . . you know, it isn't music. And also, if I may say so, it doesn't have a lot of class.

JOHNNY FONTANE: That stuff all comes from a primitive side of people. It was dead artistically from the get-go, so all that's really left is for it to get gone.

FRED CORLEONE: Good to hear. Your opinion, I mean. So let me—let's really get into it, all right? Things the people want to know.

JOHNNY FONTANE: Let 'er rip.

FRED CORLEONE: In your experience, in all of show business and including all of the women, right? Out of them all. Rating them that way one to ten, ten being high—

JOHNNY FONTANE: *(pointing to the host's coffee cup):* That ain't the *only* thing that's high.

FRED CORLEONE: —and in two categories, looks and then also talent. So one to twenty. Or else one to ten, then add the two and divide for the average. The scale's not important.

JOHNNY FONTANE: You never told me I'd need a Ph.D. in mathematics to do this show.

FRED CORLEONE: For objectivity let's say excepting your fiancée, Miss Annie McGowan, who can do it all, by the way—sing, dance, tell jokes, even act. Plus there's the puppets, which I never saw but I heard good things about. Hold on, though. I need to stop right here.

JOHNNY FONTANE: I didn't know you started.

FRED CORLEONE: So, Annie. You know what they say. About . . . *them.* Help me out, John. We got the family market to consider. People know what I'm talking about, believe me. How should I say it? Her what?

JOHNNY FONTANE (*grinning*): Her chest?

FRED CORLEONE: Chest! Right. It's a very famous chest, no disrespect to you or her in any way.

JOHNNY FONTANE: None taken. What was the question?

FRED CORLEONE: Who's the best combination of talent and looks in all of Hollywood?

JOHNNY FONTANE (*performing an exaggerated double-take*): Your interview style's gonna give me whiplash.

FRED CORLEONE: Hoo boy! The razzing, giving folks the business, just like from your stage show. We need to get you back onstage here at the world-famous Castle in the Sand.

JOHNNY FONTANE: Thanks. Thank you. I haven't been able to do shows in Vegas for a while. I do have some gigs locked up in L.A. and Chicago, if people want to come see me there.

FRED CORLEONE: Our show just goes to here in Vegas, and not even all of it, either. This channel doesn't quite make it to my own house, can you believe that?

JOHNNY FONTANE: You got a tower or just the rabbit ears?

FRED CORLEONE: You kidding? Tower. Back to business matters, though, if you will. All kidding aside, you're telling me you're not singing here? Today? For us? I was told we had a little combo coming in to back you.

JOHNNY FONTANE: I'd love to, but I gotta rest the pipes. Those are big shows comin' up. Sorry.

FRED CORLEONE: That's disappointing. Really disappointing. You're making me look bad.

JOHNNY FONTANE: That ship already sailed before I came on deck.

FRED CORLEONE (*cracking up*): Funny guy!

JOHNNY FONTANE: I try.

FRED CORLEONE (*to someone offstage*): Did anyone call that combo and . . . Right. You did? You did. Why am I the last to know these things? (*Turns to Fontane.*) So, all right, what? Let's start. Any thoughts on the Dodgers and Giants moving to California?

JOHNNY FONTANE: Nothing that'll fly with the family market. That ripped people's hearts out.

FRED CORLEONE: I don't know. Businesses relocate all the time. My brother's business, which I am also a partner in, that business—hotels and entertainment, construction, cement—it moved west, too. That move led to us being here together on this show. Why is baseball different? I got sentimental feelings about New York just like you, but at the same time, why should the national pastime operate in a way that's not un-American?

JOHNNY FONTANE: Baseball's tied in to neighborhoods and with the faith of the common people. All the times I been to Ebbets Field . . . well, I can't imagine that place empty or torn down. They tear it down, and a piece of me'll get torn down, too.

FRED CORLEONE: You yourself relocated from New York to the West.

JOHNNY FONTANE: That's different. People can play my records anywhere, see my pictures anywhere. Sooner or later I end up performing everywhere.

FRED CORLEONE: I bet you'll go. To Dodgers games out in Los Angeles. These days, you've got more ties to L.A. than you do New York.

JOHNNY FONTANE (*pausing to light another cigarette*): I'll go, sure. But they'll never be the real Dodgers. They cut themselves off from what made them the real Dodgers.

FRED CORLEONE: Okay, look, no more about that touchy subject. We could talk about politics. I hear you already got a fella you're backing for president next time. Little bird tells me.

JOHNNY FONTANE: How's Deanna?

FRED CORLEONE: She's fine. Though that ain't the bird I'm talkin' about.

JOHNNY FONTANE (*winking at the camera*): Because to answer your previous question, I think that if both looks and talent are the categories used, I can't think of anyone who outclasses Deanna Dunn. No disrespect to you or her, but she's a real barn burner.

FRED CORLEONE: Thank you, Johnny. That's very kind and not to mention in my opinion also a true fact. For those of you who may have just joined us, this lucky bum here, yours truly, is happily married to the lovely and talented Deanna Dunn.

JOHNNY FONTANE: Academy Award–winning.

FRED CORLEONE: Two times, though you won one also. Were you surprised how heavy it was?

JOHNNY FONTANE: An honor like that, coming from your peers, that's what *this* cat found heavy.

FRED CORLEONE: Speaking of awards, you're backing Governor Shea from New Jersey for president? He won that big award for his book, you know the one I mean.

JOHNNY FONTANE: If he runs, I'm leaning that way, yes. I hope he does run. He's a good man, and he'd be good for our country. Did you read his book?

FRED CORLEONE: It's on my nightstand as we speak. I'll read it before he comes on the show.

JOHNNY FONTANE: He's coming on the show?

FRED CORLEONE: We're working on it. Listen, John, let me ask you something. You ever see a picture called *Ambush in Durango*?

JOHNNY FONTANE: Did I *see* it? *(Laughing)* Are you for real?

FRED CORLEONE: Johnny was *in* that picture, folks, in case you got there after the first reel.

JOHNNY FONTANE: You were in it, too. And also your wife.

FRED CORLEONE: Blink, and you missed me. Blink twice, and folks missed you, too.

JOHNNY FONTANE: In which case they'd be in good company. Most people missed the movie altogether. They can't all be masterpieces, y'know. Or big hits at the box office.

FRED CORLEONE: I hear you may be getting away from making motion pictures?

JOHNNY FONTANE: No, not at all.

FRED CORLEONE: But it's not where your heart is anymore, is it? You've got your own production company, and yet—

JOHNNY FONTANE: There's pictures in the works that should be hits. A gladiator movie, for one.

FRED CORLEONE: A musical?

JOHNNY FONTANE: That's right. Top songs. How'd you hear that?

FRED CORLEONE: I know half of the songwriting team a little. Listen, we gotta pay some bills.

JOHNNY FONTANE: You're not paying your bills?

FRED CORLEONE: I meant going to commercial, as you know.

JOHNNY FONTANE: We'll be right back.

FRED CORLEONE: Whose show is this, huh?

JOHNNY FONTANE: So you say it. How'd a bum like you get a television show in the first place, not to mention a chick like Deanna Dunn?

FRED CORLEONE: See what I mean, everybody? You're a national treasure! We'll be right back.

From the penthouse window of the Château Marmont, Fredo Corleone stood alone in the dark and looked down at the Sunset Strip, waiting for his wife to come home. This place cost Fredo more each week than what his pop had paid for that whole mall of houses back on Long Island, but it

was probably worth it. He could stay here without fans bugging Deanna or bodyguards breathing down his neck. He looked at his watch. Almost two. They'd had dinner reservations at eleven. Shooting usually finished around nine, though he'd been in three movies himself (all bit parts) and knew that you could never tell. Deanna hadn't been in a hit for five years— which in Hollywood time might as well have been five hundred. She'd landed this part after several younger actresses had passed, and every day she came back from shooting talking about what a dog the movie was going to be, what a horrible actor her pretty-boy costar was.

Even as Fredo turned away from the window and toward the phone, he told himself he wasn't going to dial it, he was just going to test himself. He dialed. The switchboard put him through to Bungalow 3. The deep, sleepy voice that answered belonged to Wally Morgan, half of one of the most in-demand songwriting teams in the business. He'd been in the navy, raced motorcycles, liked to hunt: no one you'd have figured for a fairy. Fredo was learning that you can't go by that. Guy paints a room in his house, it doesn't make him a painter. Just a guy who painted a room is all. Also, this was Hollywood. Things were different here. Fontane called fags *buttfuckers,* right to their face, but he always had plenty of them at his parties to keep conversation with the ladies moving when he and the boys were talking football or chucking M-80s into the ravine behind his house. And where was Fredo when this was happening? With the boys, maligning quarterbacks and pissing off the neighbors. So he was certainly no fag.

Fredo cleared his voice and asked if it would be okay if he swung by for a drink.

"Swung by?" Morgan chuckled. "Nice euphemism, tiger. But sure. I'll make some martinis. Be a sport and bring a few of our green friends, too, mmkay?"

Euphemism. Our green friends. Tiger. It was hard for Fredo to believe he had anything to do with anyone who talked like that. He grabbed his bathing suit and a bottle of pills and left. The trunks were for later, after- ward, a swim to clear his head.

By the time he finally did get to the pool, it was four in the morning and there was a couple fucking in the deep end. No lights. Fredo changed in the bathhouse, hoping that while he did they'd finish, but when he opened the door they were still there. He hadn't taken a shower back in Bungalow 3. He had to do something before he went back to the pent- house, to clean up, just in case. The couple had stayed more or less in the same place—against the wall, next to a ladder—and seemed to be in no hurry. What did Fredo care? He jumped into the shallow end and swam back and forth a few times. He hadn't eaten anything, but the pills had given him all the energy in the world. As he was gathering up his clothes,

he glanced over at the couple, still going at it in the deep end. That was when he realized that the woman was his wife.

"Dee Dee?"

She laughed. The man laughed, too. The man was her costar, Matt Marshall. "Be right with you," Deanna called. "Little busy right now."

Fredo put his head down and strode to the elevator. In the penthouse, he strapped on the gun belt he'd stolen from the set of *Apache Creek* (his second movie; he'd played an Indian) and two loaded Colt Peacemakers. Despite the pills, he felt an abiding calm. Revenge was justified, and in a few moments he'd have it.

But when he got back to the pool, they were gone.

The next thing Fredo knew, he was standing in the garage of the Château Marmont, leveling a pistol at the Regal Turquoise 1958 Corvette he'd bought Deanna for their first anniversary. He heard his heart beating. He took several deep breaths, keeping his arm steady, squeezing but not quite pulling the trigger. They'd gone to Flint together to pick up the car. Their publicist had gotten the photos of that smiling moment into newspapers and magazines across the world—good ink for all involved.

Fredo opened fire: into the rear window, the left rear tire, two in the driver's door, one through the driver's window and out the passenger's, one in the windshield. It felt good to kill a car. Glass shattered, and tires and upholstery exploded. The echoes of metal on metal and the aftershock tinkling of who knew what.

He holstered the first Colt, opened the Corvette's hood, and took out the other. The hotel manager and several of his people showed up, but they knew Fredo and knew that this was Deanna Dunn's car. They'd seen many more famous people engaging in stranger and more clearly criminal behavior. In an even voice the manager asked if there was anything he could do.

"Nope." Fredo fired a slug into the four-barrel carburetor. "Got it covered, thanks."

The next one provoked a small explosion and a puff of white smoke. The first gawkers were showing up now.

"It's rather late, Mr. Corleone. As you can see, several of the other guests—"

He put another bullet in the engine block.

"—have unfortunately been disturbed."

Two more into the passenger side. His final bullet missed the car.

Behind him, a lady screamed and shouted shrill nonsense in what might have been French. When Fredo turned around, there was Matt Marshall—shirtless, barefoot, and in chinos, charging toward him, his blandly handsome face contorted in rage.

Fredo drew the other gun, too, and pointed them both at Marshall—who either was nuts or knew Fredo was out of bullets, because he kept coming. Fredo had never experienced a moment of such clarity. He stood his ground. Marshall lunged toward him, and Fredo dodged him, deftly as a matador. Marshall hit the pavement. He rose, bloodied, and charged again, head stupidly down. Fredo wanted to laugh but instead threw a roundhouse pistol-whip haymaker. It made a sound like dropping a roast from a tall building. Marshall crumpled.

As one—except for the shrieking French lady—the crowd that had gathered said, "Ooh."

Fredo holstered the guns. "Self-defense," he said, "pure and simple."

It was Hagen who came to bail him out.

"You made good time," Fredo said as they walked out of the police station. "You fly?"

"Only in a manner of speaking. Jesus, Fredo. I'm not sure anyone in that hotel ever managed to get themselves arrested."

"Stray bullets," he said. "It could happen to anyone. I feel rotten about that dog, though."

The French lady was a deposed countess, out walking her toy poodle. One of the bullets had blown all but a few stringy remnants of its head off. The other problematic shot was one that had somehow passed through the Corvette and torn up the grille of the car behind it, a white DeSoto Adventurer, the pace car for the 1957 Indy 500. The winner of the race had made a mint selling it to Marshall, best known to moviegoers as the cocky gearhead with a heart of gold in *Checkered Past, Checkered Flag*. That asshole wasn't fighting for Deanna or on her behalf. What set him off had been the acrid smoke coming from his precious car.

"It's worse than stray bullets, Fredo. Those guns—"

"They're clean. Neri said they were as clean as they come."

"They better be, because the LAPD is bringing in the FBI to help check 'em out."

"They're clean."

They got into Hagen's Buick—everyone in the Family was driving boring cars all of sudden—and they drove in silence to the Château Marmont. Not only hadn't the management kicked Fredo out, but Hagen had taken a room there, too. There's a lot to be said for a place with a discreet staff. There was also a lot to be said for tipping well, paying for one's room in advance, and being married to a VIP. Hagen and Fredo took a walk together on the secluded tropical grounds.

"So what about those pills they found in your pocket?" Hagen said.

"Prescription. Segal gave 'em to me." That was true, at least indi-rectly. He'd sent Figaro, his guy in Vegas, out to get the pills. Jules Segal, an old friend of the family, was head of surgery at the hospital the Cor-leones had built.

"They tell me they were in an aspirin bottle."

"I dumped 'em in there and then took all the aspirin. There's no law that says you gotta carry pills a certain way."

"I don't know. Segal got suspended once for that, a long time ago, and before he worked at our hospital. But now . . . well, the hospital makes us look good, and if—"

"Get a different doc at that hospital to say he prescribed it, then. Make it worth his while. You've fixed problems a hundred times worse than this. Jesus, Tommy. Pop always called you the most Sicilian one. What the fuck happened? They remove that from you with a special act of Congress? I *told* you what that guy did! It was my *wife!*"

"You told me on the phone. Which wasn't smart, Fredo."

Fredo shrugged, in concession. "Marshall didn't die or nothin', did he?"

"No, thank God." Hagen said. "He'll be fine. His face is another mat-ter, though."

"Pretty bad, huh?"

"Pretty bad. Matt Marshall makes a living with his cheekbones, one of which is now more of a liquid than a solid. Which would be bad enough, but as you know he's in the middle of shooting a movie. They don't seem to think they can finish it without him. It's possible we can take care of things, but L.A. is a tough town for us anymore, with the Chicago—"

"We got peace with those guys. They know me, they like me. I can handle 'em."

"At any rate, you've given me a lot of things to take care of."

"C'mon, Tom. What would you have done if it had been Theresa?"

"Gee, I don't know. Kill a car, a poodle, and a major motion picture?"

"At least you didn't say it would never be Theresa."

"It would never be Theresa."

"Fuck you, you fucking holier-than-thou fuck."

"How many pills you take today, Fredo?"

"None." He didn't think like that, about the number. "I only take 'em off and on." He didn't want to go by Bungalow 3, and he didn't wasn't to go by the pool. "Better view this way," he said. "Of Sunset Boulevard and all."

"I know," Hagen said. "I've stayed here. I was the one who told you about this place."

"So you know, then. Better view this way."

They went that way.

"I been meaning to ask," Fredo said. "Did Kay go nuts when you told her about the bugs?"

"She doesn't know," Hagen said.

Fredo had guessed right: Mike hadn't even told her himself. He'd have Tom do it. There was some pilgrim who'd lost his woman. "Kay's smart. She knows things. Even if she don't know, sooner or later but probably sooner you'll tell her."

"What are you talking about?"

"I'm not saying you're sweet on her or nothin', but everyone knows she's got a way of getting things out of you."

"That's the most ridiculous thing I ever heard."

"You told me my idea about cornering the cemetery racket in New York like out in Colma was the most ridiculous thing you ever heard."

"That *cemetery* idea? You're still talking about that? Mike told you, it's not a project we can get into now. We're staying away from rackets of any sort. We don't want to be beholden to the Straccis for anything. We'd need to call in favors from all kinds of politicians in New York, and the last thing we want to do right now is spend those kind of favors on a project like this—one that has a lot of holes in it, I might add."

They rounded a corner and ran into Alfred Hitchcock, out for a walk along with Annie McGowan and her agent. Fredo introduced Hagen as "Congressman Hagen." Annie asked Fredo if he was okay. Fredo said it was a long story and he'd give her a call later. No, Johnny wasn't in town, Annie said. He was in Chicago. Hitchcock insisted he had to go, and they went.

"What holes?" Fredo said, again alone with Hagen.

"It's got holes," Hagen said. "Look, the way things are is this: The operation in New York is going to maintain things as is. The only new ventures have to be legitimate businesses."

"That's the beauty of my plan, Tom. It's no racket. It'll all be completely legal."

"Fredo, you can't have this both ways. You can't on the one hand be in the public eye, married to a movie star, running the entertainment side of our hotels in Las Vegas, and starting up your own television show—which I hear went well, by the way."

"Thanks. We try."

"But you can't do all that and at the same time be the force behind something like your cemetery plan. And you can't do *any* of it if you don't clean up your act. Wake up, huh?"

Waking up would be great, except that the cops had taken his fucking pills. "So let someone else take care of the dirty work," Fredo said. "Rocco

could do it. Or you know who'd be perfect? Nick Geraci. After it's all legit, I'd be in charge. It was my *idea*, Tom."

"Ideas," Hagen said, "are shit. It's knowing what to do with an idea that matters."

"I know what to fucking do with my idea, okay? I know how to put it in place. I know how to run the fucking operation once it's in place. My problem is, you won't let me do it."

Hagen started to say something.

"Say it," Fredo said. "Say it's not you stopping me, it's Mike. Goddamn it, Tom, he takes advantage of you worse than he does me. We're both older than him. We both got passed over, and why?"

Hagen frowned.

"You're not Italian," Fredo said, "and you're not blood either, so fine, that complicates things, but not to the point of making you automatically into his errand boy."

"I should have let you cool your heels in there, you ungrateful prick. Maybe you'd like it in jail."

"Fuck's that supposed to mean?"

Hagen closed his eyes. "Nothing."

"What's wrong, you afraid?"

Hagen didn't say anything.

"I asked you a question, goddamnit."

"Are you going to hit me, Fredo? Go ahead."

"I know what you're trying to say, Tom. Just say it. This is about that kid, the thief in San Fran." Fredo hadn't had to kill a guy to get initiated into the business. Dean the beatnik was the first person Fredo had ever killed. If only the kid hadn't remembered that old photo of Fredo crying on the curb. Fredo had pretended not to know anything about it. He had the kind of face that looked like a lot of people, he'd told Dean. But the kid wouldn't drop it. Fredo smothered the kid with a pillow, got him dressed, and beat up the corpse to make it look good. Nice kid, but the fact remained, he was a pervert. Not someone just messing around but a guy who thought of himself as a faggot. It was sick. At the time, Fredo had been in such a panic about being recognized that the whole business had been easy. Getting out of it had been harder, but that had come out all right, too. "Don't keep looking at me like that. Say it."

"I'm not trying to say a goddamned thing," Hagen said. "San Francisco, as far as I'm concerned, is ancient history."

"You're really starting to piss me off, Tom."

"Starting?"

Fredo threw a punch. Tom caught it with his left hand, wrenched Fredo's arm around, then buried his fist in Fredo's gut with such force

Fredo left his feet. Tom let go of the arm. Fredo staggered and then fell to his knees, gasping for breath.

"I fucking hate you, Tom," Fredo finally said, still panting.

"You what?"

"The minute you walked in our house," Fredo said, "you were Pop's favorite."

"C'mon, Fredo. How old are you?"

"Mike was Ma's," he said, his breathing slowing. "Sonny didn't need nobody, and Connie's a girl. You know, *I* was Pop's favorite until you got there. Did you know that? You ever think of that? Did you ever care? What you took was *mine*."

"This is a hell of a thing to say to the guy you're counting on to fix the mess you made."

"What's it matter what I say?" Fredo said. "You'll do it anyway. You'll do whatever Mike tells you to."

"I'm loyal to this family."

"Bullshit. You're just loyal to him."

"Listen to yourself, Fredo."

He stood up, then charged. Hagen's second punch caught Fredo square on the chin and dropped him flat on his back in a bed of Asian jasmine.

"Had enough?"

Fredo sat up and rubbed his hands over his gray, stubbly face. He took several deep breaths. "I haven't slept," he said, "y'know, really *slept*, for I don't know. Days."

Hagen took out a cigar and lit it. He got a good draw going and then extended his hand. Fredo, still kneeling, looked up at it for a long time, then finally took it.

"Cigar?" Hagen asked, reaching for his breast pocket.

"No thanks," Fredo said.

Hagen nodded. "Go up and see your wife, Fredo."

"Don't tell me what to do. Anyway, she's not up there."

"Where else would she be? They're not filming today."

"She's up there?"

Hagen patted Fredo on the shoulder. "I love you, Fredo. You know that, right?"

Fredo shrugged. "I love you, too, Tommy," he said, "but at the same time—"

"We've been over that," Tom said. "Forget about it."

"I guess how could it be any other way, with brothers, huh?"

Hagen cocked his head in a way that indicated *maybe, maybe not.*

"Nice reflexes, by the way," Fredo said. "Catching that punch."

"Lots of coffee," Hagen said.

"Oughta cut back on that stuff," Fredo said. "It'll kill you."

"Just go. Rest up. Everything's going to be fine."

For a time, however briefly, Hagen was right.

Deanna greeted him at the door. She kissed him again and again and ran a hot bath in the huge tub. He soaked in it as she shaved him.

She was, yes, one of the most honored actresses of her generation, but Fredo was convinced that the ardor he'd sparked by standing up for her, by fighting for her, couldn't be faked. In their whole time together, they'd never had a better time in bed.

"So how'd a bum like me wind up with you, huh?" he asked afterward.

She sighed in a way that sounded happy. "Don't look a gift horse in the mouth," she said.

"What about here?" he said.

"*Definitely* look there. Get close and take a good lick around. I mean look."

"No, you don't."

"You're right," she purred, hands pressed firmly against the back of his head. "I don't."

Chapter 18

THAT MARCH, Nick Geraci's father came to New York—the first time he'd been there since Nick moved from Cleveland. Naturally, he drove. All however many thousand miles from Arizona, which he somehow did alone and in three days. To the end, he'd be Fausto the Driver.

When he first arrived, he seemed content to simmer in the self-contained cocoon of his own sulky regret, staring out at his son's swimming pool. He ran out of Chesterfield Kings. Charlotte offered him a carton of hers, which he said would be fine. They were a ladies' brand, but he said a friend of his smoked this kind and he was used to them, in a pinch. Nick winked and asked if that meant Miss Conchita Cruz. "Shut up about things you don't know nothin' about, eh? You want money for these?" He reached for his money clip.

"It's fine, Dad. No."

"You're a big shot, but I pay my own way, understood?"

"We just want you to have a good time, okay?"

"That's a lot of pressure on me," he said. "Why don't you all just mind your own business? And take the money, unless my money's no good."

"It's no good in this house, Dad," Nick said. "You're our guest."

"Guest?" he scoffed. "Don't be stupid, you big stupid. I'm family."

"It's nice to see you," Nick said, still refusing the money and embracing his father, who did in fact embrace him back, and they kissed each other's cheeks.

In the morning, there were five bucks under Charlotte's purse.

The next day, unseasonably warm for New York in March, they went as a family for lunch at Patsy's, Geraci's favorite Italian restaurant in the city, where he practically had his own table upstairs, and then for a cruise on the Circle Line, which had been Charlotte's idea. It offered views of New York that even a native like her never got to see otherwise, plus it seemed like a congenial afternoon for a man who spent every day brooding and staring at the water. Nick and Charlotte had taken the cruise on an early date, but their girls had never done it before. Barb was a freshman in high school now and could barely go anywhere without her friends, a

squadron of whom met her at the pier. Bev, though, who looked as old as Barb but was only eleven, stayed next to her grandfather, asking him things about Ellis Island—which, as a little boy, was the last time Fausto had been to New York. By the time they got to Roosevelt Island, she'd somehow gotten him to give her lessons in Sicilian dialect.

After they'd passed the Polo Grounds but before the desolation of the northern tip of Manhattan had segued from hard to believe to deathly boring, Fausto, his spirits as buoyant as they got, took his son aside and said that he'd actually come to New York on business.

Nick frowned and cocked his head.

"Message from the Jew," he said, meaning Vince Forlenza. "Long story. This ain't the place. How far are we from Troy?"

"Troy what? Troy, New York?" Nick Geraci was pretty sure his father had never told him a long story of any kind.

"No, big shot. Troy with Helen and the big fuckin' horse. Yes, Troy, New York."

"We need to go to Troy for you to tell me what you need to tell me?"

"We don't need to go to Troy at all. We could do what we need to do at your house or at your precious Henry Hudson Political Club, any place we can talk that's—"

"Patrick Henry," Nick corrected. His headquarters in Brooklyn. His office.

"Wherever. Let me tell you something. I *want* to go to Troy. All right? Think you can begrudge a dying old man that one little thing?"

"Since when are you dying?"

"Since the day I was born."

"I thought you were going to say since the day *I* was born."

"You give yourself too much credit, hotshot."

Turned out, Fausto had heard that there were cockfights in Troy, supposedly the top place in the country. It was upstate, and thus presumably under the direct or indirect control of the Cuneo Family. Fausto had always been a fan of cockfights and over the years had dropped enough money at a joint in Youngstown that by rights his name should have been on the deed. Tucson had cockfights, but they were run by Mexicans, and Fausto thought they were crooked.

"You're kidding," Nick said. "That place in Youngstown had birds with cocaine on their feathers, birds pumped full of blood thinner so they'd bleed like mad in a loss and become a huge underdog and then go off the drugs and win. Birds with any of a thousand kinds of poison on their spurs. I can't begin to remember all the different ways they made birds look sick when they were ready to kill and made others look healthy when they were about to die."

"You're naive. Mexicans are worse. Geniuses, though, gotta admit."

They didn't need to leave until midafternoon, but Fausto Geraci was up the next morning at four, studying road maps and ministering to the pampered engine of his Olds 88. He insisted on driving, of course. Geraci's usual driver—Donnie Bags, his third cousin—was just a guy who drove the car, but Nick Geraci's father was a true wheel man. Someone looking at him behind the wheel and ignoring everything else would have said he drove like an old man: huge eyeglasses, head bent over the wheel, gloved hands at ten and two, radio off so he could concentrate on the road. But he'd always driven like that. Meanwhile, he weaved that Rocket 88 through traffic like the Formula One racer he should have been, swerving from lane to lane, cutting into spaces that seemed too small but never were. Except for the cars and trucks he'd wrecked on purpose and notwithstanding the stretch he did in Marion for vehicular homicide (a cover-up he participated in, loyally, after the Jew's joyriding fourteen-year-old niece accidentally greased an old lady), Fausto Geraci had never had an accident. He had a sixth sense for where the cops were, too, and, on the rare occasions he was pulled over, could size up the officer and know instantly whether to hand him the badge indicating that he was a retired member of the Ohio Highway Patrol (the badge was real, picked up, crazily enough, at a yard sale) or whether to slip him the badge with a folded-up fifty underneath it. He kept one, prefolded, in the glove box, between the badge and the car's registration. Once, when Nick was twelve, he took the money. His father gave him an epic beating: the motivation, in fact, for him to start calling himself "Nick" (until then he'd been "Junior" or "Faustino") and to sign up for boxing lessons.

Nick waited his father out. Whatever the story was, he'd tell it when he was good and ready. Whatever it was, it was something big. He had an air about him like he'd finally been given the kind of job suitable for a man of his obvious talents.

Finally, as they got to the other side of the George Washington Bridge and whipped onto the shoulder to pass two semis, Fausto Geraci veered back onto the road, took a deep breath, and began to tell his son everything he'd learned—personally, by the way—from Vinnie Forlenza.

"You listening?"

"All ears," Nick said, tugging his ears.

Apparently, Sal Narducci got tired of waiting around for the Jew to die. But even though Laughing Sal probably killed a stadium full of men in his time, he didn't have the balls to kill his boss. What he did was, he tried to humiliate Forlenza into stepping down, first by getting someone to sabotage that plane—yes, *that* plane—and then by coming up with the idea of kidnapping Nick from the hospital and hiding him, which was sup-

posed to make Forlenza look reckless and weak, and which probably at least to a point did the trick.

"But look, *Ace*," Fausto said, using the nickname, as always, with an edge to his voice, "don't go running to your boss, either, okay? That *pezzonovante* is behind the whole thing."

Nick Geraci found this more than a little hard to believe.

"Why you think you're alive, you big dummy?' Fausto said. "You think they'd've kept you alive if they thought you fucked up? How many guys you know pulled a stunt like you did in the lake there and didn't wind up taking two in the head, a meat hook up the ass, butta-beepa-da-boppa-da-boop?"

There were plenty of reasons. Michael needed him. "The crash was ruled an accident."

Fausto sighed. "Everyone tells me what a genius son I got, can you believe it?"

It only then occurred to Nick that he had no idea what sort of men worked for the FAA, how easy it might or might not be to bribe them. Though there was always some underpaid, powerless shmoe you could get to: a diver, some assistant in the crime lab, somebody who'd lie about life-and-death matters for a little cash or a night with a classy hooker.

He didn't say anything for a long time. He listened. His father went over it. Everything added up. There *had* been something dumped in those gas tanks. Don Forlenza had figured it out when he'd heard about a guy who'd gone to Las Vegas on vacation and disappeared. Guy was a mechanic but also a *cugin'*, wanted to be a qualified man with all his heart. Fausto laughed. "I can tell you personally, those people ain't let nobody in since who knows fucking when."

Fausto kept the car at a steady eighty-eight, as if the car's model name decreed it.

"Anyway, the *cugin'* don't come back from Vegas, and this pal of his, another *cugin'*, he gets on his high horses, comes to the social club, trying to find out what happened. For the Jew, a light goes on. A mechanic. Missing, probably—" He made a gun with his hand, reached over, and pretended to blow his son's brains out. "So Forlenza takes the pal in back for a talk. A question here, question there, butta-beepa-da-boppa-da-boop. The pal knew everything. The rest you can guess."

"What do you mean, the rest I can guess? You mean like what's left of the pal is underneath a freshly poured basement in Chagrin Falls?"

"Smart guy. Forget the pal. Long story short, your boss and Laughing Sal had this dead mechanic slip something in your fuel tank. Look in the glove box, smart guy."

Nick gave him a look. "Go on," Fausto said. "I won't beat you."

Thirty years ago, that beating was, and they'd neither one mentioned it since. Thirty years between a father and a son can work like that. In fact, it usually does.

Like the rest of the car, the glove box was immaculate: the badge, neatly stacked atop the fifty (which Nick was careful not to touch), the registration, two white envelopes, and the owner's manual. One envelope contained service records for the car. "The other one," Fausto said. "That one there."

Inside it were six train tickets to Cleveland, for Nick and five of his men, which made it unlikely there'd be any kind of ambush there.

Fausto explained in detail about where to go and the security measures to take to meet with Don Forlenza, which would happen in a part of the Cleveland Art Museum that was in between exhibits and closed off to the public. "Probably you don't remember that Polack Mike Zielinsky, used to run my old local?"

"You serious, Dad? Of course I remember." That Polack Zielinsky had been a friend of the family for years. He was Nick's sister's godfather and one of Fausto's best and only friends.

"Well, all right then. Get to the museum nine-fifteen sharp. You see that fat fuck standing out by that Thinker thing—"

"The sculpture?"

"Sculpture, statue. In front there."

"I know it."

"He's there—the Polack, not the statue—you'll know things are jake, go on in. No Polack, go back to the hotel, he'll be in the lobby."

For Nick Geraci, this whole matter had gone from hard to believe to hard to accept. But what could Michael's motives have been? Why would he want to kill him?

"I know what you're thinking." Fausto shook his head. "You really *are* naive."

"How you figure?"

"How long you been in this line of work?"

"Your point?"

"My point is," said his father, "*no* point. Shit gets done for no reason that makes sense to anybody but the doer and the fellas he has do the shit for him. Most of the time they don't know shit, either. They just *do* shit. It's a miracle you didn't die a long time ago, big shot."

It was a good thing that the drive to Troy was so long and that his father wasn't much of a talker. The long silences gave Nick Geraci time to figure out what to do. Even so, he struggled. He'd look into things, verifying what he could verify without sending up any flags. He'd move slowly. He'd learn more. He'd consider every move, from every angle.

One thing he knew for certain: if what his father said was indeed true, Nick Geraci would figure out how to do something to Michael Corleone that would do more harm than death.

They made it to Troy. The cockfights were in an old icehouse. The front of the place had been turned into a bar. There was a huge gravel parking lot behind the building and out of sight from the road.

"How'd you know about this place, Dad?"

Fausto Geraci rolled his eyes. "You know all the ins and outs and what-have-yous, right? But your old man, *he* don't know his ass from his elbow."

Nick let it go. They got out. His father complained about the cold. He'd been the toughest sonofabitch there was about the cold back in Cleveland.

"It's March in New York, Dad."

"Your blood thins." He nonetheless stopped to light one of Charlotte's cigarettes, gave a little scornful chuckle, muttered something, and headed for the door.

"What's that?"

"I said, 'I can see that aerial warfare is actually scientific murder.' " He was moving pretty fast for an old guy.

"You can what now?"

"From your Eddie Rickenbacker book, genius," Fausto said. "He said it. You left it. The book. Do me a favor, stop looking at me like you think I can't read."

Nick seemed to remember that the line had been on the book's flyleaf.

Inside, men Nick didn't know recognized him and made way for him. This happened a lot in New York, but it was nice to see it here, through his father's eyes.

They went to the men's room. "Last words on the subject," Fausto whispered, his eyes on the wall above the urinal trough. "You want me to take care of you-know-who"—he let go of his dick, turned to his son, and snapped his fingers, both hands—"I'll do it tomorrow."

Nick smiled. "Thanks," he said. "I'll let you know."

"Don't take him lightly," Fausto said, zipping up. "In his day he sent more men to meet the Devil than—"

"I won't." Nick washed his hands and held the door for his father. "First bet's on me."

He placed it with the same five his father had left under Charlotte's purse. It went on a big ugly Blueface stag, a ten-to-one underdog that they first saw in its pen, shitting all over itself. Fausto looked at the diarrhea and even stuck his finger into a gob that had fallen on the floor and smelled it. Thirty seconds in, the shit-tailed cock leapt up and hit the other

bird's carotid artery. As Fausto the Driver had guessed, the diarrhea had been a sham, induced with Epsom salts.

The Geracis were fifty to the good, playing it cool, trying to find the angles that would decide the next deadly fight, no matter how much rage beat in the hearts of the next two chickens.

Chapter 19

PETE CLEMENZA was holding court at a diner just outside the Garment District, a place with a back dining room where no one who was not with Clemenza was ever seated. The man who owned the place was old enough to be Pete's father, and Pete was seventy. They'd been friends longer than either man could remember. This particular morning, the boss was home sick and Pete was in the kitchen, an apron tied over his silk suit, cooking peppers and eggs, redoing the chopped onions (the ones already prepared were "a million times too coarse"), and showing the ropes to the punks who worked for his friend, keeping them in line. Two of Clemenza's men sat at a metal table crammed in the corner, listening to Clemenza do what he'd done for the better part of his waking life, which was tell a story. It had been what had sealed his bond with Vito Corleone. Pete was a born storyteller, Vito a born listener.

This one happened five years ago, right after Pete got out of prison for a short stretch he'd had to do for extortion (the case was overturned on appeal). Pete had gone to see Tessio's new TV. "Compared to the TV sets in the joint," Pete said, "this one's got a picture so pretty it made your dick hard. It's Friday night, and Tessio's got a few of us over to watch the fights, hoist a couple, place a friendly wager or two. Tessio had inside dope on every fight in creation, but he's extending his hospitality, so losing money to him, it's like slipping the house a little something for a good seat. Only guy there I don't know is this one kid—new guy, wound tight as a squirrel. For somebody who's not well known, he's asking a lot of questions, and at a certain point I say something about it. Kid goes white, but Sally says, 'Let him ask, how else does a guy learn?' A little later I'm in the hall comin' out of the can when Richie Two Guns asks what the squirrel's story was. I didn't know shit, I said, which maybe oughta be on my tombstone. The first fight starts, and Sally tells Richie to turn the sound off, that he can't stand the announcer. Then Sally tells the squirrel to announce the fight. Kid laughs, but Sally pulls out a gun and waves it at him like get on with it. Kid looks like he might piss himself. 'Welcome to Madison Square Garden,' he says, and, I shit you not, his voice comes out of the TV! 'Who's in the dark trunks?' Sally says. The squirrel says, 'In the dark

trunks, we have Beau Jack,' which again comes through the TV. Sally smiles and says he don't like this announcer, either. Richie rips the squirrel's shirt off, and damned if this hairy bastard ain't wearing a wire. First one I ever saw with a transmitter. Primitive government piece of shit played right through Sally's new TV. Sally goes over, leans into the microphone part, and says, '*Fatta la legge, trovato l'inganno.*' For every law, there's a loophole, I guess you'd say. Anyway, this cop or whatever he was must have known Italian and figured out that despite the rule against killing cops, Sally was going to get the job done anyway. So then the squirrel really *does* piss himself. It shorts out the fucking transmitter. Squirrel starts jerking and screaming. Swear to God, his *nuts* are on fire. His nuts!"

Everyone in that cramped kitchen laughed.

Clemenza keeled over onto the grill.

They must have thought he was going for a bigger laugh yet. For a moment—as the big man's great big heart blew like a bald truck tire—he got one. Then the flesh of his fat face seared and crackled and his suit coat burst into flame. His men leapt up and pulled him from the grill. They smothered the fire in no time.

All the last original employees of Genco Pura Olive Oil—its president, Vito Corleone; its manager, Genco Abbandando; and its two salesmen, Sal Tessio and Pete Clemenza—were dead.

The train station in Cleveland was near enough to the lake that gusts of icy wind were knocking down disembarking passengers. Nick Geraci fell, as did two of his men. Eddie Paradise broke his arm, though it was a few days before he figured that out.

The Polack was out by the Thinker.

It was the day before Clemenza's funeral and an hour after the Cleveland Museum of Art closed. Geraci was shown into a white room, utterly empty except for Vincent Forlenza—the largest anonymous donor in the history of that great museum—and his wheelchair. He called to his men to get Mr. Geraci a chair or a bench, but Geraci insisted that it was fine, he'd stand. Forlenza's nurse and all the bodyguards waited at the end of a long hall.

Geraci admitted that his first impulse had been to have Laughing Sal's car sabotaged and make it look like an accident. Tit for tat, more or less. Forlenza's idea had been to car-bomb Narducci into a hundred corners of oblivion. Car bombing was the midwestern Families' style. It was a labor saver, eliminating any need to dispose of the bodies.

They discussed the merits of torturing Narducci, as Forlenza had the dead pal of the dead mechanic. But there was nothing Narducci could tell

them that they hadn't already confirmed. If they were going to kill him, they might as well just give him two to the head or, sure, wire up his car.

But Geraci talked Forlenza into keeping Narducci alive. For now.

First of all, if Narducci died or disappeared, Michael Corleone would be onto them. And Narducci hardly seemed to pose a threat. He'd made the most indirect move on Forlenza possible. Furthermore, as far as Geraci knew, no *consigliere* had ever betrayed his boss. This could be a terrible embarrassment to the Cleveland organization. Narducci would have to be disposed of in a way that wouldn't look as if it had been ordered or even condoned by Don Forlenza.

Killing Michael Corleone would have been another option, and, like killing Narducci, a satisfying one. But where would it have led? Mayhem, war, millions of dollars in lost profits in the meantime. Even if they won, they'd lose.

For now, they'd keep a close eye on the men who'd betrayed them but turn their efforts to building a new set of allegiances. Geraci already worked with Black Tony Stracci and his organization. Forlenza had ties to Paulie Fortunato. With Clemenza's death, Geraci would be controlling the day-to-day operations of the Corleone Family in New York. He was practically a boss himself now. So that was three of the five New York Families.

The key after that would be Chicago. Louie Russo already had a coalition involving Milwaukee, Tampa, Los Angeles, New Orleans, and Dallas. Put that together with what Geraci and Forlenza could build, and Michael Corleone will *wish* he was dead.

The best revenge on Michael Corleone *was* tit for tat.

They would use Fredo as a pawn, the same way Michael had tried to use Nick Geraci.

They'd stay above the fray and let their enemies kill each other off.

They'd take it slowly. Carefully.

When it was over, Cleveland and Chicago and the other midwestern Families would again control the West. Nick Geraci would be the boss of what used to be the Corleone Family, doing business in and around New York. All they needed to do was put Fredo in the middle between Michael and Hyman Roth.

Don Forlenza shook his frail head. Morgues are full of new arrivals who look more vital than the ancient Don. "Tell me this, Fausto," he said. "Why would this Fredo do it?"

Fausto. Only he and Michael Corleone called Geraci *Fausto* and it always threw him, just a little. The real Fausto called him no name at all, just names. *Genius. Big shot. Ace.*

"That time he cried on the street in New York after his father was

shot?" Forlenza said. "Didn't that come after his brother Sonny took sides against the Family on the issue of narcotics?"

Don Forlenza had no idea his own godson was the biggest heroin importer in the United States. "I don't know," Geraci said. Though he did, of course. "Something like that."

"Sonny more or less got Vito shot, is the story I heard. I don't see this Fredo, after an experience like that, doing something even worse."

"First of all," Geraci said, "Fredo's on the booze and has an unbelievably bad marriage. He's out of control. Second, and this is how we get him to hang himself—"

"Hang himself?"

"Figure of speech."

Forlenza shrugged. "If he hangs himself, he hangs himself."

"Right, well. Sure. Anyway. Here's the deal: Fredo's got this idea about building a city of the dead in New Jersey. He's like a guy who had a religious vision or something."

"City of the dead?"

"Big cemetery scam. Long story. Michael's not for it, and he's probably right. How is Fredo, out west and married to a movie star, going to run a big new operation—on another Family's turf, more or less? Point is, Fredo thinks he came up with a billion-dollar business and that Mike's too caught up in his Cuba thing to give him the time of day. Or too sick of what a fuckup Fredo is to give him more than a symbolic title and a legal whorehouse to run."

Geraci heard himself say all this and knew there was no turning back. He was taking sides against the Family, too. Fuck it. Loyalty's a two-way street. Nick Geraci never breathed a disloyal breath—up until the point Michael Corleone tried to kill him.

Revenge, in Nick Geraci's book, was not the same thing as betrayal.

Don Forlenza closed his eyes and sat in silence so long that Geraci looked at the man's chest to make sure he was still breathing.

"Hyman Roth's been in partnership with the Corleones," Geraci said, "even longer than he has with you, but the deal he and Mike are working on in Cuba is so big that they've reached some sort of stalemate." Geraci came closer. He raised his voice, enough to wake Forlenza up if need be. "We can use Fredo to break it. Roth still has plenty of political pull in New York. If Fredo thinks that Roth will back this cemetery thing, it'll get his attention in a hurry."

Forlenza kept breathing. His fingers tugged ever so slightly at the blanket on his lap.

"What we do," Geraci said, "is go through Louie Russo for everything. The L.A. guys are Russo's puppets. Fredo's chummy with a lot of

'em. What happens is, you get Russo to get the word to L.A. Gussie Cicero or somebody can set it up so that one of Roth's guys—Mortie Whiteshoes, Johnny Ola, a party boy like that—just happens to bump into Fredo out in Beverly Hills. Fredo'll give Roth's guys any info about Mike they want so long as he thinks that the payoff will be that if you die in New York City, Fredo'll get a piece of it."

Finally, Forlenza looked up. "Why the fuck would I die in New York City?"

"Godfather, I have every confidence that you'll never die anywhere."

Forlenza waved him off and laughed. "*La testa di cazzo*, eh?" What makes you so sure Fuckface will want to go along with all this?"

"He'll benefit from it. That's the main thing. But the other reason is that the person he'll be dealing with is you—the only Don who's not Russo's puppet or his enemy."

"That's what you think, huh?" Forlenza said, clearly flattered.

"I didn't get as far as I have by being a guy who doesn't do his homework, you know?"

Forlenza smiled. He knew. He agreed to the plan and sealed it with a kiss.

If anything went wrong, the blame would fall on Russo. If that layer of insulation failed, the blame would fall on Forlenza, who could be counted on, in his dealings with Russo, to leave all mention of Geraci out of it—both to protect his godson and because he'd want to take credit for the plan himself. Geraci didn't *want* blame to fall on Forlenza, but better him than Nick Geraci.

At great length, they discussed the details.

"Trust me," Geraci said as they were finishing. "Fredo's so dumb, he'll betray his brother and think he's helping out."

"Never say *Trust me*. Because no one will."

"Oh, yeah?"

"Trust me."

Geraci grinned "You trust *me*, don't you, Godfather?"

"I do, of course. Of course!"

"Enough to grant me a favor? One final detail we haven't yet covered?"

Forlenza pursed his lips and turned his hands palms up, a let-me-hear-it gesture.

"When the time is right," Geraci said, "I want to kill that rat Narducci myself."

That rat. In his mind's eye, Geraci saw the river rat slithering out of the rectum of that stiff Laughing Sal had planted down by the river, the corpse the world had mistaken for Gerald O'Malley.

"Let me be honest with you," Forlenza said. "I was already gonna have you do it."

Clemenza had been Vito Corleone's oldest friend, but the only member of the late Don's immediate family who went to New York for the funeral was Fredo. Carmela had had a flare-up of her blood clots—this time in her legs—and couldn't travel. Michael had business. Kay, a lot of people seemed to think, was on the edge of leaving him. Connie had dumped her second husband, that sadsack accountant Ed Federici, and was off in Monaco, consorting naked on the beaches with Eurotrash. It was un- clear—to Nick Geraci, anyway—why Hagen couldn't come, but he wasn't here. The same went for all the members of the organization out in Nevada, even Rocco Lampone, who'd made it all the way from a gimpy war vet with few prospects all the way to *caporegime,* every step of it with Clemenza's backing. Nobody but Fredo, dispatched for symbolic value, presumably, though when Geraci picked him up at the airport, Fredo said he wouldn't have missed the chance to pay his respects to Pete Clemenza for anything.

On the way to the funeral, during a snowstorm, Fredo Corleone and Nick Geraci stopped for a walk through the Brooklyn Botanic Garden. This had been Tessio's favorite place to talk business, and it had become Geraci's. The place was never so crowded on a weekday that it was hard to talk privately. Plus, it would have been an impossible place to bug.

The snow fell in wet flakes, four inches or more expected. The Rock Garden looked like the lumpy surface of the moon. Trailing several paces behind were four of Geraci's men, Momo the Roach, Eddie Paradise, and two zips (recently arrived Sicilians, in other words, considered ruthless even by other wiseguys). Two others (Tommy Neri, who'd come with Fredo, and Geraci's driver, Donnie Bags, so named for the colostomy bag he'd needed since he was gutshot by his own wife) had stayed with the cars.

"What I hear," Fredo said, "is that maybe Pete's heart attack was no heart attack."

"The autopsy said heart attack," Geraci said. "Making someone *have* a heart attack? Christ. Know what I think? People watch too much TV. Rots their brains. No offense."

"None taken," Fredo said. "Plus which you may be right." The pre- vailing rumor was that the men who said they pulled Clemenza from the grill had actually pushed him onto it, that they were trying to burn him up and along with it, the diner, too, but lucked out: he had a heart attack, which streamlined things. There were men both inside and outside his

own crew who were suspected of the killing, if there had been a killing, which was highly debatable.

That didn't stop other rumors from flying. Many seemed to think Clemenza had been killed by Hyman Roth, the Jewish gang leader, if only because Roth was in the middle of negotiations with Michael Corleone for control of Cuba. Louie Russo's Chicago outfit couldn't be ruled out, either. If it *had* been murder, Geraci would have bet on the Rosato Brothers, a rogue element in Clemenza's *regime* with ties to Don Rico Tattaglia. All that said, both Ockham's razor and Clemenza's diet pointed to an unadorned heart attack. An autopsy showed that his heart was twice the size of a normal man's.

"Hagen said he thought that all the rumors were ridiculous, too," Fredo said.

"What did the Don say?" asked Geraci.

"Mike agreed with Hagen," Fredo said. "I talked to him personally about it." He bounced on the balls of his feet as he said it.

A semi-illiterate reader of human beings could have guessed that this was a lie, though Geraci didn't even have to guess. Fredo's top bodyguard used to be Geraci's barber. Everyone called him Figaro. Figaro's cousin was a welder and fabricator—Geraci's guy for tricking out storage spaces in cars and trucks to transport goods from the docks in Jersey. According to Figaro and the cousin, Fredo had barely said hello to Michael since Francesca's wedding.

Fredo was shivering almost to the point of convulsion. He'd lived out west for twelve years and said he couldn't handle the cold anymore. Pathetic. If he wanted to experience real cold, he ought to take the fucking train to Cleveland sometime. But out of pity, Geraci steered him into a greenhouse, full of orchids in full bloom and a troop of Girl Scouts.

"How's your ma?" asked Geraci. "Doin' all right?"

"She's tough. The move was hard on her, though. Her place in Tahoe is a million times nicer than that house on the mall, but she and Pop built that place together. Lot of memories."

"If she's anything like my mother," Geraci said, crossing himself and looking out at the falling snow, "the change of scenery might do her a world of good."

"Not to mention the warmer weather," Fredo said. "I never seen an orange orchid before," he said, pointing.

The Girl Scouts left, and the two men were alone together in the greenhouse.

"Mike really wanted to come," Fredo said, "but he's all tied up with something big. He loved Pete like an uncle. Christ, we all did."

Geraci nodded, willing his face into impassiveness. "I'm sure the Don

knows what's best." Geraci presumed that the real reason Michael hadn't come was that he didn't want to be seen at the funeral by any New York reporters or the FBI. His mania to become quote-unquote legitimate overrode his loyalty to his father's oldest friend, a man he himself had seemed to love—to the extent he was capable of love, or any other emotion. "Something big, huh?"

"To be honest with you," Fredo said, "I don't know much about it."

That was probably true. But Geraci knew plenty. Michael and Roth were apparently unaware that their negotiations for control of Cuba were pointless, since the Batista government was doomed to fall, and had no real importance other than to make them cogs in a bigger wheel involving a coalition of the midwest Families, led by Chicago and Cleveland. Louie Russo had a deal worked out with the rebels. Even if Batista somehow stayed in power, Fredo's weakness could be used to turn Roth and Michael against each other. All that would be left of their deal was the deal itself, the terms of which Russo and his associates were fully prepared to assume.

Geraci nodded toward the door. They had to keep moving.

He gave Fredo an update on the project they were calling Colma East. He'd worked out the turf issues in Jersey with the Straccis. He had a front, someone impossible to connect to the Corleone Family, who had a contract on a big swampy parcel of land. Also, since Geraci was already shipping most of his heroin from Sicily in between slabs of marble too heavy for customs inspectors to move, getting into the stonecutting business would be a snap. "What about on your end?"

"It's in the bag. Me and Mike just need to sit down and hammer out a few particulars."

"You haven't done that yet?" Geraci said, pretending to be surprised. "Because this is as far as I can take this thing. Ordinances, rezoning, et cetera—those aren't fields of the law I know about. I know *who* to ask, how to get all that rolling, but first you have to get the Don's blessing. The politicians—again, his call and not mine. There's also the matter of how the public might react to this, how to sell it to them. How to keep it off the ballot and so on. Fredo, I respect what you're trying to do, but don't you think that if the Don thought these problems were easy to fix, we'd probably be moving forward already?"

"Nah. The problem is the timing. Mike's focus for the time being is on other things. Knowing you're on board, though, that'll get it done. From Mike's way of thinking, me and you are perfect for a thing like this. His brother and the guy he's got the highest opinion of."

Geraci put his big hand on Fredo's shoulder. "Mike never said that, Fredo."

It was a show of disrespect, a calculated risk, but of course Geraci was right.

"Did I *say* he said that?" Fredo said. "What I said was what his way of thinking was."

"I'm just a mook from Cleveland." Geraci tightened his grip; Fredo flinched. "I do what I'm told, run my own things, spread the wealth, everybody's happy. Here and there, I see an opportunity, and I take it. But don't make me into more than I am. I'm not *on board,* either. You asked me to look into some things, and I looked. Period. We clear?"

Fredo nodded. Geraci let go of his shoulder. They started walking again. The sun came out, but the snow kept falling.

"I hate that," Fredo said. "The snow and the sun. It's unnatural. Like the bomb's been dropped and the world's gone screwy on us."

"I need to be clear on something else, Fredo," Geraci said. "I don't want to get into the middle of things between you and your brother."

"Things are fine between me and my brother."

"Just so it's understood. I'm not taking sides. Under no circumstances."

"There's no sides to take. C'mon. We're on the same side about everything. Anybody says different, they don't know me. They don't know Mike."

" 'Methinks thou dost protest too much.' "

"What the fuck?"

Geraci jerked his thumb toward where they came from. "Shakespeare. The garden back there made me think of it. You're an actor now, Fredo. Maybe you should learn that stuff."

"Don't college-boy me, Mr. Just-a-mook-from-Cleveland. You think you're *better* than me?"

"Easy," Geraci said. "I don't think anything. Shakespeare was just on my mind."

"Because I've been to see Shakespeare. I've even seen Shakespeare in Italian."

"Which ones? Which plays?"

"I don't know which ones, right off. What are you, my fucking English teacher? Don't tell me what I need to *learn.* It may come as news to you that I got a lot of different things going on. I'm not sittin' on my ass sipping sherry and making lists of all the plays I ever been to. I've been to plays. All right? Smart guy? Plays."

"Fine," Geraci said.

They kept walking. He gave Fredo time to calm down.

"Look," Geraci finally said. "I'm edgy, all right? I don't like to go behind Michael's back even to take a leak."

"Don't worry about it. Our operation's too big for any one man to be aware of every little thing or even want to."

If Fredo really believed that, he certainly didn't know his brother.

"Problem with Mike," Fredo said, "he's smart but he's bad with people. He don't understand, it's natural for people to want to do things for themselves, create things. All I want is to have something that's mine. My legacy, if you will. If you didn't feel the same way—"

"This is getting us nowhere, Fredo. I've said what I have to say." Geraci had been right. Fredo was a sweet guy but dumb enough to take his thirty pieces of silver and betray his brother without even knowing that was what he'd done. It was a sad moment. Despite everything, he really liked Fredo. "The next step is one hundred percent between you and Mike. End of story."

Fredo shrugged, then looked down at his loafers. "I tell you what," he said. "These sure aren't the right shoes for this slop."

"Should've worn your cowboy boots," Geraci said.

"What cowboy boots?"

"I thought all you guys out there wore cowboy boots, carried six-shooters, the whole bit. Shoot up cars and little dogs."

Fredo laughed. He usually took it well when you needled him, further proof what a good guy he really was. How sad using him as a pawn in all this was going to be. "If there were ever two cars that had it coming," Fredo said, "those were it. Too bad about the dog, though."

"True it took the head right off?"

Fredo raised his eyes in woe and lamentation. "Clean. I couldn't have made that shot in a million years if I was trying."

"We need to get going," Geraci said, pointing toward the lot where they'd parked. "This is not a thing I'm going to be late to."

"We're a lot alike," Fredo said, "you know that?"

"I'll take that as a compliment," Geraci said, looping an arm around him, cuffing him playfully, the way a brother or an old friend would.

They crossed a small wooden bridge across a barely frozen pond.

"You should see this place in the spring," Geraci said. "Cherry blossoms like you can't believe, pinker than pink."

"I probably should."

"You know," Geraci said, "I've always wanted to ask you something."

"Anything, my friend."

"Tell me if I'm out of line for even asking, but what exactly are your responsibilities as *sotto capo*? What did Mike tell you they were?"

"Are you serious? What are you talkin' about? What are you askin' me here?"

"Because I don't think it's clear to anyone. To a lot of people, and

here I confess that what I really mean is *to me,* but I'm not alone, no offense, but it seems mostly symbolic."

"Symbolic? What the fuck you talking about, symbolic? I got a lot of different things I do. How is it that you don't understand that there's a bunch of it I can't talk about?"

"That, I understand. It's just that—"

"I imagine that, with Pete gone, I'll even be going along with Mike to the meeting of the heads of all the Families, in upstate New York there."

I imagine. Which meant, of course, that he had no idea. It was a shocking and pathetic thing even to be talking about, both because Pete wasn't even in the ground yet and because this was not the sort of speculation Fredo should be making to anyone but his brother.

"It's just that a lot of what's going on with you," Geraci said, "is awfully public."

"Come on. Bit parts. Little local TV show. It's nothin'. No harm in any of it, and maybe some help."

"I don't disagree," Geraci said. "I see the value of it to the organization if the only aim is to get out of any businesses that might be considered crimes, victimless and otherwise. But there are other parts of the business to consider."

They got back into the car.

"Don't worry about nothin'," Fredo said. "Me and Mike, we'll work out the details."

What Nick Geraci would like to know is this: If Michael wanted the organization to be more like a corporation, bigger than General Motors, in control of presidents and potentates, then why run it like some two-bit corner grocery store? Corleone & Sons. The Brothers Corleone. When Vito Corleone was shot, incapacitated, who took over? Not Tessio, Vito's smartest and most experienced man. Sonny, who was a violent rockhead. Why? Because he was a Corleone. Fredo was too weak for anything important, yet even then, symbolic or not, Michael made that empty suit his underboss. Hagen was the *consigliere* even when he supposedly wasn't, the only non-Italian *consigliere* in the country. Why? Because Michael grew up in the same house with him. Michael himself had all the ability in the world, but in the end he was the biggest joke of all. Vito, without even consulting his own *caporegimes,* made Mike the *boss*—a guy who never earned a red cent for anyone, who never ran a crew, who never proved himself at all except for the night he whacked two guys in a restaurant (every detail of which was arranged by the late, great Pete Clemenza). Only three people ever even got initiated into the Corleone Family without first proving themselves as earners. That would be, yes, the Brothers Corleone.

So now the whole organization was under the control of a guy who'd never done anything but think big thoughts and order people killed. Yes, he was smart, but didn't anybody besides Sally Tessio, Nick Geraci, and possibly Tom Hagen realize that, as long as Michael thought he was smarter than everybody else, the whole organization was at the mercy of the guy's ego?

True: Geraci had barely allowed himself to think these things before he learned that Michael Corleone had tried to kill him. Still. That didn't mean that he was wrong.

Though no one could have known it at the time, Peter Clemenza's was the last of the great Mafia funerals. The air inside St. Patrick's Cathedral was almost unbreathably thick with the scent of the tens of thousands of flowers, blanketing the altar and spilling down the aisles, signed less cryptically than any such flowers would ever be again. In the pews, for the last time, were dozens of unself-conscious judges, businessmen, and politicians. To this day, singers and other entertainers show up at such funerals, but never in the numbers in evidence for Clemenza. Anyone in the know—and for now there were still very few such people—could have scanned the scores of mourners and put together a pretty impressive all-star team of New York wiseguys and assorted heavy people from out of town—including Sicily. Never again would a Don attend a funeral for a member of another Family. Never again would the presence of law enforcement be at such a manageable level. And only one more time, ever, would so many high-ranking figures in La Cosa Nostra gather in one place. All this, for an olive oil importer who'd shunned attention and barely known many of the most famous people who had convened to see him off. The most famous person he knew well—Johnny Fontane—wasn't even there.

Nick and Charlotte Geraci took a seat in the pew directly behind Laughing Sal Narducci, his wife, and Narducci's son Buddy, who was in the shopping center business along with Ray Clemenza—like the Castle in the Sand, a wholly legitimate, privately held enterprise in which elements of the Corleone and Forlenza organizations were legal investors. (That is, irrespective of where that money had come from in the first place, although where does *any* money come from in the first place? How would one define "first place"?) Sal turned and reached over the back of the pew to give Geraci an enormous, lengthy embrace. Throughout the homily and several eulogies, at every pause, Laughing Sal, characteristically, muttered the speaker's last few words, and not in a whisper, either. Charlotte had barely known Clemenza, but it got her goat.

After the service, Laughing Sal turned to face the Geracis, tears streaming down his face. "So young," he said. "Such a tragedy."

Nick Geraci nodded grimly, as anyone at a funeral would do. Narducci and Clemenza were about the same age.

As a soprano from the Metropolitan Opera sang "Ave Maria," Charlotte crossed her arms and turned to face the back of the church. The huge oak double doors were open. The pallbearers started down the steps. Clemenza's rosewood casket disappeared into the falling snow.

Chapter 20

EXPERTS CITE MANY factors that led from the heyday of La Cosa Nostra in the fifties and sixties to the mannered, treasonous shadow of itself it is today. Various Senate and congressional hearings. The FBI's shift in focus from the Red Menace to the Mob. The tendency in all businesses created by first-generation immigrants to be destabilized by the second generation and ruined by the third. The widespread supposition on the part of average Americans (brought into mainstream thought by the Mafia and hammered home by the Watergate scandal) that laws and regulations are for other people, i.e., the suckers. The greater profits to be had by running "legal" corporations that get no-bid contracts from their powerful friends in the government. Most of all, the Mob was kneecapped by the RICO statutes, which gave the weapon of racketeering charges to federal prosecutors everywhere, which resulted in lengthy jail terms for mobsters and the feeling in many dark corners of the American underworld that *omertà* was becoming a law observed mostly in the breach.

These things were all hugely important, of course, but they flowed from a common source, the single most devastating blow ever dealt to organized crime in America: the order, placed less than a month before that first meeting of all the Families in a white clapboard farmhouse in upstate New York, for two dozen custom-built maple tables.

If, say, they'd just bought or stolen or even rented tables, the stain wouldn't have been so fresh. The vapors wouldn't have forced the men to open the windows. The aroma of the roasting pig wouldn't have had all afternoon to waft inside and work its succulent magic. The Dons and their *consigliere*s wouldn't have lingered. They might never have scheduled further meetings of the heads of all the Families.

Even if the tables *had* been custom-made at the last minute but the head carpenter had been anyone other than a Mr. Floyd Kirby, we might all be living in a very different America. This was not only because another carpenter might have favored a less noxious brand of stain but also because Mr. Kirby was married to a cousin of a New York State trooper. That Christmas, the trooper had heard about all those tables and what kind of people he thought they might have been for. The trooper knew that the

brewing company owner who lived in the house was suspected of having the local police in his pocket. The trooper and his partner talked to several residents in the area, but no one had seen anything unusual, or so they said.

The trooper made a note to keep an eye on things there, but who knows if he'd have followed through on it if he hadn't been recently divorced and if the woman who lived in the rusty trailer near the road that led to the farmhouse hadn't been so friendly. They began dating. By the time the Families met the second time, they were married. She'd moved out of the trailer, but they kept it because she owned the land. They planned to build something nice on it someday. They happened to be there, in fact, making love in the trailer for old times' sake, when the parade of Cadillacs and Lincolns came thundering down the gravel road, past the trailer.

Again: to build power, sometimes one must control the least powerful. The trooper slipped tenners to motel desk clerks in the area, with instructions to let him know if they had a flurry of reservations by out-of-state people with Italian names (he was also an instinctive racial profiler). The next year he had enough advance notice to get an operation going.

It nearly didn't happen. His own commander didn't see enough merit in the investigation to allocate anyone to it other than the trooper and his partner. No one at the FBI would return his phone calls. In a last-ditch effort, he contacted the Bureau of Alcohol, Tobacco and Firearms. The man he talked to was young and gung ho. The trooper also took it on himself to make a few calls to reporters. The next day, he and his partner were sitting in his wife's old trailer with binoculars. Twenty ATF agents were poised in their gray government Chevrolets at a truck stop out on the main highway, waiting for a call. In rented cars behind the Chevys were the press, a platoon of shooters and scribes, and even a radio guy from Albany.

What happened next made the front page of every major newspaper in America and the cover of *Life* magazine. Even these many years later, most readers will be familiar with it: the raid on that white farmhouse and the seventy-odd men who saw them coming and scattered.

The pictures are famous: heavy men in silk suits and white fedoras hauling ass through the woods. Fat Rico Tattaglia and even fatter Paulie Fortunato being handcuffed as a half-carved hog turns on a spit behind them. ATF agents crouched beside sawhorses at a roadblock on that tree-lined road, guns drawn, as the Dons of Detroit, Tampa, and Kansas City emerge from their respective vehicles (armored, a fascinated public learned). The state trooper, grinning like he's just caught the biggest wall-

eye in the lake, while the man next to him—Ignazio Pignatelli, aka Jackie Ping-Pong (those nicknames! God, how the public loved the nicknames!)—covers his big round face with both hands.

The men were taken to the nearest state police barracks and charged with—what? That turned out to be a problem. It looked bad, all those men in that farmhouse together, but looking bad was in itself no crime. "It's safe to say," an ATF agent told a New York newspaper, "that all those Italians in fancy suits didn't come from all over the country just to roast a pig." Maybe. But what *had* they come there to do? No one but the men themselves had any idea, and they weren't talking.

Eminent lawyers swooped in (including a former assistant attorney general of the United States, the senior partner of what was then the largest law firm in Philadelphia, and onetime U.S. congressman Thomas F. Hagen of Nevada). They were good enough to point out that the U.S. Constitution guaranteed the right to free assembly.

Those detained invoked their constitutionally guaranteed right not to testify against themselves. As a consequence, a few were charged with obstruction of justice—charges that were later literally laughed out of court. Despite the efforts of countless state and federal attorneys, the only direct result of the raid was the deportation of three of the detainees to Sicily, including one, Salvatore Narducci of Cleveland, who'd lived in America since he was a baby, more than sixty years. He claimed he was unaware that he'd never become a citizen.

The indirect results, however, were legion. When the newspapers with the stories about the raid hit the front stoops up and down Main Street, USA, it was the first time many people heard the words *Mafia* and *La Cosa Nostra*. The stories speculated about the heretofore undreamt of existence of an international crime syndicate. Many headlines used that word: *syndicate*. It is not a word that soothes the American ear. It sounds vaguely mathematical, and America is not a mathematical country.

A public outcry went up: *Who are these men?*

Before the raid, beat cops and precinct captains, beholden politicians, and writers for magazines like *Manhunt* and *Thrilling Detective* all knew more about the men in that white farmhouse—and about the *uomini rispettati* who worked for those men, and about the legion lesser street toughs who worked for *those* men—than did the FBI.

That time was about to end.

Today, twenty-three of those lovely, almost indestructible maple tables are crated and stacked in a warehouse at an undisclosed location in or near the District of Columbia. By rights, the twenty-fourth should be on permanent display in the Smithsonian. *This table,* the plaque would read, *helped deliver the single most devastating blow ever dealt to organized crime*

in America. With a pig skull on top, alongside a scale model of the rusted house trailer.

Instead, the table was sent from one white house to another. Since 1961, it has been in constant use in or near the Oval Office.

Tom Hagen didn't swoop in, of course. It only looked that way. When detectives asked how someone who lived in Nevada had gotten there so fast, Hagen said that he had already been in New York, that he often was, which was true.

Hagen was among the younger men there. He made it to the bottom of the hill and followed a rocky stream until he got to a town. He walked into a diner. No one was looking for anyone who looked like Tom Hagen, and the car he'd driven there, now parked behind the farmhouse, was registered to a ghost. He sat in a booth and calmly had lunch. Then he went to Woolworth's, bought a suitcase, and got directions to the county courthouse. It was in the next town over. He walked back to the diner and called a cab. Luggage in hand like any ordinary, unremarkable traveler, Hagen checked into a hotel in the county seat. He walked to the barbershop closest to the courthouse. By the time he paid the barber, Hagen had learned the broad outlines of what had happened. He called in to the phone service in Las Vegas. He went back to the hotel and took a nap. A few hours later, the phone woke him. It was Rocco Lampone, calling from Tahoe. Hagen took a taxi to the nearest state police barracks. Michael had not been among those arrested, but, as a goodwill gesture, Hagen provided legal assistance to a few friends of the Family.

In 1959, under oath and before a subcommittee of the U.S. Senate, Michael Corleone testified that he had not been in that farmhouse. He denied having been among those who had escaped what was undoubtedly an illegal police action.

Strictly speaking, Michael Corleone was telling the truth.

He and Hagen had driven there separately, for various business and security reasons (though they did have the archaic and, in the face of a police raid, worthless insurance policy provided by holding a Bocchicchio hostage at a whorehouse in the desert). Had Michael been as punctual as his father, he'd surely have been among those who, dignity be damned, went scrambling down the hill. Yes, he had escaped from more harrowing situations, with the air full of bullets and bombs and Jap Zeros heading his way on a divine tailwind. But that was a dozen years and a hundred thousand cigarettes ago. Who knows if he'd have been able to run fast enough and far enough to elude capture?

He did not have to find out—only because, as per usual, he was late:

so egregiously late, in fact, that they'd started their business without him. A split second before Michael flicked on his turn signal to go down the gravel drive, he glimpsed something yellow in the bushes, not far from that rusted trailer. He put his hand back on the wheel and kept going. He passed the drive and began to round a bend. In his rearview mirror, he saw two men—cops of some kind—dragging yellow sawhorses from those bushes.

The car he was using was a blue Dodge, a few years old, equipped with a police scanner (Al Neri had been a cop; both the bland car and the scanner were his idea). Michael found the frequency the ATF agents were using.

He pounded the steering wheel as hard as he could and let out an anguished roar.

This was supposed to have been Michael's last appearance at a meeting of the Commission or of all the Families. He'd planned to negotiate his retirement. After today, after he nailed down the deal in Cuba, he'd have been a completely legitimate businessman. He hit the wheel once more.

Calm down, he thought. *Think.*

He lit a cigarette. He sat back in his seat, forcing himself to take long and even breaths, listening to the raid he had so narrowly escaped. It was the sound of a world coming to an end. He'd heard about Pearl Harbor on a radio, too.

Michael Corleone had no idea where this narrow, winding road would lead. The sun was straight overhead, and he couldn't even tell what direction he was going. Still he kept driving, scrupulously observing the traffic laws and looking for signs. What choice did he have? He sure as hell couldn't turn around and go back the way he came.

Fredo Corleone did not wake up thinking, *This is the day that I betray my brother.* He did not set out to do it, and, as Nick Geraci had predicted, Fredo didn't know what he'd done even after he'd sealed his fate by doing it. His day began, instead, when, in the suite at the Château Marmont, Deanna Dunn got out of the shower and, still smelling of last night's gin, slipped into bed beside her sleeping husband.

"C'mon, lover," she purred, starting to tie his wrist to the bedpost with a hand towel.

Fredo jerked his arm free. "What are you doing?"

"Be a sport," she said.

"What time is it? I had an hour's sleep, tops."

She frowned and tossed the towel aside. "You don't want me to be hungry for love on my first day of work with a new costar, do you?"

He had it on good authority—Wally Morgan, who'd know—that Deanna's costar was hardly the sort of man who'd want to lay a hand on her.

Fredo nonetheless gave her what she wanted.

"Try doing more than up-down, up-down," she said.

He was on top. "That ain't exactly music to a guy's ears." He tried giving her a little side-to-side, or whatever it was she wanted. "Not in the middle of things."

"Want me to roll over?" Before he could answer, she'd already done it. That was how she was about everything. "Not in the ass, though." She was on all fours. "Not first thing in the morning."

"I wasn't going to," he said. "Jesus." Why did she keep bringing that up? Even with Wally Morgan, all Fredo usually did was get his dick sucked. Last night, for example, that was all he'd done. Fredo lost his erection. He threw himself down on the mattress, disgusted.

"Don't be like that," she said, reaching for his prick. "It's nothing."

Fredo slapped her hand away. "It's something to me."

"You're just drinking too much," she said.

"You should know," he said.

They lay side by side, staring at themselves in the mirror she'd paid the hotel to install on the bedroom ceiling. After a while, Deanna took matters into her own hands. She was rough with herself. Fredo lit a cigarette and watched. The idea of it was dirty and excited him. He tried to keep his eyes off the round-bellied balding man in the mirror, whose limp prick lolled uselessly against his thigh. Deanna planted her feet on the bed, raised up her ass, and made a big show of bucking her hips and coming. It was like looking at a nature program on TV. Afterward, she kissed him. He rolled away. They lay there and rode out another long silence.

"Fredo," she finally said. "Baby. I want you to know that I know. I've always known."

"Known what?" Fredo got out of bed and went to take a piss. He knew what she meant, though. Rage washed over him.

"This is Hollywood. That's entertainment, y'know? Plenty of people have marriages that are covers for . . . well, *that*. It's fine. All I ask is a warm place to come at night—pun intended—and maybe some nice things once in a—"

"What the fuck are you talking about?"

"Nothing." She sighed. "Forget it."

Fredo washed his hands and stood in the doorway to the bathroom. "I want to know." He raised his fist and bounced it lightly against the doorframe. "Tell me."

"What are you going to do? Are you going to hit me? Shoot another

little dog? I'm telling you that I understand how you are. I don't know if *forgive* is the right word, but—"

"Forgive me for *what*?"

He could toss her out the window. She was a drunk bitch with a fading career. People like that jump out of windows every day.

"Really," she said. "Forget it. I'm sorry I brought it up."

His brothers would have beaten her up. Fredo knew that. They thought he was weak. Everyone did, but he wasn't. He was *strong*. It took strength not to throw her out the window or beat her. Fredo kept his breathing perfectly even and ordered room service. When it came he did not smash his grapefruit in her face. He calmly ate his food and waited for her to leave.

Once she was out of earshot, he hurled his orange juice glass at the door.

He picked up the table lamp and slammed its iron base into the television screen. He threw a green glass ashtray against the row of liquor bottles behind the bar. He took out a knife and, taking his time, shredded the sofa, the chairs, the bed, the pillows, even the drapes.

He took running starts and stomped dozens of holes in the walls.

For no particular reason, the only things in the suite he was careful to leave alone were Deanna's clothes and jewelry. And his own clothes. Otherwise, he destroyed whatever he could. People must have heard, but no one came to stop him.

Finally, he took out his gun. Some crummy off-brand piece of shit, nothing nice like those Colts. He went into the bathroom and fired a round at the bidet, which he'd never figured out how to use or whether it was just for women. Who the fuck wanted to pay prices like what this joint cost and feel stupid? A porcelain shard gashed his cheek, but he barely felt it.

He looked at himself in the bathroom mirror. He put a bullet in the reflection of his balding head. Then he shot the mirror over the bed, too. The shower of glass was spectacular. His life up to now had been but forty-three years of bad luck; if he'd just brought on another seven, another fourteen, so what?

Fredo looked at his watch. The whole day had gotten away from him. He was supposed to meet Jules Segal and some possible investors at Gussie Cicero's supper club in an hour. Fredo called the front desk and said that his wife had had a wild party last night. "You might want to send someone up to figure out the damage," he said. "Just put it on my bill."

The clerk asked if Fredo had heard shots fired.

"Oh, that," Fredo said. "I had a Western on the TV full-blast."

He hung up. He gave the ruined TV set a kick. He went into the

flooded bathroom and turned off the water to the toilet. He looked around the suite. A hell of a goddamned mess, but in the end, all he'd wasted on this one was a day. He'd spent forty-three years on the mess he'd made of his life. He grabbed his tux and his Mary Janes. He could get dressed at Cicero's.

After two encores, J. J. White, Jr., left the stage, drenched in sweat and to a standing ovation. Fredo and Jules Segal were at a table in front, along with two Beverly Hills attorneys, Jacob Lawrence and Allen Barclay—friends of Segal's and also the registered owners of a Vegas casino that really belonged to Vincent Forlenza. Fredo had wrangled gorgeous young starlets as dates for the two married lawyers. Segal's date was Lucy Mancini, who used to be Sonny Corleone's *goumada*. The ladies all went to powder their noses.

Figaro and Capra were at the next table with dates of their own, watching Fredo's back.

"All right, Doc," Fredo said, sitting down. "I got this theory."

"I know what you're going to say," Segal said. "J.J.'s better when he's solo and not kissing Johnny Fontane's ass with all the Uncle Tomming."

"My theory," Lawrence said, "is that Jews are the best entertainers. It's in our blood."

This cracked Barclay and Segal up. White, a Negro, had married a Jew and converted. Lawrence, Barclay, and Segal were all born Jewish, though the lawyers had changed their names.

Fredo frowned. "J.J.'s great, but I'm not talking about nothin' like that," he said. "I'm talking about our possible business arrangement in New Jersey. My theory is, the trick to getting anybody to do anything is that you gotta get 'em to think it was their own idea in the first place."

"You're just figuring that out?" Segal said. "How old are you?" A few years ago, his hair had been gray. Now it was brown as milk chocolate. His suntanned face was only a shade lighter.

Fredo forced a smile. "Point is, I could twist things around and make you think you were the ones who thought of this cemetery thing, but that's not how I do business. I'm not trying to sell you on nothin'. You don't want to get in on the ground floor here? Believe me, I know a hundred guys who will. But Jules, you've helped me out of a lot of tight spots with the ladies; the least I could do was give you this chance. You fellas, too. Friends of Jules are friends of mine. I'm friends with your Cleveland friends, too. Me and Nick Geraci, probably you know him, we're like this. Tight. When the time comes, he'll be in on this, too, believe me. And the Jew?" he said, meaning Forlenza. "Personal friend." Fredo had actually

never laid eyes on the guy. "Long story short, this was my idea, all right? But put your pride aside, and you'll see that if you go in on this, we'll all make a mint."

Capra buried his head in his date's hair. His English was too shaky for him to pick up on what was going on at the next table. Figaro, on the other hand, was stunned that Fredo would go to civilians for money—even though Geraci had said that this was probably what would happen. Figaro used to cut Geraci's hair; his original connection to the Family had been Tessio (another customer). The longer Figaro was out in Nevada and California, the more he was convinced that Vito's sons were wrecking everything. The base of the Family's power was New York—where Figaro was born, and where his loyalties remained. He was Nick Geraci's guy, all the way.

Gussie Cicero and Figaro made eye contact from across the room. Figaro nodded. Gussie went to tell Mortie Whiteshoes and Johnny Ola they had the opening they'd need to get Fredo to help them get their boss and Michael to wrap up some sort of mutually beneficial negotiations. As far as Gussie knew, he himself was doing a harmless favor, and Figaro was just confirming that Fredo was talking about whatever it was that he'd supposedly come there to talk about. As far as Gussie Cicero knew, the idea for putting Ola and Whiteshoes together with Fredo Corleone—for whatever reason—had come from Jackie Ping-Pong. As far as Ping-Pong knew, the idea was Louie Russo's. As far as Russo knew, it was Vincent the Jew's idea.

"It may well be a good idea, Fredo," Segal said. "But good ideas are for suckers."

Fredo cocked his head.

"What makes an idea valuable," Segal said, "is knowing what to do with it."

This was a lot of disrespect to swallow from a self-important, cunt-happy Jew who'd have never even gotten his medical license back if the Corleones hadn't made the head of the review board an offer he couldn't refuse. "I know," Fredo said in a near-whisper, consciously aping the quiet menace his father and brother came by so naturally, "what to do with it."

The men at his table showed no sign of being intimidated.

"Maybe so," Lawrence said, "but we've looked into the details. The ordinances will be next to impossible to pass. Even if you do, the existing cemeteries and related businesses are sure to file suit to get any new laws overturned. I don't know how things were done in San Francisco or why, but it doesn't matter. Different state, different century. Today, you have to worry about the likes of Allen and me. The lawyers. If you want to go ahead with this, trust me, there'll be plenty of . . . what's the term you people use? Plenty of beaks to wet."

" 'You people'?" Fredo said.

Lawrence shrugged. The women were making their way back to the table.

"There's other problems," Segal said. "Tell him, Allen."

"Cemeteries," Barclay said, "have to able to be maintained until the end of time with only the interest from a trust. In other words, you're tying up a fortune up front, which from what I know about your business, I can't imagine you'd want to do. Also, don't take this the wrong way, Mr. Corleone, but the money would need to be so clean you could eat off it."

"Don't worry about that," Fredo said. He couldn't believe they were going to keep talking about this in front of their dates. "I got all that covered." Though he didn't.

The women took their seats and kissed their dates.

"I won't even get into all the problems you'd face," Lawrence said, "trying to transport millions of dead bodies across state lines. Or the impossibility of sewing up any kind of monopoly on all this out in New Jersey."

"Dead bodies!" said Lucy Mancini.

Fredo shot a look at the other men, who at least had enough sense not to explain things. The other women averted their eyes. Lucy flushed, redder than her fresh Singapore Sling. She'd been around long enough not to say a thing like that, and she obviously knew it.

Segal put an arm around Fredo and patted him on the shoulder. "As get-rich-quick schemes go," Segal said, "this is the worst I've ever heard."

Segal extended an arm toward his friends, and they told Fredo that Segal was right.

Fredo stood. He called out to their waitress to bring another round of drinks. "Ladies," he said, "if you'll excuse me?" He made it seem like he was just going to take a leak, but he had no intention of coming back to the table. It'd be a good way to ditch the bodyguards, too, and have a decent night on the town.

Across the room, Johnny Ola—Hyman Roth's token Sicilian—rose and at a discreet distance followed him to the men's room.

Maybe, Fredo thought, *I'll just go home.* Although where was that? Home? He'd spent most of the last dozen or so years in hotel suites. His father was dead. His mother was in Tahoe, where Fredo had a house, too. But that wasn't home. That was just a lake cottage in the country. A fishing cabin. Fredo Corleone was a city boy, stifled in Vegas, but Tahoe? Suffocating.

He saw Gussie Cicero and slipped him a Cleveland. For the tab. Gussie told Fredo his money wasn't good here. "Aw, buy your wife flowers or something," Fredo said. "Or put it in the offering plate at Mass tomorrow."

"Mass tomorrow!" Gussie said, pocketing the thousand dollars. "You crack me up."

At the urinal, he wondered what Deanna would do if she got back to the wreckage of their room before he did. It sent a chill through him. Though maybe it was just a piss shiver.

Fredo zipped up, spun around and slammed into Johnny Ola so hard Ola's hat went flying and Fredo fell on his ass. The men's room attendant rushed over to help, but Ola was already apologizing and helping Fredo to his feet.

"Did I do that?" Ola said, pointing to Fredo's gashed cheek.

Fredo shook his head. "Cut myself shaving."

"You're Frederico Corleone, aren't you? Johnny Ola," he said, offering his hand. "We have some friends in common. I've been hoping to run into you. I didn't expect it'd be so literal, you know?" He grinned. "We should talk. Sometime soon."

Deanna was no doubt already there, had already seen what he'd done. If Fredo hadn't balked at the thought of going to face up to that, it might have saved his life.

"No time like the present," Fredo said.

Moments later, he was in his car, following Ola and Mortie White-shoes to Hollywood. They stopped at the Musso & Frank Grill. The place was packed, but one of those high-backed mahogany booths with the padded red leather seats miraculously opened up.

"My kind of place," Fredo said. "Best martinis in L.A. if not the whole world. Stirred, not shaken, which, take it from an Italian, is the right way to make a martini."

At a place with lesser martinis or less private booths, on a day that had gone better for Fredo than this one, who knows what might have happened? Fredo didn't think of himself as a weak man, but he'd certainly look back on this as a weak moment. Ola and Whiteshoes explained that their boss and Fredo's brother were involved in a big deal of some sort. They claimed not to know what it was about; Cuba wasn't mentioned. Ola said that Michael was being unreasonable in the negotiations. On a better day, Fredo might have understood that was a fancy way of saying that Roth wanted Michael killed. All Fredo could think of at the time was that, when it came to his own big brother, Michael was unreasonable about everything. Fredo tried to poker-face it, but even under the best of circumstances, he was no good at that.

Ola said that if Fredo could help out with things—just some simple information that might help confirm things about the Family's position and assets, nothing major—that there'd be something in it for him. They were open to talking about what that might be. A cash bonus, maybe.

That was when Whiteshoes chimed in and said that a little bird told him something about some kind of city of the dead Fredo was planning out in New Jersey. "I only know what my friend Jules Segal told me," Mortie said, "but from the sound of it, I gotta say, I like the sound of it."

(*From* The Fred Corleone Show, *March 23, 1959 [final episode].*)

FRED CORLEONE: Ladies and gentlemen, on our show tonight we were supposed to have a very special guest, but as you can see we don't. We're going to *have* a guest, that is, and I said the wrong thing in implying that this other guest—I'm getting ahead of myself. That the other one's not special. He is. Great fella. I'm not . . . (*Looks down; rubs his face with both hands.*) I should keep this simple. Nobody wants me to make it complicated. Miss Deanna Dunn, who as you may know . . . What I mean to say is that despite what was in the newspaper there, our guest tonight is not Miss Deanna Dunn. (*Looks offstage.*) I don't need to say more than that, do I?

VOICE OF DIRECTOR: (*Inaudible*)

FRED CORLEONE: Not really. (*Turns back to face the camera.*) Don't worry, folks. With no further to-do, not to mention that there hasn't been any to-do here in the first place, let's welcome our first guest. Here he is, a fine actor who is now making a movie with Mr. Johnny Fontane and that whole crew, about robbing casinos, they tell me, which I can't wait to hear more about, put your hands together for Mr. Robert Chadwick.

(*Recorded applause. This is the only episode that used it, even though the show had dispensed with the live audience several episodes earlier.*)

ROBERT CHADWICK (*waving at the nonexistent audience*): Thanks, everyone. Thanks, Freddie.

FRED CORLEONE: No, thank *you*, Bobby. You're a lifesaver, comin' in at the last minute.

ROBERT CHADWICK: Don't mention it. Believe me, I've been second choice to movie stars a lot less legendary than Deanna Dunn.

FRED CORLEONE: You're obviously being ironical, and I appreciate it. Though in seriousness, a good-lookin' guy like you, leading-man material, classy British accent, I wouldn't think that'd be the case. Most of the roles you get, you're the first choice, right?

ROBERT CHADWICK: The scripts I see have been read by so many other actors, they have more coffee stains on the pages than words. But I must say, it does beat working for a living.

FRED CORLEONE: What?

ROBERT CHADWICK: I said, it's a living.

FRED CORLEONE: Sorry. I'm sorry. I was just—

ROBERT CHADWICK: It's fine. By the way, I wanted to say I was sorry to hear about your mother. I lost my own mother last year, so I know what you're going through. It's not something you really ever get over.

FRED CORLEONE (*frowning*): You know what *I'm*—? (*Closes his eyes, nods, stops frowning.*) Right. Of course . . . thanks.

ROBERT CHADWICK: I tell you what I truly believe, though. A philosophy of life, if you will. Between losing your mother and—I know you don't want to talk about it on the air, but I just want to say I'm also sorry things didn't work out with your lady.

FRED CORLEONE: Thank you.

ROBERT CHADWICK: But between those two misfortunes, I can just about guarantee you that your luck's about to change.

FRED CORLEONE: Just about, huh?

ROBERT CHADWICK (*looking into the camera*): So, ladies, line up! This galoot next to me's on the open market again!

FRED CORLEONE: That'll be a while yet. Before I—

ROBERT CHADWICK: Sure. But there's a lot of fish in the sea.

FRED CORLEONE: That's what they say. You're a happily married man these days, I hear.

ROBERT CHADWICK: I am. Seven years this month, actually.

FRED CORLEONE: To a great girl. She's the sister of Governor Jimmy Shea, if I'm not mistaken.

ROBERT CHADWICK: She is.

FRED CORLEONE: Whattaya think, our next president?

ROBERT CHADWICK: Margaret?

FRED CORLEONE: No, Governor Shea. Oh, right. Good one.

ROBERT CHADWICK: I do. I certainly hope so. I've actually known him since prep school. He's a great leader, a great friend. A war hero, as you may know. He's done wonderful things for New Jersey, and I think in all honesty that America needs a man like this, someone young and smart who can inspire people and take us into the space age. Not to get on a soapbox, but you asked.

FRED CORLEONE: What? Oh. I did. No, I agree with you. This is not a political show, but I'm an American, and so I have my opinions. The opinions expressed by guests on this show or even the host do not necessarily represent blah, blah, blah. However that goes. Anyway, maybe we should get into another topic.

ROBERT CHADWICK: I'm an American, too, old boy.

FRED CORLEONE: You are? I thought—

ROBERT CHADWICK: Since I was twelve years old.

FRED CORLEONE: That's tremendous. I want to hear about how it is that you and Fontane and all your buddies—Gene Jordan, J. J. White, Jr.—

ROBERT CHADWICK: Morrie Streator, Buzz Fratello.

FRED CORLEONE: Right. You guys are staying up all night doing your act onstage at that casino which I don't want to name right now—

ROBERT CHADWICK: The Kasbah.

FRED CORLEONE: —and then filming a movie all day?

ROBERT CHADWICK: It sounds like a lot of work, but it's been a total gas.

FRED CORLEONE: What do you do in a nightclub act?

ROBERT CHADWICK (*laughing*): Precious little.

FRED CORLEONE: Seriously?

ROBERT CHADWICK: I don't sing, and I certainly can't dance. What I do is, I go up onstage, have a few drinks, and tell a few blue jokes. I assure you, they're *ba-a-a-a-ad* jokes. People laugh, though. When you're having that much fun, it's contagious.

FRED CORLEONE: I'll get back to that in a minute, but before we go to commercial, I want to ask you about the movie you're making, because I hear that you and Fontane, Gino, Buzz, all your friends—that you think you're gonna rob all the casinos in Vegas.

ROBERT CHADWICK: It's only a movie, old boy.

FRED CORLEONE: No, I understand that, obviously, having—

ROBERT CHADWICK: You were brilliant in *Ambush at Durango,* by the way. Gave me chills.

FRED CORLEONE: Thank you. What I'm saying is that I wonder how you're going to pull off your big caper. My thinking is that either you'll do it in a way that could never work in real life, in which case it'll seem ridiculous to people. Or *else*—and here's my question—you do have a realistic way of doing it, but then you run the risk of someone copying you.

ROBERT CHADWICK: You're having me on, right? Is that a question?

FRED CORLEONE (*shrugging*): It's a valid point, I think.

ROBERT CHADWICK: You want me to tell you how we do it? How they do it? In the movie?

FRED CORLEONE: I do. That would be interesting.

ROBERT CHADWICK: It would be. But then who'd go see the movie?

FRED CORLEONE: Lots of people would see a movie like that. Whattaya say, folks, you want to hear how they pull their, whatever. Their *heist,* I think is the right word. How 'bout it?

(Recorded applause)

ROBERT CHADWICK: Cute. The problem is, Freddie—and all you good people out there, too—the problem is that I *could* tell you, but then I'd have to kill you.

FRED CORLEONE (*stares at him, frowning; an excruciatingly long silence*)

ROBERT CHADWICK: Yikes. (*Calling out.*) Footwear! Bring me a 12D Italian loafer in a nice gray cement, extra heavy. Send the bill to this fellow.

FRED CORLEONE: We'll be right back.

ROBERT CHADWICK: At least one of us will.

Two days later, Fredo Corleone went to Lake Tahoe to attend to some details in the wake of his mother's death. He had also promised to take his nephew Anthony fishing.

The boy lived on a lake, but his own father never took him. Uncle Fredo took him whenever he was in town. Anthony was eight years old and crazy about Uncle Fredo.

Anthony loved to fish, but he'd never wanted to go fishing more than he did that day. His parents were splitting up, and he had a sneaking suspicion that it was somehow his fault. If he'd been a better boy, maybe none of the bad things that happened would have happened. Now he and his little sister weren't even allowed to stay with their mother. She was moving away. He was staying here, with his father who was gone all the time, in this scary house that a few months earlier had been fired upon by men with tommy guns. A lot of the bullet holes were still there if a person knew where to look. Anthony was the kind of boy who knew where to look.

An hour after his mother said good-bye to him, Anthony got into the boat with Uncle Fredo and Al Neri, who worked for Anthony's father. Mr. Neri had said to call him Uncle Al, but he wasn't really Anthony's uncle. Anthony thought that might be a sin and so never did it. That was how the Devil caught you, he'd learned at Sunday school. With little tricks like that.

Mr. Neri fired up the motor. Uncle Fredo had a secret way of catching fish that they were going to try out. Anthony didn't like the idea of letting Mr. Neri in on the secret, but he was so eager to get out on the water he wasn't about to complain. Anthony was as happy as a completely miserable little boy could be.

Right as they were about to shove off, Aunt Connie came running down the dock, shouting that Anthony's father needed to take him to Reno. Anthony started to complain, but Uncle Fredo got a hard look on his face and said that Anthony had to go. He promised to take him tomorrow instead. The boy, devastated, nodded and tried not to let on.

Aunt Connie took Anthony back to the house. Everyone had said bad things about her until a few months ago. Now she was going to be the person who took care of Anthony and his little sister every day. She was no good at taking care of her own kids, as far as Anthony could see.

Once they got inside, Aunt Connie sent him to his room. He asked about Reno. She said she didn't know about Reno, just go. He went.

From his bedroom window, the boy watched Mr. Neri and Uncle Fredo ride away. After they disappeared from view, he stayed there, even though there was nothing to see. Anthony was alone. He didn't cry. He promised himself he'd never cry, no matter what happened to him. He would be a good boy always, and maybe his parents would love each other again.

Minutes later, he heard a gunshot.

Soon after that, Mr. Neri came back in the boat alone.

Anthony sobbed. He didn't stop crying for days.

During his parents' contentious divorce, the boy summoned the courage to confront his father with what he'd seen. Michael Corleone dropped his demand for custody of his two children, which was awarded to Kay Adams Corleone.

The cold waters of Lake Tahoe often prevent the formation of the internal gases that make corpses float. The body of Frederico Corleone was never found. His nephew never again went fishing.

BOOK VI

1920–1945

Chapter 21

It is said that babies bring their own luck, and so it was with Michael Corleone. The Corleones were mired in poverty, living in a Hell's Kitchen tenement. Railroad tracks ran right down the middle of the street. Day and night, freight trains rumbled by, loaded with animals headed for slaughter. Children clamored for the chance to play cowboy, to mount a horse and warn pedestrians to get out of the way. Every week, one or two failed to hear.

Since Santino's birth ten years earlier, Carmela had suffered four miscarriages. The baby who'd survived, Frederico, had been sickly all five years of his life. Vito was working six days a week in a corner grocery store owned by his adoptive parents. To make ends meet, he'd helped his friends Clemenza and Tessio hijack a truck, only to find that a bullying neighborhood dandy named Fanucci expected an extortionist portion of the proceeds. Weeks before Michael was born, Vito's murder of Fanucci—widely suspected but only furtively discussed—brought Vito the respect of a grateful neighborhood. With a minimum of words, he began sorting out conflicts and protecting store owners from hoodlums and the police.

Michael's birth itself was as painless as such a thing might ever be. He had ivory skin, long black eyelashes, and a head of lustrous hair. When the midwife spanked him, he took a deep breath but didn't cry. She sighed like a girl at a Valentino movie. The moment he was at his mother's breast, he was her favorite child. Vito had barely crossed the threshold to the room when he saw Michael's noble features. The baby was the image of Vito's own father, who'd fought alongside Garibaldi. Vito dropped to his knees and wept with joy.

The next day, thoughts of his father's beloved olive grove inspired Vito to go into the olive oil business. Tessio and Clemenza would be his salesmen. Prohibition—which provided other profitable uses for their delivery trucks—was another stroke of luck that came into the world about the same time as Michael Corleone. Soon they were all rich.

Michael's babyhood passed without his temperature ever climbing above ninety-eight. It was often cooler. He had a confidence about him, as if he knew people would love him and do what needed to be done and saw

no need to make a fuss. His christening party was held in the street, which the police closed as a favor to the generous young importer. It seemed every Italian in New York was there. Michael's godfather, the saturnine Tessio, spent the afternoon making silly faces at the baby, who was already able to smile. It was Vito's smile, drained of menace.

After a year or so, the older boys saw that Michael had usurped them and become the favorite of both parents. Fredo reacted by putting mice in the baby's cradle and, briefly, regressing into a period of bed-wetting. Once he even went to school and told everyone his baby brother had been sliced in two by the cowcatcher of the Eleventh Avenue freight train.

Sonny took bolder action, complicating Michael's claim on Vito's affections by bringing home a new rival, one Sonny chose himself—a sick and filthy kid whose parents had died of drink. At the age of twelve he'd been on the street, living by his wits—which, it turned out, were considerable. His name was Tom Hagen. Sonny ceded his narrow bed to his orphaned friend and slept on the floor. No one discussed making this arrangement permanent. But like so many of the Don's affairs, a need presented itself and with a minimum of words was resolved.

Michael's earliest memory was of the day his family moved to the Bronx. He was three. His mother was on the stoop, hugging neighbors good-bye and crying just as hard as baby Connie. Tom and Sonny must have been up at the new apartment. Michael was in the car with his father and a driver. Fredo stood at the curb, looking toward the trains. "What's wrong?" Vito shouted. Fredo wanted to play cowboy. Sonny got to do it at least a hundred times. Fredo hadn't done it once, and now they were leaving the neighborhood. Vito saw the misery on Fredo's face. He took Michael by one hand and Fredo by the other and marched them down the narrow street. The man with the horse saw Vito, and a moment later Fredo was in the saddle, waiting for a train. When one appeared in the distance, Vito hoisted Michael onto his shoulders. Fredo rode the horse across the tracks, screaming his warnings, happy and unafraid.

The Corleones' new apartment was in the Belmont section of the Bronx, on the second floor of an eight-story redbrick building. The apartment itself was humble but had a new icebox, good heat, and enough space for everyone. Vito owned the whole building, though so discreetly not even the super knew it. To young Michael, Belmont seemed like paradise. The streets were filled with boys playing stickball and the cries of men with laden pushcarts. The air shimmered with the tang of simmering onions and the sugary haze of rising breads. After supper, women carried chairs down to the sidewalks and gossiped away the twilight. Men shouted affectionate taunts to one another. There were more Italians in Belmont than in most of the towns they'd originally come from. They'd go years at a time without leaving the borough.

Outside the Corleones' apartment was an iron fire escape. On hot nights they slept on it, an adventure tempered only when the wind shifted and sent the smell from the Bronx Zoo wafting down Arthur Avenue. "Enough," Vito would say to his complaining children. "That zoo? It was built by Italians. What you smell is the fruit of their labor. How can a child of mine refuse fruit, which is a gift from God?" The others still complained sometimes, but not Michael. There were lions in that zoo, too. He loved lions. The Corleones. The lionhearted.

The Corleones became active in their new church. At first even Vito attended. Fredo went with his mother to Mass almost every day. When he was ten, he stood up at supper and announced that he'd had a talk with Father Stefano, his mother's favorite celebrant and also his boxing coach, and decided to become a priest. The family exploded in congratulations. That night, Michael sat on the fire escape and watched his mother parade Fredo around the neighborhood. By the time Fredo returned, his face was covered with smeared lipstick.

At school, when Michael's friends practiced that age-old ritual of bragging about their father, Michael would walk away. He'd been raised not to boast. He also had no need for it. Even the worst schoolyard bully knew that Michael's quiet father was a man of respect. When Vito Corleone walked down the street, people backed away, almost bowing, as if he were a king.

One night at dinner, when Michael was six, there was a knock at the door. It was Peter Clemenza. He apologized for interrupting dinner and asked to have a word with Vito alone. Moments later, from behind the locked parlor door, Vito began to yell in Sicilian dialect, which Michael understood, but imperfectly. His father's rage was clear enough. Michael's mother fed olives and calamari to Connie and pretended to be oblivious. Tom smirked and shook his head. "It's Sonny," Tom said. Sonny wasn't at dinner—which had become less and less unusual—but Tom's smirk seemed to indicate that nothing truly grave had befallen him.

Still, Michael was terrified. Only Sonny—and, years later, Michael— would ever provoke Vito Corleone enough to shatter his legendary patience and reserve. There was no greater measure of the depth of his love for them. If the dead could speak, many would testify that it was Vito's patience and reserve a person should fear most.

"What'd he do?" Michael said.

"Some stupid *cafone* stunt," Tom said. "Typical Sonny."

Tom and Sonny were both students at Fordham Prep. Since the move they'd run with different crowds. Tom was on the tennis team and an honor student. Perhaps because he wasn't really a member of the family, perhaps out of gratitude, he'd quietly become the perfect son—the smartest, the most loyal, the best behaved, the most ambitious, and, at the

same time, the most humble. The most ardent student of Vito's code of behavior, he spoke Italian like a native, and was in every way but blood the most Sicilian.

As for Sonny, he'd been kicked off the football team after shouting at the coach (when Sonny had asked his father to intercede, Vito slapped the boy and said nothing). He sneaked bootleg gin and slipped into Harlem to hear jazz. Even at sixteen, Sonny was already getting a reputation as a ladies' man, and not only from girls his age.

"What kind of stupid *cafone* stunt?" Michael asked Tom.

"A rubar poco si va in galera, a rubar tanto si fa carriera." Steal a little, go to jail; steal a lot, make a career of it. "Sonny and two idiots he thinks are his friends pulled a stickup—"

"Ah-ah-ah!" Carmela clamped her hands over Connie's ears. "Enough!"

The parlor door opened. Vito was shaking, red-faced, visibly angry. He and Clemenza left without saying a word. Connie broke into tears. Michael forced himself not to follow suit.

Years later, Michael would learn that Sonny had robbed a filling station that received protection from the Maranzano Family, though Sonny hadn't known that. The robbery had been a lark. That night, Vito went to make things right with Maranzano and dispatched Clemenza to go look for Sonny. A few hours later, Pete found him atop a lonely and demonstrative housewife and dragged the boy to the office at Genco Pura Olive Oil to face his father's wrath.

When Vito confronted Sonny about his stupid act, what Sonny said in his defense was that he'd seen his father kill Fanucci. Vito sat down, heavily, defeated, unable to talk to his son about how he should behave. When Sonny asked to quit school and join the family business, Vito relented and called it destiny.

Vito believed that he himself had done what he had to do in a world that offered little to a man who looked like he did and came from where he came from. He did so steadfast in the belief that life would be different for his children. He'd promised himself that none of them, not even Hagen, would follow in his footsteps. It was the only promise Vito Corleone ever broke.

At the time, though, all Michael knew was that, for the first time in his life, he'd seen his stoic father lose his temper, and that Sonny had somehow caused it. Moments after Vito and Clemenza left, Tom, obviously disgusted, excused himself and headed for the door. "Need anything, Ma? I'm going for a walk."

She didn't. Her face was gray and drawn.

Michael caught the door as Tom was closing it and followed him

down the stairs. When they got to the street it was raining. A downpour. Tom leaned against the glass door, hesitating.

"Tell me what's happening, Tom," Michael said. "I have a right to know. We're family."

"Where'd you learn to talk like that, kid?"

Michael hardened his expression as best he could.

Tom glanced over his shoulder. The super and a few tenants were milling around. "Not here." He motioned toward an awning a few doors down. Together, they ran for it.

At sixteen, Hagen didn't know everything. But he knew how to read Sonny, and he worshiped Vito, so he knew more than anyone would have guessed. The things he told Michael that night, under the striped awning in front of Racalmuto Meat, were candid and true.

From that day on, Sonny became one of the men who accompanied Vito everywhere. He came home late if at all. When he *was* home, he doted on Fredo, who looked up to him the way Michael did Tom. For Michael's seventh birthday, Tom gave him a tennis sweater. Michael wore it tied around his neck, the way Tom did.

Within weeks of one another, Sonny left home and got his own apartment in Manhattan, just off Mulberry Street, and Tom moved into a dormitory at NYU. Whether because of their departure or his own maturation, Fredo emerged quite unexpectedly at thirteen as a strong and powerful young man. Though undersized, he played guard on the freshman football team. After years of being knocked around, he won a small CYO boxing tournament. He was getting better grades and excelling in his religious studies under Father Stefano. Fredo was still shy around girls, but to them this shyness was suddenly endearing, an allure made more profound because they all knew he wanted to be a priest.

Michael couldn't have pinpointed a moment when all this changed, when Fredo's clumsiness became something darker, when the self-sufficiency became sullen self-absorption. It must have happened gradually, but to Michael, it seemed that one moment Fredo was a weakling, the next he was a strong, serious young man, and the next he was locked in his room for hours at a time. At sixteen, Fredo announced what everyone but his mother already assumed: he no longer wished to become a priest. He started flunking classes. He had dates, but only because girls found him harmless. Soon he, too, joined his father's business, though Vito gave him only menial tasks: relaying messages, fetching coffee, unloading actual olive oil.

Vito Corleone kept stressing the importance of education, and sometimes at night he and Michael sat on the fire escape and dreamed big dreams about the boy's future. Vito had had such conversations with the

other boys, too, and only Tom—who was about to start law school at Columbia—even finished high school. Michael loved and respected his father, but he was scared that he'd turn sixteen and something in his blood would send him into the world Tom told him about.

Michael's understanding of that world was still that of an eleven-year-old. During the summer, when Michael was home from school, his father—undoubtedly on days he expected to be uneventful—sometimes took him along as he made his rounds. Vito seemed mainly to go from meal to meal, at various social clubs, restaurants, and coffee shops, shaking hands, saying he'd already eaten, and then eating anyway. He'd leave without seeming to have conducted any business at all, unless it somehow all got done in brief whispers.

On one such day, Vito was suddenly called to meet with some people at the Genco Pura warehouse. He told Michael to wait outside. Michael found a baseball in the trunk of the car and went into the alley to throw it off the wall. When he got there, a boy he'd never seen before was already doing the same thing. The boy's features were aggressively Irish.

"This is my alley," Michael said, though he didn't know what provoked him to say that.

"Aw, c'mon," the boy said. "No one owns alleys." He flashed a dazzling white smile and laughed. The laugh was kind of braying, but it somehow put Michael at ease.

Still, they didn't say much more than that for a long time. They stood alongside each other in that alley, and each threw his scuffed baseball against the wall over and over, trying to outdo each other, though neither one was a born ballplayer.

"You know," the Irish boy finally said, out of breath and taking a break, "my dad's boss of all those trucks out there, and you know what's in 'em, don'tcha?"

"Some of those trucks are my dad's. All the ones that say 'Genco Pura Olive Oil.' "

"Likkah!" The boy's accent sounded like Katharine Hepburn's: neither American nor British yet both. It took Michael a moment to realize he'd said *liquor.* "Enough likkah to get all of New York drunk tonight, and half of New Jersey, too."

Michael shrugged. "It says *olive oil.*" Though he knew that most of those trucks carried liquor. He'd seen inside them before. "Where'd you learn to talk like that?" Michael said.

"I might ask you the same thing," the boy said. "You're Italian, right?"

"I don't talk like anything."

"Sure you don't. Listen, you want to know why the coppahs aren't

here right now arresting everyone for selling all that bootleg likkah? Do you?"

"You're off your nut. All those trucks have in 'em are olive oil."

"Because my dad bribes every coppah in New York!" the boy said.

Michael looked up and down the alley. There was no one in earshot, but he still didn't like the boy talking so loud about such things. "You're lying," Michael said.

The boy explained in detail how his father bribed all the cops. He spoke in specific terms about the murders and beatings necessary to make a profit selling liquor. Either he had a great imagination or he was telling the truth. "You're makin' it all up," Michael said.

"Your people are worse, from what I hear."

"You're just talkin' big. You don't know anything."

"Think what you want," the boy said. "In the meantime, I dare you to go get a bottle of likkah off the truck and bring it back here and split it with me."

This was nothing that had ever occurred to Michael to do, but he just nodded and went to get one. Fredo was helping another man unload a truck. Michael told them his father wanted to see them. When they left, Michael took a bottle of Canadian whiskey back to the alley.

"I thought you'd chicken out," the boy said.

"You thought wrong. Maybe you're just bad at thinking." Michael opened the bottle and took a swig. It burned, but he didn't embarrass himself. "Hey, what's your name?"

"Jimmy Shea," said the boy, taking the bottle. He drank a big gulp of it, and it triggered an immediate coughing fit. He sank to his knees and started to vomit.

Moments later, their fathers caught them, two eleven-year-olds drinking whiskey in broad daylight at the height of Prohibition, and there was hell to pay. The boys—though their lives would run parallel—never spoke directly to each other again.

When Prohibition was repealed, Vito Corleone faced yet another fork in the road. He had, without suffering so much as an arrest, made a small fortune, enough to provide for his family and live the rest of his days in comfort. He chose, instead, to seek a partnership with Salvatore Maranzano, the New York underworld kingpin. Was that Vito Corleone's one destiny? A cunning act of venal opportunism? Or did he do what he did simply because he was brilliant at doing it? Perhaps Vito had no choice. Sonny and Fredo were young men with little education and few skills. Left to their own devices, either son would probably have been dead in a year. Still,

weren't there legitimate businesses that a wealthy, brilliant man like Vito might have run? If there was ever a time for the Corleones to move to Las Vegas and go legit, this was it.

What happened instead is the stuff of history.

Maranzano scoffed at becoming an equal partner with Vito Corleone, and it touched off the Castellammarese War. Maranzano's ally Al Capone sent two top men to New York to kill Vito Corleone. One was Willie "the Icepick" Russo, older brother of the future Don. Vito Corleone's ability to derive power from the powerless paid off yet again. A railroad porter in Chicago sent information about what train the men were on, and a porter in New York led the gunmen into a taxi whose driver worked for Luca Brasi. Brasi tied the men up, and while they were still alive he hacked off their arms and legs with a fireman's ax and calmly watched them die. Then he beheaded them. On New Year's Eve, Tessio walked into a restaurant and shot Maranzano. Vito took over the Maranzano organization, reorganized other interests in New York and New Jersey into the Five Families we know today, and became *capo di tutti capi*. Boss of all bosses. He'd done so with a minimum of bloodshed and with hardly a mention of his name in any newspaper.

The young Michael Corleone had noticed more of his father's men standing guard than usual, and his father had been gone at night more often. Otherwise, the upheaval didn't touch that apartment building in the Bronx. When, years later, he learned what had happened, he was astonished. He'd remembered that as a good time for the family. Sonny got married. Tom finished law school. Connie got her first pony. Michael was elected president of his class. Fredo had come out of his shell and often took Michael with him into the city to shoot pool. Michael was a natural, able to see the angles on the table as if in a vision. Fredo was a capable player but a natural hustler, able to see the metaphorical angles several steps ahead of all but the best sharks. Anyone who underestimated the quiet, unflappable boy and his endearing loudmouth big brother left the table broke. The one time Fredo and Michael were rolled, Sonny found the two sore losers who'd done it and stomped them to death in broad daylight, in the middle of 114th Street, and left them there. The murder was investigated by a detective on the Corleones' payroll. A dishonest Family shylock was convicted for it. Michael didn't know a thing about any of that until he heard the story, years later, from Sonny himself, who thought the whole thing was hilarious. Why did they think they'd only been rolled once?

For more than ten years, peace reigned. The country foundered through the Great Depression and rose up to fight a just war, but during these hard times, Vito Corleone kept amassing power and riches. He brought a crew of stonecutters from Sicily to fashion mausoleums for

nonexistent people that were in fact surprisingly commodious places to keep millions of dollars in cash. The Corleones continued to live modestly.

One day, well after this peace was under way, Michael was at the blackboard in his high school geometry class when there was a knock at the door. It was Fredo. He told the teacher there'd been a family emergency. Fredo didn't say anything until they got in his car. "It's Pop," he said. "They shot him. In the chest. He's gonna be okay, they said, but—"

Michael could barely hear him. The car was still double-parked in front of the school, but Michael felt like it had just gone over a huge dip in the road. "*Who* shot him?"

"They're nobody," Fredo said. "Gang of Irish shitbirds too dumb to know the difference between Pop and some nothing you'd get into a turf war with. This dumb Mick walked right up to Pop on the street and shot him, and a second later we all opened fire on him."

"On Pop?" *Turf war? Gang?* Nobody ever said this kind of thing in front of Michael.

"What? *No.* Jesus, Mikey. Don't be stupid." He put the car in gear and tore off.

"Where are we going?"

"Home. The hospital's too crowded."

Crowded was a euphemism. Michael didn't know for what and didn't push it.

Carmela put on a brave front for her children, but Michael saw through it. After everyone went to bed, he could hear her through the wall of his room. She was praying when he finally fell asleep and when he woke up, too. He hurried to the kitchen to make the whole family breakfast, to spare her that tiny burden. She shooed him out of her kitchen, but on his way out she hugged him and started chanting something in Latin that he didn't understand.

Later that morning, when Fredo said it was time to go to the hospital, Michael refused.

"He's going to be okay, right?" Michael said.

"Right," Fredo said.

"Then I'll see him when he gets home."

His mother's face fell.

"I got a test coming up," he said. "As long as Pop's okay, I should go to school."

His mother patted Michael on the cheek and told him what a good boy he was, that his father would be proud.

The next morning, Michael again refused to go. Fredo told his mother to take Connie and wait in the car. Then he pulled Michael aside and asked what the fuck he was trying to prove.

"I don't know," Michael said. "Nothing."

"Nothing? C'mon."

"He probably had it coming," Michael said.

"He *what?* What's wrong with you?"

"Nothing's wrong with me. He's a criminal. Criminals get shot. He's lucky he never got shot before. You all are."

Fredo's punch caught him squarely in the cheek. Michael fell into his father's favorite armchair and heard a dull crash. It was the big ceramic ashtray with a mermaid on a ridged island in the middle. It had broken into two clean pieces, right down the middle.

Still Michael refused to go to the hospital. Fredo gave up. When the glue dried, the crack in the middle of the ashtray was barely visible.

The day Vito was discharged, Carmela had been up since dawn, cooking a dinner to welcome him home. The whole family came: Sonny and his new wife, Sandra, Tom and his fiancée, Theresa, everyone. Vito looked more weary than weakened. He seemed to be doting on Michael in particular. No mention was made of Michael's failure to go to the hospital.

As courses came and went and glasses were raised high again and again, anger rose in the breast of young Michael Corleone. He was less than a year from his sixteenth birthday and remained fearful that he would somehow be drawn into working for his father. Even in times of peace and prosperity in the world his father ran, Vito was never safe from the countless men who thought they'd benefit from killing him. Michael loved his family with the depth and breadth of his soul, yet at the same time he wanted to get out of there: this apartment, this neighborhood, this city, this life. Where he wanted to go, he had no real idea. Why he wanted to do it was beyond reckoning. Only as a very old man would he attain enough wisdom to realize the folly of trying to divine why any human being does anything.

As Carmela nodded to Connie to help her clear the table for dessert, Michael clanged his wineglass with a spoon. He stood. He hadn't made a toast all night. Michael looked at no one but his father, fork in midair. When their eyes met, his father gave a tiny smile. Seeing his father smile like that in the face of such trauma made Michael's anger boil over.

"I would rather die," Michael said, raising the glass, "than grow up to be a man like you."

A stunned silence fell over the table like a heavy wool shroud. From where Michael stood, they had all disappeared. There were only two people in the world.

Vito ate the last bite of his chicken scaloppine and set his fork down. He reached for his napkin and wiped his face, almost daintily, then set the napkin down, and, with a coldness in his eyes that had never been directed at anyone in his own family, he stared down his youngest son.

Michael's throat tightened. He clutched the wineglass. He remained standing, but he braced himself, ready for his father to laugh at him or say something about the long way Michael had to go to become a man like anyone.

Instead, his father continued to stare him down.

Michael felt chills run over him, and his legs begin to tremble. The knuckles of his right hand were white against the wineglass. The glass broke. Wine, blood, and broken glass fell to the table, and still no one said anything. Michael tried not to move, but he was shaking.

At last, Vito Corleone reached for his own wineglass.

"I share your wish," he said, his voice barely above a whisper. He drained the glass, set it down noiselessly. "Good luck to you," he said, and he held his stare.

Michael's knees buckled. He sat.

"Please." Vito pointed at the broken glass. "Do your mother a favor. Clean that up."

Michael did as he was told. Connie and his mother rose to clean everything else up and get dessert, but no one said anything. The *sfogiatelle* and the coffee hit the table, and the only sounds were clanking spoons and chewing. Michael wrapped his napkin around his bloodied hand and ate with his head down. Not even Fredo tried to make light of things and make peace.

The other Corleone children never even seemed tempted to rebel against their father. Santino was like a dog fiercely loyal to his keepers. Fredo was slavishly in pursuit of his father's approval. Though Tom wasn't blood, he sought Vito's approval as fervently as Fredo and ultimately with more success. Connie, the only girl, enjoyed her role as the docile, doting daughter until long after Vito had died. Only Michael felt the need to rebel—as, perversely, the favorite child in most families can be counted on to do.

It was the rebellion of the good Italian son. None of it was directed at his mother. Michael doted on her so much that for a time Vito was concerned about his youngest son's masculinity. Nothing he did embarrassed the family. He did not disobey his parents, yet his every choice seemed calculated to present some kind of affront to his father.

For example, when Fredo first told Michael that their father had been asking questions about Michael's masculinity, Michael stopped bringing his dates by the apartment, just to keep his family in the dark. When Sonny offered to get him a hooker for his seventeenth birthday, Michael said he didn't think his girlfriend would like it, and when Sonny asked, "What girlfriend?," Michael showed up at Sunday dinner with a big-breasted blonde he'd been dating off and on for months. He started bringing a new

girl home every couple weeks. None of them was Italian. The one time his father ever said anything to him about it, Michael said that he loved his mother, but there was no one else like her in all the world and never would be. "It's none of my business," Vito whispered to him later, but clearly with approval. Michael didn't bring another girl home for seven years, when he took Kay as his guest to Connie's wedding.

Michael applied to Princeton and Columbia and got into both. He went to Columbia because Tom had gone there for law school. Halfway through his first term, he learned that his father had given a sizable anonymous gift to the university's endowment fund. He met Tom for lunch at the Plaza Hotel and told him he was dropping out. He asked if he could stay with Tom and Theresa after he did. Tom was working on Wall Street, and they had an apartment downtown. "Get a tutor," Tom said. "A lot of people struggle their first year."

"I'm getting straight A's," Michael said. He told Tom why he was dropping out.

"If all the students at that place whose fathers are in a position to support the school—"

"I don't care about everyone else. I want to be there on my own merits."

"You're being so naive I can hardly stand to look at you."

"So is it all right?" Michael said. "I'm sure you'll have to ask Theresa."

Tom shook his head and said, no, he could speak for Theresa. If Michael wanted to make the biggest mistake of his life, Tom wasn't going to stop him.

At the end of the term, Michael, with straight A's, dropped out of an Ivy League school and tried to find a job. Frustrated, he finally asked Tom one night at dinner if he could borrow enough money to take some classes at City College. When Tom told him that if he was going to borrow money anyway, he should borrow it for Columbia, Michael didn't say anything.

"That's just what the old man would have done," Tom said. He paused, but Michael didn't ask what he meant. Tom answered. "The silence."

Which Michael maintained. Theresa cleared the table before anyone said anything more.

"You can't run from who you are," Tom said.

Michael laughed. "This is America, my orphaned friend," he said. "Running from who we are *is* who we are."

For a moment, Tom's eyes flashed with anger. He composed himself. "You want money, you know where to get all the money you could ever need for anything. I'm not getting in the middle of this any more than I already have."

Michael felt trapped. He could defy his father's wishes by asking to join the family business, which was out of the question. Going to school and doing well and becoming a doctor, a lawyer, a professor: that was what his father *wanted*. He *wanted* Michael to follow another path entirely. But what path could Michael take that he wouldn't find had been blazed by the invisible hand of his father? Most paths wouldn't just be blazed, either. They'd be blacktopped, lit by floodlights, and flanked by sturdy handrails.

Where could he go?

His father was building a house on Long Island, and that spring the family would be moving—Connie, of course, who was sixteen, but also Fredo, who was still living at home. Sonny and Sandra had just had twin girls, and they'd have a house right next door. On the blueprint for his father's house was a room labeled "Michael's Bedroom." When he saw it, he got the same suffocating feeling he'd had when he'd thought the family business would claim him at sixteen.

Michael had fallen prey to that curse of the young; he knew only what he *didn't* want. A life driven by avoidance is like a team trying not to lose. Like a skydiver trying to land anywhere but in that one tree over there. Like the traveling salesman who can sleep in the barn so long as he *doesn't*. Like two naked lovers in Paradise free to do anything at all *except*.

So Michael Corleone did what thousands of foundering young men in the 1930s did: he joined the Civilian Conservation Corps.

Most of the other men in the corps, of course, were people with no advantages, no opportunities at all, men who told tales of a kind of desperate poverty that Michael (despite his parents' tales of living through similar circumstances) had never before understood. He was stationed in the Winooski River Valley in Vermont. He planted countless trees and moved untold tons of earth. Unlike the other Italians, he ate the tasteless food without complaining. His name was constantly mispronounced, and he never corrected anyone. He volunteered to help the tutors who came in to give night classes, and before long he was running the camp's education program. He taught hundreds of men to read, many of them Italians who could barely read *Italian* when Michael started working with them. Like everyone else, he was paid thirty dollars a month, twenty-two of which were automatically sent home to his family. At night, Michael lay in his bunk and tried to imagine his father's face each month when that check arrived. Only during the courtship of his wives, Kay (his second wife and first true courtship) and Apollonia (first wife, second courtship), was Michael Corleone ever happier.

There were about a thousand men in his camp. Most were only a generation or two removed from their roots in Europe. If one thing united them, though, it was their pride in being Americans—a pride enhanced by

their shared, daily mission. So when the Germans annexed Czechoslova-
kia, those who came from Germany felt no animosity from their Czech or
Slovak campmates. Similarly, the only nationalistic fervor touched off in
the Winooski Valley by the Italian invasion of Albania or the Soviet-
Finnish War was a shared dread of what might happen next and how it
would affect the USA.

"It's going to be different for us," said Joe Lucadello one night. He
was a tutor, too. They were the last ones in the classroom building, lock-
ing it up. "Italians. Just wait."

Joe's people were from Genoa by way of Camden, New Jersey. He'd
wanted to be an architect, but his family had lost everything in the stock
market crash. Now he designed retaining walls and picnic shelters. Smart
as a whip and about as skinny, Joe was Michael's best friend in the corps.

"I've been thinking the same thing," Michael said. If America was
drawn into the European war, everyone of Italian descent would be suspect.

"The German fellas look just like—"

"I know," Michael said. "You're right."

"Don't laugh, but I've been working on a plan to kill Mussolini."

"Come on," Michael said, laughing. "How are you going to do that?"

"I didn't say I knew how. I said I'm working on a plan."

Joe was that rare combination: a resourceful schemer who was prepared to act. Ordinarily, he was practical, too, but he had an idealistic
streak.

"You couldn't get within five miles of Mussolini. Nobody could."

"Think about it. You read a lot of history books. There's never been
anyone—any hero, any villain, any king, any leader of any kind—that it
was impossible to kill."

It was a sobering thought. Michael did think about it, and he admitted that maybe Joe was right. "I suppose when you're done with Mussolini you'll go after Hitler."

"I know I'm just dreaming," Joe said. "I'm not a fool. I know I'm not
really the man for the job. It's just hard to watch the way the world is
going and not do anything about it."

On this they agreed. The ancient rift between northern and southern
Italians had no effect on their friendship or their shared contempt for
Mussolini. They dreaded war. At the same time—because it would crush
Mussolini and at the same time be a chance for men like them once and for
all to prove themselves in the eyes of the American people—they yearned
for it.

Then there was the matter of Ustica. About the same time Mussolini
signed the Axis treaty with Hitler, he ordered his army to Sicily to round

up all known or suspected Mafiosi and imprison them on the tiny island of Ustica (Vito continued to regard Mussolini as just another vainglorious oppressor whose time would come and go). When Michael and Joe talked about the men imprisoned at Ustica, they lamented the lack of American due process. Michael gave no indication of his father's allegiance with those men. Joe knew the Corleones as olive oil importers. There were cases of the stuff in the camp's mess kitchen.

In June of 1940, when Italy declared war against the Allies, Joe Lucadello had a plan. "We go to Canada," he said.

"What's in Canada?"

Joe pulled out a newspaper clipping. According to the article, the Royal Canadian Air Force was seeking experienced American pilots. A World War I ace named Billy Bishop—"the Eddie Rickenbacker of Canada," the article called him—would oversee their training personally.

"That's great," Michael said, "but we're not experienced pilots."

Joe had it all worked out. He had a friend, a Polish Jew from Rhode Island, who was a pilot for the CCC, dumping water to fight forest fires and spraying DDT on bug-infested areas where crews were about to work. Joe got the guy to give them lessons, and they all three went to Ottawa to join up. Joe convincingly forged licenses for him and Michael. They were all initially accepted. Two days later, Billy Bishop himself walked into the barracks and asked to see Michael Corleone (which he pronounced correctly—a tipoff something was up). He asked to see Michael's pilot's license. There were a number of men in that room without licenses, some of them crop dusters and barnstormers who a few months later would be holding their own against the Luftwaffe. The license wasn't the point. Somehow, Michael knew, his father had found out he was here. There was no sense using the forged license and possibly getting Joe kicked out, too. "I'm sorry, sir," Michael said to Billy Bishop. "I don't have one."

Michael took a bus back to the camp and got his job back. Six months later, he was on another bus, heading to New York for a surprise birthday party for his father, when the driver heard the news about Pearl Harbor. Shaking, he pulled over to the shoulder and turned up the radio. Eventually, they got back on the road. Michael walked straight from the bus terminal to Times Square. The place was teeming with men bragging about the killing they were about to do. Michael got in the line for the Army Air Corps, but as he waited an officer walked down the line and told everyone who was under five ten that he'd have to seek his revenge in another branch of the service. Michael missed the height requirement by an inch. The Marines, too, appealed to his ideals. An elite fighting squad, tougher than the rest, with a rigorous initiation and a sacred code of honor. They had the same height requirement, but emotions were running high, and

Michael and the lieutenant signing him up gave each other a look and an understanding passed between them. Michael caught a cab to his father's house.

Vito Corleone's favorite child was the last person at the party to say "Surprise!"

Vito was stoic about Michael's news. He asked the questions any loving and concerned father would. It was clear that he did not approve, though he never said so.

In the days that followed, the U.S. government rounded up the Italian citizens within its borders and held them as prisoners of war (Enzo the baker, for example, would spend two years in a prison in New Jersey). In addition, more than four thousand American citizens with Italian names were arrested. Theresa Hagen's parents were among them, though they were not charged and were quickly released. Hundreds of people with less sophisticated legal representation were detained much longer—months, years—even though they, too, were charged with no crimes.

Before Christmas, the government issued an edict that restricted the participation of Italian Americans in war-related industries. All over the country, hardworking, law-abiding American longshoremen, factory workers, and civilian clerk-typists were summarily fired.

By then, Michael was at Parris Island, crawling like a reptile across a parking lot covered with broken oyster shells.

Four percent of the American population came from Italy. They were destined to make up ten percent of the casualties.

Everything the government issued Michael Corleone was too big—his helmet, his uniform, even his boondockers. He barely noticed. He was proud to be a Marine, and he saw what he wanted to see. But the first time his mother saw the picture of her youngest son, hair shorn, dressed in ill-fitting dress whites that looked more like a costume than a uniform, she burst into tears and didn't stop crying for three days. She then put the photo on the mantelpiece. Every time she passed it, the tears began anew. No one dared to move the picture, though.

Michael Corleone's platoon at Parris Island had forty-seven men, all from the East, with a fairly even split between northerners and southerners. Michael had never been in the South before. He knew more about the rivalry between north and south in Italy than the one here, and was surprised by how similar those two rivalries turned out to be. Being from southern Italy and northern America, he could see both sides. And the arguments were over nothing. Music, for example. The southerners liked what the northerners called shit-kicker music. The northerners liked Cole Porter,

Johnny Mercer, classy numbers they could dance to. Though Michael had known Johnny Fontane all his life, he kept that to himself during the many arguments waged over his music. Any time some petty squabble made the men even for a moment forget about the real enemy, their DI made them regret it—by *becoming* the real enemy. They'd all arrived most afraid of being afraid, of failing to do their duty when the time came. An hour later, they were more afraid of Sergeant Bradshaw than anything. Michael was a quiet, able soldier, but he spent his days convinced that at any moment his DI might kill him. At night, Michael lay sweating in his bunk, thinking about what a brilliant system boot camp was.

Michael's suspicion that the Corps's height requirement had been instituted in part to keep Italians out of the elite forces was borne out when he found only one other person of Italian origin in his platoon. Tony Ferraro, also from New York, was a minor-league ballplayer—a catcher. He looked it: stocky, bald on top. Like Michael, he'd volunteered as soon as he heard about Pearl Harbor, but what he really wanted was to go into Italy and send Mussolini to hell.

Tony and Michael were the two shortest men in the platoon. They were slow-footed and weak marksmen, but they'd arrived at PI in better physical condition than most of the other men—happily, since everything they'd ever heard about Marine boot camp was true. Men collapsed, vomited, vomited blood. Michael learned to love it. He felt sorry for the platoons whose DIs sent them back to their barracks after only four hours of marching in the knee-deep sand instead of the eight Sergeant Bradshaw made them do. When boot camp ended, he addressed the platoon—for the first time—as *men.*

Every Marine in the platoon loved him. Many shed unashamed tears.

Michael, who shed nothing in boot camp but a few harmless pounds, again marveled at the genius of what had been inflicted upon him.

A few months later, Tony Ferraro was securing an island so small it didn't have a name or a military purpose either when a Japanese sniper shot him right in the heart.

Before dawn, the men grabbed their rifles, shouldered their seabags, and stood at attention beside a row of idling trucks. A corporal with a thick southern accent called out names and assignments. He butchered *Corleone,* which Michael had expected. He was shocked, though, about what the corporal said next.

Camp Elliott, M1 rifle, infantry. Michael Corleone was going to the Pacific.

His dream of helping to liberate Italy was shattered. But what was he

going to do, write his congressman? It was probably his congressman (after no more than a nod from Michael's father) who'd rigged this in the first place.

Michael let nothing show. A Marine goes where he's sent.

A southerner already on the Camp Elliott truck extended his hand. "Welcome aboard, Dago boy!" he said, pulling Michael up.

That was the Marine name for San Diego: *Dago*. Michael knew how else the man meant it, but he didn't rise to the bait. They were Marines first, Americans second. Whatever else they were came after that.

Michael had never seen the West before, either. He spent the better part of the trip at the troop-train window, mesmerized. It was a good way to see what he was fighting for. Nothing could have prepared him for the size, grandeur, and beauty of this country. The farther west he went, the more he fell in love with the craggy, improbable landscape.

They stopped for a desert training session about thirty miles from Las Vegas, where the first big casino had opened months earlier. That night, Michael killed a rabbit with his bare hands and ate its stringy meat in a cold arroyo, staring at the otherworldly glow from the town that visionary men like him were destined to transform into an industry that would still be there, thriving, long after the fall of the Axis powers, the British Empire, and the Soviet Union, after most of America's factories and steel mills went broke or moved to Southeast Asia.

In San Diego, Michael went through another few weeks of lectures and training, hand-to-hand combat, swimming tests, all the finishing touches, but when it came time to ship out, his heart again sunk. He'd been assigned to guard detail. Indefinitely.

The first chance he got, he went to a pay phone and called Tom. The Hagens were having dinner. A baby screamed in the background.

"I'm going to ask you something, Tom. If you lie to me, I'll know. Things will never be the same between us."

"Any question that starts out like that," Tom said, "is one a man shouldn't ask."

Michael was young and undeterred. There would come a time when he'd have understood that Tom had just answered the question Michael was about to ask: "Did Pop have anything to do with my assignment?"

"Your assignment to do what?" Tom said.

Michael lowered his voice. "I did *not* join the Corps to be a cop."

"You're a cop?" Hagen said.

Michael hung up on him. A few days later, Michael pulled shore patrol and stood on the docks with his rifle shouldered, watching as men

he'd come to trust shipped out, the air thick with bragging about all the Japs they were about to kill. He never saw any of those men again.

The worst guard detail job was making civilians follow the blackout law. People think their circumstances are special, and it's impossible to reason with them. The first few exasperating nights of this, Michael wanted to smash in their smooth, self-important faces with the butt of his rifle, but he soon came up with a better idea. His CO, who had an even lower opinion of civilians, thought it was brilliant. "I never thought I'd say this to an Italian fella," the CO said, "but you may be officer material."

Michael took two other men and went to an oil storage facility north of the city, right on the coast. Two big oil tanks, both empty. It was a nice change of pace to be away from the whiny civilians and also to have a chance to make use of the training he'd had in explosives.

The next day, the newspapers and the radio (their anonymous source was Michael himself, pretending to be the CO) reported that the oil tanks they'd blown up had been hit by a Jap sub that—because of the illegal city lights—had no trouble hitting its target.

The blackout was much easier to enforce after that.

Michael went up the chain of command at Camp Elliott, trying to get reassigned. He applied for pilot training. At the beginning of the war, pilots had to be college graduates, but the rule was changed so that anyone with a 117 on his college entrance exam was eligible. Michael took the test, got a 130, but nothing happened. After one of the many times he stood at attention for a four-hour shift outside Admiral King's office, Michael managed to get a word with him. The admiral promised to look into it personally. He even sounded optimistic about a transfer to the European theater. Nothing came of it. Michael was there a year but it felt like ten.

Finally it dawned on him that the admiral's clerk filled out all the admiral's paperwork and signed most of it. Michael noticed the clerk's taste in music and arranged front-row seats at the Hollywood Bowl for the clerk and his wife to see the one and only Mr. Johnny Fontane.

Days later, Michael was reassigned to a combat battalion.

It shipped out on a converted luxury liner, painted battleship gray and fitted with guns. The troops were packed on that ship for weeks. They were almost in the harbor before there was any official word they'd be going ashore at Guadalcanal.

The fighting had been going on for months, Jap cruisers still lobbed shells onto the beach at night, and there were still pockets of resistance, in-

cluding hundreds of men in underground tunnels, but the battle was all but over.

The beach at Guadalcanal was a junkyard of burned vehicles of all kind—tanks, jeeps, amtracs—but when Michael first set eyes on the place, with all those green coconut trees and white sand, it still looked to him like a tropical paradise, minus the girls.

Michael climbed down the cargo nets into a Higgins boat. He heard shelling in the distance, but no one shot at him as they landed. When he reached the beach, he tripped on something soft and went flying. He got up and ran for the tree line. He dove for cover next to a heap of tangled fencing wire and a pile of blackened corpses. The stench wasn't so much a smell as a taste—burned, decaying meat, far up the nose and back in the throat. Michael looked back at the beach and realized that what he'd tripped on was a body, too.

The Japs left their dead to rot or wash out to sea. Those corpses were the first dead bodies he'd ever seen outside a funeral home.

The salty Marines who greeted the new troops seemed identically filthy, bearded, and tired. They said little. All the loud talk the new arrivals had done in their clean uniforms suddenly seemed like boys playing cowboys and Indians. Those men were *warriors*. When they took Michael on his first patrol, he blasted away at every rustling leaf. They just smirked and kept humping through the jungle. When they hit the dirt, Michael hit it, too. He could be sure a split second later there'd be tracers, bullets, shells, bombs—something coming to kill him.

Michael's second day on Guadalcanal, he was on sentry at the perimeter of the airstrip. He heard a plane coming. A Navy Hellcat, scraping the treetops and spewing smoke. The pilot crash-landed a hundred yards away. The plane burst into flame. Michael broke into a sprint to try to help the pilot out of there. By then two jeeps full of people had pulled up, and Michael's platoon leader, Sergeant Hal Mitchell, yelled at him to get back. The flames were too hot. Their fire truck had been bombed. The equipment they used instead could have barely put out a campfire. Michael could see into the cockpit. The pilot, trapped and screaming, looked right at Michael and begged to be shot. Michael gripped his rifle, but his sergeant gave no orders. The screams stopped soon after that. Michael needed to get burn treatment just from standing nearby.

Victory was declared at Guadalcanal a week or so later. The Marines who'd done most of the fighting were rotated out, sent home or at least for some R and R in New Zealand. The replacement troops were left behind to secure the island. On the map Guadalcanal's just a dot, but it's a hundred miles long and twenty miles wide, heavily forested with rough terrain and the destruction left behind by a battle that went on for months. Not to mention all the caves.

The caves were a nightmare. Dead bodies of course, deep crevices full of sewage, biting ants an inch long, rats the size of raccoons. The Marines went into the caves in groups of four plus a Doberman. Michael loved the first dog, but after a couple of them got blown up by booby-trapped corpses, he stopped getting attached.

Michael himself captured a grand total of one Jap, emaciated and near death. He propped the man up. The Jap pointed at Michael's Ka-Bar. "Knife," he said. He pantomimed shoving it in his guts. Michael wouldn't give it to him. The man looked relieved.

At first, like nearly all the men on that caves detail, Michael saw it as a salvage operation. He learned to field-strip booty from a dead Jap faster than you could pull out your watch and check the time. Back at camp, the market for these things was flooded, and the best items left the island with the Marines who'd done most of the fighting. But an enterprising man can find a way. For Michael Corleone, it was the native people. Any gear that was useful in the home was easy to sell locally. Michael traded a lot of what he found for fresh fish. All Marines love a brother in arms who can improve on the lousy food, especially in a war zone.

One morning, though, Michael woke up and saw a pet cockatoo he'd gotten from a native for a carton of smokes get swallowed whole by one of those rats. He shooed the rat out of the tent, and when he did he looked up and saw the biggest spiderweb he'd ever seen, stretched between two coconut trees. The spider had caught a seagull in it. The gull was wrapped up, and the spider was eating it. Also, another dog died. Some days go that way. They were about to blow one last cave and go back to the base camp when Michael noticed a crayon drawing on the ground. It struck him as odd that some Jap was in here passing the time coloring a picture. Michael bent over. There was a whole stack of drawings. The one on top had an airplane in the sky with a meatball on the side and smiling people on the ground waving up at it. There was one of a family at a dinner table with an empty place setting, one of a princess, and several more of ponies. Just a regular little girl drawing pictures of ponies to send to her daddy, who probably died fighting a war whose course he couldn't have changed one way or the other. Michael smoothed them out and set them down. He gave the signal to blow the cave.

He got back to camp and heard that Sicily had been liberated. Michael Corleone never again took anything off the enemy that he didn't need for his own survival.

Compared to a lot of others, Michael's battalion had it easy on Guadalcanal. They fared well during skirmishes on some of the surrounding islands, too.

Peleliu was another story. They were going in first. Cannon fodder.

The convoy that loaded onto the ship for the invasion looked like the Okies heading west. Every inch of the deck was crammed with men and machines, stacked high and covered with a patchwork of tarps. The heat was unbearable, a hundred and ten in the day and ninety at night. There wasn't enough room below for everyone to sleep. They bunked on the deck, in or underneath trucks, anywhere they could find shade. Michael only pretended to sleep. Even the saltiest veterans on the ship looked pale and shaky.

By the time Peleliu came into view all there was to see was a wall of smoke and flame. Dozens of battleships pounded the island with sixteen-inch shells that sounded like airborne freight trains. Cruisers peppered it with smaller mortars. Soon the sound of all the guns bombarding Peleliu became one deafening thunder. The noise felt like it was pressing down on him. The whole ship throbbed with it. The air smelled like diesel fuel. The invasion force piled into amphibious tractors and Higgins boats and squatted down below the gunwales.

They went right into the middle of it. The air was full of the snapping of bullets. The smoke was so thick Michael couldn't imagine how the driver knew where to go. Michael felt the amtrac scrape coral. Sergeant Mitchell shouted the order to hit the beach. Michael jumped out and ran. Everything was smoke and chaos. He was aware of men falling all around him and screams of pain, but he kept his head down and hit the deck alongside two other Marines behind a fallen tree. Up and down the beach, amtracs exploded and burned and sometimes men staggered out of them and were cut to pieces by machine-gun fire. Michael saw the deaths of at least a hundred of his brothers in arms. Men he loved and trusted, and he was not, even then, a man much given to trust. But all he felt was nothing. A blur. He'd been shot himself, on the side of his neck. Just a nick, but it bled like mad. Michael had no idea until the man beside him, a corporal from Connecticut named Hank Vogelsong, asked if he was all right.

In combat, no one ever really knows what's going on. Somewhere far behind them was a colonel in charge of all this who didn't know which way their guns were pointing. Someone Michael didn't know and who'd probably never lay eyes on him had decided he was expendable. Not Michael *personally*. It's not personal, just war. And Michael was a pawn. All he tried to do at Peleliu was not die. Nothing smart or brave. He was just luckier than the thousand other guys from his division who died that day.

Once enough of them made it across the beach, they were able to advance inland and start stacking rocks and debris so they could return fire. Enemy fire slowed, but still Michael was pinned down that whole first night. They'd apparently given up on those banzai attacks Michael had trained for, and there was never any chance to mow them down.

At first light, Sergeant Mitchell organized an assault on the ridge where most of the shooting was coming from. Michael and ten others made a run for it, about fifty yards to a clump of trees and scrub. Two were killed and two more were wounded before they got there. An American tank advanced to the other side of the ridge, and it drew fire the way tanks always do. Then the shooting stopped. They were twenty feet from the crest of the ridge. Hal Mitchell sent three men with automatic rifles and two with flamethrowers up to the crest. As they were about to scorch it, the Japs opened fire. Sergeant Mitchell ordered Vogelsong and Michael to help him get the wounded out of there and retreat. As Michael covered them, Vogelsong and Sergeant Mitchell carried one of the wounded men back to where Michael stood. As they were going back for the other one, an 80mm mortar killed him and wounded Vogelsong and Mitchell.

Later, when he was questioned about what he did next—both by his superiors and later by a reporter from *Life* magazine—Michael couldn't explain what had possessed him to come to get his brothers in arms, or how he got out of there alive, either. Maybe there was too much coral dust from the mortar. Maybe they thought they'd already killed all the foot soldiers and were focused on taking care of the tank, which they blew up as Michael was charging their bunker. Michael had no training at all on that flamethrower. He just grabbed it without thinking and recoiled as a fat tongue of flame shot over the ridge.

There was machine-gun fire from a cave to his right, and Michael felt like his leg had been shot off. He fell and scrambled for cover—alone at the crest of the ridge, a sitting duck. The odor of burned flesh and napalm was horrible. He had a bullet in his thigh and one that went through his calf.

Right in front of him were six enemy soldiers with their eyes boiled out and their lips burned off. Their skin was mostly gone. Their muscles looked like a sketch from a science book.

Michael was pinned down for only twenty minutes before the Japs in that cave were taken out, too, and a corpsman covered head to toe with blood came over that ridge and got Michael out of there. He'd had whole years go by faster than those twenty minutes.

He had no memory of how he got from there to Hawaii.

His first thought when he came to his senses was that his mother must be worried sick. He wrote her a long letter, and he sweet-talked a nurse into picking out something as a gift to send along. The nurse chose a coffee mug with a map of the Hawaiian Islands painted on it. The day Carmela Corleone got it—along with the news that her son was coming home—she filled it with wine, raised the mug, and thanked the Virgin Mary for answering her prayers. From then on, each time she passed Michael's photo on the mantelpiece, Carmela smiled.

Michael and Hal Mitchell both recuperated. Hank Vogelsong wasn't so lucky. Right before he died he told the corpsman he wanted Michael Corleone to have his watch. When it arrived, Michael, who barely knew the man, wrote to Vogelsong's parents, told them how brave Hank had been under fire, and offered to give them his watch back. They wrote back and thanked him but said they wanted him to have it.

While Michael was still in the hospital, he learned that he'd been accepted for pilot training. He was also promoted to second lieutenant. But the promotion was just symbolic, and he never did go to flight school. That was the end of Michael Corleone's first war.

Just before Michael was discharged, a reporter from *Life* magazine came to interview him. Michael, who presumed that the story had been set up by his father, thanked the reporter for his interest but said that he was a private person. He already had a medal and he could do without the attention. But Admiral King personally told Michael to do it. Good for morale, he said.

Michael was photographed in a uniform that fit. The story ran in a special issue about the American fighting man. Audie Murphy was on the cover. On the facing page was James K. Shea, the future president of the United States.

BOOK VII

January–June 1961

Chapter 22

Via a maze of intermediaries, Nick Geraci had been told to come in. To see the Boss. Geraci had a pretty good idea what it was about. He'd suggested the Brooklyn Botanic Gardens. Too public, he was told. Don Corleone couldn't possibly risk doing anything that would make his appointment to the presidential transition team any more controversial than it already was—especially the day before the inauguration. It would have to be in the car, a limo.

Which cinched it: they were going to kill him.

In a situation like this, though, there's no choice but to go where you're told. It's a part of the life. Geraci knew that a long time ago. A wiseguy who's called in, if he's smart, is like a lawyer preparing a case. You anticipate every question you might get asked and hope for the best. If you're able to talk your way out of it, walk away pissed off, not grateful.

Asking to bring his guys along for the ride would arouse suspicion. That was out. Packing a gun or a knife was a bad risk. If he's searched, he's done for. Even if he's not, there's not much chance he'd have enough time to whip out a concealed weapon at the moment of truth.

He waited all morning at a corner table in a tavern on First Avenue along with Donnie Bags, Eddie Paradise, and Momo the Roach. A few connected guys milled around outside. A row of pallid men from the neighborhood drank breakfast at the bar. The place was owned by Elwood Cusik, a boxer who'd done enforcer work for the Corleones.

Michael had tried to kill him once before, and Geraci had retaliated beautifully. He'd used Forlenza to let Russo know what was going on with Fredo and down in Cuba; after that, Geraci hadn't had to lift a finger. Fredo had unwittingly betrayed Michael, over nothing. Anyone could see that Cuba was unstable and going to blow. Yet Michael was so blinded by the millions he could make as an almost-legitimate businessman there that he had allowed himself to get sucked into a situation where he'd killed his own brother. His *wife* had left him over it, took the kids, and moved a continent away. He'd lost two *capos*—Rocco and Frankie Pants, both rivals of Geraci's—fighting over an empire in Cuba that was destined never to exist. If there really was a fate worse than death, Geraci had inflicted it on Michael Corleone.

As he waited, Geraci tried to figure out how Michael could have learned about this. He was at a loss.

Two hours late, Donnie Bags, near the window, signaled that Michael's limo was there. The Roach and Eddie Paradise flanked Geraci as he crossed the sidewalk. He was ready for anything. He pictured his daughters' faces. And he reached for the door handle.

"Hello, Fausto."

"Don Corleone." Geraci got into the car alone and climbed into the seat facing Michael. Al Neri, behind the wheel, was the only other person in the car. "You have a nice trip?"

Geraci nodded to the Roach, who closed the door. Neri put the car in gear.

"Outstanding. You should go up again. These new planes practically fly themselves."

"I'll bet," Geraci said. One of Michael's thank-you gifts from Ambassador M. Corbett Shea had been a new airplane. "I have dreams that I'm flying. Funny thing is, they're never nightmares. But once I wake up, I can't even imagine being a passenger again. Hey, congratulations, by the way. Next best thing to having a *paesan'* in the White House."

"It's just the transition team," Michael said. "I only served as an adviser. One of many."

Over the years, the Corleones had granted the Sheas many favors, including several that had helped get the new president elected. In return, Michael had asked for this appointment. Geraci had it on good authority that Michael had never met face-to-face with anyone in the new administration. It was understood that he would participate in name only. All Michael wanted was the credibility the appointment gave him.

"Think we'll live to see it?" Geraci said. "An Italian in the White House?"

"I'm certain of it," Michael said.

Geraci had positioned himself on the seat so that Neri would have to stop the car before killing him. There didn't seem much chance that Michael would do the job himself. If it happened, it would happen someplace they took him, probably by men waiting for him there. "I hope you're right, Don Corleone."

"Just Michael, okay? We're old friends, Fausto, and I'm retired now."

"That's what I hear." The rumors that Michael was going legit had been swirling around for years and intensified after Shea's election. "But I didn't think we had retirement in this thing of ours. Whatever happened to 'You come in alive and you go out dead'? We all swear to that."

"I swore to it, and I'll uphold it. I'll always be a part of the Family my father built," Michael said. "But my relationship to it will be the same as

it is for some of the men my father's age who've served us well and moved to Florida or Arizona. Men from whom we ask nothing."

"Explain to me how this is going to work," Geraci said. "I've heard different things, but I wrote a lot of it off as just talk."

"It's simple. As you know, I promised Clemenza and Tessio they could have their own Families when the time was right. Tessio betrayed us and Pete's dead, but the promise still lives."

"*Ogni promessa è un debito*, eh?" Geraci said. "As my old man used to say."

"Exactly," Michael said. "Today I pay that debt. In every respect, you're our best man in New York. As of today, I have no further need for the businesses you run, not even the income from them. I'm out. I'm the one who should call *you* Don. Don Geraci. Congratulations."

That's it. I'm dead. "Thank you," Geraci said. "Just like that?"

"How else?" Michael said.

Despite himself, Geraci shot a glance at Neri. They were heading west on Seventy-ninth Street, into Central Park. Neri was looking straight ahead. "I'm deeply honored. Overwhelmed."

"You earned it."

Geraci held up his ringless right hand. "If I'd known, I'd have bought a ring."

"Take mine," Michael said. "It was blessed by the pope himself." He started taking it off. It was tasteful, classy: a big diamond surrounded by sapphires.

He wouldn't give that ring to a man he was about to kill, would he? And who'd give away a ring that had been blessed by the fucking pope?

"I was kidding," Geraci said. "I couldn't possibly accept. You've been too generous already." Geraci held up his big right hand, half again the size of Michael's and gnarled from the many punches it had landed, with and without boxing gloves. "Also, I don't think it'll fit."

Michael laughed. "I never really noticed." He slid the ring back on his finger.

How could he never have noticed? "You know what they say. Big hands—"

"Big rings."

"Exactly. Really, Michael, this is incredible news. A dream come true."

"You didn't know?"

"Of course I knew. But I heard there was some trouble with the Commission."

"You have good sources. The Commission has asked that I stay on. I was opposed to this, but their decision is binding. I will remain in an advisory capacity, both to them and to you. It should go without saying that

this arrangement will be maintained in the strictest confidence. Anyone you appoint as *capo* must be cleared with the Commission, and I advise you to clear it with me first. I assume you'll want to keep Nobilio?"

"I need to think about it." Richie Two Guns had taken over Clemenza's old regime. Everything Geraci knew about Richie was good—he'd helped put together the monopoly the New York Families now had on cement, for example, and had a big presence down in Fort Lauderdale, too—but saying yes, just like that, didn't seem smart. If all this was on the level, that is. "Think Richie'll be sore you picked me?"

"You don't think he'll be a lot more sore if you bust him down?"

"I'm not talking about busting him down. I'm just wondering how he'll take the news."

"I'm sure it won't come as much of a surprise."

"You talk to him?"

Michael shook his head. "It's out there, though. If there's a problem, I can talk to him."

"I'm sure it'll work out great." He and Richie had talked about the rumors. Richie had said he'd be happy to see Geraci become the new Don and was pulling for the Commission to approve it. Probably he was telling the truth. "Richie seems like a good man."

"For your own *regime*, I won't presume to make suggestions. Just talk to me first."

"Will do."

"I'll be providing limited counsel to you, but I won't be serving as your *consigliere*. I have another sort of life I wish to lead. I don't want my past to intrude on that life."

"I understand." Though he didn't, not entirely. "Do I run that choice past you as well?"

"Up to you."

"If you don't mind," Geraci said, "I'd like Tom Hagen to be my *consigliere*."

"Unfortunately," Michael said, "I do mind. My brother Tom will continue to work closely with me as my attorney."

Another good sign. If Geraci really was about to be killed, Michael could have said yes.

"Thought I'd take a shot. You always want the best man you can get."

"You don't like me," Michael said. "Do you, Fausto?"

Geraci quickly decided that lying would be more dangerous than telling the truth. "That's true. I don't. No disrespect, but I don't know many people who do."

"But you fear me."

"Fear is the enemy of logic," Geraci said, "but you're right. I do.

More than death. I know what you're trying to say, Michael. I'm ready. I know what it means to you, the sacrifices your family has made to build this organization. I'll give it all I have. Everything."

Michael reached over and slapped Geraci on the knee, affectionately.

They got onto Broadway, uptown.

No mention had been made of what had used to be Rocco Lampone's *regime.* Rocco had gotten himself killed two years ago in Miami and still hadn't been replaced. There were made guys out in Nevada—Al Neri, his nephew Tommy, Figaro, four or five others, plus the connected guys underneath them. If they were a part of this deal, Michael would have said so. Especially with Neri right there, Geraci wasn't going to push his luck. Fuck Nevada.

Geraci rubbed his chin. "Maybe I took a couple punches too many," he said, "but I'm confused. You honest to God have no further need for my businesses? You're gonna just, what, control a couple casinos in Nevada and call it a career?"

Michael nodded. "Fair question," he said. "I made my family a promise that I'd get out, and I'm keeping my promise. As a matter of fact, I had this in place two years ago. Between the casinos in Nevada and the ones in Cuba and our various real estate holdings, I had a business empire that would've sustained itself for a hundred years. But then the Communists took over Cuba and we lost everything there. The various misfortunes that came our way at about the same time meant both that the organization as a whole needed the income from those legitimate businesses and that I couldn't yet step down. But two years and Jimmy Shea's election have changed everything. Losing our legal gambling revenues in Cuba was terrible, but now we have influence in New Jersey. We got their governor elected president, but I'd say what was even more important there was the mutually beneficial arrangement you've built with the Stracci Family. For as long as I can remember, there's been talk of legalizing gambling in Atlantic City, and I plan to stay on the Commission until that happens—probably in a year—so that we can get in there, too. How long is a Communist country a hundred miles off our shore going to last? If it wasn't for the Russians, we'd have taken the place back the moment they started stealing from us, but the difference between Cuba and every other Communist country is that they're so close to the richest country in the world they can taste it and already have. I give it two years, maybe three, and we'll be back in business there, too. I have assurances from the Shea government that they'll enforce the return of all properties to their previous owners. The point I'm trying to make is that if we don't have considerable resources banked, we can't run casinos without the likes of Louie Russo crushing us. We don't quite have those resources yet. Between what

we *do* have, both financial and in terms of personnel, together with what now seems inevitable—well, it's better to get out a year too early than a minute too late."

"So who feeds the meat eaters?" Geraci asked. The Corleone Family's greatest asset was the network of people it kept on its payroll. "I know a lot of the cops and union people we have, some of the judges and the D.A.s, but I'm sure I don't know the half of it. And the politicians, forget it. All I know is rumors."

Geraci had been running most of the Family's business in New York, but the connection guys were under Michael and Hagen.

"Tom will be in touch with you," Michael said. "There will be a transition period. When I took over from my father, it took him and Tom six months to explain everything to me."

"I guess if it's possible to make the transition from one leader of the free world to another in two months, I can figure all this out in six."

Michael chuckled.

"You're really not going to use our judges and cops and so on?" Geraci asked. "You're giving that up?"

"Did I say that? I said I have no more need for the income from the businesses you run."

"Sure," Geraci said. "I understand. You're out."

"Don't be naive, Fausto. There are plenty of men on the president's transition team who are feeding more meat eaters than we do."

So there's retired and then there's whatever it is that you are, Geraci thought. *Got it.*

"And the seat on the Commission. Do I have one, or is that you?"

"That's me for now. You'll have one eventually. Get yourself organized, and after that the Commission will take care of it. I don't think there's going to be any problem with that."

They discussed several other specific issues. The car crossed the park again and started back down Lexington Avenue—hardly a neighborhood for a murder. They really weren't going to kill him. Michael still hadn't learned who was really behind his brother's betrayal. But Geraci wasn't taking any chances.

"Speaking of excellent sources," he said, "I want you to know something. They tried to kill your brother."

"Who tried to kill my brother?"

"Louie Russo. Fuckface."

"My brothers are dead."

"A while ago. I just learned about it."

"Which brother?"

It unnerved Geraci that Michael could call Hagen *my brother* one mo-

ment and say *My brothers are dead* the next. "Fredo. It was a botched hit, and Russo called it off. Remember Labor Day?"

Geraci didn't need to say which Labor Day. Michael nodded.

"After Pete's kid's wedding, Fredo wound up in a motel in Canada. With—I don't know how to say this—with another man. The button guys were supposed to make it look like Fredo killed himself out of shame or what-have-you. I'd tell you that it was a setup, a frame-up, except for a few things."

The problem with Michael's poker face was that when he put it on, you noticed it.

"First," Geraci said, "when Russo's men got to the motel, Fredo was gone but there was still someone there—a salesman; nice job, wife, kids—and he's naked on the bed. Second, the button guys open the door, and the salesman pulls a gun and shoots them. The gun's a Colt Peacemaker with the serial number filed off. It may have been Fredo's gun, maybe not, but he definitely lost a gun on that trip—Figaro told me that—and Fredo loved those Colts. Anyway, the salesman kills one guy, wounds the other. Next day, someone chloroforms a nurse, slits the wounded guy's throat, then buries the knife in his eye up to the hilt and leaves it there. The day after *that,* the salesman goes to meet with his lawyer, and that's the last anybody ever sees him. Other than his hands, that is, which someone chopped off and mailed to his wife."

"You're saying Don Russo covered his tracks."

"I'm saying that, yes."

"Why didn't they come after Fredo again?"

"The idea was to embarrass the Family. You named Fredo *sotto capo,* and right after that it turns out he's queer. I'm not saying he was, all right? I'm just giving you information."

Michael nodded.

"If they made it look like he offed himself," Geraci said, "that would've been the end of it. No revenge, no nothing. Our organization is hurt, and they benefit. They were mad about Las Vegas. They thought of it as their turf. But then after . . . you know. The crash. *My* crash. It wasn't necessary anymore, at least for a while. I can't prove it, but it stands to reason that Russo was behind the tragedy with your brother. Fredo was out in L.A. half the time, and L.A. was where he betrayed us." Geraci raised his eyebrows, shrugged. "L.A. equals Chicago, right?"

It was no secret among the made members of the Family that Michael had ordered his own brother killed.

"How do you know so much?" Michael said. "How did you learn these things?"

"I've got a guy," Geraci said. "Somebody inside the FBI."

"The FBI?" Michael said, clearly impressed. The FBI—the director's peccadillos notwithstanding—was considered incorruptible.

"The gun Fredo was arrested with in L.A. when he killed that dog? Also a Colt with its serial number filed off. In the lab they were able to use acid and bring the number back up. Same with the gun from Windsor. They were both part of a shipment that our guy in Reno got and sold to nonexistent people. Thank God not to Gerald O'Malley. Oh, and one more thing."

Geraci reached in his coat pocket for the closest thing he had to a concealed weapon—a cigarette lighter: jeweled, made in Milan, engraved CHRISTMAS 1954. He tossed it to Michael.

"Recognize this?"

Michael's face reddened. He turned the lighter over in his small, perfectly manicured hand, then made a fist, covering it. Almost covering it.

"The salesman said it belonged to the other guy," Geraci said. "Listen, Michael, I feel awful about this. If you want me to go after Russo, say the word and it's done. I'll come at him with everything we got."

Michael turned to face the window. For several blocks he tapped the fist with the lighter in it against his chin.

Geraci was bluffing. He didn't have anyone in the FBI. He'd heard those Colts all came from the same dealer and hoped that was right. He'd gotten the lighter from Russo, who'd gotten it from the salesman's killer.

But Geraci was serious about going after Russo. He'd had peace in his *regime* for five years. He had a hell of a war chest. The last few years, Cesare Indelicato, the Sicilian *capo di tutti capi,* had been providing Geraci not only with heroin and other drugs but also personnel. Geraci had a whole crew of zips now, over in Bushwick, there on Knickerbocker Avenue, and he'd been setting up some of the legal immigrants with jobs in pizza parlors all over the Midwest, quietly tossing dough and making a little of it until the time may come for them to do Nick Geraci a favor. Men like that, living as law-abiding good neighbors for years in Kenosha, Cleveland Heights, or Youngstown, could go on "vacation," do a job on somebody, come home, and nobody would ever in a million years connect them to some dead gangster eight hundred miles away. If Richie Two Guns was as good as he seemed, Geraci was confident the Corleones could cripple the Chicago outfit and make those animals answerable to the New York Families again. And, of course, Geraci could in the process cover his tracks for his role in manipulating Fredo to betray his brother. Better to do it on Michael's say-so (with Michael having to answer to the Commission for it) than for Geraci to worry about whether to do it later.

"Thank you just the same," Michael finally said. "But as I told you, I'm retired."

The car stopped. They were back on First Avenue, in front of the Roach's bar. Geraci wondered if Michael had really been thinking all that time or if he'd simply waited until the end of the drive to answer.

Nick Geraci held out his left hand, palm down, in front of his chest and held his right underneath, pointing at the bottom of his palm. *"Qui sotto non ci piove."* Under here you won't be rained on. *"Un giorno avrai bisogno di me."* One day you'll need me.

An old expression. Tessio would say it when pledging his protection, and Michael must have heard his father say it, too.

"I appreciate that, Fausto," Michael said.

"Don't mention it."

Michael smiled. A chill went through Nick Geraci.

"You thought I was going to kill you," Michael said, "didn't you?"

"I think everyone's trying to kill me all the fucking time," Geraci said. "Force of habit."

"That's probably why you're still alive."

How did he mean that? That it was probably why no one had ever killed him or why Michael wasn't killing him now? Geraci wasn't about to ask for a clarification.

"Anyway, Michael, what reason would I have to think you were going to kill me?" Geraci said. "Like you said, you're retired. Good luck to you in your new life."

Michael still had the lighter in his fist.

They kissed and embraced, and Geraci watched the limo pull away. When he walked inside the bar, his men had somehow known to gather, a good thirty or forty of them. Shaking, Nick Geraci went upstairs and slumped in a big leather chair in the corner. His men followed. He slipped his wedding ring onto the little finger of his right hand, and his men lined up to kiss it.

Chapter 23

Mr. Fontane! Have you been promised a job in the Shea administration?"

The lobby of Constitution Hall was full of reporters. Johnny Fontane was sitting behind a table on a crowded dais, flanked by a dozen stars of stage and screen. There would be many more onstage tomorrow. They were making history. No one he'd asked to perform at the inaugural ball for Jimmy Shea had said no. If the Russians dropped the bomb on Washington, there'd be little left of show business but school plays, rock music, and stag films. "A *job?*" Johnny said, in mock horror. "I became a saloon singer so I'd never have to *have* a job."

This got a decent laugh. He wanted them to think the answer might be yes. The Ambassador had talked about setting Fontane up to run for office. Jimmy himself—at Fontane's place in Vegas, on a break from going at it with Rita Duvall, who was also on the podium now—had suggested making Fontane the ambassador to Italy. Or how about some little tropical paradise with blue skies and limitless pussy? He and Johnny had both been pretty drunk at that point.

"What does it say about the Shea presidency," a voice shouted, "that the inaugural ball is being produced by someone like yourself with reputed Mafia ties?"

Johnny couldn't believe it. When was this shit going to stop?

The jerk-off who asked the question was with a paper in New York. Johnny had punched him out once. The out-of-court settlement had been ten grand and worth every cent.

Bobby Chadwick—the brother-in-law of the president-elect—leaned over his mike. "By someone *like* Johnny Fontane? Forgive me if you're a correspondent from the planet Uranus and unfamiliar with our ways, but here on Earth, it's safe to say there's nobody *like* Johnny Fontane."

He got a laugh, too, but the laughter subsided and the other reporters still looked at Johnny for an answer. If this had been a restaurant or a nightclub, Johnny could have merely arched an eyebrow and this jerk-off would have been out on his ass.

"*Reputed* is a word lazy reporters use so they can make things up," Johnny said. "Let me give you some facts. There are more than five million Americans of Italian descent. According to a report the U.S. Senate put out two years ago, there are at most four thousand people associated with the quote-unquote Mafia. I'll do the math for you, buddy-boy. That's thirteen-hundred-to-one odds. You're more likely to get eaten by a bear. Yet every time somebody whose name ends with a vowel gets ahead, bigots like you ask if we're in the Mob."

"*Are* you in the Mob?"

Well, he'd walked into that one. "I'm not even going to dignify a question that ignorant."

"I could be wrong," said Sir Oliver Smith-Christmas, the distinguished British actor, seated at the edge of the podium, "but aren't you confusing the sort of gentlemen who oftentimes own American nightclubs with those like my friend Mr. Fontane, who simply perform in them? Where is a nightclub singer to perform if not in a nightclub?"

"Ollie makes a good point," Johnny Fontane said. "Once the big-band era was over—"

"Isn't it a fact that the late Vito Corleone was your godfather?" the reporter said.

Not that kind of godfather, you stupid fuck. "He stood for my baptism, yes. He was a friend of my parents."

"Does President-elect Shea have ties to organized crime?" another reporter asked. "Michael Corleone, who was among those called to testify before the Senate two years ago, served as a member of the transition—"

"Why don't you ask that to Michael Corleone, huh?" Johnny said. "Better yet, why don't you ask all the sick kids Mr. Corleone's hospital and charities have helped? Look, folks, this is an exciting time for our country. I think I can speak for everyone up here when I say that we're behind President Shea one hundred percent. But let's keep the questions a little more on the subject of the inaugural ball itself, all right?"

"You grew up in New York," the jerk-off shouted, "but you're friendly with Louie Russo in Chicago and Ignazio Pignatelli in Los Angeles." The shithead pronounced it *Pig-natelli*, rather than *Peenyatelli*. "Pignatelli's sister is listed as a shareholder in the new record label you started. My question is, is it possible to transfer your membership—"

"Don't make me come down from here and show you some manners," Johnny said.

"Are you going to have me whacked? That's the Mafia word for it, right? Whacked?"

"Now, how the fuck would I know that?" Johnny said. Obviously, everyone knew that, but that wasn't the point.

A murmur went through the room.

"How on *earth*," Johnny rephrased it, "would I know that?"

After Kay Corleone left her husband and left Nevada, she landed a teaching job at a first-rate boarding school in Maine. She and her children lived in a stone cottage on the grounds of the school. Michael didn't like it, but she needed a job, not financially but as a means of creating an identity separate from all she'd been with him. She'd applied only to schools thousands of miles from Lake Tahoe. She hadn't expected Michael to fight so hard for custody and had been even more surprised when out of the blue he told her he'd looked into the school where she was teaching and decided that the children's education would be best served by going there. Kay had no idea what changed his mind. He claimed he simply realized he was using the kids as pawns in the divorce and putting his feelings ahead of what they really needed. She wanted to believe that. She'd curbed her impulse to tell him that if he'd paid more attention to his heart than his cold mind, he might not have found himself in this mess in the first place.

Michael didn't see Tony and Mary often. When he did, he usually picked them up in his plane and flew them to New York for a weekend of frenzied activity: ice-skating, carriage rides, museums, movies, the zoo—everything he could cram in. They'd come home exhausted. For weeks afterward, Mary, who was seven now and worshiped her father, would tell endless stories about their time together. Tony, who was nine, rarely talked about him at all.

When Michael first told Kay his schedule was tight and asked her to take the kids to New York herself this time, she'd said it was impossible. When he told her about the inaugural ball and said Kay could go, too, she declined. Washington had a lot of bad memories for her. Though she hoped he'd find a way to make it work so he could take Mary and Tony. And, no, having some button man come to Maine and drive them to New York was not an option.

Everything changed when Kay heard about Jules Segal. He'd been her doctor in Nevada. She'd recommended him to a friend who'd moved there and learned that he'd been shot more than a year ago—the victim of a botched burglary, according to the newspapers.

So now, the day of the ball, Kay waited in a room at the Essex House, in a suite overlooking Central Park. The kids were watching TV. They didn't have a set at home anymore. Seeing them transfixed by it here confirmed for her that this had been a good idea. She looked at her watch. He was late. Some things never changed.

Finally, she heard voices in the hall. Michael and—of course!—Al Neri opened the door.

"Why isn't he dressed?" Michael asked, pointing at Tony. Michael already had his tux on.

"I'm not *going* to your stupid ball," Tony said.

Kay had been so distracted that she hadn't noticed that Tony had taken off his suit and changed back into the blue shirt and chinos he wore to school every day.

Mary leapt from the bed to go hug her father. "I'm going!" Mary said. "Don't I look like a beautiful princess? Because that's who goes to balls is why."

"You do, sweetheart. You really do. C'mon, Tony. You're going. You'll love it."

Kay told Tony to put his suit back on. The boy snatched it up and trudged to the bathroom, muttering. Neri sat down on the sofa, apparently content with the cartoon program that was on. Mary twirled around, showing off her dress. Kay told her to go watch the rest of the show on TV, she needed to have a word alone with Daddy. Then she steered Michael into the adjoining bedroom and closed the door.

"I did it, Kay. I've retired from—well, from the dangerous aspects of the business I inherited from my father. I promised you that I'd make all my business dealings legitimate, and I've done it."

She frowned. "You made that promise *ten years ago*." She presumed it was a clumsy ploy to get her to come back to him. Still, she hoped for the kids' sake he was telling the truth. Sooner or later, he was going to be killed or go to jail, and she hated to think how it would affect Tony and Mary when he did. "I'm happy for you, though, Michael. I really am."

"You look great, Kay. Maine, teaching: it's really agreeing with you."

"Michael, I have to ask you something. I want you to tell me the truth."

In a split second, his face became an expressionless mask.

"Did you have Jules Segal killed?"

"No."

No hesitation. Just *no*. Isn't that exactly what a liar would do when the answer is *yes*?

"I don't think I believe you," Kay said.

"I told you a long time ago not to ask me about my business, Kay."

"This isn't your business, it's *our* business. You had Dr. Segal killed because of me, didn't you? Because of the—"

"Don't say it." At least now he had an expression on his face. "I don't want to hear it."

"Abortion. Are you going to slap me again?" The way he had when

she'd told him: the slap that had ended their marriage, in a different hotel, but in Washington, where he was about to go.

"No, Kay," he said. "I'm not."

"Because if that *burglary* was your handiwork—"

"I don't want to talk about this subject."

"—you should know that it wasn't him."

"Kay, stop it. We both know that when you—when that happened, he was the doctor you went to. We own that hospital, Kay."

"So it shouldn't have been too hard to get my records and see that I had a miscarriage."

"Oh, sure. You flew to Las Vegas so you could have a miscarriage, and the attending doctor just happened to be the same man who performed the abortions every time Fredo—"

Her stomach felt like it had been twisted by a pair of strong hands. "Oh, God, Michael. I *knew* it. I knew it. You just . . . I was so *angry*. I was *scared*. It was terrible to live in fear of what might happen to you, but I realized there was nothing I was more afraid of than you—"

"Me? I have protected this family, *our* family, ahead of anything and everything else."

"Michael, you married into another kind of family a long time before we started ours. Even your first wife was your second wife. I was your third."

"Nothing could have ever happened to you. Or our children. Nothing ever will."

"Come on, Michael. Our house in Nevada was attacked, like some target in a war zone. Did you promise *Apollonia* nothing would ever happen to her, too? I suppose we should count our blessings we weren't blown to smithereens."

"Kay—"

"And what do you mean, *Nothing ever will*? What sort of *protection*, what kind of *goons* do you command in your capacity as a legitimate businessman? *Legitimate businessman*. We'll see. Do you really expect me to believe that anything about you has changed, that anything about you will *ever* change? Calling yourself *legitimate* won't change what you've done."

He kept his eyes on her as he reached into his jacket pocket. For a terrible moment she thought he was reaching for a gun or a knife. He took out a cigarette and lit it.

"Are you through?" he said.

"You don't *understand*. I'm not *like* you, Michael. I could have never killed our . . . our son. I flew to Las Vegas to help organize a fund-raiser for the art museum, and right after I got there I had a miscarriage. I didn't have any word from you for *two weeks* after that happened. *Two weeks*. No

woman should have to live through that alone. I decided to leave you. I had other reasons, bigger reasons, all the reasons we've talked about, but that was the last straw. I knew you'd never give me a divorce. So I told you I'd had an abortion. I wanted to hurt you, and I told a lie to do it. I wanted to see that look on your face, and I saw it. I wanted to see what you'd do, and you hit me."

Michael lowered his head and, very slightly, nodded.

"Jules Segal was my *regular doctor,* Michael. Do you really think that *anybody,* especially him, a man who knew who you are as well as anyone in Las Vegas, would have performed an abortion on the wife of a—of a man in your position? Segal wouldn't have . . . I don't know . . . lit a cigarette without your blessing. I never in my wildest dreams, my wildest nightmares, thought you'd send your goons—"

"We need to go," Michael said. "I'm going." He turned and went into the other room. "Come on, Mary, Tony. Who wants to go for an airplane ride?"

Mary shouted that she did, she did, and Tony didn't say anything, but within moments her children had both kissed her and said their goodbyes. No one turned off the television.

Kay Corleone—an accessory to murder before the fact—collapsed onto the bed.

She had no one to blame but herself. Michael was a killer. She'd fallen in love with him not in spite of that but—as he told her about what he'd done in the war—because of it. She knew in her heart that he'd killed those two men in the restaurant. She knew about a lot of other killings, too, and pretended not to. She married him and *changed religions*—leaving one that allowed divorce for one that prohibited it—so that she could go to confession and try to live with herself for loving a killer. When she'd finally worn Tom Hagen down and gotten him to tell her that the house in Lake Tahoe had in fact been torched and bulldozed because the FBI had bugged the beams and foundation, she'd actually thought, *This is the last straw.* But no. She'd stayed. She'd rebuilt. When men with machine guns opened fire and nearly killed her children, she left the house but stayed with him. Not until he abandoned her when she lost the baby *and* hit her *and* killed his own brother did she do what a truly innocent person would have done years ago.

A news broadcast came on. The lead story of course was the swearing in of the toothy new president. Kay looked up. In a shot of the crowd, she saw Tom and Theresa Hagen. She put her head back down, profoundly alone, and cried herself to sleep.

Chapter 24

Dʀᴇssᴇᴅ ɪɴ a pink ball gown that barely contained her swollen breasts and clutching a pair of Superman pajamas, Francesca Van Arsdale, six months pregnant with her second child, chased her first one (two-year-old William Brewster Van Arsdale IV, whom they were calling Sonny) through the maze of boxes in their apartment on Capitol Hill. Sonny was naked except for the gold Notre Dame football helmet he'd gotten for Christmas from her brother Frankie. She heard Billy's Dual-Ghia and looked out the kitchen window. The sight of the woman getting out of Billy's ridiculously expensive car stopped Francesca in her tracks.

She dropped the pajamas. It wasn't the babysitter. It was *her*. That Woman.

Francesca braced herself against the kitchen sink. But no. It wasn't. On second glance, the babysitter was about fifteen and looked no more like the woman Billy had cheated on her with—another member of the Floridians for Shea staff—than would have any other willowy blond beauty who was everything Francesca was not.

"Ready, Francie?" Billy called, opening the door.

Sonny, ecstatic, sprinted toward his father and gave him an inadvertent but savage header to the crotch. As Billy moaned and crumpled into a chair, Francesca scooped up the pajamas and then Sonny, too, and gave the girl—the little sister of someone Billy knew from Harvard Law School—an agonizingly thorough set of instructions.

"You look fantastic," Billy said, holding the car door open. "Gorgeous."

Francesca was quite clear on the fact that she looked like a big pink cow. She struggled to get into that low-slung car with some semblance of dignity. Billy didn't seem to notice. When she was in, he leaned down and kissed her, chastely at first, and then passionately. When the kiss was over, he thanked her. Thanked her!

It had been like this for weeks. *Her own mother* had told her to forget about the affair. Men are going to have their *goumadas*. You know why surveys say that fifty percent of men cheat on their wives? she'd asked. Because the other fifty are liars. But once in a while, she'd said, you can pre-

tend to be surprised to learn about some woman—which, if you don't do it too often, can spark enough guilt to make your husband treat you like you were courting. In contrast, Francesca's sister's advice had been to kill him. But Kathy had never liked Billy. She was also (despite a string of boyfriends in London, where she was getting her Ph.D. in Continental literature) not a mother. Being a mother changed things more than anyone who was not a mother could possibly imagine. What was Francesca supposed to do, get a divorce? Raise two children alone? So far, her mother seemed to have been dead-on. But Francesca didn't trust Billy's newfound devotion. Despite all his penitential tenderness, he'd made love to her maybe twice since she started to show. When she'd been pregnant the first time, Billy had been turned on by it, had wanted to do it all the time.

"You should see my office, babe," Billy said. Right after the inaugural address, Daniel Brendan Shea—the president's brother and new attorney general—had assembled his staff and had a meeting. This didn't bode well for Billy working fewer hours than he had during the campaign (though maybe in this case those hours would be more exclusively devoted to work). "It's small, but it's on the same floor as Danny's."

"You're calling him *Danny*?" *You're calling me* babe?

"That's what he said to call him." Billy actually stuck his chest out with pride. This was not a gesture she found endearing, though maybe she once had.

"On a first-name basis with the attorney general," she marveled. Did he call That Woman *babe*, too? "I'm proud of you."

Which, despite everything, was true.

"The third youngest attorney general in the history of the United States," Billy said. "Before he's done, don't be surprised if he's considered the best one, too. He has an incredible combination of intelligence and—this doesn't sound like a compliment, but it is—ruthlessness."

"Sounds to me," she said, "like he's the right man for the job."

On the way to the ball, they made quick stops at parties at several different embassies and hotels. As if by magic, Billy knew where to go, where the valet parking would be, the names of the hosts, and how to find them. When Francesca got inside, she had to pee—she *always* had to pee; it was like having a truck parked on her bladder—and she always guessed wrong about which way the bathroom was. She couldn't help but be dazzled to be in these ornate mansions—especially the *French embassy*, which gave her an evil thrill, thinking about how jealous Kathy would be when she heard about it. And everywhere she turned, she saw a famous face or met a powerful person. But at the same time, she was miserable. Strangers kept pawing her, presuming that they could touch her belly, and Billy never once told them to keep their filthy hands to themselves. Her back was

killing her. And she felt inadequate and out of place, as she had for most of her marriage. The pregnancy aside—and it was *never* aside; this kid was going to be a giant—no one looked like her (the Italian embassy was not among their stops). The women were either tall, WASPy, and glamorous, with their hair piled high and sprayed perfectly in place (like That Woman, in other words), or they were *Washington wives:* elegant matrons in fat pearls who somehow managed to be both unobtrusive and lively.

At every party, though, except for during her trips to the restroom, Billy stayed by her side. It was painful to watch him thwart his instinct to abandon her and work the room, but not so painful that Francesca was ever tempted to tell him to go do what he needed to do.

They finally arrived at Constitution Hall and were walking up the steps when she heard a high, unfamiliar voice calling her name. She turned and couldn't see where it was coming from.

"Bee-Boy! Bee-Boy!"

Francesca's heart soared. It was Mary Corleone and Uncle Mike. She hadn't seen them since her wedding day, more than three years before. Her uncle looked like he'd aged ten years.

She reached down to pick Mary up and then thought better of it. "I hardly recognized you," Francesca said. "You're huge."

"You're huge, too," Mary said, rubbing Francesca's belly. Mary was her cousin. She could rub until her heart's content. "We both have on the same-colored dress. That's a baby in there, right? I'm smart. I'm seven years old."

Uncle Mike asked if he could touch it.

"Of course," she said. "You *are* smart," she told Mary. "It is a baby. A big one, I think."

When the baby kicked and Michael recoiled in delight, Francesca noticed her cousin Tony, standing behind his father. She bent down to hug him, too. He smiled but didn't say anything. There was a man in a long coat behind them, too, who must have been a bodyguard.

"My brother doesn't talk much," Mary said. "But he's not retarded. When he sings he can say anything. People are going to sing at the fancy ball, did you know that?"

"*You're* retarded," Tony said, perfectly well.

"I was hoping I'd see you here," Francesca said. "When did you get in?"

Michael looked at his watch. "Fifteen minutes ago."

"Are you staying long?" Francesca asked. "We're not really moved in, but I'd love to have you come see our apartment."

A look passed between Billy and Michael, then Billy turned the other way. The only other time they'd seen each other had been at the wedding;

Billy had acted funny then, too. She knew it had to do with how her family's past might affect his political future. Every marriage has taboo conversations, she thought, and this, really, was their only one. They were lucky.

"Just for the night," Michael said. "Next time I'm in town, maybe. The work with the transition team is over, obviously, but I should still be back here on business fairly often."

Billy extended his hand to the bodyguard. "Billy Van Arsdale."

"We met," Al Neri said. But that was all he said.

"C'mon, Uncle Mike," Francesca said. "You sure you don't have time for a home-cooked breakfast?"

"Yeah, are you sure?" Mary said. "Mommy says breakfast is the most importantest meal of the day."

"All you eat for breakfast is cheese," Tony said.

"That's from a *song*," Mary scoffed. "I eat everything. *Please*, Daddy? Can we go?"

Marguerite Duvall took the stage with ten women in red lingerie and ten slim men in tight-fitting simulated chaps, to re-create the big production number from *Cattle Call*, complete with the burning bordello and her famous risqué-but-classy finish. Rita played the French madam, the best friend of the sheriff. It was a small role, but this number had helped get her a Tony award nomination (that and the rumor that she was sleeping with the man who was now president).

Johnny Fontane stood in the wings, dressed in a white cape with a purple satin lining and a striped swallowtail tuxedo designed especially for tonight's event by the best designer in Milan. He was sipping what looked like bourbon but was really tea and honey in a rocks glass.

"The lovely and talented Miss Done-'Em-All Duvall," said Buzz Fratello, shaking his head in admiration. He and Dotty were on next. "I hear she's fucking Fuckface, too."

Johnny had introduced her to both Jimmy Shea and Louie Russo. But Fontane had included Rita in the inaugural ball on his own, with no word from either of them. The talent roster had been his call. The Ambassador made some suggestions, but Johnny ignored him. Rita might not be the biggest star here, but she'd been nominated for a Tony award, for Christ's sake. For Fontane, she was a good luck charm. He'd met her when Hal Mitchell rounded her up—back when she was just some struggling French showgirl—for a threesome the night before the first sessions on *Fontane Blue*. Ever since then, Johnny Fontane's life had been mostly Saturday nights. Even when things had gone south with Annie McGowan, a week

in Acapulco with Rita and a Golden Globe for that picture about the alkie detective, and everything was so jake it was jacob.

The fake bawdy house was in flames now. The audience seemed to be eating it up.

"Look at him," Fratello said, meaning the president: front and center, holding hands with his wife and beaming at the taut-legged, high-kicking ersatz hookers. "I'll sleep a lot better tonight knowing the leader of the free world is a man who appreciates fine pussy," he said.

"Relaxes the hand that's on the button," Johnny agreed.

Buzz made his inimitable leering noises. "Which button we talkin' about?" Buzz asked, which cracked Johnny up.

"Let me ask you something, Buzz," Johnny said. "You're a *paesano*. You sing in all the same joints I do. You know the same guys I know. Why don't they ask *you* that Mafia shit?"

"You know the definition of *dirty Guinea*? An Italian gentleman who just left the room."

"I'm serious."

"I'm funny," Buzz said. "Who ever heard of a funny gangster?"

"I got news for you, pally. You're not that funny."

"I love you, too, you wop bastard."

Not a lot of other people could talk to him this way, but from Buzz it was different.

"C'mon. You own a part of a casino, Johnny. Who else owns casinos but wiseguys?"

"A lot of people, and you know it."

"I know it, but that's not how people see it," Buzz said. "Look, I hear it, too. What you said to that reporter yesterday, you were right."

"I never read that about you."

"You probably sold more records since we been talkin' than I will all year. Crook your little finger, and any chick alive follows you home. *And* you're a movie star. If that ain't enough, you got your pussy-chasing partner there elected president, and he owes you. When you're on top of the world, my dago friend, little people sit home at night, dreaming about knockin' you down. Forget it. You'll live longer."

Jimmy Shea was a man of vision who'd inspired the country and gotten the most votes. Nobody *got him elected*. Johnny had worked hard to help him, but so had a lot of people. Still, he was proud Jimmy had won, and he had high hopes for what it would be like to be one of the best friends of the president. He'd already redone his estate in Las Vegas, expanding the main house and building bungalows for guests and Secret Service. There was a second pool now and even a helicopter pad. Jimmy had said it would be his western White House.

Now came the big finish. The stage was full of fake smoke, and Rita

tore off her dress. She was wearing a body suit. The squares in the cheap seats might have sworn they saw her bird, but from where Johnny Fontane stood, it was pure cornball, not to mention a lousy substitute for Rita in the genuine altogether.

"You know the other reason they don't ask me as often if I'm in the Mafia?"

"What's that?" Johnny was backing away, ready to take the stage.

"Because I'm not."

"What's that supposed to mean?"

Buzz lowered his head. "I am sorry if I have displeased you." He dropped to his knees, grabbed Johnny Fontane's right hand, and kissed the signet ring Annie McGowan had given him during their brief marriage. "Forgive me, Godfather."

Only once did Billy Van Arsdale ask Francesca Corleone if her family was in the Mafia. It was the day before his graduation from Florida State. His parents had taken them to dinner at the Governor's Club, gotten into a noisy, drunken argument, and left separately. "I love your family," she'd said, deadpan, hoping to lighten the mood. It had come out wrong.

"At least," he said, "they're not in the Mafia."

"Is that supposed to be a joke?" she said.

"I don't know." He brightened, as if he'd been waiting to ask the question from the time they'd met and finally had his opening. "*Is* your family in the Mafia?"

"That's what you think, isn't it? That all Italians are in the Mafia? That we eat-a the pizza, we squeeze-a the tomatoes, and we—"

"Not *all* Italians," he said. "I'm only asking about the male members of your family."

"Of course not." She threw down her napkin. She stood up, punched him in the mouth, and stormed out.

She knew that her family *was* in the Mafia—Kathy had convinced her—but Francesca hadn't meant to lie. What she'd heard was her own anxiety, the anxiety that lurked *behind* his question: the fear that Billy was with her only because she seemed exotic. He was always looking for something new and different: foreign movies, the latest records, beat poetry in a coffeehouse in Frenchtown, the Negro neighborhood in Tallahassee. Once, they had driven six hours to the Seminole Reservation so he could learn to wrestle alligators. Every few weeks, it seemed, he started some new hobby. Every haircut was a little different than the one before.

Can't you see Billy's just here, Kathy had said, *to experience a gen-u-ine Mafia Christmas?*

Francesca started running through the hot night, determined not to

cry. It was over. Fine. Good. He'd been her first love, but so what? He wouldn't be her last. He was going off to Harvard Law School in the fall, and she'd be back here. It probably wouldn't have worked out anyway. Also, he was a jerk. A phony. It had felt great to hit him. It had made a great smacking noise that had sounded more impressive than what people would expect from a girl. Her hand still tingled. She'd have to thank her brother Frankie for being such a pain in the ass over the years and giving her the chance to hone her skills.

The same mysterious ability Billy deployed to breeze into and out of all those inauguration-night parties had been on display that night in Tallahassee, too. She'd had no destination. She'd run down a hill and into a residential neighborhood unfamiliar to her, and at the exact moment she realized she might be lost, she heard a car slow down beside her and there was Billy, in his Thunderbird. He'd known just where to go.

"*Wow*, what a punch!" He was smiling, laughing through his big, undamaged white teeth. She was a girl who could knock your block off, another way she was exotic and new. "I love you, slugger."

"How did *your* family get so rich?" she asked. "Behind every great fortune there's a crime." She'd read that in a book by one of the French writers Kathy was studying. Balzac, maybe.

"Several, I'm sure," he said. "Those assholes are capable of anything."

Those assholes were his father and grandfather. It was bizarre to hear anyone talk about his family that way.

She got in the car.

They made up that night, but the drama of that evening set the tone for their courtship.

The long-distance romance had all the melodrama such things do among the young, fraught with ten-page letters, sneaking suspicions, and tearful phone calls—at least on Francesca's part. Billy claimed to be so busy at Harvard that he barely had time to eat or sleep, much less write her letters or talk on the phone long distance. Then he sent her a *postcard*, of all things, a *typed* postcard, to tell her he'd gotten an internship with a firm in New York and wasn't coming back home to south Florida that summer. She borrowed her roommate Suzy's VW bug and drove all night to Cambridge, to end the whole mess in person. Naturally, she and Billy slept together. She went home more confused than ever and, it turned out, pregnant.

He wanted her to get an abortion.

Then he even made arrangements for a doctor in Palm Beach to do it.

Francesca couldn't bear the thought of it. But she certainly didn't want to have the baby, either. Marrying Billy—not that he'd asked or even mentioned the possibility—was out of the question. She told Kathy—the

first and only person she'd confided in—that she wouldn't marry that snake if he was the last man on earth. Everything that could happen was something Francesca Corleone definitely would not do.

Billy broke his leg skydiving (the end of another new hobby), and while he was in the hospital he had a sudden change of heart—inexplicable, from Francesca's perspective, though who can explain a change of heart? The day he was discharged, he flew to see her and proposed.

Overjoyed, she accepted.

They were married in July with him still on crutches. She'd been upset that he'd have to slit the leg of his tux, and he assured her he could afford the small tailoring charge. She got upset about a lot of things—a pregnant bride's prerogative, perhaps, but all of it a substitute for the two things she was really upset about: her walks up and down the aisle. Down would be pathetic, with Billy on crutches. But up would be impossible. Who could *ever* take her father's place? Not her little brothers, and certainly not Stan the Liquor Man (who was still engaged to her mother and who still hadn't married her). Uncle Fredo was older than Uncle Mike, and she knew Uncle Fredo better. She was drawn to Uncle Mike, though, and always had been. He was a war hero, a romantic figure, a man who looked great in a tuxedo. She knew some of his dark secrets—at least via the imperfect conduits of Kathy and Aunt Connie—but despite this, in the end he was the only man she could imagine giving her away. "It's who Pop would want," she told Kathy, her maid of honor, expecting her twin sister to disagree. "Obviously," Kathy said instead. No one said *obviously* with more withering scorn than Kathy. "Who else?"

Uncle Mike balanced Francesca's jittery nerves with his dignified and regal bearing. He told her that her father would have been proud, that Santino *was* here, watching, be sure of that. But he was smart enough to say this a long time before they went up the aisle, so that they could cry together and get those tears out of the way. When they were finally alone in the narthex, he took her arm and told her not to worry. He shrugged. "It's only the rest of your life."

She laughed. It was the perfect thing to say.

She went down the aisle happy. Only when Michael gave her hand to Billy did she see that it was her uncle whose face was streaked with tears.

On the trip back down the aisle, she steadied Billy, and he managed to make it without crutches. At the reception, he even danced. He was such a bad dancer in the first place, at least with the cast he had an excuse.

They moved to Boston. When he finished law school, he turned down a job making a fortune on Wall Street (he already had a fortune) in favor of being a clerk for a judge on the Florida Supreme Court. It was tough to be back in Tallahassee as her class graduated (she went to Suzy Kimball's

graduation party and hardly knew the poised young woman who was bound for missionary work in China). But Francesca had a family now and truly did think she was happy—at least until Billy quit his job with the court to work for Floridians for Shea. He was gone all the time. Eventually Francesca found out that he was doing more than campaigning.

How did she find out about That Woman?

Francesca was a Corleone. It was a maxim, much repeated in her family, that it was impossible, over time, to deceive a Corleone. That was one theory. She was also that most dangerous of adversaries to philandering: a woman whose darkest fear is that her husband doesn't think she's good enough for him.

Ernest Hemingway is not Papa, that guy with the white beard. He's not the voice of a lost generation. He's not a straw man to be dismissed as sexist by tweedy frauds whose lives will give less to the world than any of several of Hemingway's lesser afternoons. He's those great early books. Nothing else matters.

Einstein is not a poster boy for genius. Picasso is not a swarthy bald womanizer. Mozart isn't an *enfant terrible*. Virginia Woolf and Sylvia Plath aren't tragic affronts to the oppressive male hegemony. Mahatma Gandhi and Martin Luther King aren't harmless, lovable little brown guys white people can feel comfortable endorsing. Babe Ruth isn't a fat slob who ate hot dogs and visited sick kids in the hospital. Yes, the Mafia fixed the Sonny Liston fight that allowed Muhammad Ali to become the heavyweight champ in the first place, and, yes, Ali stood up for what he believed in. But first and foremost, he was a man who could knock the toughest motherfucker in the valley on his ass and make it seem like poetry.

Johnny Fontane was a fine actor when he felt like it. He had an enviably large penis that he put to great use. He helped transform Las Vegas from a desert stopover into the fastest-growing city in the United States. He was the son of immigrant parents, the embodiment of the American dream. He looked great in a hat. He invented American cool (Caucasian division).

Big deal.

What difference does it make that Fontane gave the Shea campaign a half-million bucks in a satchel that had been a personal gift from Jackie Ping-Pong? Ping-Pong had nothing to do with the money itself. Johnny had to carry it in something. (And, anyway, he lived in a world where people gave a lot of gifts. Once, he'd had an accountant who told him to cut back on all that. Fontane sent him a Rolex.) Fontane raised millions for that campaign, so what does it matter that this particular half million was

part of the skim from the Kasbah, a Chicago-owned casino in Las Vegas? What difference does it make who in West Virginia wound up with it, or how exactly those recipients might have used it to ensure that Jimmy Shea won a state that he might have won anyway?

Fontane introduced Rita Duvall to both Louie Russo and Jimmy Shea (not to mention Fredo Corleone, whose baby she put up for adoption in 1956, right before her career took off). What happened after the introductions had to do with her, not Johnny Fontane.

Once, a sheriff's deputy who'd taken a swing at Johnny Fontane after Fontane had fucked the guy's wife died mysteriously in the desert. So what? Fontane fucked a lot of men's wives. People die mysteriously in the desert every day. There was never a shred of evidence of any causal connection between those two terrible but commonplace truths.

Sure, Fontane was Vito Corleone's godson. He got along with Michael, too. He was friendly with Russo, with Tony Stracci, with Gussie Cicero, and so on. So were a lot of people (Ambassador M. Corbett Shea, for example). He wasn't a *member* of anyone's quote-unquote crime family. Johnny Fontane was just loyal to people who were loyal to him when his life was nothing but Mondays.

Butta-beepa-da-boppa-da-boop.

In the end, Johnny Fontane was a singer. The world will not see his like again.

He called himself a saloon singer, but at first that was Sicilian humility, then false modesty, then—after the masterpieces of American song that he released in the late fifties and early sixties—a disingenuous joke that the whole world was in on.

Take, as only one of many examples one might cite, his performance at James K. Shea's inaugural ball.

That famous striped tux would have looked clownish on anyone else, but on Fontane it seems perfectly natural, one of the signal moments in twentieth-century style. All evening, he's a charming and funny master of ceremonies, with none of the boys-will-be-boys dicking around from his nightclub act or the ponderous showbiz patter of his late-career arena shows. He is, when called upon, a brilliant duet partner—most notably with Ella Fitzgerald on a quiet, stirring a cappella version of "The Battle Hymn of the Republic."

Fontane's own set consists of just three songs. The occasion would not seem to play to his strengths. His greatest recordings were either torch songs sung from a singularly male perspective or anthemic renditions of numbers about battered losers who endure—neither of which would have struck the right note for the occasion.

We first see him alone, in a pool of light. The top hat sits on a stool

beside him. The music starts, just a piano and drums. Brushes. It's a slow, loping arrangement of "It Had to Be You." Fontane holds the micro-phone away from him at an angle and sings with his head cocked toward the ceiling. Throughout the song, Fontane moves the mike to alter his tone, playing it as well as Charlie Parker played his horn. Great voices abound, but Johnny Fontane is something rarer: a great singer.

The crowd bursts into applause. Fontane grabs his top hat and rips into "Ridin' High," stalking the stage with an animal ferocity Cole Porter could never have imagined. When Fontane finishes, breathless, the crowd leaps to its feet. Fontane's grin is unmistakably that of a kid who grew up with nothing and looks out to see he's got more than everything.

While there may be little to redeem the earnest version of "Big Dreams" that the Shea campaign co-opted as its official theme song (with new lyrics written by Wally Morgan), Johnny Fontane, suffused with the triumph of the moment, gives it a hero's try. He certainly seems sincere. After the opening verse, a curtain behind him rises, and the rest of the night's acts stride forth and join in for the chorus. When the camera cuts to the audience, the houselights are up and everyone's standing and singing along, too. The president kisses his first lady. Fontane throws them his top hat. The president catches it and puts it on. It fits.

Chapter 25

I KNOW YOUR NAME IS BILLY," Mary said. "I only call you Bee-Boy because my cousin Kathy who looks just like Francie only without a baby inside calls you that too, even though I thought of it first, back when I was a baby. But I'd been born, of *course*."

"I like it," Billy said, showing everyone inside the apartment, "coming from you."

Francesca had been up since four, unpacking the kitchen boxes, going to the grocery store, and cooking breakfast. She was exhausted but used to it. The baby kicked so much she hadn't been getting much sleep anyway.

"Everything's just about ready," she said. "Excuse the mess. We've only been here two days. Billy, why don't you give them the ten-cent tour and then we'll eat. Hey, *Sonny*! Get over here, right now! We have guests!"

Her son got up from in front of the TV and ran and tackled Tony. Sonny was just shy of his third birthday. Tony was nine. Tony took it well. Uncle Mike noted his son's patience with obvious approval. She'd never noticed much resemblance between Uncle Mike and Grandpa Vito, but suddenly it was there in her uncle's weary eyes, so much so it was spooky.

"So this is Sonny," Michael said, picking him up. "I'm your Uncle Mike. You're pretty tough, huh?"

Francesca rolled her eyes. "Sonny won't take that helmet off. Half the time he even sleeps in it. It's Frankie's fault. At Christmas, all he did was teach Sonny how to play football."

Billy, for no apparent reason, eyed Uncle Mike as if he thought he might drop Sonny.

"Good teacher, I bet," Michael said. Frankie Corleone, as a sophomore, had started at linebacker for Notre Dame.

"You like football, sport?" Billy asked Tony.

Tony shrugged.

"That's the way I am, too," Billy said, mussing the boy's hair.

"He hates that," Mary said.

"I don't mind," Tony said.

She reached for his hair herself, and he slapped her hand. Michael set Sonny down, scooped Mary up in one arm, and held Tony by the hand with the other.

"Sorry," Michael said. They immediately calmed down. He was an amazing father.

"Don't be," Francesca said. "They're just being kids. I bet you fought with your brothers and Aunt Connie worse than that. I'm lucky I never killed my sister."

"Nice apartment," Michael said.

The building was more than a hundred years old. It was once a mansion and had been divided into four big apartments. Theirs was on the ground floor and included most of what must have been a ballroom and was now their living room, dining room, and kitchen. The wooden floors were sloped and buckled enough that Sonny's toys and marbles were forever rolling across rooms. Francesca loved it. She'd never lived anyplace that was more than twenty years old before, and certainly nowhere so elegant, however faded. Several times a day she'd walk to the curb just to look at it and marvel that *this* was where she lived.

Thinking of this, she looked out at the curb and saw Al Neri still sitting in the car. "Your driver can come in, too, you know," she said as everyone sat down. "I bet he's hungry."

"He ate already," Michael said. "He gets up early."

Francesca wasn't really that anxious about breakfast—after all, other than Uncle Mike, it was just Billy and three kids. Still, she apologized for the sausages, which were the best she had been able to find on short notice—she had no idea where to shop—but everyone else seemed to think they were fine. The rolls she'd found weren't what she'd have chosen, either, but they went over all right, too. She could only blame being pregnant for the box of jelly doughnuts.

Her fretting gave her something to talk about other than Aunt Kay. She couldn't figure out how to bring that up. The Corleones were *Catholic,* yet in the last few years both Aunt Connie (who'd been married to Ed Federici for less than a year before they'd split up) and Uncle Mike had gotten divorced. And there must be some reason her mother and Stan the Liquor Man had never gotten married. All that, plus Billy's situation. It had Francesca worried. She couldn't think of much that would be more horrible than living a continent away from your kids.

"I was sorry to hear about you and Kay," Billy said. Blurted it out, just like that. Francesca didn't know whether to admire him for his bluntness or slap him.

Michael answered with a rueful nod.

Francesca reached across the table and gave her uncle's arm a squeeze in sympathy.

"I spent my whole childhood rooting for my parents to get a divorce," Billy said. "But you and Kay didn't—"

She kicked him under the table.

"You never know, I guess," Billy said. "How often do you get to see Tony and Mary?"

Just like that, right in front of them. Slapping him seemed like the way to go.

"Not as often as I'd like," Uncle Mike said. "I'm trying to rearrange some of my responsibilities with my businesses so that I'll have more time for that."

"Daddy has a new *airplane*!" Mary said. "He's going to fly and see us *all* the time now."

Tony took another jelly doughnut, though he hadn't eaten the one that was on his plate.

"I keep a small apartment in New York for when I'm there on business," Michael said. "I may get something bigger so that they can stay there, too, whenever I come east."

"I still think of all of you as being in New York," Francesca said. "It seems like you just moved to Nevada."

"Six years," Michael said. "Almost four in Tahoe. I kept both houses, in Vegas and Tahoe, too. They're both bigger than I need, but for Mary and Tony they're home. They've been home."

"It's different these days," Billy said. "People move around a lot more. Look at us, sweetie. Three years of marriage, three addresses."

"It's funny," she said, "all those years in Florida, and I still think of New York as home. I should have gone to college there, the way Kathy did. She loved being back."

"But then we'd have never met," Billy said.

Francesca cocked her head. He was completely sincere, crestfallen, as if he really were imagining never meeting her. It was so impossibly vulnerable, she just melted.

"The love of my life," she said, completely sincere, too, reaching out to stroke his cheek.

"Francie and Bee-Boy sittin' in a tree," Mary said. "C'mon, Tony. *Sing* it with me."

"Dad," Tony said. "Tell her to cut it out."

Michael Corleone raised his coffee cup. "To love," he said.

It was the perfect thing to say.

The kids stopped squabbling and everyone raised a glass, and no one, Francesca thought, could have felt anything *but* love.

Except Billy, whose participation in the toast couldn't have been more halfhearted.

When they left, Francesca sent a plate of food along for the bodyguard.

They stood on the white marble front steps, waving as the car pulled away. "You always say you love my family," she said to Billy. Sonny was running in circles, arms pumping, carrying his teddy bear like a football. "So why don't you like my uncle?"

They'd been through so much. Why not get rid of this taboo, too?

But Billy didn't say anything. He called to Sonny to stay away from the street. Sonny wasn't all that close to the street, actually, but Billy picked him up and went inside.

That night, after Sonny was asleep, Francesca came to bed, exhausted, to see that Billy had her side covered with file folders. He was propped up on his side, reading.

"Want me to sleep on the sofa?"

He looked up, startled, then immediately scooped up the folders and dropped them to the floor. She got into bed, and he turned off the light and started giving her a massage: unhurried, careful, lingering on her swollen feet and sore lower back. She'd come to bed with barely enough energy to close her eyes, but when he finally took her nightgown all the way off, she turned toward him, and when his tongue slid between her lips, she let out a low, hungry gasp.

"What was that?" he said.

"Shut up and love me," she said.

For a few moments, minutes, she forgot everything she was worried about and just *was*.

Out of breath afterward and slick with sweat, she felt enormous again. Billy rested his tanned arm on her mountainous fish-white belly. They lay like that for a long time.

The baby started kicking, harder than ever.

"Why don't I like your uncle, huh?" Billy asked.

"Forget it," she said. She knew, anyway, or thought she did. "I shouldn't have said anything."

She felt the searing pain of a contraction.

"Wow. I felt *that*," Billy said. "What a kick!"

She clenched her jaw to endure the pain. It started to ease.

"Remember when I broke my leg skydiving?" Billy said.

"Of course I do," she said, her breathing slowing now.

"I lied. I've never been skydiving in my life."

Her hips bucked with another contraction, sharper this time.

"I think this is it," Francesca said. "I think I'm having the baby."

That night, Francesca fell victim to her family's grim history. Her paternal grandmother always refused to talk about it, but she'd had at least four

miscarriages. Her maternal grandmother went to Mass every July 22 to mourn the one she had. Her mother and two of her aunts had suffered them, too.

Francesca's baby, born three months prematurely, was a fighter. She lived for almost a day. She was named Carmela, after her great-grandmother. Francesca wanted to bury her next to her as well, on the family burial plot on Long Island. Billy disagreed. He thought the baby should be buried in Florida. Circumstances—the horror of losing the baby and Billy's all-around contrition even before that—ensured that this was a disagreement, not an argument, and that Francesca would prevail.

Michael Corleone paid for everything. Francesca knew that Billy objected, but she was pleased that he had the good sense not to insult her uncle by refusing his help. The ceremony was small and held at the cemetery, in a driving snowstorm.

Billy's parents didn't even come. Her own twin sister didn't come, either—just sent a telegram from London saying she was sorry to learn the bad news. Her brother Frankie missed the spring intersquad football game for it and never complained. Her brother Chip missed his own sixteenth birthday party for it, also without a second thought. Family.

It was a traditional Italian cemetery, with pictures of the dead in cameo frames mounted on the marble monument. As Francesca left, she bent to kiss the cold images. Grandma Carmela. Grandpa Vito. Zia Angelina. Uncle Carlo. Her father, Santino Corleone. She looked into his laughing eyes and thought, *See you next time, Daddy.*

Uncle Fredo was missing and presumed dead, but there was no picture of him here. There was no picture of baby Carmela, either. None had been taken. She'd lived, briefly, but had had no life.

Uncle Mike, as busy as he undoubtedly was, came early, stayed late, and was a tremendous comfort. Not even her mother was able to talk to Francesca as openly about the nightmare of losing a child as Uncle Mike did. And seeing Sonny playing with Tony and Mary at the reception afterward, watching how well they got along, what buoyant spirits they all seemed to have, gave Francesca hope she could go on.

Billy was struggling with the baby's death and, understandably, was having a hard time talking about it.

She was having a hard time not blaming him. It was irrational, she knew. But it seemed like a kind of justice being visited on them for his having wanted her to get an abortion when she had been pregnant with Sonny. And what on *earth* had possessed him to think that telling her he'd been so disinclined to marry her in the first place that he'd only done it after her uncle had sent men to break his leg would make *him* seem like the good guy in the story?

On top of that, every time she looked at him, she imagined that he was worrying about being photographed by the police or the FBI while attending *a gen-u-ine Mafia funeral.* That was probably unfair. She had no idea what he was thinking. But they *had* been photographed. Evil, heartless bastards. She was starting to understand the oppression her uncle faced every day, that her father had faced every day, too.

Suddenly, on the day she buried her own daughter, it clicked. He'd used his parents' money and his efforts in the Shea campaign to get the job in the attorney general's office *so he could destroy her family.*

That was ridiculous, she immediately realized. She wasn't thinking clearly. She was emotional, distraught, with crazy hormones running amok from head to toe. This was *Billy.* Whatever his faults—and who doesn't have faults?—this was the one true love of her life.

Still.

When she'd accused Billy, once, of there having been a crime behind his own family's fortune, he'd nonchalantly said he was sure there'd been several. *Those assholes are capable of anything,* he'd said, and he hadn't been joking. So why was he worried about whatever *her* family might or might not have done? She knew what her sister would say: *Because we're Italian.* It was Kathy who'd found out that the new president's father had been in business with Grandpa Vito. Bootlegging. A crime that no longer exists. A crime that never should have been a crime, but a crime nonetheless. A generation later, James K. Shea is in the White House and Michael Corleone (again, according to Kathy, who'd gotten it from Aunt Connie, who'd sobered up and seemed a more reliable source than she used to be) had cut himself off from criminal activity of any kind and yet was still being trailed by the heartless maggots from law enforcement *at the family-only funeral of his baby niece.* Why? *Because we're Italian.*

A few weeks later, on a transatlantic call Francesca had been working up to since the funeral, she woke her sister up from a deep sleep and told her how much she'd been hurt that Kathy hadn't come home.

"You had a *funeral?*" Kathy said. "I thought it was just a miscarriage."

"*Just* a miscarriage? And anyway, she lived for—"

"Do you know what time it is here?"

"How could you *not* know we'd have a funeral? When I lost baby Carmela—"

"You *named* it? Oh, honey. Honey. You named it after *Grandma?*"

It.

Francesca hung up.

Even though Jimmy Shea had said that he probably wouldn't be able to get out to Las Vegas until after his administration's first hundred days,

from the moment Johnny Fontane got back from Washington, he took time out of his frantic professional schedule to oversee preparations at his newly expanded estate as if the president's first visit would be tomorrow. Johnny added ten people to his staff, including a retired member of the Secret Service, whose job was to stay in constant contact with his old agency, to be ready at a moment's notice if the president needed to come west and blow off a little steam. There was now a guest room accessible through an ingenious recessed panel from what would be the president's office as well as from a stairway in the floor of the closet, which would allow the Secret Service to show women in and out via the new underground garage. Louie Russo had given Rita Duvall her own suite at the Kasbah, but as a backup, Fontane had at least three of Hollywood's reigning sex goddesses clamoring to be of service as well, again at a moment's notice. Danny Shea had started back up with Annie McGowan, who'd been his mistress before she had been married to Johnny, and Johnny had made it clear to them both that they'd be welcome anytime, together or separately. He'd given several of the best chefs in L.A. fifty thousand apiece just to agree to drop everything and come when Johnny called. Johnny didn't go for drugs himself, but Bobby Chadwick and the president both had a thing for cocaine; the stuff Gussie Cicero had gotten him was supposedly as pure as it gets.

Johnny's career was at its commercial peak. The record label he owned might or might not have been bankrolled to some extent by Louie Russo and Jackie Ping-Pong. Johnny tried to stay out of that kind of thing and let his team of lawyers and accountants take care of it. Same thing went for his movie production company and the Corleones' investment. What he did know was that both companies were making a mint. His own records sold like mad—for which he got three times the royalty rate he'd made back at National Records. He'd hired Philly Ornstein away from National to run the company, and the acts Philly had signed were piling up gold records, too. Even the bad pictures his company released were packing the theaters (perhaps *especially* the bad ones; the only film the company released from 1959 to 1962 that lost money in its initial run was *Fried Neck Bones,* with Oliver Smith-Christmas playing a terminally ill southern lawyer and J. J. White, Jr., playing a Negro juke joint singer falsely accused of raping a white girl, a film now considered a classic). If Johnny Fontane bought a stock, it went up. If he bought land, same deal. The casino he owned twenty percent of in Lake Tahoe, the Castle in the Clouds? Forget about it: full of suckers every day of the year, hottest joint in town. Sure, it was good to be the president's pally. It was better to be Johnny Fontane's.

Johnny hadn't spoken to either Shea brother since the inauguration. He understood, of course, but a few days before the Shea administration's

hundred-day mark, Johnny finally broke down and called the private number he'd been given. The secretary refused to put him through.

"Can you take a message?"

"Of course, Mr. Fontane."

"Here it is: *Get your bird out here before it falls off. Love, JF.* In those exact words."

Later that day, as the news started to get out that the crazy little invasion of Cuba wasn't just the work of a bunch of angry expatriates but instead had been undertaken with the backing of the U.S. government, Johnny felt bad about leaving such a frivolous message. His retired Secret Service man said there was no use calling to tell the secretary to tell her to toss the message. If it was on the log, it stayed on the log.

Soon, though, the worst of the controversy passed—the whole operation had been approved by Jimmy's predecessor anyway, something he'd inherited that was too far along to stop—and Corbett Shea sent word that the president was planning his first trip to the West. He'd signed a bill for a new national park not far from Las Vegas, and he wanted to give a speech at the site. He had a few other stops to make—other smiley feel-good moments for the boys on the nightly news—but primarily this was going to be a vacation.

"Much deserved, I might add," Johnny said, which was true. Even Jimmy's political opponents had to admit that aside from the Cuban escapade, the young charismatic president was off to one of the finest starts in American history. "Come on out early if you want," Johnny said. "Bring your wife or come alone. Stay as long as you'd like."

"My wife!" the Ambassador said, guffawing. He'd been to Fontane's place in Beverly Hills a few times and was as randy an old guy as you'd ever want to meet.

He arrived a few days later with only his Secret Service detail. He sat out by the pool in the nude, making long distance calls almost nonstop, visibly pissed off nearly all the time but keeping his voice down. Here and there, he took a few minutes off and went up to his room for a session with one of the high-class pros Johnny had arranged. The Ambassador never went into town to see a show or place a friendly bet, never even played tennis, even though he supposedly still played and Fontane had put in a lighted court.

Truckloads of food and beverages arrived for the impending visit. The day before the president left for his trip west, Johnny took a handcart and rolled the latest delivery out beside the larger pool to show to his guest. It was a thick bronze plaque, four feet by three feet, that read PRESIDENT JAMES KAVANAUGH SHEA SLEPT HERE.

"What in hell are you going to do with that?"

"What do you think, Corbett? I have a crew on their way over right now to bolt it over the headboard in the room where Jimmy's staying. I was going to put quotation marks around *slept,* but I didn't want to be disrespectful."

The Ambassador frowned. "Kind of big, don't you think?"

"Look around, Corbett. The biggest and the best of everything. My friends are worth nothing less."

The Ambassador shook his head. "There must have been a misunderstanding, John. Jimmy's not coming."

That cracked Johnny up. "Seriously, though. Any idea what time they're getting here tomorrow? I have some arrangements I need to take care of."

"You deaf, you stupid Guinea? He's not coming. I never said he was. You invited me out here, and I came. Jimmy has too many other matters to contend with right now. He's going to make that speech, but there's not going to be time for a vacation. Even if there is, it's a bad idea for him to be seen in a town like Las Vegas or at the home of . . . well, at your home."

"What's wrong with my home? What are you talking about?"

But Fontane had it figured out now.

"You know we all appreciate everything you've done for us," the Ambassador said.

"That sounds a hell of a lot like a kiss-off."

"I'm sorry if there was a misunderstanding, John. Blame that cocksucker in Cuba. He *embarrassed* my boy. We're looking into what we can do for revenge. You Italians understand that, though, right? Revenge?"

What did *that cocksucker in Cuba* have to do with such a titanic act of rudeness? "Who did you think all this food was for? All these—"

"How the hell would I know?" He stood up, letting his towel fall, stark naked with his arms outstretched. He was a large but frail man. Why an old goat like this was determined to go around all the time with his shriveled prick flapping in the wind, Johnny couldn't imagine. "Do I look like I have your social calendar hidden on me here somewhere?"

Johnny Fontane shook his head. He swallowed the firestorm of anger rising in him. He left the plaque where it was, turned around, and went inside. He didn't think it would have been a good move to beat the president's father to a bloody pulp. He was tempted to make a few calls and send up some girl with a disease for Corbett Shea's nightcap, but he thought better of that, too. He just avoided the despicable old coot.

Early the next morning, the Ambassador left without saying goodbye.

On the outside, Johnny seemed to be taking this snub with impressive

Sicilian stoicism. He even rented a semi and helped his staff load up the food. He gave the driver directions to a soup kitchen in one of the poorest neighborhoods in Los Angeles, with strict instructions to tell the staff only that it was from an anonymous donor.

The president gave the speech. Johnny Fontane watched it on television. It was hard to be angry at a man who could make you feel that good about your country's future.

But at the end of the story, the reporter said the president would be spending the next week in Malibu, vacationing at the home of a Princeton classmate of his, a lawyer who—according to the reporter—"is a direct descendent of President John Adams."

Fontane watched in stunned disbelief.

You stupid Guinea.

Then he flicked off the television and went out to the workshop the construction crews had been using. The crate of TNT they'd used to blow a hole in the rock that had been where the second pool now was had only two sticks left. He'd never used TNT before but was far too furious to be afraid, at least until he lit the first stick and saw the flame racing down the wick. He heaved it, and it landed dead bang in the middle of the helipad. The air rained sand and fist-sized chunks of cement.

You stupid Guinea.

After the second stick, the helipad was pretty much a crater.

Chapter 26

TOM HAGEN, early for his tee time, ducked into the country club restaurant for coffee. He ordered two cups, as was his habit, so he wouldn't be at anyone's mercy for a refill.

"Mr. Hagen!" a voice called.

Hagen turned around. "Mr. Ambassador," he said, approaching the old man's table, hand outstretched. Corbett Shea was at a table with Secret Service men. "What a pleasant surprise." It was a secret, apparently, that he'd been staying at Johnny Fontane's, but there were few secrets in Nevada that Hagen didn't know about. "What brings you to Las Vegas?"

"My foundation is considering a request to build a theater building at the university here," he said. "I was so shocked Las Vegas even had a university, much less a theater department, I had to come out and see it for myself. Sit."

Like he was a goddamned dog. But that was the Ambassador. Hagen got the waiter's attention, then sat. "I just have a minute. Early tee time."

The Ambassador raised his cup. "Never too early for tea."

Hagen smiled. "Coffee man, myself," he said. "You a member here?"

The Ambassador cringed, as if Hagen had asked him if he'd ever fucked a chicken.

"Your son's doing a magnificent job," Hagen said. "I wasn't in Washington long, but it was long enough to know how hard it is to get things done, especially things that might really make a difference in the lives of average Americans."

This launched the Ambassador into a litany of (Cuba-free) fatherly bragging. Hagen had been sincere, though. His kids had pictures of President Shea on their walls, next to rock-and-roll singers, movie stars, and Jesus. As tainted as the election had been and as callow as Jimmy Shea seemed, Hagen had been astonished to see how swiftly he'd become a great leader. It reminded Hagen of when he was teaching Michael to take over for his father.

Hagen finished his second cup. He had to go. "Are you in town long?" he asked.

"On my way out, actually," he said. "Couple quick meetings, and I head out of this desert hellhole for California."

"We still need to get that tennis game in sometime," Hagen said.

"What tennis game?"

"Forget it," Hagen said. "Please give the president my regards. Anything he ever needs, consider it done."

"I'll do that."

Tom Hagen spent his patience on his business and his family and had none left over for the game of golf. He rented a cart whenever possible. He walked up to the ball, addressed it, smacked it. Just hit it and forget it.

He had a knack for knowing where his ball went, and it drove him nuts—as was the case now—when one of his playing partners hacked through undergrowth with his seven-iron like some great explorer trying to find the headwaters of the Nile. *You're just a duffer with custom clubs,* he thought, drumming his hands on the steering wheel of the cart. *Take the fucking drop.*

"Take a *drop,* for God's sake!" Hagen shouted. On the rare occasions he had to spend more than ten seconds looking for his ball, he took the penalty and got on with it. Life's short.

"Found it!" Michael Corleone called. Michael had heard that Corbett Shea was in town, too. Supposedly the president had been planning to stay at Fontane's but had had to cancel. Which didn't mean the story about the proposed Corbett Hall was entirely false.

"You'd get your handicap down to nothing," Michael said, taking his sweet time lining up his shot, "if you took more time on your shots and weren't so quick to take a drop."

"Forget it," Hagen said. "I'd just be trading one sort of handicap for another." As it was, his handicap was a six, best in the foursome. Hal Mitchell was a fifteen, Mike was at best a twenty. Mike's friend Joe was playing with borrowed clubs and would be lucky to break a hundred on the front nine. "You found your ball; hit the fucking thing and let's go."

Beside him in the cart, Hal Mitchell shook his head and chuckled. In any other context, even Hagen wouldn't have dared to speak to Michael this way. But it was understood that when it came to sports, Tom was still the big brother, no different than when they were kids and he was trying to teach Mike to play a decent game of tennis. Their playing partners didn't seem as startled by this as other people were. Both had known Mike almost as long as Tom had—Mitchell since the war and Joe Lucadello even longer, since Mike's days in the CCC. Joe was a skinny guy from Philadelphia with loud clothes and an eye patch. He was in Vegas on vacation, a guest at the Castle in the Sand. This was the first Hagen had met him.

"Mike tells me you and him joined the Canadian Air Force together,"

Mitchell said. Joe had just cheerfully four-putted the flattest, slowest green on the course. They were on the way to the next tee.

"That's the *Royal* Canadian Air Force, Mr. Mitchell," Joe said, winking.

"Call me Sarge," he said. "All my fwiends do."

"Thanks, friend."

"Should've seen us, Sarge," Michael said. "Couple of punk kids who could barely handle this little plane we'd taken lessons on, and somehow we thought we were ready to bring down the Red Baron."

"Youth," Joe said. "That's your somehow. The Red Baron's from the wrong war, by the way. He was the Great one. We were the Good one."

"The wrong war," Michael muttered.

Ever since the situation with Fredo, Michael had been like this, these shifts in mood. It weighed on Hagen, too. As *consigliere,* he'd always believed that there were things that had to be done and you did them. Once you did them, you never talked about it. You forgot about it. Even a tiny gap between believing a thing and doing it was enough space to harbor nightmares.

Snap out of it. Hit it and forget it.

Hagen had honors. He blasted the ball, more than two hundred fifty yards and straight as a Kansas Rotarian.

"I didn't catch what you do, Joe," Mitchell said on the way to the next hole, their two carts abreast on the path. "Still a piwot?"

"Very funny," Joe said. "You're a funny guy. I knew you managed the casino, but I had no idea you were one of the comedians, too."

Pilot, the sarge had meant, but it did, Hagen realized, sound a lot like *pirate.* He didn't want to embarrass Mitchell by correcting Joe, and he couldn't make eye contact with Mike. For a long, painful moment, no one seemed to know what to say.

It was in that moment that Hagen first wondered if Joe Lucadello was really an old buddy from the CCC and not a member of another Family.

"Not piwate," the Sarge barked. *"Piwot."* He held out his arms to pantomime *airplane.* His golf cart nearly swerved into a sand trap. "Pwanes."

"Oh, right," Joe said. "Sorry. Um, no. Right after the war I was with Eastern. But no."

"You get that in the war, did you?" Mitchell said. "The eye?"

"More or less," Joe said.

More or less? Hagen got out and grabbed his driver. Maybe that wasn't as odd as it sounded. A lot of veterans were funny about talking about the

war. Hagen wasn't a veteran, but those three were. Mitchell seemed to accept the nonanswer as nothing unusual.

Hagen teed up his ball.

"So what wine of work *are* you in?" Mitchell said.

"This and that," Joe said. "Different deals in the works, you know? Mostly I take it nice and easy, like the song says."

Hagen backed off the ball. He'd been about to tee off, but that got his attention. It wasn't the breach of golf etiquette that bugged him. Chatter all you want, he didn't care. It was that Joe had said what a wiseguy would say. Michael was supposedly in town for shareholders' meetings of two of their companies, and Joe was supposedly here on vacation. What did it mean if Joe *was* with another Family? Hagen had always presumed there was something other than the desire to be a law-abiding citizen that was behind Michael's making Geraci the boss. If Mike *was* sincere about stepping down, why did he do it with all those strings attached? The Commission? They'd have been glad to see him go. Michael had said that it was for protection: for himself, his family, his business interests. Or maybe Michael couldn't bring himself to let go of the connection racket, which had always been the Corleones' most valuable asset.

Or maybe it had something to do with this Joe character.

Hagen addressed the ball.

He continued to believe that Michael had created the kind of intricate, brilliant riddle that Vito had often constructed and Hagen had enjoyed trying to solve (why Hagen resented having to do this with Michael, he both did and didn't understand). Could this pirate in orange Sansabelt slacks be a key to it all? Hagen hadn't checked him out in advance. Michael had said that he and Joe had been in the CCC together, and Hagen had accepted it at face value. Joe said he was from Jersey, just outside Philly, but Hagen didn't really know the Philly people. They were a thing unto themselves. New Jersey might be a lead, though. The president was from New Jersey. Michael had his head so far up the Ambassador's ass he could sing out of that pink bastard's navel. It didn't all add up—Eastern Airlines? *not* what a wiseguy would say—but there were plenty of numbers to plug in and see if they'd help Tom Hagen solve for *x*.

Still in his golf clothes, Tom Hagen flicked on the lights of his office in Las Vegas, above a shoe store near Fremont, and sat down at his desk—the rolltop that had once been Genco Abbandando's, shipped here from Vito Corleone's house on the mall. At this point in Hagen's career, he had the connections to get anybody's story on his desk and gift wrapped, generally with three or four calls, nearly always in no time at all. An hour, by his

standards, was a pretty lousy showing. He already had the information Lucadello had given to register at the Castle in the Sand and what he'd learned about the guy during a morning on the golf course. He estimated that Joe Lucadello would be a three-call, twenty-minute job. Hagen looked at his watch, noted the time, and picked up the phone.

Four hours later, Hagen had nothing. No one by that name had ever worked for Eastern Airlines, flown for the RCAF, or been a member of the CCC. The Philly people had never heard of him. He'd never been fingerprinted anywhere in the United States. He'd never registered a car, a boat, a gun, or a legal complaint. He'd never paid federal income tax. Sure, the identity was probably a fake, but even a fake ID left more of a trace than this. As far as Hagen could tell, there *was* no Joe Lucadello. He'd played golf all morning with Casper the One-Eyed Ghost.

Just to have anything at all to show for his afternoon, he checked out the Ambassador's story. All of it was true: he'd been at Johnny's but left; he had in fact met with the people at the university, who were *very* eager to know if Mr. Shea seemed inclined to approve the building. "The Ambassador's a hard man to read," Hagen said. "Good luck to you, though."

He looked at his watch again. He'd barely have time to change and make it to the opening at the art museum.

He sped to the hotel and ran around getting ready to go out for the night as if he were dreadfully late, but he arrived at the museum early, as usual. The opening didn't start for twenty minutes. Theresa, the chairwoman of the museum's acquisitions committee, was at the airport picking up the artist. The wizened docent minding the velvet rope wagged her finger at Hagen and told him to hold his horses, but the museum director rushed over and apologized profusely.

Tom had never heard of this artist, but he saw right away that the exhibit was Theresa's idea of a compromise, garnished with a wicked joke. He couldn't help but smile. She had a degree in art history, and her taste ran toward abstract painting. Many of the ladies on her committee were blue-haired ranchers' wives who didn't know art but knew what they liked. They liked lugubrious oil paintings of Indians. They liked Norman Rockwell. They liked some of Picasso's early work. The show was called "Cats, Cars, and Comics: The Pop Art of Andy Warhol." The cars looked like they'd been copied from magazine ads, with the same image of a sports car repeated in neat rows and many colors. The comics were blotchy enlargements of Popeye and Superman. The bluehairs loved the cats, though, even the green one with red eyes that gave Hagen the willies.

The rope came down. Still no Theresa. A sparse crowd began to gather.

"Nice car," Michael said, pointing. He'd arrived along with a group of

stockholders and fronts in their biggest real estate company, plus Al Neri and some other muscle. After this they were all going to a private dinner Enzo Arguello was serving up in the rotating ballroom at the Castle. "All those different colors make it hard to choose, though."

"I think maybe that's sort of the point," Hagen said.

Finally, Theresa arrived with what had to be the artist, a frail, blank-faced young man with pinkish blond hair and red-lensed glasses. The blue-hairs swarmed him.

"Your friend Joe seemed like a good man," Hagen said.

"He is," Michael said. "One of the best I've ever met."

"Is that right?" Hagen said.

"You have a nice afternoon?" Michael said.

It was not said kindly.

How the hell could he have learned about that blackjack dealer in Bonanza Village? Hagen had taken every precaution. Had it been the flowers? A phone tap?

"You didn't find a thing, did you?"

Lucadello. That's what he was talking about. "I just made a few calls on him," Tom said. "I had some other paperwork. But to answer your question, no. I didn't."

"If you wanted to know about my friend Joe, why didn't you ask me?"

"I was just curious," Hagen said.

Michael raised his wineglass and nodded toward the green cat. "To curiosity," he said, but did not drink.

"Did something get back to you?"

"Nothing got back to me," Michael said, switching to Sicilian. "I know how you think, Tom. I knew what you'd do. It's who you are, why you're such a good lawyer."

"So what Family is he with?" Tom asked, in Sicilian, too. "I contacted Nunzio in Philly—"

"Why do you leap to the conclusion that Joe is a part of this thing of ours, Tom? Because he has an Italian name? I'm disappointed in you."

"Not because he has an Italian name, no. Who do you think you're talking to?"

"Look, it's fine. Everything you want to know about Joe he'll tell you himself." Michael switched back to English. "Actually, more like everything you *need* to know. At any rate, we're meeting with him at midnight in my suite."

Theresa had escaped from the ring of people surrounding the artist and made a beeline over to her husband and Michael. "What do you think?"

"Great," Michael said.

"Visionary," Tom said.

She put her arm around him, as if they were still schoolkids.

"I hate it, too," Theresa said. "But, believe me, it'll be big. Him, too."

"Late plane?" Tom asked, holding out his arms the way the sarge had, which did manage to get a smile out of Mike.

Theresa shook her head. "He made me stop so he could get out and walk down the Strip. He stared at one marquee, just stared without moving, for—God, I don't know. Forever. He did it again at a gift shop window. He took every whorehouse leaflet he could get his hands on, too. Hundreds of them, for art purposes obviously, but who ended up carrying them? *Moi.*"

"Obviously?" Tom said.

"I don't think he likes girls," Theresa stage-whispered.

Tom averted his eyes from Michael's.

"Anyway," Theresa said, "now he's over there telling everybody that in the future, America will be Las Vegas. Not be *like* Vegas. *Be* Vegas. The man's been here three hours."

Michael shrugged. "Some people catch on quick."

After the dinner meeting, when they got to Michael's suite, Joe Lucadello was already there, shirtless, still in his orange pants, sitting at the bar and playing solitaire.

"Tom! What a treat. C'mon in." As if it were his suite. "Mike tells me you were interested in getting to know me better. I'm flattered."

Tom had been with Michael the entire time since the art museum. There would have been no time Michael could have told Joe anything.

Al and Tommy Neri had followed them in. Michael gave them a nod, and they headed to the adjoining room, closing the door behind them.

"Mike tells you that, huh?" Hagen looked around the room and realized why it seemed so familiar. The pool table. This was the same suite where Fredo had lived before he had been married. It had been redecorated, but the pool table was the same. Michael turned on the television, loud. The TV was also new. Fredo had kept the TV on all the time just for the sake of having noise around, but these days they turned it on to provide cover from possible wiretaps. The late show was on, some old picture with people in togas.

Joe raised an open bottle of Pernod in one hand, a sealed bottle of Jack Daniel's in the other, and arched his eyebrows. As he did, Hagen tried to see behind the eye patch, but no dice.

"I'll pass," Tom said. "Look, I don't want to sound disrespectful, but

I've had a long day, and it's not over yet, so would you mind telling me what's going on? Whoever you are."

"He's Joe Lucadello," Michael said, racking the balls on the pool table. "That's God's honest truth."

"Though I haven't been Joe Lucadello in fifteen years," Joe admitted.

"Oh yeah?" Hagen said. "So who are you?"

"Nobody. Anybody. Mike knows me as Joe Lucadello, which was who I was back when we first met. It still is who I am, of course, but as you took it upon yourself to learn, other than the hotel registration last night—which will disappear, by the way—there's no record of me anywhere. A few people have memories of that young man, but that's all."

"Right," Hagen said. "You're a ghost."

Joe laughed. "Excellent guess, Tom! You're *very* warm."

The shattering sound of Michael Corleone's break startled Tom off his bar stool.

Then it hit him. What's close to ghost? Spook. Joe was a spook. CIA.

"Sure you don't want a drink?" Joe said. "You're pretty jumpy."

"He drinks a lot of coffee." Michael sank two balls off the break. He kept shooting. "Like you can't believe. Gallons."

"Stuff'll kill you," Joe said.

Hagen turned on the bar stool to face Michael. "What's going on here? This one-eyed guy you haven't seen since Christ left Chicago stops by on vacation claiming he's in the—"

"Company," Joe said.

"And we're supposed to believe him? Without checking—"

Michael slammed the two ball into a corner pocket, much harder than necessary.

"You're off your game, Tom," Michael said in Sicilian. "All this jumping to conclusions. Why do you assume I haven't seen him in years? I simply told you he was my friend Joe that I met in the CCC. Why do you assume I haven't verified who he works for? Why do you assume he's stopping by and not that he came here with business to discuss with us?"

Hagen frowned. *Us?*

And how did Hagen—or Michael, for that matter—know for certain that Joe couldn't understand Sicilian dialect?

Michael lined up a tough bank shot on the three ball and stroked it in like it was nothing. "Tom, you were my lawyer at those Senate hearings," he said in English, "and you did a first-rate job, but—"

Three ball, side pocket.

"—I was fortunate enough to have another line of defense."

"Defense overstates it," Joe said, gathering up the cards from the bar. "Insurance; that's all it was. Friends helping friends. You did such a good job, Tom, that we didn't have to do much of anything."

Much of anything?

Michael set down the cue stick.

What happened, he said, was that Joe had contacted him not long after the raid on that farmhouse in New York, when the FBI established the Top Hoodlum Program and it became clear they'd be putting more pressure on the so-called Mafia. He and Joe hadn't seen each other since the day Billy Bishop had asked to see Michael's pilot's license and Michael had protected Joe by saying he had no license. In the meantime, Joe had been shot down over Remagen, escaped from a prison camp, then been assigned to a U.S. intelligence detail. After that, one thing led to another. Lots of jobs in Europe. The last few years back on home soil. Long story short, Joe—who'd remained grateful to Mike for what he did—had thought he might be able to help an old friend. He had various ways of keeping a man out of jail, protecting him from prosecution. If it ever came to that, the FBI wouldn't know who was responsible, wouldn't even know what had happened. What's the catch? Michael had wanted to know. No catch, Joe said. We're not looking for an informant the way the FBI would. Nothing that could get you into trouble within your world. Anything we'd ever ask would be a purely cash-and-carry, services-rendered deal. If Michael was ever asked to do a job he didn't want to send men to do, Joe promised, that'd be fine. Say no, and that would be the end of it. Joe wasn't in the market for a slave or a terrified supplicant. Just a vendor.

Hagen started going over all the jobs the past three years that he'd wondered about, but he stopped himself. He couldn't think about that.

"So why all of a sudden are you bringing me into this?" Hagen said.

"Joe has a proposal," Michael said. "And I need your counsel. It's a big step. One step backward from what we've been trying to do in order to take a dozen steps ahead. If we accept, I'll need your full involvement."

"A proposal?"

Michael picked up his stick, pointed it at Joe, giving him the floor, then started sizing up angles on the impossible shot the four ball seemed to be.

Joe clapped a hand on Tom's shoulder. "What I'm going to tell you here, you're either going to like it and be a part of it or else it never happened. One or the other. Obviously, I'm talking to men who understand how to conduct themselves under conditions like that."

Michael missed the shot, but not by much.

"A long time ago," said Joe Lucadello, "I told Michael—I'll bet you remember this, Mike; we were talking about Mussolini—I said that in all of history there's never been any hero, any villain, any leader of any kind who was impossible to kill."

Michael nodded. "It made an impression."

"So here's your government's proposal, in a nutshell. This comes di-

rectly from Albert Soffet himself"—Soffet was the director of the CIA—
"and it has presidential approval. How would you—meaning your business interests—like to be able to go back down to Cuba and pick up right
where you left off? How would you like to get paid to do a job for us
down there that would make that happen? Supremely well paid, I should
add. Every dime is a hundred percent legal, and we can do things so that
it's effectively tax-free. We'd even help train your people. In fact, we'd
have to insist on that point."

"Train them?"

"The revolution changed many things. The men you send to do the
job need to know about those things. There are Cuban patriots living in
exile who will be able to help as well. We know these people. We're familiar with their skills and limitations. There's procedure to follow, too, so
that, as I say, nobody goes to jail, be it one in America or, God forbid,
Cuba. The risk—let me be clear—is that if and when anything goes wrong,
we had nothing to do with it. If the Russians think we're behind it, as
a government, we could be looking at World War Three. Naturally, if your
people get into trouble, we'll do everything possible to help, but not at
the expense of revealing our connection with the project. You—your
people—will have acted as private citizens. You never met me. I don't
exist."

Hagen would have been amused by Joe's spelling all this out—he *definitely* wasn't a connected guy of any sort—except for the enormity of the
scheme he was suggesting. Killing a lowly beat cop was against the rules of
their tradition, Hagen thought. How in the hell were they going to get
away with assassinating the leader of another country?

And contrary to what the public and FBI and apparently the CIA
seemed to think, killings happened for some *reason*—self-preservation, revenge—not for a *fee*.

But wasn't it revenge? Men had died for stealing a hundred bucks
from a Corleone shylock. When the Cuban government had taken over or
closed down their casinos—how had that been any different from stealing
millions?

And what exactly *were* the rules that governed a retired Don?

In a spectacular combination shot, Michael Corleone sank the four in
the side pocket. The six rolled after the five like a man trying to apologize
to an angry lover, and they disappeared into the corner pocket together.

"Wow," Joe said. "Now I've seen everything."

Just then, there was a knock at the door.

"We expecting someone?" Hagen said.

"He's late," Joe said, though it was Michael who went to get the
door. "My apologies. As perhaps you know, he's nearly always late."

It was Ambassador M. Corbett Shea.

"Sorry, gents," he said. The Secret Service men stayed in the hall, which meant they'd been allowed to search the room earlier. "I had some business with my sons. So can I tell the president and the attorney general we have a deal? Or do you have questions you'd like me to pass on? How'd you put it, Mr. Cahn-sig-lee-airy? Anything the president needs, consider it done?"

Chapter 27

AFTER LUCADELLO and Shea left, Hagen made himself a stiff drink and went out onto the balcony. Johnny Fontane's name was in lights on the marquee of the casino across the street, the Kasbah. The Chicago joint. No performer "belonged" to a certain Family, but for years it had rankled Hagen that they'd let the biggest draw in Las Vegas cross the street to play the casino of the Corleones' biggest rival. Hagen didn't *like* Johnny, the way Vito and Fredo did, and even, to an extent, Michael. Michael was right that Families couldn't be fighting over matters so small as what singer was booked in what casino, but in truth Michael was also covering for Fredo, who'd been responsible for overseeing the entertainment at the Corleone hotels at the time. Thinking his friendship with Johnny was a substitute for negotiation, Fredo had been caught flat-footed when Fontane—who was friendly with Russo, too, after all—had signed a six-year exclusive deal with the Kasbah. Fuck friendly. It was business.

This was business, too. He took a deep breath. He couldn't let his emotions enter into it.

The door opened, and Michael joined him on the balcony. There was a built-in hi-fi unit, and Michael turned on a radio station, again as cover, presumably. Opera. Hagen didn't particularly care for opera, which Michael knew. Hagen didn't bother objecting.

"That wasn't the first time you heard that offer," Hagen said. "How long have you known about it?"

Michael flipped open his lighter, a jeweled one with something engraved on it. His face glowed in the flame. He took a long drag off his cigarette. "Since the last time I was in Cuba."

"The last time you were in Cuba, you—" *Were there with Fredo.* Hagen didn't want to get into that at all. "The revolution was just under way. They knew then? *You* knew then?"

"We talked about it then," Michael said. "At the time, it was more of an idea than an offer. His idea. Just talk. At the time, I believed that the revolution was far bigger than the charisma of one man. I didn't think killing him would make any difference."

"And now?"

"The same. Only now I don't think it makes any difference if it makes a difference."

More riddles. Tom took a slug of his drink.

"I love you," Tom said, "but it may be time for you and me to go our separate ways. Professionally, at least."

"I was thinking just the opposite," Michael said.

"*Whatever* you're thinking, I can tell you, I've had it up to here with being kept in the dark, enough of being in, then I'm out, then I'm in, then I'm out. I'm your brother, then I'm just your lawyer. I'm your *consigliere*, then I'm just another politician on your payroll, then I'm in charge of things while you're out of the country, then I'm some fucking nothing that you don't consult about a thing like this. You *knew* I wasn't going to say anything one way or the other about—anything, really, in front of a man I've known since this morning, without talking to you about it first. Not to mention Corbett Shea. Yet for some secret reason I'll have to puzzle out on my own, you set it up that way."

"Look, Tom, there's nothing to puzzle out. I wanted you to hear it from him first because it's his operation. Not mine. We'd be performing a service. Mickey Shea is your reassurance that the president is behind this, too. You saw how angry Mickey was. For us, it's business. Money, opportunity, power. For them it's revenge. I wasn't sure about that myself, but there was no better way to see it firsthand."

Mickey Shea. Hagen had never heard anyone call him that but the Don, Vito.

"You want to talk about it, Tom, let's talk. Doing this job at all is a big step. The fact that we need to do it with Geraci's people makes it a bigger step. Theoretically we could use our men here in Nevada, but the only one who's ready for something like this would be Al Neri, and we can't risk losing him. This is more than likely a suicide mission. If we have Geraci's men do it, either they succeed or they don't. If they don't, we'll have set it up so that we have nothing to do with it. Any repercussions would be felt by him but not us. I'm retired, after all."

Hagen crunched an ice cube from his drink, his eyes on the nearby darkness of the desert.

"It's possible that they'll succeed," Michael said, "and yet the Communists stay in power. So what? The world is neither better nor worse, and we wind up with a little something for our trouble. But think of it, Tom. Think if it *does* make a difference. Freedom is restored, we're back in business in Cuba. *Legal,* bigger than anything we have now. Our government and whatever sort of puppet regime the U.S. installs in Cuba will be indebted to us, enough to ensure that we get re-established down there

ahead of any other Family. We can easily convince the others on the Commission that Geraci and his men were just *our* puppets. Any resentment for our having cooperated with the government will be quelled by the millions they'll make because of us when Cuba reopens. In any case, though, no matter how all this plays out, we'd get half the money the government is prepared to pay and Geraci'd get the other half. He'll never know that the whole thing came through us. Joe and his associates will approach him without mentioning us. We'll get half what they're paying, same as if Geraci gave us our share of any big deal, only in this case Joe will bring it to us directly. Geraci is too opportunistic, too aggressive, to turn down a chance like this. And he's got all those Sicilians he can use on this job— brave, single-minded people with the added bonus of not having the rule about killing cops or government officials. In the unlikely event that Geraci *does* come to us and ask for our advice or our blessings, we simply say that we're out of such things. If he offers us a share of the money, we politely decline. Only if his efforts are successful will he ever learn a thing—probably via his godfather, Don Forlenza. Again, so what? By then Geraci will be a hero, and he'll owe it all to us. But the bottom line is this, Tom: I need someone beside me so smart and loyal that I'll be—we'll be— thinking with two brains. I can't, and won't, go ahead with this without you at my side."

"You've already thought it out pretty well without me," Hagen said. "You'd have your old pal Joe at your side. Neri at your side. Nick Geraci doing the dirty work. I'm not indispensable, Mike. Look at the body count in this thing of ours, and it's been going on for centuries, turning a profit every year. None of it needs any of us."

"Well, *I* need *you*, Tom. You've been dealing with the Ambassador for years. The president won't do anything to us against the old man's wishes."

"You could send someone else. A lawyer, a judge, somebody like that."

"You're the only person on this earth I trust. You know that. There's nothing I've ever done that cut you out because I didn't value you or need you. I was only trying to protect you."

"Protect me, huh?" he said. "Thank you very much."

"What do you want me to say? You want me to say I'm human? That I've made mistakes, particularly when it comes to you, and that I'm *sorry*? Is that what you want?"

Tom sighed. "Of course not. What I want are some straight answers."

Michael extended his arm in an after-you gesture. "Ask away, counselor."

"Is that eye patch for real?"

"That's your question?"

"I'm working up to the big ones."

"He told me war wound. I never gave it a thought after that."

"And he's for real, too? This whole thing, you're certain it's on the level? The Ambassador may have helped get his son elected, but he has no official position. I've never trusted him, and I'm sure you don't either."

"Joe was my initial contact," Michael said, "but when I decided we might go ahead with this, I insisted on meeting with Albert Soffet. When I was in Washington for the transition meetings, I didn't meet with those people at all, as you know. But I did meet with Director Soffet. Even then, I thought this might be too big a risk. Like that bungled invasion, it was approved by the previous administration. What Joe said was true. Soffet told me the same thing. The U.S. military can't invade Cuba because then the Russians will retaliate. If all the U.S. does is use economic sanctions, fifty years from now the place will still be in the hands of the Communists. But our government doesn't dare do *anything* directly. So they need to come up with other means. They tried Plan A, and it failed. We're Plan B."

"So am I to assume this was somehow the real reason you quote-unquote retired?"

"Yes and no. Look, you already know nearly everything. You know more about the finances of the legitimate businesses than I do. There's nothing about the things we did to help get the president elected that you don't know. And as far as putting all the connection guys we have in one crew so that both Geraci and I can use them, independently of each other—hell, Tom, we'd call that a *regime* if you were Sicilian."

Tom took another long drink.

"That was supposed to be a joke," Michael said.

Hagen rattled the ice in his glass. "Hear that? That's me laughing."

A siren wailed, and then another. Two fire trucks sped by. There was a big fire on the far edge of town.

"Okay. So you're right. I didn't tell you everything. I had two other things I had to address. I couldn't do those things as a completely private citizen, so I engineered the deal with the Commission that—well, Jesus, Tom, you put that together, too."

"So one of those two things you're talking about is this job in Cuba?"

"No. Cuba is just a means to an end."

Tom patted his coat, looking for a cigar, and found one in his breast pocket. He was softening. He had an orphan's distrust of the stability of all human bonds, yet he knew in his heart he was destined to be Michael's *consigliere,* now and forever.

Michael flicked his lighter. He kept the flame awfully high for a cigarette smoker.

Hagen bit off the tip of his Cuban cigar.

"Thanks," Hagen said. "Nice lighter."

"It was a gift," Michael said.

"The other two things?" Hagen said.

As Michael lit a new cigarette for himself, he pointed to the Kasbah. "Number one."

"Fontane?" Hagen said. "I'm getting tired of the guessing."

"Fontane?" Michael scoffed. "No, no, no. I meant *Russo*. If I retired, truly retired, Louie Russo's gotten so much power the last few years that the Commission would end up making him boss of bosses, which would be a great blow to our interests, particularly here and in Lake Tahoe. Cuba, too, if and when it opens up. He'd come after us, and we'd be powerless to stop him. We have a whole crew of men here, but it's relatively small and primarily muscle. Without a seat on the Commission and with Russo as *capo di tutti capi*, we'd get outfought politically, which would be the end of us."

"True," Hagen agreed.

The deejay came on the radio, said they'd been listening to a selection from Mascagni's *Cavalleria Rusticana*, then grew very excited about the beer commercial he was doing.

"Not to mention, if Russo does become boss of bosses, knowing the way the Ambassador thinks, I'm concerned that Fuckface would have better access to the president than we would."

"I guess I had that one half figured out already," Tom said. "I never heard you call him that before, though. I never heard you call any Don by a nickname."

"Well, the reason for that leads me to my second thing." Michael smiled. It was not a smile with any mirth at all. "You want to know who gave me this lighter?"

"Let me guess. Russo."

"All of a sudden you want to take guesses? No, Tom. Not Russo."

Michael told him about Geraci.

He told him about trying to kill Geraci.

He told him about the need to try again, when the time was right.

Hagen listened in silence, knowing he should be angry for having been kept out in the cold for so long, fighting back the elation he was feeling instead.

He got himself another Jack Daniel's. Michael, who almost never drank, not even wine, asked him to make him one, too.

"Question," Hagen said, handing Michael his glass. "What's to keep the CIA from doing the same thing to us that you're planning to do to Geraci? Use us for the job and then dispose of us when it's done?"

"Good to be working with you like this again," Michael said.

"And?"

"Touché," Michael admitted. "That's the tricky part. But we have the connections to pit the Bureau against the Company and vice versa, at least to an extent. And, don't forget, we do have a family member at the Justice Department."

"Who, Billy Van Arsdale?" Hagen scoffed. "That kid still thinks he got the job because of his parents' connections. He's going to do everything he can to keep his distance from us."

"He'll do what we need him to do," Michael said, "which is to be our personal canary in the coal mine. He's ambitious, and he resents us. He's afraid his connection to us by marriage is why he's stuck in the law library instead of holding press conferences or going to court. We don't need to use our connections to get him promoted to something better. He'll use us—what he thinks he knows about us—to get the job done. After *that*, we ask him, politely, for his help."

"In other words," Hagen said, biting his lip to keep from grinning, "we make him an offer he can't refuse. It's brilliant, Mike. The old man would be proud."

Vito Corleone had never set foot in Las Vegas, but the two men on that balcony felt the force of his legacy press down on them like a warm, firm hand.

"We'll see," he said. "The final test of any plan is its execution."

"To execution," Hagen said. They clanked glasses and drank to his grim pun.

BOOK VIII

1961–1962

Chapter 28

So it was that Michael Corleone and Nick Geraci began their final year in business together in a state of perfect Cold War stalemate.

They'd each attacked the other and thought, mistakenly, that the other didn't know.

They were both frozen by a secret they thought they were harboring, wary at all times of tipping their hands.

They might have been eager to kill each other now, too, but they couldn't.

It wasn't safe for Geraci to make a move against Michael (or Russo, for that matter) without the blessings of the Commission, which would be essentially impossible without being *on* the Commission. Just as important, killing Michael Corleone might also mean killing the most powerful army of on-the-take politicians, judges, union officials, cops, fire marshals, building inspectors, coroners, newspaper and magazine editors, TV news producers, and strategically placed clerk-typists the world has ever known. No one but Michael and Hagen knew everyone the Family had on the payroll and everything about how that operation worked, and Hagen seemed incorruptible. Michael had toyed with Hagen's dignity, but those two needed each other the way old married people do. Even if Geraci was wrong about this, he was right: the risk of trying to flip Hagen was too great. Maybe one chance in a thousand it'd work, nine hundred ninety-nine it'd get Geraci killed. Even if Geraci did get rid of Michael, it was hard to imagine Hagen—out in Nevada, not even Italian, no chance of taking over the operation—saying, *Okay, Nick, here's how this thing works.* Even the indirect access Geraci now had to that machine of connections was too valuable to jeopardize.

As for Michael, he needed Geraci far too much to kill him. Who else could oversee this business in Cuba? Michael needed someone who'd pick the right men, get the job done, and yet after the job was done be disposable: Geraci to a T.

More important, who else would, during this transition phase, seem like a credible boss to the other Dons? Kill Geraci now, and Michael would kill any chance he had of keeping the pledge he'd made to his wife and his father.

His ex-wife. His dead father.

No matter. Divorce and death are terrible things, but a man who uses them to break a promise cannot consider himself a man of honor.

Nick Geraci hadn't noticed his shaking problem until the day Michael Corleone told him he was the new Boss. It didn't completely go away after that, but it was barely noticeable, easily explained away (chills, coffee jitters) until that summer, about the time he first went out to New Jersey with Joe Lucadello (whom he believed to be "Agent Ike Rosen") to visit the swampy tract of land Geraci had found when he and Fredo had been planning Colma East. Whatever the merits of Fredo's plan, the land had been a steal. Geraci had used the barn for various storage needs and otherwise sat on the property. Anytime he wanted to, he could sell it for twice what he paid.

They all drove there together, Donnie Bags at the wheel and Carmine Marino, the baby-faced zip, also up front. Rosen wore an eye patch and didn't seem Jewish at all. He'd brought another agent, a tight-jawed WASP whose name was supposedly Doyle Flower. The same congressman who'd told Geraci that Michael never met with anyone on the presidential transition team had spoken about all this with Director Albert Soffet, who'd apparently confirmed that Rosen and Flower were indeed CIA field agents. Nonetheless, Geraci used a trail car, with Eddie Paradise and some muscle, just as a precaution.

They turned down the rutted, muddy road to the barn. Rogue garbage trucks and private citizens had for years been using this place as a dump. The property was pocked with stoves, toilets, and the rusting hulks of cars and farm machinery. That island of debris in the scum pond was a portion of what had once been Ebbets Field.

"Good place to plant your stiffs, I bet," Rosen said.

"I wouldn't know about that," Geraci said, which was true. Any recent bodies on the property would have been the work of civilians. Mob guys out here—Stracci's people, for the most part—knew who owned the place and respected that. "We're the best boogeyman the cops ever invented. Every time you guys find a body rolled up in a carpet, we get blamed."

"We're not cops," Rosen said.

"My granny had one of those things," Flower said, meaning Donnie's colostomy bag.

"You get used to it," Donnie said. "Probably like your friend's pirate thing there."

"Did you shit?" Rosen said. "It smells like shit in here."

Donnie rounded a bend so hard a flume of mud shot up and was about to say something stupid when Carmine interrupted him. "Is not his shit, that smell. Is New Jersey."

Flower and Geraci both laughed, which cooled things off. Carmine was a born leader. He was almost thirty but looked ten years younger. He was related to the Bocchicchios on his mother's side and was also a godson of Cesare Indelicato, the Palermitan Don who'd been Geraci's partner in the narcotics business from the beginning. The kid had originally come over to be a hostage during the first meeting of all the Families. Five years later, and he was already running a crew of fellow zips over on Knickerbocker Avenue.

Two cars were parked behind the barn. It was broad daylight, but they were both bobbing with illicit coitus.

"The only real problem we have out here," Geraci said, "as far as the locals go, is this."

The trail car pulled up behind them. Only Eddie Paradise got out.

"You're shaking as much as those cars are," Rosen said. "You okay?"

"Donnie and his fucking air-conditioning," Geraci said, though it hadn't been particularly cold in the car. He got out of the car. Moving around helped make the shaking stop.

Carmine got out, too. In one fluid motion, he drew a pistol from the waistband of his pants and fired three hollow-point slugs into the barn siding.

The trespassing cars began to lurch in place; inside, the terrified fornicators clawed at their strewn-about clothing. Carmine fired another shot.

"Four in a row into the broad side of a barn," Flower said. "Impressive start, friend. I should warn you, though. The tests do get harder."

Carmine waved as the cars sped away.

They all had a good laugh, even the agents. Geraci's shaking had stopped.

"Last time he did that," Donnie said, "the fuckers got stuck in the mud. We went to give 'em a push, but they got out and ran. That was one of the cars getting chopped when a friend of ours got pinched, which I don't know if you can call a car abandoned by sex perverts stolen."

Momo the Roach had happened to be in his chop shop when it got raided. He was now doing a stretch for grand theft.

"Tits on that girl in the Ford like no tomorrow," Agent Flower said.

"Tits like that, and tomorrow can go fuck itself," Carmine said, by way of agreement.

Rosen nodded, a faraway look in his eyes, muttering, "Not bad, not bad," and it took Geraci a moment to realize he wasn't talking about the redhead's tits but rather sizing up the property.

"How's it look?" Geraci said.

Rosen kept nodding, too lost in thought to answer. Geraci showed them into the barn. Rosen grunted in appreciation. It only looked dilapidated from the outside. Inside, the building had been fortified by the guy who fabricated armored cars for the Corleone Family.

"Anyone have any paper?" Rosen asked. He held up a pencil.

Flower pulled out a little pad of paper from his shirt pocket.

"Bigger." Rosen drummed the pencil in midair with a speed Buddy Rich might envy.

"We got a bakery box," Eddie Paradise said.

Rosen frowned. When he did, you could practically see in there, whatever was behind the patch. "Needs to be *paper*."

"Sorry," Eddie said. "I don't write things down. That way I don't lose nothin'."

Geraci looked in the car and found Bev's biology notebook. "How's this?"

Rosen thanked him. He sat on the floor of the barn and drew plans to convert the inside into a gymnasium. He seemed to draw as fast as he could move his hand. He went back outside, found a spot where a barracks could go, and he drew those plans, too. Inspired no doubt by the sight of Carmine and Donnie Bags on the ridge above the scum pond, shooting seagulls and rats, Rosen walked off some measurements and sketched a rifle range.

Donnie was missing everything, but Carmine looked like Buffalo Bill out there, vaporizing gulls in explosions of blood-pinked feathers. Other than those who'd been cops or in the war, most of the men in this business, Geraci included, really couldn't hit the broad side of a barn. The shooting that needed to be done got done at close range. Geraci had never even heard of anyone who'd been killed with a rifle, which was probably what this job down in Cuba would take. Who ever heard of a Mob sniper? That said, who better to go down to Cuba and whack an avowed enemy of freedom than Carmine Marino?

"Damnedest thing you ever saw, eh?" Flower said, elbowing Geraci and nodding at his partner's manic drawing style.

Rosen handed him Bev's notebook. The drawings were miraculously neat, given how fast he'd done them. They were easily good enough to build from. The design of the barracks was simple and clean.

"I'm a frustrated architect," Rosen said, as if in apology.

Geraci said he had a crew that could knock this job out in three days. Rosen frowned and said it was a lot more complicated than that. It turned out there were all kinds of government regulations that made that impossible, for money reasons (Geraci could get it done, but he had the right to make a buck in the process) just as much as security.

That was when Geraci felt sure this whole thing was for real. These clowns really did work for the government.

Rosen took the notebook back and paged through it like a spinster fogging the window of a bridal shop. "I don't know, though," Rosen said. "If only the locals weren't such a problem."

"Problem how?" Geraci said.

"Taking away the place people shitcan their most inconvenient trash or go to fuck their babysitters," Flower answered, "definitely gets noticed in a community."

"Especially in New Jersey," said Carmine. He'd come back to the car to get more ammo.

"I'm *from* New Jersey, sir," Rosen said.

"So then you know," Carmine said, shrugging and slamming the trunk shut.

"I like you," Flower said, patting Carmine on the back. "Just the kind of man we need."

"My back?" Carmine said. "Don't touch it no more."

"He's funny about that," Geraci said. "The back patting."

"Funny," Carmine said. "Many dead men are laughing about this, I think."

"Now I'm even more sure," Flower said. "Mr. Marino, you're at the very top of my list. Between all those dead rats and your attitude, you're going to be hard to beat."

Carmine smiled broadly and slapped Flower on the back, and Flower feinted a return slap that stopped short, and they both laughed like hell.

"Only Italian I ever saw who had a thing about being touched," Rosen muttered, which made Geraci wonder if he was really Italian or if that was what someone who wasn't Italian would say.

"The locals won't be a problem," Geraci said. "Trust me."

The next day, a sign went up out by the highway, announcing an exclusive new subdivision. DELUXE LOTS ON SALE JUNE 1962! it read underneath. A year away. This should turn whatever curiosity the locals had into a plus. The anticipation might make it worth really developing the place—draining it, hiring lawyers and architects, bribing the planning commission: the usual subdivision drill, no different for a Mafia Don than anybody else.

That night at dinner Nick Geraci started shaking, enough to scare Barb and Bev. Charlotte wanted to call an ambulance. "It's nothing," he said. "Coffee jitters." She said she thought he'd stopped. "That's the problem," he said. "I had an espresso at the club this afternoon." Which he hadn't. He concentrated on the movement of his hands and jaw as he

ate, and the shaking stopped. But when it happened again in the morning, Char said if he didn't go see a doctor she'd get a knife and stab him in the leg so he wouldn't have any choice. He said he was fine, it'd pass. She went and got the biggest knife in the kitchen. He smiled and told her he loved her. She wagged it and said she was serious. "Me, too," he said. He was. He held up his quavering hands. "Be a doll and dial him for me, huh?" Though the moment she set the phone back down he was fine.

His regular doctor prodded him with tools and questions, but he was stumped.

"I wonder if maybe it's in your head," he said. "Are you having a tough time at work? Pressure, stress, that sort of thing? Or at home, things okay there?"

"You think I'm a fucking nut, is that what you're saying?"

He referred Geraci to a specialist.

"If *specialist* is just another word for shrink, I'll be back, only not as a patient."

The doctor said he certainly understood that.

The specialist was supposedly a world-famous neurologist and tiny, barely five feet tall. He diagnosed Geraci with a mild form of Parkinson's disease, related to getting hit in the head all those times as a boxer and triggered by a serious concussion.

"I didn't get hit in the head all that often," Geraci said.

"You boxers are all the same," the doctor said. "All you remember is what the other guy looked like. Tell me about that concussion, though. Pretty recent, right?"

Geraci hadn't told the doctor a thing about the plane crash that had nearly killed him. "I guess so," Geraci said. "If six years ago qualifies as recent."

"What happened six years ago?"

"I fell down," Geraci said. "Knocked myself cold. Damnedest thing."

The doctor looked into Geraci's eyes with his flashlight gizmo. "Fell down from where?" he asked. "The Empire State Building?"

"Something like that," Geraci said.

From an upstairs window of the Antica Focacceria, Nick Geraci watched a wiry, moustached man—his friend and business partner Cesare Indelicato—cross the Piazza San Francesco, theoretically alone. The piazza was an oasis of light tucked deeply in a neighborhood of dark, narrow streets in the oldest part of Palermo.

Don Cesare was never really alone. He'd trained his *soldatos* and bodyguards to blend in. A casual observer wouldn't have guessed that the

young men leaning on Vespas in front of the cathedral were Don Cesare's men, as were the four milling around outside the restaurant arguing about soccer. A casual observer might have guessed that the nondescript man in the off-the-rack suit walking across the piazza was a history teacher a few years shy of retirement, rather than a hero of the Allied invasion of Sicily and the most powerful Mafia boss in Palermo.

Though it's also true that Palermo is a city where little is observed casually.

It was three in the afternoon, and the restaurant was closed. The waiter seeing to their table had been approved and searched by Don Cesare's men, one of whom was stationed in the doorway. There were men downstairs, too, keeping an eye on the cooks and the back door.

Over wine and the restaurant's legendary beef spleen sandwiches, Geraci and Indelicato discussed various details of their thriving narcotics business. They spoke entirely in English, not as any sort of security measure but because, even after all these years coming to Sicily on business, all these years surrounded by native Sicilians, Geraci's Italian was atrocious and his Sicilian even worse. He understood it but couldn't speak it. He couldn't explain why. A mental block or something.

"It is good to have you in my city, my gigantic friend," Don Cesare said, finishing his last bite and licking his fingers. "But these matters, I don't know, I think they are not why you came all this way to speak with me?"

"I brought the family this time," he said. "My wife and daughters. The older one is off to college in the fall. To university, I guess you'd say. It might be our last family vacation. They'd never been to your beautiful island before, and now they've been all over it, at least as best you can in ten days." They'd have spent more time, but they'd had to come on an ocean liner. Nick Geraci had no intention of ever getting into an airplane again. "I actually never took the time to sightsee before. First time I've ever been to Taormina, if you can believe it."

Don Cesare raised his hands in lamentation. "I own the finest hotel in Taormina. Why didn't you tell me you were going to be there? I would have seen to it that you and your family was treated like royalty."

"You do so much for me already, Don Cesare, I wouldn't think of imposing further."

But Don Cesare wouldn't let it drop until Geraci promised he'd come back to Taormina no later than next year and stay at Indelicato's mountaintop resort.

"I do have another reason to see you in person, though, Don Cesare. It involves your young godson Carmine Marino."

The Don frowned. "He's all right?"

"He's doin' great," Geraci said. "Possibly the best man I have. Which is why I wanted to talk to you about a job I want to give him. A valuable, important, but very dangerous job."

Geraci was tempted to confide in him. Indelicato was a valuable, even trusted, ally. More to the point, he was the only person Geraci knew who'd worked with the CIA before. During the war, the Mafia members not banished to Ustica by the Fascists had functioned in Sicily as the Resistance had in France. Indelicato quickly emerged as one of the leaders of this violent, effective underground. Via Lucky Luciano, the deported American Don, Indelicato met with operatives from the OSS—the forerunner of the CIA— to provide intelligence that laid the groundwork for the invasion of the island. It was supposedly Indelicato who came up with the stunt of air-dropping tens of thousands of red handkerchiefs emblazoned with Luciano's famous script *L* to alert the Sicilian people—but not the Fascist invaders from the north—to what was coming. The British, who did not collaborate with the Mafia, suffered heavy casualties in their battles to take the eastern third of the island, but on the western two thirds, particularly in the regions that were Mafia strongholds, the Americans profited from superior intelligence and sustained relatively few casualties. After the invasion, in many of the cities occupied by the Americans, the civilians installed as provisional mayors were mafiosi. When the Allies withdrew, most of the mayors stayed. And when the Dons were freed from Ustica, they returned home to find that, courtesy of the USA and the OSS, the political power of the Mafia had increased exponentially. Soon thereafter, Cesare Indelicato was elected to the Italian Parliament and helped spearhead a surprisingly popular movement to secede from Italy and become America's forty-ninth state.

Ultimately, Geraci decided not to risk it. "I can't give you any details," he said. "I can only say that Carmine wants to do the job and that he'd be the leader of the other men I send."

"You tell me this why? What reason? You want my blessing, how can I do that if I don't know what I bless, eh?"

"If you tell me to take Carmine off this job, I'll do it. But I can't be specific about what we're doing. What we have to do."

Don Cesare considered this. "I think you are asking me to approve that my godson Carmine, who sends his mother money home every month, that he go do something where you think he will be killed, eh? If not that, you don't need to ask me nothing."

Geraci answered this only with silence.

"And you know he's related to the Bocchicchio clan? I wouldn't want to be the man who got blamed for anything that happened to him."

Don Cesare said this with no conviction, clearly grasping at straws. Geraci knew full well who Carmine Marino's people were.

In silence, Geraci waited Don Cesare out.

"One question, then," Don Cesare finally said. "Carmine, he knows as much about this as you, the danger and also the reason for it, and still he want to do it, *sì*?"

"That's right. Absolutely he still wants to do it."

The Don bobbed his head back and forth, as if to show he was thinking about the repercussions of anything he might say. "Carmine is a man," he said. "He does not need me to tell him what brave deeds he can or cannot do."

"Thank you, Don Cesare." Geraci felt the tremors coming on and excused himself to go to the bathroom, though all he really wanted to do was move around and concentrate on the moving so that the shaking would stop. For some reason, very little worked better in this regard than any action he could make his prick do. Urinating was in general handier than the other.

"For many reasons," Geraci said as he sat back down at the table, "one of which being that Carmine will be in charge, I think it's best that all the men we put on this job be Sicilians." Another of the many reasons was that the Sicilians did not have rules against killing cops or government officials.

"You want people," Indelicato said, "I'll get you people."

"I appreciate that. But I can't risk bringing men in just for this job. I need men who've been in the States awhile. I don't want to use too many of Carmine's people either, especially, God forbid, if something should happen to the guy. I'm going to call in the pizza men, the best ones. Any objections?"

"If not for a tough job, then when, huh?"

Nearly all the men stashed in the pizza parlors had been directly or indirectly dispatched to America by Cesare Indelicato.

"A lot of those people I don't know at all," Geraci said.

"Of course you don't. They don't get in trouble, don't have problems, what's to know?"

"Exactly. I've got guys who've been out there seven years. Guys I've never laid eyes on. I need your advice, Don Cesare. If you were to recommend, say, the four best men you've sent over—best in terms of toughness, character, smarts—who would that be?"

Geraci had expected him to have to think about this awhile, but Don Cesare answered immediately, complete with brief descriptions of the men's skills. If they were half the men he said they were, Geraci would have no trouble getting this done without sending Carmine.

"There's another, unrelated matter," Geraci said. "It involves a traitor in your midst. A man sent here from America. An inconvenient man to our Commission, or so they ruled."

Geraci couldn't do it himself, as of course Don Cesare understood. He was a Boss. Such things must be done by others.

The frail Capuchin monk struggled down the stairs to the convent's catacombs. He had glaucoma and an arthritic hip, but he was determined not to become a burden to the order. He could still do all the tasks he'd done when he first came to Palermo as a young man—from the sublime of tending the garden, preparing meals for his brothers in Christ, and embalming the dead to be interred in the city cemetery next door, to the ridiculous of selling postcards to tourists and picking up the filth they left behind. Soda cans, wine bottles, spent flashbulbs (photography was explicitly forbidden), and even, once, a used prophylactic.

It was after lunch: almost three, when the catacombs would reopen to the public. A German tour group milled around outside the barred iron doors. As the monk descended farther, their vulgar noise receded. He smiled and thanked almighty God for allowing him to recognize that even diminished hearing can be a gift from on high.

At the base of the stairs was a candy wrapper. The monk's knees cracked as he stooped to pick it up.

In the tunnels before him were the crumbling, finely dressed remains of eight thousand Sicilians. Many were hung from hooks in long rows, their skulls bowed in what the monk liked to think of as humility. Others lay on shelves and tucked into recessed alcoves, floor to ceiling. A few reclined in wooden coffins, heads resting on pillows covered by a film of dust that had once been flesh. In life, they'd been dukes and countesses, cardinals and important priests, military heroes who fought alongside Garibaldi and those who drew their swords against him. Some, including the monk's own grandfather, had been defiled in their mortal lives by their association with what Sicilians call the Friends. Eight thousand dead: people who paid the order handsomely so that their remains or those of their loved ones could be displayed here. The folly of this was not lost on the old monk. With one exception—*La bambina*, whose presence the monk had helped arrange—the order had stopped accepting bodies in 1881, eighty years ago, two years after the monk was born. For the most part, these people who'd wanted so badly to be remembered had been forgotten by all but their Creator. Few if any of the children in these catacombs—including an entire chamber filled with them—were mourned by a living soul. The corporeal rot of these eight thousand had been slowed by skilled Capuchin embalmers and by the cool, dry air, but, except for *La bambina*, rot and earthly oblivion had come nonetheless.

He bore left, scanning the floor for debris or fallen body parts. His grandparents, who came from the tiny town of Corleone, were among

those hung vertically. His grandfather wore a green velvet coat (underneath, the gunshot wound in his back gaped open and a steel rod was all that kept the powdery-boned torso from collapsing). His grandmother (an arm had dropped off some time ago and been loosely reattached with wire) wore her wedding dress. When the monk had first arrived, they, like many of the dead, still had faces. For a half century he'd watched the day-by-day disappearance of their eyes and skin. He kissed his fingertips, applied them spider delicately to the foreheads of his ancestors, mumbled a prayer for their souls, and hurried on.

At the end of the tunnel was *La bambina,* the lovely two-year-old girl who'd died in 1920 and become one of Sicily's most popular tourist attractions. The doctor who embalmed her had taunted the monks about the new procedure he'd invented. Before anyone learned his secret, he, too, died (from the deadly sin of pride, the monk would tell the younger brothers, though the prosaic cause was a ruptured spleen). The old monk had spent many reflective hours studying the doctor's pitiful notes and the girl herself, fruitlessly trying to guess what the doctor had done. The baby with the long blond hair in that glass-covered coffin had been in there for forty-one years. She looked as though she'd died a few days ago.

As the monk approached *La bambina,* his cloudy eyes seemed to be playing tricks on him. Against the wall near the poor babe was a body as well preserved as hers.

He rubbed his eyes. It was a bald man in a raincoat. Diamonds gleamed from the rings on his fingers and the bar across his fat tie. The dead were not interred here wearing jewelry. Then the monk saw the distinct black lines on either side of the man's mouth and felt a wave of relief.

It was a huge marionette. The jewelry must be fake. An odd prank, but the monk had lived in Palermo a long time and had learned not to be surprised by anything that happened here.

He drew nearer.

The puppet lines beside Laughing Sal Narducci's mouth were actually rivulets of blood.

The rope used to garrote him—just before noon, when the catacombs closed for lunch—lay on the floor beside the dead man's shiny shoes.

The monk took in this grim tableau, in this strange and holy place, and something inside his heart broke. A common thief would have taken the jewels. An ordinary killer would have hidden the body, not left it *here,* in the same chamber with *La bambina*! The monk shouted a stream of curses at the Friends. Who else would do such a thing? He had devoted his life to paying penance for his family's violent tradition, but again and again it sought him out. And now, so late in life, this atrocity. It felt cruelly inevitable. Rage filled him like a poison. His curses grew louder.

The brothers who ran to his aid told the authorities that when the

beloved old man collapsed and died, his face was as red as the rightmost stripe of the Italian flag.

When, from the killer himself, Cesare Indelicato heard what had happened—on the terrace of his cliffside villa, overlooking the medieval city he essentially ruled—he marveled at God's bleak sense of humor. Don Cesare had never met the poor monk, but he recognized the man's name. It had been Don Cesare's grandfather, Felice Crapisi, who killed the monk's traitorous grandfather. Even more strangely, Don Cesare had been asked to kill Narducci twice (first by Thomas Hagen, then by Nick Geraci). The trusted *soldato* he'd sent had killed Narducci only once, yet the bloody poetics of the Creator saw fit to transform that lone killing into two deaths.

Don Cesare thanked the killer and dismissed him.

Alone, shaking his head in wonder and awe, Don Cesare raised a glass of grappa toward Palermo and toward the darkening heavens.

What toast might he give to such a world, such a God, that had made him so happy, so rich, that had rewarded his every duplicitous act while punishing the superstitious little ants down there striving to do good?

What else?

"Salut'," he cried. He drank.

The toast echoed off the cliff. He heard it again, and again he drank.

Chapter 29

At the Corleone compound at Lake Tahoe, Theresa Hagen and Connie Corleone (who'd gone back to using her maiden name) were cooking dinner together, as they did most nights they were both home, which was most nights. They alternated kitchens, by no pattern Michael could see, some nights in his house, others (like tonight) at the Hagens'. There had been a remarkable change in Connie in the two years since she'd stopped trying to be a part of the jet set and come home to serve her brother—just as unmarried relatives have served as de facto first ladies to widowed or bachelor presidents. Theresa was no small part of Connie's turnaround. She'd become the big sister Connie never had—complete with constant sisterly bickering, true, but they clearly loved each other. Because of Theresa, Connie had taken an interest in art and was helping Theresa raise funds to establish a permanent symphony orchestra in Lake Tahoe. They both held office in the League of Women Voters. The last year or so, Connie had even started dressing much more conservatively. They used the same designer the real first lady did.

In Tom Hagen's office, the stone cottage behind the house, Tom and Michael were lying low until dinner was ready. Connie's kids drove Michael nuts, even his godson, Mickey Rizzi, who was six years old and cried constantly. Connie ran things around the house, but Michael could have hired people to do that. Having someone else's children living in his house made him miss Tony and Mary even more, he thought, than if he'd been rattling around over there alone. Not to mention the Hagen kids, right next door. Gianna Hagen and Mary were the same age, had gone to the same schools, and been best friends. It was impossible to look at Gianna and not feel a pang of yearning for the simple pleasure of reading a bedtime story to his daughter.

He and Tom also had business to discuss, of course. Tom had spoken to the Ambassador about getting Billy more responsibility in his job at the Justice Department; the Ambassador claimed to have spoken to his son Danny, the attorney general, but Tom had his doubts. Billy was apparently still being kept away from anything in the office that might be useful to the Corleones.

There was also the matter of Vincent Forlenza's trumped-up rationale for killing his long-deported *consigliere* and the word Nick Geraci had sent that he needed to speak with Michael Corleone, in person, one on one.

"Did Geraci say what it was about?" Michael presumed it had to do with Narducci.

"He didn't," Tom said. "He said he could come out here if you'd rather—Aw, shit."

On the putting green outside Tom's office, Victor Rizzi—his twelve-year-old nephew, freshly suspended from school for fighting and drinking—executed a flying tackle of Andrew Hagen, seven years older and about to begin his sophomore year at Notre Dame. Andrew—a divinity major who planned to become a priest—was probably not the instigator. Victor came up swinging. Andrew tossed his putter aside and pinned Victor to the green.

Michael cocked an eyebrow.

"Forget it," Tom said. "Andrew can handle it."

"It's not Andrew I'm worried about."

The Hagens' alarmed, obedient collie raced to the back door of the house, barking. A moment later, Connie came running out in a filthy apron, screaming at Victor. Andrew used his longer arms to his advantage and essentially handed Victor over to his furious mother.

"Remind you of anybody?" Tom said.

Michael knew Tom must have meant either him or Fredo, but it didn't seem like something either of them would have done. Also, neither he nor Tom ever spoke Fredo's name. There were things that had to be done, and you did them, and you never talked about it. You didn't try to justify them. They can't be justified.

"You mean me?" Michael said. "When did I ever—"

Tom rolled his eyes. So this *had* been his attempt to talk about Fredo.

"When did . . . he ever take on you and Sonny?"

Tom shook his head, gravely. "I shouldn't have said anything. I'm getting old."

A few beats late, Michael realized that Tom hadn't meant Fredo. He'd meant Carmela, who'd broken up more petty fights in their neighborhood than ten beat cops combined.

"Anyway," Tom said, "getting Geraci out here's going to take a while. He'll have to drive or take a train."

"I'm supposed to go see the kids the week after next."

"If you're going to do it at all," Hagen said, "I think that's when. But—"

"I'm going to do it."

"It could be a trap. Especially in New York, I think."

"It's fine," Michael said. "I'll take care of it. I'll be sure Al takes every precaution."

"What'll happen when they find out we had the job done on Narducci before they did?"

Sal Narducci hadn't seemed like the sort of man who'd hold up well if he were tortured. It hadn't been a chance Michael was willing to take. They could suspect whatever they wanted from Narducci, but they weren't going to hear it from that horse's ass's mouth. "How would they find out?" Michael said. "We contacted the same man they did. Indelicato waited to hear from them, as we told him he would, and then he did the job to our specifications."

"You're that confident in Cesare Indelicato? This was the first time I'd ever met the man. He's worked with Geraci for years."

"He's been in business with the Corleone Family for many more years," Michael said. "If it hadn't been for the help of my father during the war, Cesare Indelicato would still be hijacking tomato carts. Anyway, what incentive does he have to side with anyone but himself? He was contacted twice, received two tributes, all for one simple job. He won't give the matter a second thought."

"After all the bullshit Forlenza fed the Commission about Narducci's activities in Sicily," Hagen said, "I'm surprised he didn't send his own men to do the job. Or at least to contact Don Cesare."

"Forlenza will just say that Geraci's from Cleveland—his godson, et cetera—and was going to Sicily on business anyway, which is true. It's suspicious, but Don Forlenza made no secret of it. He told the Commission that this was how he was going to handle it. Brilliant. It looked like he had nothing to hide."

"And you're still certain they *do* have something to hide." *They* meaning Forlenza, Geraci, and Russo.

"What in this life is certain?" Michael said. "I'm certain enough."

"If it was anyone else," Hagen said, "I'd say be careful."

Michael smiled. "If it came from anyone else, I'd take offense."

"I think I have an idea," Tom said, "about how to handle things with Russo."

He was interrupted by Connie banging the dinner gong as if she were seeking rescue, not serving up the evening meal.

When they got to the table, it was a bruised and chastised Victor who led them in grace.

Francesca Van Arsdale had spent all morning making a picnic lunch to surprise her husband, but when she and little Sonny showed up at his office,

Billy grumbled about all the tourists on the Mall and how hot it was before he finally thanked her for the gesture and agreed to go. "It's not as if I'm too busy to get away," he said.

Billy had probably begun working at the Justice Department with unrealistically high hopes, although, after seven miserable months on the job, he still seemed unready to admit that to himself, much less to his wife. He was only two years out of law school, Francesca reminded him, but that only launched him on some litany of names she didn't know—people who, like Billy, had been president of law review at Harvard and what glamorous and/or lucrative things those strangers were doing two years later.

"Exactly," she said, "and someday some other, younger presidents of law review will have *you* on the same kind of list. 'Do you know what Senator Van Arsdale—'"

"C'mon, Francie."

"'—was doing two years out of law school? Working for the United States Justice Department, that's what, and not just under *any* attorney general. No! Under Daniel Brendan Shea! The greatest attorney general in American history and our, y'know, thirty-seventh president or whatever number he'd be.'"

Sonny was jumping around in the grass of the Mall doing the famous Monkey Dance from *Jojo, Mrs. Cheese and Annie*. Except for the gold football helmet bobbing on the boy's head, it was a dead-on impression of Jojo. Tourists paused to watch.

"When did he learn to do that?" Billy whispered, spreading out the blanket.

"It's from TV," she said. *Months ago* was the answer. He frowned, either confused or disapproving, Francesca didn't want to know which. Sonny finished, and bystanders applauded. Francesca firmly told him he couldn't do an encore like Jojo, because it was time to eat.

They sat down as a family. Why couldn't he appreciate *this*? she thought. Why couldn't he accept *this* as the point of life and take pleasure in it? Between his unhappiness at work—which he talked about all the time—and their joint unhappiness about losing the baby—which they never really talked about—she was feeling more and more like they had to get out of this godforsaken city. Billy had been so good to her from the time she'd found out about the affair until the night they'd lost the baby, but he'd barely touched her since then. The only time they'd tried to make love, he couldn't get hard and she was too fragile herself to make it happen for him. He rolled off her, onto his back, and used his hand. When he came, she started crying, though she was also strangely relieved. About half the nights since then, for no apparent reason, he'd spent the night on the couch with the TV test pattern on.

"You don't understand, Francie," Billy said. "It's complicated." He'd folded several napkins to sit on, even on top of the blanket, so he wouldn't get his seersucker suit dirty. "All day I sit on my duff in the library," he said, slapping said duff, "checking other people's citations. Some of the lawyers who wrote those things are my age, and most of them wouldn't know a decent English sentence from—I don't know, the Monkey Dance, but—"

"Monkey Dance!" Sonny cast aide his bologna sandwich, grabbed his football helmet, and shot up, dancing. Billy didn't even budge. Francesca got up, got Sonny under control, and, with the minor concession of allowing him to keep the helmet on, got him back to eating lunch.

"When I was on law review," Billy said, "I had people doing this kind of job for *me*."

It took her a second to realize he meant the work in the law library, not her efforts to subdue a four-year-old with a Monkey Dance fixation. Billy had people for that, too: her. A normal, healthy four-year-old boy was wearying enough without having to contend with a whiny husband, too. She'd only been eleven when her father died. She knew she'd probably built him up into someone who never existed, but she hadn't even the vaguest memory of him whining to his wife, not once. "Well, you're not on law review anymore," Francesca said, "are you?"

"How can I talk to you about this? You didn't even finish *college*. Nobody in your family ever did."

"That's ridiculous. Aunt Kay did, and so did Uncle Tom and Aunt Theresa."

Billy laughed. "They're not *blood*, though, are they? Other than Theresa, they're not even Italian."

Francesca would have let him have it—verbally, at *least*—if Sonny hadn't been sitting right there. "My *twin sister* finished, and she's getting her *doctorate*. My brother Frankie is doing great at Notre Dame, and—"

"Your brother Frankie plays *football*. What's the toughest class he's taking, Theory of Gym Class?"

"That's low." Frankie was in fact a phys ed major and had never been good in school. She was proud he was doing as well as he was, even in a gut major. "I'd have finished my degree, too, if you hadn't—" Sonny was devouring his sandwich now, but Francesca didn't want to risk saying anything in front of him. "You know."

Billy shrugged. "Takes two to tango," he said. "If you took exception to that, you had your chance to have it taken care of."

A look of horror crossed his face; he immediately realized what he'd said.

"*Taken care of!*" she said.

"I'm sorry!" He reached out to her, and she pushed his arm away. He spent most of the rest of lunch apologizing. He was a talker. Eventually, he wore her down.

"It's the job," Billy said. "It's gotten to the point that it's affecting the way I am with you. I need to be making more of a difference in the world, and what it comes down to, I guess, is that I'm not going to be happy until I am. Can you understand that?"

She told him she did understand, as she'd told him before, and told him he really needed to talk to the attorney general and make his unhappiness known, as she'd been saying for weeks. She didn't understand why he wouldn't do it. She was raised to believe that if you had a problem, you went to the man at the top. Billy had been raised with all the advantages, so she'd have thought he'd believe in that, too. All she could figure was maybe he was intimidated by Daniel Brendan Shea, though that, too, mystified her. Danny Shea, a pale and scrawny version of his brother, possessed the startled, blinking manner of a man whose eyeglasses have just been yanked from his face, though in fact his eyesight, if not his vision, was perfect.

When they finished eating, he kissed Sonny and then told Francesca that he'd do it: if it was what she wanted, he'd march straight to the attorney general's office and see if he could talk to Danny Shea.

"I only want you to be happy," she said, which was a lie. She was starting to want a lot of things beyond the horizons of her entitled husband's happiness. "Like you said."

They walked back to the Justice Department together. He carried his sleeping son in one arm and the helmet in the other, with which he hailed a taxi so Francesca wouldn't have to carry the boy home. Billy kissed her good-bye, but with no more passion than if he were a friend of the family. He did say "Thank you," but he never did remember what day it was.

The cab merged into the traffic on Constitution. "Happy anniversary," she whispered.

"What's that, ma'am?" the cabbie said.

"Nothing," she said, pulling Sonny closer, willing herself not to cry. "Nothing at all."

That afternoon, Billy did in fact get in to see Danny Shea. According to the notes taken shorthand by the attorney general's secretary, what happened was this:

At 15:37, AG [Attorney General Daniel Brendan Shea] fit junior staff attorney Bill V. Airdale [*sic*] into a ten minute break in his

P.M. schedule so long as BVA could accompany AG as he went for his daily run 10X up and down the building's main stairwell. [Many books about the Sheas include accounts of her trailing behind AG as he held meetings in this manner, though her technique for managing to take shorthand this way has been lost to history.] BVA agreed.

BVA discussed his qualifications for this job and his desire to be involved more with prosecutorial matters that would result in more time in the courtroom and less in the library. BVA wondered if his Harvard degree had anything to do with his present dissatisfactory assignment, seeing as so many top officials in AG's office were from Princeton. AG categorically denied any such bias, citing several Jews and Negroes from state-supported schools who held high office in the JKS administration, as well as the job with Senator [censored] that AG personally helped secure for Miss [censored] from the University of Miami, whom the AG referred to as BVA's "girlfriend." BVA apologized. AG accepted.

BVA nonetheless expressed unhappiness with his current assignment and asked about the possibility of a transfer. AG referred BVA to BVA's own unit supervisor. BVA expressed disappointment with AG's reluctance to act personally in the matter, especially given [several heavily censored lines follow; among the few words not blacked out are "Van Arsdale Citrus Co.," spelled correctly, despite the earlier gaffe with Billy's name].

AG said he did not understand.

BVA explained that his parents [two more censored lines].

AG expressed surprise, insofar as no such factors had accompanied AG's decision to hire BVA. AG admitted that MCS [his father, former ambassador to Canada M. Corbett Shea] was the first to urge AG to hire BVA. AG's understanding was that this had primarily to do with BVA's excellent record at Harvard but also was aided by BVA's fine service alongside the aforementioned Miss [censored] during the JKS election campaign.

BVA, somewhat breathless and thus difficult to understand, seemed to express skepticism that family connections hadn't played a role and couldn't play a role now.

AG admitted that this was true, but that those connections existed between MCS and the family of BVA's wife, whose maiden name was [censored].

BVA asked if he'd been "foisted off" on the AG.

AG said it was more complicated than that. While reminding BVA of his sworn responsibilities, vis-à-vis confidentiality, AG said

that he was in fact preparing a comprehensive plan to [prosecute] "the [censored name of BVA's wife's family] and people like them."

BVA responded that he fondly hoped for the same thing, and certainly would not pass said information on to his wife or any member of her family.

AG expressed surprise and asked if that was really true.

Exercise session was completed.

BVA said he was committed to doing "anything and everything" to see to it that any crimes being committed by his wife's family be prosecuted to the fullest extent of the law, and that otherwise his own political future would be [nonexistent]. BVA said he had firsthand knowledge of secret aspects of her family's illegal activities that could be of use in AG's comprehensive prosecutorial plan.

AG expressed his pleasure at this news and said he was optimistic he could work something out, vis-à-vis BVA's proposed reassignment. He handed BVA a fresh white towel and thanked him for his time and candor. Meeting concluded at 15:47 EST.

The airport Michael Corleone used when he came to New York was nearly at the end of Long Island. It had once been a private airport but had been under government control since World War II. Several years before, Nick Geraci, who of course no longer flew, had rigged it so that various planes owned or operated by the Corleone Family could land there.

Michael taxied toward the hangar where Geraci was waiting. He stopped about fifty yards short of it. Geraci walked across the tarmac alone. Al Neri got out and searched him. Geraci took a deep breath and climbed the stairs.

"Leave that door open," Geraci said to Neri.

Neri glanced at Michael, who nodded. Neri left the door up and positioned himself outside it.

"So that's how it is between us now?" Michael said.

"What's how it is?"

"I have you searched," Michael said, "and you won't meet with me behind closed doors."

"The searching, I can't speak to," Geraci said, "though I have no argument with it. And since I'm sure the lovely and talented Mr. Al Neri out there is packing one or more deadly weapons, I think it's clear that my trust in you remains as solid as ever. It's just . . . I don't know if you realize this, but this is the first time I've been inside an airplane since . . . you know."

Michael did know. He said nothing. He filled out a flight plan for the next leg of his trip.

"Even when I take my kids to Coney Island," Geraci said, "if a ride leaves the ground, it leaves without me. I'd consider it a personal favor if we could keep the door open and, if you don't mind too much, while you're sitting right there, if you could kill the engine."

Michael had heard about Nick Geraci's tremors, but this was the first time he'd seen them. They weren't as bad as he'd imagined.

"We'll split the difference," Michael said, finishing the form and tossing it to Neri so he could run it over to the tower. "You keep the door open, and I'll keep the engine running."

Did Geraci really think that Michael would take off without Neri? With the door open? That Michael would be so reckless he'd try to pull something like that in an enclosed space with a former heavyweight boxer who, tremors notwithstanding, kept himself in good shape and looked like he could knock Michael Corleone into a brain-damaged tomorrow?

"All right," Geraci agreed. "Let me just say this, and I'll go. It's just something that I wanted you to know about. I don't know where to start, so I'll just say it. I've worked out a deal for us to get back into Cuba."

Michael's surprise was genuine, even though nothing Geraci was saying came as any news. Not the offer from the one-eyed "Jewish" CIA agent, not fenced-off land in New Jersey, guarded by a crew of federal agents and a pack of rottweilers. Not the combustible mix of mercenary Sicilians and aggrieved, once-wealthy Cubans who'd overcome their differences (language, culture, motives, you name it) and an unfortunate stabbing incident (one of Geraci's men, recuperating nicely back in Toledo, Ohio) and were only a few weeks away from trying to sneak onto the island, in assassin squads of two or three, in the hope that the killing of one man would produce certain desirable results. What shocked Michael was that Nick Geraci was telling him about it at all.

"When you say you've worked out a deal for *us*," Michael said when Geraci finished, "I'm not sure I know what you mean."

"Let it mean what you want it to mean. I know you're out and all that bit, but I'm not in the casino business and you are. I thought you'd be interested to know in advance about the opportunities that might be coming up, and also to be sure you knew about the competition."

Competition? "Competition for what?"

"Well, this is where, if I'd have known everything that was going on, I'd have come to you right away. I was led to believe that my thing out in Jersey was the whole operation, but I started hearing different things. Come to find out, Sammy Drago down in Tampa's got something just like it, training right on the beach way south of Miami. That didn't bother me

half as much as when I happen to learn that there's fifty or so men train-ing at a closed-off part of the navy base in Jacksonville, which I actually use from time to time in my own business. All the wiseguys I could find any-thing out about at that base are connected to Carlo Tramonti and New Orleans, but—" He turned his trembling palms over and smirked in an of-course way. "Tramonti's a puppet. Drago's an empty suit. Put it all to-gether, what's it spell?" Geraci spelled it out on the fingers and thumb of his left hand, as if he were counting. "R. U. S. S. O."

Michael presumed that *come to find out* and *I happened to learn* were Geraci's way of covering up his obvious sources for this—either Vincent Forlenza, who was down in Key Biscayne for the winter, or Louie Russo himself.

"Stop right there," Michael said. "I know that you're telling me these things out of your respect for me and for our friendship, and for that I'm grateful. But you've said too much already. I can't be a part of this. I appreciate the awkward position that puts you in, but all I can tell you is that in spite of what you may have heard from your godfather in Cleveland, I assure you I'm doing everything I can to move this along so that you can have my seat on the Commission and I can be out alto-gether. I'm close. We're close. You and I want the same things. This would be a terrible time to start up any trouble at all with any of the other Families."

Michael couldn't tell if Geraci was nodding or trembling.

"I know I don't need your blessing," Geraci said, getting up to leave. "I'm just trying to make sure I avoid the opposite. Your curse, I guess."

Michael would have thought that a move that cravenly defensive was beneath him. "Good luck to you and your men in Cuba," Michael said. "Say hello to all the things that were stolen from us. Are we clear?"

"Will do," Geraci said, descending the stars. "And yes."

A week later, back in Lake Tahoe, Joe Lucadello showed up alone, as promised, in a crummy little boat and tied up to the Corleone dock. Capra and Tommy Neri met him and frisked him and gave Michael the all clear. Michael called Tom Hagen and told him Joe had arrived, then waited until Hagen was already out there before making his own way down the slop-ing lawn to the aluminum bench at the end of the dock, taking his place in the middle.

"Tom didn't seem to want to tell me," Joe said. "Maybe you know, Mike. Who thought up that pizza parlor trick? Because I must say, I'm im-pressed."

It had been Geraci's idea, but Michael couldn't see anything to gain

by telling this to Joe. "Tell me if what Fausto Geraci said is true," Michael said.

"That always throws me," Joe said. "No one else calls him that."

Michael stared his old friend down.

"All right, yes," he said. "There are others. I mean, I never said there *weren't* others."

"You *knew* about this, and—"

"No, I didn't. Not at first. The more I learn about your . . . whadda-yacallit," Joe Lucadello said. "Your tradition. The more similarities I see. Secret societies, with vows of silence and a code of honor, et cetera. But this situation here is a way we differ. You seem to have ways of finding out everything you need to know, but in my line of work, nobody knows everything about anything."

"That's not acceptable," Michael said.

"I don't make the rules. Though, honestly, I don't think it affects you. You're part of the project. Once anybody gets the job done, it's safe to say that everyone on the project will get a big dose of Christmas for their troubles. Plus, our operation is *by far* the best. They're not willing to lose a few men if necessary as part of the war on communism, and because of your military training, you are, which gives us an enormous advantage. I don't know all the ins and outs of the other plans, but I hear stories. They're talking about going to the radio station where our target gives his speeches to the Cuban people and putting aerosol spray in the air, some hallucinogenic drug called LSD that'll make him sound crazy. They're working on ways of poisoning his cigars or shining his shoes with a chemical that'll seep into his skin and make his hair fall out, beard included, to embarrass him that way. They've killed a hundred pigs and monkeys field-testing pills that are supposed to dissolve right away in frozen daiquiris. The newest idea I heard about was having a midget submarine drop a pretty seashell on the reef where the guy goes scuba diving. The seashell will be attached to a bombshell, and when he picks the thing up, he'll be hamburger. In other words, they're a bunch of pussies. We're taking a straightforward route. We're going to shoot the Commie bastard."

The men sat silently on the bench for a long time.

"So what's the deal?" Joe said. "You want to pull the plug? Because the others won't, I can tell you that."

"Can you guarantee us that our people will be the first ones in?"

"Guarantee?" Joe said. "What do I look like, Sears and Roebuck? I can tell you that your man Geraci is the best person we have on this, though. He was the first to get his facility organized, and he has the best people. I have it from the top that they're the most ready to go. I have to be honest with you, I'm wondering if some of your competition here is

just taking the money with no intention of doing anything ever. So, yes, I'm confident our people will be first, but I won't *guarantee* you the sun will come up in the morning. If and when Geraci's men are dispatched, I'll let you know. A promise, not a guarantee."

"Understood," Michael said.

They discussed the details of what would happen when the men got to Cuba until Michael was satisfied that he should go ahead and let what was going to happen happen.

"I never thought we'd have men on our side as good as the ones we're going up against in Cuba," Joe said. "Not because our men are inferior— they're not—but because our people just work for money. If something goes wrong, they're out some cash, a promotion, what have you. But the men that SOB in Cuba has, if they fuck up, they know he'll kill them. That's what makes his intelligence so good. But *your* people?" Joe shook his head in admiration. "With them, we've got the best of both worlds."

Michael didn't know what else to say but to thank him.

Joe got up to go.

"Whoever thought of the pizza parlor thing, by the way," he said as Hagen untied the boat for him, "it's a hell of a good idea. I'm not saying what I'm saying, but we have the same kind of thing. Fairly new. Most Special Fellows, they're called. Doesn't matter if I tell you, because, believe me, you'll never hear about it. The Company sets them up, makes sure they prosper, but for the most part we leave 'em alone for years until we need 'em for something. I'm not involved with it at all, but mark my words, there will come a time when the American president will be a Most Special Fellow. Of course, you won't know it when it happens."

As Michael watched the boat pull away, the flicker of a smile played across his face. Already, he knew of at least three such Fellows, including the man who lost to Jimmy Shea in the last election; the son of a senator on the Family's payroll, now bumbling around in Texas, pretending to be an oilman; and Peter Clemenza's son Ray, the shopping mall magnate.

"It's time," Michael said to Hagen. "Go see Russo. This gives you a reason."

"You're sure?"

Michael nodded. "Geraci's men are either going to succeed or fail, and we have it worked out either way. This news of Joe's throws us a curve, but it's nothing we need to worry about. It just means that we need to move forward. The only thing that's not ready is our canary in the Justice Department, but we know Billy used the chance to betray us as a means of getting the attorney general's trust. He needs a little more time there before he'll know enough for it to be worth turning him to our advantage. So, yes. Start with Russo. Presuming you're ready."

"I'm ready."

"It's a big step."

"I've been waiting for this," Tom said, "I don't know how long. A long time."

"Well, that's it, then," Michael said, kissing his older brother on the cheek and then trudging up the lawn to his empty house.

Chapter 30

LESS THAN a year after the facility on Geraci's land was built, a crew came to tear it down. Your tax dollars at work. Geraci said he had demolition guys who could do the job for a reasonable price, but "Agent Ike Rosen" said they had to do it to certain specifications. Also, there were security issues. The remaining trainees had been sent home, to be called upon when needed to a staging area at a villa in the Bahamas.

Three Cuban expats were the first to be dispatched, apparently on the orders of CIA Director Allen Soffet himself, the logic being that the Cubans knew the country and if something went wrong they'd be better able to disappear than Geraci's men would. Geraci was furious. He'd wanted a Cuban (for the language and general navigation) and two Sicilians (so the job would get done right the first time). Do it that way, Geraci told his contacts, and nothing *will* go wrong. The Cubans landed on an unnamed coral island just outside Cuban waters, were picked up in a speedboat that had been seized from the estate of Ernest Hemingway, and were killed on the way to shore, when the boat exploded under suspicious circumstances. The thinking was that the pilot had been a spy for the Cuban government, but everything Geraci heard about it was far from firsthand. Geraci told Agent Rosen he'd told him so. Geraci didn't want to lose a man, but he also didn't want one of the other operations to be the ones to murder that thieving dictator, and there seemed to be no reliable way to find out what was going on in those other camps. Why even train his men, Geraci said, if they were only going to send the Cubans to do the job?

About a week later, Rosen told Geraci he'd been authorized to send another three men in, this time on a low-flying seaplane, under the radar, delivered right to a trusted operative who'd be waiting on the beach. Geraci was told he could recommend one man. Geraci insisted on two. One or nothing, the agent said. Geraci picked Carmine. The Sicilian *soldato* told Geraci not to worry; he was as good as two men, any two.

A few days after that, Geraci was out in his office behind the pool, reading the same two-volume history of Roman warfare that had been defeating him off and on for seven years, when Charlotte knocked on the

door. "There was a call." She was ticked off. The longer they'd been married, the more she seemed to resent taking messages for him, especially from callers who didn't identify themselves. "Whoever it was, he wanted me to tell you that they're in. That's it. 'They're in.' Does that mean anything to you?"

"Yes." In Cuba, of course. And from where he sat it meant everything.

"How's that book coming?" she said.

"*Books*," Geraci said. "Two volumes. When's the last time you read anything that wasn't flashed up on a television screen? And as a matter of fact, I'm making headway."

It was still dark outside as Tom Hagen left the Palmer House and caught a cab to go see Louie Russo. Theresa was asleep in their hotel room upstairs. Later this morning she had a meeting at the Art Institute of Chicago—some kind of national museum board consortium. Tomorrow they'd drive over to South Bend, to see not just Andrew but also Frankie Corleone, Sonny's oldest kid, who was starting at middle linebacker for the Fighting Irish and had gotten them tickets for the last home game of the year, against Syracuse, Theresa's alma mater. Hagen had been looking forward to this weekend for a long time.

Hagen would have rather taken a limo, but he couldn't risk taking anything so prearranged. The cabbie was classic Chicago, spewing profanity and cheerful complaints about some sports team. Hagen had a lot on his mind. He'd had only two cups of coffee. He was sweating. He didn't feel nervous, and it wasn't hot in the car. Probably it had to do with his blood pressure, so high his doctor might not have been joking when he'd said that one day Hagen might just pop, like an engorged tick. The driver kept yapping. Hagen did nothing to discourage it. The more the guy talked, the less he'd remember his passenger.

Russo had a private supper club out in the sticks, almost in Wisconsin. Even against the flow of morning traffic, the drive took more than an hour. It seemed almost as long from the gate and across the expanse of parking lot to the club itself—a white barn made of painted cinder blocks. Though it didn't seem like much, this place managed to book singers like Johnny Fontane, all the top comics, even the Ice Capades. A sign over the door read HECTOR SANTIAGO, THE KING OF RUMBA! The shows were never advertised but always sold out. Next to the barn was a square pond about the size of four city blocks and surrounded by pine trees. The water was barely visible and black as tar. On the other side of the pond was a nondescript, windowless, three-story warehouse that had been converted

into a casino. At night, gondoliers poled guests back and forth across the pond. Russo was unduly proud of the place; by all accounts, it was impossible to come see him here on business and leave without getting a tour of his precious casino. Even so, Hagen had to admire the amount of work that had gone into bribing all the cops it would have taken so that Louie Russo's customers could arrive at his illegal gambling joint right out in the open, in something as slow as a gondola.

Behind the club, an old farmhouse had been expanded and converted into a guesthouse. Russo kept an office in the biggest room upstairs. To get there, Hagen had to go through some kind of metal-detecting device and then though a steel door, the kind they have on bank vaults. As Hagen expected, two of Russo's goons sat in an outer room, each with a tommy gun across his lap. One got up, gave him a lazy search, and waved him into his boss's lair.

"If it ain't the world's only Mick *consigliere*!" Russo said. He had on a pair of diamond cuff links. "What an honor."

Hagen thanked him and sat down in the offered seat. Russo remained standing, a crude and petty assertion of control.

"Michael Corleone," Hagen said, "is prepared to support you as *capo di tutti capi* and to resign his seat on the Commission, which will go to Nick Geraci, so long as you and I can reach an understanding on a few small matters."

"Hey, you hear this guy?' Russo called down the hall to the men with guns. "Listen, Irish. Where I come from, we don't get fucked without first we get kissed. Get my meaning?"

Hagen did. "I'm German-Irish," he corrected. "And I meant no offense, Don Russo. I know you're a busy man, and I thought you'd appreciate it if I got right to the point."

"Coffee? Shit, where are my manners? How about a cocktail, Irish?"

"Coffee's perfect," Hagen said. It was from a percolator, but it would have to do. "Thank you."

Russo frowned. "Hey, are you okay? Because it ain't hot in here."

"I'm fine."

"My ma used to say being *fine* is more a decision than a condition."

"Smart woman."

"Yeah, well, you look like either you're scared out of your wits or else you got some kind of whatchacallit. Tropical fever. Like from the jungles. Hey, boys?" he called. "My Mick friend in here could maybe use a towel."

"All I need is coffee," Hagen said, downing the cup in two long swallows.

"Only person I ever had in here who sweated the way you are was wearing a wire."

"Is that right?"

Russo nodded.

Hagen raised his arms. "Search me," he said. "I don't mind."

Russo wasn't too proud—or respectful—to do it, either. Russo searched him. No wire, of course. Russo again motioned for Hagen to sit. Hagen paused, waiting for Russo to sit, too.

"A few small matters, eh?" Russo settled in behind his desk. "Like for instance what?"

From the small third-story balcony of a boarded-up library in downtown Cienfuegos, Carmine Marino loaded the Russian-made rifle he'd been set up to use and waited for the motorcade to come his way. He'd lost the two angry Cubans he'd come with the night they all landed. The only Spanish he spoke was corrupted Italian, but he managed to make his way across two hundred miles of a dictatorship to the two women spies who gave him the rest of his instructions. Carmine was naturally disappointed when he did not have hot sex with them in the dark and sultry Cuban night. Who ever heard of a female spy who didn't have sex with a dashing assassin such as himself? Why else *be* an assassin such as himself? There were *two* of them, and still nothing. It was confusing. Maybe they were dykes. Maybe he wasn't the man he thought he was. If he got out of this alive, he thought, he'd go back to that one-eyed Jew and tell him that if he knew what was good for him, he'd find the brave Carmine Marino a buxom, randy spy, and pronto. Carmine was nobody's fool. He knew that girls like that were out there.

The streets were lined with soldiers and cheering Cubans. As the motorcade approached, the sound the people made was oddly metallic, like a record of a cheering crowd played too loud and a little too fast. As a toddler in Sicily, Carmine had heard another despot, Mussolini, cheered this way.

Now the motorcade turned the corner by the cathedral and came toward him, a row of American cars, which was hilarious. These people hate the Americans, yet look. Carmine shouldered his rifle.

In the fourth car—a blue convertible, as promised—was the bearded target, in full military uniform, smiling beatifically and waving to his oppressed people.

Marino inhaled smoothly and squeezed the trigger.

The bearded man's head jerked backward. A shower of blood and gore arced over the trunk. The driver hit the gas.

Screams filled the air. Police waved the rest of the motorcade—including the black sedan two cars behind the convertible, in which the leader of Cuba was riding—down a side street and out of the city.

The man in the blue convertible, the dictator's favorite double, was dead.

Carmine Marino was captured on his way to Guantánamo Bay, dressed like a woman.

Louie Russo agreed to everything. The Corleones could, with no interference from Chicago, operate their hotels and casinos in Nevada. Atlantic City, too, if, as expected, things opened up there. Hagen admitted that Geraci's assassin squad operation was ultimately controlled by the Corleones, and Russo admitted, in so many words, that he controlled the ones run by Tramonti and Drago. They might be rivals, these Families, but they had more in common with one another than with the cynical opportunists at the CIA and in the White House.

After a brief discussion of the particulars, Russo agreed that if his people did the job in Cuba first, the Corleones could resume control of the Capri and the Sevilla Biltmore and operate them within the law and with no interference from Russo or any other organization—power Russo would certainly have once Michael helped make him the first formal boss of all bosses since the death of Vito Corleone seven years before.

Hagen himself would personally oversee the organization of the people on the Corleone payroll. Some of this operation would be gradually given to Nick Geraci, but it would also be available to Louie Russo on occasion and in consideration of his help in allowing Michael Corleone to become an entirely legitimate businessman.

Russo was so cooperative that it became increasingly clear to Tom Hagen that Fuckface didn't plan to let him out of here alive. It was something he and Michael had thought might happen. Knowing that a thing like that *might* happen is a world apart from feeling it edge closer to happening. The sweating hadn't slowed down. He'd have given a thousand bucks for a chance to shower and put on some dry clothes.

"This is a great day, Irish," Russo said. "We should celebrate. I'll join you, too, only I was kidding about the cocktail before. I don't have nothing here stronger than that coffee and the bad breath of those gentlemen out in the hall. The bar in the club there's all right, but the really top-shelf stuff, best selection in the state of Illinois, is right across Lake Louie there."

It wasn't even nine A.M.

"I appreciate that," Hagen said. "But tempting as it is, I need to be getting back."

"Aw, c'mon, Irish. You don't drink on it, it ain't a deal. On top of which, since you people are going to be in the legal casino business—I pity you the money you ain't gonna make, but no one asked you to go down

that road—anyway, you ought to get a last look at my establishment here, which at the risk of not being humble I have to say I'm proud of. It don't open up for a while yet, but—" Russo took off his black glasses. His eyes were solidly red with a green ring in the middle. He smiled.

The chill that went through Tom Hagen was not a result of the sweating and the air-conditioning, though that's what he told himself.

"—I know some people," Russo said. "Ever take a gondola ride?"

"Can't say I have," Hagen said.

Russo herded him out the door. The men with the tommy guns stood. "Get this," Russo said. "Irish here ain't ever been on a gondola ride. If that ain't one of those things a man ought to do before he dies, I'd like to know what is."

Joe Lucadello walked to the front door of Nick Geraci's house, in the middle of the night, and rang the bell. Geraci had fallen asleep in the chair in his den out back. Charlotte had taken a sleeping pill and was dead to the world. Barb was off at college. After several rings, Bev Geraci answered, but only through the intercom.

"Tell your father it's Ike Rosen."

"Will he know what this is about?"

"Sure, why not?"

"What happened to your eye?" she asked. "Is that real?"

"It is. It's from a war wound."

"I don't believe you," Bev said.

Lucadello flipped the eye patch up. Even through the peephole, the absence of an eyeball was gory enough to make the girl scream and run away. Lucadello sighed, sat down on the porch steps, and waited for the police to come. That was another brilliant thing these people had worked out. The police functioned as their private security force, and other people—civilians—would summon them when needed.

Two squad cars responded. Cops piled out of them, guns drawn. Lucadello raised his hands. He provided them with his Ike Rosen driver's license and told them he was in the import-export business with Mr. Geraci. He was there at such an ungodly hour only because of an unfortunate customs incident. By then, the commotion had awakened Nick Geraci, who thanked the cops and calmed his daughter down. Then he and the agent went back out to his den.

Lucadello sat down on one of the seats Geraci had salvaged from the wreckage of Ebbets Field and gave Geraci the news about Carmine.

"Rest assured," Geraci said, "whatever they do to him, that kid's not going to talk."

"Whether he talks may be the least of your problems."

"Oh yeah?" Geraci wasn't sure what the agent was talking about, but his choice of pronouns—*your problems,* not *our problems*—didn't bode well.

"The Cuban government would be nuts to torture him. They'd be nuts to do anything but make a big fuss about this foreign national who tried to kill their bearded, beloved revolutionary sweetheart. The Russians will be on their side. The U.N. will get dragged in. When they deport him, there won't be anything for us to do but put him in jail, maybe execute him."

"Don't worry about it," Geraci said. "Carmine Marino's still an Italian citizen. If they send him back there, he's got a pretty powerful godfather."

Lucadello shook his head. "You don't understand. *We* need to execute him a long time before any of that happens. But that's just where your problems start, I'm afraid."

Geraci would be goddamned if he was going to let this one-eyed bastard kill him in his own backyard. "Stand up," Geraci said. "I need to search you."

"Suit yourself. But if I wanted to kill you, you'd be dead. And if you waste precious time on things like this, you may wind up that way."

Geraci searched him anyway and liberated him of a gun and two knives.

"Keep 'em with my compliments," Lucadello said. "I'm on your side, remember?"

Geraci motioned for him to sit back down. "It's late. I was sleeping. Forgive me if I'm confused about why this is my problem and not yours, too."

"Oh, it's mine, too. Look, I've already heard from somebody at the top—not my boss but his—that the FBI knows about the camp Tramonti was operating in Jacksonville. They already had an investigation going. I'd heard a rumor floating around that the Bureau was somehow tipped off to our operation, too, but it didn't seem credible. But after this incident, it doesn't matter. The risk of someone at the Bureau putting it all together is high."

"And you can't protect me from that? There's nothing you can do?"

"Very little, under these circumstances," he said. "I'd like to kill those guys."

"Kill 'em, then," Geraci said. "I'm not stopping you."

"Unfortunately," Lucadello said, "that's not an option. It wouldn't solve everything for you anyway. We have reliable intelligence that your former associate Michael Corleone has been planning to kill you. The only

thing he's been waiting for was for you to do this job. Now that you're not going to get it done at all, we believe your life is in immediate danger. In addition, we have somewhat less reliable intelligence that Louie Russo is planning to kill you as well, apparently because . . . well, I don't know how everything works for you people, but apparently there's some sort of Commission?"

Geraci shrugged. "Never heard of it."

"Of course not. At any rate, everything Russo's doing had their approval and unfortunately your operation didn't. Apparently that's a breach of protocol severe enough for them to authorize . . . well, we're not certain who. Presumably Mr. Russo. To kill you, that is. You're not shaking."

"It comes and goes."

"If something like this was happening with me, I'd be shaking."

"It's a type of Parkinson's. Not fear. It has nothing to do with fear. And anyway, how do you know something like this *isn't* happening with you?"

"Oh, I'm sure it's happening," he said. "At any rate, things are going to move fast, and you need to move faster."

"Not we?"

"No," Lucadello said. "Not *we*. We never had anything to do with anything. You and I have never met. There is no *we*. There is no me, either. Agent Ike Rosen doesn't exist."

Lucadello said that the best he could do was get Nick Geraci and his family out of there. One-way tickets under assumed names, to any destination on earth. It might be possible to have an agent meet them at the airport and give them some quick pointers about starting a new life in wherever they happened to be. This wouldn't be possible everywhere, but if Geraci wanted to run a few locations by him, he could probably say if they were a good choice.

Geraci looked at the gun on his desk. It would have been nice to kill the guy. It might not make anything worse than it was.

Then, in a flash, almost a vision, he saw his way out of this, or at least how to buy some time.

"All right," Geraci said, extending his hand, consciously imitating his godfather, Vincent Forlenza. "Four things. First"—index finger—"I'm going to Sicily. I don't need your people. I *have* people. Second"—middle finger—"I don't fly. Period. But you're going to help me get where I want to go, and my family, too, if they'll join me, which I doubt. Third"—ring finger—"I promise you, my good friend Michael Corleone isn't going to kill me, so you might want to check into your reliable intelligence and see what went wrong. And fourth"—pinkie—"I'd strongly advise you not to kill Carmine Marino or to have him killed."

"Three out of four we can do. As for Carmine, I love him, too. He didn't do anything wrong. He went where he was supposed to, he made a great shot at the target we told him to hit, and he was smart enough to swallow his manly pride and dress like a woman and try to escape that way. If it was up to me, I'd hire him, but . . . well, all I can say is that it's out of our hands."

Geraci smiled. "Carmine's mother's maiden name was Bocchicchio."

Even after he explained about the peerless, weirdly mercenary ability of the Bocchicchio clan to exact revenge, Lucadello was unmoved.

"So who are they going to come after, huh?" Lucadello said. "The United States government?"

Geraci shook his head. "They'll take it personally."

"Meaning what? Me? Or wait, I know! They'll go after the president!"

Abruptly, Geraci started shaking. To steady himself, he crossed the room, grabbed a fistful of Lucadello's shirt, and pulled him to his feet. "Carmine's still alive," he whispered. "Keep him that way, and they won't come after anybody."

Only one gondolier was at work this early, but the gondolas were large. There was plenty of room. As Hagen expected, Russo's men took their tommy guns on board.

"Don't look like that, Irish," Louie Russo said, taking a seat at the front. "I know you ain't on the muscle side of things. Hell, you people aren't even gonna *have* no muscle side of things. Anyhow, loosen up. Take it from me, you'll live longer."

The gunmen found this pretty funny. The gondolier averted his eyes and didn't say anything. He began poling them across the fetid, man-made pond. Finally, he and Hagen made eye contact. Almost imperceptibly, the gondolier nodded.

Hagen had stopped sweating. A sense of peace washed over him. Russo was telling the story of how he had gotten this place, but Hagen wasn't listening. He studied the tree-lined shore, anticipating the moment they'd get to the halfway point across, bending over enough that no one would notice him unbuckling his belt.

Halfway across, the gondolier brought his pole out of the water. He'd made tens of thousands of trips across this pond, and it had given him forearms a pile driver might envy. As Hagen straightened up and yanked off his belt, the gondolier swung the pole, unleashing the pent-up anger of a man who'd spent years wanting to do this to every self-important ass-hole who'd ridden in his gondola. It connected with the skull of one of the gunmen.

The other whipped around, but before he could get off a shot, he was jerked backward. Tom Hagen's belt dug into his neck.

The gondolier grabbed the first dead man's gun and trained it on Louie Russo.

The second man kicked and turned purple. Hagen felt his windpipe rupture. The man went still. Tom shoved him to the floor of the boat.

Russo started to jump, to try to swim for it, but before he got out of the boat the gondolier grabbed him by the back of the shirt and held him fast. His sunglasses fell into the water.

The tiny-fingered Don started to cry. "I gave you everything you wanted. Now this?"

"Don't insult me," Hagen said. He fished a .22 with a silencer out of the coat pocket of the man he'd killed. The assassin's tool of choice. His arms tingled from the effort it had taken to garrote a man. "You were going to kill me," Hagen said, waving the gun in front of Russo.

"You're crazy," Russo whimpered. "That's just a gun. It don't mean nothin'."

"Even if you weren't, I don't care. You gave Roth the idea of getting Fredo to betray the Family, and you set it all up with your people in L.A. You've done a hundred other things that give me cause to kill you."

"*You?*" Russo's tears muted the effect of his devilish eyes. Snot ran freely from his phallic nose. "Kill *me*? You're not in this side of the *business,* Irish. You were a fucking congressman. You think they're gonna let you make your bones, Irish? You're *Irish.*"

Tom Hagen's whole adult life, everyone had gotten him wrong. He was first and foremost a poor Irish kid from the streets. He'd lived under bushes and in tunnels for an entire New York winter and won fistfights with grown men over half a loaf of moldy bread. Hagen raised the pistol. Now it was his turn to smile.

"If you live in the wolf's den long enough," Hagen said, "you learn to howl."

He fired. The bullet tore into Russo's brain, ricocheted around in his skull, and did not make an exit wound, the way a bigger-caliber bullet would have.

Hagen tossed the gun into the pond.

He and the gondolier quickly, silently tied weights to the three dead men and threw them overboard. No one saw them. The gondolier took Hagen back to shore and went to work scouring the boat with a bleach solution. He didn't see any blood, but it paid (well) to play it safe. Hagen drove away in Louie Russo's own car. The gondolier would swear on the immortal soul of his sainted mother that he'd seen Russo's car drive away.

The car was found two days later in the airport parking lot. The newspapers reported that passengers with any of several aliases known to have been used by Louie the Face had boarded planes that day. None of these leads had turned up an actual person.

The gunmen had been loyal, trusted Russo *soldatos*, men it would have been difficult if not impossible for the Corleones to bribe. This gondolier, on the other hand, made less in a year than what Louie Russo's cuff links cost. Russo and his men were found a month later. They were hardly the only corpses there, either. The acidic pond accelerated decomposition. When the state police had it drained and the top layer of mud excavated, they found bones galore, most of them in weighted gunnysacks, suitcases, and oil drums.

By then the gondolier had disappeared.

Neither the authorities nor anyone from the Chicago outfit ever found him. He lived out his days under a different name in a small town in Nevada, running a gun shop and private cemetery on land purchased (with other people's money) from the federal government, only twenty miles from the windy, irradiated outskirts of Doomtown.

Joe Lucadello called from a pay phone less than a mile from Geraci's house and told Michael Corleone everything. The lie he'd told about Russo, the truth he'd told about Michael. The details about the ship that would take Geraci to Sicily. Alone. His wife and kids weren't going with him, which ought to make things even easier.

"Sorry we didn't get it done down there," Lucadello said, meaning Cuba. "I know you were counting on it."

"We've lived to fight another day," Michael said. "What more can a person ask of life?"

"Quite a bit," Joe said. "But only if you're young."

At his mansion in Chagrin Falls, Vincent Forlenza awoke in the dark barely able to breathe, with the familiar and excruciating sensation of an elephant standing on his chest. He managed to ring the bell for his nurse. He knew a heart attack when he had one. It wasn't his first, and with any luck it wouldn't be the last, either. It wasn't as bad as the others. More like a baby elephant. Though maybe he was just getting used to it.

The nurse called for an ambulance. She did what she could and told him he'd be fine. She wasn't a cardiologist, but she meant what she said. His vital signs were good, considering.

Vincent Forlenza was a cautious man. God seemed to be having a hard time killing him, and he'd be damned if he was going to make the job easy for mere mortals. His estate here and his lodge on Rattlesnake Island were heavily guarded and fortified. It had been years since Forlenza had gotten into a car or boat without his men checking it thoroughly for bombs. Ordinarily, he had two guys do the job who were known to dislike each other, so they'd each be eager to catch the other betraying his Don. He'd stopped eating anything that wasn't prepared as he watched. But even Don Forlenza, in his hour of medical need, wouldn't have thought to question the men who arrived to save his life. Neither did anyone guarding the estate. Neither did the nurse, who noticed nothing unusual in the way the men administered to the old man. There was nothing unusual about the ambulance, either—until it left and, moments later, another one just like it showed up.

The first ambulance was found the next day, a block from where it had been stolen. Vincent "the Jew" Forlenza was never seen again.

In the family section of the stadium, Tom and Theresa Hagen and their handsome son Andrew rose for the playing of the national anthem. Tom clamped his hand over his breast and found himself singing along.

"You usually just mutter," Theresa said.

"This is such a great country," Tom said. "No one should ever just mutter."

Frankie Corleone was the smallest man on the entire Notre Dame defense, but on the first play from scrimmage, he shot through the line and hit the Syracuse Orangemen's gigantic fullback so hard his head snapped back and his body followed. The crowd went wild, but Frankie jogged back to the huddle like he hadn't done anything unusual.

"Frankie!" Andrew shouted.

"My nephew!" Theresa said.

Tom and Theresa hugged each other, and the fullback made it off the field without the need of a stretcher.

On the next play, Syracuse tried to pass. The receiver was wide open over the middle. Just as the ball got there, Frankie came out of nowhere and batted the ball away.

"Woo-hoo!" Theresa yelled. "Go, Frankie!"

"The Hit Man!" Tom shouted. It was his nephew's nickname. He didn't allow himself to give it a second thought.

"Aren't you supposed to be cheering for Syracuse, Ma?" Andrew teased her.

It was a perfect November day for football, crisp and struggling to be

sunny. Everyone should see a football game at Notre Dame. The Golden Dome. Touchdown Jesus.

"This is different," she said. "This is family."

In the Palermo harbor, Michael Corleone sat on the deck of a yacht belonging to his father's old friend Cesare Indelicato. Michael had never traveled with as many men for security as he had on this trip, but Don Cesare had not taken offense. They were living in troubled times.

Michael settled in now, comfortable that he would not suffer a double cross, willing to risk the recklessness of being only a few hundred meters away from Geraci when he arrived in Sicily for the satisfaction of watching him taken from the boat by the best assassins in Sicily.

Michael would have to return to New York. Other than Hagen, the best people the Corleone Family had left posed unacceptable risks because of their ties to Geraci. The next best people were mediocrities like Eddie Paradise and the DiMiceli brothers. Michael would have to run the Family again, every aspect of it. He'd be able to make it look as if he were returning in triumph, he was certain—the elimination of Louie Russo and Vince Forlenza would see to that, at least in the eyes of the top men from the other New York Families. But so much of what Michael had wanted— legitimacy, peace, the love of his wife and children, a life different and better than the one his father lived—was now beyond his reach: for years, perhaps forever.

The terrible sting of this would not go away by killing Geraci. He knew that.

There was no pleasure to be taken from such a thing. He knew that, too.

Still.

As they waited, Don Cesare—in his brilliantly indirect Sicilian way— was discussing the benefits of membership in a Roman Masonic organization, the name of which, *Propaganda Due,* he did not utter but which was understood between these men. P2, as it was usually called (though Indelicato did not say this either), was a secret society rumored to be more powerful than the Mafia, the Vatican, the CIA, and the KGB put together. Michael was being proposed for membership, and if all went well, he would be the first American admitted. Not even his father had been considered for this. It was a sign that, even in the wake of the Carmine Marino debacle, the true powers understood that Michael Corleone was destined to resume this role as the most dominant force in the American underworld. Any other man in Michael's position would have been flattered, and he gamely pretended to be just that.

Finally the ship came into view. Michael sipped a glass of ice water and kept his eyes on the men Indelicato had positioned at the foot of the pier.

The ship docked.

The passengers gradually disembarked.

There was no sign of Nick Geraci.

Indelicato nodded to a man on the roof of the yacht, who waved an orange flag, signaling the men on shore to board the ship and look for their target.

"They'll find him," said Don Cesare. "They're good men, and he has nowhere to go."

But soon the ship-to-shore radio crackled with bad news. Their target had apparently eluded them.

Enraged, Michael used the radio to call the United States.

He was unable to reach Joe Lucadello, but his assistant assured Michael that nothing had gone wrong. They'd had to use several layers of intermediaries to conceal the man's identity, but the assistant assured him that, unless the guy jumped off somewhere in the Mediterranean, he was on that ship. "I assure you it was him," the assistant said. "I have the paperwork right in front of me. Fausto Geraci. Passport, pictures, everything."

Whistling a tune his Palermitan mother sang him as a little boy, Fausto Geraci, Sr., disappeared under the ancient stone arch near the dock, into what was once the walled city of Palermo.

Cesare Indelicato professed to be as flummoxed by the situation as Michael was.

Chapter 31

Michael Corleone's phone rang in the middle of the night. He was still jet-lagged from the punishingly long trip home from Palermo.

"Sorry to wake you, Uncle Mike. It's just . . . there's been an accident."

He could never tell Francesca and Kathy apart, on the phone or in person.

"Francie!" Kathy Corleone called from the kitchen. She had Billy's typewriter and several neat piles of books set up on Francesca's kitchen table —which, only hours after her train arrived in D.C., she'd already commandeered so she could work on her dissertation. "Phone!"

"Who is it?" Francesca asked. She was giving Sonny a haircut on a chair in the bathroom.

From Kathy's lips came words Francesca and Billy had agreed would never be spoken in this apartment, the name of the tall blond whore from Floridians for Shea.

Francesca dropped her scissors. For a crazed moment, she was furious with her sister for this cruel joke, but of course it was no joke. Kathy didn't even know Billy had had an affair. "Don't move," she told Sonny. "Stay right there."

The boy must have heard something in his mother's voice. He froze.

For most of their lives, Kathy and Francesca had known the most trivial details of each other's lives. When had that changed? It wasn't just going away to different colleges, Francesca thought, standing over the black telephone in her bedroom, blood roaring in her ears. *Boys,* she thought. *Men.* What of life's biggest problems are caused by anything else? Francesca wanted to go back into the bathroom, lock the door, take her son in her arms, and hold him tight, willing him not to become one of those charming, selfish sociopaths.

Instead, she stopped stalling, took a deep breath, and picked up the phone.

"I'm sorry to call you at your home." The voice of That Woman

sounded as if she'd just stopped crying. It also didn't sound long distance. "This isn't easy for me."

"Where are you?" Francesca said.

"Look, it would have been easier for me not to call than to call," the woman said. "Much easier. I'm only trying to do what's right."

"You're a little late for that, you whore," Francesca said. "Don't lie to me and tell me you're not in Washington."

"I have no intention of lying," she said. "I wouldn't put myself through this for anything but the truth."

Francesca resisted the urge to hang up. Instinctively, she knew that whatever the woman was about to say, it was something Francesca should hear, and wouldn't want to. "Hold on," she said. She put her hand over the mouthpiece and asked Kathy if she'd go finish up Sonny's haircut. Francesca closed and locked her bedroom door. She slammed the heel of her hand against the plaster wall. She put a hole in it. Kathy called out to see if she was okay. Francesca lied and said she was. She picked up the phone and sat down. "Now talk," Francesca said. She covered her eyes with her throbbing right hand as if avoiding the sight of a dead dog on the road.

"To begin with," the woman said, "you're right. I'm in Washington. I work in a congressman's office. When I first moved here, it wasn't for Billy, it was for this job, but—"

"Do you really think," Francesca said, "that *you* have the right to cry about this?"

The woman regained her composure and succinctly confessed. She and Billy had started up again not long after Francesca had lost the baby. They'd been at it off and on until lately, when Billy had gotten her pregnant and been so casual about her getting an abortion that she'd gone ahead with it. She was having a hard time living with herself, though, and had decided to quit her job and move back home to Sarasota.

Francesca clenched her teeth and pressed her swelling hand firmly against the bedpost, trying to use pain to keep the rage that was rising in her from exploding. *Not yet. Don't give this whore the satisfaction.*

The woman said she was calling from her office. She and Billy had gone to a hotel at Dupont Circle on their lunch hour. There—what does it matter how it had happened?—whatever they'd had had come to a tearful end. She claimed that Billy had cried as much as she had.

"Feel better, do you?" Francesca said between her clenched teeth. "Can you live with yourself now?" She was shaking. If she'd been in the same room with this woman, it would have been nothing to kill her. Knock her down and stomp her pretty skull until it popped like a grape. Better yet, thrust a butcher knife through her heart.

"Not really," the woman said. "Listen, say anything to me you want. I deserve it. I really don't—" More tears. "I mean, I'm not the sort of person who—"

"Bad people," Francesca said, "never think they're the sort of person who did the things they did. I've got news for you, you whore. You're not what you think you are. None of us are. You're what you did, nothing more. You act like a whore, you're a whore. I have to go."

"Wait, don't," the woman said. "There's something else I have to tell you. As bad as what I already said, this might be even worse. *I* think it's even worse."

"You don't impress me as someone who knows the difference between good and bad."

"It's about your family."

"I know that look," Kathy said. "Don't think I don't know that look."

"Help me bandage my hand," Francesca said.

"You need to see a doctor," Kathy said. "What happened that—"

"Help me."

After years of petty conflict and drifting affection, the sisters felt a shock of understanding shoot through them. They'd had their differences the past few years, but the bond they had as twins never went anywhere. Summoned, it obeyed. There is nothing more complicated and less so than family, nothing easier to understand and at the same time unknowable. With twins, that all goes double.

Francesca didn't explain any of the particulars to Kathy, yet Kathy understood what she needed to understand. She helped Francesca with her hand, helped her get dressed, listened to her instructions about Sonny (*get dinner at Eastern Market Lunch, he loves that, loves the market, too, but dress warm, it's supposed to snow later tonight*). Kathy tried to soothe her but not counterproductively so.

Francesca kissed Sonny and grabbed the keys to Billy's Dual-Ghia. They had only one car (though it cost more than two nice ones), and *of course* it was his, the selfish prick, a big fancy custom-built thing he was ordinarily reluctant to let her drive. At least he'd left it for her today so she could go pick up Kathy at the train station.

"Don't do anything I wouldn't do," Kathy called as Francesca slammed the apartment door behind her.

"Maybe I *am* you," Francesca shouted back.

When she got there, since only Billy himself was allowed to use the parking garage, she had to circle round and round the building, looking for a space. Her tightly wrapped hand throbbed. Pain shot through it each

time she had to shift. The pain wasn't exactly unpleasant. It was somehow keeping her from crying. The last thing she wanted to allow herself to do was cry.

She banged her unbandaged fist on the leather-wrapped wheel, trying to quell her anger. It only made it worse. *You are what you do, nothing more.* Francesca was disgusted to be the kind of person who'd look for a legal parking space at a time like this. She growled, feral as a cornered wolf, and whipped the car into an empty space in a loading zone.

She strode but did not run up the steps to the Department of Justice.

"I'm sorry, Mrs. Van Arsdale," said the receptionist in Billy's office. "Mr. Van Arsdale is in an off-site meeting with the attorney general. I don't expect them back until tomorrow."

Which Francesca knew. She was supposed to meet Billy at a bar he and his friends from work liked, down by the river in Georgetown, then go out for dinner and a movie. "Billy needed some files," Francesca said. "He forgot them. He told me right where to look."

The next thing Francesca knew, she was alone in Billy's office, going where the whore had told her to go, looking where the whore had told her to look: in the backmost file in the top drawer. The file was thick and battered; the handwritten label—Billy's handwriting—read *Insurance.*

Francesca couldn't be seen going through it, not there. She tucked it under her arm, thanked the receptionist, and left. She went back to the car. It had not been towed. It had not been ticketed. A good omen, she thought, with no sincere hope it would be.

Inside the folder, as the whore had promised, was information about her family. Newspaper clippings that anyone might have kept, but from papers all over the country. Hundreds of carefully arranged and catalogued snapshots, including quite a few Francesca had taken with her own camera, even before Billy had met her: photos of everyone in her family, but especially those on her father's side. There was the picture of her uncles and grandfather at Aunt Connie's wedding that used to be on their dresser and had supposedly been lost in one of their moves. There were four notebooks, the same kind Francesca had been required to use for her freshman English themes, filled with notes about her family, and a several-page typewritten summary of the contents of those notebooks. She tried to figure out when he'd started doing this. The first began in December 1955, the day after they first made love. It wasn't about that; it was everything that happened at Grandma Carmela's house, not a journal of any sort, but notes, as if from a class. They weren't faked. There were things in there only Billy could have known, rendered in handwriting that was unmistakably his (right down to the cursive-style capital *A*'s and *M*'s that he'd used then and replaced with printed style a few years later).

Can't you see Billy's just here to experience a gen-u-ine Mafia Christmas?

Billy *told* his whore blonde from Sarasota that he had this file. He probably *showed* it to her. They probably had a good laugh about it, naked in a hotel room overlooking Dupont Circle.

Dizzy, she collapsed, falling sideways against the gearshift and not caring. She let herself cry. That made nothing better. She wanted to *do* something, not sit in her cheating husband's fancy car, crying like some helpless woman.

She was *not* some helpless woman.

She was a Corleone.

She was the daughter of a great warrior king, Santino Corleone.

By the time she noticed she was murmuring "Daddy, help me" over and over, she'd been doing it awhile.

A Capitol Police traffic cop stopped to write her a ticket, but when Francesca sat up—her face contorted in anguish, her hair and eyes wild—the cop put the summons book away. He looked like he'd seen a ghost. He turned and walked the other way, shaking his head.

In a dark parking lot down by the Potomac River, Francesca waited in her husband's red car, watching the bar across the street, where she was supposed to meet Billy. She'd been there for a long time, long enough to read every speculation, half-truth, and condescending comment in that hateful file. She wasn't wearing a watch, and the clock in the Ghia kept lousy time. There had been a handful of aspirin in her purse (next to the kitchen knife, a wedding present from Fredo Corleone and Deanna Dunn), but they'd worn off. Her hand was throbbing worse than ever. But the emotional and physical pain were working together to keep her from passing out, the way two deadly poisons in the bloodstream can keep a person alive.

Maybe an hour ago, Billy had gone into the bar with several other young lawyers. He hadn't seen her. If he had, they'd have probably had this out already. She wouldn't really have used that knife (would she?), and she wasn't above making a scene. But she couldn't bring herself to do it. Every moment since then, she'd been a moment away from getting out of the car. She would have, she thought, if she knew what she was going to do or even what she wanted.

She kept going back and forth between wishing she hadn't brought the knife at all and fearing that she couldn't possibly do this with her left hand.

She kept thinking about her tough and funny little boy, which made her alternately more and then less inclined to act.

She kept thinking that if only she could calm down, she'd think better.

She realized, now, that this was as absurd as thinking that if only her father were here for her, her whole life would be different and better.

She thought she might soften when she saw Billy again, but when he finally came out of the bar, alone and unsteady on his feet, turning up the collar of his coat against the cold, the opposite happened.

Insurance.

Her heart raced. Her hand hurt so badly she whimpered like a dying animal. Billy turned the corner and started up a steep, narrow cobblestone alley toward M Street. She knew what he was doing. He was a rich boy who'd bought this fancy car because it was what Johnny Fontane, Bobby Chadwick, and Danny Shea drove, but he was also too cheap to hail a cab if it meant having to ride around an unnecessary block. On M Street, he'd be able to get one that wouldn't have to turn around.

Francesca turned on the ignition. It was a fast car, that Dual-Ghia, one of the fastest made. A perfect hybrid of Italian engineering and American flamboyance.

In the blink of an eye and a few agonizing thrusts of the gearshift, Francesca had it rocketing up that alley.

Billy turned, shielding his eyes from the glare of the headlights. She braced her arms against the big, faux-wood steering wheel. Billy was directly in front of her. There was a split-second flash of what might have been a smile, and she hit him. On impact, his shoes exploded off his feet, his legs buckled, his torso whipped forward, and his head slammed into the hood as hard as if he'd dove from ten stories above. The car fishtailed but kept going. She slowed down but did not slam on the brakes. Billy stayed on the hood as if he were imbedded there.

Francesca grabbed the folder and jumped out of the car. She closed the door as if nothing unusual had just happened and, without hesitating, walked away from the car.

She wasn't hurt. No one seemed to have seen her. The only thing she felt was awe. She wasn't screaming or crying. She'd had the mental strength to go through with this and the physical strength to brace herself against the wheel, even with a badly injured hand. The hand was killing her now, but on impact she hadn't felt a thing.

About fifty yards from the wreck she saw one of his shoes but didn't even break stride.

She told herself not to look. But as she was about to turn onto M Street, she couldn't help but look back.

From the top of the hill, the damage to the car didn't look bad at all. Billy was still on the hood, motionless. A pool of blood was spreading

across the cobblestones. At first she couldn't tell where all that blood was coming from, until she realized that his legs were not crumpled underneath the front bumper. Far behind the car, under the alley's lone streetlight, lay the severed bottom half of his body.

She felt no remorse whatsoever.

The walk home might have taken her a minute or a day, Francesca couldn't have said. All the way home, enduring the pain in her hand and the almost as severe pain from the lurches her heart made every time she heard a siren, she didn't look behind her, not once.

Kathy was at the table, lost in her writing, and Sonny was asleep in his room.

Francesca sat heavily down on the sofa.

"Did Billy call?"

"I don't know," Kathy said, not looking up. "I unplugged the phone to work. I hope you weren't worried. Sonny was a blast. A doll. Everything went great. How's your hand?"

"Remember when I found out Billy was cheating on me, and you said I should kill him? Well, I did it."

Kathy started to laugh, then looked closer at her sister and, eyes wide, stifled it. She rushed over to the sofa. "Oh, my God, you—"

"Look at this," Francesca said, extending the folder to her sister.

"Tell me everything," Kathy said. "Tell me everything *fast*."

The police showed up about an hour after Francesca did, maybe five minutes after Kathy got on the bus that would take her to Union Station and the night's last train back to New York. There was no trace of her in Francesca's apartment. Kathy hadn't even told her mother and her mother's fiancé, Stan the Liquor Man, that she'd gone to Washington for fear Sandra would immediately start laying on the guilt about how long it had been since Kathy had come to see them in Florida.

When the police gave Francesca the news, she ran down the hall to her bedroom, screaming in not-quite-mock hysteria. She hit the wall with the palm of her left hand—hard but of course not hard enough to hurt anything. Still, the noise it made was convincing. When they caught up to her, there was a hole in the wall and Francesca's hand was, in their opinion, broken and starting to swell. The ice that had in fact just brought the swelling down dramatically had been flushed down the toilet.

Miraculously, Sonny slept through all of this. After the police left, and after the doctor sent over by Danny Shea's secretary left, too, Francesca

unplugged the telephone and stood over her son's bed and watched him sleep, his golden football helmet on the pillow beside him.

She would have to tell him. She would call Kathy in New York, and Kathy would call everyone else: their mother, even Billy's brother and his parents. But Francesca would, somehow, have to shoulder the burden of telling Sonny.

She went back out to the kitchen and took the file out from behind her pots and pans, where she'd hidden it. She paged through it again, marveling that anyone would betray his own family like this. And for what? His career? He was rich. Francesca's family had connections. Her family could have *been* Billy's insurance.

Francesca knew what it was to grow up without a father. She did not know what it was like to grow up with a father who was willing to destroy his own family.

She still felt no remorse.

For now, she'd tell Sonny that Daddy had had an accident and was in Heaven with baby Carmela. But someday, she vowed, she'd tell the boy the truth.

She plugged the phone back in and called Kathy to tell her what had happened. As part of the plan she'd worked out a few hours before, Kathy had told Francesca to betray nothing on the phone, in case Billy had had them bugged. Kathy and Francesca had a fake conversation about what happened and a real one about who Kathy should call.

It was getting close to dawn. It would be late in Nevada now, too. Even so, Francesca called. He'd want to know.

"Sorry to wake you, Uncle Mike. It's just . . . there's been an accident."

The next day—as Kathy had predicted—the secretary at Billy's office mentioned that Francesca had come by to get a file for Billy. There was nothing incriminating or unusual about this. She hadn't left the office angry or distraught. Billy had several different files at home, and Francesca produced them. The one marked *Insurance* was a personal file of Billy's. No one outside her immediate family ever asked to see it.

Francesca's whereabouts after the trip to the Justice Department were easy to prove. The counter people at Eastern Market Lunch said that of course they'd seen Francesca and little Sonny there the night before.

The people in the apartment upstairs said they'd seen Francesca and Sonny come home not long after dark. For at least two hours after that there had been typing coming steadily from below.

Francesca confirmed this. She said that she'd been writing a letter to

her sister in New York, which she'd mailed not long before the police arrived. She said this in the presence of the best criminal defense lawyer in New York (an arrangement quietly made by Tom Hagen). A few days later, Kathy (by now ably represented by the same lawyer) said she'd received the letter but had thrown it away. As several friends and relatives (including their mother, Sandra) could and did attest, the twins had grown apart in recent years. One happy consequence of this unhappy story would be the way it served to bring the twins together again, as close as they'd ever been.

The steering wheel and gearshift of the Dual-Ghia seemed to have been wiped of fingerprints (the effect of Francesca's Ace bandage, actually). Still, detectives identified four sets of prints. Three came from the members of the family for which this was the only car—Billy, Francesca, and Sonny Van Arsdale (Kathy had both kept her gloves on for the short drive from Union Station to her sister's apartment and remembered that she'd kept them on). The fourth set—found in both the front seat and back—came from a woman with whom Billy Van Arsdale had had an ongoing affair.

The police were able to find several people who'd seen this woman on the very afternoon of Billy's death, checking into a hotel on Dupont Circle and leaving in tears approximately ninety minutes later. The woman had confessed to several people in her office that Billy had ended his relationship with her that day. Several months before, she'd confessed to many of these same friends that Billy had impregnated her and coerced her into having an abortion.

When detectives questioned her about this, she was openly distraught. They arrested her and charged her with second-degree murder.

BOOK IX
Summer 1962

Chapter 32

CARMINE MARINO'S ARREST turned out to be the international incident that everyone involved with his trip to Cuba had feared.

The scope of what the CIA was trying to do in Cuba came as a shock to President Shea. Publicly, he made it clear that the United States would cooperate in any way it could to bring Marino, an Italian national, to justice (for its part, the Italian government said that it had several Carmine Marinos on record, but none matching the description of the notorious killer). Marino had been living in the United States for six years. The Cuban dictator said that he held President Shea personally responsible. The Soviet premier issued no public statement on the matter, but he did come to Havana for the double's lavish funeral.

Privately, President Shea spent many long hours meeting with his national security team and screaming at his CIA director. But before the president got the chance to confront his father with his suspicions of the old man's involvement in the matter, the Ambassador had a massive stroke. He'd live for several more years, but he'd had his last conversation.

Marino's affiliation with what the newspapers had never stopped calling "the Corleone crime family" was easy enough to document. Even the papers still controlled by the Family had little choice but to follow suit with their competitors and investigate the many rumors that the young gangster had not acted alone.

In public, the attorney general scoffed at any notion of a connection between the federal government and what he was now calling "the Mafia." In a private meeting with his staff, he unveiled an aggressive new plan to prosecute organized crime. Billy Van Arsdale was irreplaceable, he told them, but their efforts would be dedicated to his memory.

The FBI director had not forgotten his meeting with Tom Hagen many years before, when the future congressman had produced that grainy black-and-white image of the director on his knees, fellating his top assistant. His current situation gave grimly comic new meaning to being caught between a rock and a hard place. Still, the director had no choice, for now, but to go along with the attorney general's bold initiative.

At the United Nations, the usual sorts of intermediaries—small coun-

tries with good educational systems and disbanded armies—were dispatched to conduct negotiations to deport or extradite Carmine Marino either to the supposed country of his birth or to the United States, where he'd been months away from becoming a citizen. At minimum, the negotiators wanted to ensure that Marino was given a swift and fair trial in Cuba. The Cuban government made a big show of meeting with these men, but Marino was of most use to Cuba where he was: safely imprisoned, the sword of justice suspended indefinitely over his bare neck.

Whether Marino was tortured remains to this day a matter that can spark debate. But by all accounts, he never told anyone anything.

Soon, other crises, including another, more ominous one between the United States and Cuba, shoved the assassination of the dictator's double and its thorny aftermath off the pages of the world's newspapers. It reemerged on the front page of the official state newspaper of Cuba when Carmine Marino tried to escape and was shot. Few American newspapers ran the story anywhere close to the front. It barely rated a mention on TV. In no case was the official story questioned.

Concealed in a tunnel underneath Madison Square Garden, two hours before Johnny Fontane's sold-out concert, Michael Corleone, in a new but classically styled tuxedo, waited for his *consigliere*. Michael lit a cigarette with his brother's old lighter. This was, he thought, the problem with being early. Waiting.

Michael's return to New York had been rumored for months. The men in his and other Families wanted him back. And why not? Those who stayed on Michael's good side got rich. But it wasn't just those men who engaged in speculation about Michael's next move. The public was just as intrigued. The rumors were reported by every newspaper in the city. He had, to his horror, become something of a folk hero. Hundreds of crimes were rumored to be his doing, and he'd never once been charged with any of them. Thugs like Louie Russo and Emilio Barzini were gone, and Michael was still kicking. Most of the Dons in America had been arrested in upstate New York, and Michael—who, common sense decreed, must have been there—wasn't seen within a thousand miles of the place. Brilliant men in his own Family—Sally Tessio, Nick Geraci—had questioned his authority and were no longer around to question it further.

He had also, not incidentally, grown into his good looks. His suits were exquisitely tailored. His hair was as perfect and his teeth were as white as the president's. He was a war hero. He flew his own airplane. If he said *Jump*, even an icon of cool like Johnny Fontane would say *How high?* He'd withstood the grief of losing his two likable brothers. He'd

loved and lost, twice, and managed to go on. Barely a day went by without the newpapers mentioning or picturing the progress of his new romance with the glamorous Tony award–winning actress Marguerite Duvall. She lived in New York now. Only a matter of time before he did, too, right?

For savvy New Yorkers, there was another tantalizing matter, the legendary ability of people like Michael Corleone to make urban neighborhoods safer than small Lutheran towns in Iowa. All over the city, developers tried to figure out how to give away property to him, knowing they'd make it up when everything around it appreciated.

Michael heard Tom Hagen call his name.

Tom left his bodyguards with Michael's and came down the tunnel alone. They embraced.

"You ready?"

Michael nodded. "It's just dinner, right?"

"Just dinner," Tom said. "Right. It's this way."

They headed toward what was ordinarily the locker room of the basketball team that would come to play the New York Knicks, where the heads of the Five Families of New York and their respective *consiglieres* were meeting for a catered, celebratory dinner. For the first time, all four of the other Dons—Black Tony, Leo the Milkman, Fat Paulie Fortunato, and the newest one, Ozzie Altobello, who'd taken over for the late Rico Tattaglia, who'd died of natural causes—were friends of the Corleones.

"C'mon, Mike." Tom put an arm around him. "Everything's going to be all right. You tried to do things that had never been done. You tried to do the impossible, and you almost did it. Damn close. You can't kick yourself over it."

"Do I look like I'm kicking myself over it?"

"Not to the untrained eye." Tom squeezed his shoulder, in the same tender way Vito Corleone had when he was asking for a favor. "You're the sort of man who only pays attention to what he doesn't have. Which is what makes you a great man, but there comes a time when you have to step back and appreciate what you do have."

Michael was tempted to say that there wasn't anything he had that he really wanted. But that was wrong. He knew that. He had two great kids, a brother and a sister who loved him. The memories of a happy childhood. The will to regroup and try again. Untold riches, in the greatest country on earth, which practically demands that a person reinvent himself.

Tom let his arm drop. They were on the threshold of where the dinner would be.

"If he's out there," Tom said, "we'll find him." He did not say Geraci's name. It was unspeakable now. "No one can hide forever."

Michael said that he wasn't so sure. They'd both heard stories of Mafiosi in Sicily who'd gone underground and weren't heard from for twenty or even thirty years, and America was a lot bigger place than Sicily.

"It's also full of people with a hell of a lot bigger mouths. If he's out there, I have to believe that we'll eventually find him."

"You have to believe that, huh?"

"A boy's gotta have hope, Mikey."

From upstairs came the sound of Fontane's sound check. His big arrogant anthem, the one he'd always professed to hate.

"I have hope," Michael said.

Tom Hagen opened the door.

The other Dons shouted Michael's name and, beaming, rushed to greet him.

In a ballroom-sized cavern underneath the lodge on Rattlesnake Island, where he was prepared to stay as long as he could, Nick Geraci finally finished that two-volume history of Roman warfare, the only books he'd had time to take with him. There were others down there, but they were dime novels and pornos, things Geraci couldn't bring himself to read even in weak moments. He'd lost track of day and night, but, bored, he went to sleep, and in what functioned for him as morning, he made himself a pot of coffee, took out a notebook, and started to write. *Fausto's Bargain,* he'd call it. It would blow the lid off the world of American crime.

What did he know about writing a book?

Fuck it. What did anyone know? Begin. That's what a person needs to know. He began.

"We live by a code," he wrote, "which is more than you can say for your government, which I've seen enough of from the inside to speak about with some authority. In the time it will take you to read this book, your government will take part in more killings and other crimes than the men in my tradition have done in its seven centuries of existence. Believe me. Probably you won't. Suit yourself. No disrespect, but that's what makes you, dear reader, a sucker. On behalf of my former associates, and if I may be so bold also your president, we thank you."

He stopped. He couldn't stay here forever, but arrangements had been made so that he could stay here a hell of a long time. Certainly long enough to write a book.

Sometimes at night, he thought he could hear drilling—the crew that was digging the tunnel that, supposedly, would one day connect him to Cleveland. Maybe he was imagining things. Maybe by the time they fin-

ished, he'd be gone, or dead. His chances weren't good. Slim and none, and the word on the street was, slim just got whacked.

Nick Geraci laughed. Miserable as he was, he had it all over slim.

Michael Corleone and Francesca Van Arsdale emerged from the elevator into an empty, blindingly white penthouse apartment. Roger Cole followed. Al Neri punched the red button and waited in the elevator. Kathy Corleone had stayed downstairs with little Sonny, in the suite that, if Michael bought the building, was earmarked for the twins.

The penthouse took up the whole top floor, the fortieth, but it was a small building. Michael strode across the gleaming marble floor to the windows overlooking the East River and Queens. The building was plain, almost ugly, from the outside, tucked behind a bigger building on a cul-de-sac at the end of Seventy-second Street. The lower floors were filled with offices. Security guards were stationed by the elevator to the apartments on the top floors; it would be easy to have those people replaced by men Neri chose himself. And the penthouse required a special key. This place would be more secure than either the complex at Lake Tahoe or the mall in Long Beach. Cole's own company had gutted and remodeled the apartment, long before Michael told him what he was looking for, so there was no chance of a repeat of the bugging debacle in Tahoe.

Francesca was gasping at the beauty of the view and the apartment. For weeks, Michael had expected the shock of what happened with Billy to bring her low, but it never happened. He was beginning to realize it never would. She had become, even more than her all-American football-star brother, the closest living embodiment of her father's single-minded toughness. Killing her husband was just the kind of hotheaded thing Sonny would have done. She'd had no way of knowing that Michael had already taken care of this. Tom Hagen had made Billy an offer he couldn't refuse. He'd have been a resource for the Corleones, not a nemesis. For a brief, shining moment, they'd had a person inside the Justice Department. And then he'd been cut in half by his own wife, with his own car. Michael would make certain Francesca never learned the truth.

Michael pointed down the hallway. "The kids' bedrooms would be . . . ?"

"Right," Cole said. "That way."

Cole was probably the most famous developer and real estate speculator in New York. Born Ruggero Colombo, he grew up in a Hell's Kitchen tenement near the Corleones. He often told the heartwarming story of the day Vito Corleone convinced their landlord not to evict the Colombos, ignoring the no-pets clause in the lease (and foregoing the opportunity to

rent the apartment for more money to another family) so that little Rug-gero could keep his beloved but noisy mongrel puppy (the namesake of Cole's company, King Properties). Vito also paid for Roger Cole to get his business degree from Fordham. Cole had made Michael Corleone mil-lions—silently at first and now publicly. If Michael had only had more time to develop a few more relationships like the one he had with Cole, he might have been able to stay true to his promise to Kay and his father. It wasn't too late. He could try again. But for now, he was back.

"How often do you get to see them?"

"Who?"

"Your family," he said. "Tony and Mary."

For a moment, Michael had thought Roger meant his theoretically former business associates. "I'm seeing them tomorrow."

The rooms were big for Manhattan, small compared to what they'd had in Tahoe. "They'll like this, I think."

"What about you?" Cole asked. "Do you like it? Because if you don't I've got a couple other places that could work. If you have time."

"Who's the seller?" Michael said.

Cole smiled. "King Properties, every square foot."

Which meant that as Cole's silent partner Michael already had a piece of it. "And the whole building's for sale?"

"Not officially. Just the apartments. But for you, of course."

He could draw his family closer to him than ever. Kathy had gotten a teaching job at City College; she and Francesca would live together and raise little Sonny. Connie and her kids would move into the other big suite on that floor. Tom and Theresa could have the whole floor under that. Anyone who moved here, he could make room for them and keep them safe.

They discussed terms.

"This is perfect, Roger."

Francesca applauded. The men kissed each other on the cheeks. They all headed for the elevator.

"Once a New Yorker, huh?" Cole said. "I knew you'd come back. Welcome home, my friend!"

"It's good to be back," Michael said, louder than he'd meant to say it. As the elevator doors closed, his hollow words still echoed in the stone hallway of his empty new home.